ADVANCES IN DECISION ANALYSIS

Decision analysis consists of a prescriptive theory and associated models and tools that aid individuals or groups confronted with complex decision problems in a wide variety of contexts. Decision analysis can offer workable solutions in domains such as the environment, health and medicine, engineering, public policy, and business. This book extends traditional textbook knowledge of decision analysis to today's state of the art. Part I covers the history and foundations of decision analysis. Part II discusses structuring decision problems, including the development of objectives and their attributes, and influence diagrams. Part III provides an overview of the elicitation and aggregation of probabilities and advances in model building with influence diagrams and belief networks. Part IV discusses utility and risk preferences, practical value models, and extensions of the subjective expected utility model. Part V consists of an overview of advances in risk analysis. Part VI puts decision analysis in a behavioral and organizational context. Part VII presents a selection of major applications.

Ward Edwards (1927–2005) received his Ph.D. in psychology from Harvard University. He was the recipient of many awards, including the Frank P. Ramsey Medal from the Decision Analysis Society of INFORMS in 1988 and the Distinguished Scientific Contributions Award in Applied Psychology from the American Psychological Association in 1996. He wrote more than 100 journal articles and books, including *Decision Analysis and Behavioral Research* and *Utility Theories: Measurement and Applications.*

Ralph F. Miles, Jr., received his Ph.D. in physics from the California Institute of Technology and is a consultant in risk and decision analysis. He was the editor and coauthor of *Systems Concepts* and has written many articles. Until 1991, he worked as an engineer, supervisor, and manager in the Jet Propulsion Laboratory (JPL) at the California Institute of Technology. At JPL he was the Spacecraft System Engineer for two flights to Mars. He was awarded the NASA Exceptional Service Medal for his contributions to early mission design and spacecraft development in the role of Mission Analysis and Engineering Manager for the Voyager Mission to Jupiter, Saturn, Uranus, and Neptune.

Detlof von Winterfeldt is Professor of Industrial and Systems Engineering and of Public Policy and Management at the University of Southern California (USC). He is also Director of the Homeland Security Center for Risk and Economic Analysis of Terrorist Events at USC. He received his Ph.D. in psychology from the University of Michigan. He cowrote *Decision Analysis and Behavioral Research* with Ward Edwards and has published more than 100 articles and reports on decision and risk analysis. He is a Fellow of the Institute for Operations Research and the Management Sciences (INFORMS) and of the Society for Risk Analysis. In 2000 he received the Frank P. Ramsey Medal for distinguished contributions to decision analysis from the Decision Analysis Society of INFORMS.

Advances in Decision Analysis

FROM FOUNDATIONS TO APPLICATIONS

Edited by

Ward Edwards

University of Southern California

Ralph F. Miles, Jr.

Detlof von Winterfeldt

University of Southern California

CAMBRIDGE
UNIVERSITY PRESS

CAMBRIDGE UNIVERSITY PRESS
Cambridge, New York, Melbourne, Madrid, Cape Town, Singapore, São Paulo, Delhi

Cambridge University Press
32 Avenue of the Americas, New York, NY 10013-2473, USA

www.cambridge.org
Information on this title: www.cambridge.org/9780521863681

First published 2007

Printed in the United States of America

A catalog record for this publication is available from the British Library.

Library of Congress Cataloging in Publication Data

Advances in decision analysis : from foundations to applications / edited by Ward Edwards,
Ralph F. Miles, Jr., Detlof von Winterfeldt.
   p.   cm.
Includes bibliographical references and index.
ISBN-13: 978-0-521-86368-1 (hardback)
ISBN-10: 0-521-86368-6 (hardback)
ISBN-13: 978-0-521-68230-5 (pbk.)
ISBN-10: 0-521-68230-4 (pbk.)
1. Decision making.   I. Edwards, Ward.   II. Miles, Ralph F., 1933–
III. von Winterfeldt, Detlof.   IV. Title.
BF448.A38   2007
153.8′3 – dc22   2006025610

ISBN   978-0-521-86368-1 hardback
ISBN   978-0-521-68230-5 paperback

Contents

List of Contributors

PHILLIP C. BECCUE Strategy, Baxter BioScience

DAVID E. BELL Harvard Business School, Harvard University

VICKI M. BIER Department of Industrial and Systems Engineering, University of Wisconsin-Madison

TERRY A. BRESNICK Innovative Decisions, Inc.

DENNIS M. BUEDE Innovative Decisions, Inc.

JOHN C. BUTLER A.B. Freeman School of Business, Tulane University

ALEXANDER N. CHEBESKOV State Scientific Center of Russian Federation, Institute for Physics and Power Engineering

ROBERT T. CLEMEN Fuqua School of Business, Duke University

JAMES L. CORNER Waikato Management School, University of Waikato

LOUIS ANTHONY COX, JR. Cox Associates and University of Colorado

JAMES S. DYER McCombs School of Business, University of Texas-Austin

THOMAS A. EDMUNDS Systems and Decision Sciences Section, Lawrence Livermore National Laboratory

WARD EDWARDS Department of Psychology, University of Southern California (deceased)

DAVID HECKERMAN Machine Learning and Applied Statistics Group, Microsoft Research

STEPHEN C. HORA College of Business and Economics, University of Hawaii-Hilo

RONALD A. HOWARD Department of Management Science and Engineering, Stanford University

JIANMIN JIA Faculty of Business Administration, The Chinese University of Hong Kong

DONALD L. KEEFER W. P. Carey School of Business, Arizona State University

RALPH L. KEENEY Fuqua School of Business, Duke University

CRAIG W. KIRKWOOD W. P. Carey School of Business, Arizona State University

DON N. KLEINMUNTZ School of Policy, Planning, and Development, University of Southern California

CONNSON LOCKE Haas School of Business, University of California, Berkeley

DAVID MATHESON SmartOrg, Inc.

JAMES E. MATHESON SmartOrg, Inc., and Department of Management Science and Engineering, Stanford University

BARBARA MELLERS Haas School of Business, University of California, Berkeley

RALPH F. MILES, JR. Jet Propulsion Laboratory, California Institute of Technology (retired)

ROBERT F. NAU Fuqua School of Business, Duke University

VLADIMIR I. OUSSANOV State Scientific Center of Russian Federation, Institute for Physics and Power Engineering

M. ELISABETH PATÉ-CORNELL Department of Management Science and Engineering, Stanford University

LAWRENCE D. PHILLIPS Department of Operational Research, London School of Economics and Political Science

HOWARD RAIFFA Harvard Business School and the Kennedy School of Government, Harvard University

JAMES K. SEBENIUS Harvard Business School, Harvard University

ROSS D. SHACHTER Department of Management Science and Engineering, Stanford University

CARL S. SPETZLER Strategic Decisions Group

JEFFREY S. STONEBRAKER Decision Sciences, GlaxoSmithKline

ROBERT L. WINKLER Fuqua School of Business, Duke University

DETLOF VON WINTERFELDT Viterbi School of Engineering, University of Southern California

Preface

Decision analysis consists of models and tools to improve decision making. It is especially useful when decisions have multiple conflicting objectives and when their consequences are uncertain. The theoretical foundations of decision analysis can be found in the three areas of decision theory: *individual decision theory*, *social choice theory*, and *game theory*. In addition, disciplines including the behavioral sciences, economics, operations research, philosophy of science, and statistics have contributed to the foundations of decision analysis.

Several introductory decision analysis texts have been written since Raiffa's *Decision Analysis* (1968); including Bell and Schleifer (1995); Brown (2005); Brown, Kahr, and Peterson (1974); Clemen (1996); Keeney and Raiffa (1976); Kirkwood (1997); Skinner (1999); von Winterfeldt and Edwards (1986); Watson and Buede (1987); and Winkler (2003). Nevertheless, none of these books cover all of the recent developments in decision analysis. These developments include advances in risk analysis, the use of Bayesian networks and influence diagrams, analysis with multiple stakeholders, generalizations of the expected utility model, and much more. The purpose of this book is to fill this gap with the present state of the art of decision analysis.

This book is intended for two audiences: (1) students who are taking a second course in decision analysis, following an introductory course using any of the texts listed above; and (2) decision analysts or managers who are already familiar with the subject and wish to know the present state of the art. The word "Advances" in the title is meant to convey the significant advances since the first decision analysis books were published, but that we also expect there to be many more to follow in the twenty-first century.

This book came about as a result of weekly meetings between the editors while discussing a future paper on the distinction between normative, prescriptive, and descriptive decision analysis (see Chapter 1: "Introduction" for our resolution) and putting forth our praise of prescriptive decision analysis in support of decision making. We were also discussing possible revisions for a second edition of Detlof's and Ward's *Decision Analysis and Behavioral Research* (von Winterfeldt and Edwards, 1986). It became clear that expanding Detlof and Ward's book to cover recent advances was just not possible. Decision analysis has expanded to encompass such a wide range of theories and applications that we lacked the intellectual resources to master it. Nevertheless, we recognized the need for such material in text form. Thus the idea for this book was born.

Our first task was to identify the advanced areas of decision analysis that should be included in this book. We identified roughly twenty advanced topics and developed an outline in the form of chapters. We also thought that some chapters on the foundations and applications of decision analysis were important and included several chapters on these topics. We then organized the chapters into the seven principal parts of the book. Our second task was to find the most knowledgeable authors for each of the chapters. Much to our delight, nearly every author we approached agreed to participate, and all recognized the need for this book. Almost everyone followed through and delivered their chapters by our deadlines. With few exceptions, if these authors were asked if they were, along with other talents, a decision analyst, the answer would firmly be "yes." Finally, Cambridge University Press agreed to publish this book.

Following are the seven principal parts. Part I covers the history and foundations of decision analysis. Part II discusses structuring decision problems, including the development of objectives and their attributes. Part III presents an overview of probabilities and their elicitation and aggregation across experts, model building with belief nets and influence diagrams, and learning causal networks. Part IV discusses utility and risk preferences, practical value models, and extensions of the subjective expected utility model. Part V reviews engineering risk analysis and risk analysis for health risk management. Part VI puts decision analysis in a behavioral and organizational context, including behavioral research, decision conferencing, resource allocation decisions, transitioning from decision analysis to the decision organization, and negotiation analysis. Part VII presents case studies of applications based on the discussions of decision analysis throughout the book.

Some subjects are conspicuous by their limited appearance. Social choice theory has its own disciples and many excellent texts. It does appear in the context of Part VI: "Decision Analysis in a Behavioral and Organizational Context." Likewise for game theory, which provides theoretical support for Sebenius' Chapter 23," Negotiation Analysis: Between Decisions and Games." The reader will find little on nonexpected utility theory, except as it has a bearing on decision analysis – see Nau's Chapter 14, "Extensions of the Subjective Expected Utility Model." We believe that the theoretical foundations for decision-making support should come from expected utility theory, and that the role of nonexpected utility theory lies in understanding the heuristics and biases that one encounters in decision making (Kahneman and Tversky 1982; Kahneman, Slovic, and Tversky 2000; Gilovich, Griffin, and Kahneman 2002) and in understanding market behavior (Glaser, Nöth, and Weber 2004). We had hoped for chapters on the growing use of decision analysis in the medical field and on the subjects of options pricing and decision analysis innovations in finance, but for various reasons these chapters were not written.

Finally, decision analysis is an emerging discipline, having existed by name only since 1966 (Howard 1966). As a result there remains much in contention among decision analysts. Even the nomenclature is in debate. See the June 2004 (Vol. 1, No. 2) issue of *Decision Analysis* and the articles by Brown (2004), Clemen and Kleinmuntz (2004), Howard (2004, 2004a), Keeney (2004), Kirkwood (2004), and Smith (2004).

It is interesting to reflect on the views of the three founders of decision analysis, as each provides a different perspective and emphasizes different aspects of decision analysis. Ronald Howard emphasizes the uncertainty part of decision analysis over the multiple objective part, criticizing some of the simpler applications of multiattribute utility theory. Ward Edwards considered multiple objectives as the key problems in decision analysis, while he worked on probability problems in the 1960s and in the 1980s. Howard Raiffa, who pioneered multiattribute utility theory with Ralph Keeney, also sees a major role of decision analysis as solving multiattribute problems. In addition, Howard Raiffa always had a strong interest in expanding decision analysis to bargaining and negotiation problems, and he expressed regret that these aspects of decision analysis have not become more prominent.

There are even different views about history. Ronald Howard traces the history of subjective probability back to Laplace (1814), who introduced probability by partitioning an event space into equally likely events. Many other decision analysts and philosophers have criticized Laplace's definition of probability and instead see the foundations of subjective probability in the works of Bayes (1763), Ramsey (1926), de Finetti (1931, 1937), and Savage (1954).

As editors, we believe that taking a position on these issues is not our role. Thus all opinions of the authors are presented without restriction in this edited book. We leave it to future generations to resolve these issues. Quoting Kirkwood (2004), "In the long run, the answers to these questions will be determined by the research, teaching, and practice of those who view themselves to be in the field."

Ralph Miles wishes to thank Ron Howard and James Matheson for introducing an engineer to decision analysis in a course taught for Caltech's Jet Propulsion Laboratory in the mid-1960s. Detlof von Winterfeldt wishes to thank Ralph Keeney for many years of friendship and collaborations on decision analysis projects. He also acknowledges the support of the Department of Homeland Security under grants EMW-2004-GR-0112 (FEMA) and N0014-05-0630 (ONR). However, any opinions, findings, and conclusions or recommendations in this document are those of the authors and do not necessarily reflect the views of the United States Department of Homeland Security. Unfortunately, Ward Edwards died on February 1, 2005, before this book could be completed. We believe he would be proud of the product that he initiated.

R. F. Miles, Jr.
D. v. W.

REFERENCES

Bayes, T. (1763). An essay toward solving a problem in the doctrine of chances. *Philosophical Transactions of the Royal Society of London, 53*, 370–418. Reprinted in 1958 with biographical note by G. A. Barnard in *Biometrika, 45*, 293–315.

Bell, D. E., and Schleifer, A. Jr. (1995). *Decision making under uncertainty*. Boston, MA: Harvard Business School.

Brown, R. (2004). Naming concepts worth naming. *Decision Analysis, 1*, 86–88.

Brown, R. (2005). *Rational choice and judgment: Decision analysis for the decider*. New York: John Wiley.

Brown, R., Kahr, A., and Peterson, C. (1974). *Decision analysis for the manager*. New York: Holt, Reinhart & Winston.

Clemen, R. T. (1996). *Making hard decisions: An introduction to decision analysis* (2nd ed.). Belmont, CA: Duxbury Press.

Clemen, R. T., and Kleinmuntz, D. N. (2004). From the editors.... *Decision Analysis, 1*, 69–70.

de Finetti, B. (1931). Sul Significato Soggettivo della Probabilità. *Fundamenta Mathematicae, 17*, 298–329. Translated in 1993 in P. Monari and D. Cocchi (Eds.), On the Subjective Meaning of Probability. *Probabilità e Induxione*. Bologna: Clueb, pp. 291–321.

de Finetti, B. (1937). La prévision: Ses lois logiques, ses sources subjectives. *Annales de l'Institut Henri Poincaré, 7*, 1–68. Translated in 1980 by H. E. Kyburg, Jr., Foresight. Its logical laws, its subjective sources. In H. E. Kyburg, Jr. and H. E. Smokler (Eds.), *Studies in subjective probability* (2nd ed.). Huntington, NY: Robert E. Krieger, pp. 53–118.

Gilovich, T., Griffin, D., and Kahneman, D. (Eds.). (2002). *Heuristics and biases: The psychology of intuitive judgment*. Cambridge, UK: Cambridge University Press.

Glaser, M., Nöth, M., and Weber, M. (2004). Behavioral finance. In D. J. Koehler and N. Harvey (Eds.), *Blackwell handbook of judgment and decision making*. Malden, MA: Blackwell Publishing, pp. 527–546.

Howard, R. A. (1966). Decision analysis: Applied decision theory. In *Proceedings of the Fourth International Conference on Operational Research*. New York: John Wiley, pp. 55–71.

Howard, R. A. (2004). Speaking of decisions: Precise decision language. *Decision Analysis, 1*, 71–78.

Howard, R. A. (2004a). Response to comments on Howard. *Decision Analysis, 1*, 89–92.

Kahneman, D., and Tversky, A. (Eds.). (1982). *Judgment under uncertainty: Heuristics and biases*. New York: Cambridge University Press.

Kahneman, D., Slovic, P., and Tversky, A. (Eds.). (2000). *Choices, values, and frames*. Cambridge, UK: Cambridge University Press.

Keeney, R. L. (2004). Communicating about decisions. *Decision Analysis, 1*, 84–85.

Keeney, R. L., and Raiffa, H. (1976). *Decisions with multiple objectives: Preferences and value tradeoffs*. New York: John Wiley.

Kirkwood, C. W. (1997). *Strategic decision making: Multiobjective decision analysis with spreadsheets*. Belmont, CA: Duxbury Press.

Kirkwood, C. W. (2004). Prospects for a decision language. *Decision Analysis, 1*, 84–85.

Laplace (P. Simon, Marquis de Laplace). (1814). *Essai philosophique sur les probabilities*. Translated by F. W. Truscott and F. L. Emory and reprinted in 1951 with an introductory note by E. T. Bell as *A philosophical essay on probabilities*. New York: Dover Publications.

Raiffa, H. (1968). *Decision analysis: Introductory lectures on choices under uncertainty*. Reading, MA: Addison-Wesley.

Ramsey, F. P. (1926). Truth and probability. In R. B. Braithwaite (Ed.). 1931. F. P. Ramsey, *The foundations of mathematics and other logical essays*. London: Routledge and Kegan Paul. Reprinted in 1980 in H. E. Kyburg, Jr., and H. E. Smokler, *Studies in subjective probability* (2nd ed.). New York: John Wiley. Reprinted in 1990 in D. H. Mellor, *Philosophical papers: F. P. Ramsey*. Cambridge, UK: Cambridge University Press.

Savage, L. J. (1954). *The foundations of statistics*. New York: John Wiley. Revised 2nd ed. in 1972. New York: Dover Publications.

Skinner, D. C. (1999). *Introduction to decision analysis: A practitioner's guide to improving decision quality* (2nd ed.). Gainesville, FL: Probabilistic Publishing,

Smith, J. E. (2004). Precise decision language. *Decision Analysis, 1*, 79–81.

von Winterfeldt, D., and Edwards, W. (1986). *Decision analysis and behavioral research.* Cambridge, UK: Cambridge University Press.

Watson, S. R., and Buede, D. M. (1987). *Decision synthesis: The principles and practice of decision analysis*. Cambridge, UK: Cambridge University Press.

Winkler, R. L. (2003). *An introduction to Bayesian inference and decision* (2nd ed.). Gainesville, FL: Probabilistic Publishing.

1 Introduction

Ward Edwards, Ralph F. Miles, Jr., and Detlof von Winterfeldt

This first chapter of *Advances in Decision Analysis* presents definitions for decision analysis that will be used consistently throughout this volume and provides a list of references on the subject of decision analysis. As this is an edited volume on "advances" in decision analysis, it is assumed that the reader is familiar with the subject to the level presented in one or more of the introductory decision analysis texts listed in the Preface.

This book attempts to maintain consistent distinctions among normative, prescriptive, and descriptive decision theories—distinctions that we find inconsistent in the literature. There is a rich and related literature on microeconomics, decision theory, behavioral psychology, and management science, which is only touched on in the following chapters.

Advances in Decision Analysis presents methodologies and applications of decision analysis as derived from prescriptive decision theory. Each of the first six parts of the book concentrates on different aspects of decision analysis. Part VII is devoted to applications of decision analysis.

The Rational Decision Maker

Many books in economics and decision analysis propose theories and methodologies that claim to be "rational." Philosophers disagree on what is rational (Mele and Rawling 2004; Searle 2001). Many decision theories define the "rational decision maker" through mathematical principles or axioms, which, if combined, imply rational behavior (e.g., to maximize expected utility). But how compelling are these axioms? We would be remiss not to define what we mean by rationality.

For the purposes of this book, "rationality" will be interpreted as "Bayesian rationality," with an emphasis on (1) decision making guided by maximizing subjective expected utility, and (2) the importance of information and the processing of that information through Bayes' theorem. We take a pragmatic view of why this position is compelling. By pragmatic, we mean that systematic and repeated violations of these principles will result in inferior long-term consequences of actions and a diminished quality of life. See also Chapter 5: "Pragmatism" in McClennen (1990).

Pragmatism

The pragmatism of Peirce (1878) and James (1907) was preceded by that of Kant (1781), who, in his *Critique of Pure Reason,* makes two essential points: (1) The justification for reason is ends for happiness and (2) it cannot be obtained a priori from logic:

> The sole business of reason is to bring about a union of all the ends, which are aimed at by our inclinations, into one ultimate end – that of *happiness* – and to show the agreement which should exist among the means of attaining that end. In this sphere, accordingly, reason cannot present to us any other than pragmatical laws of free action, for our guidance towards the aims set up by the senses, and is incompetent to give us laws which are pure and determined completely *á priori.*

In many ways, the behavioral movement of psychology and economics and the philosophical inclinations of the founding fathers of decision analysis aligned with this pragmatic philosophy. Many decision analysts today subscribe to the pragmatic idea that beliefs, values, and actions should serve the pursuit of happiness, whether this be wealth, health, quality of life, or an aggregation of those attributes into a general notion of utility.

Subjective Expected Utility (SEU)

There are three fundamental principles that are rational because they are pragmatic in the sense just discussed. These principles apply to choices with certain consequences as well as to choices with uncertain consequences (gambles). For generality, these principles are presented here for gambles, because sure things are simply degenerate gambles. The three principles are:

1. Transitivity.
2. The sure-thing principle.
3. Additivity of probability.

TRANSITIVITY. Transitivity states that if gamble f is preferred to gamble g, and gamble g is preferred to gamble h, then gamble f must be preferred to gamble h. The pragmatic argument for transitivity is that its intentional, systematic, and persistent violation subjects the decision maker to the possibility of becoming a "money pump" (Davidson, McKinsey, and Suppes 1955), and, in market situations, to be vulnerable to arbitrage opportunities.

SURE-THING PRINCIPLE. The *sure-thing principle* states that the preference between two gambles f and g, which have the same set of events and which have identical consequences in one of the events (but not necessarily in others), should not depend on what that identical consequence is. Much has been written about the rationality status of this principle since it was introduced by Savage (1954). To us, the convincing pragmatic argument is that violations of the sure-thing principle contradict a slightly generalized version of the monotonicity principle. The specific version of the monotonicity principle states that replacing a *consequence* in a gamble with a preferred consequence, creates a new gamble that is preferred to the original one. Luce (2003) refers to this condition as "consequence monotonicity," to distinguish it form other types of monotonicity. The generalization applies this principle to the situation in which a consequence in a gamble can be a gamble itself (i.e., a second-stage gamble). It states that the replacement of a *gamble* with a preferred gamble creates a new gamble that is preferred to the original one. Violations of this principle can be shown to lead to money pump arguments similar to those of violating transitivity.

The power of the sure-thing principle is that it allows the separation of probabilities of events from the utilities of the consequences associated with these events. Technically, the principle allows the construction of an additive function over a series of events, where the consequences for each event are evaluated separately. Other technical principles ensure that the functions for evaluating events are related by positive linear transformations, thus leading to the interpretation of weights attached to events.

ADDITIVITY OF PROBABILITY. The weights attached to events can have very different interpretations. In decision analysis, these weights are interpreted as probabilities. The most important feature of these probabilities is that they are additive, that is, the probability of two mutually exclusive events is equal to the sum of the two probabilities. The principle underlying additivity of probability is what Luce (2003) calls "event monotonicity." Event monotonicity requires that when we replace an event associated with a preferred consequence with an event that is more likely, and, at the same time, replace an event with a less-preferred consequence with a less likely one, we should prefer the new gamble over the original one.

Violation of event monotoncity or additivity subjects the decision maker to the sure long-term loss implied by the *Dutch Book argument* (de Finetti 1931, 1937; Kemeny 1955; Lehman 1955; Ramsey 1926; Shimony 1955). In other words, if you believe in nonadditive probabilities, someone can create a series of gambles that will lead to your eventual sure losses. Aside from avoiding the Dutch Book, the power of additive probabilities is that they open the door to the use of the whole apparatus of probability theory.

Acceptance of transitivity, the sure-thing principle, and the additivity of probability (plus some less important technical assumptions) inevitably leads to the acceptance of the *subjective expected utility model* of decision making (Savage 1954). Denying any of these principles leads to "nonexpected utility theories" that attempt to model descriptive decision making. Nau discusses these nonexpected utility theories in Chapter 14 in this volume.

Bayes' Theorem

Bayes' theorem is a trivial consequence of the definition of conditional probability, although calling it a "definition" is inadequate because there are intuitive notions as to what "conditionalization" means (Hájek 2003). Define $p(A|E) = \frac{p(A \cap E)}{p(E)}$ to be the probability of Event A conditional on Event E, where A and E are events and $p(A)$ and $p(E)$ are unconditional probabilities of the events and where $p(E) \neq 0$.

Let A_i ($i = 1, \ldots, m$) and E_j ($j = 1, \ldots, n$) be partitions of the same event space. Then it can be shown that

$$p(A_i \mid E_j) = \frac{p(E_j \mid A_i)p(A_i)}{\sum_{i=1}^{m} p(E_j \mid A_i)p(A_i)}.$$

Credit is given to Thomas Bayes (1763) for the theorem, although the story is more complicated than that (Bernardo and Smith 1994; Dale 1999). The richness for conditionalization becomes apparent when $p(A_i)$ is interpreted as the unconditional probability of Event A_i prior to observing the Event E_j, $p(E_j \mid A_i)$, which is interpreted as the probability of Event E_j conditional on observing Event A_i and called the "likelihood function." The terms in the denominator are a normalizing function that equates to $p(E_j)$.

The pragmatic argument for a bettor to use Bayes' theorem as a rule for updating probabilities is that otherwise a bettor updating by Bayes' theorem can construct a Dutch Book against a bookie who does not likewise update. Roughly, the bettor observes the bookie's fair odds before and after the evidence obtains and places a series of fair bets such that the bettor is guaranteed to win no matter the outcome of the bets. For the details on how the Dutch Book is constructed, see Freedman and Purves (1969), Skyrms (1987, 1990, 1993), and Teller (1973, 1976).

Decision Theory

Decision theory, the foundation of decision analysis, has a long history, some of which is discussed in the next chapter. Briefly, decision theory started with two streams of thought: modification of the expected value model to account for nonlinear utilities and the introduction of subjective probabilities and use of Bayes' theorem for updating probabilities. Both streams of thought date back to the eighteenth century. Daniel Bernoulli (1738), responding to several criticisms of the expected value model, proposed the use of a logarithmic utility function to replace the direct monetary consequences in an expected utility calculation. Although the notion of subjective probability was known since the 1660s (Hacking 1975), its implementation lay fallow until Thomas Bayes (1763) used subjective probability when he proposed an algorithm to update probabilities based on new data. It took two centuries for these ideas to culminate first in the *expected utility model* (von Neumann and Morgenstern 1947), and soon thereafter in the *subjective expected utility model* (Savage 1954). Many books on decision theory followed (see Chapter 2, in this volume). Subjective expected utility theory is the foundation of decision analysis to this date. The first conference on "decision processes" was held at the RAND Corporation in 1952 (Thrall, Coombs, and Davis 1954).

Another precedent of decision analysis was created in *game theory* by von Neumann and Morgenstern (1947), which was popularized by the very influential book by Luce and Raiffa (1957). Game theory is very much alive today in experimental economics and terrorism research, although it does not appear to have much direct impact on decision analysis.

Social choice theory is concerned with the rules that govern aggregate choices by individuals, including voting and selection of aggregate decision rules (Arrow 1963). Some of social choice theory has been used in multiple stakeholder applications of decision analysis (e.g., Dyer and Miles 1976).

Normative, Descriptive, and Prescriptive Decision Theories

Following Bell, Raiffa, and Tversky (1988), we can distinguish among three different perspectives in the study of decision making. In the *normative* perspective, the focus is on rational choice and normative models are built on basic assumptions (or axioms) that people should consider to provide logical guidance for their decisions. In the domain of decision making under risk or uncertainty, the traditional expected value model, the expected utility model of von Neumann and Morgenstern (1947), and the subjective expected utility model of Savage (1954) are the dominant normative models of rational choice. In the domain of beliefs, probability theory and Bayesian statistics in the presence of evidence for updating beliefs provide the normative foundation.

The *descriptive* perspective focuses on how real people make judgments and decisions, and some descriptive researchers develop mathematical models of actual behavior. Such models are judged by the extent to which their predictions correspond to the actual judgments and choices people make (Allais and Hagen 1979; Gilovich, Griffin, and Kahneman 2002; Kahneman, Slovic, and Tversky 1982; Kahneman and Tversky 2000). One of the most prominent descriptive models of decision making under uncertainty is the *prospect theory model* of Kahneman and Tversky (1979), later refined in Tversky and Kahneman (1992). The model captures many of the ways in which people deviate from the normative ideal of the expected utility model in a reasonably parsimonious form.

The *prescriptive perspective* focuses on helping people make better decisions by using normative models, but with awareness of the limitations of human judgment and of the practical problems of implementing a rational model in a complex world. Regarding the limitations of human judgment, the prescriptive perspective attempts to ensure that the tasks presented to experts and decision makers are sufficiently simple and are not affected by biases and errors known from descriptive studies. Training, tools, and debiasing techniques are used to avoid such biases and errors. To implement rational models in a complex world, it is important to simplify a complex decision environment to a manageable size for analysis. Savage (1954) recognized this issue when discussing the issues related to "small" and "large" worlds.

Decision Analysis

Decision analysis is unabashedly normative in theory and thoroughly prescriptive in practice. Its purpose is to assist decision makers to make better decisions.

Decision analysis draws on the disciplines of mathematics, economics, behavioral psychology, and computer science.

The fundamentals of decision analysis were developed in the late 1950s and the ideas first appeared in book form with Schlaifer's *Probability and Statistics for Business Decisions* (1959). Decision analysis came to early maturity in the 1960s when Howard (1965, 1966) merged *decision theory* and *systems modeling*. Howard named the new discipline "decision analysis." Quoting Howard (1983): "Specifically, decision analysis results from combining the fields of systems analysis and statistical decision theory." Howard edited the *Special Issue on Decision Analysis* (Howard 1968), in which he wrote "The Foundations of Decision Analysis" (Howard 1968a). Raiffa (1968) published the first book titled *Decision Analysis*. It is amazing that, with the help of Ward Edwards, in the same year Lusted, an M.D., published a book on medical decision making (Lusted 1968).

For the state of statistical decision theory at that time, see Raiffa and Schlaifer (1961) and much later, Pratt, Raiffa, and Schlaifer (1995). For an overview of systems analysis during that period, see Miles (1973). There are many books that are truly dedicated to decision analysis (Baird 1989; Bell, Keeney, and Raiffa 1977; Bell and Schleifer 1995; Brown 2005; Brown, Kahr, and Peterson 1974; Bunn 1984; Clemen 1996; French 1989; Golub 1997; Goodwin and Wright 1991; Hammond, Keeney, and Raiffa 1999; Howard and Matheson 1983a; Jeffrey 1983; Keeney 1978, 1992; Keeney and Raiffa 1976; Kirkwood 1997; Lindley 1985; Marshall and Oliver 1995; Morgan and Henrion 1990; von Winterfeldt and Edwards 1986; Watson and Buede 1987; Zeckhauser, Keeney, and Sebenius 1996). The Decision Analysis Society of the Institute for Operations Research and the Management Sciences (INFORMS) also has a quarterly journal, *Decision Analysis*.

What does decision analysis have to offer that other related disciplines do not? Research on the mathematical foundations of decision theory that are largely normative, in the sense that we have defined "normative," can contribute to decision analysis, but is not decision analysis per se (Fishburn 1964, 1968, 1970, 1982; Jeffrey 1983, 1992; Kreps 1988; Luce 1959; Wakker 1989). Research that is axiomatic in nature, but violates the three fundamental principles of rationality (transitivity, sure-thing, and additivity of probabilities), cannot serve as a foundation of decision analysis (Bacharach and Hurley 1991; Fishburn 1988; Hooker, Leach, and McClennen 1978; Quiggin 1993; Stigum and Wenstøp, 1983).

Descriptive decision theory or behavioral psychology are important for their insight into the cognitive limitations of decision makers, but their conclusions are not always guidelines for rational decision making we have discussed. Some publications are a mixture of normative, prescriptive, and descriptive decision theory (Dawes 1988; Edwards 1992; Edwards and Tversky 1967; Gärdenfors and Sahlin 1988; Hogarth 1990; Kleindorfer, Kunreuther, and Schoemaker 1993; Shanteau, Mellers, and Schum 1999; Zeckhauser, Keeney, and Sebenius 1996). Management science combines economic and social science theories with analyses of real-world results, but these analyses are not always studies framed within the paradigm of decision analysis (Bazerman 1998; HBS 2001; Hoch and Kunreuther 2001; March 1994; Russo and Schoemaker 1989).

Philosophical studies cannot be construed as decision analysis (Eells 1982; Eells and Skyrms 1994; Gibbard 1990; Joyce 1999; Kaplan 1996; Kyburg and Teng 2001; Kyburg and Thalos 2003; Levi 1986; Maher 1993; Resnik 1987; Skyrms 1990; Sobel 1994; Weirich 2001). Microeconomics concentrates on theory and not on how decision makers would actually implement the theory (Kreps 1990; Mas-Colell, Whinston, and Green 1995). The same can be said for excellent studies on Bayesian statistics (Berger 1985; Bernardo and Smith 1994; Berry 1996; Gill 2002; Leonard and Hsu 1999; Robert 2001; Zellner 1971) or operations research (Hillier and Lieberman 2001).

Decision analysis is normative at its roots, but becomes prescriptive in recognizing the limitations of human decision makers and the complexity of the environment in which it has to be implemented. See Gigerenzer and Selten (2001), Simon (1982), and Rubenstein (1998) for a discussion of *bounded rationality*.

REFERENCES

Allais, M., and Hagen, O. (Eds.). (1979). *Expected utility hypothesis and the Allais paradox.* Dordrecht, The Netherlands: D. Reidel Publishing.

Arrow, K. J. (1963). *Social choice and individual values.* (2nd ed.). New Haven, CT: Yale University Press.

Bacharach, M., and Hurley. S. (Eds.). (1991). *Foundations of decision theory: Issues and advances.* Cambridge, MA: Blackwell.

Baird, B. F. (1989). *Managerial decisions under uncertainty.* New York: Wiley.

Bayes, T. (1763). An essay towards solving a problem in the doctrine of chances. Published posthumously in 1763 in *Philosophical Transactions of the Royal Society, London, 53,* 370–418 and *54*, 296–325. Reprinted in 1958 in *Biometrica, 45*, 293–315.

Bazerman, M. (1998). *Judgment in managerial decision making.* (4th ed.). New York: John Wiley.

Bell, D. E., Keeney, R. L., and Raiffa, H. (Eds.). (1977). *Conflicting objectives in decisions.* New York: John Wiley.

Bell, D. E., Raiffa, H., and Tversky, A. (Eds.). (1988). *Decision making: Descriptive, normative, and prescriptive interactions.* Cambridge, UK: Cambridge University Press.

Bell, D. E., and Schleifer, Jr., A. (1995). *Decision making under uncertainty.* Cambridge, MA: Course Technology.

Berger, J. O. (1985). *Statistical decision theory and bayesian analysis.* (2nd ed.). New York: Springer-Verlag.

Bernardo, J. M., and Smith, A. F. M. (1994). *Bayesian theory.* New York: John Wiley.

Bernoulli, D. (1738). Specimen theoriae novae de mensura sortis. *Comentarii academiae scientiarum imperiales petropolitanae, 5*, 175–192. Translated into English by L. Sommer in 1954. Exposition of a new theory on the measurement of risk. *Econometrica, XXII,* 23–36.

Berry, D. A. (1996). *Statistics: A Bayesian perspective.* Belmont, CA: Wadsworth Publishing.

Brown, R. V. (2005). *Tools of rational choice.* New York: John Wiley.

Brown, R. V., Kahr, A. S., and Peterson, C. (1974). *Decision analysis for the manager.* New York: Holt, Rinehart, & Winston.

Bunn, D. V. (1984). *Applied decision analysis.* New York: McGraw-Hill.

Clemen, R. T. (1996). *Making hard decisions: An introduction to decision analysis.* (2nd ed.). Belmont, CA: Duxbury Press.

Dale, A. I. (1999). *A history of inverse probability.* (2nd ed.). New York: Springer.

Davidson, D., McKinsey, J. C. C., and Suppes, P. (1955). Outlines of a formal theory of value. *Philosophy of Science, 22,* 140–160.

Dawes, R. M. (1988). *Rational Choice in an Uncertain World.* Orlando, FL: Harcourt Brace Jovanovich.

de Finetti, B. (1931). Sul significato soggettivo della probabilità. *Fundamenta mathematicae, 17,* 298–329. Translated into English in 1993 in P. Monari and D. Cocchi (Eds.). On the subjective meaning of probability. *Probabilità e induzione.* Bologna: Clueb, pp. 291–321.

de Finetti, B. (1937). La prévision: Ses lois logiques, ses sources subjectives. *Annales del'Institut Henri Poincaré, 7,* 1–68. Translated with corrections by H. E. Kyburg, Jr. Foresight. Its logical laws, its subjective sources. In H. E. Kyburg, Jr. and H. E. Smokler (Eds.). (1980). *Studies in subjective probability.* (2nd ed.). Huntington, NY: Krieger, pp. 53–111.

Dyer, J. S., and Miles, Jr., R. F. (1976). An actual application of collective choice theory to the selection of trajectories for the Mariner Jupiter/Saturn 1977 Project. *Operations Research, 24,* 220–244.

Edwards. W. (Ed.). (1992). *Utility theory: Measurements and applications.* Dordrecht, The Netherlands: Kluwer Academic Publishers.

Edwards, W., and Tversky, A. (Eds.). (1967). *Decision Making: Selected Readings.* Middlesex, UK: Penguin Books.

Eells, E. (1982). *Rational decision and causality.* Cambridge, UK: Cambridge University Press.

Eells, E., and Skyrms, B. (Eds.). (1994). *Probability and conditionals: Belief revision and rational decision.* Cambridge, UK: Cambridge University Press.

Fishburn, P. C. (1964). *Decision and value theory.* New York: John Wiley.

Fishburn, P. C. (1968). Utility theory. *Management Science, 14,* 335–378.

Fishburn, P. C. (1970). *Utility theory for decision making.* New York: John Wiley.

Fishburn, P. C. (1982). *The foundations of expected utility.* Dordrecht, The Netherlands: D. Reidel Publishing.

Fishburn, P. C. (1988). *Nonlinear preference and utility theory.* Baltimore, MD: Johns Hopkins University Press.

Freedman, D. A., and Purves, R. A. (1969). Bayes' method for bookies. *Annals of Mathematical Statistics, 40,* 1177–1186.

French, S. (Ed.). (1989). *Readings in decision analysis.* Boca Raton, FL: Chapman & Hall/CRC.

Gärdenfors, P., and Sahlin, N.-E. (Eds.). (1988). *Decision, probability, and utility: Selected readings.* Cambridge, UK: Cambridge University Press.

Gibbard, A. (1990). *Wise choices, apt feelings.* Cambridge, MA: Harvard University Press.

Gigerenzer, G., and Selten, R. (Eds.). (2001). *Bounded rationality: The adaptive toolkit.* Cambridge, MA: MIT Press.

Gill, J. (2002). *Bayesian methods: A social and behavioral sciences approach.* Boca Raton, FL: Chapman & Hall/CRC.

Gilovich, T., Griffin, D., and Kahneman, D. (Eds.). (2002). *Heuristics and biases: The psychology of intuitive judgment.* Cambridge, UK: Cambridge University Press.

Golub, A. L. (1997). *Decision analysis: An integrated approach.* New York: John Wiley.

Goodwin, P., and Wright, G. (1991). *Decision analysis for management judgment.* New York: John Wiley.

Hacking, I. (1975). *The Emergence of probability.* Cambridge, UK: Cambridge University Press.

Hájek, A. 2003. What conditional probability could not be. *Synthese, 137,* 273–323.

Hammond, J. S., Keeney, R. L., and Raiffa, H. (1999). *Smart choices: A practical guide to making better decisions.* Boston, MA: Harvard Business School Press.

HBS. Harvard Business School Publishing. (2001). *Harvard Business Review on decision making*. Boston, MA: Harvard Business School Publishing.

Hillier, F. S., and Lieberman, G. J. (2001). *Introduction to operations research*. (7th ed.). Boston: McGraw-Hill.

Hoch, S. J., and Kunreuther, H. C. (Eds.). (2001). *Wharton on making decisions*. New York: John Wiley.

Hogarth, R. M. (1990). *Insights in decision making: A tribute to Hillel J. Einhorn*. Chicago, IL: University of Chicago Press.

Hooker, C. A., Leach, J. J., and McClennen, E. F. (Eds.). (1978). *Foundations and applications of decision theory. Vol. I: Theoretical foundations. Vol. II: Epistemic and social applications*. Dordrecht, The Netherlands: D. Reidel Publishing.

Howard, R. A. (1965). Bayesian decision models for system engineering. *IEEE Transactions on Systems Science and Cybernectics, SSC-1*, pp. 36–40.

Howard, R. A. (1966). Decision analysis: Applied decision theory. In *Proceedings of the Fourth International Conference on Operational Research*. New York: John Wiley, pp. 55–71.

Howard, R. A. (Ed.). (1968). Special issue on decision analysis. *IEEE Transactions on Systems Science and Cybernetics, SSC-4*. New York: IEEE.

Howard, R. A. (1968a). The foundations of decision analysis. In R. A. Howard, (1968). *Special issue on decision analysis. IEEE Transactions on Systems Science and Cybernetics, SSC-4*. New York: IEEE, pp. 211–219.

Howard, R. A. (1983). The evolution of decision analysis. In Howard, R. A., and Matheson, J. E. (Eds.). (1983). *The principles and applications of decision analysis. Vol. I: General collection, Vol. II: Professional collection*. Menlo Park, CA: Strategic Decisions Group, pp. 5–15.

Howard, R. A., and Matheson, J. E. (Eds.). (1983a). *The principles and applications of decision analysis. Vol. I: General collection, Vol. II: Professional collection*. Menlo Park, CA: Strategic Decisions Group.

INFORMS. Institute for Operations Research and the Management Sciences, Hanover, MD.

James, W. (1907). *Pragmatism: A new name for some old ways of thinking*. New York: Longmans, Green, & Co. Reprinted in 1995 with new footnotes as: *Pragmatism*. Mineola, NY: Dover Publications.

Jeffrey, R. C. (1983). *The logic of decision*. (2nd ed.). Chicago, IL: University of Chicago Press.

Jeffrey, R. C. (1992). *Probability and the art of judgment*. Cambridge, UK: Cambridge University Press.

Joyce, J. M. (1999). *The foundations of causal decision theory*. Cambridge, UK: Cambridge University Press.

Kahneman, D., Slovic, P., and Tversky, A. (Eds.). (1982). *Judgment under uncertainty: Heuristics and biases*. Cambridge, UK: Cambridge University Press.

Kahneman, D., and Tversky, A. (1979). Prospect theory: An analysis of decision under risk. *Econometrica, 47*, 263–291.

Kahneman, D., and Tversky, A. (Eds.). (2000). *Choices, values, and frames*. Cambridge, UK: Cambridge University Press.

Kant, I. (1781). *Critique of pure reason*. Translated in 1900 by J. M. D. Meiklejohn. London: Colonial Press. Reprinted in 2003 by Dover Publications, Mineola, NY, p. 449.

Kaplan, M. (1996). *Decision theory as philosophy*. Cambridge, UK: Cambridge University Press.

Keeney, R. L. (1978). Decision analysis. In J. J. Moder and S. E. Elmaghraby (Eds.), *Handbook of operations research*. New York: Van Nostrand Reinhold, pp. 423–450.

Keeney, R. L. (1992). *Value-Focused thinking: A path to creative decision making*. Cambridge, MA: Harvard University Press.

Keeney, R. L., and Raiffa, H. (1976). *Decisions with multiple objectives: Preferences and value tradeoffs*. New York: John Wiley.

Kemeny, J. G. (1955). Fair bets and inductive probabilities. *Journal of Symbolic Logic, 20,* 263–273.

Kirkwood, C. W. (1997). *Strategic decision making: Multiobjective decision analysis with spreadsheets*. Belmont, CA: Wadsworth/Thompson International.

Kleindorfer, P. R., Kunreuther, H. C., and Schoemaker, P. J. H. (1993). *Decision sciences: An integrative perspective*. Cambridge, UK: Cambridge University Press.

Kreps, D. M. (1988). *Notes on the theory of choice*. Boulder, CO: Westview Press.

Kreps, D. M. (1990). *A course in microeconomic theory*. Princeton, NJ: Princeton University Press.

Kyburg, H. E., Jr., and Teng, C. M. (2001). *Uncertain inference*. Cambridge, UK: Cambridge University Press.

Kyburg, H. E., Jr., and Thalos, M. (Eds.). (2003). *Probability is the very guide of life*. Chicago, IL: Open Court.

Lehman, R. S. (1955). On confirmation and rational betting. *Journal of Symbolic Logic, 20,* 251–262.

Leonard, T., and Hsu, J. S. J. (1999). *Bayesian Methods: An analysis for statisticians and interdisciplinary researchers*. Cambridge, UK: Cambridge University Press.

Levi, I. (1986). *Hard choices: Decision making under unresolved conflict*. Cambridge, UK: Cambridge University Press.

Lindley, D. V. (1985). *Making decisions*. (2nd ed.). New York: John Wiley.

Luce, R. D. (1959). *Individual Choice Behavior: A Theoretical Analysis*. New York: John Wiley. Reprinted in 2005 by John Wiley, NY.

Luce, R. D. (2003). *Rationality in choice under certainty and uncertainty*. In S. L. Schneider and J. Shanteau (Eds.), *Emerging perspectives on judgment and decision research*. Cambridge, UK: Cambridge University Press, pp. 64–83.

Luce, R. D., and Raiffa, H. (1957). *Games and decisions: Introduction and critical survey*. New York: John Wiley.

Lusted, L. B. (1968). *Introduction to medical decision making*. Springfield, IL: Charles Thomas.

Maher, P. (1993). *Betting on theories*. Cambridge, UK: Cambridge University Press.

March, J. G. (1994). *A primer on decision making: How decisions happen*. New York: Free Press.

Marshall, K. T., and Oliver, R. M. (1995). *Decision making and forecasting: With emphasis on model building and policy analysis*. New York: McGraw-Hill.

Mas-Colell, A., Whinston, M. D., and Green, J. R. (1995). *Microeconomic theory*. New York: Oxford University Press.

McClennen, E. F. (1990). *Rationality and dynamic choice*. Cambridge, UK: Cambridge University Press.

Mele, A. R., and Rawling, P. (Eds.). (2004). *The Oxford handbook of rationality*. New York: Oxford University Press.

Miles, Jr., R. F. (1973). *Systems concepts: Lectures on contemporary approaches to systems*. New York: John Wiley.

Morgan, M. G., and Henrion, M. (1990). *Uncertainty: A guide to dealing with uncertainty in quantitative risk and policy analysis*. Cambridge, UK: Cambridge University Press.

Peirce, C. S. (1878). How to make our ideas clear. *Popular Science Monthly, 12,* 286–302. Reprinted in 1955 in J. Buchler (Ed.), *Philosophical writings of Peirce*. New York: Dover Publications, pp. 23–41. Reprinted in 1992 in N. Houser and C. Klosel. *The essential Peirce:*

Selected philosophical writings (Vol. 1: 1867–1893). Bloomington, IN: Indiana University Press, pp. 124–141.

Pratt, J. W., Raiffa, H., and Schlaifer, R. (1995). *Introduction to statistical decision theory*. Cambridge, MA: MIT Press.

Quiggin, J. (1993). *Generalized expected utility theory: The rank-dependent model*. Dordrecht, The Netherlands: Kluwer Academic Publishers.

Raiffa, H. (1968). *Decision analysis: Introductory lectures on choices under uncertainty*. Reading, MA: Addison-Wesley.

Raiffa, H., and Schlaifer, R. (1961). *Applied statistical decision theory*. Cambridge, MA: MIT Press.

Ramsey, F. P. (1926). Truth and probability. In R. B. Braithwaite (Ed.) (1931). *Foundations of mathematics and other essays*. London: Routledge & P. Kegan, pp. 156–198. Reprinted in 1980 in H. E. Kyburg, Jr. and H. E. Smokler (Eds.), *Studies in subjective probability* (2nd ed.). Huntington, NY: R. E. Krieger Publishing, pp. 23–52 Reprinted in 1990 in D. H. Mellor (Ed.), *Philosophical Papers: F. P. Ramsey*. Cambridge, UK : Cambridge University Press, pp. 52–109

Resnik, M. D. (1987). *Choices: An introduction to decision theory*. Minneapolis, MN: University of Minneapolis Press.

Robert, C. P. (2001). *The Bayesian choice*. (2nd ed.). New York: Springer-Verlag.

Rubinstein, A. (1998). *Modeling bounded rationality*. Cambridge, MA: MIT Press.

Russo, J. E., and Schoemaker, P. J. H. (1989). *Decision traps: Ten barriers to brilliant decision-making and how to overcome them*. New York: Simon & Schuster.

Savage, L. J. (1954). *The foundations of statistics*. (2nd ed.). New York: John Wiley. Reprinted in 1972. New York: Dover Publications.

Schlaifer, R. (1959). *Probability and statistics for business decisions*. New York: McGraw-Hill.

Searle, J. R. (2001). *Rationality in action*. Cambridge, MA: MIT Press.

Shanteau, J., Mellers, B. A., and Schum, D. (Eds.). (1999). *Decision science and technology: Reflections on the contributions of Ward Edwards*. Dordrecht, The Netherlands: Kluwer Academic Publishers.

Shimony, A. (1955). Coherence and the axioms of confirmation. *Journal of Symbolic Logic*, *20*, 1–28.

Simon, H. A. (1982). *Models of bounded rationality* (Vol. 2). Cambridge, MA: MIT Press.

Skyrms, B. (1987). Dynamic coherence and probability kinematics. *Philosophy of Science*, *54*, 1–20.

Skyrms, B. (1990). *The dynamics of rational deliberation*. Cambridge, MA: Harvard University Press.

Skyrms, B. (1993). Discussion: A mistake in dynamic coherence arguments? *Philosophy of Science*, *60*, 320–328.

Sobel, J. H. (1994). *Taking chances: Essays on rational choice*. Cambridge, UK: Cambridge University Press.

Stigum, B. P., and Wenstøp, F. (Eds.). (1983). *Foundations of utility and risk theory with applications*. Dordrecht, The Netherlands: D. Reidel Publishing.

Teller, P. (1973). Conditionalization and observation. *Synthese*, *26*, 218–258.

Teller, P. (1976). Conditionalization, observation, and change of preference. In W. Harper and C. Hooker (Eds.), *Foundations of probability theory, statistical inference, and statistical theories of science*. Dordrecht, The Netherlands: D. Reidel Publishing, pp. 205–253.

Thrall, R. M., Coombs, C. H., and Davis, R. L. (Eds.). (1954). *Decision processes*. New York: John Wiley.

Tversky, A., and Kahneman, D. (1992). Advances in prospect theory: Cumulative representation of uncertainty. *Journal of Risk and Uncertainty*, *5*, 297–323.

von Neumann, J., and Morgenstern, O. (1947). *Theory of games and economic behavior.* (2nd ed.). Princeton, NJ: Princeton University Press.

von Winterfeldt, D., and Edwards, W. (1986). *Decision analysis and behavioral research.* Cambridge, UK: Cambridge University Press.

Wakker, P. P. (1989). *Additive Representations of Preferences.* Dordrecht, The Netherlands: Kluwer Academic Publishers.

Watson, S. R., and Buede, D. M. (1987). *Decision synthesis: The principles and practice of decision analysis.* Cambridge, UK: Cambridge University Press.

Weirich, P. (2001). *Decision space: Multidimensional utility analysis.* Cambridge, UK: Cambridge University Press.

Zeckhauser, R. J., Keeney, R. L., and Sebenius, J. K. (1996). *Wise choices: Decisions, games, and negotiations.* Boston, MA: Harvard Business School Press.

Zellner, A. (1971). *An introduction to Bayesian inference in econometrics.* New York: John Wiley.

2 The Emergence of Decision Analysis

Ralph F. Miles, Jr.

ABSTRACT. Decision analysis emerged as a discipline separate from decision theory or operations research following World War II. It could not have emerged earlier. It required a stable society with the appropriate philosophy and culture, and a sufficiently rich mathematical language to think logically about decision making. It required the understanding of subjective probability of Ramsey (1926) and de Finetti (1931, 1937), and the appropriate measure of preference under uncertainty of von Neumann and Morgenstern (1947) and later of Savage (1954). It formally came into being with the naming by Howard and his merger of decision theory and systems analysis (1966).

This chapter draws on several historical reviews on the development of probability and utility cited in this chapter and on reviews of the emergence of decision analysis (Edwards 1954, 1961; Raiffa 1968, 2002; Smith and von Winterfeldt 2004; von Winterfeldt and Edwards 1986). This chapter starts with the first intellectual awakenings of the mind of humans. From there it traverses through the origins of mathematics, Greek philosophy, the Renaissance, and on into the twentieth century. It concludes with the significant publications of Howard (1965, 1966, 1968) and Raiffa (1968). This book is only a way point in the progress of decision analysis. Decision analysis can be expected to experience significance advances throughout the twenty-first century and beyond.

From *Homo sapiens* to the Renaissance

The mind of modern humans (*Homo sapiens*) emerged in sub-Saharan Africa between 100,000 and 200,000 B.C.E. At this point humans gained the mental capacity to plan, to think about alternatives, and to have a vision of a future even after death. Their brains were not significantly different from ours today.

To put the potential of this brain to use, a stable social environment was required. This required the presence of a civilization, which occurred between 10,000 and 5,000 B.C.E. More than that, a written language was required, along with mathematics of a form capable of capturing the richness of the analysis of decision making.

The Greeks raised their thoughts from survival and religious activity to thoughts about the nature of the universe, man's place in it, and societal issues.

They were the first to develop schools of intellectual inquiry. They founded the metaphysical studies of ontology (what exists) and epistemology (to what extent we can know it). We associate the names of Socrates (c. 469–399 B.C.E.), Plato (c. 429–347 B.C.E.), and Aristotle (384–322 B.C.E.) with this period. Out of this period came the Socratic method of inquiry and deductive reasoning. Although the Greeks did much to advance philosophy and mathematics, there is no evidence they applied this knowledge to the analysis of games or decision making.

The introduction of universities of learning, first in Spain and then in the rest of Europe between the tenth and twelfth centuries, was a necessary precursor for the dissemination of knowledge of the kind necessary for the analysis of decision making. The invention of the printing press about 1450 by Johann Gutenberg rapidly spread what knowledge existed at that time and provided an efficient medium for dissemination of new knowledge. Also required of the civilization was a philosophy that the fate of the citizens resulted more from their actions than from the dictates of gods. Furthermore, the culture of the civilization had to be relatively free of repression of new and controversial ideas. This could not have occurred until after the time of Galileo (1564–1642) and Copernicus (1473–1543).

The Renaissance

The Renaissance Period in Europe, from the fourteenth century through the early seventeenth century, was an intellectual awaking from the Dark Ages. *Humanism*, the philosophical movement originating during this period, has come to represent a nonreligious worldview based on man's capacity for progress and that man's choices can influence his life and society. The most important development for decision analysis during this period is Bacon's *Novum Organum* (1620) for inductive logic. Bacon's "scientific method" attempted to bring together the rationalist philosophy of an a priori approach to truths about nature and the empiricist philosophy that truths of nature are obtained through experience. Quoting from the *Concise Routledge Encyclopedia of Philosophy* (Routledge 2000), "...*Novum Organum* remained unfinished.... Perhaps his most enduring legacy, however, has been the modern concept of technology – the union of rational theory and empirical practice – and its application to human welfare."

Given that a stable civilization existed with the appropriate philosophy and culture, then intellectual concepts were needed for thinking logically about decision making – mathematics for modeling decision problems, a measure of uncertainty, a suitable measure of preference, and an approach to integrate all this.

Mathematics

The origins of mathematics undoubtedly go back to primitive man, for whom nothing much more was required than the concepts of *1*, *2*, and *many*. All the early systems of displaying numbers were clumsy until the Arabic system of numeration came into general use in Europe by the end of the thirteenth century. By the early sixteenth century, the Arabic system was, for practical purposes, the same as ours.

Mathematics as an organized discipline does not predate that of the Greeks. Thales (c. 640–550 B.C.E.) is credited with introducing deductive reasoning in mathematics. Pythagoras (c. 570–500 B.C.E.) is given credit for developing deductive reasoning in geometry. The Alexandrian School, where Euclid (c. 330–275 B.C.E.) wrote his *Elements*, existed from about 300 B.C.E. to as late as 604 B.C.E. The Arabs contributed little to the development of mathematics, which was largely derived from the Greeks and the Hindus. The Hindus are credited with the further development of arithmetic and algebra, starting with their "high period" as early as 200 B.C.E.

The continuing development of mathematics languished until well into the Middle Ages (fifth to thirteenth centuries C.E.). Arabian mathematics arrived in Europe via the Moors of Spain in the twelfth century. During the thirteenth century there was a revival of learning in Europe. The first notable mathematician of this period was Leonardo Fibonacci, the author of *Liber Abaci* (1202). In *Liber Abaci*, Leonardo introduces Christian Europe to the Arabic system of numeration and also discusses algebra, geometry, and the solution of simple equations.

The required mathematics for decision analysis continued to develop through the Renaissance (fourteenth century into the seventeenth century) and on into the nineteenth century. This would include the works of Descartes, Fermat, Newton, Leibniz, the original eight Bernoullis, Euler, Lagrange, Laplace, Gauss, and others, as discussed in Bell's *Men of Mathematics* (1937). These mathematical achievements would include the development of mathematical notation, advances in arithmetic, algebra, geometry, and trigonometry, the function concept, analysis, and calculus. The history of mathematics is well documented in the books of Ball (1908), Boyer (1968), Cooke (1997), and Kline (1972).

Early Analysis of Games

Records of games played date back to 4,000 B.C.E. (David 1962). It can be assumed that many players developed a high level of skill, yet undoubtedly it came from experience and intuition and not from an analysis of the games. Even as late as 1,600 C.E., David reports that "gamblers could detect a difference in probabilities of about 1/100 without being able to demonstrate the reason for it." Luce Pacioli is remembered for his *Summa de arithmetica, geometria, proportioni e proportionalità* published in 1494. In *Summa*, Paciolo discusses the fair game of *balla*, the first record of the "Problem of Points" to be discussed in the next section, although he did not get the right answer. Cardano is credited as the first to formulate probability in gambling in *Liber de Ludo Aleae* (1664). The big advance that Cardano made was to use combinatorics to enumerate all the elementary events of a game. Cardano was an inveterate gambler. While a student, after squandering his inherited money, he turned to card games, dice, and chess for an income. His knowledge of probability came primarily from intuition and experience. He understood the "classical" concept of probability, based on symmetry and equiprobable events. He would have known that there were thirty-six ways that two dice could land, and that the probability of rolling a 7 was 6/36, and not 1/11. The next advance in the use of probability in gambling was to await the correspondence between Pascal and Fermat.

Probability and Statistics

Until the 1660s, "probability" meant "worthy of approbation" (Hacking 1975). Soon thereafter, probability took on its modern meaning as a measure of uncertainty (Arnauld and Nicole 1662).

Probability was first presented in mathematical form in the 1654 correspondence between Blaise Pascal and Pierre Fermat, although axiomatization did not happen until three centuries later in Kolmogorov's *Foundations of Probability* (1933). Pascal's and Fermat's correspondence concerned the "Problem of Points," the fair division of stakes in an interrupted game presented to Pascal by a gambler, Chevalier de Méré. David and Edwards (2001) give credit to Pascal for introducing the concept of expectation in the correspondence. See Daston (1988), David (1962), and Hacking (1975) for further discussions of this game and the Pascal–Fermat correspondence.

Huygens' *De Ratiociniis in Aleae Ludo* (1657) is the first published probability textbook and was for nearly half a century the only introduction to the theory of probability. Huygens' work was not superseded until the turn of the eighteenth century. At that time there was an outpouring of work in probability, culminating in Montmort's *Essai d'analyse sur les Jeux de Hasard* (1713), Jakob (James) Bernoulli's *Ars Conjectandi* (1713), and de Moivre's *Doctrine of Chances* (1718). Arbuthnot (1710) is given credit for the first formal test of significance.

In the nineteenth century, Laplace published *Essai philosophique sur les probabilities* (1814). John Venn published *The Logic of Chance* (1866).

Hacking (1987) argues that the nineteenth century and the early twentieth century did not see a probabilistic revolution in the Kuhnian (1996) sense. Nevertheless, there were significant changes in philosophical thought involving metaphysics, epistemology, and pragmatics. In metaphysics, nature was no longer under the control of rigid mechanical laws, but instead was dominated by quantum indeterminacy. In epistemology, learning and the foundations of knowledge could be expressed by probabilistic models. In pragmatics, probability would play an important role in determining the benefits and risks of endeavors. Hacking lists the works of Fourier, Quetelet, and Galton as being significant in this period. See Krüger, Daston, and Heidelberger (1987). Although there may not have been a Kuhnian revolution, significant advances were made in psychology, sociology, economics, physiology, evolutionary biology, and physics (Krüger, Gigerenzer, and Morgan 1987). To pick just one of these disciplines, quoting Krüger (1987), " . . . we may distinguish three thresholds in the development of probabilistic ideas in physics: (1) The discovery of the law of errors at the end of the eighteenth century, (2) the emergence of classical statistical mechanics around 1870, and (3) the establishment of quantum mechanics around 1926."

Between 1883 and 1918, much of modern mathematical statistics was developed, including the correlation coefficient, contingency analysis, the chi-squared test, the t-test, and analysis of variance. For this period, see Porter's *The Rise of Statistical Thinking 1820–1900* (1986).

Pearson and Neyman transformed Fisher's statistical inference into confidence intervals during the first half of the twentieth century. The merger of their work became known as "classical" statistics. It must be emphasized that although many of the analysis techniques of "classical" statistics (the Fisher, Neyman, and Pearson school of the twentieth century) are similar to those of decision analysis, the philosophy is fundamentally different. Quoting Gigerenzer et al. (1989), "Fisher's theory of significance testing, which was historically first, was merged with concepts from the Neyman–Pearson theory and taught as 'statistics' per se. We call this compromise the 'hybrid theory' of statistical inference, and it goes without saying that neither Fisher nor Neyman and Pearson would have looked with favor on this offspring of their forced marriage." The intensity of the difference between classical statisticians and decision analysts is perhaps best stated by Raiffa and Schlaifer in *Applied Statistical Decision Theory* (1961): "We believe, however, that without this [decision analysis] formalization decisions under uncertainty have been and will remain essentially arbitrary, as evidenced by the fact that, in most statistical practice, consequences and performance characteristics receive mere lip service while decisions are actually made by treating the numbers .05 and .95 with the same superstitious awe that is usually reserved for the number 13." The history of the development of probability and statistics up to World War II is recorded in many other books (Gigerenzer et al. 1989; Hacking 1990; Hald, 1990, 1998; Stigler 1986, 1999; Todhunter 1865). See also Jaynes (2003) for a mixture of history and theory. David, in an appendix to David and Edwards (2001), lists the first known occurrences of common terms in probability and statistics. By World War II, nearly all the probability and statistics required for decision analysis had been developed.

Inverse Probability

Bayes' theorem allows one to invert a conditional probability: given $p(E \mid A)$, we can calculate $p(A \mid E)$, provided we also have $p(A)$ and $p(E)$. Bayes' theorem is especially useful when E is some event and A is a particular hypothesis. In this case, $p(E \mid A)$ is called a "likelihood." Thus, given a likelihood and the prior probabilities of the event and the hypothesis, the theorem allows us to calculate the conditional probability of the hypothesis, given the probability of that event.

Credit for the first writer to do this is given to Thomas Bayes (1763). Bayes' theorem has played an important role in probability theory, statistics, decision theory, and philosophy. Whether to call Bayes' mathematical result for inverse probability a theorem or a formula is open to discussion as it follows directly from the definition of conditional probability. As discussed and terms defined in Chapter 1 in this volume, Bayes' theorem is typically written as:

$$p(A_i \mid E_j) = \frac{p(E_j \mid A_i)p(A_i)}{\sum_{i=1}^{m} p(E_j \mid A_i)p(A_i)}.$$

In decision theory, Bayes' theorem provides the mathematics to update probabilities based on new information. Bayesian statistics requires all probabilities to be subjective; all statistical reasoning is based on this supposition, and much statistical inference is decision oriented (Berger 1985; Bernardo and Smith, 1994; Berry 1996; Box and Tiao 1973; Gelman et al. 1995; Gill 2002; Jensen 2001; Lindley 1969, 1970, 1972; O'Hagen 1994; Press 1989; Robert 2001; West and Harrison 1989; Winkler 2003; Zellner, 1971). For an extended discussion of inverse probability and Bayes' theorem, see Dale (1999).

Interpretations of Probability

Kolmogorov's axioms (1933) are accepted by most probabilists as the appropriate axioms for probability. Nevertheless, it is quite another issue to decide on an interpretation of those axioms. Among others, the most frequently cited interpretations of probability are the "classical," the "frequentist," the "logical," and the "subjective."

The classical interpretation, credited to Laplace (1814), is based on the absence of any information. Quoting Laplace, "The theory of chance consists in reducing all the events of the same kind to a certain number of cases equally possible, that is to say, to such as we may be equally undecided about in regard to their existence, and in determining the number of cases favorable to the event whose probability is sought. The ratio of this number to that of all the cases possible is the measure of this probability.... "

The *frequentist interpretation* considers the probability of an event to be the ratio of favorable outcomes of trials to total number of trials that are observed and is credited to Venn (1866). Quoting von Mises (1957) for the frequentist interpretation, "We state here explicitly: The rational concept of probability, which is the only basis of probability calculus, applies only to problems in which either the same event repeats itself again and again, or a great number of uniform elements are involved at the same time."

The *logical interpretation* considers probabilities to be nothing more than the logical relation between propositions and has been presented by Keynes (1921), Carnap (1950), and others.

The *subjective interpretation* of probability, the interpretation accepted by all Bayesian scholars, holds that probabilities are states of mind and not states of objects. The subjective interpretation is an integral part of decision analysis and is the subject of the following section. The subjective interpretation runs counter to the very concept of probability in classical and frequentist statistics that has, for more than a century, attempted to purge statistics of all subjective components.

See Fine (1973) and Weatherford (1982) for extended discussions on interpretations of probability.

Subjective Probability

In the 1660s and following, it was recognized that there could be a subjective interpretation of probability. Jakob (James) Bernoulli presented a subjective interpretation in *Ars Conjectandi* (1713) by suggesting that probability could be interpreted as a degree of belief. Quoting Bernoulli, "All other things have a less perfect measure of certainty in our minds, greater or smaller according as the probabilities ... are greater or smaller. For probability is a degree of certainty. ... " Scholars debate whether Poisson (1837) meant "subjective probability" when he used "chance" for one interpretation and "probabilité" for something close to subjective probability.

The subjective interpretation of probability rose to prominence in the twentieth century through the works of de Finetti (1931, 1937, 1970, 1972), Jeffreys (1961), Ramsey (1926), and Savage (1954). Quoting Ramsey as the first to bring subjective probability into prominence, "The subject of our inquiry is the logic of partial belief, and I do not think we can carry it far unless we have at least an approximate notion of what partial belief is, and how, if at all, it can be measured. ... We must therefore try to develop a purely psychological method of measuring belief." Ramsey then describes the sort of bet that would meet his measurement criteria. Quoting de Finetti, "The only relevant thing is uncertainty – the extent of our own knowledge and ignorance. The actual fact of whether or not the events considered are in some sense *determined*, or known by other people, and so on, is of no consequence." Quoting Savage, "Personalistic views hold that probability measures the confidence that a particular individual has in the truth of a particular proposition, for example, the proposition that it will rain tomorrow." See Fishburn (1986) for an axiomatic development of subjective probability, with comments by others. See Bernardo and Smith (1994), Fellner (1965), Good (1983, 1987), Wright and Ayton (1994), and references therein for further discussions.

Preference and Risk Aversion

In 1713 Nicolas Bernoulli proposed a gamble named "The Saint Petersburg Paradox." The *Saint Petersburg Paradox* shows that if the utility of a monetary gamble can be measured by the expected value of the gamble, then a gamble can be constructed such that the utility of the game is infinite. Any amount of money would be paid to play this game. Twenty-five years later, Daniel Bernoulli (1738) resolved the paradox by claiming that the utility of money decreases with increasing amount, thus introducing the mathematical concept of risk aversion. He assumed that the utility of money increases with the logarithm of the amount. There is no particular reason that the utility of money should increase with the logarithm. The important fact is that the utility must be bounded, else other similar games can be constructed that will have infinite value (Menger 1934).

See Jeffrey (1983), Weirich (1984), and Jorland (1987) for discussions on this subject.

Operations Research

Operations Research as a discipline arose during World War II in response to a requirement for analyses of military operations. Philip Morse and George Kimball were members of the Operations Research Group of the U. S. Navy. During and immediately after World War II, many of the analyses were documented. When the documents were declassified, Morse and Kimball (1951) added some organizing and explanatory material and published *Methods of Operations Research*, the first book on the subject. They defined "Operations Research" as "a scientific method of providing executive departments with a quantitative basis for decisions regarding the operations under their control."

Operation Research teams employed mathematics, probability theory, statistics, and systems modeling in the study of many military operations. It was recognized that the analyst did not have to be an expert in all the disciplines involved, but he did have to understand how to conduct scientific research. The first step in an analysis was to understand the true nature of the problem. A proper measure of effectiveness was crucial to the value of an analysis. For example, an analysis showed that while antiaircraft guns on merchant ships were not successful at shooting down enemy aircraft – a reason not to employ them – they did decrease the accuracy of the enemy aircraft sufficiently to make their employment cost effective. Procedures were developed to collect and analyze large amounts of data for use in the analyses. It was recognized that the enemy would change tactics in response to improvements in operations.

Some of the analyses were undertaken to determine:

- The optimal distance under the sea for antisubmarine depth charges to explode. This involved probability studies using both knowledge of the properties of depth charges and the likely depth of the submarines.
- The optimal size of convoys transporting troops and material from the United States to England. This involved studies that showed that, with larger convoys, a fewer percentage of ships would be sunk by submarines. The increased size of the convoy had to be traded off against restrictions on the size of a convoy that could be assembled.
- The optimal search patterns for aircraft to locate enemy submarines. Probability entered into the "sweep rate" as a measure of effectiveness of the search. The quantities that appeared in the sweep rate formula were numbers of contacts, the size of the area search, the total search time, and the probable number of enemy submarines in the area.
- Optimal exchange rates between enemy and American aircraft. The exchange rate was defined as the ratio of enemy aircraft destroyed compared with American in air-to-air combat. Results of the analyses confirmed that increased training resulted in higher exchange rates. The exchange rate of 10:1

between Japanese planes shot down and American planes could be explained partially on the greater experience of the American pilots. What was also revealed in the analyses was that "sometimes it is worthwhile even to withdraw aircraft from operations for a short time in order to give the pilots increased training."
- The optimal use and maintenance of aircraft bomb sights. Statistical surveys were done of the effectiveness of bombing missions. The analyses involved considerations of equipment performance, crew training, and maintenance.

Since that time, the analytical tools and organizational applications have greatly expanded, and departments have been formed in universities. But were these World War II activities decision analyses in the modern sense of the discipline? Here the answer has to be "no." Although probability played an important role in the analyses, the numbers were interpreted as "objective" probabilities. Expert opinion was found to be of only limited usefulness owing to psychological biases, and data from experience and experiments dominated the analyses. There is no record of the use of Bayes' theorem to update probabilities based on new data. Measures of effectiveness did not use utility theory, and there is no evidence that risk aversion was considered. The major contribution to decision analysis may have been the validation of analytical models for optimizing the performance of systems.

Decision Theory

Pascal's *Pensées* (1670), containing his famous "Wager," was never completed, and what exists today is a set of notes. Hacking (1975) describes Pascal's Wager as "...the first well-understood contribution to decision theory." Hájek (2004) states that the Wager is an exercise in "...decision theory, used for almost the first time in history..." Pascal is skeptical that reasoning alone can settle whether or not God exists. But he believes that choosing to believe or not to believe in God is a *decision problem*, and that rationality dictates the former. There are at least three arguments in the Wager (see Hájek), but the one relevant to decision analysis can be read as an exercise in decision theory: You either believe in God or you don't, and you either have an infinity of an infinitely happy life (if God exists and you believe) or you have your earthly life and die (otherwise). So the expectation of believing in God, which is infinite, exceeds the expectation of not believing, which is finite. In the Wager there is no quantification of probability and there is no gradation of preference.

Decision theory continued to develop through economics in the eighteenth century. Bentham, in his *Principles of Morals and Legislation* (1789), first suggested that utility in terms of pleasure and pain could be measured. He assumed the measurement to be made on what today would be a called a cardinal scale (numerical scale unique up to a linear (affine) transformation), so that he could make interpersonal comparisons and use arithmetic to aggregate individual utilities into a social utility – the greatest good for the greatest number of individuals. Initially utility in economics was measured on this cardinal scale. Nevertheless, through the works of writers such as Edgeworth (1881) through Hicks and Allen (1934), economics was purged of all requirements for cardinal scales. They showed that the riskless economic theories of indifference curves required only ordinal utilities (numerical scales unique up to positive montonic transformations). Stigler (1950) gives a history of utility theory from 1776 until 1915. See Fishburn (1982) for a unified treatment of his research in the foundations of expected utility theory from 1965 to 1980.

In 1944, von Neumann and Morgenstern published their first edition of *The Theory of Games and Economic Behavior.* In their second edition (1947), they included an appendix that gave an "axiomatic treatment of utility," and with that cardinal utility reappeared to treat decision making under uncertainty. This was followed by Marschak's similar formulation of decision theory in "Rational behavior, uncertain prospects, and measurable utility" (1950), Wald's *Statistical Decision Functions* (1950), Chernoff and Moses' *Elementary Decision Theory* (1959), Raiffa and Schlaifer's *Applied Statistical Decision Theory* (1961), and Pratt, Raiffa, and Schlaifer's "The foundations of decision under uncertainty: An elementary exposition" (1964).

Now that decision theories could treat uncertainty, the modern form of game theory emerged, with publications by Nash (1950, 1951) and others. Luce and Raiffa published *Games and Decisions* (1957). In addition to the classical publications (Kuhn 1997), game theory has been applied to economics (Bierman and Fernandez 1998; Gibbons 1992), analysis of conflict (Myerson 1991; Schelling 1960), bargaining and negotiation (Brams 1990), dispute resolution (Brams and Taylor 1996), political theory (Ordeshook 1986), the social contract (Binmore 1994), and business decisions (McMillan 1992). Camerer (2003) uses experiments in psychology and neuroscience and the resulting models to explain "behavioral economics."

In philosophy, decision theory plays an important role in epistemology and scientific reasoning (Bacharach and Hurley 1991; Earman 1992; Hartigan 1983; Howson and Urbach 1993; Kaplan 1996).

Psychology of Decision Making

The groundwork was in place following World War II for psychologists to ask (1) to what extent did decision making in the real world actually correspond to the axioms of decision theory and (2) how could both decision theory and decision making be improved? The first conference was held by the RAND Corporation of Santa Monica, California, in the summer of 1952. Papers from this conference were subsequently published in *Decision Processes*, edited by Thrall, Coombs, and Davis (1954). The conference was attended by mathematicians, statisticians, psychologists, economists, and philosophers interested in decision making. The preface of the book starts with "The past few years have seen a rapid development in the mathematical formulation and testing of behavioral science theory." The purpose of the conference was to bring together the many diverse approaches to the analysis of decision making.

Edwards (1954) published "The theory of decision making." That same year, Savage (1954) published *The Foundations of Statistics*, in which he simultaneously axiomatized both probability and utility, and placed the combination of subjective probability and utility theory on a firm axiomatic basis. Three years later, Luce and Raiffa (1957) published *Games and Decisions*, initially based on a series of seminars undertaken at Columbia University as part of its Behavioral Models Project.

Edwards (1961) was the first to use the words "Behavioral Decision Theory" in print as the title of his paper. Edwards (1954, 1961) has surveyed the state of the art up to 1954 in his "The theory of decision making" paper and extended the survey up to 1960 in his 1961 paper. Edwards, Lindman, and Savage (1963) published "Bayesian statistical inference" to "introduce psychologists to the Bayesian outlook in statistics." Four years later, Edwards and Tversky (1967) published *Decision Making*, an edited volume of significant papers addressing "... the key questions of decision theory." By this time the division between normative, descriptive, and prescriptive decision theories, as discussed in Chapter 1, was well recognized. Out of this post-World War II work, subjective utility theory has emerged as the normative standard for decision making. This emergence has been reviewed by von Winterfeldt and Edwards (1986) in *Decision Analysis and Behavioral Research*.

Modifications to the normative theory are made in prescriptive theories to accommodate the intellectual and resource limitations of decision makers, such as can be found in Savage's "small worlds" concept (1954) and the literature on Simon's "bounded rationality" (Gigerenzer and Selten 2001; Mele and Rawling 2004; Rubinstein 1998; Simon 1956, 1982). For the current state of behavioral decision making, see Connolly, Arkes, and Hammond (2000), Goldstein and Hogarth (1997), Schneider and Shanteau (2003), and Shanteau, Mellers, and Schum (1999).

Descriptive decision theories were developed in parallel to this effort in normative and prescriptive decision theories, based on the observations and experimental evidence that decision makers, by and large, were not normative or prescriptive decision makers. This led to the heuristics and biases work of Tversky and Kahneman (1974), the "prospect theory" of Kahneman and Tversky (1979), and the work of others as surveyed in Kahneman, Slovic, and Tversky (1982), Kahneman and Tversky (2000), and Gilovich, Griffin, and Kahneman (2002). The application of this work to decision analysis appears in Chapter 14 in this volume.

Foundations of Measurement

"Measurement," in the sense discussed here, consists of establishing a correspondence between empirical objects and a mathematical structure. Euler's *Elements* (c. 300 B.C.E.) represents the first attempt to axiomatize mathematics. His interest was in the empirical objects of geometry – points, lines, and planes. Examples of measurement abound, from length (both nonrelativistically and relativistically) to color perception.

In the physical sciences and engineering, measurement is, by and large, so intuitive and based on tradition that the subject is relegated to philosophy. Not so for the social sciences, where the satisfactory resolution of measurement can determine the very existence of a particular empirical relation. Following World War II, the discipline of the foundations of measurement emerged through research appearing in a large number of publications scattered throughout the literature. This was brought together in *Foundations of Measurement*, the all-encompassing three-volume collection by Krantz, Luce, Suppes, and Tversky published in 1971 (*Vol. I: Additive and Polynomial Representations*), Suppes, Krantz, Luce, and Tversky published in 1989 (*Vol. II: Geometrical, Threshold, and Probabilistic Representations*), and Luce, Krantz, Suppes, and Tversky published in 1990 (*Vol. III: Representation, Axiomatization, and Invariance*).

Quoting Krantz, Luce, Suppes, and Tversky (1971):

> We conclude, then, that an analysis into the foundations of measurement involves, for any particular empirical relational structure, the formulation of a set of axioms that is sufficient to establish two types of theorems: a representation theorem, which asserts the existence of a homomorphism ϕ into a particular numerical relational structure, and a uniqueness theorem, which sets forth the perissible transformations $\phi \rightarrow \phi'$ that also yield homomorphisms into the same numerical relational structure. A measurement procedure corresponds to the construction of a ϕ in the representation theorem.

The interest in foundations of measurement for decision analysis lies primarily in the measurements of uncertainty, preference, and their conjunction. It made its initial appearance in Ramsey's work (1926) to measure subjective probability through preference relationships. It was followed by the work of von Neumann and Morgenstern (1947) and Savage (1954) and others for utility – the conjoint measurement of uncertainty and preference. It also appears in the conjoint measurement theories for multiple attributes of Krantz (1964) and Luce and Tukey (1964).

The incomplete – or at least debatable – parts of the foundations of measurement for decision analysis lie in prescriptive decision theory, descriptive decision theory, and social choice theory. This cuts such a wide sweep through decision analysis that theoreticians can be assured of serious research for generations.

Decision Analysis

This chapter concludes with the arrival of decision analysis, a discipline distinct from decision theory in that it focuses on the application of decision theory to real-world, complex problems. By the early 1960s, the stage was set for decision analysis to arrive in its present form. Mathematics existed in a sufficiently developed form for the modeling and analysis of complex systems in the presence of uncertainty, Operations Research of World War II validated the usefulness of that modeling, and utility theory existed to encode preferences in the presence of risk. Then von Neumann and Morgenstern (1947), followed by two articles by Friedman and Savage (1948, 1952), made cardinal utility analytically respectable, at least for "objectively known" probabilities. As discussed in an earlier section, Savage extended this work to incorporate subjective probabilities.

Quoting French (1989) on the development of decision analysis out of decision theory, "When it was first developed, Bayesian decision theory provided such an idealized, simplified view of decision making that it was difficult to believe that the theory had anything to offer practice in the complex, ill defined world of real decision making. Gradually it has become apparent that it has."

Schlaifer published *Probability and Statistics for Business Decisions* (1959), which might be called the first book on decision analysis. Nevertheless, a decade later by Schlaifer's own words in his *Analysis of Decisions Under Uncertainty* (1969), it was not decision analysis in the modern sense: "Whereas the earlier book was primarily concerned with decision problems in which the stakes were so small that each problem could be considered in isolation and solved by maximization of expected monetary value, the present book is primarily concerned with large-scale problems in which risk aversion must be taken into account.... "

Raiffa wrote the first book titled *Decision Analysis* (1968). It contained decision trees, a method for eliciting utilities, and a chapter on "judgmental probabilities." Nevertheless, it did not explore the decision analysis of complex problems of the scale that Howard first considered in "Bayesian decision models for system engineering" (1965) and "Decision analysis: Applied decision theory" (1966). Howard (1968) published "The foundations of decision analysis."

REFERENCES

Arbuthnot, J. (1710). An argument for divine providence, taken from the constant regularity observ'd in the births of both sexes. *Philosophical Transactions of the Royal Society of London*, 27, 186–190. Reprinted in 1977 in M. G. Kendall and R. L. Plackett, *Studies in the History of Statistics and Probability* (Vol. 2). London: Griffin, pp. 30–34.

Arnauld, A., and Nicole, P. (1662). *La logique ou l'art de penser,* aka *Port-Royal logic.* Translated in 1964 by J. Dickoff and P. James. Indianapolis, IN: Bobbs-Merrill.

Bacharach, M., and Hurley, S. (1991). *Foundations of decision theory.* Cambridge, MA: Blackwell Publishers.

Bacon, F. (1620). *Novum organum.* English translation in 1863 in J. Spedding, R. L. Ellis, and D. D. Heath, *The works* (Vol. VIII). Boston: Taggard and Thompson. Translated and edited in 1994 by P. Urbach and J. Gibon, *Francis Bacon, Novum Organum, with other parts of the great instauration.* La Salle, IL: Open Court.

Ball, W. W. R. (1908). *A short account of the history of mathematics.* (4th ed.). New York: Dover Publications. An unabridged and unaltered republication of the 1908 (last) edition.

Bayes, T. (1763). An essay towards solving a problem in the doctrine of chances. *Philosophical Transactions of the Royal Society of London*, 53, 370–418. Reprinted in 1958 with biographical note by G. A. Barnard in *Biometrika*, 45, 293–315.

Bell, E. T. (1937). *Men of mathematics.* New York: Simon & Schuster.

Bentham, J. (1789). *An introduction to the principles of morals and legislation.* Reprinted in 1968 with notes in A. N. Page (ed.), *Utility theory: A book of readings.* New York: John Wiley, pp. 3–29.

Berger, J. O. (1985). *Statistical decision theory and Bayesian analysis.* (2nd ed.). New York: Springer-Verlag.

Bernardo, J. M., and Smith, A. F. M. (1994). *Bayesian theory*. New York: John Wiley.

Bernoulli, D. (1738). Specimen theoriae novae di mensura sortis. *Commentarii academiae scientiarum imperialis petropolitanea, 5*, 175–192. Translated in 1954 by L. Sommer, Exposition of a new theory on the measurement of risk. *Econometrica, 22*, 23–36.

Bernoulli, J. (1713). *Ars conjectandi*. Thurnisius, Basilea. Reprinted in 1975 in *Die Werke von Jakob Bernoulli* (vol. 3). Basel: Birkhäuser.

Berry, D. A. (1996). *Statistics: A Bayesian perspective*. Belmont, CA: Duxbury Press.

Bierman, H. S., and Fernandez, L. (1998). *Game theory with economic applications*. (2nd ed.). Reading, MA: Addison-Wesley.

Binmore, K. (1994). *Playing fair: Game theory and the social contract* (Vol. 1). Cambridge, MA: MIT Press.

Box, G. E. P., and Tiao, G. C. (1973). *Bayesian inference in statistical analysis*. Reading, MA: Addison-Wesley.

Boyer, C. B. (1968). *A history of mathematics*. Princeton, NJ: Princeton University Press.

Brams, S. J. (1990). *Negotiation games: Applying game theory to bargaining and negotiation*. New York: Routledge, Chapman & Hall.

Brams, S. J., and Taylor, A. D. (1996). *Fair Division: From cake-cutting to dispute resolution*. Cambridge, UK: Cambridge University Press.

Camerer, C. F. (2003). *Behavioral game theory: Experiments in strategic interaction*. Princeton, NJ: Princeton University Press.

Cardano, G. (1664). *Liber de ludo aleae*. English translation in 1953 in O. Ore, *Cardano, the gambling scholar*. Princeton, NJ: Princeton University Press.

Carnap, R. (1950). *Logical foundations of probability*. London: Routledge & Kegan Paul.

Chernoff, H., and Moses, L. E. (1959). *Elementary decision theory*. New York: John Wiley. Reprinted in 1986 by Dover Publications, NY.

Connolly, T., Arkes, H. R., and Hammond, K. R. (Eds.). (2000). *Judgment and decision making: An interdisciplinary reader*. (2nd ed.). Cambridge, UK: Cambridge University Press.

Cooke, R. (1997). *The history of mathematics: A brief course*. New York: John Wiley.

Dale, A. I. (1999). *A history of inverse probability: From T. Bayes to K. Pearson*. (2nd ed.). New York: Springer-Verlag.

Daston, L. (1988). *Classical probability in the enlightenment*. Princeton, NJ: Princeton University Press.

David, F. N. (1962). *Games, gods and gambling: A history of probability and statistical ideas*. London: Charles Griffin. Reprinted in 1998 by Dover Publications, Mineola, NY.

David, H. A., and Edwards, A. W. F. (2001). *Annotated readings in the history of statistics*. New York: Springer-Verlag.

de Finetti, B. (1931). Sul Significato Soggettivo della Probabilità. *Fundamenta Mathematicae, 17*, 298–329. Translated in 1993 in P. Monari and D. Cocchi (Eds.), On the Subjective Meaning of Probability. *Probabilità e Induxione*. Bologna: Clueb, pp. 291–321.

de Finetti, B. (1937). La prévision: Ses lois logiques, ses sources subjectives. *Annales de l'Institut Henri Poincaré, 7*, 1–68. Translated in 1980 by H. E. Kyburg, Jr., Foresight. Its logical laws, its subjective sources. In H. E. Kyburg, Jr. and H. E. Smokler (Eds.), *Studies in Subjective Probability*. (2nd ed.). Huntington, NY: Robert E. Krieger, pp. 53–118.

de Finetti, B. (1970). *Teoria delle probaililtà* (Vol. I and II). Torino, Italy: Giulio Enaudi. Translated in 1974 and 1975 by A. Machi and A. Smith, *Theory of probability: A critical introductory treatment*. New York: John Wiley.

de Finetti, B. (1972). *Probability, inductions and statistics: The art of guessing*. New York: John Wiley.

de Moivre, A. (1718). *Doctrine of chances: Or a method of calculating the probability of events in play*. London: W. Pearson. Facsimile reprint in 1967 of the 3rd ed. (1767). New York: Chelsea Publishing.

Earman, J. (1992). *Bayes or bust? A critical examination of confirmation theory*. Cambridge, MA: MIT Press.

Edgeworth, F. Y. (1881). *Mathematical psychics: An essay on the application of mathematics to the moral sciences*. London: Kegan Paul.

Edwards, W. (1954). The theory of decision making. *Psychological Bulletin, 51*, 380–417.

Edwards, W. (1961). Behavioral decision theory. *Annual Review of Psychology, 12*, 473–498.

Edwards, W., Lindman, H., and Savage, L. J. (1963). Bayesian statistical inference for psychological research. *Psychological Research, 70*, 193–242.

Edwards, W., and Tversky, A. (Eds.). (1967). *Decision making*. Middlesex, UK: Penguin Books.

Fellner, W. (1965). *Probability and profit: A study of economic behavior along Bayesian lines*. Homewood, IL: Richard D. Irwin.

Fibonacci, L. (1202). *Liber abaci*. Translated in 2002 by L. E. Sigler in *Leonardo Pisano's book of calculation*. New York: Springer.

Fine, T. L. (1973). *Theories of probability: An examination of foundations*. New York: Academic Press.

Fishburn, P. C. (1982). *The foundations of expected utility*. Dordrecht, The Netherlands: D. Reidel.

Fishburn, P. C. (1986). The axioms of subjective probability. *Statistical Science, 1*, 335–358.

French, S. (1989). From decision theory to decision analysis. In S. French, *Readings in decision analysis*. Boca Raton, FL: Chapman & Hall, pp. 158–174.

Friedman, M., and Savage, L. J. (1948). Utility analysis of choices involving risk. *Journal of Political Economy, 56*, 179–304.

Friedman, M., and Savage, L. J. (1952). The expected utility hypothesis and the measurability of utility. *Journal of Political Economy, 60*, 463–475.

Gelman, A., Carlin, J. B., Stern, H. S., and Rubin, D. B. (1995). *Bayesian data analysis*. London: Chapman & Hall.

Gibbons, R. (1992). *Game Theory for Applied Economists*. Princeton, NJ: Princeton University Press.

Gigerenzer, G., and Selten, R. (Eds.). 2001. *Bounded rationality: The adaptive toolkit*. Cambridge, MA: MIT Press.

Gigerenzer, G., Swijtink, Z., Porter, T., Daston, L., Beatty, J., and Krüger, L. (1989). *The empire of chance: How probability changed science and everyday life*. Cambridge, UK: Cambridge University Press.

Gill, J. (2002). *Bayesian methods: A social and behavioral sciences approach*. Boca Raton, FL: Chapman & Hall.

Gilovich, T., Griffin, D., and Kahneman, D. (Eds.). (2002). *Heuristics and biases: The psychology of intuitive judgment*. Cambridge, UK: Cambridge University Press.

Goldstein, W. M., and Hogarth, R. M. (Eds.). (1997). *Research on judgment and decision making: Currents, connections, and controversies*. Cambridge, UK: Cambridge University Press.

Good, I. J. (1983). *Good thinking: The foundations of probability and its applications*. Minneapolis, MN: University of Minnesota Press.

Good, I. J. (1987). Subjective Probability. In J. Eatwell, M. Milgate, and P. Newman (Eds.), *Utility and probability*. New York: W. W. Norton, pp. 255–269.

Hacking, I. (1975). *The emergence of probability: A philosophical study of early ideas about probability, induction, and statistical inference*. London: Cambridge University Press.

Hacking, I. (1987). Was there a probabilistic revolution 1880–1930? In L. Kruger, L. J. Daston, and M. Heidelberger. (Eds.), *The probabilistic revolution: I: Ideas in history*. Cambridge, MA: MIT Press, pp. 45–55.

Hacking, I. (1990). *The taming of chance*. Cambridge, UK: Cambridge University Press.

Hájek, A. (2004). Pascal's Wager. In E. N. Zalta (Ed.), *The Stanford encyclopedia of philosophy*. Retrieved on May 31, 2005 from http://plato.stanford.edu/archives/spr2004/entries/pascal-wager.

Hald, A. (1990). *A history of probability and statistics and their applications before 1750*. New York: John Wiley.

Hald, A. (1998). *A history of mathematical statistics from 1750 to 1930*. New York: John Wiley.

Hartigan, J. A. (1983). *Bayes theory*. New York: Springer-Verlag.

Hicks, J. R., and Allen, R. G. D. (1934). A reconsideration of the theory of value. *Economica*, *14*, 52–76, 197–219.

Howard, R. A. (1965). Bayesian decision models for system engineering. *IEEE Transactions on Systems Science and Cybernetics*, *SSC-1*, 36–40.

Howard, R. A. (1966). Decision analysis: Applied decision theory. In *Proceedings of the Fourth International Conference on Operational Research*. New York: John Wiley, pp. 55–71.

Howard, R. A. (1968). The foundations of decision analysis. *IEEE Transactions on Systems Science and Cybernetics*, *SSC-4*, 211–219.

Howson, C., and Urbach, P. (1993). *Scientific reasoning: The Bayesian approach*. (2nd ed.). Chicago, IL: Open Court.

Hugyens, C. (1657). De ratiociniis in aleae ludo. In *Oeuvres complètes de Christiaan Huygens* (Vol. 14). The Hague: Nijhoff, pp. 49–179.

Jaynes, E. T. (2003). *Probability theory: The logic of science*. Cambridge, UK: Cambridge University Press. Edited by G. Larry Bretthorst.

Jeffrey, R. C. (1983). *The logic of decision*. (2nd ed.). Chicago, IL: University of Chicago Press.

Jeffreys, H. (1961). *Theory of probability*. (3rd ed.). New York: Oxford University Press. Reprinted in 1998 in the Oxford Classics series with corrections and amplifications through 1966.

Jensen, F. V. (2001). *Bayesian networks and decision graphs*. New York: Springer-Verlag.

Jorland, G. (1987). The Saint Petersburg paradox. In L. L. Krüger, J. Daston, and M. Heidelberger (Eds.), *The probabilistic revolution, Vol. 1: Ideas in history*. Cambridge, MA: MIT Press, pp. 157–190.

Kahneman, D., and Tversky, A. (Eds.). (2000). *Choices, values, and frames*. Cambridge, UK: Cambridge University Press.

Kahneman, D., and Tversky, A. (1979). Prospect theory: An analysis of decision under risk. *Econometrica*, *47*(2), 263–291.

Kahneman, D., Slovic, P., and Tversky, A. (Eds.). (1982). *Judgment under uncertainty: Heuristics and biases*. Cambridge, UK: Cambridge University Press.

Kaplan, M. (1996). *Decision theory as philosophy*. Cambridge, UK: Cambridge University Press.

Keynes, J. M. (1921). *A treatise on probability*. London: Macmillan. Reprinted in 2004 by Dover Publications, Mineola, NY.

Kline, M. (1972). *Mathematical thought from ancient to modern times*. New York: Oxford University Press.

Kolmogorov, A. N. (1933). *Foundations of the theory of probability*. Second edition translated in 1956 by N. Morrison and published by Chelsea Publishing, NY.

Krantz, D. H. (1964). Conjoint measurement: The Luce–Tukey axiomatization and some extensions. *Journal of Mathematical Psychology*, *1*, 248–277.

Krantz, D. M., Luce, R. D., Suppes, P., and Tversky, A. (1971). *Foundations of Measurement (Vol. I: Additive and Polynomial Representations)*. New York: Academic Press, p. 12.

Krüger, L. (1987). The probabilistic revolution in physics – an overview. In Krüger, L., Gigerenzer, G., and Morgan, M. S. (Eds.). *The Probabilistic Revolution, Vol. 2: Ideas in the Sciences*. Cambridge, MA: MIT Press, pp. 373–378.

Krüger, L., Daston, J., and Heidelberger, M. (Eds.). (1987). *The Probabilistic Revolution, Vol. 1: Ideas in history.* Cambridge, MA: MIT Press.

Krüger, L., Gigerenzer, G., and Morgan, M. S. (Eds.). (1987). *The Probabilistic Revolution, Vol. 2: Ideas in the Sciences,* Cambridge, MA: MIT Press.

Kuhn, H. W. (Ed.). (1997). *Classics in Game Theory.* Princeton, NJ: Princeton University Press.

Kuhn, T. S. (1996). *The Structure of Scientific Revolutions.* (3rd ed.). Chicago, IL: University of Chicago Press.

Laplace, P. S. (1814). *Essai philosophique sur les probabilities.* Translated by F. W. Truscott and F. L. Emory and reprinted in 1951 with an introductory note by E. T. Bell as *A philosophical essay on probabilities.* New York: Dover Publications.

Lindley, D. V. (1969). *Introduction to probability and statistics from a Bayesian viewpoint. Vol. 1: Probability.* London: Cambridge University Press.

Lindley, D. V. (1970). *Introduction to Probability and Statistics from a Bayesian Viewpoint. Vol. 2: Inference.* London: Cambridge University Press.

Lindley, D. V. (1972). *Bayesian Statistics: A Review.* Philadelphia, PA: Society for Industrial and Applied Mathematics.

Luce, R. D., Krantz, D. H., Suppes, P., and Tversky, A. (1990). *Foundations of Measurement (Vol. III: Representation, Axiomatization, and Invariance).* San Diego: Academic Press.

Luce, R. D., and Raiffa, H. (1957). *Games and decisions: Introduction and critical survey.* New York: John Wiley.

Luce, R. D. and Tukey, J. W. (1964). Simultaneous conjoint measurement: A new type of fundamental measurement. *Journal of Mathematical Psychology, 1,* 1–27.

Marschak, J. (1950). Rational behavior, uncertain prospects, and measurable utility. *Econometrica, 18,* 111–141.

McMillan, J. (1992). *Games, strategies, and managers: How managers can use game theory to make better business decisions.* New York: Oxford University Press.

Mele, A. R., and Rawling, P. (Eds.). (2004). *The Oxford handbook of rationality.* New York: Oxford University Press.

Menger, K. (1934). The Role of Uncertainty in Economics. Reprinted in 1967 in M. Shubik (Ed.), *Essays in Mathematical Economics in Honor of Oskar Morgenstern.* Princeton, NJ: Princeton University Press, pp. 211–231

Montmort, P. R. de. (1713). *Essai d'analyse sur les jeux de hasard.* (2nd ed.). Paris: Jacque Quillau. Reprinted in 1721 in *Histoire de l'Académie royale des sciences pour l'année 1719,* pp. 83–93.

Morse, P. M., and Kimball, G. E. (1951). *Methods of operations research.* New York: John Wiley.

Myerson, R. B. (1991). *Game Theory: Analysis of Conflict.* Cambridge, MA: Harvard University Press.

Nash, J. F. (1950). The bargaining problem. *Econometrica, 18,* 155–162.

Nash, J. F. (1951). Non-cooperative games. *Annals of Mathematics, 54,* 286–295.

O'Hagen, A. (1994). *Kendall's advanced theory of statistics. Vol. 2B: Bayesian inference.* New York: John Wiley.

Ordeshook, P. C. (1986). *Game theory and political theory: An introduction.* Cambridge, UK: Cambridge University Press.

Pascal, B. (1670). *Pensées.* Translated in 2003 by W. F. Trotter. New York: Dover Publications.

Poisson, S. D. (1837). *Recherches sur la probabilité des jugements en matière criminelle et en matière civile.* Paris: Bachelier.

Porter, T. M. (1986). *The rise of statistical thinking 1820–1900.* Princeton, NJ: Princeton University Press.

Pratt, J. W., Raiffa, H., and Schlaifer, R. (1964). The foundations of decision under uncertainty: An elementary exposition. *Journal of the American Statistical Association, 59,* 353–375.

Press, S. J. (1989). *Bayesian statistics: Principles, models, and applications*. New York: John Wiley.

Raiffa, H. (1968). *Decision analysis: Introductory lectures on choices under uncertainty*. Reading, MA: Addison-Wesley.

Raiffa, H. (2002). Decision analysis: A personal account of how it got started and evolved. *Operations Research, 50*, 179–185.

Raiffa, H., and Schlaifer, R. (1961). *Applied statistical decision theory*. Cambridge, MA: MIT Press.

Ramsey, F. P. (1926). Truth and Probability. In R. B. Braithwaite, (Ed.). 1931. F. P. Ramsey, *The foundations of mathematics and other logical essays*. London: Routledge and Kegan Paul. Reprinted in 1980 in H. E. Kyburg, Jr. and H. E. Smokler, *Studies in subjective probability*. (2nd ed.). New York: John Wiley. Reprinted in 1990 in D. H. Mellor, *Philosophical papers: F. P. Ramsey*. Cambridge, UK: Cambridge University Press.

Robert, C. P. (2001). *The Bayesian choice: From decision–theoretic foundations to computational implementation*. New York: Springer-Verlag.

Routledge. (2000). Francis Bacon. *Concise Routledge encyclopedia of philosophy*. London: Routledge, p. 73.

Rubinstein, A. (1998). *Modeling bounded rationality*. Cambridge, MA: MIT Press.

Savage, L. J. (1954). *The foundations of statistics*. New York: John Wiley. Revised second edition published in 1972 by Dover Publications, New York.

Schelling, T. C. (1960). *The strategy of conflict*. London: Oxford University Press.

Schlaifer, R. (1959). *Probability and statistics for business decisions: An introduction to managerial economics under uncertainty*. New York: McGraw-Hill.

Schlaifer, R. (1969). *Analysis of decisions under uncertainty*. New York: McGraw-Hill.

Schneider, S. L., and Shaneau, J. (Eds.). (2003). *Emerging perspectives on judgment and decision research*. Cambridge, UK: Cambridge University Press.

Shanteau, J., Mellers, B. A., and Schum, D. (1999). *Decision science and technology: Contributions of Ward Edwards*. Boston, MA: Kluwer Academic.

Simon, H. A. (1956). Rational choice and the structure of the environment. *Psychological Review, 63*, 129–138.

Simon, H. A. (1982). *Models of bounded rationality* (Vol. 2). Cambridge, MA: MIT Press.

Smith, J. E., and von Winterfeldt, D. (2004). Decision analysis in management science. *Management Science, 50*(5), 561–574.

Stigler, G. J. (1950). The development of utility theory. *Journal of Political Economy, 58*, 307–327, 373–396.

Stigler, S. M. (1986). *The history of statistics: The measurement of uncertainty before 1900*. Cambridge, MA: Harvard University Press.

Stigler, S. M. (1999). *Statistics on the table: The history of statistical concepts and methods*. Cambridge, MA: Harvard University Press.

Suppes, P., Krantz, D. M., Luce, R. D., and Tversky, A. (1989). *Foundations of Measurement (Vol. II: Geometrical, Threshold, and Probabilistic Representations)*. San Diego: Academic Press.

Thrall, R. M., Coombs, C. H., and Davis, R. L. (Eds.). (1954). *Decision processes*. New York: John Wiley.

Todhunter, I. (1865). *A history of the mathematical theory of probability from the time of Pascal to that of Laplace*. Cambridge. Reprinted in 1949 and 1965. New York: Chelsea Publishing.

Tversky, A., and Kahneman, D. (1974). Judgment under uncertainty: Heuristics and biases. *Science, 18*, 1124–1131.

Venn, J. (1866). *The logic of chance*. Reprinted in 1962. London: Macmillan.

von Mises, R. (1957). *Probability, statistics, and truth*. (2nd revised English ed.). Originally published in 1928 (3rd ed.) in German by J. Springer. Reprinted in 1981 by Dover Publications, New York.

von Neumann, J., and Morgenstern, O. (1947). *Theory of games and economic behavior.* (2nd ed.). Princeton, NJ: Princeton University Press.

von Winterfeldt, D., and Edwards, W. (1986). *Decision analysis and behavioral research.* Cambridge, UK: Cambridge University Press.

Wald, A. (1950). *Statistical decision functions.* New York: John Wiley.

Weatherford, R. (1982). *Philosophical foundations of probability theory.* London: Routledge and Kegan Paul.

Weirich, P. (1984). The St. Petersburg gamble and risk. *Theory and Decision, 17,* 193–202.

West, M., and Harrison, J. (1989). *Bayesian forecasting and dynamic models.* New York: Springer-Verlag.

Winkler, R. L. (2003). *An Introduction to Bayesian inference and decision.* (2nd ed.). Gainsville, FL: Probabilistic Publishing.

Wright, G., and Ayton, P. (Eds.). (1994). *Subjective probability.* New York: John Wiley.

Zellner, A. (1971). *An introduction to Bayesian inference in econometrics.* New York: John Wiley.

3 The Foundations of Decision Analysis Revisited

Ronald A. Howard

ABSTRACT. For centuries people have speculated on how to improve decision making without much professional help in developing clarity of action. Over the last several decades, many important contributions have been integrated to create the discipline of decision analysis, which can aid decision makers in all fields of endeavor: business, engineering, medicine, law, and personal life. Because uncertainty is the most important feature to consider in making decisions, the ability to represent knowledge in terms of probability, to see how to combine this knowledge with preferences in a reasoned way, to treat very large and complex decision problems using modern computation, and to avoid common errors of thought have combined to produce insights heretofore unobtainable. The limitation to its practice lies in our willingness to use reason, rather than in any shortcoming of the field. This chapter discusses the sources of the discipline; the qualities desired in a decision process; the logic for finding the best course of action; the process of focusing attention on important issues in attaining clarity of action; the need for clear and powerful distinctions to guide our thinking (because most decisions derive from thought and conversation rather than from computation); and the challenges to the growth of the discipline.

Introduction

Revisiting the foundations of decision analysis means seeing what those foundations have been, how they have evolved, and how well they will serve in the future. Since the entire book is generally concerned with this subject, this chapter will be a personal view of the development of decision analysis. Other chapters will discuss many of the topics commented on here in greater depth. Some of my opinions may be idiosyncratic, as you will see as you read further. I will briefly repeat comments from original writings, which should be consulted for a deeper understanding of decision analysis.

Origins

When I was asked to write this chapter, I thought of it as an opportunity to review the progress of the field since its inception. I decided to return to my paper presented in 1965 titled "Decision Analysis: Applied Decision Theory" (DAADT) (Howard 1966) wherein I define the term "decision analysis" for the first time:

> The purpose of this article is to outline a formal procedure for the analysis of decision problems, a procedure that I call "decision analysis." We shall also

discuss several of the practical problems that arise when we attempt to apply the decision analysis formalism.

By the way, I decided to call the field "decision analysis," rather than "decision engineering," because the latter term sounded manipulative, though, in fact, it is more descriptive.

The following paragraph from DAADT provides a definition of decision analysis:

> Decision analysis is a logical procedure for the balancing of the factors that influence a decision. The procedure incorporates uncertainties, values, and preferences in a basic structure that models the decision. Typically, it includes technical, marketing, competitive, and environmental factors. The essence of the procedure is the construction of a structural model of the decision in a form suitable for computation and manipulation; the realization of this model is often a set of computer programs.

Not having read the paper for some time, and expecting it to be antiquated, I was pleased to see how relevant some of the comments are today. For example, here is the discussion of the most fundamental distinction underlying decision analysis:

> Having defined a decision, let us clarify the concept by drawing a necessary distinction between a good decision and a good outcome. A good decision is a logical decision – one based on the uncertainties, values, and preferences of the decision maker. A good outcome is one that is profitable or otherwise highly valued. In short, a good outcome is one that we wish would happen. Hopefully, by making good decisions in all the situations that face us we shall ensure as high a percentage as possible of good outcomes. We may be disappointed to find that a good decision has produced a bad outcome or dismayed to learn that someone who has made what we consider to be a bad decision has enjoyed a good outcome. Yet, pending the invention of the true clairvoyant, we find no better alternative in the pursuit of good outcomes than to make good decisions.

The distinction between *decision* and *outcome* is still not clear for most people. When someone makes an investment, and then loses money, he often says that he made a bad decision. If he would make the same decision again if he did not know how it would turn out, then he would be more accurate in saying that he made a good decision and had a bad outcome. Jaynes traces this distinction back to Herodotus (Jaynes 1986):

> From the earliest times this process of plausible reasoning preceding decisions has been recognized. Herodotus, in about 500 B.C., discusses the policy decisions of the Persian kings. He notes that a decision was wise, even though it led to disastrous consequences, if the evidence at hand indicated it as the best one to make; and that a decision was foolish, even though it led to the happiest possible consequences, if it was unreasonable to expect those consequences.

Let me now turn to what motivated the writing of this chapter.

The Motivating Application

I taught in electrical engineering and industrial management at MIT from 1958 through 1964. One of my mentors at MIT, Bill Linvill, had taken a position at Stanford University. He invited me to visit him there for the 1964–1965 academic year. While I was at MIT, I taught statistical decision theory and Markov decision processes in the General Electric Modern Engineering Course, which they gave to middle engineering management. When one of the participants learned I was going out to Stanford, he asked if I could teach the same course in San Jose to employees of the GE nuclear power division, and I agreed.

At the end of the third weekly lecture in decision theory presented in San Jose, one of the engineers said that the division was facing a major decision problem with both technical and business implications. The question was whether to install a superheater of steam on their nuclear power reactors. He asked whether what we were discussing in class could help with this problem.

I replied, "Why not?" We spent eight months working on how to put together the dynamic, preference, and uncertainty issues they faced, marking the beginning of decision analysis and providing the material that motivated the first decision analysis paper (Howard 1966).

Pillars of Decision Analysis

It is certainly true that we stand on the shoulders of giants. I used to think that there were two pillars supporting decision analysis, but I came to realize that there were three, and then four. I will briefly discuss the first two pillars and emphasize the last two.

The First Pillar: Systems Analysis

Bill Linvill introduced me to systems analysis. Systems analysis grew out of World War II and was concerned with understanding dynamic systems. Key notions were those of state variables, feedback, stability, and sensitivity analysis. The field of systems engineering is currently in a state of resurgence. Decision analysis and systems engineering have many complementary features (Howard 1965, 1973).

The Second Pillar: Decision Theory

Decision theory is concerned primarily with making decisions in the face of uncertainty. Its roots go back to Daniel Bernoulli (Bernoulli 1738) and Laplace (Laplace 1812). Bernoulli introduced the idea of logarithmic utility to explain the puzzle called the St. Petersburg paradox. In the most influential book on probability ever written (Laplace 1812), Laplace discusses the *espérance mathématique* and the *espérance morale*. Today we would call these the mean and the certain equivalent.

Howard Raiffa showed how to treat many of the problems of statistics in Bayesian form, and how to use tree structures to select the best alternative. I learned much from Howard while I assisted him in teaching the year-long program *Institute of Basic Mathematics for Application to Business* at the Harvard Business School.

The Third Pillar: Epistemic Probability

I did not appreciate the importance of this pillar until well after I began teaching statistical decision theory. My epiphany began with a manuscript sent to me by Myron Tribus, Dean of Engineering at Dartmouth. It was a paper by Ed Jaynes (Jaynes 2003), a professor of physics at Washington University. Because I needed a haircut, I took it with me to a small barbershop on Massachusetts Avenue in Cambridge, Massachusetts. As I sat in the barber's chair, I read the first few pages and thought, "This is pretty silly." When I arose from the chair 20 minutes later, I had become completely converted to Jaynes' way of thinking about probability, and I have been in his debt ever since (Howard 2005).

Jaynes taught that there is no such thing as an objective probability: a probability reflects a person's knowledge (or equivalently ignorance) about some uncertain distinction. People think that probabilities can be found in data, but they cannot. Only a person can assign a probability, taking into account any data or other knowledge available. Because there is no such thing as an objective probability, using a term like "subjective probability" only creates confusion. Probabilities describing uncertainties have no need of adjectives.

This understanding goes back to Cox (1961), Jeffreys (1939), Laplace (1996), and maybe Bayes, yet somehow it was an idea that had been lost over time. A famous scientist put it best more than 150 years ago:

> The actual science of logic is conversant at present only with things either certain, impossible, or entirely doubtful, none of which (fortunately) we have to reason on. Therefore the true logic for this world is the calculus of probabilities, which takes account of the magnitude of the probability which is, or ought to be, in a reasonable man's mind. (Maxwell 1850)

I ask students who have taken a probability class about the origin of the probabilities that they use in the classroom and in their assignments. It turns out that these probabilities originate from the professor or from a very simple rule based on coin tossing, balls in urns, or card playing that says to make all elemental probabilities equal. Probability class then teaches you how to transform this set of probabilities into probabilities of derivative events, like two heads out of ten tosses of a coin or a royal flush – from inputs to outputs. There is very little discussion of where probabilities come from, and where they come from has everything to do with the use of probability. I have never seen an actual decision problem where the assignment of probabilities could be done using the probability class rule.

DAADT emphasized the importance of the epistemic view:

> Another criticism is, "If this is such a good idea, why haven't I heard of it before?" One very practical reason is that the operations we conduct in the course of a decision analysis would be expensive to carry out without using

computers. To this extent decision analysis is a product of our technology. There are other answers, however. One is that the idea of probability as a state of mind and not of things is only now regaining its proper place in the world of thought. The opposing heresy lay heavy on the race for the better part of a century. We should note that most of the operations research performed in World War II required mathematical and probabilistic concepts that were readily available to Napoleon. One wonders about how the introduction of formal methods for decision making at that time might have affected the course of history.

Over the years, many people have tried to modify the probability theory of Bayes, Laplace, Kolmogorov, and Jaynes for some purpose. Perhaps someday we will see a useful contribution from such efforts; I believe that, at present, they only serve to make these giants roll over in their graves.

The Fourth Pillar: Cognitive Psychology

In the 1960s few appreciated the important role that cognitive psychology would play in understanding human behavior. At the time of DAADT, we just did our best to help experts assign probabilities. In the 1970s the work of Tversky, Kahneman, and others provided two valuable contributions. First, it showed that people making decisions relying only on their intuition were subject to many errors that they would recognize on reflecting on what they had done. This emphasized the need for a formal procedure such as decision analysis to assist in making important decisions. The second contribution was to show the necessity for those who are assisting in the probability and preference assessments to be aware of the many pitfalls that are characteristic of human thought. Tversky and Kahneman called these heuristics – methods of thought that could be useful in general but could trick us in particular settings. We can think of these as the "optical illusions" of the mind.

An important distinction here is that between "descriptive" and "normative" decision making. Descriptive decision making, as the name implies, is concerned with how people actually make decisions. The test of descriptive decision-making models is whether they actually describe human behavior. Normative decision making is decision making according to certain rules, or norms, that we want to follow in our decision-making processes.

To illustrate, I might make mistakes, descriptively, in carrying out operations in arithmetic. I know they are mistakes because I want to follow the norms of arithmetic. I call any violation of the norms a mistake.

We know there is a conflict between our reasoning (normative) and our temptations (descriptive) that can resolve in favor of either, as illustrated by the person eating a bowl of peanuts at a cocktail party and saying, "I know I am going to regret this tomorrow."

Many theorists have attempted to change the norms of decision making to make the norms agree with descriptive behavior. Every attempt to do so that I have seen creates more problems than it solves (Howard 1992a).

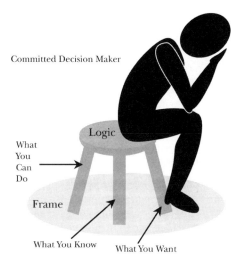

Figure 3.1. Decision essentials.

Edifice of Decision Analysis

General Concepts

You can think of a decision as a choice among alternatives that will yield uncertain futures, for which we have preferences. To explain the formal aspects of decision analysis to both students and to executives I use the image of the three-legged stool shown in Figure 3.1 (Howard 2000).

The legs of the stool are the three elements of any decision: what you can do (your alternatives); what you know (the information you have); and what you want (your preferences). Collectively, the three legs represent the decision basis, the specification of the decision. Note that if any leg is missing, there is no decision to be made. If you have only one alternative, then you have no choice in what you do. If you do not have any information linking what you do to what will happen in the future, then all alternatives serve equally well because you do not see how your actions will have any effect. If you have no preferences regarding what will happen as a result of choosing any alternative, then you will be equally happy choosing any one. The seat of the stool is the logic that operates on the decision basis to produce the best alternative. We will soon be constructing the seat to make sure that it operates correctly.

The stool can be placed anywhere and used to make a decision. However, the most important choice you make is where to place it. Placement of the stool represents the frame of the decision, the declaration by the decision maker of what decision is under consideration at this time. The frame will influence all elements of the decision basis. Framing a decision of where to live as a renting decision rather than a buying decision will affect the alternatives, the information, and the preferences appropriate to the decision basis.

The decision hierarchy of Figure 3.2 shows how the frame separates what is to be decided on now from two other potential sources of decisions.

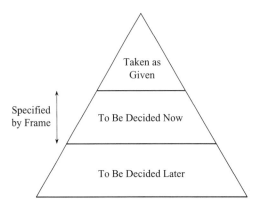

Figure 3.2. The decision hierarchy.

The top of the hierarchy in the figure represents higher-level decisions with the alternatives that are taken as given at this time. The bottom of the hierarchy represents decisions that will be made in the future following the decision under consideration. Selection of a proper frame is perhaps the most important task in decision analysis.

Finally, note the person seated on the stool. This figure reminds us that the frame, and every element of the decision basis, must be a declaration by the decision maker. Decisions are not found in nature, they are creations of the human mind.

Decision Quality

Decision quality comprises the six elements of the stool. A high quality decision has a proper frame, a selection of alternatives that respond to the frame, reliable information to an extent appropriate to the frame, and considered preferences on possible futures. The logic to arrive at a course of action must be sound, and the decision maker must be committed both to the process and to the significance of the decision.

The decision quality spider shown in Figure 3.3 is a graphical representation of the qualitative attainment of these elements in any particular decision. Individuals and groups find it helpful in assessing their decision process. The distance from the inner circle to the outer one represents the degree of achievement for each element. The outer circle represents the proper balancing of these elements for this particular decision. The analysis is not balanced if too many alternatives are considered, or too much information of little value relative to cost is gathered. The resulting picture displays the deficiencies in any of the elements of decision quality.

Group Decision Making

Any person, and an organization operating under the direction of a person, can use decision analysis. An organization using decision analysis is agreeing to act as if it were a single entity using the logic of a person. Separate groups might have the assignment of creating the frame and the elements of the decision basis. (Howard

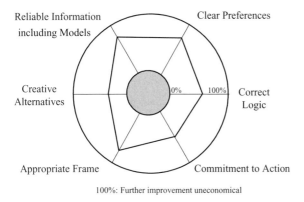

Reliable Information
including Models

Clear Preferences

Creative
Alternatives

0%   100%

Correct
Logic

Appropriate Frame

Commitment to Action

100%: Further improvement uneconomical

Figure 3.3. The decision quality spider.

1975). The analysis must use the same high-quality logic appropriate for a person soon to be described.

Even when the decision maker is one person, that person may consider the consequences of the decision on other people. It is useful to define a stakeholder in a decision as "someone who can affect or will be affected by the decision." Stakeholders can be as disparate as regulators and customers.

Clairvoyance

A useful construct in achieving clarity in all the dimensions of uncertainty in a decision is that of the clairvoyant. The clairvoyant can tell us the resolution of any uncertain distinction past, present, or future as long as (1) the clairvoyant need not exercise any judgment in stating this resolution and (2) the resolution does not depend on any future action of the decision maker unless that action is specified. We say that a distinction meeting these conditions has met the *clarity test*. We cannot understand what a distinction like "technical success" means unless it meets the clarity test. Assigning probabilities to distinctions that do not meet the clarity test is an exercise in futility.

Once we have the notion of clairvoyance, we can speak of the improvement that we might make in a decision if clairvoyance on one or more of the uncertainties in the decision were available. If the prospects of the decision are completely describable by a value measure we can compute the value of clairvoyance (Howard 1966a). The most that should be paid for any information gathering activity or experiment is the value of clairvoyance on the results of that activity.

As stated in DAADT:

> Thus the decision analysis is a vital structure that lets us compare at any time the values of such alternatives as acting, postponing action and buying information, or refusing to consider the problem further. We must remember that the analysis is always based on the current state of knowledge. Overnight there can arrive a piece of information that changes the nature of the conclusions entirely. Of course, having captured the basic structure of the problem, we are in an excellent position to incorporate any such information.

Desiderata

In developing any theory, it is useful to specify the desirable properties we would like to have: desiderata. Here we will present desiderata for a theory of decision (Howard 1992a). We define the decision composite as the axioms supporting the theory plus all of the theorems that follow from them.

1. The decision composite must allow me to form inferences about uncertain distinctions even in the absence of a decision problem. This means that probability must stand on its foundation, in accordance with our discussion of epistemic probability.
2. The decision composite must be applicable to any decision I face regardless of type or field.
3. The decision composite must require that I be indifferent between two alternatives I consider to have the same probabilities of the same consequences. In other words, I must be indifferent between two alternatives for which I have created the same descriptions.
4. Reversing the order of contemplating uncertain distinctions should not change inference or decision. This means, in particular, that changing the order of receiving a given body of information, including alternatives, should not change any inference or decision. This property is sometimes called "invariance to data order."
5. If I prefer alternative 1 over alternative 2 when the uncertain event A occurs and if I prefer 1 over 2 when event A does not occur, then I must prefer alternative 1 over 2 when I am uncertain about the occurrence of event A.
6. Once I have ordered my alternatives from best to worst, the noninformative removal of any of them does not change the preference order of the remaining alternatives. "Noninformative" means that the removal of the alternative does not provide new information about the remaining alternatives.
7. The addition of a noninformative new alternative to the basis cannot change the ranking of the original alternatives.
8. The ability to obtain free clairvoyance on any uncertainty cannot make the decision situation less attractive.
9. At this epoch, my thoughts about how I will behave and choose in the future must be consistent.
   If the consequences of a decision are completely describable in terms of a value measure chosen so that more will always be preferred to less, then the desiderata can be further refined.
10. If an alternative has various value consequences with associated probabilities, then I must be able to compute the amount of the value measure I would have to receive in exchange for the alternative to be indifferent to following it. This selling price of the alternative I will call the certain equivalent. This amount will be negative for undesirable alternatives.
11. I must be able to compute the value added by a new alternative: the value must be nonnegative.

12. I must be able to compute the value of clairvoyance on any uncertain distinction or collection of uncertain distinctions; the value of clairvoyance cannot be negative.
13. Payments of value that cannot be changed must have no effect on future decisions.
14. Because I am choosing among uncertain futures, there must be no willingness-to-pay to avoid regret.

The Rules

How could we construct a systematic logical process to serve as the seat of the stool in Figure 3.1? The answer is that we have to agree in our decision making to follow a set of rules, or norms, for our decision process. I consider them the rules of actional thought, thought about action. These norms – some would call them axioms – are the foundation of the decision composite. I will state them here as requirements that the decision maker is placing on himself, rather than as requirements imposed on him. The rules apply at one instant in time – there is no notion of temporal consistency. Although every decision made using this normative process must follow the rules, once they are acknowledged they will seldom be referred to in a formal analysis. Just as a carpenter relies on the axioms of geometry, perhaps without even knowing them, the decisions made using decision analysis procedures should be so self-evident in their correctness that there is rarely a need to mention the rules.

RULE 1: THE PROBABILITY RULE. The *probability rule* requires that I be able to characterize any alternative I face in a decision to my satisfaction by introducing uncertain distinctions of various kinds and degrees and assigning probabilities to them. Once I have done this for all alternatives I wish to consider within my present frame, I have completed the requirements of the probability rule.

RULE 2: THE ORDER RULE. The *order rule* requires that, for each alternative I face, I construct the possible futures formed by selecting the alternative and then one degree of each distinction used to describe it. I call the result a "prospect." Sequential decisions following revelation of information require prospects that describe each alternative and the distinctions that follow it. When I have a complete list of prospects formed by the alternatives and their possible consequences, I must then order them in a list, starting with the one I like best at the top and the one I like worst at the bottom. I may have one or more prospects at the same level in the list. It is possible that when I attempt to create this ordering, I will find it difficult because I discover uncertainties that I did not represent in the probability rule. This means that I must return to the probability rule, add distinctions to represent the uncertainties, and then repeat the process. Notice that the order rule is an ordering of prospects in a certain world: no consideration of uncertainty is allowed.

RULE 3: THE EQUIVALENCE RULE. The *equivalence rule* applies, in principle, to any three prospects at different levels in the list. Suppose I like prospect A better than prospect B, and I like prospect B better than prospect C. The equivalence rule requires that I be able to assign a probability of the best prospect A and one minus that probability of the worst prospect C such that I would be indifferent to receiving this probability mixture of the best and worst prospects on the one hand and the intermediate prospect B for certain on the other. I will call the probability that establishes this indifference a "preference" probability because it is not the probability of any uncertainty that the clairvoyant could resolve.

When satisfying the equivalence rule, I may find that some of the prospects ordered in the order rule require refinement to allow the proper assessment of preference probabilities. For example, I may know that I prefer a steak dinner to a lamb chop dinner to a hamburger dinner. However, my preference probability for a steak dinner versus a hamburger dinner that would make me just indifferent to a lamb chop dinner may well depend on further specification of each dinner, a task that will require returning to the probability rule and creating new distinctions.

Because an actual decision could have hundreds if not thousands of prospects, and three at different levels could in such cases be chosen in even more ways than there are prospects, you can see why we said that the equivalence rule must apply in principle. Rarely will we have to carry out the assignment of so many preference probabilities.

RULE 4: THE SUBSTITUTION RULE. The *substitution rule* requires that:

> If I should face in life any of the situations for which I assessed a preference probability in the equivalence rule, *and*

> If I assign a probability to receiving the best of the three prospects rather then the worst that is equal to the preference probability I assigned, *then*

> I remain indifferent between receiving the uncertain deal and the intermediate prospect.

This rule is necessary because the preference among uncertain prospects expressed in the equivalence rule is not some hypothetical preference, but one that reflects my actual preferences for uncertain deals. This means that probabilities and preference probabilities may be used interchangeably in the analysis of decision problems.

RULE 5: THE CHOICE RULE. The *choice rule* applies whenever I have two prospects at different levels in my ordered list. If I prefer prospect A to prospect B, and if I face two alternatives with different probabilities of only those two prospects, then I must choose the alternative with a higher probability of receiving prospect A. In other words, I must choose the alternative with a higher probability of the prospect I like better.

Note that this is the only rule that specifies the action I must take, and that it is so self-evident that if I told someone I was violating it, they would think they had misheard me. Every aspect of this choice is under my control: my preference and my probability.

I can make any decision using only these five rules. You can think of the process as transforming an opaque decision situation into a transparent one by a series of transparent steps. The transparent steps are the rules applied systematically. Using the first four rules, the choice between any two alternatives can be reduced to an application of the choice rule. If there are several alternatives, the repeated application of the choice rule will order them (Howard 1998).

The application of the rules simplifies considerably if I can describe all the prospects completely in terms of a value measure, for example, money. If I prefer more money to less, as I do, the rules require that I be able to construct a nondecreasing curve on the money axis, which I will call the u-curve and any point on it a u-value. This curve summarizes my preferences for receiving different amounts of the value measure with different probabilities, my risk preference.

The rules require that I order the alternatives in terms of their mean u-values, the sum of the u-values of each prospect multiplied by the probability of that prospect. This computation yields the u-value of any alternative. The certain equivalent of the alternative is then the amount of money whose u-value equals the u-value of the alternative. Rather than having to be concerned with assigning the preference probabilities in the order rule to the many possible threesomes of prospects at different levels, I need only deal with the u-curve. We will have more to say on the terminology for this curve at the end of the chapter.

If there is no uncertainty in a decision situation, the rules are considerably simplified. The probability rule does not require any assignment of probabilities because every alternative now has a certain consequence. The order rule is still required because it expresses preferences in a deterministic world. There is no need for either the equivalence or substitution rules because they are concerned with preferences when there is uncertainty. The choice rule would still come into play; however, the probabilities involved would be 1 and 0. For example, would I rather have $20 or $10?

The rules are required for systematic decision making in an uncertain world. Simpler procedures, some of which we will later discuss, cannot handle uncertainty.

Practice of Decision Analysis

The purpose of decision analysis is to achieve clarity of action. If you already know what to do beyond any doubt, do it. If you do not know what to do, then apply the philosophy of decision analysis at an appropriate level. The process can be as simple as realizing that you are incorrectly including sunk costs or failing to recognize an alternative available to you.

Decision Engineering

The professional practice of decision analysis is decision engineering. The rules dictate the norms, but not how to create the representation of a decision that

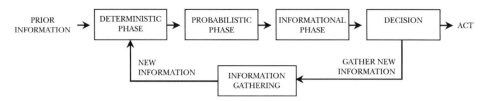

Figure 3.4. Early decision analysis cycle.

will skillfully and efficiently yield clarity of insight to the decision maker. What often happens when people try to analyze decisions using a structure like a decision tree is that they are tempted to include every possible uncertainty they can think of and thereby create an unanalyzable bush rather than the spare structure desired.

Creating a focused analysis requires the continual elimination of every factor that will not contribute to making the decision. This winnowing has been a feature of decision analysis since the beginning (Howard 1968, 1970). Since DAADT, the process has been described as a decision analysis cycle, depicted in Figure 3.4 (Howard 1984a).

A brief description of the cycle is this. After the problem is framed and alternatives are specified, the uncertainties that appear to have an effect on the decision are given nominal ranges. The deterministic phase explores the sensitivity of alternatives to these uncertainties to determine which alternatives are worthy of probabilistic analysis. The probabilistic phase encodes probability distributions on these uncertainties, including necessary conditional distributions. It also requires assessing the risk preference to be used for the decision. At this point, the best alternative can be determined, but the process continues to the informational phase to find the value of eliminating or reducing any or all of the uncertainties. The result is not only the best decision up to this point, but also clear knowledge of the cost of ignorance. This may lead to new information gathering alternatives and a repeat of the cycle, or simply lead to action.

By the way, this process was used in DAADT. Probability assignments were needed for a material lifetime and three experts were knowledgeable. The probability distributions they assigned individually and the one they agreed on collectively are shown in Figure 3.5. It turned out that the effect of this uncertainty, deemed of great concern at the start of the analysis, could be minimized by design changes and that the decision hinged on time preference.

There have been many refinements to the cycle over the years (Howard 1984a, 1988). For example, in preparing for probabilistic evaluation, the "tornado diagram" (so named by a client observing its shape) shows the sensitivity to uncertainties by the width of horizontal bars, ordered from the widest to the narrowest. Because the variance of the resulting payoff usually grows as the square of the length of the bars, only a few uncertainties with the longest bars are typically needed in the probabilistic evaluation.

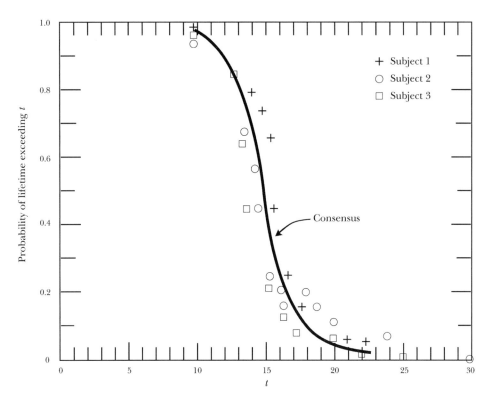

Figure 3.5. Probability assignment.

Influence, Relevance, and Decision Diagrams

A development that has aided practice and research over the past three decades is the introduction of diagrams that contribute to the understanding, communication, and computation of decision problems. The influence diagram (Howard and Matheson 1980, 2005) provides a structure that on the one hand is readily understood by decision makers and yet is formally defined so that it can serve as the basis for machine computation. I have found it to be an invaluable tool in the classroom and in executive conversations.

Unfortunately, the use of the word "influence" has led some people into difficulty in creating the diagrams. I have found it useful to introduce other forms. I call the special form of the influence diagram that contains only uncertainties represented by uncertain nodes (usually represented by a circle or oval) a "relevance diagram" (Howard 1989, 1990). *Relevance diagrams* directly address the question of inference in probabilistic networks, by representing the conditional probability structure of distinctions. Arrows between uncertainties represent the possibility that the probability of the successor uncertainty is conditional on the originating uncertainty. Every relevance diagram expresses an assessment order

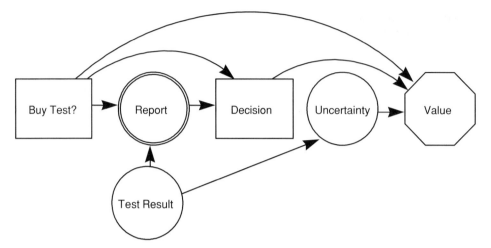

Figure 3.6. A decision diagram.

for all uncertainties in the diagram. A missing arrow is an assertion of the irrelevance of one uncertainty to another given all uncertainties that are predecessors to both. Many puzzling problems in probability become transparent when viewed in the form of a relevance diagram.

A *decision diagram* contains decision nodes (rectangles) and the value node (hexagon or octagon). It may also contain one or more relevance diagrams. Arrows into a decision node are called "informational" arrows; they signify that the node originating the arrow is known when that decision is made. Arrows into the value node are called "functional" arrows; they show the nodes on which value depends. Sometimes a special case of the uncertain node called a deterministic node (double walled circle or oval) is created. The arrows into such a deterministic node are functional arrows; the value of the node is computable from its inputs. You can consider the value node as a special deterministic node.

Figure 3.6 shows a decision diagram for a test that is relevant to an uncertainty. The test costs money; value resides in the decisions and the uncertainty.

Note that this decision diagram contains a relevance diagram on Test Result and Uncertainty that has no arrows entering it. Decision diagrams that contain relevance diagrams with this property are said to be in canonical form.

Why is canonical form important? Arrows that go from a decision node to an uncertain node are called "influence" arrows. They assert that the probability assignment to an uncertain node depends on how a decision is made. They are problematic because they blur a separation we have made between actions that are under our control, alternatives, and the uncertainties that might be resolved by a clairvoyant that are not under our control. Although influences do not pose significant problems in computing the best decision, they do increase the difficulty of computing the value of clairvoyance (Howard 1990). The simple reason is that if a clairvoyant could tell you something about an uncertainty affected by an influence, he would be telling you something about an action on which you have not yet decided and thereby would call into question your free will. One can avoid this difficulty by eliminating all influences from the decision diagram, thus placing it in canonical form. If necessary, this can be done by creating more nodes in the relevance diagram conditioned on the influencing decisions. If this has been done, or if there are no influences in the original diagram, then the diagram is in canonical form.

Options

I consider one of the most important concepts in the practice of decision analysis to be that of an option, properly defined (Howard 1996). I do not restrict the term to financial options or even to so-called real options that people attempt to replicate by portfolios of marketed securities. By option, I mean an alternative that provides a new decision situation after the revelation of information. Thus obtaining clairvoyance is an option because it is permitting you to make a decision you face after resolving one or more uncertainties. The option may be obtained only at a price, and there may be an additional cost, the *exercise price*, of using any alternative after receiving the information. In computations involving clairvoyance, we typically assume that the same alternatives will be available after the information is provided – although this is not necessary, we might have more or fewer. We also assume that there will be no additional cost to exercising any of our original alternatives. All these comments apply to the option of performing an information gathering activity, like an experiment, because we know that the experiment can be valued by valuing clairvoyance on its results.

Sometimes options must be bought, like a fire extinguisher for your car; sometimes, they are free of additional cost, like choosing what movie to see after driving to a multiscreen cinema.

Failure to recognize options and to incorporate them as sequential decisions is one of the most important and consequential mistakes of decision analysis.

Cogency versus Verisimilitude

In representing a decision of professional size there is sometimes controversy about how much detail to include. Notice that the standard of excellence for model representations, like model trains, is verisimilitude: the correspondence of the model in detail to the real situation it is intended to represent. At a model train exposition you might notice a tiny passenger train with a bar car. In examining the bar car you might see that there are people inside holding drinks; this is surely a detailed model. Further scrutiny shows that one of the drinks is clearly a martini containing an olive; this will be a prize-winning train. Using a magnifying glass, you see that the olive contains a pimento. Surely, this train will be "best of show."

Is verisimilitude the criterion for decision models? Is a decision model that includes "the sales tax in Delaware" better than one that does not? The answer is no, unless that factor is material to the decision. The criterion for decision models is cogency: whether the model leads to crisp clarity of action for the decision maker.

You should eliminate any feature that does not contribute to this goal. If the decision maker insists on adding such embellishments, they should be regarded as a professional courtesy, like giving the decision maker a ride to the airport, rather than as part of professional decision analysis.

Ethics

Decision analysis is amoral, as is an adding machine. Like any other powerful tool, people can use decision analysis for good or ill. They can justify any course of action by manipulating the elements of the analysis: the alternatives, information, and preferences. As organizations increasingly accepted decision analysis, I became concerned about its ethical use (Howard 1980, 1991, 2001), as should anyone teaching or practicing the discipline. The study of decision analysis is an excellent precursor to ethical discussions for it illuminates both utilitarian (consequence-based) and formalist (action-based) ethics. We find that characterizing actions as to whether they are prudential, legal, and ethical is a helpful step in resolving ethical choices.

Language of Decision Analysis

Once again, decision analysis is more about clear thinking than about any of its detailed procedures. Because even when thinking about a decision by ourselves we are going to use a language to help us, it is extremely important that the language contain the proper concepts. This is even more essential if we are discussing our decision with others. Whether supported by modeling and computation or not, the decision conversation will become the basis for action. My concern with the language of decision analysis goes back to DAADT:

> One aid in reducing the problem to its fundamental components is restricting the vocabulary that can be used in discussing the problem. Thus we carry on the discussion in terms of events, random variables, probabilities, density functions, expectations, outcomes, and alternatives. We do not allow fuzzy thinking about the nature of these terms. Thus "The density function of the probability" and "The confidence in the probability estimate" must be nipped in the bud. We speak of "assigning," not "estimating," the probabilities of events and think of this assignment as based on our "state of information." These conventions eliminate statements like the one recently made on a TV panel of doctors who were discussing the right of a patient to participate in decision making on his treatment. One doctor asserted that the patient should be told of "some kind of a chance of a likelihood of a bad result." I am sure that the doctor was a victim of the pressures of the program and would agree with us that telling the patient the probability the doctor would assign to a bad result would be preferable.

Some of the communication advantages in using decision analysis were also spelled out:

Table 3.1. Suggested terminology changes

Conventional term	Preferred term	Purpose of change
Dependence	Relevance	To emphasize the informational rather than the causal nature of conditional probability assignments.
Outcome	Prospect	To emphasize that decisions choose uncertain futures rather than only an immediate result.
Expected value	Mean	To recognize that the expected value is seldom to be expected. In discussing probability distributions, use "mean" to describe the first moment.
Expected value	Certain equivalent	To recognize that the expected value is seldom to be expected. In describing the value of an alternative with uncertain values, use certain equivalent.
Utility	*u*-curve	To avoid confusion with other uses of the word utility in related subjects, for example, "marginal utility." The *u*-curve says nothing in a deterministic world.

One of the most important advantages of decision analysis lies in the way it encourages meaningful communication among the members of the enterprise because it provides a common language in which to discuss decision problems. Thus engineers and marketing planners with quite different jargons can appreciate one another's contributions to a decision. Both can use the decision-analysis language to convey their feelings to management quickly and effectively.

My concern for precise language continues to the present. Refer to a recent paper on this subject (Howard 2004) for a thorough discussion of this issue. My intention is to have the language we use in describing decisions consist of the simplest, least confusing, most accurate terms for the concepts under discussion. Table 3.1 summarizes some of the recommended changes in language that I have found useful in dealing with students and clients.

Confusions

UNCERTAINTY ABOUT PROBABILITY. As we previously discussed, the language of probability is sufficient for describing the phenomenon of uncertainty. Yet people keep trying to build another level they might call uncertainty about probability to describe any uneasiness they might feel in the process of probability assignment. This is akin to the previous quote from DAADT where the doctor said that the patient should be told of "some kind of a chance of a likelihood of a bad result."

Once you have internalized the thinking of Laplace and Jaynes, any notion of uncertainty about probability becomes unnecessary (Howard 1988a).

DEAL CHARACTERIZATION AND DEAL DESIRABILITY. I recently consulted with a Board of Directors concerned about whether to follow an alternative with highly uncertain value prospects that ranged from great profits to serious losses. There had been much previous discussion about whether this alternative was "too risky" for the company. The members of the Board were highly educated and experienced business people.

The Board might see an alternative like this as too risky for two logically separate reasons. There might be a belief that the chances of large profits were overstated, or perhaps the chances of losses understated. This would be a concern about the characterization of the deal, about whether the analysis assigned proper probabilities to each level of profit and loss.

Once the deal has a proper characterization, the question is whether it is attractive given the company's attitude toward risk: does the company have the "stomach" for this deal? Failure to separate issues of characterization and desirability has been a perpetual source of confusion. From DAADT:

> Often arguments over which is the best decision arise because the participants do not realize that they are arguing on different grounds. Thus it is possible for *A* to think that a certain alternative is riskier than it is in *B*'s opinion, either because *A* assigns different probabilities to the outcomes than *B* but both are equally risk-averting, or because *A* and *B* assign the same probabilities to the outcomes but differ in their risk aversion. If we are to make progress in resolving the argument, we must identify the nature of the difficulty and bring it into the open. Similar clarifications may be made in the areas of time preference or in the measurement of the value of outcomes.

Challenges of Decision Analysis

Classical Statistics Persists

In spite of the clear perspectives on uncertainty provided by Laplacian probability, much of the teaching about uncertainty takes place in statistics classes where students are taught concepts that can only confuse them. They learn about confidence intervals and confidence statements and come to believe that a confidence statement is a probability assignment, even though the professor is careful not to say so. If ever there was a "wolf in sheep's clothing" it is a confidence statement posing as a probability assignment. Other classical statistics concepts have similar problems. Hypothesis testing tells you nothing about how to form the hypothesis or how to determine the probability level at which it can be rejected. Furthermore, if a hypothesis is rejected, there is no procedure for what to do next. Maximum likelihood procedures are based only on the data from an experiment and have no place for any preceding knowledge. None of these methods are what Maxwell had in mind.

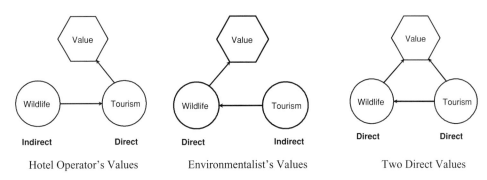

Figure 3.7. Values for tourism and wildlife.

Dealing with Multiple Attributes

Decision problems can have prospects with many attributes that the decision maker would like to consider. I will here consider some of the procedures that have been developed to address this problem.

DIRECT AND INDIRECT VALUES. Sometimes the decision maker needs to assess preferences on many fewer attributes than he or she would think. To see why, let us define direct and indirect values. A direct value is one to be traded off by the decision maker against other direct values. An indirect value is a distinction that is relevant to a direct value, but is not a direct value itself.

To illustrate, let us consider preferences for tourism and wildlife in Africa. A resort hotel operator might have values like those shown on the left of Figure 3.7.

We suppose that he does not care at all about wildlife, but is very concerned about tourism. He places a direct value on tourism and an indirect value on wildlife. Notice that the arrow connecting wildlife and tourism in this diagram is a relevance arrow. This means that the importance of wildlife depends on the information of the hotel operator. If a convincing study showed that tourism would be unaffected by the amount of wildlife, then the operator would not have an indirect value on wildlife. But if he believes, as is likely to be the case, that the tourists come to see wildlife, then he would support measures preserving wildlife habitat and preventing poaching.

The center diagram in Figure 3.7 shows how an environmentalist might value the same distinctions. The environmentalist places a direct value on wildlife and an indirect value on tourism. The importance of tourism to the environmentalist will depend on his beliefs about how the presence of tourists enhances or harms wildlife by, for example, providing funding for game wardens or interfering with habitat.

Notice that both of these people have only one direct value and therefore no reason for value trade-offs. Alternatives are judged by their effect on the one direct attribute. The right diagram in Figure 3.7 shows a value function for someone who places a direct value on both wildlife and tourism. Alternatives that produced different levels of these attributes would require trade-offs between them.

I once conducted a session with oil company executives who believed they had to deal with about thirty different attributes in making their decisions. After about an hour of discussion, and of direct and indirect values, they finally agreed that there were only two direct values. One was the profitability of the company, and the other was harm to people surrounding their facilities as the result of company operations.

Focusing on direct values considerably simplifies analysis of multiattribute decision situations.

TREATING MULTIATTRIBUTE PROBLEMS USING A VALUE FUNCTION. Suppose I have reduced a multiattribute problem I face to n attributes that have direct value. I would want one of these attributes to be a value measure so that I can compute the value of clairvoyance, or of any experimentation, in terms of this measure. In this n-dimensional space I now construct isopreference surfaces, combinations of attribute levels that are equally desirable to me. I can then identify each surface by its intercept with the value function. If I now have a joint distribution on the $n - 1$ other attributes, I will have a derived distribution on the value measure. I can then assign a u-curve on the value measure and determine the certain equivalent of any alternative that could produce these attributes, and thereby make my choice. The u-curve on the value measure would imply preferences under uncertainty for each of the other attributes. No additional information would be contained in these preferences. Proceeding in this fashion will allow establishing trade-offs within the attributes and, in particular, between any two attributes when the value of all others are specified. The incorporation of the value measure permits the decision maker to see the implication of choices in terms of a value scale of common experience. The benefit of being able to compute the value of clairvoyance or of any other information is attainable only by using a value measure (Matheson and Howard 1968).

OTHER APPROACHES TO MULTIATTRIBUTE PROBLEMS. Other approaches for multiattribute problems divide into two classes: those that satisfy the rules and those that do not. One that satisfies the rules is the approach of placing a *multidimensional utility function* directly on the attributes (Keeney and Raiffa 1976). This approach does not use a value function and as a result cannot have the advantage of computing the value of clairvoyance unless a value measure is one of the attributes. A check (Keeney and Raiffa 1976) reveals that there is no discussion of the value of information gathering in that book.

The other class of approaches to the multiattribute valuation problem consists of simplifications that do not offer all the benefits of the rules or methods that do not follow the rules and hence may not meet some of the desiderata.

WEIGHT AND RATE. A simple way to handle many attributes is to assign, say, 100 points total and then assign them to each of the attributes in accordance with their importance. The next step is to rate each of the alternatives by seeing how many of the points of each attribute are earned by that alternative. The point value of the alternative is obtained by summing over all attributes. This procedure is very simple and may be helpful in choosing a car or a stereo. It is not so helpful when there is uncertainty. Weight and rate assumes that preference for these deterministic attributes is linear in the attributes: there can be no interaction among them. When I construct my preferences for a peanut butter and jelly sandwich, I find they do not meet this condition. In summary, weight and rate methods can be helpful, but cannot bear the weight of decisions with uncertainty like choosing treatment by drugs or an operation, pharmaceutical development, or planning finances for retirement.

ANALYTIC HIERARCHY PROCESS. A widely used process that does not obey the rules is the analytic hierarchy process (AHP) (Howard 1992). The result of the process is a weight and rate system that is derived on the basis of comparative judgments of importance, preference, and likelihood. The process has an air of mathematical sophistication, but its results are easily produced in a spreadsheet by averaging or, equivalently, and with much more ado, by eigenvalues from matrix iteration. AHP can incorporate uncertainty only approximately, has a major difficulty in incorporating experimental information, cannot compute the value of information, and can provide no warranty that the alternative it recommends is the best one. Because it does not follow the rules, it is subject to failing a desideratum, like the one requiring that removing a noninformative alternative cannot change the ordering of the existing alternatives (Dyer 1990).

Why, then, do inferior processes find favor with decision makers? The answer is that they do not force you to think very hard or to think in new ways. Because we rarely find epistemic probability in our educational system, even in engineering, medical, and business schools, it is not surprising that people generally find it challenging to follow the dictum of Maxwell. In decision making, as in many other pursuits, you have a choice of doing something the easy way or the right way, and you will reap the consequences.

Risk Preference

The notion of risk preference and its representation is still a problem for people and organizations. I once heard a distinguished decision science professor give a brilliant presentation to business school professors on the necessity of having a personal risk attitude to guide decisions. After the lecture, and in private, a graduate student asked the professor what his personal risk attitude, that is, u-curve, was. The professor admitted that he did not have one.

The issue of risk preference in my experience goes back to DAADT:

> . . . for example, although we have tended to think of the utility theory as an academic pursuit, one of our major companies was recently faced with the question, "Is 10 million dollars of profit sufficient to incur one chance in 1 million of losing 1 billion dollars?" Although the loss is staggering, it is realistic for the company concerned. Should such a large company be risk-indifferent and make decisions on an expected value basis? Are stockholders responsible for diversifying their risk externally to the company or should the company be risk-averting on their behalf? For the first time the company faced these questions in a formal way rather than deciding the particular question on its own merits and this we must regard as a step forward.

Life and Death Decisions

One area in which I have a special interest is the use of decision analysis for making safety decisions, and in general decisions involving a risk of death or serious bodily harm (Howard 1978, 1980a, 1984, 1989a, 1999). I distinguish three stages of analysis. The first is *risk assessment* to assess the magnitude of risks to life in a proper unit. The second is *risk evaluation* to determine the importance of the risk in monetary terms. The third is *risk management*, or *decision making*, to choose what course of action best balances the advantages, disadvantages, and safety consequences.

By using a properly sized probability unit, the microprobability, defined as a probability of one in one million, small risks of death can be appreciated. A micromort, one microprobability of death, is a handy unit of measure for the death risks faced from accidents. Placing a value on a micromort permits making many safety decisions such as whether to take a beneficial drug with possible deadly side effects.

Future of Decision Analysis

Is it possible that the discipline of decision analysis developed over the last 40 years is no longer necessary because of improvements in decision making? Has the phenomenal growth in computation and the availability of information obviated the need for decision analysis? Unfortunately, that is not the case. Executives today are making the same mistakes their parents and grandparents used to make. I hear consultants who observe poor executive decision making say, "If we could have only 1 percent of the waste." Even the field of science has not learned the lesson. Scientific journals are still accepting hypotheses that cannot be rejected at the 95 percent confidence level. I believe that if Laplace could see the state of modern decision making, he would be appalled by our failure to use the systems we have been discussing, especially now that we have the computational and communication tools he could only have dreamed of. With few exceptions (e.g., Decision Education Foundation), students in elementary, secondary, college, and graduate schools do not learn how to think in an uncertain world.

Decision analysis has thrived in certain environments. Some consulting companies rely extensively on it. Decision analysis is entrenched in major industries like petroleum and pharmaceuticals, and is heavily employed in electric power. There is hardly an industry from paper to movie making that has not made use of decision analysis.

It has been said that any strength is accompanied by a weakness, and that is true of decision analysis. One of its greatest strengths is its transparency: the decision basis is laid out for all participants to see – the alternatives considered, the information used and its sources, and finally the preferences. Organizations wanting to use the full capability of their members to improve the quality of a decision find this to be a great advantage. However, transparency is equally a threat to executives and organizations wishing to limit alternatives, control information, and hide preferences. The more open the organization, private or public, the more it will value the process of decision analysis.

Epilogue

To me, incorporating the principles and philosophy of decision analysis is not just learning the subject, but more like installing a new operating system in your brain. You can no longer run your old thought programs.

Acknowledgment

I thank Ali Abbas for many helpful suggestions in preparing this chapter.

REFERENCES

Bernoulli, D. (1738). Specimen Theoriae Novae de Mensura Sortis (Exposition of a New Theory on the Measurement of Risk). *Commentarii Academiae Scientiarum Imperialis Petropolitanae, Tomus V (Papers of the Imperial Academy of Sciences in Petersburg, Vol. V)*, pp. 175–192.

Cox, R. T. (1961). *Algebra of Probable Inference*. Baltimore: Johns Hopkins University Press.

Decision Education Foundation. http://decisioneducation.org.

Dyer, J. S. (1990). Remarks on the Analytic Hierarchy Process. *Management Science, 36* (3), 249–258.

Howard, R. A. (1965). Bayesian Decision Models for Systems Engineering. *IEEE Transactions on Systems, Science and Cybernetics, SSC-1*(1) 36–40.

Howard, R. A. (1966a). Decision Analysis: Applied Decision Theory. *Proceedings of the Fourth International Conference on Operational Research*. New York: Wiley-Interscience, pp. 55–71. Reprinted in R. A. Howard and J. E. Matheson, J. E. (Eds.). (1984). *Readings on the Principles and Applications of Decision Analysis*. Menlo Park, CA: Strategic Decisions Group, April.

Howard, R. A. (1966b). Information Value Theory. *IEEE Transactions on Systems, Science, and Cybernetics, SSC-2* (1), 22–26.

Howard, R. A. (1968). The Foundations of Decision Analysis. *IEEE Transactions on Systems, Science, and Cybernetics, SSC-4*(3) 211–219.

Howard, R. A. (1970). Decision Analysis: Perspectives on Inference, Decision, and Experimentation. *Proceedings of the IEEE, 58*(5), 632–643.

Howard, R. A. (1973). Decision Analysis in Systems Engineering. In R. F. Miles, Jr. (Ed.), *Systems Concepts: Lectures on Contemporary Approaches to Systems*. New York: John Wiley, pp. 51–85.

Howard, R. A. (1975). Social Decision Analysis. *Proceedings of the IEEE, 63*(3), 359–371.

Howard, R. A. (1978). Life and Death Decision Analysis. *Proceedings of the Second Lawrence Symposium on Systems and Decision Sciences*, Berkeley, CA, October.

Howard, R. A. (1980). An Assessment of Decision Analysis. *Special Issue on Decision Analysis, Operations Research, 28*(1), 4–27.

Howard, R. A. (1980a). On Making Life and Death Decisions. In R. C. Schwing, W. A. Albers, Jr. (Eds.), *Societal Risk Assessment, How Safe Is Safe Enough?* General Motors Research Laboratories. New York: Plenum Press.

Howard, R. A. (1984). On Fates Comparable to Death. *Special Issue of Management Science*, April.

Howard, R. A. (1984a). The Evolution of Decision Analysis. In R. A. Howard and J. E. Matheson (Eds.), *READINGS on the Principles and Applications of Decision Analysis*. Menlo Park, CA: Strategic Decisions Group, pp. 7–11.

Howard, R. A. (1988). Decision Analysis: Practice and Promise. *Management Science, 34*(6), 679–695.

Howard, R. A. (1988a). Uncertainty about Probability: A Decision Analysis Perspective. *Risk Analysis, 8*(1), 91–98.

Howard, R. A. (1989). Knowledge Maps. *Management Science, 35*(8), 903–922.

Howard, R. A. (1989a). Microrisks for Medical Decision Analysis. *International Journal of Technology Assessment in Health Care, 5*(3), 357–370.

Howard, R. A. (1990). From Influence to Relevance to Knowledge. In R. M. Oliver, and J. Q. Smith (Eds.), *Influence Diagrams, Belief Nets, and Decision Analysis*. New York: John Wiley & Sons Ltd., pp. 3–23.

Howard, R. A. (1991). Business Ethics: Tell the Truth. *Journal of Management Development, 11*(4), 4–10.

Howard, R. A. (1992). Heathens, Heretics, and Cults: The Religious Spectrum of Decision Aiding. *Interfaces, 22*(6), 15–27.

Howard, R. A. (1992a). In Praise of the Old Time Religion. In W. Edwards, (Ed.), *Utility Theories: Measurements and Applications*. Boston: Kluwer Academic Publishers, pp. 27–55.

Howard, R. A. (1996). Options. In R. Zeckhauser, R. Keeney, and J. Sibenius (Eds.), *Wise Choices: Decisions, Games, and Negotiations*. Boston: Harvard Business School Press.

Howard, R. A. (1998). Foundations of Professional Decision Analysis: A Manuscript in Process. Stanford University Course Notes. Publication in preparation.

Howard, R. A. (1999). Life and Death Decisions for Individuals and Couples. In J. Shanteau, B. Mellers, and D. Schum (Eds.), *Decision Science and Technology: Reflections on the Contributions of Ward Edwards*. Boston: Kluwer Academic Publishers, pp. 227–254.

Howard, R. A. (2000). Decisions in the Face of Uncertainty. In C. Alexander (Ed.), *Visions of Risk*. London: Pearson Education Limited.

Howard, R. A. (2001). The Ethical OR/MS Professional. *Interfaces, 31*(6), 69–82.

Howard, R. A. (2004). Speaking of Decisions: Precise Decision Language. *Decision Analysis, 1*(2)), 71–78.

Howard, R. A. (2005). An Appreciation of Ed Jaynes. *Proceedings of the Twenty Fifth International Workshop on Bayesian Inference and Maximum Entropy Methods in Science and Engineering*. AIP Conference Proceedings 803, pp. 53–66, San Jose, CA.

Howard, R. A., and Matheson, J. E. (1980). Influence Diagrams. Private Report. Reprinted in R. A. Howard and J. E. Matheson (Eds.). (1984). *READINGS on the Principles and Applications of Decision Analysis*. Menlo Park, CA: Strategic Decisions Group, April.

Howard, R. A., and Matheson, J. E. (2005). Influence Diagrams. *Decision Analysis, 2*(3) 127–143

Jaynes, E. T. (1986). Bayesian Methods: General Background. In J. H. Justice (Ed.), *Maximum-Entropy and Bayesian Methods in Applied Statistics*. Cambridge, UK: Cambridge University Press, p. 1.

Jaynes, E. T. (2003). *Probability Theory: The Logic of Science*. Cambridge, UK: Cambridge University Press.

Jeffreys, H. (1939/1961). *The Theory of Probability*. (3rd ed.). New York: Oxford University Press.

Keeney, R. L., and Raiffa, H. (1976). *Decisions with Multiple Objectives*. New York: John Wiley & Sons, Inc.

Laplace, P. S. (1812). *Analytical Theory of Probability*. Paris.

Laplace, P. S. (1996). *A Philosophical Essay on Probabilities*. Dover Publications.

Matheson, J. E., and Howard, R. A. (1968). An Introduction to Decision Analysis. In R. A. Howard and J. E. Matheson (Eds.), *The Principles and Applications of Decision Analysis, Vol. I.* Menlo Park, CA: Strategic Decisions Group.

Maxwell, J. C. (1850). Letter to L. Campbell. See www.ewartshaw.co.uk/data/jehsquot.pdf.

4 Decision Analysis: A Personal Account of How It Got Started and Evolved

Howard Raiffa

EDITORS' NOTE. In this chapter Howard Raiffa discusses the evolution of decision analysis and his personal involvement in its development. He describes the early days of Operations Research (OR) in the late 1940s with its approach to complex, strategic decision making. After reading John von Neumann and Oskar Morgenstern's *Theory of Games and Economic Behavior* (1947) and Abraham Wald's two books (1947, 1950), he became involved in statistical decision theory. A few years later, after reading Leonard Savage's *The Foundations of Statistics* (1954), he became convinced that classical statistics was not the right approach to analysis for decision making. In 1957, with R. Duncan Luce, he published *Games and Decisions* (1957), which presented the theory of von Neumann and Morgenstern to a wider audience. In 1961, with Robert Schlaifer, he published *Applied Statistical Decision Theory* (1961) to prove that "whatever the objectivists could do, we subjectivists could also do – only better." In 1968, he published *Decision Analysis* (1968), the first book on the subject, and, in 1976, he published *Decisions with Multiple Objectives* (1976) with Ralph Keeney. These two books laid the foundation of decision analysis as it is practiced today. His interests then tuned to negotiation, resulting in the publication of *The Art and Science of Negotiation* (1982) and *Negotiation Analysis* (2002).

The Operations Research Antecedent

I am no historian, and whenever I try, I get into trouble. I invariably forget some insignificant figures like Newton, Pascal, or Gauss, or – what is a bit more tragic – I forget some really significant figure like the fellow whose office is next to mine. What I propose to do is much more modest: I am going to concentrate on myself – on who influenced me and why, how my thinking changed over time.

I was one of those returning G.I.s who resumed their college studies at the end of World War II. I studied mathematics and statistics at the University of Michigan in the late 1940s, and as a graduate student in mathematics worked as an operations researcher on a project sponsored by the Office of Naval Research. In those days, Operations Research (OR) was not so much a collection of mathematical techniques but an *approach* to complex, strategic decision making. Typically the decision entity was some branch of government – usually one of the armed services – and they were confronted with an ill-formed problem. Part of the task of the OR expert was to crystallize the problem and structure it in such a way that systematic thinking could help the decision entity to make a wise choice. My impression is that, during the war, the OR practitioners were mostly engineers and physicists with only a sprinkling of mathematicians. The problems were usually complex and required some systems thinking. Embedded in these complexities were elements of uncertainty and of game-like, competitive interactions. The most practical analyses resorted to simulations to decide which strategies were reasonable. Very often, profound insights might flow using mathematical analysis not more sophisticated than high school algebra. Indeed, there was a bias against the use of advanced mathematics. The simpler the analytical tool, the better.

As the field of OR matured, mathematical researchers isolated key recurrent problems – like queueing problems – and used advanced mathematical techniques to get analytical solutions. The name of the game became simplification of reality to make mathematical analysis feasible. Then these analytically motivated abstractions were gradually made more intricate as the body of mathematical techniques grew. The trend went from elementary analysis of complex, ill-structured problems to advanced analysis of well-structured problems. In OR departments, mathematical elegance displaced the old quest for making empirically based contributions to messy real problems. A sign of maturity, I suppose.

In the early days of OR, descriptions of complex realities used probabilities and one did not worry too much if these were judgmentally biased, but as the field "matured," probabilities were increasingly confined to the objective domain and interpreted as long-run frequencies. There was no hint of how to best elicit subjective, judgmental information from experts about uncertainties or in identifying and structuring multiple conflicting objectives.

I suspect that my continuing interest in *prescriptive* decision analysis had its roots firmly planted in that first academic type of job I had as a so-called "operations researcher." In that role, I was initiated into the cult that examined the world through decision-enhancing binoculars: *What's the problem? Who are the decision makers? What advice would I give?* A blatant, prescriptive, advice-giving orientation.

From OR to Game Theory to Statistical Decision Theory

Back to my personal odyssey. In the academic year 1948–1949, I switched from the study of statistics to pure mathematics (at the University of Michigan) and as an OR research assistant working on detection of submarines, I read parts of von Neumann and Morgenstern's (1947) epic volume and started working in the theory of games. Meanwhile, in 1949–1950, the statistics seminar started working through Abraham Wald's two books, *Sequential Analysis* (1947) and *Statistical Decision Theory* (1950), and I gave a series of seminars on those books – especially on those esoteric topics that made extensive use of game theory. About that time, a tragedy occurred: Abraham Wald was killed in an air crash over India and Jacob Wolfowitz, Wald's close associate at Columbia, took a post at Cornell, so what was left at Columbia in the domain of statistical decision theory were a few Ph.D. students with no faculty leaders. Because I reputedly knew something of

Wald's work, I got my first academic appointment in the Mathematical Statistics Department at Columbia. I was supposed to guide those students of Wald, who knew more about the subject than I.

My Gradual Disillusionment with Classical Statistics

Besides teaching decision theory à la Wald, I also had to teach the basic courses in statistics – the usual stuff on testing hypotheses, confidence intervals, unbiased estimation. These courses were mostly concerned with problems of inference, and little attention was paid to the integration of inference and decision. When I studied those problems more carefully, I felt that the frequency-based material on inference was not so much wrong but largely irrelevant for decisional purposes. I began not to believe what I was teaching.

It's not surprising that the rumblings against the Neyman–Pearson school were most pronounced at the University of Chicago, the home of the Cowles Commission, which mixed together mathematical economists (like Jacob Marschak and Tjalling Koopmans) with statisticians (like Jimmy Savage, Herman Chernoff, and Herman Rubin). It was the articulation of Rubin's sure-thing principle in a paper by Chernoff (1954) that led me to embrace the subjective school. My religious-like conversion did not come lightly, since all I was teaching about (tests of hypotheses, confidence intervals, and unbiased estimation) was, in my newly held opinion, either wrong or not central. But my colleagues in the statistics departments were so violently opposed to using judgmental probabilities that I became a closet subjectivist. To them, statistics belonged in the scientific domain, and the introduction of squishy judgmental probabilities where opinions differed did not belong in this world of hard science.

The seminal book by Savage (1954) did not so much convert me to the subjectivist camp – I was already converted intellectually by the time I read this bible – but it convinced me that I was on the right track.

At Columbia, I was a member of the interdisciplinary Behavioral Models Project – actually, as the junior faculty member of the project, I was appointed the chair of that project – and Duncan Luce and I worked on what was supposed to be a 50-page expository article (one of many on different topics) and this turned into our book, *Games and Decisions* (Luce and Raiffa 1957). It took us two years to write and in those days, sans e-mail, we spent at most seven days working on the same coast of the United States. Luce was at the Stanford-based Center for Advanced Study and I was back at Columbia or vice versa.

Go to Harvard or Stay at Columbia?

In 1957, I received an offer to go to Harvard to take a joint appointment between their Business School (the B-School henceforth) and a newly formed statistical department. I had a tough time deciding between Columbia and Harvard because neither alternative dominated on all objectives. It was rumored that when

I told one of my colleagues I was having trouble deciding, he quipped: "Trouble? But, Howard, you are supposed to be an expert in making decisions!" "But," I supposedly answered, "this is for real!" Nope, this is not true. I never said such a thing. Actually, my wife and I subjected this decision to a primitive, multiple-value analysis involving ten objectives. In the formal analysis, Harvard won easily.

Splitting My Time Between Statistics Department and the B-School

I knew so little about business, that in my mind I planned to spend far more time in the statistics department than at the B-School. But the opposite time allocations prevailed for two reasons: (1) My introduction to the case method, and (2) Robert O. Schlaifer.

I was introduced to the case method of instruction, and it blew my mind. The MBA student prepared two or three different cases each day, and most of these were *real* decision problems – each replete with competing objectives, with loads of uncertainties, and all embedded in a game-like environment. A veritable treasure trove of real-world examples that cried out for theoretical attention. *All those cases to be mined*, and I had the wrong set of tools. And then I met the amazing R. O. Schlaifer.

Schlaifer was hired by the B-School as a flexible resource who was smart enough to learn and teach any one of a number of subjects. For one semester he taught marketing, then financial control, and then, because the B-School's only statistician retired, Schlaifer was called in to fill that void. He was trained as a classical Greek scholar and never had a previous course in statistics or any mathematics beyond one semester of the calculus. So he read the classics in statistics and independently, without any outside coaching, decided that Fisher and Neyman and Pearson had it all wrong: The way to go was to closely knit the study of uncertainties with business decisions. He also was not aware of the rumblings in the field. So he began teaching his own version of statistical decision theory based on subjective probability assessments of expert, business managers – making it up as he went along. I recognized genius when I saw it and I became his personal mathematics tutor – the best student I ever had – and we worked together on developing statistics for an astute business manager.

From Closet Bayesian to Proselytizer

It didn't take long, working with Schlaifer, that I too got religion and gained the necessary conviction that the subjective school was the right school – certainly for business decisions – and I came out of the closet and began preaching the gospel according to Bayes' disciples.

It was now 1958, and we were convinced that our mission was to spread the gospel. Even statisticians who were on our side in the philosophical debates about the foundations were skeptical about implementing it. They felt: (1) *The subjective (Bayesian) approach is all too complicated*, and (2) *real experts won't cooperate by giving judgmental information*.

In 1958, Schlaifer and I set out to prove that whatever the objectivists could do, we subjectivists could also do – only better – and in 1961, we published a compendium of results entitled *Applied Statistical Decision Theory (ASDT)* (Raiffa and Schlaifer 1961). It was much more a reference volume than a textbook. We deemed our efforts a success.

At the same time, during this period, we and some of our students did get out into the field and collected judgmental probabilities galore from real experts about real events. (A good many of these experts were design engineers and marketing specialists from DuPont and Ford.) We proved to ourselves that we were on the right path. We were not troubled by the problem of expert cooperation but about the quality of their judgmental inputs. We learned how to ask for the input data we needed by the proper framing of questions. We told our experts to expect incoherencies in their responses to our hypothetical questions and those incoherencies should only prompt them to think even more deeply about their expertise. We learned not to ask questions one way or another way, but to ask both ways and to confront resulting incoherencies in an open manner. We learned that the experts calibrated better if questions were posed in terms of assets rather than in incremental monetary amounts and that by and large their judgmental inter quartile ranges were too tight – rather than capturing half the true uncertain quantities, they were capturing only a third. We became experts in the art of soliciting judgmental information. I'm reminded here of the complaint that it seems wrong to build a logical edifice on such imperfect input data, to which Jimmy Savage responded, "Better to construct a building on shifting sands than on a void." Here, the "void" being no use of judgment inputs.

Our book, *ASDT*, had at best a very limited circulation when published in 1961, but in the year 2000 it was republished by John Wiley & Sons in their Classic Series.

Decision Trees

Because many of our business students were bright but mathematically unsophisticated, I formulated most problems in terms of decision trees, which became very standard fare. The standard statistical paradigm, involving a decision whose payoff depended on an uncertain population parameter, was presented in a four-move decision tree:

Move 1 (*decision node*). Choice of an experiment (e.g., sample size).
Move 2 (*chance node*). Sample outcome.
Move 3 (*decision node*). Choice of a terminal act.
Move 4 (*chance node*). Revelation of the true population parameter.

Associated to any path through the tree was a known payoff value.

When I taught objectivist-based statistical decision theory at Columbia, I had little need for the decision tree because objectivists shunned the use of any probabilistic assessment at Moves 2 and 4. The only probabilities the objectivists would allow were conditional probabilities of sample outcomes given assumed population values. The subjectivists use not only this class of probabilities, but also prior probabilities over the population parameters – *prior* meaning before the revelation of sample evidence – and from these inputs and the use of Bayes' formula the subjectivist can derive appropriate probabilities to enter at Moves 2 and 4. Hence the appellations of "Bayesian." I got so used to the use of decision trees in communicating with my students that I couldn't formulate any problem without drawing a decision tree and I was referred to as "Mr. Decision Tree," and what I did was "Decision-Tree Analysis." It took a few years to drop the "tree" from that appellation.

From Statistical Decision Theory to Managerial Economics (1961–1964)

The three years from 1961–1964 were frenetic, and in retrospect, quite productive. First, Schlaifer and I were joined by John Pratt and we wrote a more user-friendly version of *ASDT* for classroom consumption, replete with hundreds, if not thousands, of exercises and caselets. McGraw-Hill distributed a preliminary version of this unfinished book (1965), all 1,000 pages, in a cardboard blue binder and the book was called the "blue monster" or *Introduction to Statistical Decision Theory* (ISDT). It was not published as a finished book until a delay of four decades, only after Schlaifer's demise in 1994 and after my retirement in 1994, and the reason is a bit crazy in retrospect. We (Schlaifer and I, and not Pratt) simply lost interest in pursuing the standard and much too binding statistical decision theory paradigm. We no longer thought of ourselves as applied statisticians but as "managerial economists." We thought the transformation in outlook was profound, and no longer did we have time to polish a book that was too narrow in scope. After publishing *ASDT*, I had time to study case after case in the MBA repertoire of cases, and it was crystal clear that managers galore needed some systematic way of thinking about their decision problems, which were overwhelmingly concerned with uncertainties that needed the judgmental inputs of managers. The statistical paradigm was out of kilter, was hobbling. A typical business decision problem might involve several uncertainties, and some of them required the judgments of production managers or marketing specialists or financial experts with no possibility of accumulating sampling evidence. To force those problems into a statistical decision format was too cumbersome. At about that time, I also supervised the thesis of Jack Grayson, who was interested in describing how oil wildcatters made decisions. I got him to adopt a more prescriptive orientation that dealt not only with physical uncertainties – is there oil down there and how much – but the sharing of risks and the formation of syndicates (Grayson 1960).

Schlaifer not only agreed with my assessment for the need of paradigmatic shift in emphasis away from the statistical model, but in his inimitable style he went to the extreme and would have nothing to do with that blue monster that was holding back progress. We became "managerial economists." In a prodigious effort, he developed, without my involvement, a case-based MBA course in managerial economics for all our 800 entering MBA students. I spent my time on other things, but my admiration for Schlaifer remained steadfast.

From Business and Statistics to Business and Economics (1964–1968)

I received an offer I could hardly refuse: a joint chair endowed by the Business School and the Economics Department, and because these two behemoth organizations could not agree on a name for the professorship I was invited to select a name. I became the Frank P. Ramsey Professor of Managerial Economics. I never had a course in economics and was a bit apprehensive, but they appointed me because they realized, as I did, that the theory of risky choice should be an integral part of economics. I also must admit that I needed to establish some space between Schlaifer and myself.

From Managerial Economics to Decision Analysis

Although I now was a member of the Economics Department and my title dubbed me a managerial economist, I increasingly became interested in classes of problems that had little to do with management or economics – problems in governmental policy, in science policy, in public health, in clinical medicine. I no longer thought of myself as a managerial economist but more generally as a *decision analyst*.

Starting in 1964, in the Economics Department, I taught a graduate-level course in decision analysis and started preparing material for a book under that title (Raiffa 1968). Much later, I learned that Professor Ronald Howard of Stanford, one of the key developers of the field now called *decision analysis*, had independently adopted that name for his enterprise (Howard 1966). Evidently the time was ripe. I essentially taught the same thing in the Economics Department that I taught at the B-School, but the cases were different. Instead of maximizing expected profits, the objective functions became more complex and group decision making needed more attention.

My RAND Experience and the Development of Multi-attribute Utility Theory (MAUT)

I was invited by Charles Wolfe to spend the summer of 1964 at RAND studying and critiquing the methodology used in their reports. Not infrequently, I found that not enough attention was given to the recognition of competing, interrelated objectives of the analysis, and this resulted in a misspecification of the objective function to optimize. Also all too often, the hard drove out the soft. I wrote a RAND report on decisions with multiple objectives, and in that report I first introduced notions of preferential and utility independence (Raiffa 1969). With my very capable doctoral student Ralph Keeney, we further expanded on these primitive RAND results and we – mostly Ralph – helped develop the field of multi-attribute utility theory (MAUT) (Keeney and Raiffa 1976).

Clinical Medicine

In the mid-1960s, I worked closely with the Chief of Medicine at the New England School of Medicine, Dr. William Schwartz. Bill was an enthusiastic convert to decision analysis and wanted physicians to be trained in its use for diagnostics and treatment of individual patients in real time. If he had his way, all doctors would be required to take a course in decision analysis. He himself, with a hand calculator, made the medical rounds surrounded by a half a dozen eager students, and he would all but lay out a decision tree and work his way backward. I had more modest aspirations: I wanted a group of medical research specialists to write textbooks about the desirable treatment of categories of illnesses and to support their analyses through the use of detailed decision analyses. I envisioned standard reference books with lots of decision trees in the appendixes. In 1970, I think I had the better of the debate, but with the astounding development of computing capacity and speed and with the miniaturization of computers, Bill Schwartz has been vindicated. Today there is a professional society for medical decision analysis that is more than 20 years old.

From Business and Economics to Business and The Kennedy School of Government (1966–1970)

As a member of the Department of Economics I was asked by President Bok of Harvard to comment on a report that advocated a program for the revitalization of the School of Public Administration at Harvard. I criticized that report as suggesting a watered-down applied economics program with a little public policy thrown in. I suggested the development of a new School of Public Management patterned on the model of the B-School. I opined that the new school should have its own faculty, lay primary stress on a professional master's program, feature about 50–75 percent of its instruction by the case method, and have its own mini-campus. In rapid order, I became part of a committee of four that designed the new Kennedy School of Government, and I transferred the economics share of my joint professorship from the Economics Department to the newly formed Kennedy School of Government. Decision analysis became part of the core curriculum for the master's degree in public policy, and a required course in statistics was initially taught with a distinctly Bayesian orientation. That is no longer the case. New faculty, new curricula; what professors teach is primarily dictated by what they were taught.

The Decision and Control Nonprogram (1965–1975)

Harvard never had a department or center in operations research, and there was no substantial support to create such a center. So a few of us dedicated faculty decided to act on our own. Without any clearance from the faculty of arts and sciences or the B-School, a dozen of us met informally and mapped out a coordinated set of eight one-semester courses in what we dubbed *decision and control* (D&C) to be given regularly and spread out over three departments: the Division of Engineering and Applied Physics (now the Division of Applied Science), the Department of Statistics, and the Department of Economics. The courses were designed to be given in different departments, all with the same strong mathematical prerequisites, and care was taken to avoid scheduling conflicts. The courses were decision analysis, statistics, probability models, game theory, mathematical programming, control of dynamic systems, and an integrative seminar. There was no budget, no formal committee, no secretary, no request for any approval of any faculty. Ph.D. students who took these coordinated sets of courses were enrolled in different departments. It was all low key, and students who completed this program were given a letter from me, as the honcho organizer, attesting to their superior training. Imagine – it worked like a charm for a whole decade. It took a bit of chicanery to have these eight courses listed together in the division's course catalogue.

The D&C program worked, but not perfectly because we had no fellowship money to compete with Stanford or Chicago for talented students. So a group of us fought in the 1980s for the creation of a funded Ph.D. program in the decision sciences. We succeeded to get the arts and sciences faculty to approve this program, and initially the B-School funded the program to sustain a yield of four or five doctorates a year. However, the B-School withdrew its support a few years later because not enough of these completed Ph.D.s chose a business school career; several opted for public policy or public health or the environmental sciences. The Ph.D. in the decision sciences is still on the books as a Harvard program, but it desperately needs to be funded and reinvigorated. More about this later.

On Becoming a Negotiation Analyst

Negotiating the Creation of IIASA (1967–1972)

From 1967 to 1972 I was a member of the U.S. team that negotiated with the Soviet Union and ten other countries, both east and west, in establishing the International Institute for Applied Systems Analysis (IIASA). This took place during the height of the Cold War and was a confidence-building gesture. I learned a lot about the theory and practice of many-party negotiations in the presence of extreme cultural differences.

Directing IIASA from 1972 to 1975

As the first director of IIASA, I continued in my apprenticeship role as negotiator but I added the skills of an intervener in disputes (facilitator of group interactions, mediator, and arbitrator). I had, I believe, some natural talents, but it was a self-discovery method of learning. I lacked any prior expertise from a program of training in the art and science of negotiation. In 1975, I decided to return to

Harvard to learn about negotiations, rather than continue at IIASA or becoming a dean at some other university.

Back to Harvard and Learning about the Art and Science of Negotiation (1975–1981)

I taught a very popular course on negotiations at the B-School in the late 1970s that was for me a laboratory with well-motivated student-subjects. The students were partially graded on how well they did on various simulation exercises, and I learned enough about negotiations to write a book about it (Raiffa 1982). This was not decision analysis, but perhaps a claim can be made for its inclusion in the broader field of decision sciences. After all, negotiations are all about group decision making.

The Program on Negotiation (1982–)

In the early 1980s, Roger Fisher, coauthor of *Getting to Yes* (Fisher and Ury 1981) and I – more Roger than myself – established another administrative innovation. We created an interdepartmental, interuniversity consortium of academics interested in negotiations (broadly interpreted) and launched the Program on Negotiation (PON), located – note the delicacy of language – located at (but not part of) the Harvard Law School. PON is not an integral part of Harvard's infrastructure and draws no funds from the university. Initially, it was funded by the Hewlitt Foundation, but for the last ten years it earned its own way by offering executive educational programs with largely donated faculty time. It is financially secure enough now to offer pre-doctoral and some post-doctoral research fellowships, run a clearinghouse for the distribution of simulated exercises, sponsor a journal on negotiations, offer a prestigious award for the Negotiator of the Year, and run ongoing seminars.

From Decision Analysis to Policy Analysis and to Societal Risk Analysis

Nuclear Energy Policy Study (NEPS)

When I returned to Harvard from IIASA in 1975, I was invited by McGeorge Bundy, then president of the Ford Foundation, to join a group of scholars to prepare a report for the incoming president of the United States – it turned out to be Jimmy Carter – on what to do about nuclear energy (NEPS 1977). For the purposes of this article, there were two lasting impressions from my NEPS experience: (1) it served as a model for me about how to structure facilitated group interactions leading to a group report – not necessarily to group consensus; and (2) it kindled my interest in really broad public policy issues and how an analyst like myself could contribute to such an endeavor. Is this decision analysis or societal risk analysis? It is not statistical decision theory or managerial economics. It certainly belongs in a broad program of decision sciences.

The Committee on Risk and Decision Making (1980–1982)

Following my experiences at IIASA, following my participation in the NEPS group and my ongoing involvement in an independent committee overseeing the Three Mile Island cleanup, in 1980 I chaired the Committee on Risk and Decision Making (CORADM 1982) for the U.S. National Research Council of the U.S. National Academies. The committee's task was to report about the status of societal risk in the United States, about how large societal risks are handled and how they might be handled better, and how we should be preparing future analysts to cope with these problems. I found my task daunting and in the end completely frustrating, although along the way the experience was absolutely fascinating. Besides my disappointment with the discontinuance of the Ph.D. program in the decision sciences at Harvard, my CORADM experience was my only other major disappointment in my professional life. I give myself only a marginally passing grade as facilitator, mainly because the members of the committee were not completely engaged in the problem – after all they had their own responsibilities back home – and I was too involved in the substance to be both chairman and facilitator of meetings. Along with the help of John Graham, a master's degree candidate at Duke who has had a distinguished career since that time, I wrote a draft of a behemoth report of close to 700 pages on the deliberations of our distinguished committee. That report had difficulty with the peer review system, and the only tangible product was a watered-down report of about fifty pages. It didn't say what I thought should have been said, and the pressures of the time kept me from fighting the system. Secretary Ruckelshaus, who was a member of the CORADM and who later became the leader of the EPA, was most enthusiastic about the original draft report, and he adopted several of the recommendations found in that report. Some comfort can be taken from the observation that each reviewer professed different reasons for their unhappiness. The satisfying part of that experience is that I learned a lot about the group decision-making process – a lot of what should and should not be done.

Post-Retirement Reflections

Decision Making – A Critical Life Skill

I completely missed the boat when I published *Decision Analysis* (Raiffa 1968). I was so enamored of the power and elegance of the more mathematical aspects of this emerging field that I ignored the nonmathematical underpinnings: how to identify a problem or opportunity to be analyzed, how to specify the objectives of concern, and how to generate the alternatives to be analyzed. All this was given short shrift. All that nonmathematical starting stuff was ignored. Well, John

Hammond, Ralph Keeney, and I, in *Smart Choices* (1999), try to correct that. This book reaches out to the general public and offers coaching advice to practically everybody on how to make better personal and workplace decisions.

A New Look at Negotiation Analysis

The boundaries among individual decision making (decision analysis), interactive decision making (game theory), behavioral decision making, and joint decision making (as in negotiations) should be porous but are not. A partial synthesis of these strands is attempted in Raiffa (2002). How negotiators and interveners (facilitators, mediators, arbitrators) do and should behave (most should) in seeking equitable joint gains in exploiting deals as well as in resolving disputes. For example, a negotiator who has to decide whether he or she *should* continue negotiating or break off and pursue an independent strategy (a prescriptive orientation) typically must address an individual decision problem in an interactive (game-like) environment, not knowing what others might do (a descriptive orientation).

The Need for a New Field Called Decision Sciences

I truly believe that decision making – both individual and group; descriptive, normative, and prescriptive – is an important life skill that can be and should be taught broadly in our society. I think the right umbrella term for what I have in mind is *decision science*, and I hope that in your lifetime, if not mine, there will be departments of decision sciences created in our universities that will give undergraduate and graduate courses in this subject with many, many electives. Game theory (extended far beyond equilibrium theory) and negotiation theory (broadly interpreted to include conflict management, resolution, and avoidance, as well as the growing field of alternate dispute resolution) should be a part of this developing discipline. In this department of decision sciences there should be courses on societal risk analysis, and even on organizational design and on the structure of constitutions. There's a lot to be taught and a lot more to be learned: two prerequisites for a field of study. The decision sciences department should establish strong ties to the professional schools (especially business, public policy, public health, medicine), to the engineering school, to the departments of economics, psychology, government, mathematics, statistics, philosophy, and especially to the school of education. So let's get on with it.

Acknowledgment

Reprinted by permission, Raiffa, H. 2002. Decision analysis: A personal account of how it got started and evolved. Operations Research 50, pp. 179–185. Copyright 2002, the Institute for Operations Research and the Management Sciences, 7240 Parkway Drive, Suite 310, Hanover, MD 21076 USA.

REFERENCES (CHRONOLOGICALLY ARRANGED)

von Neumann, J., and Morgenstern, O. (1944, 1947). *Theory of games and economic behavior*. Princeton, NJ: Princeton University Press. (I read parts of this epic book in 1949 working for my Office of Naval Research Contract on submarine detection. My first introduction to utility theory.)

Wald, A. (1947). *Sequential analysis*. New York: John Wiley. (A quasi-decision oriented book that I studied alone in 1948 as a student in statistics.)

Wald, A. (1950). *Statistical decision theory*. New York: McGraw-Hill. (The pioneering book that sets up the statistical decision paradigm. I read this book as soon as it appeared and gave a series of seminars on it for the statistical seminar at the University of Michigan.)

Raiffa, H. (1951). *Arbitration schemes for generalized two-person games*. Report M-720–1, R30 Engineering Research Institute, University of Michigan. (Unpublished report written for an ONR contract that became the basis for my doctoral dissertation.)

Chernoff, H. (1954). Rational selection of decision functions. *Econometrica, 22*. (Chernoff makes use of the sure-thing principle of Herman Rubin that I adopt as one of my basic axioms in my struggle with foundations of statistics. It helped convert me into the subjectivist school.)

Savage, L. J. (1954). *The foundations of statistics*. New York: John Wiley. Revised 2nd edition in 1972. New York: Dover Publications. (The "bible" of the Bayesians.)

Luce, R. D., & Raiffa, H. (1957). *Games and decisions: Introduction and critical survey*. New York: John Wiley. Republished by Dover. (Reports on much of the unpublished results in my engineering report (1951). It compares the objectivist and subjectivist foundations of probability, but it doesn't openly endorse the Bayesian camp.)

Grayson, J. C. (1960). *Decisions under uncertainty: Drilling decisions by oil and gas operators*. Cambridge, MA: Harvard Business School. (This dissertation that I supervised made me realize that the statistical decision theory paradigm was too confining and I shifted from being a "statistical decision theorist" to being a "managerial economist.")

Schlaifer, R. O., and Raiffa, H. (1961). *Applied statistical decision theory*. Cambridge, MA: MIT Press. Republished in Wiley Classic Library Series (2000). (It introduces families of conjugate distribution that make it easy to go from prior distribution to posterior distributions and shows that Bayesianism can be made operational.)

Pratt, J. W., Raiffa, H., and Schlaifer, R. O. (1965). *Introduction to statistical decision theory*. Distributed by McGraw-Hill in mimeographic form. Published in finished form by MIT Press, New York, 1995. (A textbook version of *ASDT*. While widely adopted in mimeographic, unfinished form, it was not finished until 1995.)

Howard, R. A. (1966). Decision analysis: Applied decision theory. In *Proceedings of the Fourth International Conference on Operational Research*, New York: John Wiley. Reprinted in Howard & Matheson (1983). (First published paper referring to decision analysis and outlining its applicability.)

Raiffa, H. (1968). *Decision Analysis: Introductory lectures on choices under uncertainty*. Reading, MA: Addison Wesley. Reprinted in 1970. (Documents the paradigmatic shift from statistical decision theory to decision analysis.)

Raiffa, H. (1969). *Preference for multi-attributed alternatives*. RM-5868-DOT/RC. Santa Monica, CA: The RAND Corporation. (Earlier versions of this report were circulated in 1967 and influenced the early work by Keeney alone and with me.)

Raiffa, H. (1973). *Analysis for decision making*. An audiographic, self-instructional course. Ten volumes. Encyclopedia Britannica Educational Corp. Revised and republished by Learn, Inc. (1985).

Keeney, R. L., & Raiffa. H. (1976). *Decisions with multiple objectives: Preferences and value tradeoffs*. New York: John Wiley. Republished by Cambridge University Press, New York, 1993. (First serious attempt to develop analytical techniques for the value side of decision problems. Introduces ideas of preferential and utility independence.)

Nuclear Energy Policy Study. (1977). *Nuclear power issues and choices*. Pensacola, FL: Ballinger Publishing. (A model of a group policy exercise on an important, current, complex problem.)

Fisher, R., and Ury, W. (1981). *Getting to yes: Negotiating agreement without giving in.* New York: Houghton-Mifflin. Republished by Penguin Books, New York, 1983. (Helps establish the field of negotiations as a growth industry. Sold close to 4 million copies. Emphasis is on negotiating joint gains.)

Raiffa, H. (1982). *The art and science of negotiation*. Cambridge, MA: Harvard University Press. (Early attempt to show how analysis can be an integral part of the theory and practice of negotiations.)

The Committee on Risk and Decision Making (CORADM). (1982). *Report for the National Research Council of the National Academy of Sciences*. (Unpublished report on the status of societal risk analysis that failed to pass peer review. Chair: Howard Raiffa.)

Howard, R. A., and Matheson, J. (Eds.). (1983). *The principles and applications of decision analysis. Vol. I: General collection. Vol. II: Professional collection*. Menlo Park, CA: Strategic Decisions Group. (Documents the impressive evolution of decision analysis as it developed at Stanford by Ronald Howard and his student disciples.

Keeney, R. L. (1992). *Value-Focused thinking: A path to creative decisionmaking*. Cambridge, MA: Harvard University Press. (Stresses the importance of objectives and values in analyzing problems of choice. I think of it as an often neglected and much undeveloped part of decision analysis. Ralph Keeney thinks of it as a new specialty of its own that is separate from decision analysis.)

Lavalle, I. H. (1996). The art and science of Howard Raiffa. In Zeckhauser, R. J., Keeney, R. L., and Sebenius, J. K. (Eds.). *Wise choices: Decisions, games, and negotiations*. Cambridge, MA: Harvard University Press.

Zeckhauser, R. J., Keeney, R. L., and Sebenius, J. K. (Eds.). (1996). *Wise choices: Decisions, games, and negotiations*. Boston, MA: Harvard University Press. (Festschrift in honor of Howard Raiffa.)

Hammond, John S., Keeney, R. L., and Raiffa, H. (1999). *Smart Choices: A Practical Guide to Making Better Decisions*. Boston, MA: Harvard Business School Press. (An attempt to show the universality of decision analysis, broadly interpreted to include value analysis. An emphasis on problem identification and formation. Written for a broad audience. What should have been included in Raiffa (1968) but wasn't.)

Raiffa, H. (2002). *Negotiation Analysis: The Science and Art of Collaborative Decision Making*. Cambridge, MA: Harvard University Press, 2002. (With J. Richardson and D. Metcalfe) (A revision of Raiffa (1982) stressing the analysis of deals in contrast to disputes. It synthesizes the use of individual decision making (as in decision analysis), interactive decision making (as in game theory), and behavioral decision making in the analysis of negotiations (broadly interpreted).)

5 Reflections on the Contributions of Ward Edwards to Decision Analysis and Behavioral Research

Lawrence D. Phillips and Detlof von Winterfeldt

ABSTRACT. This chapter is based on the writings of Ward Edwards and the recollections of two of his graduate students whom he influenced deeply. Larry Phillips was his student from 1960 to 1966 and Detlof von Winterfeldt was his student from 1970 to 1975. Both continued their interactions with Ward until his death in February 2005. Larry interviewed Ward in February 2003 to record his early days and contributions to decision analysis and behavioral research. Video clips from this interview were shown at a special session of the Decision Analysis Society meeting in San Francisco in 2005, and the presentation will be posted on the Decision Analysis Society web site (www.fuqua.duke.edu/faculty/daweb). Detlof met Ward together with Ralph Miles almost weekly in 2003 and 2004, mostly planning new activities, like editing this book, but also conducting interviews and discussing the early days of behavioral decision research and his work at the University of Southern California (USC). A videotaped recording of Detlof's interview with Ward can be obtained from USC. Much of this chapter summarizes these interviews and our personal memories of Ward.

Ward Edwards: Founder of Behavioral Decision Theory

In 1954 and 1961 Ward Edwards published two seminal articles that created behavioral decision research as a new field in psychology (Edwards 1954, 1961). The topics of this research include how people make decisions and how these decisions can be improved with tools and training. In his 1954 *Psychological Bulletin* article (Edwards 1954) he introduced the *expected utility model* to psychologists and he asked if people actually behave this way, balancing the desirability of an outcome against its chance of occurring, as economists had assumed. That paper identified the issues, but it wasn't until Ward's 1961 *Annual Review of Psychology* paper (Edwards 1961) that we see in the title, "Behavioral Decision Theory," the formal beginnings of the new field. In just six years, 139 papers relevant to the discipline had appeared, and subsequent exponential growth prevented any comprehensive tracking of research.

Ward fueled the growth, but not by proselytizing. He was a listener, working hard at trying to understand colleagues and students as they talked about their research ideas, commenting and criticizing where it was needed, typically with good humor, sometimes expressed in limericks. He was helpful to his students, finding hundreds of thousands of dollars over the years in gifts, research contracts, and grants, to fund their studies. He was generous in authorship; if his students had done more work on a paper than he, they were made first author. He traveled extensively, seeking out new sets of people to communicate with, and he told Larry that suffering fools and bastards helps a lot, for it avoids making enemies. He did not seek honors, finding them pleasant if they arrived, but taking most delight in being included in the reference lists of other people's papers. His own papers are a delight to read. Eschewing jargon, he communicated complex ideas in simple language, using analogies and metaphors, laced with humor.

The Early Days

Ward was born in Morristown, New Jersey, in 1927. His father was an economist, and as a young man Ward enjoyed overhearing the discussions in his home by economists, who were concerned with real-world issues, a concern that stayed with Ward all his life. After studying psychology at Swarthmore College, he went to Harvard as a graduate student the same year B. F. Skinner arrived, giving Ward a worm's eye view of behaviorism. But, being "a snotty-nosed kid, happy to take a disparate point of view," he found it easy to "reject that as what psychology shouldn't do."[1] Ironically, he married Ruth, Skinner's first Ph.D. student.

At Harvard he studied under Fred Mosteller, who introduced him to the work of von Neumann and Morgenstern and the expected utility model. He was also influenced by S. Smith Stevens, whose work on psychophysics examined the relationship between an objective stimulus and the corresponding sensation experienced by a person. Ward thought it odd that the expected utility model assumed nonlinear evaluations of money, but linear evaluations of probabilities. In his thesis (Edwards 1954), he studied people's preferences for gambles that differed in probabilities and found preferences for some probabilities, especially 50–50 gambles, other things being equal.

In his first job, at Johns Hopkins University, Ward asked for a carrel in the economics library, assembled the literature he had not read at Harvard, and eventually produced his landmark 1954 paper. In the meantime, he was supposed to be teaching social psychology, a topic of little interest to him, and his less-than-diligent attention to those duties led Clifford Morgan, then the head of the psychology department, to fire him. His direct supervisor, Walter "Tex" Garner, then on sabbatical, introduced Ward to Arthur W. Melton, who was head of research at the U.S. Air Force Personnel and Training Research Center (AFPTRC). Art found a job for Ward in Denver, where he created the Intellectual Functions section, which was expected to be relevant. He discovered a huge field of unsolved problems to which decision theory is relevant, and he later considered that the most fortunate thing that ever happened to him, for it brought him into direct contact with real-world problems. He soon found his métier, exploring the intellectual side of the problem being faced, as he had heard his father's colleagues do. He also played a lot of poker, a game that was to assume increasing relevance in his career.

[1] The statements in quotation marks are direct quotes of Ward's interview with Larry Phillips in February 2003.

A personal conflict with the head of the AFPTRC led Melton to leave for the University of Michigan, with an agreement he could take one person with him. He chose Ward, who was not given a faculty appointment, but could teach one course. Art also brought contacts, funds and contracts to a department that was growing to be the largest in the world. Ward and Ruth found an old farmhouse to live in at Ann Arbor, with their daughter, Tara, newly arrived son, Page, and two dachshunds, one named Willy, after Wilhelm Wundt, the founder of experimental psychology. It was the beginning of an era fondly remembered by his graduate students, for the heady evening seminars at the farmhouse, exploring in great depth the latest developments, requiring an original discussion paper by a graduate student at each meeting. Or the dinners at the farmhouse, at which his students savored Ruth's excellent, if often exotic, cooking, with the early arrivals required to light dozens of candles placed on every horizontal surface in living and dining rooms.

In their offices and "back at the lab," his students had the pick of more than 200 graduate students with whom to interact, providing a stimulating intellectual atmosphere supported by a busy social life. These included Amos Tversky, Paul Slovic, Sarah Lichtenstein, and many others who carved out distinguished careers. However, it was partly an uneasy time for Ward, as he had not yet secured a tenured post, and his occasional colorful and forthright behavior led to rumors that he might not achieve it. Paul, Sarah, and Larry organized a letter of support, and though we do not know what effect the letter had on the final decision, tenure was granted. As the reputation of the then Engineering Psychology Laboratory grew, it attracted postdoctoral students Lee Roy Beach, Cameron Peterson, and Jim Shanteau, among others.

Bayesian Statistics for Psychologists

Ward, too, brought research funds to the university from several sources, allowing him the flexibility to move activities from one to another. "Ideas could be pursued, and were." He had reviewed Jimmy Savage's book, *The Foundations of Statistics*, and was so impressed with the Bayesian point of view that he later said that if he could take only one book with him to a desert island, that would be the book. And on his return, he would ask, "What new book has Jimmy written?" Ward helped to lure Savage to Michigan, to the Mathematics Department, as there was then no statistics department, perhaps fortunately, as there was no particular opposition to the Bayesian point of view.

Ward asked one of his seminar students, Harold Lindman, to write a paper on Bayesian statistics, and on its receipt persuaded Jimmy to engage with him to revise and improve the paper. That began a series of weekly meetings between Ward and Jimmy, resulting in what Ward considered the third of his "blockbuster" papers (after the 1954 paper and the 1961 "Behavioral Decision Theory" review), "Bayesian Statistical Inference for Psychological Research," another *Psychological Review* paper (Edwards, Lindman, and Savage 1963). The paper showed that classical and Bayesian statistical inferences may diverge, with the classical approach too willing to reject a true null hypothesis, that the classical and Bayesian views are sometimes incompatible, and that certain characteristics of vague prior opinion can justify taking a uniform prior as the starting point – the still-unappreciated Principle of Stable Estimation. More generally, they concluded:

> Adoption of the Bayesian outlook should discourage parading statistical procedures, Bayesian or other, as symbols of respectability pretending to give the imprimatur of mathematical logic to the subjective process of empirical inference.

Ward explained to Larry how they worked together:

> We became good friends. He would say this isn't quite right, I would ask him how, he would tell me, and I'd try to fix it. He was a good mathematical consultant, he would listen and listen, ask questions; only when he was satisfied he understood the problem would he make any suggestions. Our interactions were built around the assumption that I would do the work and he would have the ideas. It worked out very well. There might have been more collaborations if he hadn't died when he did. He was fun to work with, bright, light-hearted, willing to listen, all the things you would like.

Probabilistic Information Processing Systems

During this period, Ward and his students conducted several experimental studies to determine how well the Bayesian model described human behavior in revising opinion as new information was received (Phillips et al. 1966; Edwards et al. 1968). Wilson "Spike" Tanner, one of the originators of signal detection theory (SDT) as a theory of human perception, was also at Michigan, and Ward knew that SDT had successfully challenged threshold theories, so perhaps it would also describe human inference. It didn't. After Larry had plotted numerous graphs of the posterior probabilities assessed by subjects in a complex task involving four hypotheses and twelve types of data, he pointed out that the subjects had indeed paid attention to prior probabilities, the question the experiment had been designed to answer. "Yes," replied Ward, looking at the graphs, "but they don't seem to do much after that." And so, conservatism was born. This finding reinforced Ward's enthusiasm for a system he had proposed in 1962, that a computer could use Bayes' theorem to put together the pieces of information, with people providing the likelihood inputs, later dubbed a "PIP" system (for probabilistic information processing), the forerunner of what would later be called a simple Bayesian net, with only one level in the hierarchy (Edwards et al. 1968).

Throughout his life, Ward continued to champion this idea, with his last attempt to demonstrate it shown in his Hailfinder project, a Bayesian net designed to predict severe weather conditions in eastern Colorado (Abramson et al. 1996). He saw the relevance of that early research to the design of Bayesian nets, and to the task of eliciting likelihoods from experts. He recalled a visit to the North American Aerospace Defense Command (NORAD) at Colorado Springs, before the control center was moved inside a mountain. He was amazed at the complexity of the information gathering, from radars here and abroad, from ships at sea, and many other sources, all displayed on a huge theater-screen size transparent map of North America, with a four-light threat level indicator in the upper left (only one lamp lit on the day of our visit!). When Ward asked what was done with all this information, the officer escorting us looked puzzled, so Ward asked what was the output. The officer pointed to a red telephone. Later, he asked Larry, "Do you think the ratio of input to output information should be like that?" This sense that a better way should be found stayed with him all his life.

That sense motivated a massive study at the University of Michigan, using one of Digital Equipment Corporation's first computers, a PDP-1, an investigation to determine if the PIP idea was viable. It was. The PIP system, pitted against several other ways of obtaining and combining information, consistently reached firmer conclusions earlier on the basis of the same evidence than the other systems, and this finding was replicated in several experiments in different laboratories. It soon became obvious that inference structures in the real world are hierarchical; they involve intervening indicators and events between the observable data and the object of the inference, and so a program studying hierarchical inference began in the later 1960s, with many studies reported in a special issue of *Organizational Behavior and Human Performance* in 1973. It was the PIP findings that encouraged Dave Schum, then a graduate student at Ohio State, to begin his productive, life-long study of evidence and inference.

Ultimately, the notion of hierarchical inference was superseded by Bayesian networks and, in a decision making context, influence diagrams. Chapters 10 and 11 of this book cover the most recent developments.

Early Tests of the Subjective Expected Utility Model

Throughout his Michigan days, Ward spent many evenings playing poker with Art Melton and other colleagues. Little did he know that one day his telephone would ring to invite him to a meeting of people interested in studying gambling behavior. The sponsor was a multimillionaire lawyer named Charles B. G. Murphy, who later decided to support Ward's work to the tune of several hundreds of thousands of dollars. Some of this research was carried out at the Four Queens Casino in Las Vegas, a condition of Murphy's providing financial support to the new owner of the casino. As the approval of the Nevada Gambling Commission was needed, a meeting was arranged for Ward with the head of the commission, Dr. Wayne Pearson, whose Ph.D. from Cornell University, Ward discovered, was on gambling behavior. Pearson, as it turned out, had read all of Ward's published work. He was very helpful to the project then, and later on. With the help of Paul Slovic, Sarah Lichtenstein, Amos Tversky, Dave Krantz, Mark Saltzman, and in particular Barbara Goodman, the project went ahead, with a corner of one room devoted to a task giving, truthfully, "the best odds in Las Vegas." A professional croupier by the name of John Poticello ran the game, using a roulette wheel and a computer, and a variety of specially developed gambles, that one way or another offered zero expected-value bets. Ward reported:

> I learned some interesting things. I learned that the absolute level of the stakes make less difference than I thought they would; people pay attention to the

differences, to the structures of the gambles. It also came to be very clear that my original conclusion from my thesis experiments, that people prefer gambles at some probabilities rather than others, showed up very clearly in the results, like preferences for 50–50 gambles.

He also found that the expected value model describes people's choices very well for two-outcome bets, so that model is descriptive of simple situations, good news for decision analysts who break problems into small pieces, though research is sparse on whether this also works for more complex problems. Looking back on this research, Ward told Larry:

> It's impossible for me to say how much of the thinking back at Michigan was influenced by this research, but there was a lot of influence for the people on the project, the custodians of the ideas. It's one of those situations in which the paths of influence are complex and not easily traced, but there nevertheless.

In the mid-1960s, Ward and Art Melton joined forces with Paul Fitts, considered by many to be the "father of engineering psychology," and Bill Hays, author of the thoughtful and accessible *Statistics for Psychologists*, to form the Human Performance Center. The mixture of theoretical and applied work conducted by the Center attracted graduate students and postdocs, including Daniel Kahneman, thereby bringing together the team of Kahneman and Tversky.

By the late 1960s, Ward's marriage ended in divorce, and in 1970 he married Sylvia, a lively Brazillian who tolerated but never much liked the cold winters of Ann Arbor. In the meantime, Paul Fitts died suddenly and unexpectedly, Bill Hays became a dean at another university, and stars like Dick Pew moved on. Ward realized that Art Melton's imminent retirement would leave him in charge of the Center, whose focus had become blurred. Recognizing he could probably not maintain the viability of the Center, Ward moved on to become the Associate Director of the Highway Safety Research Institute in 1971, a position he held for only two years, before moving to the University of Southern California (USC).

Transitions

Detlof von Winterfeldt joined Ward's Engineering Psychology Laboratory in Michigan in the summer of 1970. At this time Ward was still in the midst of developing and implementing probabilistic information processing systems and he also continued the Las Vegas experiments testing the descriptive validity of the SEU model. He continued his first line of research throughout his academic life, trying to engineer solutions to human judgment and decision making problems, very much in the spirit of engineering psychology.

The second line of descriptive research proved frustrating to him. He discovered the usual descriptive deviations from the SEU model, though no other model did much better (in fact, the SEV model, which he favored throughout his life, did very well). Had he been more intrigued by the deviations from the SEU model, he may well have joined forces with Amos Tversky and Danny Kahnemann to develop a new descriptive theory. Instead, he was more interested in making the

SEU model work in practice rather than in discovering its descriptive violations. So he gave up on this line of research altogether.

Two things happened around 1970. On the probability side, Tversky and Kahnemann conducted and published their first experiments on probability biases and heuristics (for a summary, see Kahneman, Slovic, and Tversky 1982). On the utility side Keeney and Raiffa developed multiattribute utility theory (Keeney 1968, 1971; Keeney and Raiffa 1976). Ward was enthusiastic about the ideas inherent in multattribute utility theory. However, he thought that the Keeney and Raiffa version was too difficult to use in practice. Always the engineering psychologist, he wanted to create a simple version of this method – which later came to be known as SMART – the Simple Multiattribute Rating Technique. This method is still around, though it went through some metamorphoses.

As much as Ward liked the multiattribute utility research, he had fundamental issues with the research on cognitive heuristics and biases in probability and utility judgments:

1. He deeply believed that people, using appropriate tools, could excel in cognitive tasks. He thought that the heuristics and biases work mischaracterized people's abilities. He was especially incensed by an ill-chosen characterization of "man as a cognitive cripple" in one of his colleagues' papers.
2. He was concerned that the cognitive illusions literature would be used to argue against the use of decision analysis. (In fact, in a review of one decision analysis application, a reviewer wrote that "Tversky and Kahneman have shown that people can't make these sort of probability judgments," and used this as an argument to reject the paper.)

Ward struggled with the heuristics and biases research for many years and he never made peace with this research, which, to the present, continues to focus on describing behavior rather than improving it.

USC and the Social Science Research Institute

Ward always liked problem solving and making a difference with applied research. He also liked to manage research. In 1973 he was presented with a unique opportunity to create the Social Science Research Institute (SSRI) at USC, an interdisciplinary institute spanning several schools, with a commitment to bring social science research to bear on important societal problems. Support came from Zohrab Kaprelian, then USC's Provost and Dean of the Engineering School, whom Ward found to be a highly successful combatant, and with whom he "hit it off beautifully." Ward was given a budget and a brief to build an organization, which he did, with the help of several very good people, managing its rapid growth from 1973 to the mid-1980s. Two of his Michigan students, David Seaver and Detlof von Winterfeldt, joined him as research assistants at USC. The initial research of this small group at SSRI consisted of tests of multiattribute utility and probability assessment methods. The groups also conducted some studies attempting – with mixed success – to validate multiattribute utility and expected utility models in experimental settings.

SSRI grew quickly, partly because of Ward's management style and philosophy. He often said that his job was to find the brightest researchers, support them well, and then get out of their way. Excellent researchers like Robert Kalaba (mathematics), Malcom Klein (criminal justice), and Sarnoff Mednick (genetic research) joined SSRI, because they shared Ward's approach to applied research and because of the supportive environment the institute provided. Another aspect of Ward's management style was that he liked to work on a one-on-one basis, avoiding committees or large group meetings. During the ten years Detlof worked at SSRI, he remembers only two large meetings. The first came in the early days of getting to know the existing faculty and staff and the last occurred, sadly, during the demise of the Institute.

Ward's research in the 1970s and 1980s continued to focus on developing decision analysis tools, now with a major emphasis on using multiattribute utility theory. He developed several versions of SMART and applied them to social problems (Edwards 1971, 1977). One quite remarkable application was an evaluation of school desegregation plans for the Los Angeles Unified School District (LAUSD), which was under a court order that required it to develop and evaluate alternative plans (Edwards 1980). This application of SMART involved 144 evaluation criteria – a feat that he, wisely, never repeated.

Detlof rejoined Ward in 1978 after a three year appointment at the International Institute of Applied Systems Analysis in Austria. The result of this collaboration were two major accomplishments: The publication of *Decision Analysis and Behavioral Research* (von Winterfeldt and Edwards 1986) and the development of a more formal approach to multiattribute utility analysis in situations involving multiple stakeholders (Edwards and von Winterfeldt 1987).

The book *Decision Analysis and Behavioral Research* was meant to be an in-depth examination of the behavioral research that was relevant for decision analysis. Ward spent months working on a chapter covering the by-then-famous work of Kahneman, Slovic, Tversky and others on cognitive errors in human probability and utility judgments. He was unable to suppress his feelings about this research in many early drafts. He wanted to get it right and therefore solicited comments and criticisms of the early drafts by the authors he criticized – and he got an earful. The experience was painful for him, but eventually this chapter became one of the most important ones in the book. Titled "Cognitive Illusions," it put the literature on probability and utility biases into the perspective of many other biases in human cognition. It also emphasized the usefulness of tools and argued that these biases can be overcome with proper use of tools.

The work on decision analysis with multiple stakeholders generated several papers. Perhaps the most important ideas of this work are that a common value structure can be created, even when stakeholders violently disagree about the issues at hand; that conflicts are often about specific value tradeoffs or facts; that conflicts about values can be expressed as different weights; and that conflicts about facts can be modeled by using judgments from different experts. Most importantly perhaps was the finding that decision analysis can be useful to help multiple stakeholders understand what they agree and disagree about, focus on the things that they disagree about, and explore options that are better for everyone involved.

In the late 1980s and early 1990s, Ward developed an interest in the generalization of the expected utility model. He brought together a stellar group of scientists to discuss advances in utility modeling (Edwards, 1992). Ward's own conclusion from this meeting was that generalized expected utility models were unlikely to replace the SEU model as the dominant prescriptive model, but he did recognize the need to incorporate the status quo and relative evaluations of gains and losses more explicitly into utility theory.

A change in the university administration caused Zohrab Kaprelian to resign in the mid-1980s, and money from the U.S. government's Department of Justice vanished, resulting in a 50 percent downsizing over two years for SSRI. In addition, SSRI, which was originally designed to be a self-standing unit reporting to the provost, was moved into the School of Letters, Arts, and Sciences, and Ward had to report to the dean of that school. Aside from the financial implications, this also restricted Ward's ability to hire faculty from other schools and reduced his ability to develop interdisciplinary proposals focused on solving urgent social problems. Ward managed, not without pain, to keep the organization afloat, and it continued to exist until 2002, though in Ward's view it never recovered from the loss of Zohrab.

Retirement

After his retirement in July 1995, Ward remained active in many projects, though as he had been suffering from Parkinson's disease for many years, his energy was increasingly limited. For the next eight years Ward continued a tradition he started at Michigan in 1962: the annual Bayesian Conference. Researchers and decision analysts from around the world gathered to present their latest ideas. Not, as Ward insisted, their hackneyed old papers, but new thoughts, research, ideas, anything relevant to the theory and practice of decision making. You sent in a brief summary of what you wanted to say, and Ward turned it into a humorous title for the agenda. You talked, participants discussed, and we waited for Ward's wise words, typically encouraging, looking beneath the surface for the intellectual issues, usually finding things you hadn't thought of, but never embarrassing you in front of colleagues. It was all good fun, and intellectually stimulating.

Two weeks before the 35th Bayesian Conference, in 1997, planned as a Festschrift honoring Ward, Sylvia suddenly died. Although Ward was heartbroken, he decided she would have wanted the celebration to go ahead, and it did. Jim Shanteau, Barbara Mellers, and Dave Schum (1998) edited the Festschrift volume, *Decision Science and Technology: Reflections on the Contributions of Ward Edwards*, which delighted Ward for the quality of contributions from his colleagues worldwide. Within a year he married Sandy, whose loving care enabled him to continue through to the 41st Conference, in 2003, which was the last. Ward's energy was draining from him, soon confining him to a wheelchair, but his mind was still active, supported by weekly meetings at his house with Detlof and Ralph

Miles. The three of them worked on this book, tentatively titled *Advances in Decision Analysis*, which they hoped to publish in 2006 by Cambridge University Press. Active to the end, Ward died on February 1, 2005. We can think of no better tribute to Ward than finally to see *Advances* in print.

REFERENCES

Abramson, B., Brown, J., Edwards, W., Murphy, A. H., and Winkler, R. L. (1996). HAIL-FINDER: A Bayesian system for predicting extreme weather. *International Journal of Forecasting, 7*, 57–78.

Edwards, W. (1954). The theory of decision making. *Psychological Bulletin, 41*, 380–417.

Edwards, W. (1961). Behavioral decision theory. *Annual Review of Psychology, 12*, 473–498.

Edwards, W. (1971). Social utilities. *Engineering Economist, Summer Symposium Series, 6*, 119–129.

Edwards, W. (1977). How to use multiattribute utility measurement for social decision making. *IEEE Transactions on Systems, Man and Cybernetics, SMC-7*, 326–340.

Edwards, W. (1980). Reflections on and criticism of a highly political multiattribute utility analysis. In L. Cobb and M. Thrall (Eds.), *Mathematical frontiers of behavioral and social sciences*. Boulder, CO: Westview Press, 157–186.

Edwards, W. (Ed.). (1992). Utility theories: Measurement and Applications. Boston, MA: Kluwer Academic.

Edwards, W., Lindman, H., and Savage, J. (1963). Bayesian statistical inference for psychological research. *Psychological Review, 70*, 193–242.

Edwards, W., Phillips, L. D., Hays, W. L., and Goodman, B. C. (1968). Probabilistic information processing systems: Design and evaluation. *IEEE Transactions on Systems Science and Cybernetics, SSC-4*, 248–265.

Edwards, W., and von Winterfeldt, D. (1987). Public values in risk debates. *Risk Analysis, 7*, 141–158.

Kahneman, D., Slovic, P., and Tversky, A. (1982). *Judgment under uncertainty: Heuristics and biases*. New York: Cambridge University Press.

Keeney, R. L. (1968). Quasi-Separable Utility Functions. *Naval Research Logistics Quarterly*, 551–565.

Keeney, R. L. (1971). Utility Independence and Preferences for Multiattribute Consequences. *Operations Research*, 875–893.

Keeney, R. L., and Raiffa, H. (1976). *Decisions with multiple objectives*. New York: Wiley.

Phillips, L. D., Hays, W. L., and Edwards, W. (1966). Conservatism in complex probabilistic inference. *IEEE Transactions on Human Factors in Electronics, HFE-7*, 7–18.

Shanteau, J., Mellers, B., and Schum, D. (Eds.). (1998). *Decision research from Bayesian approaches to normative systems: Reflections on the contributions of Ward Edwards*. Norwell, MA: Kluwer.

von Winterfeldt, D., and Edwards, W. (1986). *Decision analysis and behavioral research*. New York: Cambridge University Press.

6 Defining a Decision Analytic Structure

Detlof von Winterfeldt and Ward Edwards

ABSTRACT. This chapter is a revision and update of the chapter "Structuring for Decision Analysis" of our book *Decision Analysis and Behavioral Research* (von Winterfeldt and Edwards 1986). More than 20 years have passed since we wrote this chapter and during this time we gained substantial experience with applying decision analysis to many different government, business, and personal problems. The one lesson that has not changed is that structuring decision problems is the most important and, at the same time, least well understood task of a decision analyst. The three-step structuring process (identifying the problem; selecting an appropriate analytical approach; refining the analysis structure) also has survived the test of time. However, more than 20 years of applying decision analysis have taught us many new lessons, some new tools, and a variety of refinements when it comes to structuring decision problems. We liberally use the text of the 1986 chapter and weave in new materials and ideas as we go along.

This chapter focuses on progressing from an ill-defined problem, articulated often vaguely by decision makers and stakeholders, to a clear definition of the problem and the associated analysis framework. Other chapters in this volume discuss specific structuring techniques using objectives hierarchies (Chapter 7), and belief networks and influence diagrams (Chapter 10). We therefore will touch only briefly on the specifics of structuring problems with these tools and will focus on the general ideas and principles guiding the decision analyst's structuring task.

The Structuring Problem

Three Steps of Structuring

Textbook examples of decision problems are usually neatly structured, with pre-specified options, objectives, events, and uncertain variables. Although they are written in text, the underlying structure (a decision tree or a multiattribute structure) are usually obvious. In the experience of most decision analysts, problems just do not come so neatly packaged. Typically, one of the following conditions motivates a decision maker to ask for decision analysis support:

1. Opportunity – for example, a privately held company considers a buyout offer from another company as opposed to staying private or going public.

2. Need – for example, a utility company needs to increase its electricity production capacity because of population growth.
3. Controversial choice – for example, the board of a company wants to relocate its headquarters to be closer to its client base, but it faces opposition by its employees.
4. Confusing facts – for example, a regulatory agency is urged to set standards for a pollutant, but the facts about the health effects of the pollutant are not known, are conflicting, or both.
5. Requirement of accountability – for example, a government agency wants to make sure that its choice of a contractor is well documented and accountable.

As initially presented, many problems do not offer an opportunity for choice among specific alternatives. The most common initial condition is a set of often vague concerns, needs, or opportunities and a sense of perplexity about how to find a sensible course of action that at least partially addresses them all. In such cases the first and most important step in structuring must be to translate the problem into a set of alternatives and objectives. A subsequent step is to identify uncertainties about the outcomes of the available options and to think about acts that may help to reduce some of these uncertainties or allow the decision maker to hedge against them.

In this chapter, we are primarily concerned with the initial tasks of identifying alternatives and objectives. After presenting some general ideas about problem structuring, we present tools for structuring objectives: means–ends diagrams and objectives hierarchies, also known as value trees (see Chapter 7 in this volume). We have much less to say about inventing or structuring options. Identifying alternatives and objectives is the key, and by no means trivial, structuring task. Dealing with uncertainties is another important task. We will discuss structuring tools for this task by describing decision trees, influence diagrams, and belief networks, among others.

Trees and diagrams are the major structuring tools of decision analysis. However, building trees and diagrams is itself a fairly specific activity. To understand structuring within a broader perspective, it is useful to think of it as a three-step process:

1. *Identify the problem.* In the first step the following questions are addressed. What is the nature of the problem? Who is the decision maker? What are the decision maker's values? What are the generic classes of options? Which groups are affected by the decision? What is the purpose of the analysis? At this stage only rough formal relationships between the variables are created. Simple lists of alternatives, objectives, and events are the typical products of this task.
2. *Select an analytical approach.* In the second step, the analyst must choose the appropriate analytic framework, answering questions such as: Is uncertainty the key problem, or are conflicting values more important? Is it worthwhile to model parts of the problem with nondecision-analytic techniques

like linear programming or simulation models? How can different models be combined creatively? It is useful to avoid an early commitment to a specific decision analytic approach (e.g., multiattribute versus decision tree) and to explore alternatives in some detail. Often, the best solution is to combine approaches.

3. *Develop a detailed analysis structure.* This step involves the more familiar territory of developing trees, diagrams, and networks. Guidance about building these structures is scattered throughout this book. In this chapter, we will focus on some of the generic lessons for building means–ends diagrams, objectives hierarchies, consequence tables, decision trees, influence diagrams, event trees, fault trees, and Bayes' nets.

Although these three steps are reasonably distinct, the intellectual work behind them is extremely recursive. The analyst should expect to go through each step several times – and indeed should worry about whether the problem has been thought through carefully enough if it has not been restructured at least once or twice. A good way of checking an initial structure is to make some preliminary numerical assessments and run through some rough calculations. Often the results produce insights for restructuring and simplification.

The analyst should be reasonably certain that the current structure is acceptable before eliciting numbers in detail. Only a well-defined and acceptable structure will provide a sense for what numbers are important and require refined assessment. Moreover, number elicitation is expensive, time consuming, and irksome for some clients. It is unpleasant as well as wasteful to elicit numbers that later turn out to be irrelevant.

Identify the Problem

Becoming Educated About the Problem Environment

Problems that lead an organization or individual to seek outside help are almost always difficult, substantively and organizationally. The worst frustrations an analyst encounters are likely to occur early in the process of discovering the nature of the problem. The initial contact person, typically a member of the analysis or program staff of the client organization, is eagerly explaining what the problem is, and the analyst finds that different members of the organization often disagree on the nature of the problem.

At this early stage of an analysis it is important to answer three questions: (1) Who is the decision maker(s)? (2) What are the key alternatives and objectives? and (3) Who are the stakeholders involved in this problem? This requires quick learning about the problem and the organizational environment. The requirement that the analyst learn quickly has several consequences. One consequence is increased specialization within the field regarding specific classes of problems and organizations. This trend towards specialization is likely to continue in decision analysis, as it has in other forms of operations research. Another consequence is that generic problem structures for specific problem classes are both inevitable and useful; we return to generic problem structures at the end of this chapter.

Identifying the Decision Makers and Their Values

One task the analyst must face in interacting with any client is to figure out who the client is. Virtually all clients are organizations. The contact person is typically very familiar with the organization's institutional culture. Is there a boss? Sometimes yes, sometimes no. The real boss may not be the one who formally approves decisions. Or the leadership role may be partitioned. Invariably the boss delegates decision-making power, and invariably he or she retains some degree of ex post facto evaluative (and perhaps veto) power over the result.

Although the analyst will, later in the structuring process, elicit in detail the values related to the specific decision problem at hand, early clarity about the overall objectives of the client organization is essential. Superficial definitions of an organization's function are inherent in its mission statement and organization chart. Ford makes cars; the Environmental Protection Agency polices the environment. But Ford's organizational style and goals are different from those of General Motors, Chrysler, or (especially) Nissan. Every organization's personality is unique.

A myth to watch out for is that a single value dominates all others. This myth is more common in corporations than in government agencies, because corporation executives are so often taught in business schools that corporations exist to make money. Though no entity, corporate or individual, is averse to making money, no value structure is that simple. Instead, the corporate myth that profit is the goal serves as a useful structuring tool for much more complex corporate objectives: maximizing market share, meeting future demand, reducing unnecessary overhead costs, upgrading the quality of personnel and of production processes and products, and even enhancing corporate flexibility. If you encounter this myth or any other similar oversimplification of values, it is usually easy to endorse it and elicit the real values that lie beneath it. Myths could not exist if they prevented effective interaction with the realities underneath.

Hunting for the Decision

An analyst is usually called in because the organization has a problem, which requires a solution that internal staff cannot provide. It is very common for an analyst to discover that the organization does not know what its problem is. Perhaps the most useful task during early exploration is to hunt for the decision. Almost always there is one, or more. Contact people usually know what it is, though they may have different perspectives on what the relevant options and values are. Often, if the problem is not brand new, a helpful question is: how did they deal with this problem in the past, and why won't that method still work? The corresponding question for new problems is: if they were to rely only on internal resources, what would they do, and how well would they fare? Once the analyst can get the contact person and key others in the organization to agree on what the decision is and to agree that the job is to work on it or some aspect of or input to it, half the structuring is done.

It is important to understand the preferences and possible biases of decision makers and stakeholders early. In some cases decision makers have preconceived preferences for one alternative and understanding these preferences can help reveal underlying values and hidden agendas. In one of our analyses a decision maker expressed a strong preference for one of several technology alternatives prior to the detailed study. Some of the values that motivated this preference were quite reasonable and could be incorporated into the analysis. Other values were related to providing employment for the client's favorite subsidiary and could not be made explicit in the analysis. Other stakeholders and decision makers had different values, balancing the client's views. In the end, the alternative that the client preferred became a contender, but it ultimately lost to a better alternative.

Defining the Purpose of the Analysis

The analyst and the relevant people in the organization have identified the decision or decisions to be made – and all have breathed a sigh of relief. Now the analyst's task is to help the organization make that decision as well as it can, right? Often dead wrong! There are a variety of factors that can stand in the way:

1. The organization may not be in a position to make the decision. The Central Intelligence Agency needs decision-analytic help, badly, but (according to its rules) makes no decisions; it merely provides well-structured information to remote decision makers. Such problems are typically, but not always, diagnostic. They may require hypothesis invention.
2. To make decisions, a list of options must exist. The real problem may be producing that list. If a dominant option emerges during the decision structuring, the decision problem may vanish, with or without the analyst's help.
3. The task may be not to make a decision, but to design and install a decision-making mechanism or procedure. The rules for picking the winner or winners in a competitive situation must usually be in place before the competition starts. Such problems are typically evaluative.
4. Time pressure or other constraints may make it necessary to complete all analysis before the decision problem arises. Crisis management is the most common example. The analyst must substitute scenarios about the future for information about the real decision problem and must package the output either as rapid, easy-to-use decision aids, often in the form of interactions with computers, or as system design for the quick-response system, or, ideally, both.
5. Decision makers do and should resist the idea that machines or computational procedures should or can replace them. By definition, a decision maker is the person who takes the blame if the decision leads to a distressing outcome.

So he or she must feel and should insist on feeling that that responsibility is deserved. The output of any decision-analytic procedure is at best an input to a decision. It is almost never the only one.

6. Sometimes the reason for asking a decision analyst for help is confusing and conflicting facts. Occasionally, it turns out that the decision maker really does not need a complete decision analysis, but some other kind of model or data. In one case, we helped a decision maker substantially by building a simple life-cycle cost model of a multimillion dollar effort to decommission a nuclear power plant. This model did not lead to any specific decision, but provided substantial clarity to the cost and risk accounting as the project moved along.

7. The decision may already have been made or may be made independently while the analyst is working on the problem. A common and sometimes legitimate purpose of an analysis is to justify a decision, which the decision maker has been committed to prior to the analysis. In this case the analyst must first ensure that the preferred decision is at least a contender and that there is no interference by the decision maker with putting all the facts about all alternatives on the table. If these conditions are met, sensitivity analysis can clarify when the alternative preferred by the decision maker is also favored by the analysis and when this is not the case. If either of these conditions is not met, the analysis is likely to be compromised or lead to an inevitable conflict between the decision maker and the analyst.

Select an Analytical Structure

Multiple Alternative Structures

Having identified the decision maker(s), alternatives and objectives, and stakeholders, the next step is to determine which of the various decision analysis structures is most appropriate for a given problem. For example, the problem might lend itself to a multiattribute utility analysis, requiring a refinement of objectives and attributes; or it could be a decision problem in which significant events change the nature of the consequences, suggesting a decision tree; or it could be a problem involving uncertainties connected in a causal chain, suggesting an influence diagram.

Our recommendation is to keep an open mind in the early steps of structuring a decision problem and consider multiple alternative structures. To illustrate this, we examine two examples. The first example is a problem that falls under the category "need." This addresses the question of how apartment building owners should respond to regulations that require significant improvements in seismic safety. This regulation was passed by the city of Los Angeles in the aftermath of the 1993 Northridge earthquake in the Los Angeles area. The provisions for retrofitting some apartments were extensive and expensive. The second example falls under the category "controversial choice." In this example, the Department of Energy considered several technologies and sites for producing tritium for

Figure 6.1. Typical "tuckunder parking" apartment building in Los Angeles. A. Before an earthquake. B. After an earthquake.

nuclear weapons. In both examples, we considered alternative structures, began with one structure, and later modified the approach significantly.

The Northridge earthquake in California occurred in 1993 and it showed that some apartment buildings with "tuckunder" parking spaces were particularly vulnerable to collapse (see Figures 6.1A and 6.1B). In response, many cities considered ordinances requiring these types of apartment buildings to be seismically reinforced. One of us (von Winterfeldt) was asked to assist in evaluating the cost and benefits of alternative seismic retrofits in response to this regulation. This project was conducted as part of an effort by the Multidisciplinary Center for Engineering Earthquake Research (MCEER), an NSF funded center at the University of Buffalo. The project focused on an individual apartment owner as the decision maker, but the idea was to make the model sufficiently generic to apply to many types of apartment buildings and regulations. The analysis was intended to provide direct decision support for apartment owners, but also to suggest policy ideas to regulatory agencies (see Benthien and von Winterfeldt 2001).

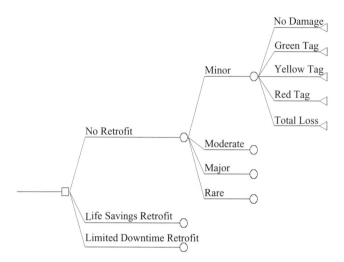

Figure 6.2. Decision tree for the seismic rehabilitation problem.

One formulation of the problem is to look at the costs, benefits, and risks of alternative retrofitting decisions. Usually, there are several alternatives that can be implemented – for example a life saving alternative that reinforces the building to prevent a collapse or an alternative that ensures that the building can remain occupied, even after a major earthquake (limited downtime). Although the "do nothing" alternative is often not acceptable due to the legal requirements, it also was considered in this analysis to provide a benchmark for the decision analysis.

Because we are dealing with events (earthquakes of various magnitudes) that can produce dramatically different consequences (from minor damage to a total collapse of the building) we started with a decision tree as the main analytical structure. This tree, shown in Figure 6.2, discretizes the seismic events and their consequences. At the end node of the tree, consequences were assessed in terms of multiple objectives: minimize retrofitting costs, minimize damage cost, minimize life losses, and minimize downtime of the apartment. Preliminary analyses showed that this analysis structure was useful in identifying the sensitive parameters of the problem and the analysis was helpful for guiding decisions by apartment owners.

However, the decision tree analysis was based on expected value calculations and it did not have the ability to focus on the tails of the distribution. We therefore explored an alternative structure, based on a simulation model using influence diagrams (see Figure 6.3).

In this influence diagram, the seismic event is characterized by three uncertain variables: Time, location, and strength. Each of these variables is modeled as a continuous probability distribution. The damage states are modeled discretely using standard engineering damage classifications (no damage, green tagged, yellow tagged, red tagged, total loss). The relationship between the seismic event variables and the damage states are modeled using standard fragility curves. The

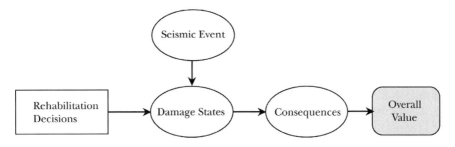

Figure 6.3. Influence diagram for the seismic rehabilitation problem.

consequences are modeled as point estimates using data of losses in the case of the five damage states. Included in the consequence assessments are the cost of retrofitting, the cost of damage and repair, the lives lost, and the loss of income due to damage and repair. These component costs are rolled up into an overall value, which was calculated as the total equivalent cost. This framework allowed us to produce probability distributions over total equivalent costs as a function of retrofitting alternatives and thereby explore the tails of these distributions.

Both frameworks have strengths and weaknesses. The decision tree framework facilitates sensitivity analyses focusing on a simple expected value criterion. Through its use, we quickly learned that the time horizon of ownership and the financing parameters made the main difference in the decision of whether or not to retrofit – at least in the expected value sense. This framework and model would make most sense for an owner who has many apartment buildings in different areas of the city and can afford to lose one or two of them. The simulation model gave us a much more refined answer on the various possible outcomes of an earthquake and the damage it can do to buildings. It also was more appropriate in exploring the tails of the distribution and thereby guiding possible insurance decisions. This model would be more useful for an owner of a single apartment building, who is concerned about catastrophic losses. In the end, we continued to pursue both types of analysis, recognizing the pros and cons of each.

The second example is an evaluation of several technologies and sites for producing tritium for nuclear weapons (for details, see Chapter 25 in this volume and von Winterfeldt and Schweitzer 1998). Tritium is a necessary ingredient to increase the yield of nuclear weapons. In 1989 the last tritium production facility was shut down in the US because of environmental problems. Because tritium decays, a new tritium supply was urgently needed by 2011 to replenish decayed tritium in nuclear warheads. Because the lead time for siting, building and licensing a new tritium production facility is substantial, the decision had to be made by 1996. The decision maker was then Secretary of Energy Hazel O'Leary, supported by the Assistant Secretary for Defense Programs and various other stakeholders in the Department of Energy (DOE) and the Department of Defense. One of us (von Winterfeldt) was the lead decision analyst supporting this decision process from 1994 to 1996.

Initially, the problem looked very much like a multiattribute utility problem: The DOE considered five technologies for producing tritium, including several types of new reactor designs and a large linear accelerator. There were five existing DOE sites that could accommodate any of the five technologies. A minor additional concern was whether to upgrade an existing tritium recycling facility at the Savannah River Site or to co-locate the recycling facility with the new production facility. In total there were forty-five alternatives.

There also were numerous objectives. At a high level, the DOE was concerned with production assurance (can the proposed facility produce enough tritium in a timely manner?), cost (both capital and operations and maintenance over a 40–year period), and environment, health, and safety. At one point of the analysis, we developed twenty-three objectives and associated measures – three production assurance objectives (capacity, availability, and schedule); three cost objectives (total project cost, operation and maintenance cost, and electricity revenue); and seventeen environmental objectives. Because of the risks of not meeting production goals, we also included an uncertainty analysis of the production assurance aspects and expressed the results in terms of probabilities of meeting production goals and schedules.

Within this analysis framework, we had numerous teams assess the consequences of each of forty-five alternatives on the twenty-three objectives – probabilistically in some cases. This was an enormous task that took seventy-five people 6 months to complete. The conclusions were informative:

1. Production assurance depended only on the technologies. The technologies differed quite a bit in the production assurance and there was significant uncertainty about production estimates.
2. Sites differed in environmental objectives, but only in a very minor way, thus site selection was a secondary issue.
3. Technologies differed only in three environmental objectives related to nuclear accident risks and nuclear waste production.
4. Technologies differed enormously in cost estimates and there was significant uncertainty about costs.

Based on these findings, we conducted a more detailed production assurance and cost-risk analysis using a probabilistic simulation framework rather than a multiattribute framework. During this analysis five new technology alternatives were proposed and submitted to the probabilistic risk analysis framework. We characterized the risks of production assurance in several ways, including probabilistic representations of shortfalls of tritium after the required start date of 2011. We also showed the cost overrun risks by presenting exceedence probability curves and box plots to the decision makers. We did not aggregate the results to a single value, but represented the findings by showing the implications of our analysis separately in terms of the production assurance, cost, and environmental objectives. Even without making tradeoffs among these three categories, one of the new alternatives (producing tritium in an existing commercial reactor) was a clear "winner" in the analysis, and, in spite of initial opposition within the DOE, this alternative was eventually selected.

Eight Analytic Structures

We distinguish among eight analytic structures depending on the whether we are dealing primarily with a multiattribute evaluation problem, a decision problem involving significant uncertainties, or a probabilistic inference problem:

- Evaluation problems
  - Means–ends networks
  - Objectives hierarchies
  - Consequence tables
- Decision problems under uncertainty
  - Decision trees
  - Influence diagrams
- Probabilistic inference problems
  - Event trees
  - Fault trees
  - Belief networks

We describe each analytic structure briefly.

MEANS–ENDS NETWORKS. When interviewing decision makers and stakeholders to elicit objectives, the major goal is to identify a set of *fundamental* objectives (see Keeney 1992). We achieve this by repeatedly asking "why is this objective important?" Many objectives are important, because they serve other ends objectives. By pursuing the means–ends chain of objectives, we eventually arrive at objectives, whose importance are self evident – these are the fundamental objectives. For example, a decision maker may state that emissions of an air pollutant are important for a regulatory problem. If asked why, the decision maker may state that air emissions cause people to inhale polluted air and cause visibility problems. When asked why this is important, the response is likely that breathing polluted air causes health effects (asthma and less lung capacity) and that visibility problems cause psychological effects. When asked why health effects and psychological effects are important, there is no answer other than that it is self-evident in this problem. Health effects are just fundamentally important to people.

Interviews to elicit objectives typically generate many objectives that are not fundamental to the problem. These fall into two classes: means objectives and process objectives. Means objectives are those that can affect fundamental objectives (e.g., air pollution emissions are a means to creating health effects), but are not by themselves relevant for the evaluation. Process objectives are those that refer to the process by which a decision is made, rather than its consequences. Examples are "Involvement of Stakeholders," "Proper Treatment and Respect of Indian Nations and Tribes," and "Provision of Timely Information." Stakeholders expect all objectives to be represented in some form in an analysis. Process objectives

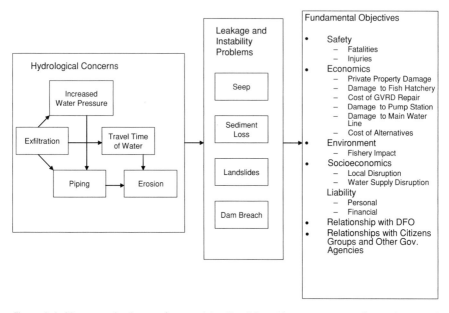

Figure 6.4. Means–ends diagram for examining the risks and consequences of an underground water tunneling project.

should be separated out and considered when designing and implementing the analysis process.

Means and ends objectives can usually be summarized well in a means–ends diagram. An example is shown in Figure 6.4. This example comes from a recent analysis (Keeney and von Winterfeldt 2005) of alternatives to mitigate the possible landslide and other risks posed by an underground water tunneling project in the Vancouver region. The problem was of interest because the tunneling project occurred near a dam and could potentially impose risks to the dam itself.

The box on the left of this diagram summarizes the hydrological concerns that may lead to leaks or slope instability problems. Exfiltration refers to water leaking out of the tunnel due to differential hydraulic pressures. This can lead to migration of water into the environment creating erosion. These processes in turn can lead to the major events of concern (middle box): seeps, loss of sediments, landslides, and a possibly catastrophic dam breach. The right-hand box contains the fundamental objectives of concern in this problem.

Structuring means and ends objectives with a means–ends diagram does not lead directly to a formal analysis. Instead, it clarifies for the decision makers and stakeholders how their concerns are being handled: Regarding means, causal and possibly probabilistic models will be used to trace the cause-and-effect relationships. Regarding ends, multiattribute models will be used to summarize the consequences of alternatives and to aggregate them to a common value metric.

OBJECTIVES HIERARCHIES. The right-hand box of Figure 6.4 is an example of the second major structuring tool for evaluation problems: *objectives hierarchies*

Table 6.1. Objectives and measures for evaluating policies for reducing exposure to electromagnetic fields from powerlines

Objectives	Measures
Health effects – EMF	
Leukemia	For cancer incidence: number of cases
Brain cancer	For fatal cancers: life-years lost
Breast cancer	For Alzheimer's: number of cases
Alzheimer's disease	
Health effects – Accidents	
Fires	For fatalities: life-years lost
Pole collisions	For injuries: number of cases
Electrocutions	
Construction	
Costs	
Total project cost	1998 dollars
Operation and maintenance	1998 dollars
Power losses	1998 dollars
Service reliability	
Contingencies	Number of contingency hours
Customer interruptions	Person-hours of interruptions
Property impacts	
Property values	1998 dollars
Fire losses	1998 dollars
Pole collision losses	1998 dollars
Environmental impacts	
Aesthetics	Aesthetics point scale
Tree losses	Number of trees lost
Air pollution	Percent of fossile fuel generation
Noise and disruption	Person-days of noise and disruption
Socioeconomic impacts	
Gross Regional product	1998 dollars
Employment	Percent change in employment

(Keeney and Raiffa 1976), also known as *value trees* (von Winterfeldt and Edwards 1986). Table 6.1 shows an example of an objectives hierarchy created for the evaluation of alternative policies to reduce exposure to electromagnetic fields from powerlines. This study was conducted for the California Department of Health Services (CDHS) and it involved many opposing stakeholders (see von Winterfeldt et al. 2004). The fundamental objectives are shown in the left-hand column. The selected measures for these objectives are shown in the right-hand column. Chapter 7 describes how to develop objectives and attributes in more detail.

CONSEQUENCE TABLES. These tables combine the fundamental objectives with the alternatives. The idea is to create a table that characterizes the consequence of each alternative with respect to each objective. This type of table is similar to tables that can be found in consumer reports. Table 6.2 shows the fundamental objectives and associated measures from a study that evaluated the quality of thirty-two decision science programs at U.S. universities (see Keeney, See, and von Winterfeldt 2006).

Table 6.2. Fundamental objectives for evaluating decision science programs at U.S. universities

Fundamental objectives	Measures
Further knowledge about decision making	Number of articles in refereed journals (last five years)
	Number of academic books in print
	Number of edited books in print
Educate about decision making	Number of graduate courses
	Number of textbooks in print
Produce doctoral students in decision fields	Number of dissertations (last five years)
Influence the making of better decisions	Number of popular audience books in print

The thirty-two decision science programs were evaluated with respect to the fundamental objectives by using the measures on the right of Table 6.2. The results are summarized in a consequence table (Table 6.3). It is often useful to lay out such a consequence table before collecting data to determine where data are easy to obtain, where difficult, and whether uncertainty assessments are required for some measures.

DECISION TREES. Figure 6.5 is an example of a simple decision tree for assessing the costs and benefits of alternatives to manage potential health hazards from exposure to electromagnetic fields (EMFs) from electric power lines. Decision trees represent the sequence of decisions and uncertain events, and they are most useful when there are discrete events that evolve over time. Decision trees can involve multiple sequential decisions, as shown, for example, in Figure 6.6.

This tree shows the sequence of decisions when contemplating research activities for studying electromagnetic fields' effects on people. In this tree decision and event nodes are mixed. For example, after funding research (first-decision node) and learning about the research results (first-event node), there still is a decision to be made on whether or not to mitigate EMF exposure (second-decision node),

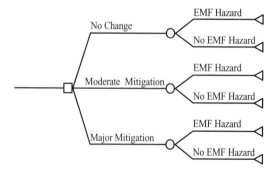

Figure 6.5. Simple decision tree.

Table 6.3. Consequence table for evaluating decision science programs

Graduate programs	Articles	Academic books	Edited books	Graduate courses	Text books	Doctoral graduates	Popular books
Arizona State University	8	0	0	6	1	0	0
Carnegie Mellon University	14	3	2	2	0	2	1
Columbia University	4	0	1	1	1	0	1
Cornell University	0	0	0	1	0	4	2
Duke University	21	3	2	7	2	1	2
George Washington University	3	0	0	8	0	2	0
Georgia Institute of Technology	1	0	0	2	0	2	0
Harvard University	21	1	2	5	2	7	0
Johns Hopkins University	8	1	0	1	0	2	0
Massachusetts Institute of Technology	4	0	0	1	0	0	0
New York University	1	0	1	2	0	0	1
Northwestern University	2	0	0	8	0	0	0
Ohio State University	5	0	0	6	0	0	0
Princeton University	2	0	0	1	0	0	0
Stanford University	9	0	1	10	1	14	1
University of Arizona	0	0	0	4	0	0	0
University of California, Berkeley	7	0	1	4	0	0	0
University of California, Irvine	9	1	0	5	0	1	0
University of California, Los Angeles	2	0	0	7	0	1	0
University of Chicago	2	0	0	1	0	0	0
University of Colorado at Boulder	0	0	0	2	0	0	0
University of Illinois, Urbana-Champaign	5	0	0	4	0	0	0
University of Iowa	0	0	0	1	0	0	0
University of Maryland	0	0	0	1	0	1	0
University of Michigan	3	1	0	3	0	2	0
University of Minnesota	1	0	0	5	0	1	0
University of North Carolina at Chapel Hill	0	0	0	3	0	0	0
University of Oregon	1	1	0	1	0	0	0
University of Pennsylvania	12	2	3	3	0	0	0
University of Southern California	1	1	0	3	0	0	0
University of Texas at Austin	6	0	0	2	0	0	0
University of Virginia	6	0	0	4	0	2	0
University of Wisconsin, Madison	9	0	0	3	0	1	0
Yale University	1	0	0	2	0	2	0

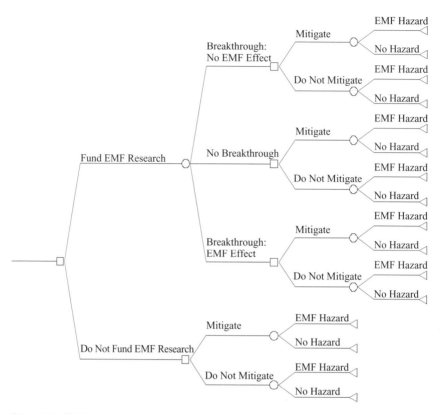

Figure 6.6. EMF research decision tree.

before one eventually finds out whether EMF is a health hazard (second-event node).

At the end of the tree are consequences. These almost always concern multiple objectives. As a result, decision trees are usually combined with a multiattribute analysis by listing the multiple consequences at the end nodes of the tree and calculating multiattribute utilities to enter into the decision tree calculations.

Influence Diagrams

Figure 6.7 shows an influence diagram for a problem involving protective action to reduce the electrocution risks of workers servicing high-voltage transmission and distribution lines. The decision variables were the length and the size of ground cables that would absorb the flow of electricity if the line that was being serviced was accidentally energized. If this occurs, the current splits between the ground and the body of the exposed utility worker, possibly leading to ventricular fibrillation and death. The likelihood of ventricular fibrillation depends not only on the two decision variables, but also on many other uncertain variables and events that are

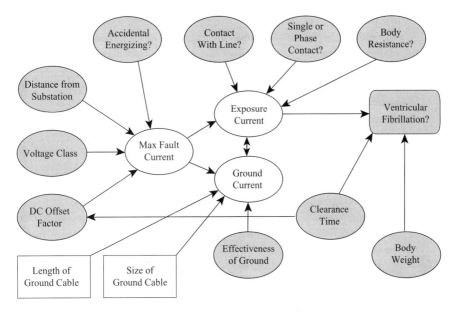

Figure 6.7. Influence diagram for electrical worker safety practices.

shown in Figure 6.7. Following influence diagram conventions, uncertain variables and events are shown by an ellipse; decision nodes are shown as rectangles; and value nodes are shown as rounded rectangles.

This diagram led to a mathematical model of the flows of electricity and the possible electrical shocks to the worker body under various risk scenarios (see von Winterfeldt 2005). It also was the starting point of a probabilistic simulation of the worker risks and helped design appropriate grounding systems that provided sufficient worker protection and safety.

FAULT TREES. Fault trees are frequently used in engineering safety analysis. A simple example is shown in Figure 6.8. This example concerns the development of a possible water leak at the surface area near a dam due to exfiltration of water from a newly constructed water tunnel (see Keeney and von Winterfeldt 2005). It builds on the means–ends diagram shown in Figure 6.4.

Leaks are important, because they are precursors to possible landslides or even a possible breach of a dam. In the fault tree there are two paths by which water can move from the tunnel to the area of a potential leak: through two aquifers OR by bypassing the aquifers and seeping directly into the open environment. Leakage through the aquifers is no problem, as long as the water pumps in the lower aquifer are working. A problem occurs only, if both a leak through the aquifers occurs AND the pumps are not working. Once probabilities are attached to the nodes of this fault tree, one multiplies the probabilities at the "AND" nodes and adds probabilities at the "OR" nodes.

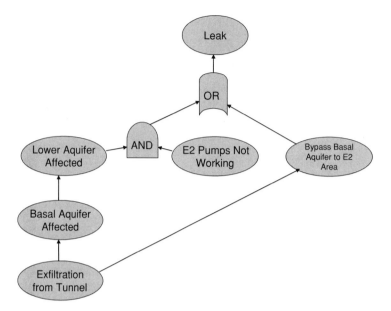

Figure 6.8. Example of a simple fault tree.

EVENT TREES. An event tree example for the leakage problem is shown in Figure 6.9. Event trees reverse the logic of fault trees – they start with initiating events and trace them to the fault or problem event. Fault trees start with the fault and trace back the causes of the problem.

BELIEF NETS. Belief networks are closely associated with influence diagrams. They represent the causal or noncausal structure of inferences going from data and inference elements to the main hypothesis or event about which an inference is

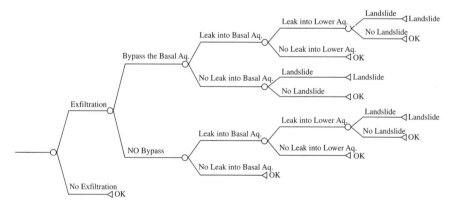

Figure 6.9. Example of a simple event tree.

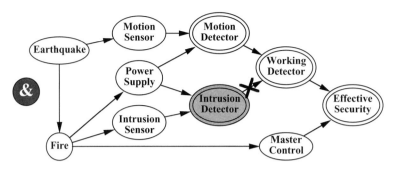

Figure 6.10. Example of a belief network. The "&" symbol indicates that all probability assessments in the network are conditional on the prior knowledge.

made. An example from Ross Schachter's Chapter 10, in this volume, is shown in Figure 6.10. This example concerns the assessment of the likelihood of being successful in fire suppression after an earthquake. More details are provided in Chapter 10.

Matching Problems and Analytic Structures

Students commonly ask: "How do you decide which analytic structure to use?" As decision analysts, we have accumulated significant experience with matching problems and analysis structures, but it is difficult to communicate this experience.

First, almost all problems have multiple objectives and thus some structuring of alternatives and objectives is always useful. Simple objectives hierarchies and consequence tables help clarify the key relationships between alternatives and objectives. If data about consequences are not readily available, ranking alternatives by objectives can be illuminating.

Second, decision trees are useful, if there are clear, important, and discrete events that stand between the implementation of the alternatives and the eventual consequences. Medical decisions, decisions dealing with major disasters, terrorism, and the like lend themselves to decision trees. The multiple consequence part of this type of problem can be handled by listing all consequences at the end of the decision tree and determining an equivalent value or utility through standard multiattribute utility analysis.

Influence diagrams are most useful when some of the uncertain variables are continuous and causally linked. In this case it may be easier to develop a deterministic model that calculates the propagation of causal effects and then to superimpose a probabilistic simulation to assess the overall uncertainties. Multiple objective aspects can easily be integrated with influence diagrams.

Fault trees, event trees, and belief nets are special to inference problems. For example, when trying to make an inference about the likelihood that terrorists have obtained and will use a nuclear bomb to deploy in the US, these tools are very useful.

Generic Problems and Analytic Structure Templates

Over the years, many decision analyses have been conducted on different classes of problems and, through the process of trial and error, some analytic structures have emerged as more appropriate than others. For example, it is generally accepted that facility siting decisions are best served by using objectives hierarchies and consequence tables. Similarly, most medical and legal decisions lend themselves to a decision tree analysis.

Keeney and other decision analysts have investigated the facility-siting problem in much detail and in a variety of contexts (see the examples in Keeney and Raiffa 1976 and Keeney 1980). A typical feature of siting problems is sequential screening from candidate areas to possible sites, to a preferred set, to final site-specific evaluations. Another feature is that they are multiattribute evaluation problems with common generic classes of objectives: investment and operating costs, economic benefits, environmental impacts, social impacts, and political considerations. Also, the process of organizing, collecting, and evaluating information is similar in many siting decisions. Keeney's prototypical structure for facility-siting decisions simply assembles the generalizable features of past applications.

Contingency planning is another recurring problem. Decisions and Designs, Inc., has addressed this problem in the military context, but it is also relevant to planning for action in the case of civil disasters, such as liquefied natural gas plant explosions or blowouts from oil platforms. Generic properties that characterize contingency planning include:

- Strong central control by executive bodies,
- The requirement that numerous decisions be made simultaneously,
- The fact that major events can drastically change the focus of the problem,
- Rapid influx of no-cost or low-cost information, and
- Organizational problems that may impede information flows and actions.

At first glance, decision trees seem to be natural models for contingency planning. But a generic structure would need special characteristics not found in many decision trees. For example, the model structure should allow rapid changes due to unforeseeable events. It should be able to update its information base quickly but should not overstress the value of information, because most information is free. It should be able to fine-tune its actions essentially instantaneously in response to rapidly changing input information.

Budget allocation to competing programs is another typical problem. In many problems such as this, different programs attempt to pursue similar objectives, and the merit of the program mix is at least as important as the direct benefits of single programs. Budgeting decisions allocate a single continuous decision variable subject to a total budget constraint. Typically, budget allocation problems also have constraints on suballocations to major budget elements and must take implicit or explicit commitments carried over from previous years very seriously. Multiattribute utility analysis is a natural structure for budget allocation decisions, because it easily handles program evaluation (see Kleinmuntz, Chapter 20 in this volume).

Environmental regulation presents a class of decision problems that has a number of recurrent themes. Three generic groups are involved (i.e., regulators, regulated, beneficiaries of regulation). Monitoring and sanction schemes are important. Those regulated and the beneficiaries of regulation usually have opposing objectives. The objectives of the regulator are often political. In a previous study we examined the specific regulation problem of standard setting and suggested decision-analytic structures for it. A decision-analytic structure for regulation in general would have many features of this model (von Winterfeldt and Edwards, 1986).

This list could be extended to include private investment decisions, product mix selection, resource development, medical diagnostic problems, and others. But the four examples suffice to demonstrate how generic decision-analytic structuring can be approached. In our opinion, such an approach to structuring will be at least as useful for the implementation of decision analysis as computerization of decision models. Generic decision-analytic structures are transferable; that is their technical advantage. More important, they enable decision analysts to be knowledgeable and concerned about problems. We find it unappealing that the too-frequently-encountered methods expert, looks for problems that can be made to fit methods on hand by lopping off some goals here, stretching some assumptions there, and distorting intuition and common sense everywhere. Decision analysts can, should, and generally do perform better.

Develop a Detailed Analytic Structure

The most important decision that a decision analyst can make is the choice of an analytic structure when addressing a decision problem. After this decision, the process of developing a detailed version of the structure is typically quite straightforward. Chapters 7 and 10 in this volume give some specific advice about how to structure objectives, influence diagrams and belief nets. Following are some general guidelines.

Means–Ends Diagrams

There are two main purposes of a means–ends diagram: To display to the decision makers and stakeholders that all of their concerns are accounted for and to separate the multiattribute modeling part (using the fundamental objectives) from the probabilistic or causal modeling part (using the means diagram). The means–ends diagram is usually only a starting point of this process, and it does not lend itself directly to modeling of either kind. The fundamental objectives often require more work to ensure completeness, and measures need to be defined for the objectives (see Chapter 7). The means part of the diagram has to be fleshed out with a decision tree or an influence diagram to make it useful for modeling.

Objectives Hierarchies

In the early days of multiattribute utility analysis, the biggest problem was an enormous proliferation of objectives, either by counting too many objectives or by providing too much detail, or both. For example, Edwards (1979) developed an objectives hierarchy to evaluate school desegregation plans that had 144 objectives. Similarly, Keeney and von Winterfeldt developed an objectives hierarchy to evaluate German energy policies that had ninety objectives. In hindsight, these early attempts were motivated by an effort to be as complete and detailed as possible and they did not focus sufficiently on the purposes of the analysis – namely to provide a more transparent and clear evaluation of the alternatives. For evaluation purposes, one should focus on the objectives that matter – both in the sense that they are the most important in the eyes of the decision makers and stakeholders and in the sense that they differentiate between alternatives. These considerations can often reduce the relevant objectives to a manageable number – for example, in the tritium analysis, the number of relevant objectives was reduced from twenty-three to four using this logic.

Consequence Tables

The main lesson about consequence tables is to keep them small both in terms of the relevant alternatives and objectives and to make sure that the consequence measures are quantitative. In general, natural scales are preferred over constructed scales, because the latter require qualitative judgments.

Decision Trees

In 1986, we proposed that decision trees should be small enough to fit on a page and still be readable. This is still a good goal and it helps the communication of decision tree results tremendously. However, we also have learned to appreciate the value and power of very large decision trees. In those cases, we suggest that the function of communicating the tree is separated from that of running it as a model. The communication tree can be in an abbreviated version, using only some paths to illustrate the main points, but the tree used for modeling and analysis has to be complete and may include thousands of branches.

One thought that we still consider valid is that a decision tree is not meant to be a complete and exhaustive representation of all future decisions and events. Instead, it is to capture the main aspects of decisions and events that can make a difference to the ultimate consequences. As a result, a guiding principle for inserting decisions is to ask: If I were at this point in the tree, what actions could I take that would truly make a difference in the consequences? Similar questions should be asked for events.

Influence Diagrams

When we wrote the original structuring chapter in 1986, we had almost no experience with influence diagrams, although we knew the principles and rules. Since then we have often faced situations in which we had to decide between using an influence diagram and a decision tree. Influence diagrams are very seductive as they can be diagrammed quickly to represent very complex situations. But we also found them to be occasionally deceptive in that the modeling and elicitation effort can turn out to be prohibitive.

We find influence diagrams to be most useful as a precursor to probabilistic simulation, when variables are causally connected through deterministic functions. We also tend to use influence diagrams when there is a mix of discrete and continuous variables. This provides additional flexibility in modeling by either assessing discrete probability distributions over some variables or by creating a probabilistic continuous simulation for other variables.

Fault Trees, Event Trees, and Belief Networks

We used these tools in different contexts, but we have much less experience with them than other authors of this book. (See Chapters 15 and 16 in this volume.)

REFERENCES

Benthien, M., and von Winterfeldt, D. (2001). *Using decision analysis to improve seismic rehabilitation decisions*. Working Paper No. WP-01-01. Institute for Civic Enterprise, School of Policy, Planning and Development, University of Southern California, Los Angeles.

Edwards, W. (1979). Multiattribute utility measuremenmt: Evaluating desegregation plans in a highly political context. In R. Perloff (ed.), *Evaluator interventions: Pros and cons*. Beverly Hills, CA: Sage, pp. 13–54.

Keeney, R. (1980). *Siting energy facilities*. New York: Academic Press.

Keeney, R. (1992). *Value-focused thinking*. Cambridge, CA: Harvard Unversity Press.

Keeney, R. L. and Raiffa, H. (1976). Decisions with multiple objectives. New York: John Wiley.

Keeney, R., See, K. E., and von Winterfeldt, D. (2006). Inventory and appraisal of U.S. graduate decision programs. *Operations Research, 25*, 1–16.

Keeney, R., and von Winterfeldt, D. (2005). *Evaluation of Capilano–Seymour tunnel project alternatives*. Report to the Greater Vancouver Regional District, Vancouver, CA.

von Winterfeldt, D. (2005). *A risk analysis of grounding practices to improve utility worker safety*. Report submitted to Southern California Edison Co., Rosemead, CA.

von Winterfeldt, D., and Edwards, W. (1986). *Decision analysis and behavioral research*. Cambridge, UK: Cambridge University Press.

von Winterfeldt, D., and Schweitzer, E. (1998). An assessment of tritium supply alternatives in support of the U.S. nuclear weapons stockpile. *Interfaces, 28*, 92–112.

von Winterfeldt, D., Eppel, T., Adams, J., Neutra, R., and Delpizzo, V. (2004). Managing potential health risks from electric power lines: A decision analysis caught in controversy. *Risk Analysis, 24*, 1487–1502.

7 Developing Objectives and Attributes

Ralph L. Keeney

ABSTRACT. The fundamental objectives of any decision problem should define why the decision maker is interested in that decision. However, listing a complete set of the fundamental objectives for a decision is not a simple task. It requires creativity, time, some hard thinking, and the recognition that it is important. This chapter offers many suggestions to help do the task well and provides criteria to appraise the quality of the resulting set of fundamental objectives. For an analysis of the alternatives in terms of these objectives, an attribute to measure the achievement of each objective is required. Good attributes are essential for an insightful analysis. This chapter also includes many suggestions to help identify or construct useful attributes as well as criteria to appraise the quality of the resulting attributes. Collectively, the fundamental objectives and corresponding attributes provide the basis for any objective function and for any discussion of the pros and cons of the alternatives.

Introduction

For any decision situation, there is a specific time when it is first recognized. Before that time, there is no conscious awareness of the decision. These decision situations can be categorized depending on how they were elevated to consciousness. Some were caused by an external event, referred to as a trigger that makes it clear that a decision will have to be made. Triggers are caused by circumstances or by people other than the decision maker, the person who needs to make a choice sometime in the future. Hence, I refer to these decision situations as decision problems. The other way that a decision comes into consciousness is that it simply pops up in the mind of the decision maker when he or she realizes that some control to influence the future can be taken by making choices. I refer to this internally generated decision situation as a decision opportunity. However it occurs, this first recognition that there is a decision to be made is the initial decision context for the situation. Examples of this initial decision context include the following: What university should I attend? What is the best way to increase the market share of product X? Where should a new power plant be located? Who should we hire as the new faculty member in our department? How should I lose fifty pounds?

The initial decision context is revised as the decision situation is better defined. For personal decisions, the revision may result from more careful thinking by the decision maker. For example, that decision maker may gather opinions of friends, acquaintances, or advisors to revise a decision context. For business or public policy problems, where many people might be directly concerned about the same decision, discussions may result in a better characterization of the decision context. This context basically bounds the decision to be faced. These bounds put a preliminary limit on the types of objectives and attributes appropriate to consider for the decision.

Once the decision context is thought to be understood, the tasks, eventually resulting in the choice of an alternative to "solve the decision," begin. This process may be very informal and basically involve trying to identify an alternative that is good or good enough to select. However, for important situations it is often worthwhile to more carefully consider the alternatives and their implications before choosing. In these cases, it is also useful to identify the set of objectives that one wishes to achieve by addressing the decision and a list of alternatives that are the contenders to best achieve those objectives. The lists of objectives and alternatives provide a well-defined decision frame for the decision context. If the decision frame is carefully constructed, the choice might be made by informally considering how well the various alternatives seem to measure up in terms of the objectives. Again, however, for some problems it is worthwhile to delve more deeply and perform an analysis of the alternatives. This involves carefully defining the objectives and identifying measures, referred to as attributes, to indicate the degree by which those objectives are met by the various alternatives. An analysis of those alternatives can then proceed quantitatively following the theory and practice of decision analysis.

Objectives and Attributes

The focus of this chapter is on three issues:

- How can we create an appropriate set of objectives?
- How can we identify an appropriate attribute to measure the degree to which each of those objectives is achieved?
- How can both of the above tasks be done efficiently and well?

Presenting two cases will help define terms and provide examples for our discussion.

A common generic decision in many businesses concerns a choice of alternatives to best meet company objectives. For certain classes of major decisions, two objectives will suffice: maximize profits and maximize market share. The profit objective might be measured by the attribute "net present value of profits" over a certain time period, and the market share objective might be measured by the attribute "percent of the total product class being sold at the end of that period." These objectives and attributes are listed in Table 7.1. The profit objective measures how well the company performs in the short term, and the market share objective indicates how well the company is poised to do from the end of the short term into the future.

Table 7.1. Objectives and attributes for a major business product decision

Objectives	Attributes
Maximize profit	Net present value of profit for 3 years
Maximize market share	Percent of product category sold in third year

A specific, more detailed, example concerns decisions of British Columbia Gas (BC Gas), a company that supplies natural gas throughout British Columbia. Tim McDaniels, of the University of British Columbia, and I worked with BC Gas to identify objectives and attributes for their integrated resource planning (Keeney and McDaniels 1999). As a result, we ended up with the set of objectives and attributes indicated in Table 7.2. It is worthwhile to briefly mention how these were obtained as it is relevant to the process for important major decisions.

Tim and I first had meetings with several executives at BC Gas, two individuals at the BC Utilities Commission, and representatives of ten stakeholder groups in the province. In all of these discussions, we asked the individuals to identify any values, interests, or concerns that they had about resource planning and choices of BC Gas. After the meetings, we summarized the individual contributions with a report personalized to the participants requesting any modifications or additions. From the original reports and additional suggestions, we made a complete list of all the values stated by the participants. This provided the basis for us to identify the objectives in Table 7.2 using processes described in this paper.

The attributes for the BC Gas objectives were developed partially based on a workshop with BC Gas personnel, including technical and regulatory specialists. Essentially, our task was to use their knowledge to help identify an attribute that would both serve to better define what was meant by each objective and adequately describe the consequences of alternatives in terms of how well they met that objective. Details about the process of identifying attributes are discussed later in this paper.

Tables 7.1 and 7.2 provide a background to understand the definitions that we use for objectives and attributes. Objectives are a statement of something that the decision makers wish to achieve by addressing that decision. They can be effectively stated using a verb and a noun (i.e., object). In Table 7.2, with "minimize service costs," the verb is *minimize*, and the object is *service costs*. With "promote job creation," the verb is *promote*, and the object is *job creation*. The attributes are measuring scales that provide a basis to indicate how well these objectives are achieved. For instance, with "promote job creation," the attribute is "net full-time job equivalents created in province." It may seem that an attribute is obvious as a match for an objective, but important choices are made in selecting appropriate attributes, as we will see later.

Identifying Objectives

The most basic advice for someone facing a perplexing decision is "list your objectives." This is logical, as the only reason for caring about any decision is to achieve

Table 7.2. Objectives and attributes for integrated resource planning at BC Gas

Objective	Attribute
Provide quality customer service	
Keep energy bill down	
Minimize service cost	Dollar change in average residential customer bill
Keep required capital expenditures low	Capital cost of DSM initiatives for a typical customer
Have smooth and predictable changes	Maximum percentage rate increase at any one time
Provide reliable service	
Minimize service outages	Number of customer outages in one year
Promptly respond to service requests	Average response time for service requests
Provide equitable service	
Avoid rate subsidies to customer classes	Ratio of long-run cost of service by customer class over rates for customers class
Minimize inequities in demand side management	Number of customers benefiting divided by number of customers paying
Promote intergenerational equity	Amount of gas consumption avoided over the planning period
Ensure health and safety	
Minimize public and employee fatalities	Number of fatalities
Minimize public and employee injuries	Number of days lost from work, school, or equivalent for public and employees
Minimize environmental impact	
Minimize loss of forests and fauna	Hectares of mature commercial forest, or equivalent, alienated hectares of high quality animal habitat lost
Minimize emissions of greenhouse gasses	Tons of greenhouse gas emissions per year (in CO_2 equivalents)
Minimize emissions of air pollutants	Tons of NO_x emissions per year
Optimize socioeconomic impacts in BC	
Minimize adverse impacts to individuals	
Minimize disruption	Person-year equivalents of significant disruption (e.g., unable to drive or park near home) due to construction or related activities
Minimize noise	Person-year equivalents of significant noise impacts on neighbors, sufficient to cause recurring complaints due to facilities
Minimize visual impacts	Person-year equivalents of significant visual impacts from viewing construction site at least once daily
Minimize adverse effects on lifestyles	Person-year equivalents of constraint on personal choices due to lack of natural gas available
Minimize property damage	Dollars of property damage claims in one year

(continued)

Table 7.2. *(continued)*

Objective	Attribute
Minimize fear and worry	Person-year equivalents of significant fear or worry about facilities, sufficient to cause complaints
Minimize odors	Person-year equivalents of exposure to odors from facilities significant enough to cause complaints
Avoid bad-tasting water	Person-year equivalents of water with bad taste from facilities
Enhance viability of communities	
Promote regional development and contribute to stable communities	Number of communities receiving service or receiving new investment in major facilities (more than five employees)
Minimize disruption of native lands	Hectares of reserves that are disrupted by construction and other activities
Provide community service	Number of BC Gas employees involved in community service
Support the province	
Provide tax revenue to province	Tax flows to province from BC Gas revenues (income tax and gas royalties)
Promote job creation	Net full-time job equivalents created in British Columbia
Keep BC industry competitive	Relative cost of BC Gas rates to industrial customers compared with Washington State industrial gas rates
Ensure quality shareholder return	
Provide high dividends	Real annual percentage return on equity
Have stock appreciation	Real annual percentage return on equity

something. The objectives state what that something is. Without knowing what you want to achieve, there doesn't seem to be any reason to care or think about a decision. Peters and Waterman (1982) refer to their "all-purpose bit of advice for management" in the pursuit of excellence as "figure out your value system."

Simple as it sounds, it is not easy to list a good set of objectives for any complex decision problem. In the BC Gas case, numerous executives of the firm, and the ten stakeholder groups, provided lists of objectives. Indeed, we analysts helped to stimulate their thoughts in order to come up with more complete lists of objectives. Yet, I think that most of the ten executives and the ten stakeholder groups listed only about half of the objectives in Table 7.2. After seeing the list of objectives in Table 7.2, they all felt the list was appropriate.

In preliminary experiments with my colleagues Kurt Carlson and Samuel Bond at Duke University, we have explored the difficulty people have in generating a complete set of objectives for their own decisions. We start by asking individuals to list objectives for a problem they have faced in the past or could easily face in the future (for example, prospective MBAs were asked to list objectives for choosing a business school for an MBA and doctoral students were asked to list objectives of their dissertation). Next, we provide these individuals with a list of objectives that we have designed to be "reasonably complete." By reasonably complete, we mean that our list contains most of the objectives that we, with help from our colleagues, thought of that were relevant to that decision. We then ask participants to indicate which of the objectives on our complete list apply to them personally. If individuals have already generated all the objectives that matter to them, they should not identify any new objectives from our complete list. However, our respondents initially list only about half of the objectives that they subsequently say are relevant after observing our list.

One might think that individuals simply list their most important objectives and miss less significant ones. Therefore, we asked respondents to prioritize the objectives that they listed or selected from our complete list. Perhaps surprisingly, objectives that people miss on their original lists are roughly as important as ones they list. Although this work is still in progress, it shows that individuals may need assistance to identify adequate objectives. Indeed, the suggestions later in this section may be helpful for that purpose.

Listing objectives can be complex because individuals often do not have a clear concept of exactly what an objective is. As a result, they will include targets, constraints, aspirations, goals, and even alternatives in their list of objectives. For instance, if a company has a goal to make a profit of $50 million in the coming year, this suggests failure if they make $49 million, and success if they make $51 million. Likely, this preference does not really represent their real values. Suppose that there were two alternatives, one that would guarantee a profit of $51 million and one that had a 50/50 chance of a profit of $49 million or a profit of $100 million. Which alternative would the company likely prefer? They would likely prefer the second alternative, and yet that alternative has a 50 percent chance of failing to meet the target, whereas the first alternative has no chance of failing. Goals that are listed with a target (i.e., the $50 million) are not very useful for evaluating alternatives or thinking about the relative desirability of alternatives.

Constraints have another shortcoming for evaluating alternatives. Namely, they eliminate alternatives that may end up being very desirable. Suppose a new product was being developed, and a constraint was that the product would need to weigh less than 5 pounds. This would naturally eliminate any alternative that would weigh 5.1 pounds. But what if that alternative performed fantastically well on all the other objectives? It might clearly be the best. By eliminating the constraint, but including an objective such as minimize weight of the product, the relative significance of being 0.1 pounds more than 5 pounds, or 12 pounds more than 5 pounds, can be appropriately included in the evaluation of alternatives.

Because of the difficulties in coming up with a good list of objectives, it is worthwhile to break the process into two steps and to provide methods to assist each step. The first step, as mentioned with the BC Gas study, is to ask individuals to write down their values, meaning anything that they care about, regarding the possible consequences of potential alternatives. The second step is to carefully appraise each value item on their list and to convert it into an objective. The first step goes from nothing to something, and it is reasonable to accept some disorganization in

Table 7.3. Devices to help articulate values

Device	Questions
Wish list	What do you want? What do you value? What would be ideal?
Alternatives	What is a perfect alternative, terrible alternative, some reasonable alternatives, the status quo? What is good or bad about each?
Consequences	What has occurred that was good or bad? What might occur that you care about?
Goals and constraints	What are your aspirations to meet the stated goals and constraints? What limitations do these place on you?
Different perspectives	What would your competitor or constituency or other stakeholders be concerned about? At some time in the future, what would concern you?
Strategic values	What are your ultimate values that may be represented in a mission statement, a vision statement, or a strategic plan? What are your values that are absolutely fundamental?
Generic values	What values do you have for your customers, your employees, your shareholders, yourself? What environmental, social, economic, or health and safety values are important?
Why do you care?	For each stated value, ask why it is important. For each response, ask why it is important.
What do you mean?	For each stated value, specify its meaning more precisely. For broad values, identify major component parts.

this process in order to stress creativity and gather as much information as possible from the minds of individuals concerned about the decision. Once values are presented in the form of a list, it is not difficult to systematically convert them into objectives. For discussion purposes, it is clearer to consider the steps separately, although there can certainly be interplay between the two steps when developing a useful set of objectives.

Listing Values

The process of developing a list of values requires creativity and hard thinking. It is often useful to stimulate this process so individuals can be as expansive as possible at this stage. The devices described in Table 7.3 have proven to be useful in this regard.

When developing a set of values for a personal decision, the stimulating questions must be considered alone. However, you may wish to brainstorm using this list with a friend even on personal problems. For business decisions or public decisions, usually there are multiple individuals who could and should be involved in developing values. In such situations, a facilitator may use the stimulating questions in Table 7.3 to generate a larger scope of the potential objectives.

At the beginning of listing values, it is useful to think freely and to list all the concerns that come to mind. Essentially, you are developing a wish list by considering what you want, what you care about, what would be ideal, and what you do not want.

Once your initial wish list is complete, using the devices in Table 7.3 may help identify additions to your list. These devices may end up stimulating values that overlap, that are the same values stated differently, or that are parts of values already on the list. However, redundancy is not a problem at this stage, as this can be recognized when one converts values to objectives and then organizes them.

It is useful to indicate how some of the devices might help.

ALTERNATIVES. One can readily identify real or hypothetical alternatives that are relevant to your decision. Using any of these alternatives, identify what you like and what you do not like about them as they are guides to potential values. You can stretch your thinking by visualizing hypothetical alternatives that would be great or terrible, and then write down the values that would make these alternatives either great or terrible.

CONSEQUENCES. Alternatives lead to consequences, and it is sometimes easier to think about consequences than those alternatives. If you can identify consequences that you like or do not like, they certainly suggest associated values. For example, someone may state that a particular health risk is unacceptable, which suggests that value might lead to the objective of minimizing those health risks.

GOALS AND CONSTRAINTS. Many individuals have implicit or explicit goals and organizations often have stated goals. If a goal of a student is to earn a B average next year, this suggests a value concerning high grades. A constraint for a certain decision problem similarly suggests a value. If a company has a constraint that potential vendors should be able to supply materials within a week, this suggests the value of delivery time.

DIFFERENT PERSPECTIVES. For some public problems, stakeholders with different perspectives should often be included. This typically leads to a broader set of potential values. The same idea can be employed when you deal with personal decisions or decisions in a company. One can ask what a person with a given perspective different from mine would think about this. In a company, one might ask what would concern a particular competitor in such a situation. It is also sometimes helpful to take your own perspective on the problem but viewed from different time. Usually, we consider decisions viewed from today looking forward. We may perceive the same decision differently from the future looking back to the present. Suppose you are considering marketing your product in Eastern Europe. You may wish to consider your values assuming that you will be in a different position 10 years from now on such a venture. This might be useful to suggest additional values for now.

STRATEGIC VALUES. Many public and private organizations have a mission state-ment or a vision statement or a strategic plan that outlines their highest level of values. One can ask, with any given decision being faced, what the ways are in which our current actions and their consequences contribute toward achieving any of these strategic values. Any response suggests additional values. It is also useful for individuals to have a mission statement for their life or for the next five years or for the time in college or for the time at a given firm. Major decisions being made now should contribute to such a mission and that relationship can suggest values.

GENERIC VALUES. On many public decisions, the categories of values concern social, economic, environmental, and health and safety impacts. Any of these can suggest specific values relevant to a given problem. For many business prob-lems, generic objectives certainly include satisfying the customer, making money, meeting responsibilities to shareholders, enhancing market share, and providing a good climate for employees. Again, any of these categories may stimulate poten-tial values for current problems.

WHY DO YOU CARE? One of the more powerful devices to articulate values is simply to ask why an item on the current list of values is important. For instance, if an individual lists air pollution as important, ask why. The response might be that less pollution would expose fewer people. Then ask again why that matters, and the response might be that some people would become ill if they were exposed to too much pollution. Again, ask why that matters. The likely response would be that we do not want people to be sick, and, in extreme cases, exposure may lead to premature death. This process suggests that values concerning exposure to pollution, illnesses caused by pollution, and potential premature death are all relevant to the list of values.

WHAT DO YOU MEAN? To better understand the concern of listed values, ask what is meant by that value. By being more specific, values are clarified and additional values are often stated. In the context of logging a forest, many individuals list that they are concerned about degradation of the environment. By asking what this means, individuals may refer to the loss of plants or animal species and habitat, as well as the aesthetic losses. One might ask about the meaning of each of these. For instance, the habitat loss may concern river habitat, lake habitat, and forest habitat. Then inquire about habitat for particular species. Any of this process to drill deeper about what matters can lead to a better list of values.

Specifying Objectives from Values

It is generally not difficult to convert a value into a corresponding objective. You essentially need a verb and an object. The verb indicates the orientation of preferences, and often can be minimize or maximize. In general this orientation is obvious. Who wants to minimize profits, maximize jobs lost, increase air pollution, receive a poorer education, or have a rotten sex life? Thus, the main essence in specifying an objective from a value is defining the object.

In the context of examining what future space missions would be appropriate for the U.S. civilian space program run by the National Aeronautics and Space Administration, stakeholders suggested values that concern national pride, international prestige, scientific advancement, and cost. In that decision context, these values were converted into objectives such as enhance national pride, promote international prestige, advance scientific knowledge, and maintain fiscal responsibility. These are clearly broad objectives, and it would be worthwhile to specify their meaning with more detail.

One concern of potential customers, regarding the design and subsequent sale of a very-large-scale-integrated circuit tester, was the quality of service from selling organizations. This value was converted to the objective "maximize the quality of vendor service." You might state that one of the important values in your personal life is to have fun. The obvious objective in this context is to simply "maximize fun." Clearly stating such an objective as to "maximize fun" does not mean it would be easy to measure or easy to create or evaluate alternatives in terms of fun. But if fun is important, and it certainly is in my life, then it definitely ought to be on the list of values and articulated as an objective when considering the decision context on how to live your life.

Structuring Objectives

After specifying objectives for each of the general values, the next step is to structure these objectives in a logical manner. In the structuring process, objectives should be categorized into four types:

- *Fundamental objectives*: the ends objectives used to describe the consequences that essentially define the basic reasons for being interested in the decision.
- *Means objectives*: objectives that are important only for their influence on achievement of the fundamental objectives.
- *Process objectives*: objectives concerning how the decision is made rather than what decision in made.
- *Strategic objectives*: objectives influenced by all of the decisions made over time by the organization or individual facing the decision at hand.

The main relationships among the types of objectives are illustrated in Figure 7.1 for a public agency facing a decision about how best to construct a dam. The process objectives contribute to better achieving the means objectives, the fundamental objectives, and the strategic objectives. The means objectives mainly influence the fundamental objectives, but also have some direct influence on the strategic objectives. The fundamental objectives, influenced by the specific decision, have an effect on the strategic objectives, which are influenced by all decisions made by that state agency.

Figure 7.1 is referred to as a means–ends objective network. The important aspects of this are to link objectives through means–ends relationships and trace

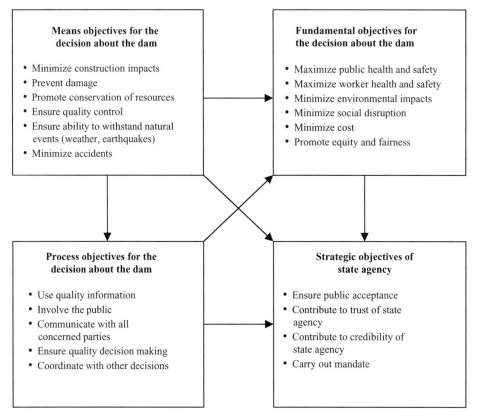

Figure 7.1. Representative objectives and their relationships for a decision concerning the construction of a dam (an arrow means "influences").

these relationships to fundamental objectives. This is done with a series of questions that follows the logic of what objectives influence the achievement of what other objectives.

Begin with an objective and ask, "Why is this objective important in the decision context?" Two answers are possible. One is that the objective reflects the essential reasons for interest in the situation: if so, it is then a fundamental objective. The other answer is that the objective is important because it influences some other objective. In this case, it is a means objective, and the response to the question identifies another objective. This "why is it important?" logic should be applied to this new objective to ascertain whether it is a means objective or a fundamental objective.

Consider a decision involving the transportation of nuclear waste. One objective may be to minimize the distance the material is transported by trucks. The answer to the question, "why is this objective important?" may be that shorter distances reduce both the chances of accidents and the costs of transportation. However, shorter transportation routes may go through major cities, exposing more people to the nuclear waste, and this may be deemed undesirable. Again, for each objective concerning traffic accidents, costs, and exposure, the question "Why is that important?" should be asked. For accidents, the response may be that fewer accidents cause fewer highway fatalities and less accidental exposure of the public to the nuclear waste. Additionally, the answer to why it is important to minimize exposure may be to minimize the heath impacts due to nuclear waste. To the question "Why is it important to minimize health impacts?" the response may be that it is simply important. This indicates that the objective concerning health impacts is a fundamental objective in the decision context.

It requires some skill to identify the fundamental objectives for a decision context, as appropriate fundamental objectives must be both controllable and essential. "Controllable" means that alternatives appropriate to the decision context influence the degree to which the objective is achieved without requiring additional decisions outside of that decision context. "Essential" refers to the fact that all of the alternatives in the decision context have an influence on the fundamental objectives. Some examples will help clarify these ideas.

If a candidate fundamental objective is too broad, alternatives, in addition to those in the decision context, are required to influence achievement. A simple illustration of this point involves the decision context of investing funds. The fundamental objective here might be to maximize the net worth of those funds in five years. The decision maker could reasonably state that the only interest she has in the funds is to use them to enhance her subsequent quality of life, which is her strategic objective. However, enhancing her quality of life is an inappropriate fundamental objective in the investment context, as it is not controllable. The consequences affecting her quality of life would depend on many decisions outside the investing decision context.

Consider a decision context where a company makes a product and states that the fundamental objective is to minimize the average cost of unit production. If the real concern of the company is to maximize profits, then minimizing the average cost of unit production is really not a fundamental objective. It is too narrow and not essential. Alternatives that help the company sell more units or sell units for a higher price do not influence unit production costs, and yet, do influence achieving the actual fundamental objective of maximizing profits. However, suppose that all such alternatives have been considered and a new decision context focuses only on product costs. In this decision context, the objective to minimize average cost of unit production is a fundamental objective.

Another, more involved example helps illustrate the notions of both controllable and essential. Consider the operation of a city ambulance service. Preliminary thinking might suggest that fundamental objectives could be any of the following: save the most lives possible, get patients to the hospital as soon as possible, get patients to the hospital in the best condition possible, minimize the time between the request for service and actual arrival to the scene where service is needed, and minimize the distance from the ambulance station to service locations. Saving lives is a strategic objective of the health system of which the ambulance system is a part. However, once a patient arrives at the hospital, whether or not he or she lives depends on decisions not under the influence of the ambulance service. Hence that objective is too broad, and not controllable in this decision context. The objective of minimizing distance to requests for service is too narrow, and not essential in this decision context. Alternatives, such as a better information system that indicates potential traffic jams or the physical state of the person for which the service is needed, would be potentially important for improving ambulance service. However, they would not have any influence on the distance of the ambulance from service requests. Zeroing in, the ambulance would have fundamental objectives of delivering the patient to the hospital as soon as possible and in the best condition possible. The objective of arriving on the scene as quickly as possible is a means to stabilizing the patient, so he or she can be delivered to the hospital in better condition, and delivering him or her sooner, as arrival time on the scene is part of the time to get to the hospital. Alternatives such as staffing ambulances with better-trained paramedics do not influence time to the accident scene, so this objective is not essential and hence not fundamental in this decision context.

Timing is also relevant in determining whether objectives are fundamental or means. If an organization is trying to improve its ability to plan, fundamental objectives now may be to "understand planning concepts" and "to develop planning skills." Obviously, these concepts and skills will be useful for planning in the future. The fundamental objective now is to learn, whereas the fundamental objective later will be to use that knowledge. For example, the fundamental objective at a job interview should be to obtain the job offer. In a subsequent decision, you can decide whether or not to accept the offer. You can always turn down an offer, but you cannot accept a job that was not offered.

In addition to the means–ends objectives network, the fundamental objectives hierarchy is a critical structure for clarifying objectives and providing a foundation for analysis. Table 7.2, which lists the objectives of BC Gas, is an objective hierarchy. The relationship between objectives is one of inclusion in a hierarchy. The objectives listed under a higher-level objective are considered a part of that higher level objective. Ideally, the lower-level objectives listed under a higher-level objective define that higher level objective and include all of its parts. This simplifies the ability to do an analysis of alternatives. It is easier to determine how well alternatives measure up in terms of detailed fundamental objectives than for broad objectives. As terminology, we sometimes refer to the highest-level objectives as "major objectives" and use the phrases subobjectives or component objectives to refer to objectives that are part of a major objective.

For some decisions, especially public decisions made by government, both what is chosen and how the alternative is chosen are important. In other words, the process of decisionmaking in these situations matters. When the process does matter, there are objectives to be achieved in managing the decision-making process, and these are referred to as process objectives. Figure 7.1 indicates how these process objectives can influence both the means objectives and the fundamental objectives in a decision context. Clearly if the process is done well, it influences how the main decision is made. It is important to recognize that the decision context of how to make the decision and the decision context of what decision to make are different. The same decision makers face both decision contexts, but the context differences are important. The objectives to be achieved and the alternatives for each are different.

Desirable Properties of Fundamental Objectives

The foundation for any analysis of alternatives is the fundamental objectives. There are desired properties of the set of fundamental objectives, with the corresponding attributes selected to measure them, which enhance the value of any subsequent analysis. A collective set of properties for the individual fundamental objectives, the set of fundamental objectives, and the attributes for those fundamental objectives was discussed in Keeney (1992). The important desired properties of each fundamental objective, mainly essential and controllable, were discussed earlier. The desirable properties of attributes are discussed later.

There are five desirable properties that pertain collectively to the set of fundamental objectives. These properties, with simple definitions for each, are the following:

- *Complete* – all of the important consequences of alternatives in a decision context can be adequately described in terms of the set of fundamental objectives.
- *Nonredundant* – the fundamental objectives should not include overlapping concerns.
- *Concise* – the number of objectives, and subobjectives, should be the minimum appropriate for quality analysis.
- *Specific* – each objective should be specific enough so that consequences of concern are clear and attributes can readily be selected or defined.
- *Understandable* – any interested individual knows what is meant by the objectives.

The property of complete is simple to understand. Referring to the ambulance service described earlier, if the fundamental objective were only to deliver an individual as soon as possible to the hospital, this would be incomplete. Clearly, paramedics with the ambulance service can affect the condition in which the patient arrives at the hospital, and such an obvious consequence needs to be addressed. Hence, a complete set of fundamental objectives for this example problem may be, as stated earlier: to deliver the patient to the hospital as soon as possible after receiving a call for service and to deliver the person in the best condition possible. Redundancy can often occur when means objectives are included inadvertently among the fundamental objectives. For instance, in a decision context to reduce a certain air pollutant, if the objective of minimizing health effects is included with another objective to minimize ambient pollution concentration, these would clearly overlap and lead to redundancy. A main impact of higher pollutant concentrations, in this context, would be more health effects.

To list health effects helps us, but it is likely not specific enough for many air pollution decisions. We would want to understand which health effects matter. There will likely be mortality and morbidity consequences, and each of these should be addressed separately. The mechanisms that might lead to health effects in children or infants may also be different from those that result in health effects to adults. These differences should be recognized, so one should state objectives that separately address the dichotomy of children and adult morbidity and children and adult mortality. In evaluating sites for the nuclear waste repository in the United States (Merkhofer and Keeney 1987), possible fatalities could occur to different populations due to different causes at different locations. Hence, eight fundamental objectives of minimizing fatalities addressed the trichotomy of eight categories that separated workers from the public, loss of life due to radiation or accidents, and fatalities during transportation or at the repository site.

There are naturally some interrelationships among the five desirable properties. Getting a concise set of fundamental objectives and having them at the right level of specification naturally conflicts. Specification pushes one to have more subobjectives, whereas concise pushes to have fewer. Collectively these two properties promote an appropriate balance. A set of objectives with many redundancies is likely less concise than those with fewer redundancies. To some degree, completeness stresses more objectives in opposition to being concise. All of the other four properties, when better met, typically contribute to greater understanding of the set of fundamental objectives.

I visualize the first four properties in terms of a Venn diagram. Completeness wants the universal set of concern to be broad enough to consider all the concerns. This universe is divided into subobjectives because a single objective for that universe would usually be way too broad and not specific enough. Completeness now requires that the subobjectives cover the universe and nonredundancy means we would like them to have no overlap. Concise refers to having as few subobjectives as needed and no subobjectives that are not needed. A set of fundamental objectives that measures up well in terms of these four properties, will likely be understandable.

Basic Concepts about Attributes

The decision frame for any analysis is the set of objectives considered and the set of alternatives for achieving those objectives. To describe the consequences of alternatives and make value tradeoffs between achieving relatively more or less on different objectives, it is necessary to identify a measure for each objective. We refer to such a measure as an *attribute*. The terms *performance measure, criterion,* and *metric* are often used as synonyms. This section and the following two present concepts, guidelines, and examples for identifying appropriate attributes to measure the achievement of objectives in analyses. These sections liberally adapt and at times repeat material from Keeney and Gregory (2005).

Previous research has identified three different types of attributes: *natural attributes, constructed attributes,* and *proxy attributes* (Keeney 1992). In some cases, an attribute may look more like a hybrid of two of these types, but this trichotomy is useful for discussing features of attributes.

Natural attributes are in general use and have a common interpretation. In the BC Gas example in Table 7.2, the objective "minimize service cost" has the natural attribute "dollar change in the average residential customer annual bill." For the objective "minimize public and employee fatalities," the attribute is "number of fatalities." Most natural attributes can be counted or physically measured. They also have the property that they directly measure the degree to which an objective is met. Proxy attributes share many qualities of natural attributes. These attributes usually involve a scale that is in general use that can be counted or physically measured. The difference is that they do not directly measure the objective of concern. For a decision involving setting speed limits, for example, one proxy attribute for the objective "minimize fatalities" is the "number of vehicle accidents." Certainly the number of vehicle accidents is related to the number of fatalities, but it does not directly measure those fatalities. A proxy attribute is less informative than a natural attribute because it indirectly indicates the achievement of an objective. Proxy attributes typically are used when it is difficult to gather information about how well various alternatives measure up in terms of possible natural attributes.

A constructed attribute is sometimes developed to measure directly the achievement of an objective when no natural attribute exists. Again referring to the BC Gas Table 7.2, the objective "promote job creation" is measured by the constructed attribute "net full-time job equivalents created in British Columbia." This is a simple constructed attribute as it weights a new job by the hours per week of work and normalizes to the standard of a full-time job (i.e., 40 hours per week). In a sense, this constructed scale is done in the same fashion as a grade point average to indicate performance in school.

Another type of constructed scale identifies two or more distinct levels of achievement of an objective and describes them with an appropriate definition. One example from a decision analysis of national strategies to manage nuclear waste from power plants concerned an objective "minimize environmental impact" (Keeney and von Winterfeldt 1994). The constructed scale indicated in Table 7.4 was developed for this decision, where terms used in the scale such as major aesthetic impact, disruption of an endangered species habitat, and historical site of major significance were carefully defined.

Once a constructed attribute has been commonly used in practice, people become familiar with it and it takes on properties of a natural attribute. The Dow Jones Industrial Average was introduced in 1896 and expanded in 1928 to include the prices of thirty stocks to measure the movement of the stock market. This originally constructed attribute is now more like a natural attribute to individuals knowledgeable about the stock market. Familiarity with an attribute and the ease of interpreting the attribute levels are the main distinguishing features between natural attributes and constructed attributes.

It is useful to recognize that the concept of an attribute has two associated notions, one qualitative and one quantitative. These can best be illustrated by example. For an objective such as minimize cost, the attribute likely would be cost

Table 7.4. Constructed attribute for environmental impact in the evaluation of national nuclear waste strategy

Attribute level	Representative environmental impact
0	No impact
1	Impact to historical or archeological site of major significance; no aesthetic or biological impact
2	Major aesthetic impact or disruption of an endangered species habitat; no archeological or historical impact
3	Major aesthetic impact or disruption of an endangered species habitat, plus impact to historical or archeological site of major significance
4	Major aesthetic impact and disruption of an endangered species habitat, no archeological or historical impact
5	Major aesthetic impact and disruption of an endangered species habitat, plus impact to historical or archeological site of major significance

in dollars. The qualitative notion is "cost," and "dollars" is a quantitative scale for cost. In this case, they almost seem like the same thing and naturally go together.

However, even in this "apparently obvious" case, important issues for applications arise. In the study done with and for the Department of Energy (DOE) to evaluate the final candidate sites for the U.S. high-level nuclear waste repository (Merkhofer and Keeney 1987), one major objective was "minimize repository costs." Base-case estimates for the five sites ranged from $7.5 billion to $12.9 billion in 1987 dollars. In doing the analysis, it seemed as though some policy makers in DOE did not consider the cost differences to be very significant. Numbers such as 7.5 and 12.9 were conceptually small and the difference seemed even smaller. To make these numbers salient within DOE and to legislators, politicians, and the public who would later see the report, the analysts chose to use the scale "millions of dollars" rather than billions in the study. It is perhaps a little awkward to always say and write numbers like 7,500 millions of dollars and 12,900 millions of dollars, but they did communicate better the magnitude of the cost estimate. They look and sound as big as they are.

In another decision, one objective might be to maximize fuel efficiency of automobiles. Here, the qualitative notion is "mileage," which can be measured by different quantitative scales. The scale typically used for mileage by an individual in the United States is miles per gallon. In Europe, the typical natural attribute for the same objective is mileage measured in liters per hundred kilometers. Note that more miles per gallon is better, whereas fewer liters per hundred kilometers is better.

Desirable Properties of Attributes

If the fundamental objectives underlying an analysis are not appropriate, even great attributes for those objectives will not make up for this inadequacy. Any

subsequent analysis will provide much less insight than when a good set of fundamental objectives is in place. When these objectives do provide a good foundation
for describing consequences, then inadequate attributes can seriously damage an
analysis. Common errors include attributes that are ambiguous, fail to account
for available information relating to consequences, or incompletely describe the
consequences of the objective they are intended to measure. Too frequently, insufficient thought is given to the identification and choice of attributes.

Keeney and Gregory (2005) extended previous work (Keeney 1992; Gregory and Failing 2002) to specify a sufficient set of five desirable properties of
good attributes. These five properties, with simple definitions for each, are as
follows:

> *Unambiguous* – A clear relationship exists between consequences and descrip-
> tions of consequences using the attribute,
> *Comprehensive* – The attribute levels cover the range of possible conse-
> quences for the corresponding objective, and value judgments implicit in
> the attribute are reasonable,
> *Direct* – The attribute levels directly describe the consequences of interest,
> *Operational* – The information necessary to describe consequences can be
> obtained and value tradeoffs can reasonably be made,
> *Understandable* – Consequences and value tradeoffs made using the attribute
> can readily be understood and clearly communicated.

There are several interrelationships among these five properties. If an attribute
is ambiguous, it will likely fall short in terms of being comprehensive or understandable. If an attribute is not comprehensive or not direct, it will be much less
operational than otherwise. If an attribute is not operational, then there cannot be a good understanding of the consequences. Subsequently, if an attribute
is not understandable, then it is naturally not very operational and likely ambiguous.

Unambiguous

An attribute is unambiguous when there is a clear relationship between the consequences that might or will occur and the levels of the attribute used to describe
those consequences. Unambiguous attributes must be neither vague nor imprecise. Consider the objective to minimize cost and the attribute cost in millions
of dollars. If the cost of one alternative is $16.3 million, analysts would simply
describe that consequence as $16.3 million. On the other hand, if the attribute
only vaguely categorized costs as high, medium, or low, it might not be obvious
which attribute level is appropriate for $16.3 million. Different people could inter-
pret high, medium, and low differently without specific ranges in dollars used to
guide interpretation of these terms.

Even if this vagueness was eliminated by defining medium cost as $10–20
million for a specific decision, such an attribute would still be ambiguous. Although
$16.3 million is clearly categorized as medium, people interpreting a medium cost

consequence would only know that the cost is in the range of $10–20 million. Because of imprecision, they would not know whether the cost was $11 million, $19 million, or $16 million. Yet, there likely is a significant difference in the desirability of consequences of $19 million and $11 million. There is no reason for loss of such useful information in describing and evaluating alternatives.

Another shortcoming arises when uncertainties are involved, which is usually the case with important decisions. Suppose the cost of a particular alternative was described with a probability distribution that ranged from $18 to 23 million. Furthermore, suppose medium cost was defined as $10 to 20 million and high cost was defined as more than $20 million. Would the consequences be categorized as a medium cost or a high cost? Of course, one might say there is a 40 percent chance of a medium cost and a 60 percent chance of a high cost in this situation, but that still does not address the issue of not knowing exactly what the medium costs or the high costs might be.

In summary, an unambiguous attribute has such properties that when you know what the consequence is or will be, you know exactly how to describe it using the attribute, and when you know the description of a consequence in terms of the attribute level, you know exactly what the corresponding consequence is or will be. With uncertainties present, a full description of consequences with respect to an objective is given by a probability distribution over the associated attribute.

Comprehensive

An attribute is comprehensive if two properties are met: its attribute levels cover the full range of possible consequences, and any implicit value judgments are appropriate for the decision problem.

Consider the decision of setting a national ambient air quality standard for carbon monoxide. One of the fundamental objectives is to minimize detrimental health effects from carbon monoxide. Breathing more carbon monoxide increases carboxyhemoglobin, which decreases the oxygen carried by the blood, which leads to detrimental health effects such as fatal and nonfatal heart attacks. Consider the attribute "number of fatalities" for this objective. This attribute does not cover the full range of possible consequences of the objective, as not all detrimental health effects are fatal heart attacks. Either a second attribute, such as the number of nonfatal heart attacks, or a constructed attribute that includes both nonfatal and fatal consequences is necessary to be comprehensive. Keeney (1992) used four attributes to completely describe detrimental health effects for the decision of setting a national ambient air quality standard for carbon monoxide. These were number of fatal heart attacks, number of nonfatal heart attacks, number of angina attacks, and number of peripheral vascular attacks.

Comprehensiveness also requires that one consider the appropriateness of value judgments embedded in attributes. Whenever an attribute involves counting, such as the number of fatalities, there is the assumption that each of the items counted is equivalent. With the number of fatal heart attacks, there is a built-in assumption that a fatal heart attack for a 45-year-old is equivalent to a fatal heart attack for a 90-year-old. Is this a reasonable value judgment for a particular decision? There is not a right or wrong answer, but its an issue that should be considered in selecting the attribute. To be extreme, consider a decision concerning automobile safety. If the objective to minimize fatalities is measured by the attribute number of fatalities, this assumes that the death of a 10-year-old is equivalent to the death of a 90-year-old. Many people think this is inappropriate, as they consider the death of the 10-year-old to be more significant. One way to account for this is to use the attribute "years of life lost" to measure the objective "minimize fatalities." If the expected lifetime of a 10-year-old is 80, then 70 years of life is lost if a 10-year-old dies in an automobile accident. If the expected lifetime of the 90-year-old is 95, then 5 years of life is lost due to a death in an automobile crash. With the attribute of "years of life lost," the death of a 10-year-old would count fourteen times as much as the death of a 90-year-old (the ratio of 70 years to 5 years). Although the implications of such value judgments rarely are made explicit, their significance is underscored by the current public policy debate regarding the different values embedded in the two attributes "number of fatalities" and "years of life lost" (Seelye and Tierney 2003).

In the medical decision-making field, many individuals have taken a further step and developed a scale called "quality adjusted life years," or QALY (Pliskin et al. 1980; Gold et al. 2000; Hazen 2004). With QALYs, a year of life lost for a healthy individual counts more than a year of life lost from a less healthy individual. Whether the number of fatalities, years of life lost, or quality adjusted years of life lost is a more appropriate attribute, any specific decision problem needs to be appraised using all five desired properties of attributes.

Direct

An attribute is direct when its attribute levels directly describe the consequences for the fundamental objective of interest. A common example where this does not occur is when guidelines have been developed to cover an issue such as worker safety. Attributes measuring how well the guidelines are being met (e.g., what number, or what percentage, of the guidelines have been met, or have been violated, during a specified period) are not direct as they do not directly provide useful information about worker deaths or injuries. More useful information could be provided by attributes that are direct such as the number of worker fatalities, the number of worker injuries of different severities, and the lost-time experienced by workers due to accidents and fatalities.

Another example concerns the BC Gas objective "keep BC industry competitive." The attribute chosen for that study is the relative cost of BC Gas rates to industrial customers compared to Washington state industrial gas rates. Although the relative cost of gas rates is perhaps the main manner in which BC Gas influences the competitiveness of BC industry, the attribute, per se, is not directly a measure of BC industry, competitiveness. This indicates two points. First, with each of these five desirable properties, there is typically a degree to which a property may or may not be met. Second, searching for attributes is a decision problem with multiple objectives, a point we consider in the next section An attribute, such as comparative gas rates, might be easier to use and understand but is less direct than another attribute that might be more direct but less understandable and operational.

Operational

Even if attributes are unambiguous, comprehensive, and direct, there is also the practical question of whether the attributes are operational. One aspect of this concerns how easy it is to obtain the information describing consequences. One example concerns the BC Gas objective "promote intergenerational equity," where the attribute is "the amount of gas consumption avoided over the planning period." Avoiding the consumption of gas now means that more gas is preserved for future generations and that seems more equitable. However, it may be quite difficult to determine how much gas consumption is avoided now as it cannot be measured. It would have to be estimated based on assumptions that should be articulated explicitly.

Another aspect of operational attributes concerns whether they enable decision makers to make informed value tradeoffs concerning how much of one attribute is an even swap for a given amount of a second attribute. These value tradeoffs are necessary to balance the various pros and cons of alternatives. Consider the objective "minimize emissions of greenhouse gases" of BC Gas, which is measured by the attribute "tons of greenhouse gas emissions per year in CO_2 equivalents." This attribute directly indicates the emissions of greenhouse gasses. However, it is very difficult to interpret how significant, say in terms of costs, any specified number of tons of emissions is, which makes the value tradeoff issue very complex. This value tradeoff involves decreasing tons of greenhouse gas emissions versus increasing cost, for example. Would one be willing to have capital costs increase by $50 million to decrease 1,000 tons of emissions, or to increase costs only by $50 thousand to avoid an increase of 1,000 tons of emissions?

It is important to recognize that the ability to make informed value tradeoffs requires more than appropriate attributes. It requires hard thinking about implications of the consequences and a willingness to express value judgments about necessary value tradeoffs. Consider, for example, the fact that a value tradeoff between economic costs and the potential loss of human lives must be made in many public policy situations. In these situations, more money can be expended to make circumstances safer and reduce the potential for the loss of lives. The issue is not whether, but rather how, this value tradeoff is made: implicitly without thought and perhaps even awareness, or explicitly with reasoned consideration. Yet many individuals, including some with responsibilities for selecting related policies, refuse to make a value tradeoff between economic costs and the potential loss of human life for proclaimed moral or ethical reasons. Value tradeoffs such as these, when many people refuse to make them, are referred to as "taboo tradeoffs" (see Fiske and Tetlock 1996).

Understandable

The fifth desirable property is that attributes should be understandable to any-one interested in the analysis. The attributes need to be understandable to those doing the analysis, to decision makers who want to interpret the analysis, and to stakeholders who want to be informed by the analysis.

Understandability is essential for clear communication. One should be able to easily communicate the pros and cons of various alternatives in terms of their consequences. The standard on understandability for an attribute is that an indi-vidual understands the consequences if they are given the attribute levels. With consequences such as cost, number of fatalities, and length of salmon spawning areas created in a river, there would likely be a high level of understandability. For an objective such as maximize mileage of automobiles discussed earlier, the attribute "miles per gallon" has a high level of understandability for people in the United States, whereas the attribute "liters per hundred kilometers" is almost incomprehensible. This is the case even though there is a one-to-one relationship between the descriptions of fuel efficiency on these two attributes.

In some cases, technical experts tend to rely on attributes that are not under-standable to the larger audience of participants concerned about alternatives for dealing with a problem. For instance, with decisions concerning nuclear power or nuclear waste, one objective is often to minimize possible cancer cases to the public due to radioactive emissions from nuclear material. Because of the polit-ical sensitivity of talking about radiation-induced cancers, many people avoid using the understandable and direct attribute "number of cancer cases induced." Instead, many studies have used the proxy attribute "person-rems of radiation exposure" for the corresponding objective. But what percentage of the public, even the technically trained public, knows whether an exposure of 4 person-rems is horrendous or insignificant in terms of health implications? Person-rems is inad-equate as an attribute in an analysis for public use in terms of understandability. As the dose-response relationship relating radiation exposure to cancer has been studied for more than 50 years, using this to convert exposure to induced can-cer cases and cancer fatalities is the appropriate way to better inform decision makers.

A Decision Model for Selecting Attributes

The selection of an attribute is a decision. The quality of a selected attribute, on average, will be better if alternative attributes are considered. This is especially true when there is no obvious attribute, such as dollars to measure an objective concerning cost. The attribute chosen for any objective should be the one that best meets the five desirable properties outlined in the previous section. These properties can be thought of as the objectives that one wishes to achieve in decisions involving the choice of attributes.

Each selection of an attribute needs to be addressed in the context of the decision problem being analyzed. That said, there is still value in looking at the generic problem of what types of attributes are generally best to use in decision problems.

There is strong prescriptive advice for the types of attributes to select. If a natural attribute can be found that is comprehensive, direct, and operational, it should be selected. When that is not the case, effort should go into construction of an attribute. If there is no time for that effort or if it does not lead to a good constructed attribute, then a proxy attribute should be chosen.

The logic for this ordering is that natural attributes have a general understanding for many people. Information often is collected in terms of natural attributes so it is readily available or can be gathered without inordinate effort. Also, because people commonly think in these terms, it is easier for them to make value tradeoffs. However, for some important objectives, there are no natural attributes. Examples include objectives that address the social disruption to small communities when large facilities are built nearby; the morale within a company or organization; the physical pain of different treatments for a disease; or a community's pride in new civic infrastructure.

Construction of attributes should involve individuals knowledgeable about the consequences of concern. This should lead to unambiguous attributes that are comprehensive and direct. If the basis for their construction is adequately described and the manner in which data are gathered and value tradeoffs are made is also clarified, then people should be able to understand and communicate about what was done and why. This typically won't be as easy as with natural attributes, but a well-constructed scale should do a good job of meeting the five desirable properties of attributes.

Only when there is no appropriate natural attribute or constructed attribute should one select a proxy attribute. In this case, it is generally best to choose a proxy attribute with a natural scale, so it likely meets the properties of being unambiguous and comprehensive. Also, it should be selected such that information can be readily gathered to describe consequences, thereby meeting that part of the operational property. A major shortcoming of a proxy attribute is that it does not directly describe the consequences. This, in turn, makes it difficult for decision makers to understand the real consequences and assess reasonable value tradeoffs involving the proxy attribute.

Reconsider the national ambient air quality standards for carbon monoxide discussed earlier. Suppose the alternatives are evaluated in terms of cost and their effects on air quality, measured in parts per million of carbon monoxide, which is a proxy attribute for minimizing health effects. How can one responsibly think about whether it is worthwhile to tighten the standards from four parts per million to three parts per million of carbon monoxide for an additional cost of $3 billion annually? The answer is that one has to think about the differences in health effects associated with four and three parts per million. However, this complexity is likely what led to the fact that a direct attribute, such as the number of heart attacks, was not used in the first place.

When no natural attribute for a corresponding objective is found, the difficulty may be that the objective is too broad. In such cases, it is useful to decompose that broad objective into component objectives and then identify natural attributes for each of those components. If natural attributes are found for only some of the components, then one proceeds to develop constructed attributes for the other component objectives.

There are several examples in the BC Gas objectives that illustrate decomposition. Consider the major objective "ensure health and safety." There was clearly no single natural attribute for this objective, as both mortality and morbidity concerns are relevant. Therefore, component objectives to address each of these concerns were identified and measured by natural attributes. The number of fatalities is the attribute for "minimize public and employee fatalities," and the number of days lost from work/school or equivalent injury time was used for the objective "minimize public and employee injuries." In a sense, this latter natural attribute is constructed also, as it equates a loss of a day from work to the loss of a day from school to a day of equivalent injury time experienced by an individual who does not work or go to school. For the major objective "minimize adverse impacts to individuals," there are eight different types of impacts categorized. Except for the objective "minimize property damage." the other seven are measured by person-years of that type of adverse impact on an individual. Property damage is measured by the natural attribute of dollars of property damage claims.

Summary

The reason that we are interested in any decision problem is represented by its objectives. We want to do better rather than worse by choosing an alternative, and the objectives characterize what is better. If one wishes to do an analysis of the alternatives, it is useful to quantify the objectives with an objective function. This objective function explicitly defines what is better, and often how much better, in a particular decision situation. An in-depth knowledge of our values, as represented by an objective function, can be of considerable help in choosing better alternatives. Even if no more formal analysis is done, it is simply the case that we have a much better chance of ending up where we want to be if we know where it is that we want to be.

The objectives and corresponding attributes are perhaps even more useful for business and public problems than for personal problems. The distinction is that those decision situations typically involve many people. With clear objectives and attributes, the communication process necessary among those individuals can be much clearer. The objectives and attributes provide a framework to discuss the pros and cons of the various alternatives in a precise way. They also provide a basis for explaining actions and justifying choices, which are often important in decisions with many stakeholders, which include almost all major governmental decisions.

REFERENCES

Fiske, A., and Tetlock, P. (1996). Taboo trade-offs: reactions to transactions that transgress spheres of justice. *Political Psychology, 18,* 255–297.

Gold, M., Siegel, J., Russell, L., and Weinstein, M. (2000). *Cost-Effectiveness in Health and Medicine.* New York: Oxford University Press.

Gregory, R., and Failing, L. (2002). Using decision analysis to encourage sound deliberation: Water use planning in British Columbia, Canada. *Journal of Policy Analysis and Management, 21*(3), 492–499.

Hazen, G. (2004). Multiattribute structure for QALYs. *Decision Analysis, 1,* 205–216.

Keeney, R. L. (1992). *Value Focused Thinking: A Path to Creative Decision Making.* Cambridge, MA: Harvard University Press.

Keeney, R. L., and Gregory, R. S. (2005). Selecting attributes to measure the achievement of objectives. *Operations Research, 53,* 1–11.

Keeney, R. L., and McDaniels, T. (1999). Identifying and structuring values to guide integrated resource planning at BC Gas. *Operations Research, 47,* 651–662.

Keeney, R. L., and von Winterfeldt, D. (1994). Managing nuclear waste from powerplants. *Risk Analysis, 14,* 107–130.

Merkhofer, M. W., and Keeney, R. L. (1987). A multiattribute utility analysis of alternative sites for the disposal of nuclear waste. *Risk Analysis, 7,* 173–194.

Peters, T. J., and Waterman, Jr., R. H. (1982). *In Search of Excellence.* New York: Harper & Row.

Pliskin, J. S., Shepard, D. S., and Weinstein, M. C. (1980). Utility functions for life years and health status. *Operations Research, 28,* 206–224.

Seelye, G.Q, and Tierney, J. (2003). EPA Drops Age-Based Cost Studies. *New York Times, Late Edition, Section A*, May 3, p. 34.

8 Eliciting Probabilities from Experts

Stephen C. Hora

ABSTRACT. Decision models sometimes require the use of expert judgments to quantify uncertainties. Modes and methods for eliciting probabilities are presented in this chapter. Criteria for selecting issues and experts are discussed and protocols for acquiring these judgments derived from research and practice are described. These protocols are designed to eliminate problems that sometimes arise when using experts for uncertainty quantification. A range of considerations for organizing a probability elicitation is presented as a guide for developing a protocol for a given situation. The identification and avoidance of psychological biases arising from the application of heuristics is discussed as important background for probability elicitation. Probability training is presented as one method for reducing these biases. Measures of the goodness of assessed probabilities and probability distributions such as calibration measures and proper scores are given. Methods for completing a distribution from assessment fractiles are shown.

The ability of decision analysis to deal with significant uncertainties is one of its most attractive features. Probabilities or probability distributions provide the primary means for integrating uncertainties into a decision model. Often times, however, the acquisition of probabilistic information is, itself, a challenge. One method of developing probabilistic input for a decision model is to engage experts who have special knowledge about the likelihood of values or events in question. In order that the judgments of these experts be integrated with other types of information in the decision analysis, they should be codified as probabilities. Probabilities are the natural mathematical language of uncertainty and lend themselves to mathematical manipulations that cannot be accomplished with less rigorous expressions of uncertainty. The process of obtaining probabilities from knowledgeable individuals is sometimes called "expert judgment elicitation."

Probabilities can be elicited in several different forms. The least complex situation is when the uncertainty is about the occurrence or nonoccurrence of an event. In such a situation a single probability summarizes the expert's judgment about the likelihood of the event. The next level of complexity involves an event that may resolve into more than two outcomes such as the winner of a horserace. Sometimes, the uncertainty is about a numerical quantity that has an infinite number of possible values. For example, the winning time in the before mentioned horse race. For such a quantity, we require the expert to provide a probability density function or its integral, the distribution function. Because there are an infinite number of potential values, one must use other means than individual probabilities to express the judgment about uncertainty.

Eliciting judgments from experts is only one method for obtaining probabilities. When there is sufficient historical data and the stability of the process that generated the data can be guaranteed, these data should be used to develop probabilities or probability distributions rather than using experts. Expert judgment is most useful in situations where the evidence for mechanically estimating probabilities or distributions is incomplete. Expert judgment should not be used, however, when there is absence of a basis for making the judgments. This basis can be composed of data, models, analogues, theories, physical principles, etc., but without such a basis the judgments are mere guesses.

The impetus for the development of theories and methods for expert judgment has come from four directions. The development of Bayesian statistical methods and the subjectivist interpretation of probability have played an important role. For the Bayesians, it is the requirement of a prior distribution in order to produce a posterior distribution that has been the impetus. The prior distribution is inherently subjective in nature (meaning its philosophical interpretation) and thus is consistent with probabilities given by experts which are also inherently subjective. Subjectivists such as de Finetti (1974) and Savage (1954) provided theoretical underpinnings for the use of personal or subjective probabilities in decision making contexts.

Bayesian statistics has become a cornerstone of statistical decision theory (Raiffa & Schlaifer 1961), which in turn, has been a major contributor to decision analysis. Decision researchers have made major contributions to the techniques used to assess probabilities. Their motivations sprang from the practical need to represent uncertainties through probabilities in order to quantify decision models.

Cognitive psychologists have studied judgment formation about uncertain events. From their studies has emerged a large literature about cognitive biases in elicited probabilities. These biases are discussed later in the chapter.

Another area that has made major contributions to probability elicitation is risk analysis. An important milestone here was WASH-1400, The Reactor Safety Study (United States Nuclear Regulatory Commission, 1975). In this major analysis of the safety of nuclear power generating stations, expert judgments were used extensively, and openly, to develop subjective probabilities of various events, opening the way for greater use of expert judgment in public policy studies.

Elicitation Modes

Probability elicitation normally entails asking questions about events or about quantities.

Probabilities of Events

The simplest case to begin with is the uncertainty regarding an event that resolves into one of two states – the event occurs or does not occur. The required response is a single probability. It is important to distinguish this situation from a sequence of events where some events in the sequence resolve one way and others resolve another way. With a sequence of events there is a frequency of occurrence that is conceptually knowable and it is proper to create a probability distribution for this frequency. This is not the case for a non-repeating event – one that can occur only once. It is tempting to assign probabilities to probabilities or to use a range for a probability as if the probability had some physical or measurable value even if this is not the case. In any event, even if one were to assign probabilities to probabilities, expectations are linear in probabilities and neither expected values nor expected utilities would differ from those obtained using the mean of the probabilities. For a discussion of second-order probabilities and their meaningfulness, see de Finetti (1977) and Skyrms (1980). It is perhaps disconcerting that the expert's probability of a non-repeating event simultaneously carries information about the likelihood of the event and its uncertainty. These two aspects of knowledge about a non-repeating event are inseparable, however.

The most straightforward approach to obtaining a probability on a non-repeating event is to ask an expert for that numerical value. An expert who replies with "I don't know the value" is most likely thinking that there is some physical/ measurable value that should be known but is not. The expert must be reminded that the probability is a degree of belief and does not have a true, knowable value. It is, instead, a reflection of the expert's knowledge about the likelihood of the event and will differ from expert to expert and over time as new information is acquired.

Sometimes indirect methods work better. Odds provide a simple re-expression of a probability and the two are easily calculated from one another. Odds require a relative judgment about the likelihood of an event and its complement rather than a direct judgment resulting in a numerical value. The judgment that an event is, for example, four times more likely to occur than not occur may be easier for the expert to feel comfortable with than is a direct judgment that the event has a 0.8 probability.

Another type of comparison is with a physical representation of the probability of an event and the probability of its complement. The probability wheel developed for use in probability elicitation by Stanford Research Institute requires such comparisons. This device provides a visual analogue to the probability of an event and its complement. The partial disks can be moved so that one segment is proportional to a number between 0.5 and 1.0 while the other segment is proportional to the complement. Which segment represents the event and which segment represents the complement is decided by which is more likely.

Beyond odds and the wheel, analysts have attempted to use verbal descriptors of likelihoods such as probable, rare, virtually certain, etc. Sherman Kent, head of the CIA's Office of National Estimates, proposed such a verbal scale (Kent 1964). But research has shown that these descriptors are interpreted quite differently by various individuals (Druzdel 1989).

Perhaps the best approach to events with multiple outcomes is to decompose the assessment into a number of assessments of events with binary outcomes. Judgments about such events are not as difficult to make. This is a "divide and conquer" approach and will result in coherent assessments. Decomposition can be accomplished through probability trees, influence diagrams (discussed in a later chapter), or even formulas. When probability trees are used, the assessed probabilities are conditional probabilities and marginal probabilities of the conditioning events or variables. Influence diagrams are discussed in Chapter 10. Expressing a target quantity as a function of several other variables has been termed algorithmic decomposition.

There are many decompositions possible for a given problem. One should look for a decomposition that requires judgments that the expert is best prepared to make. Hora, Dodd, and Hora (1993) note that it is possible to over-decompose a problem and make the assessment task more difficult. If time allows, one can look at several decompositions of a given problem and resolve inconsistencies among the recomposed probabilities. Ravinder, Kleinmuntz, and Dyer (1988) examine the propagation of error in subjective probability decompositions.

Many assessments are concerned with the value of a variable. Usually, these variables have a continuous range of potential values. Sometimes the range of a variable is bounded by physical consideration and sometimes it is unbounded. Also, one end of the range may be bounded and the other may be conceptually infinite. For example, the depth of snow at a given location is bounded below by zero but has no well-defined upper limitation. Unbounded variables are troublesome in that making judgments about the most extreme possible values is difficult.

In some instances, the decomposition of a probability assessment depends on the source of uncertainties and the resolvability of those uncertainties. Knight (1921) made the distinction between "risk" (randomness with knowable probabilities) and "uncertainty" (randomness with unknowable probabilities). Today, these components of uncertainty are termed "aleatory" and "epistemic" uncertainties. *Reliability Engineering and System Safety* devoted a special issue to this subject (Helton and Burmaster 1996). Morgan and Henrion (1992) also discuss various components of uncertainty.

Assessment for Continuous Quantities

Assessment of continuous distributions is most often accomplished by having the expert provide a number of points on the distribution function (cumulative probability function). We denote such a point by the pair (p, v), where p is the probability that the quantity in question has a value no larger than v, that is, $P(X \leq v) = p$ where X is the uncertain quantity. Of course, one is limited to assessing only a small number of such points, often fewer than ten. The pairs (p, v) may be denoted by v_p and are called fractiles or quantiles. We will use the term fractile although the two terms are used interchangeably. Fractiles can be assessed either by specifying p and asking for v or by specifying v and asking for p. Both techniques can be used in a probability elicitation although the first approach has less tendency to direct the expert toward specific values as explained later in the discussion of the anchoring bias. These two approaches, fixing p and asking for v and vice versa, have been termed the p and v methods (Spetzler and Stael von Holstein 1975).

A variation on the p method is called successively subdivision. It requires the expert to specify a value that breaks an interval into two equally likely subintervals. The process is repeated several times until enough points on the distribution function are obtained to have a good idea of its shape. At the first subdivision, the expert is asked to provide a value such that the uncertainty quantity is equally likely to be above as below this value. This assessment yields $v_{.50}$, the median of the distribution. The second stage of successive subdivision entails dividing the range below the median into two equally likely sub-subintervals and similarly dividing the range above the median into two equally likely sub-subintervals. These subdivisions yield $v_{.25}$ and $v_{.75}$, the first and third quartiles, respectively. There are now three values, $v_{.25}$. $v_{.50}$, and $v_{.75}$, that divide the range of possible values into four subintervals each having a probability of 0.25. Once again some or all of these intervals may be resubdivided until the level of fineness needed to represent the distribution is obtained.

An analyst may choose to use successive subdivision for the median and quartile values and then switch modes to direct of assessment using the p or v method for values needed to complete the distribution. Comparisons should also be made to check the consistency of results. For example, the analyst might ask whether it is more or less likely that the quantity is between $v_{.25}$ and $v_{.75}$ than outside that interval. This is a consistency check, and if the analyst finds that inside or outside the interval is more likely, it will be necessary to make some adjustments.

Once a sufficient number of points on a distribution function have been obtained, the distribution must be completed by interpolation or curve fitting, and if end points have not been obtained, extrapolation will be necessary. The simplest method of completing the distribution is to use linear segments between assessed values on the distribution function. This is shown in Figures 8.1a and 8.1b. The resulting density is a histogram as connecting the fractiles by linear segments spreads the probability evenly throughout an interval. Although the image may appear unpleasing compared with fitting some kind of curve through the assessments, it does have advantage of maximizing the entropy of the distribution subject to satisfying the assessed fractiles. Entropy (Cover and Thomas 1991) is a measure on disorganization or uncertainty and is calculated from the density function:

$$I(f) = - \int_{-\infty}^{\infty} f(x)\ln f(x)dx \qquad (8.1)$$

where $I(f)$ is the entropy of the density $f(x)$. By maximizing the entropy, the analyst has added as little information as possible into the completed distribution, that is, relative to any other distribution with the same fractiles, the distribution completed by linear segments has the least information in it.

The process of extrapolating to obtain end points is much more difficult to justify than interpolating to obtain interior values and there is no agreed-upon method for doing so. In some decision analyses, the behavior of the distribution in the tail may be rather inconsequential, while in others, the tail behavior may be critical. This is apt to be true in studies of low-probability, high-consequence

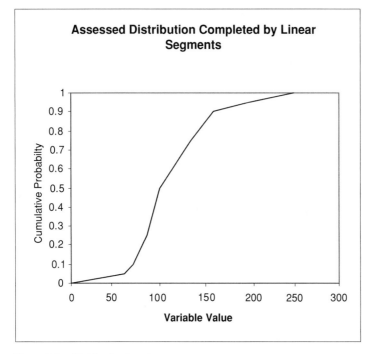

Figure 8.1a. Distribution function.

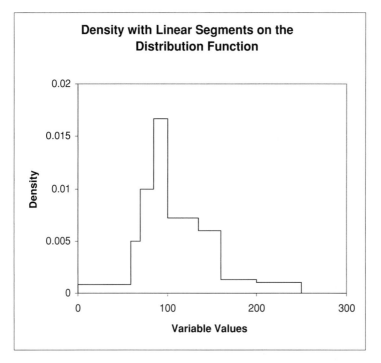

Figure 8.1b. Density function.

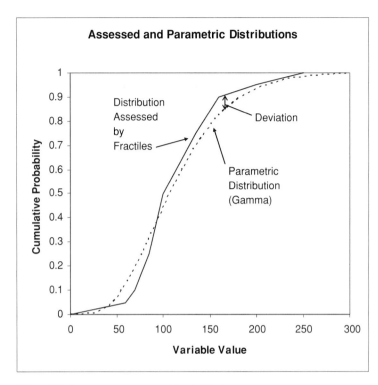

Figure 8.2. Assessed and parametric distributions.

hazards such as terrorism and technological hazards. Sadly, the behavior in the tail may be both of greatest interest and most challenging to assess.

An alternative to the p and v methods for eliciting a subjective distribution is that of selecting a parametric family of distributions and asking the expert to provide judgments about the parameters, either directly or indirectly through fractiles or other assessments. This is a shortcut method in that the number of assessments required is usually greatly reduced. The costs of this method are that an arbitrary family of distributions is imposed on the expert's judgment and the subjective estimates of the parameters may require more difficult judgments and thus greater error introduced into the assessment process. For example, judgments about a mean may be much more difficult to make than judgments about a median or mode when a distribution is asymmetric. Likewise, judgments about standard deviations may be more difficult to make than judgments about interquartile ranges.

It is sometimes desirable to encode elicited fractiles into a specific parametric family of distributions such as the gamma, beta, or normal family of distributions. A general method for making this conversion is to minimize the L_2-norm between the assessed density and the parametric density. Figure 8.2 displays a distribution assessed by fractiles and a parametric distribution, in this case a gamma distribution.

Table 8.1. Density functions

Name	Density	Expected density
Normal	$\dfrac{1}{\sqrt{2\pi}\sigma}e^{-\frac{1}{2\sigma^2}(x-\mu)^2}$	$\dfrac{1}{2\sqrt{\pi}\sigma}$
Gamma	$\dfrac{x^{\alpha-1}}{\beta^{\alpha}\Gamma(\alpha)}e^{-x/\beta}$	$\dfrac{\Gamma(2\alpha-1)}{\beta 2^{2\alpha-1}[\Gamma(\alpha)]^2}$
Beta	$\dfrac{1}{\beta(a,b)}x^{a-1}(1-x)^{b-1}$	$\dfrac{\beta(2a-1,2b-1)}{[\beta(a,b)]^2}$
Weibull	$\dfrac{\alpha}{\beta}x^{\alpha-1}e^{-(x/\beta)^{\alpha}}$	$\dfrac{\Gamma(2-\frac{1}{\alpha})}{2^{2-\frac{1}{\alpha}}}\dfrac{\alpha}{\beta}$

Denoting the assessed density function by $g(x)$ and the parametric density by $f(x\,|\,\theta)$, the problem is to find the value of the parameter vector θ that minimizes:

$$L_2[g(x),\, f(x\,|\,\theta)] = \left[\int_{-\infty}^{\infty} [g(x)-f(x\,|\,\theta)]^2 dx\right]^{\frac{1}{2}} \tag{8.2}$$

We denote the assessed fractiles by x_{p_i}, where p_i is the cumulative probability associated with the ith fractile. When the assessed distribution is completed by the method of linear segments, the L_2-norm can then be expressed as:

$$L_2[g(x),\, f(x\,|\,\theta)] = \left[\sum_{i=1}^{m-1}\frac{(p_{i+1}-p_i)^2}{(x_{p_{i+1}}-x_{p_i})} - 2\sum_{i=1}^{m-1}\frac{(p_{i+1}-p_i)}{(x_{p_{i+1}}-x_{p_i})}\right.$$

$$\left. \times\,[F(x_{p_{i+1}}\,|\,\theta)-F(x_p\,|\,\theta)] + \int_{-\infty}^{\infty} f^2(x\,|\,\theta)dx\right]^{\frac{1}{2}} \tag{8.3}$$

where m is the number of fractiles, by assumption $p_1=0$ and $p_m=1$, and $F(x\,|\,\theta)$ is the distribution function associated with the density $F(x\,|\,\theta)$.

Minimizing the L_2-norm with respect to θ is equivalent to minimizing the right-hand side of:

$$L_2[g(x),\, f(x\,|\,\theta)]^2 - \sum_{i=1}^{m-1}\frac{(p_{i+1}-p_i)^2}{(x_{p_{i+1}}-x_{p_i})}$$

$$= -2\sum_{i=1}^{m-1} d_i[F(x_{p_{i+1}}\,|\,\theta)-F(x_p\,|\,\theta)] + \int_{-\infty}^{\infty} f^2(x\,|\,\theta)dx \tag{8.4}$$

where $d_i = \frac{(p_{i+1}-p_i)}{(x_{p_{i+1}}-x_{p_i})}$ is the density in the interval between successive fractiles. Solving the minimization problem can be accomplished as a spreadsheet exercise if one has access to the distribution function and knows the parametric form of the last term in the right-hand side of (8.4). This last term, the integral of the squared density, is the "expected density" and is given in Table 8.1 for some density functions.

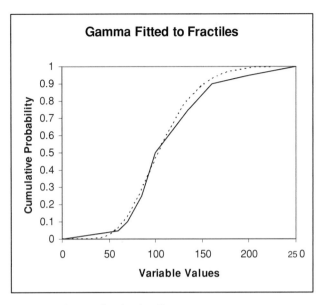

Figure 8.3. Gamma fitted to fractiles.

We note that the expected density may not exist for some parameter values. Specifically, for the gamma and Weibull densities, α must be greater than .5 and, for the beta density, both a and b must be greater than .5. The above graph shows a gamma distribution as fitted by the method to the fractiles shown in Figure 8.3.

A further complication arises when there are multiple variables that are probabilistically dependent. Dependence may be the product of a physical relationship or it may result from shared knowledge about the uncertain quantities. For example, gold and copper ores are often found together so that knowing the amount of copper present in an ore may provide information about the amount of gold in a given ore. This is an example of a physical relation. Conversely, knowing the atomic weight of copper may provide some insight into the atomic weight of gold. Thus, being informed of the atomic weight of copper, one would modify the uncertainty distribution for the atomic weight of gold.

Capturing dependence in probability assessments can be a daunting task. A general method for assessing the joint distribution of two or more variables is to break the assessment task into stages with marginal and conditional distributions being assessed. It may be necessary, however, to make many conditional assessments of the distributions give the value of the conditioning variable. Influence diagrams can provide a mechanism for organizing this effort. There are several ways to reduce the assessment effort, however. The first is to assume a particular family of distributions, such as the multivariate normal or Dirichlet, that can faithfully represent the judgments of the experts and then concentrate on assessments that will allow one to derive parameters of the joint distributions such as means, variances, and covariances. A more general approach that permits the marginal

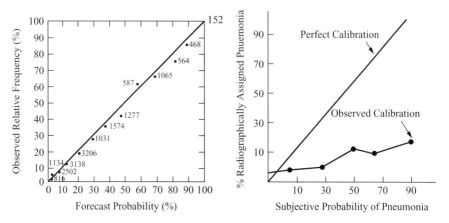

Figure 8.4. Two calibration graphs: The left panel (Fig. 8.4a) shows the calibration of weather forecasters (Murphy and Winkler, 1977); the right panel (Fig. 8.4b) shows the calibration of medical doctors (Christensen-Szalanski and Bushyhead (1981).

distributions to be general in form is to employ a *copula* (Clemen & Reilly 1999, Clemen, Fischer & Winkler 2000). Copulas are discussed in the next chapter in the context of capturing dependence among experts.

Measuring the Quality of Assessed Probabilities

Because subjective probabilities are personal and vary from individual to individual and from time to time, there is no "true" probability that one might use as a measure of the accuracy of an elicited probability. A weather forecaster who provides a probability of precipitation of .5 cannot be wholly right or wrong. Only probabilities of 1.0 and 0.0 can be held to such a standard. There are, however, two properties that are desirable to have in probabilities:

- Probabilities should be informative
- Probabilities should authentically represent uncertainty

The first property, being informative, means that probabilities closer to 0.0 or 1.0 should be preferred to those closer to .5 as the more extreme probabilities provide greater certainty about the outcome of an event. In a like manner, continuous probability distributions that are narrower or tighter convey more information than those that are diffuse. The second property, the appropriate representation of uncertainty, requires consideration of a set of assessed probabilities. For those events that are given an assessed probability of p, the relative frequency of occurrence of those events should approach p. Perhaps this is most easily understood by looking at a graph of probabilistic precipitation forecasts (horizontal axis) and observed relative frequencies (vertical axis) as reported in Murphy and Winkler (1977), Figure 8.4a, and a graph of medical diagnoses report in Christensen-Szalanski and Bushyhead (1981), Figure 8.4b, where the axes are

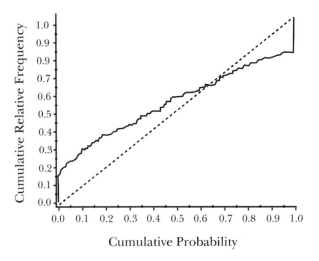

Figure 8.5. Assessment of probability.

the probability of pneumonia assigned by a physician in an initial diagnosis and a latter diagnosis by x-ray.

Ideally, each graph would have a 45-degree line indicating that the assessed probabilities are faithful in that they correctly represent the uncertainty about reality. The weather forecaster graph shows a nearly perfect relation while the graph for the physicians shows very poor correspondence between the assessed probabilities and relative frequencies. The graph is not even monotonic.

Graphs showing the relation between assessed probabilities and relative frequencies are called calibration graphs and the quality of the relationship is loosely called calibration, which can be good or poor. Calibration graphs can also be constructed for continuous assessed distributions. Following Hora (2004), let $F_i(x)$ be a set of assessed continuous probability distribution functions and let x_i be the corresponding actual values of the variables. If an expert is perfectly calibrated, the cumulative probabilities of the actual values measured on each corresponding distributions function, $p_i = F_i(x)$, will be uniformly distributed on the interval (0,1).

Figure 8.5 shows a graph of responses of experts to almanac questions (see Hora, Hora and Dodd, 1992). There is a clear departure from the ideal 45-degree line. The steep rise of the graph at both extremes is indicative of distributions that were not spread widely enough to embrace the true quantities. Hora (2004) proposes using the area between the 45-degree line of perfect calibration and the observed calibration curve as a measure of miscalibration.

Although calibration is an important property for a set of probabilities or probability distributions to possess, it is not sufficient as the probabilities or probability distributions may not be informative. For example, in an area where it rains on 25 percent of the days, a forecaster who always predicts a 25 percent chance of rain will be perfectly calibrated but provide no information from day to day about the likelihood of rain. But information and calibration are somewhat at odds. Increasing the information by making probabilities closer to zero or one or by making distributions tighter may reduce the level of calibration. Strictly proper scoring rules are functions of the assessed probabilities and the true outcome of the event or value of the variable that measure the goodness of the assessed distribution and incorporate both calibration and information into the score. The term "strictly proper" refers to the property that the expected value of the function is maximized when the probabilities or probability functions to which the function is applied are identical to the probabilities or probability functions that are used to take the expectation. An example will clarify.

A simple strictly proper scoring rule for the assessed probability of an event is the Brier or quadratic rule:

$$S(p) = -(1 - p)^2 \text{ if the event occurs}$$
$$= -p^2 \text{ if the complement of the event occurs.}$$

where p is the assessed probability. For any probability q, the expectation $Eq(S(p)) = -q(1 - p)^2 - (1 - q)p^2$ is maximized with respect to p by setting $p = q$. Thus, if an expert believes the probability is q, the expert will maximize the perceived expectation by responding with q. In contrast, the scoring rule $S(p) = p$ if the event occurs and $S(p) = 1 - p$, while intuitively pleasing, does not promote truthfulness. Instead, the expected score is maximized by providing a probability p of either 0.0 or 1.0 depending on whether q is less than or larger than 0.5. Winkler (1996) provides a discussion of this Brier rule and other strictly proper scoring rules. Also see Lichtenstein, Fischhoff and Phillips (1982) and Cooke (1991).

The concept of a strictly proper scoring rule can be extended to continuous distributions (Matheson and Winkler 1976). For example, the counterpart to the quadratic scoring rule for continuous densities is:

$$S[f(x), w] = 2f(w) - \int_{-\infty}^{\infty} f^2(x)dx \qquad (8.5)$$

Expected scores can sometimes be decomposed into recognizable components. The quadratic rule for continuous densities can be decomposed in the following manner. Suppose that an expert's uncertainty is correctly expressed through the density $g(x)$ but the expert responds with $f(x)$ either through inadvertence or intention. The expected score can be written as:

$$E_g\{S[f(x), w]\} = I(f) - C(f, g)$$

$$\text{where } I(f) = \int_{-\infty}^{\infty} f^2(x)dx \text{ and } C(f, g) = 2 \int_{-\infty}^{\infty} f(x)[f(x) - g(x)]dx \qquad (8.6)$$

$I(f)$ is the expected density associated with the assessed distribution and is a measure of information. $C(f, g)$ is a strictly non-negative function that increases as $g(x)$ diverges from $f(x)$. Thus $C(f, g)$ is a measure of miscalibration. Further discussion of decomposition can be found in Lichtenstein, Fischhoff, and Phillips (1982), Murphy (1972, 1973). Haim (1982) provides a theorem that shows how a strictly proper scoring rule can be generated from a convex function. See also Savage (1971).

Heuristics and Biases in Forming Probability Judgments

The process of expressing one's knowledge in terms of probabilities is not simple and has shown to be subject to some repeatable types of errors. Cognitive psychologists have detected, classified, and analyzed these errors in experimental settings. This work dates back to the 1970s and was led by Kahneman and Tversky (Bar-Hillel, 2001). Kahneman, Slovic and Tversky (1982) provide a compilation of research in this area up to 1982, while Gilovich, Griffin and Kahneman (2002) contains contributions from the next two decades.

Judgmental errors are thought to be related to the way information is processed, that is, the heuristics used in forming the judgments. Two predominant heuristics have been labeled the representiveness heuristic and the availability heuristic.

Representativeness is the process of using some relevant cues to associate a target event or quantity with a similar set of targets. Bar-Hillel (2001) notes, however, that similarity judgments obey different rules than probability judgments. For example, subjects given a description of what could possibly be a location in Switzerland respond with a higher probability that the location is in Switzerland than the probability that the location is in Europe (Bar-Hillel and Neter 1993). Such a judgment is irrational as one event is entirely included within another (being in Switzerland implies being in Europe.)

Another manifestation of the representiveness heuristic is termed the base rate bias. This is illustrated by the following situation taken from a CIA publication. During the Vietnam War, a U.S. fighter pilot is strafed by a fighter plane that is either Cambodian or North Vietnamese. The pilot can correctly identify a plane's nationality with 80 percent accuracy, meaning that a Cambodian will be correctly identified as Cambodian with a probability of 0.8 and a North Vietnamese aircraft would be correctly identified with a similar 0.8 probability. There are six times as many Vietnamese aircraft in the fray as Cambodian aircraft. The pilot identifies the plane as Cambodian. What probability should be assigned to the strafing aircraft's being Cambodian? The representiveness heuristic might lead one to assign a probability of 0.8, as this is "representative" of the pilot's accuracy. But this assessment fails to take into account the base rate or background frequency of the two nations' aircraft. A correct assessment would be based on Bayes' theorem and would result in a probability of the strafing aircraft's being Cambodian of 4/9.

Other effects related to the representativeness heuristic include failure to regress, failure to consider sample size, and incorrect interpretations of randomness. Failure to regress occurs when one fails to consider that values greater or lesser than the mean will tend to return to the mean as a process continues. A baseball player who hits 0.400 for the first twenty games of the season will likely end the season with a lesser batting average. Using the current batting average as a best estimate of the future average would entail this failure. Problems with sample size occur because people do not correctly adjust for the reliability of data. People will often make judgments about the accuracy of a sample by examining the proportion of a population included in the sample, rather than examining the variability within the population and the absolute size of the sample, which are proved to be the determinants of the error in an estimate. Finally, people tend to find fictitious structure in random events. For example, when asked which is more likely to occur in the flip of five coins, many will answer that TTHTH is more likely than HHHHH although both have the same probability. People often conclude that someone is on a hot streak that is likely to continue when they have made several free throws or won in craps.

A second major class of biases arises from the availability heuristic. Availability refers to the ability to access or recall information. Cues that are easier to recall tend to be given more weight in forming probability judgments. An experiment that illustrates this effect entails showing a subject a list of names of celebrities. Manipulating the list so that the members of one sex are somewhat more famous than the members of the opposite sex will result in the subject's overestimating the relative frequency of names on the list belonging to the sex having the more famous members (Tversky and Kahneman 1973). Another manifestation of availability occurs when subjects are asked to estimate the relative frequency of various causes of death in the United States. Subjects tend to overestimate the frequency of sensational causes and underestimate the frequency of mundane causes. For instance, the likelihood of death from a stroke will be underestimated while the likelihood of death from firearms will be overestimated. Information about death from firearms is more widely publicized – every such death will receive media attention while death from stroke is likely to be reported only in the case of well known individuals. Thus, the mind finds it easier to recall instances of death from firearms or, just as importantly, overestimates the frequency by overestimating the number of such instances that could be brought to mind if one really tried (Fischoff & MacGregor 1982.).

A form of availability termed *anchoring* that is particularly salient to probability elicitation occurs when a subject gives too much credit to a reference point so that other possible references or the fallibility of the selected reference is ignored (Tversky & Kahneman 1974). For example, two experts who are equally qualified and have conducted studies to determine a particular quantity are likely to give more credit to their own work and less credit than is warranted to their colleague's work. Anchoring can also occur when there is sparse evidence. The expert may rely too heavily on evidence that is available and ignore how new evidence could change our judgments. Consider a situation where there are two known sources of information, each leading to a somewhat different estimate of quantity, and there is a third source of information not known to the expert at this time. Let the three pieces of evidence be represented by dots on a line as shown in Figure 8.6.

Suppose that one of the dots is initially invisible. If the invisible dot is chosen randomly from the three dots, it is twice as likely that the invisible dot is outside

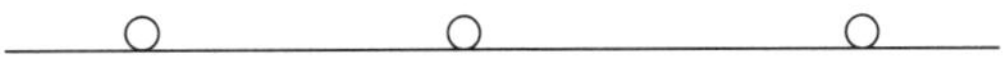

Figure 8.6. Illustration of the anchoring bias.

the range of the visible dots. Thus, the appearance of the third piece of information is twice as likely to spread the range of possibilities as to confirm the range if one "anchors" the range using the observable values. The paradox is that in judgment formation, information may result an increased expression of uncertainty so that the more we know, the less we say we know.

Anchoring can also occur as the result of a scale or instrument that suggests values for a variable. Subjects are uncomfortable going outside of the set of suggested values. Moreover, the subject is drawn to the center of the scale as a representative or central value. Hora, Hora and Dodd (1992) and Winman, Hannson and Juslin (2004) have shown that asking for probabilities of fixed intervals rather than asking for intervals with fixed probabilities can result in a loss of calibration.

Another scale effect can occur when there are discrete, mutually exclusive outcomes and one of the outcomes is a catchall, everything else category. For example, in a hospital study, a description of an admittee's symptoms was given along with a list of possible diagnoses. Two lists were used, one list with four named diagnoses and a catchall category to include all unnamed diagnoses. The second list had three possibilities, two of the four named diagnoses in the first list and a catchall category that implicitly contained the missing two diagnoses included on the first list. The result is that subjects given the second list gave a lower probability for the catchall category than the sum of the probabilities given to the two missing diagnoses and the catchall category on the first list. These probabilities should be equivalent. The availability of the additional diagnoses has been attributed as the reason for this incongruity. This has been termed the packing effect. One of the first studies in this area involved an experiment using automobile fault trees (Fischhoff, Slovic, & Lichtenstein 1978). In this study some potential causes of automobile failure were omitted from a diagram rather than being relegated to a catchall category. The subjects were asked to estimate the total probability of the missing causes and consistently underestimated this probability. In this study, the bias was termed the pruning effect. Fox and Clemen (2005) provide an alternative explanation of this bias.

The psychological bias that has received the greatest attention in probability elicitation is the tendency to assign probabilities that are too close to zero or one or to give uncertainty distributions that are too narrow. This bias is termed overconfidence or apparent overconfidence as the effect is to provide answers that are more certain than is warranted. Much of the research in this area has employed probabilities for binary events based on almanac data or sensory experiments. For example, a subject might be asked to name the higher mountain, Mt. Fuji or the Matterhorn, and then assign a probability to the subject's answer being correct (Lichtenstein and Fischhoff 1977). Keren (1988) conducts a similar experiment but asks the subjects to identify letters while manipulating the difficulty of the task. Although subjects tend to assign probabilities that are too high, the effect is much more pronounced when the questions are, in some sense, difficult rather than easy.

There have been many studies that have examined elicited distributions for continuous quantities. Lichtenstein, Fischhoff and Phillips (1982) provide a table of the findings of such studies by concentrating on the faithfulness of the tail probabilities. In each of the studies, some extreme fractiles, such as the 0.01 and 0.99 fractiles were assessed and in most of the studies the interquartile range was assessed. The studies employed almanac data with known answers or values that would be known shortly, such as football scores (Winkler 1971). Almost uniformly, each study reported that the number of times the target values occurred in these extreme tails was greater than would be indicated by the probabilities – usually much greater. For example, in a study of stock price prediction by graduate business students, Stael von Holstein (1972) reports that 30 percent of the responses fell above the 0.99 fractile or below the 0.01 fractile while 27 percent fell in the interquartile range rather than the desired 50 percent. Klayman, et al. (1999) find that overconfidence is more pronounced in assessment of continuous quantities (interval assessments) than the assessment of simple questions such as two choice questions.

Overconfidence can be very troubling where a correct expression of risk is needed. In such circumstances it is wise to educate the expert about this bias and give some training and feedback of the expert's performance. While not every individual will exhibit this bias, it appears to exist in every group of subjects, whether they be experts or students. There is ample evidence (Alpert and Raiffa 1982) to show that probability exercises and feedback will reduce this bias, although it will not entirely eliminate it.

Overconfidence is associated with the hard-easy effect wherein subjects responding to more difficult questions exhibit more overconfidence than those responding to easy questions (Lichtenstein and Fischhoff 1977). Apparent overconfidence observed in almanac tests has been explained as a manifestation of the hard-easy effect by Juslin (1994). See also Gigerenzer (1991) and Gigerenzer, Hoffrage and Kleinbolting (1991). This area is, to date, controversial and is reviewed in Brenner, Koehler and Liberman (1996).

Another active area of research is support theory which was introduced by Tversky and Koehler (1994) to explain why elicited probabilities depend on the manner of presentation of the issue and apparently do not conform to the normative principle of additivity of probabilities across mutually exclusive events. The theory envisions probability judgment formation as consisting of three sets of elements: mutually exclusive hypotheses, evidence that supports the hypotheses, and expressed probabilities. The hypotheses are descriptions of events rather than the events themselves. The evidence or support is the perceived strength of the evidence for particular hypothesis. The judged probability is the weight in favor of a particular hypothesis relative to the weights of all hypotheses.

The weight of evidence, or support for a hypothesis A is given by $s(A)$. The real content of support theory is in the assumption that support is subadditive. Mathematically, if A_1 and A_2 are a partition of A, that is $A = A_1 \cup A_2$ and $A_1 \cap A_2$

is empty, then support theory requires that $s(A) \leq s(A_1) + S(A_2)$. If the inequality holds strictly, then one will find the judged probability of an event to be less than the sum of the probabilities of the constituents elements of the partition of that event. Of course, this is relevant to probability elicitation as the way the question is posed may influence the response given.

To make things more concrete, let A be homicide, A_1 be homicide by an acquaintance, and A_2 be homicide by a stranger. Subadditivity operates if $s(A) \leq s(A_1) + S(A_2)$ and this has been shown to be the case in numerous studies (Tversky & Koehler 1994, Fox & Tversky 1998). A more subtle form of the sub-additivity is found when the question is posed with the elements of the partition stated but an assessment made of the union of the elements of the partition. For example, asking for the probability of a homicide by an acquaintance or a stranger vis-à-vis the probability of a homicide. While the events are equivalent, the implicit "unpacking" of the hypothesis "homicide" into the constituents "homicide by an acquaintance" and "homicide by a stranger" may lead to a higher probability for the first questions than the second question. The impact of suggesting additional factors and observing an increase in the given probability is termed implicit sub-additivity (Sloman, et al. 2004). These authors find that the evidence for implicit subadditivity is mixed and they demonstrate reversals of the effect when using a partition of atypical conditions.

Eliciting Probabilities

Subjective judgments permeate complex decisions (Bonano, et al. 1989). One has the choice of using these judgments in a loose unstructured manner or insisting on a more formal, more rigorous, and better documented approach. It is particularly important to employ more formal methods when the decision or risk analysis will be subjected to review. In dealing with public risk issues such as policies about the collection and distribution of medical blood supplies, there will be external reviews and perhaps challenges in the courts. Using a more structured, more formal approach will help satisfy reviewers of the study's accuracy and meaningfulness. In this section, a series of steps are given that should be considered when putting together a study using expert judgments.

Selecting and Posing Questions

Not all uncertainties are of equal consequence in making a decision. There will normally be a few major questions that drive the uncertainty about the optimal choice of actions. These questions are candidates for a more structured probability assessment activity. Other issues – those that play a minor role – can often be treated less formally or through sensitivity analysis, saving the resources for the more important issues. A sensitivity analysis using initial estimates of probabilities and probability distributions is often performed after the decision has been structured. The sensitivity analysis identifies those questions deserving of a more penetrating study.

But not all issues lend themselves to quantification through expert judgment. In addition to being important contributors to uncertainty and risk, an issue should:

- Be resolvable in that, given sufficient time and/or resources, one could conceivably learn whether the event has occurred or the value of the quantity in question
- Have a basis upon which judgments can be made and can be justified

The requirement of resolvability means that the event or quantity is knowable and physically measurable. We consider a counter example. In a study of risk from down wind radioactivity following a power plant failure, a simple Gaussian dispersion model of the form $y = ax^b$ was employed (Harper, et al. 1994). In this model, a and b are simply parameters that give good fit to the relation between x, downwind distance, and y, the horizontal width of the plume. But not all experts subscribe to this model. More complex alternatives have been proposed with different types of parameters. Asking an expert to provide judgments about a and b violates the first principle above. One cannot verify if the judgments are correct, experts may disagree on the definition of a and b, and experts who do not embrace the simple model will find the parameters not meaningful. It is very difficult to provide a value for something you don't believe exists.

The second requirement is that there be some knowledge that can be brought to bear on the event or quantity. For many issues, there is no directly applicable data so that data from analogues, models using social, medical or physical principles, etc., may form the basis for the judgments. If the basis for judgments is incomplete or sketchy, the experts should reflect this by expressing greater uncertainty in their judgments.

Once issues have been identified, it is necessary to develop a statement that presents the issue to the experts in a manner that will not color the experts' responses. This is called framing the issue. Part of framing is creating an unbiased presentation that is free of preconceived notions, political overtones, and discussions of consequences that might affect the response. Framing also provides a background for the question. Sometimes there are choices about stating conditions for the issues or ignoring the conditions and asking the experts to integrate the uncertainty about the conditions into their responses. In a study of dry deposition of radioactivity, the experts were told that the deposition surface was northern European grassland but they were not told the length of the grass, which is thought to be an important determinant of the rate of deposition (Harper, et al. 1994). Instead, the experts were asked to treat the length of grass as an unknown and to incorporate any uncertainty that they might have into their responses. The experts should be informed about those factors that are considered to be known, those that are constrained in value, those that are uncertain, and, perhaps, those that should be excluded from their answers.

Finally, once an issue has been framed and put in the form of statement to be submitted to the experts, it should be tested. The best way to do this testing is through a dry run with stand-in experts who have not been participants in the framing process. Although this seems like a lot of extra work, experience has shown (Hora and Jensen, 2002) that getting the issue right is both critical and difficult. All too often, the question that the expert is responding to differs from what was intended by the proposer. It is also possible that the question being asked appears to be resolvable to the person who framed the question but not to the expert who must respond.

Selecting Experts

The identification of experts requires that one develop some criteria by which expertise can be measured. Generally, an expert is one who "has or is alleged to have superior knowledge about data, models and rules in a specific area or field" (Bonano, et al. 1990). But measuring against this definition requires one to look at indicators of knowledge rather than knowledge per se. The following list contains such indicators:

- Research in the area as identified by publications and grants
- Citations of work
- Degrees, awards, or other types of recognition
- Recommendations and nominations from respected bodies and persons
- Positions held
- Membership or appointment to review boards, commissions, etc.

In addition to the above indicators, experts may need to meet some additional requirements. The expert should be free from motivational biases caused by the economic, political, or other interest in the decision. Experts should be willing to participate and they should be accountable for their judgments (Cooke 1991). This means that they should be willing to have their names associated with their specific responses. Many times, physical proximity or availability at certain times, will be an important consideration.

How the experts are to be organized also has an impact on the selection. Often, when more than one expert is used, the experts will be redundant of one another meaning that they will perform the same tasks. In such a case, one should attempt to select experts with differing backgrounds, responsibilities, fields of study, etc., so as to gain a better appreciation of the differences among beliefs. In other instances, the experts will be complementary, each bringing unique expertise to the question. Here, they act more like a team and should be selected to cover the disciplines needed.

Some analyses undergo extreme scrutiny because of the public risks involved. This is certainly the case with radioactive waste disposal. In such instances, the process for selecting (and excluding) experts should be transparent and well documented. In addition to written criteria, it may be necessary to isolate the project staff from the selection process. This can be accomplished by appointing an independent selection committee to seek nominations and make recommendations to the staff (Trauth, Hora, Guzowski 1994).

How many experts should be selected? Experience has shown that the differences among experts can be very important in determining the total uncertainty about a question. Clemen and Winkler (1985) examine the impact of dependence among experts using a normal model and conclude that three to five experts are adequate. Hora (2004) created synthetic groups from the responses of real experts and found that three to six or seven experts are sufficient with little benefit from additional experts beyond that point. When experts are organized in groups and each group provides a single response, then this advice would apply to the number of groups. The optimal number of experts within a group has not been addressed and is certainly dependent on the complexity of issues being answered.

Training

Most experts, even well-trained scientists, will not have a great deal of experience with probability elicitation. It is a very good idea to provide some initial training before asking for their judgments. There are different forms that this training can take but usually it will include some or all of the following items:

- Practice with forming probability judgments and feedback on results
- A discussion of personal/subjective probability and its role in the analysis
- Background information about the elicitation questions
- Discussion of biases in judgment formation

Practice is usually accomplished through the use of a training quiz composed of almanac questions.

Organizing an Expert Judgment Process

In addition to defining issues and selecting and training the expert(s), there are a number of questions that must be addressed concerning the format for a probability elicitation. These include:

- The amount of interaction and exchange of information among experts
- The type and amount of preliminary information to be provided to the experts
- The time and resources that will be allocated to preparation of responses
- Venue – the expert's place of work, the project's home, or elsewhere
- Will there be training, what kind, and how will it be accomplished?
- Are the names of the experts to be associated with their judgments and will individual judgments be preserved and made available?

These choices result in the creation of a design for elicitation that has been termed a protocol. Some protocols are discussed in Morgan and Henrion (1990), Merkhofer (1987), Keeney and von Winterfeldt (1991), and in Cooke (1991). I will briefly outline two different protocols that illustrate the range of options that have been employed in expert elicitation studies.

Morgan and Henrion (1990) identify the Stanford Research Institute (SRI) assessment protocol as, historically, the most influential in shaping structured probability elicitation. This protocol is summarized in Spetzler and Stael von Holstein (1975). It is designed around a single expert (subject) and a single analyst engaged in a five-stage process. The stages are:

- ▦ Motivating – Rapport with the subject is established and possible motivational biases explored
- ▦ Structuring – The structure of the uncertainty is defined
- ▦ Conditioning – The subject is conditioned to think fundamentally about his judgment and to avoid cognitive biases
- ▦ Encoding – This is the actual quantification in probabilistic terms
- ▦ Verifying – The responses obtained in the encoding are checked for consistency

The role of the analyst in the SRI protocol is primarily to help the expert avoid psychological biases. The encoding of probabilities roughly follows a script. Stael von Holstein and Matheson (1979) provide an example of how an elicitation session might go forward.

A distinguishing feature of the SRI protocol is the use of the probability wheel described earlier. The encoding stage for continuous variables is described in some detail in Spetzler and Stael von Holstein (1975). It begins with assessment of the extreme values of the values of the variable. An interesting sidelight is that after assessing these values, the subject is asked to describe scenarios that might result in values of the variable outside of the interval and to provide a probability of being outside the interval. The process next goes to a set of intermediate values whose cumulative probabilities are assessed with the help of the probability wheel. Then an interval technique is used to obtain the median and quartiles. Finally, the judgments are verified by testing for coherence and conformance with the expert's beliefs.

While the SRI protocol was designed for solitary experts, a protocol developed by Sandia Laboratories for the U.S. Nuclear Regulatory Commission (Hora and Iman, 1989, Ortiz et al. 1991) was designed to bring multiple experts together. The Sandia protocol consists of two meetings.

- ▦ First meeting
  - Presentation of the issues and background materials
  - Discussion by the experts of the issues and feedback on the questions
  - A training session including feedback on judgments

The first meeting is followed by a period of individual study of approximately one month.

- ▦ Second meeting
  - Discussion by the experts of the methods, models, and data sources used
  - Individual elicitation of the experts

The second meeting is followed by documentation of rationales and opportunity for feedback from the experts. The final individual judgments are then combined using simple averaging to obtain the final probabilities or distribution functions.

There are a number of significant differences between the SRI and Sandia protocols. First, the SRI protocol is designed for isolated experts while the Sandia protocol brings multiple experts together and allows them to exchange information and viewpoints. They are not allowed, however, to view or participate in the individual encoding sessions nor comment on one another's judgments. Second, in the SRI protocol, it is assumed that the expert is fully prepared in that no additional study, data acquisition, or investigation is needed. Moreover, the SRI protocol places the analyst in the role of identifying biases and assisting the expert in counteracting these biases while the Sandia protocol employs a structured training session to help deal with these issues. In both protocols, the encoding is essentially the same although the probability wheel is today seldom employed by analysts. Third, the Sandia protocol places emphasis on obtaining and documenting multiple viewpoints, which is consistent with the public policy issues addressed in those studies to which it has been applied.

REFERENCES

Alpert, M. & Raiffa, H. (1982). A progress report on the training of probability assessors in judgment under uncertainty: Heuristics and biases. In D. Kahneman, P. Slovic, and A. Tversky, (Eds.) *Judgment under uncertainty: Heuristics and biases*, Cambridge, UK: Cambridge University Press.

Bar-Hillel, M. (2001). Subjective probability judgments, in Smelser, N. J. & Baltes, D. B. (Eds.) *International Encyclopedia of the Social & Behavioral Sciences*, Amsterdam: Elsevier Science Ltd. 15248–15251.

Bar-Hillel, M. & Neter, E. (1993). How alike is it versus how likely is it: A disjunction fallacy in stereotype judgments. *Journal of Personality and Social Psychology 65*, 1119–1132.

Bonano, E. J., Hora S. C., Keeney, R. L., and von Winterfeldt, D. (1990). Elicitation and Use of Expert Judgment in Performance Assessment for High-Level Radioactive Waste Repositories. NUREG/CR-5411. Washington, DC: U.S. Nuclear Regulatory Commission.

Brenner, L. A., Koehler, D. J., Liberman, V. (1996). Overconfidence in probability and frequency judgments: A critical examination. *Organizational Behavior and Human Decision Processes, 65*, 212–219.

Christensen-Szalanski, J. & Bushyhead, J. (1981). Physicians' Use of Probabilistic Information in a Real Clinical Setting. *Journal of Experimental Psychology: Human Perception and Performance, 7*, 928–935.

Clemen, R. T., Fischer, G. W., & Winkler, R. L. (2000). Assessing dependence: Some experimental results. *Management Science, 46*, 1100–1115.

Clemen, R. T. & Winkler, R. L. (1985). limits for the precision and value of information from dependent sources. *Operations Research, 33*, 427–442.

Clemen, R. T. & Reilly, T. (1999). Correlations and copulas for decision and risk analysis. *Management Science, 45*, 208–224.

Cooke, R. M. (1991). *Experts in Uncertainty*, Oxford: Oxford University Press.

Cover, T. M. & J. A. Thomas (1991). *Elements of information theory*. New York: Wiley-Interscience.

de Finetti, B. (1974). *Theory of Probability*, Vol. 1. New York: John Wiley and Sons.

de Finetti, B. (1977). Probabilities of probabilities: a real problem or a misunderstanding? in A. Aykac and C. Brumat, (Eds.) *New Developments in the Application of Bayesian Methods*, Amsterdam: North Holland Publishing Company.

Druzdel, M. J. (1989). Verbal Uncertainty Expressions: Literature Review, Technical Report CMU-EPP-1990–02–02. Pittsburgh: Department of Engineering, Carnegie Mellon University.

Fischoff, B. & MacGregor, D. (1982). Subjective Confidence in Forecasts. *Journal of Forecasting, 1*, 155–72.

Fischhoff, B., Slovic, P., & Lichtenstein, S. (1978). Fault trees: Sensibility of estimated failure probabilities to problem representation. *Journal of Experimental Psychology: Human Perception and Performance, 4*, 330–344.

Fox, C. R. & Clemen, R. T. (2005). Subjective probability assessment in decision analysis: Partition dependence and bias toward the ignorance prior. *Management Science, 51*, 1417–1432.

Fox, C. R. & Tversky, A. (1998). A belief-based account of decision under uncertainty, *Management Science, 44*, 879–95.

Gigerenzer, G. (1991). How to make cognitive illusions to disappear: Beyond heuristics and biases. In W. Stroebe & M. Hewstone (Ed.), *European Review of Social Psychology, vol. 2*. Chichester: Wiley.

Gigerenzer, G., Hoffrage, U., & Kleinbolting, H. (1991). Probabilistic mental models: A Brunswikian theory of confidence. *Psychological Review, 98*, 506–528.

Gilovich, T., Griffin, D., and Kahneman, D. (Eds.). (2002). *Heuristics and biases: The psychology of intuitive judgment.* Cambridge, UK: Cambridge University Press.

Haim, E. (1982). *Characterization and Construction of Proper Scoring Rules*. Unpublished doctoral dissertation, University of California, Berkeley.

Harper, F. T., Hora, S. C., Young, M. L. Miller, L. A. Lui, C. H. McKay, M. D. Helton J. C., Goossens, L. H. J. Cooke, R. M. Pasler-Sauer, J. Kraan, B. & Jones, J. A. (1994). *Probability Accident Consequence Uncertainty Analysis, Vols. 1–3, (NUREG/CR-6244, EUR 15855 EN)* Brussels: USNRC and CEC DG XII.

Helton, J. C. & Burmaster, D. E., Eds. (1996). Special issue on treatment of aleatory and epistemic uncertainty. *Reliability Engineering & System Safety, 54*, 2–3.

Hora, S. C. (2004). Probability Judgments for Continuous Quantities: Linear Combinations and Calibration. *Management Science, 50*, 597–604.

Hora, S., Dodd, N. G., & Hora, J. (1993). The Use of Decomposition in Probability Assessments of Continuous Variables. *The Journal of Behavioral Decision Making, 6*, 133–147.

Hora, S. C., Hora, J. A., & Dodd, N. G. (1992). Assessment of Probability Distributions for Continuous Random Variables: A Comparison of the Bisection and Fixed Value Methods. *Organizational Behavior and Human Decision Processes, 51*, 133–155.

Hora, S. C. & Iman, R. L. (1989). Expert Opinion in Risk Analysis: The NUREG-1150 Experience. *Nuclear Science and Engineering, 102*, 323–331.

Hora, S. C. & Jensen, M. (2002). *Expert Judgement Elicitation*, Stockholm:. Swedish Radiation Protection Authority.

Juslin, P. (1994). The overconfidence phenomenon as a consequence of informal experimenter guided selection of almanac items. *Organizational Behavior and Human Decision Processes, 57*, 226–246.

Kahneman, D., Slovic, P., & Tversky, A. (Eds.) (1982). *Judgment under uncertainty: Heuristics and biases*. Cambridge, UK: Cambridge University Press.

Keeney, R., & von Winterfeldt, D. (1991). Eliciting probabilities from experts in complex technical problems. *IEEE Transactions on Engineering Management, 38*, 191–201.

Kent, S. (1964). Words of Estimated Probability, in D. P. Steury, ed., *Sherman Kent and the Board of National Estimates: Collected Essays*. Washington, DC: Center for the Study of Intelligence, 1994.

Keren, G. (1988). On the ability of monitoring nonvertical perceptions and uncertainty knowledge: some calibration studies. *Acta Psychologica, 67*, 95–119.

Klayman, J., Soll, J. B., Gonzalez-Vallejo, C., Barlas, S. (1999). Overconfidence: It depends on how, whom you ask. *Organizational Behavior and Human Decision Processes, 79*, 216–2247.

Knight, F. H. (1921). *Risk, Uncertainty, and Profit*. Boston: Houghton Mifflin Company.

Lichtenstein, S., & Fischhoff, B. (1977). Do those who know more also know more about how much they know? *Organizational Behavior and Human Performance, 20*, 159–183.

Lichtenstein, S., Fischhoff, B., & Phillips, L. D. (1982). Calibration of probabilities: The state of the art to 1980, in D. Kahneman, P. Slovic, and A. Tversky, (Eds.) *Judgment under uncertainty: Heuristics and biases*, Cambridge, UK: Cambridge University Press.

Matheson, J. E. & Winkler, R. L. (1976). Scoring Rules for Continuous Probability Distributions, *Management Science, 22*, 1087–1096.

Merkhofer, M. W. (1987). Quantifying judgmental uncertainty: Methodology, experiences, and insights. *IEEE Transactions on Systems, Man, and Cybernetics, 17*, 741–752.

Morgan, M. G., Henrion, M. (1992). *Uncertainty: A guide to dealing with uncertainty in quantitative risk and policy analysis*, New York: Cambridge University Press.

Murphy, A. H. (1973). A New Vector Partition of the Probability Score. *Journal of Applied Meteorology, 12* 595–6.

Murphy, A. H. & Winkler, R. L. (1977). Reliability of Subjective Probability Forecasts of Precipitation and Temperature. *Applied Statistics, 26*, 41–47.

Murphy, A. H. (1972). Scalar and Vector Partitions of the Probability Score (Part I) Two-state situation. *Journal of Applied Meteorology, 11*, 273–82.

Ortiz, N. R., Wheeler, T. A., Breeding, R. J., Hora, S., Meyer, M. A., & Keeney, R. L. (1991). The Use of Expert Judgment in the NUREG-1150. *Nuclear Engineering and Design, 126*, 313–331.

Raiffa, H. & Schlaifer, R. (1961). *Applied Statistical Decision Theory*, Cambridge: MIT Press.

Ravinder, H. V., Kleinmuntz, D. N., & Dyer, J. S. (1988). The reliability of subjective probability assessments obtained through decomposition. *Management Science, 34*, 186–199.

Savage, L. J. (1954). *The Foundations of Statistics*. New York: John Wiley and Sons (second edition, 1972, New York: Dover).

Savage, L. J. (1971). The elicitation of personal probabilities and expectations. *Journal of the American Statistical Association, 66*, 783–801.

Skyrms, B. (1980). "Higher order degrees of belief." In "*Prospects for Pragmatism: Essays in Honor of F. P. Ramsey*," D. H. Mellor (Ed.), Cambridge University Press, Cambridge, pp. 109–137.

Sloman, S., Rottenstreich, Y., Wisniewski, E., Hadjichristidis, C., & Fox, C. R. (2004). Typical versus atypical unpacking and superadditive judgment. *Journal of Experimental Psychology, 30*, 573–582.

Spetzler, C. S. & Stael von Holstein, C. A. S. (1975). Probability Encoding in Decision Analysis. *Management Science, 22*, 340–358.

Stael von Holstein, C.A.S. & Matheson, J. E. (1979). *A manual for encoding probability distributions*. Menlo Park, CA: SRI International.

Stael von Holstein, C.A.S. (1972). Probabilistic forecasting: An experiment related to the stock market. *Organizational Behavior and Human Performance, 8*, 139–158.

Trauth, K. M., Hora S. C. & Guzowski, R. V. (1994). *A formal expert judgment procedure for performance assessments of the waste isolation pilot plant, SAND93–2450*. Albuquerque: Sandia National Laboratories.

Tversky, A. & Kahneman D. (1973). Availability a Heuristic for Judging Probability, *Cognitive Psychology 5*, 207–232. and in an abbreviated form in D. Kahneman, P. Slovic, and A. Tversky, (Eds.) *Judgment under uncertainty: Heuristics and biases.* Cambridge: Cambridge University Press.

Tversky, A. & Kahneman D. (1974). Judgment under uncertainty: Heuristics and biases. *Science 185*, 1124–1131 and in D. Kahneman, P. Slovic, and A. Tversky, (Eds.) *Judgment under uncertainty: Heuristics and biases.* Cambridge: Cambridge University Press.

Tversky, A. & Koehler, D. J. (1994). Support theory: A nonextensional representation of subjective probability. *Psychological Review, 101*, 547–567.

U. S. Nuclear Regulatory Commission (1975). *Reactor safety study: WASH-1400, NUREG-751014.* Washington: U. S. Nuclear Regulatory Commission.

Winkler, R. L. (1971). Probabilistic prediction: Some experimental results. *Journal of the American Statistical Association, 66*, 675–685.

Winkler, R. L. (1996). Scoring rules and the evaluation of probabilities. *Test, 5*, 1–60.

Winman, A., Hansson, P., & Juslin, P. (2004). Subjective probability intervals: How to cure overconfidence by interval evaluation. *Journal of Experimental Psychology: Learning Memory and Cognition, 30*, 1167–1175.

9 Aggregating Probability Distributions

Robert T. Clemen and Robert L. Winkler[*]

ABSTRACT. This chapter is concerned with the aggregation of probability distributions in decision and risk analysis. Experts often provide valuable information regarding important uncertainties in decision and risk analyses because of the limited availability of hard data to use in those analyses. Multiple experts are often consulted in order to obtain as much information as possible, leading to the problem of how to combine or aggregate their information. Information may also be obtained from other sources such as forecasting techniques or scientific models. Because uncertainties are typically represented in terms of probability distributions, we consider expert and other information in terms of probability distributions. We discuss a variety of models that lead to specific combination methods. The output of these methods is a *combined probability distribution*, which can be viewed as representing a summary of the current state of information regarding the uncertainty of interest. After presenting the models and methods, we discuss empirical evidence on the performance of the methods. In the conclusion, we highlight important conceptual and practical issues to be considered when designing a combination process for use in practice.

Introduction

Expert judgments can provide useful information for forecasting, making decisions, and assessing risks. Such judgments have been used informally for many years. In recent years, the use of formal methods to combine expert judgments has become increasingly commonplace. Cooke (1991) reviews many of the developments over the years as attempts have been made to use expert judgments in various settings. Application areas have been diverse, including nuclear engineering, aerospace, various types of forecasting (economic, technological, meteorological, and snow avalanches, to name a few), military intelligence, seismic risk, and environmental risk from toxic chemicals.

In this paper, we consider the problem of using information from multiple sources. Frequently these sources are experts, but sources such as forecasting methods or scientific models can also be used. We will couch much of the discussion in this chapter in terms of experts, but the applicability of the aggregation procedures extends to other sources of information.

---

[*] Portions of this chapter are based on Clemen, R. T., and Winkler, R. L. (1999). Combining probability distributions from experts in risk analysis. *Risk Analysis, 19,* 187–203.

Wu, Apostolakis, and Okrent (1990, p. 170) state that "an important issue related to knowledge representation under uncertainty is the resolution of conflicting information or opinions." Although we discuss information of various kinds, including forecasts, estimates, and probability assessments, our primary focus is on the aggregation of probability distributions. The paper does not pretend to give a comprehensive view of the topic of group judgments; the accumulated knowledge in this field springs from many disciplines, including statistics, psychology, economics, engineering, risk analysis, decision theory, and psychology. Our intent is to highlight the key issues involved in combining probability distributions and to discuss a variety of combining methods.

Because the focus in this paper is on the *combination* of experts' probability distributions, we do not discuss the process by which such probability distributions might be elicited from individual experts. For general discussions oriented toward decision and risk analysis, see Garthwaite, Kadane, and O'Hagan (2005), Hora (1992 and Chapter 8, this volume), Keeney and von Winterfeldt (1989, 1991), Merkhofer (1987), Mosleh, Bier, and Apostolakis (1987), Morgan and Henrion (1990), Otway and von Winterfeldt (1992), and Spetzler and Staël von Holstein (1975). We believe that the elicitation process should be designed and conducted by a decision analysis team composed of individuals knowledgeable about both the substantive issues of interest and individuals knowledgeable about probability elicitation. Moreover, we begin with the assumptions that the experts and the decision analysis team have ironed out differences in definitions, all agree on exactly what is to be forecast or assessed, and as much as possible has been done to eliminate individual cognitive and motivational biases. In this case, of course, it is still possible for reasonable individuals to disagree for a multitude of reasons, ranging from different analytical methods to differing information sets or different philosophical approaches. Indeed, if they never disagreed there would be no point in consulting more than one expert. Morgan and Keith (1995) note that the results of expert elicitations related to climate change "reveal a rich diversity of expert opinion." Consulting multiple experts may be viewed as a subjective version of increasing the sample size in an experiment. Because subjective information is often viewed as being "softer" than "hard scientific data," it seems particularly appropriate to consult multiple experts in an attempt to beef up the information base.

These motivations are reasonable; the fundamental principle that underlies the use of multiple experts is that a set of experts or other information sources can provide more information than a single expert. Although it is sometimes reasonable to provide a decision maker with only the individual experts' probability distributions, the range of which can be studied using sensitivity analysis, it is often necessary to combine the distributions into a single one. In many cases, for example, a single distribution is needed for input into a larger model. Even if this is not the case, it can be illuminating and valuable to generate a combined distribution as a summary of the available information.

Combination, or aggregation, procedures are often dichotomized into *mathematical* and *behavioral* approaches, although in practice aggregation might involve some aspects of each. Mathematical aggregation methods consist of processes or analytical models that operate on the individual probability distributions to produce a single *combined probability distribution*. For example, we might simply take the averages of probabilities from multiple experts. Reviews of the literature on mathematical combination of probability distributions include Winkler (1968), French (1985), Genest and Zidek (1986), Cooke (1991), and French and Ríos Insua (2000). Bunn (1988), Clemen (1989), and Armstrong (2001a) review the broader area of combining forecasts. Mathematical aggregation methods range from simple summary measures, such as arithmetic or geometric means of probabilities, to procedures based on axiomatic approaches or on various models of the information-aggregation process that require inputs regarding characteristics of the experts' probabilities, such as bias and dependence.

In contrast, behavioral aggregation approaches attempt to generate agreement among the experts by having them interact in some way. This interaction may be face-to-face or may involve exchanges of information without direct contact. Behavioral approaches consider the quality of individual expert judgments and dependence among such judgments implicitly rather than explicitly. As information is shared, it is anticipated that better arguments and information will be more important in influencing the group and that redundant information will be discounted. Because our focus is on mathematical approaches for aggregation, we do not discuss behavioral methods in which experts interact in some structured way in order to reach consensus. For more information on behavioral approaches, see Wright and Ayton (1987), Clemen and Winkler (1999), and Armstrong (2001b).

In the next section we discuss mathematical methods for combining probability distributions. Some empirical results regarding these methods are then presented, followed by a brief example on the aggregation of seismic risk distributions. To conclude, we summarize our views on the key issues in the combination of probability distributions in decision analysis and risk analysis.

Combination Models and Methods

In this section, we present a variety of mathematical methods and approaches for combining probability distributions. First, we consider axiomatic approaches, which are based on certain desirable properties or axioms. Next, we consider Bayesian approaches, which treat the probability distributions as information and use Bayesian modeling to revise probabilities on the basis of this information.

Axiomatic Approaches

Early work on mathematical aggregation of probabilities focused on axiom-based aggregation formulas. In these studies, the strategy was to postulate certain properties that the combined distribution should follow and then derive the functional form of the combined distribution. French (1985), Genest and Zidek (1986), and French and Ríos Insua (2000) provide critical reviews of this literature; our summary draws heavily on these sources.

An appealing approach to the aggregation of probability distributions is the *linear opinion pool*, so named by Stone (1961), and dating back to Laplace (Bacharach 1979):

$$p(\theta) = \sum_{i=1}^{n} w_i \, p_i(\theta), \tag{9.1}$$

where n is the number of experts, $p_i(\theta)$ represents expert i's probability distribution for the uncertain quantity θ, the weights w_i sum to one, and $p(\theta)$ represents the combined probability distribution. For simplicity, we will use p to represent a mass function in the discrete case and a density function in the continuous case, and we will ignore minor technical issues involving the difference between the two cases in order to focus on the more important underlying conceptual and practical issues. As a result, we will often use "probabilities" as shorthand for "probabilities or densities" or "probability distributions."

The linear opinion pool is clearly a weighted linear combination of the experts' probabilities, and, as such, it is easily understood and calculated. Moreover, it satisfies a number of seemingly reasonable axioms. Of particular note, the linear opinion pool is the only combination scheme that satisfies the *marginalization property* (MP). Suppose θ is a vector of uncertain quantities, and the decision maker is interested in just one element of the vector, θ_j. According to the MP, the combined probability is the same whether one combines the marginal distributions of θ_j or combines the joint distributions of the vector θ and then calculates the marginal distribution of θ_j.

The weights in Eq. 9.1 clearly can be used to represent, in some sense, the relative quality of the different experts, or sources of information. In the simplest case, the experts are viewed as equivalent, and Eq. 9.1 becomes a simple arithmetic average. If some experts are viewed as "better" than others (in the sense of being more precise because of having better information, for example), the "better" experts might be given greater weight. In some cases, it is possible for some of the weights to be negative (Genest 1984). The determination of the weights is a subjective matter, and numerous interpretations can be given to the weights (Genest and McConway 1990).

Another typical combination approach uses multiplicative averaging and is sometimes called a *logarithmic opinion pool*. In this case, the combined probability distribution is of the form

$$p(\theta) = k \prod_{i=1}^{n} p_i(\theta)^{w_i}, \tag{9.2}$$

where k is a normalizing constant, and the weights w_i satisfy some restrictions to ensure that $p(\theta)$ is a probability distribution. Typically, the weights are restricted to sum to one. If the weights are equal (i.e., each weight is $1/n$), then the combined distribution is proportional to the geometric mean of the individual distributions. This is called a logarithmic opinion pool because the logarithm of the combined distribution can be expressed as a linear combination of the logarithms of the individual distributions.

Equation 9.2 satisfies the principle of *external Bayesianity* (EB). Suppose a decision maker has consulted the experts, has calculated $p(\theta)$, but has subsequently learned some new information relevant to θ. Two choices are available. One is to use the information first to update the individual probability distributions $p_i(\theta)$ and then to combine them. The other is to use the information to update the combined $p(\theta)$ directly. A formula satisfies EB if the result is the same in each case.

Cooke's (1991) *classical method* is a linear opinion pool that has been applied widely in risk assessment, primarily in Europe, beginning in the late 1980s. In order to determine weights, Cooke's method uses probability assessments by the experts on variables for which the analyst knows the outcome in order to calculate a measure of the extent to which the experts are calibrated. (An expert is empirically calibrated if, on examining those events for which the expert has assessed an x percent chance of occurrence, it turns out that x percent actually occur.) An expert's weight in the linear opinion pool is based largely on his or her calibration measure; if the expert's assessments are sufficiently miscalibrated, however, zero weight is assigned. See Cooke (1991) for full details and examples.

Combining rules such as Eqs. 9.1 or 9.2 may be quite reasonable, but not necessarily because of connections with properties such as MP or EB. Difficulties with the axioms are discussed by French (1985) and Genest and Zidek (1986). Lindley (1985) gives an example of the failure of both axioms in a straightforward example, with the interpretation that MP ignores important information, and EB requires that the form of the pooling function not change. In addition, French (1985) points out that *impossibility theorems* exist (along the lines of Arrow's classic work on social choice theory (1951)) whereby a combining rule cannot simultaneously satisfy a number of seemingly compelling desiderata. Combining rules can also affect characteristics of the probabilities; for example, Hora (2004) shows that combining well-calibrated probability distributions can lead to a combined distribution that is not well-calibrated, and it is also possible for a combined distribution to be better calibrated than the individual distributions. Moreover, despite the work of Genest and McConway (1990), no foundationally based method for determining the weights in Eqs. 9.1 or 9.2 is available.

Bayesian Approaches

French (1985), Lindley (1985), and Genest and Zidek (1986) all conclude that for the typical decision analysis or risk analysis situation, in which a group of experts provide information for a decision maker or a risk-assessment team, a Bayesian updating scheme is the most appropriate method. Winkler (1968) provides a Bayesian framework for thinking about the combination of information and ways to assess differential weights. Building on this framework, Morris (1974, 1977) formally establishes a clear Bayesian paradigm for aggregating information from experts. The notion is straightforward. If n experts provide information $g_1, \ldots, g_n$ to a decision maker regarding some event or quantity of interest θ, then the decision maker should use Bayes' theorem to update a prior distribution $p(\theta)$:

$$p^* = p(\theta|g_1, \ldots, g_n) \propto p(\theta)L(g_1, \ldots, g_n|\theta), \tag{9.3}$$

where L represents the likelihood function associated with the experts' information. This general principle can be applied to the aggregation of any kind of information, ranging from the combination of point forecasts or estimates to the combination of individual probabilities and probability distributions. Resting on the solid ground of probability theory, including requirements of coherence as explicated by de Finetti (1937) and Savage (1954), Morris' Bayesian paradigm provides a compelling framework for constructing aggregation models. In the past two decades, attention has shifted from the axiomatic approach to the development of Bayesian combination models.

At the same time that it is compelling, the Bayesian approach is also frustratingly difficult to apply. The problem is the assessment of the likelihood function $L(g_1, \ldots, g_n \mid \theta)$. This function amounts to a probabilistic model for the information $g_1, \ldots, g_n$, and, as such, it must capture the interrelationships among θ and $g_1, \ldots, g_n$. In particular, it must account for the precision and bias of the individual g_is, and it must also be able to model dependence among the g_is. For example, in the case of a point forecast, the precision of g_i is the accuracy with which expert i forecasts θ, and bias is the extent to which the forecast tends to fall consistently above or below θ. Dependence involves the extent to which the forecast errors for different experts are interrelated. For example, if expert i overestimates θ, will expert j tend to do the same?

The notions of *bias*, *precision*, and *dependence* are also crucial, but more subtle, in the case of combining probability distributions. Bias, for example, relates to the extent to which the probabilities are calibrated, as discussed above. Precision relates to the "certainty" of probabilities; a calibrated expert who more often assesses probabilities close to zero or one is more precise. In the case of assessing a probability distribution for a continuous θ, a more precise distribution is one that is both calibrated and, at the same time, has less spread (possibly measured as variance). Dependence among such distributions refers to the tendency of the experts to report similar probabilities.

Because of the difficulty of assessing an appropriate likelihood function "from scratch," considerable effort has gone into the creation of "off-the-shelf" models for aggregating single probabilities (e.g., Lindley 1985; Clemen and Winkler 1987) and probability distributions (Winkler 1981; Lindley 1983). We will review a number of these models.

Bayesian Combinations of Probabilities

Suppose that θ is an indicator variable for a specific event, and the experts provide probabilities that $\theta = 1$ (i.e., that the event will occur). How should these probabilities be combined? Clemen and Winkler (1990) review and compare a number of different Bayesian models that might be applied in this situation. Here we discuss four of these models.

Let p_i $(i = 1, \ldots, n)$ denote expert i's stated probability that θ occurs. Expressed in terms of the posterior odds of the occurrence of θ, $q^* = p^*/(1 - p^*)$, the models are Independence, Genest and Schervish, Bernoulli, and Normal.

INDEPENDENCE

$$q^* = \frac{p_0}{1-p_0} \prod_{i=1}^{n} \frac{f_{1i}(p_i | q = 1)}{f_{0i}(p_i | q = 0)}, \tag{9.4}$$

where $f_{1i}(f_{0i})$ represents the likelihood of expert i giving probability p_i conditional on the occurrence (nonoccurrence) of θ, and p_0 denotes the prior probability $p(\theta = 1)$. This model reflects the notion that each expert brings independent information to the problem. Depending on how the likelihoods are modeled, adding more experts might or might not mean more certainty (i.e., q^* closer to one or zero); e.g., see Winkler (1986). For example, if all experts say that the probability is 0.6, then under some modeling assumptions for the likelihoods p^* will tend to be much higher than 0.6, whereas under other assumptions p^* will equal the common value of 0.6.

GENEST AND SCHERVISH

$$q^* = \frac{p_0^{1-n} \prod_{i=1}^{n} p_0 + \lambda_i(p_i - \mu_i)}{(1 - p_0)^{1-n} \prod_{i=1}^{n} 1 - [p_0 + \lambda_i(p_i - \mu_i)]}, \tag{9.5}$$

where μ_i is the decision maker's marginal expected value of p_i and λ_i is interpreted as the coefficient of linear regression of θ on p_i. This model is due to Genest and Schervish (1985), and it is derived on the assumption that the decision maker (or assessment team) can assess only certain aspects of the marginal distribution of expert i's probability p_i. It is similar to the independence model, but allows for miscalibration of the p_is in a specific manner.

BERNOULLI

$$p^* = \sum_{i=1}^{n} \beta_i p_i. \tag{9.6}$$

Generally, we assume that $\sum \beta_i = 1$ to ensure that p^* is a probability. This model, which is due to Winkler (1968) and Morris (1983), arises from the notion that each expert's information can be viewed as being equivalent to a sample from a Bernoulli process with parameter θ. The resulting p^* is a convex combination of the p_is, with the coefficients interpreted as being directly proportional to the amount of information each expert has.

NORMAL

$$q^* = \frac{p_0}{1 - p_0} \exp[\mathbf{q}'\Sigma^{-1}(\mathbf{M}_1 + \mathbf{M}_0)\Sigma^{-1}(\mathbf{M}_1 - \mathbf{M}_0)/2] \quad (9.7)$$

where $\mathbf{q}' = (\log[p_1/(1 - p_1)], \ldots, \log[p_n/(1 - p_n)])$ is the vector of log-odds corresponding to the individual probabilities, a prime denotes transposition, and the likelihood functions for $\mathbf{q}$, conditional on $\theta = 1$ and $\theta = 0$, are modeled as normal with means $\mathbf{M}_1$ and $\mathbf{M}_0$, respectively, and common covariance matrix Σ. This model captures dependence among the probabilities through the multivariate-normal likelihood functions, and is developed in French (1981) and Lindley (1985). Clemen and Winkler (1987) use this model in studying meteorological forecasts.

These four models all are consistent with the Bayesian paradigm, yet they are clearly all different. The point is not that one or another is more appropriate overall, but that different models may be appropriate in different situations, depending on the nature of the situation and an appropriate description of the experts' probabilities. Technically, these differences give rise to different likelihood functions, which in turn give rise to the different models.

Bayesian Models for Combining Probability Distributions

Just as the models above have been developed specifically for combining event probabilities, other Bayesian models have been developed for combining probability distributions for continuous θ. Here we review three of these models.

Winkler (1981) presents a model for combining expert probability distributions that are normal. Assume that each expert provides a probability distribution for θ with mean μ_i and variance σ_i^2. The vector of means $\mu = (\mu_1, \ldots, \mu_n)$ represents the experts' estimates of θ. Thus, we can work in terms of a vector of errors, $\varepsilon = (\mu_1 - \theta, \ldots, \mu_n - \theta)$. These errors are modeled as multivariate normally distributed with mean vector $(0, \ldots, 0)$ (i.e., the estimates are viewed as unbiased) and covariance matrix Σ, regardless of the value of θ. Let $e' = (1, \ldots, 1)$, a conformable vector of ones. Assuming a noninformative prior distribution for θ, the posterior distribution for θ is normal with mean μ^* and variance σ^{*2}, where

$$\mu^* = e'\Sigma^{-1}\mu/e'\Sigma^{-1}e, \quad (9.8a)$$

and

$$\sigma^{*2} = (e'\Sigma^{-1}e)^{-1}. \quad (9.8b)$$

In this model the experts' stated variances σ_i^2 are not used directly, although the decision maker may let the ith diagonal element of Σ equal σ_i^2. For an extension, see Lindley (1983).

The normal model has been important in the development of practical ways to combine probability distributions. The typical minimum-variance model for combining forecasts is consistent with the normal model (e.g., see Bates and Granger 1969; Newbold and Granger 1974; Winkler and Makridakis 1983). The multivariate-normal likelihood embodies the available information about the qualities of the probability distributions, especially dependence among them. Biases can easily be included in the model via a nonzero mean vector for ε. Clemen and Winkler (1985) use this normal model to show how much information is lost because of dependence, and they develop the idea of equivalent independent information sources. Winkler and Clemen (1992) show how sensitive the posterior distribution is when correlations are high, which is the rule rather than the exception in empirical studies. Chhibber and Apostolakis (1993) also conduct a sensitivity analysis and discuss the importance of dependence in the context of the normal model. Schmittlein, Kim, and Morrison (1990) develop procedures to decide whether to use weights based on the covariance matrix or to use equal weights. Similarly, Chandrasekharan, Moriarty, and Wright (1994) propose methods for investigating the stability of weights and deciding whether to eliminate some experts from the combination.

Although the normal model has been useful, it has some shortcomings. In particular, one must find a way to fit the distributions into the normal framework. If the distributions are unimodal and roughly symmetric, this is generally not a problem. Otherwise, some sort of transformation might be required. The covariance matrix Σ typically is estimated from data; Winkler (1981) derives a formal Bayesian model in which Σ is viewed as an uncertain parameter. Assessing Σ subjectively is possible; Gokhale and Press (1982), Clemen and Reilly (1999), and Clemen, Fischer and Winkler (2000) discuss the assessment of correlation coefficients via a number of different probability transformations. (Winkler and Clemen (2004) show the value of using multiple methods for assessing correlations but argue that averaging correlation judgments from multiple judges is a better strategy.) Finally, the posterior distribution is always a normal distribution and typically is a compromise. For example, suppose two experts give $\mu_1 = 2$, $\mu_2 = 10$, and $\sigma_1^2 = \sigma_2^2 = 1$. Then the posterior distribution will be a normal distribution with mean $\mu^* = 6$ and variance $(1 + \rho)/2$, where ρ is the correlation coefficient between the two experts' errors. Thus, the posterior distribution puts almost all of the probability density in a region that neither of the individual experts thought likely at all. In a situation such as this, it might seem more reasonable to have a bimodal posterior distribution reflecting the two experts' opinions. Lindley (1983) shows how such a bimodal distribution can arise from a t-distribution model.

Another variant on the normal model is a Bayesian hierarchical model (e.g., Lipscomb, Parmigiani, and Hasselblad 1998) that allows for differential random bias on the part of the experts by assuming that each expert's error mean in the normal model can be viewed as a random draw from a second-order distribution on the error means. Dependence among experts' probabilities arises through the common second-order distribution. Hierarchical models generally result in an effective shrinkage of individual means to the overall mean and tend to provide robust estimates. Because they involve another layer of uncertainty, they can be complex, particularly when the parameters are all viewed as unknown and requiring prior distributions.

Some effort has been directed toward the development of Bayesian aggregation methods that are suitable for the use of subjective judgment in determining the likelihood function. Clemen and Winkler (1993), for example, present a process for subjectively combining point estimates; the approach is based on the sequential assessment of conditional distributions among the experts' forecasts, where the conditioning is specified in an influence diagram. Formal attention has also been given to Bayesian models for situations in which the experts provide only partial specifications of their probability distributions (e.g., moments, fractiles) or the decision maker is similarly unable to specify the likelihood function fully (Genest and Schervish 1985; West 1992; West and Crosse 1992; Gelfand, Mallick, and Dey 1995). Bunn (1975) develops a model that considers only which expert performs best on any given occasion and uses a Bayesian approach to update weights in a combination rule based on past performance.

Jouini and Clemen (1996) develop a method for aggregating probability distributions in which the multivariate distribution (likelihood function) is expressed as a function of the marginal distributions. A *copula* function (e.g., Dall'Aglio, Kotz, and Salinetti et al. 1991) provides the connections, including all aspects of dependence, among the experts' judgments as represented by the marginal distributions. For example, suppose that expert i assesses a continuous density for θ, $f_i(\theta)$, with corresponding cumulative distribution function $F_i(\theta)$. Then Jouini and Clemen show that under reasonable conditions, the decision maker's posterior distribution is

$$P(\theta \mid f_1, \ldots, f_n) \propto c[1 - F_1(\theta), \ldots, 1 - F_n(\theta)] \prod_{i=1}^{n} f_i(\theta) \qquad (9.9)$$

where c represents the copula density function.

In the copula approach, judgments about individual experts are entirely separate from judgments about dependence. Standard approaches for calibrating individual experts (either data based or subjective) can be used and involve only the marginal distributions. On the other hand, judgments about dependence are made separately and encoded into the copula function. Regarding dependence, Jouini and Clemen suggest using the Archimedian class of copulas, which treat the experts symmetrically in terms of dependence. If more flexibility is needed, the copula that underlies the multivariate normal distribution can be used (Clemen and Reilly 1999).

In other work involving the specification of the likelihood function, Shlyakhter (1994) and Shlyakhter, Kammen, Brodio, and Wilson (1994) develop a model for adjusting individual distributions to account for the well-known phenomenon of overconfidence, and they estimate the adjustment parameter for two different kinds of environmental risk variables. Hammitt and Shlyakhter (1999) show the implications of this model for combining probabilities.

A promising new direction for specifying the likelihood function uses Bayesian nonparametric methods. The typical use of such approaches is in specifying a nonparametric prior (e.g., based on a Dirichlet process) and then updating that prior. In combining experts' probability distributions, though, it is the likelihood function for the expert's probability distribution that is modeled using Bayesian nonparametric methods. West (1988) is the first to have developed such a model.

Building on West's approach, Lichtendahl (2005) combines a parameterized model of expert performance with a Bayesian nonparametric likelihood function for expert judgments that is capable of handling not only multiple experts, but multivariate judgments (for multiple uncertain quantities) as well.

In this section, we have discussed a number of mathematical methods for combining probability distributions. A number of important issues should be kept in mind when comparing these approaches and choosing an approach for a given application. These issues include the type of information that is available (e.g., whether full probability distributions are given or just some partial specifications of these distributions); the individuals performing the aggregation of probabilities (e.g., a single decision maker or analyst, a decision-analysis or risk-assessment team, or some other set of individuals); the degree of modeling to be undertaken (assessment of the likelihood function, consideration of the quality of the individual distributions); the form of the combination rule (which could follow directly from modeling or could be taken as a primitive, such as a weighted average); the specification of parameters of the combination rule (e.g., the weights); and the consideration of simple versus complex rules (e.g., simple averages versus more complex models). The empirical results discussed below will shed some light on some of these questions, and we will discuss these issues further in the Conclusion.

Empirical Evidence

The various combining techniques discussed above all have some intuitive appeal, and some have a strong theoretical basis given that certain assumptions are satisfied. The proof, of course, is in the pudding. How do the methods perform in practice? Do the combination methods lead to "improved" probability distributions? Do some methods appear to perform better than others? Some evidence available from experimentation, analysis of various data sets, and actual applications, including work on combining forecasts that is relevant to combining probabilities, is reviewed in this section.

Mathematical versus Intuitive Aggregation

Before comparing different combination methods, we should step back and ask whether one should bother with formal aggregation methods. Perhaps it suffices for the decision maker or the decision analysis team to look at the individual probability distributions and to aggregate them intuitively, directly assessing a probability distribution in light of the information.

Hogarth (1987) discusses the difficulty humans have in combining information from different data sources. Although his discussion covers the use of all kinds of information, his arguments apply to the aggregation of probability distributions. Hogarth shows how individuals tend to ignore dependence among information sources, and he relates this to Kahneman and Tversky's (1972) *representativeness* heuristic. In a broad sense, Hogarth's discussion is supported by psychological experimentation showing that expert judgments tend to be less accurate than statistical models based on criteria that the experts themselves claim to use. Dawes, Faust, and Meehl (1989) provide a review of this literature.

Clemen, Jones, and Winkler (1996) also study the aggregation of point forecasts. However, they use Winkler's (1981) normal model and Clemen and Winkler's (1993) conditional-distributions model, and they compare the probability distributions derived from these models with intuitively assessed probability distributions. Although their sample size is small, the results suggest that mathematical methods are somewhat better in terms of performance than intuitive assessment, and the authors speculate that this is due to the structured nature of the assessments required in the mathematical-aggregation models.

Comparisons among Mathematical Methods

Some evidence is available regarding the relative performance of various mathematical aggregation methods. In an early study, Staël von Holstein (1972) studied averages of probabilities relating to stock market prices. Most of the averages performed similarly, with weights based on rankings of past performance slightly better than the rest.

Seaver (1978) evaluated simple and weighted averages of individual probabilities. The performance of the different combining methods was similar, and Seaver's conclusion was that simple combination procedures, such as an equally-weighted average, produce combined probabilities that perform as well as those from more complex aggregation models. Clemen and Winkler (1987) reported similar results in aggregating precipitation probability forecasts.

In a follow-up study, Clemen and Winkler (1990) studied the combination of precipitation forecasts using a wider variety of mathematical methods. One of the more complex methods that was able to account for dependence among the forecasts performed best. Although a simple average was not explicitly considered, a weighted average that resulted in weights for the two forecasts that were not widely different performed almost as well as the more complex scheme.

Winkler and Poses (1993) report on the combination of experts' probabilities in a medical setting. For each patient in an intensive care unit, four individuals (an intern, a critical care fellow, a critical care attending, and a primary attending physician) assessed probabilities of survival. All possible combinations (simple averages) of these four probabilities were evaluated. The best combination turned out to be an average of probabilities from the two physicians who were, simultaneously, the most experienced and the least similar, with one being an expert in critical care and the other having the most knowledge about the individual patient.

All of these results are consistent with the general message that has been derived from the vast empirical literature on the combination of point forecasts. That message is that, in general, simpler aggregation methods perform better than more complex methods. Clemen (1989) discusses this literature. In some of these studies, taking into account the quality of the information, especially regarding relative precision of forecasts, turned out to be valuable.

The above studies focus on the combination of point forecasts or event prob-abilities, and mathematical methods studied have been either averages or some-thing more complex in which combination weights were based on past data. Does the result that simpler methods work better than more complex methods carry over to the aggregation of probability distributions, especially when the quality of the probability distributions must be judged subjectively? Little spe-cific evidence appears to be available on this topic. Clemen, Jones, and Winkler (1996) reported that Winkler's (1981) normal model and the more complex conditional-distributions model (Clemen and Winkler 1993) performed at about the same level. These results are consistent with a number of other studies on the value of decomposing judgments into smaller and more manageable assess-ment tasks. Ravinder, Kleinmuntz and Dyer (1988) provide a theoretical argu-ment for the superiority of decomposed assessments. Wright, Saunders, and Ayton (1988), though, found little difference between holistic and decomposed probabil-ity assessments; on the other hand, Hora, Dodd, and Hora (1993) provide empiri-cal support for decomposition in probability assessment. With regard to decompo-sition and the assessment of point estimates, Armstrong, Denniston, and Gordon (1975) and MacGregor, Lichtenstein, and Slovic (1988) found that decomposition was valuable in improving the accuracy of those estimates. Morgan and Henrion (1990) review the empirical support for decomposition in probability assessment, and Bunn and Wright (1991) do the same for forecasting tasks in general. A ten-tative conclusion is that, for situations in which the aggregation must be made on the basis of subjective judgments, appropriate decomposition of those judgments into reasonable tasks for the assessment team may lead to better performance.

Mathematical versus Behavioral Aggregation

Most of the research comparing mathematical and behavioral aggregation has focused on comparisons with a simple average of forecasts or probabilities rather than with more complicated mathematical combination methods. Results from these comparisons have been mixed. For example, for forecasting college stu-dents' grade-point averages, Rohrbaugh (1979) found that behavioral aggregation worked better than taking simple averages of individual group members' fore-casts. Hastie (1986), Hill (1982), and Sniezek (1989) reached similar conclusions. However, Lawrence, Edmundson, and O'Connor (1986) reported that mathemat-ical combination improved on the behavioral combination of forecasts. In Flores and White's (1989) experiment, mathematical and behavioral combinations per-formed at approximately the same level. Goodman (1972) asked college students to assess likelihood ratios in groups and individually; the behavioral combination showed slight improvement over the mechanical combination.

Seaver (1978) asked student subjects to assess discrete and continuous proba-bility distributions for almanac questions. Several different conditions were used: individual assessment, Delphi, Nominal Group Technique, free-form discussion, and two other approaches that structured information sharing and discussion. Both simple averages and weighted averages of the individual probabilities were also calculated. The conclusion was that interaction among the assessors did not improve on the performance of the aggregated probabilities, although the subjects did feel more satisfied with the behavioral aggregation results.

Reagan-Cirincione (1994) used an intensive group process intervention involving cognitive feedback and a computerized group support system for a quantity-estimation task. The results show this to be the only study reviewed by Gigone and Hastie (1997) for which group judgments are more accurate than a mathematical average of the individual judgments. In general, Gigone and Hastie conclude that the evidence indicates that a simple average of individual judgments tends to outperform group judgments. Moreover, they discuss ways in which groups might improve over mathematical combinations and conclude that, "there is a limited collection of judgment tasks in which groups have a legitimate opportunity to outperform individual judgments."

Larrick and Soll (2006) study how people think about averaging. Their experiments reinforce Gigone and Hastie's (1997) conclusion. Larrick and Soll point out that the strong performance of averaging results from *bracketing*, when forecasters fall on opposite sides of the actual value. The problem, however, is that people do not appreciate what bracketing implies; instead, people tend to think that averaging forecasts tends to lead to average performance, which in turn contributes to a tendency to try to identify the best expert, when averaging forecasts would be a better strategy.

Example: Seismic Hazard

In this section, we present a brief example of three methods for aggregating subjective probability distributions. In 1989, the Nuclear Regulatory Commission reported on the seismic hazard relating to nuclear power plants in the eastern United States (Bernreuter, Savy, Mensing, and Chen 1989). As part of a subsequent study to update the hazard report, probability densities were elicited from a number of seismic-hazard experts. For example, Figure 9.1 shows probability densities for seven experts, each of whom assessed the peak ground acceleration (cm/sec^2) at a distance of 5 km from the epicenter of a magnitude-5 earthquake. Lognormal densities were fitted to the assessments for each expert.

Figure 9.2 shows three aggregated distributions. The "average" curve is the simple average of the seven individual densities. The other two aggregations use Winkler's (1981) normal model and the copula model described by Jouini and Clemen (1996). Although no formal judgments regarding the quality of the experts were made following the elicitation, we assume that appropriate elicitation procedures eliminated biases as much as possible, and so the individual densities need not be recalibrated. For the normal, we assume for each pair of experts a correlation coefficient of 0.9, a value not inconsistent with empirical findings (Clemen 1989). The copula model uses a copula from Frank's family with parameter $\alpha = 0.00001104$ (see Jouini and Clemen 1996). This value of α encodes a level of dependence between any two experts that is consistent with Kendall's $\tau = 0.70$ and pairwise product–moment correlations on the order of 0.9. For both the normal and

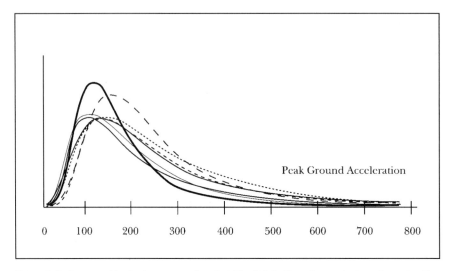

Figure 9.1. Seven subjectively assessed probability distributions for peak ground acceleration (cm/sec^2).

copula models, we transformed to log(cm/sec^2) to perform the aggregation using normal marginals, and then transformed back after aggregating.

The differences among these three models are suggestive of practical experience with aggregation methods. The average curve, which must take into account all variability in all distributions, is very spread out – in a sense understating the amount of information embodied by the experts' distributions as a whole. The model-based aggregations reflect an increase in information through the decrease in spread, placing the bulk of the aggregated density between 100 and 200 cm/sec^2,

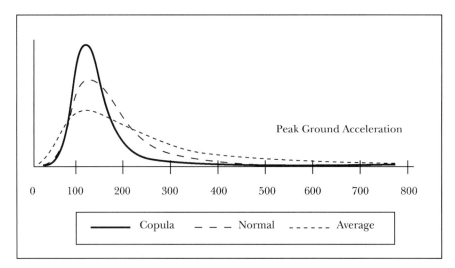

Figure 9.2. Three methods for aggregating individual probability distributions.

which is generally consistent with the individual distributions. Both are much more spread out, however, than the density (not shown) that would result from an assumption of independent experts.

Our example demonstrates how different combination methods might behave in a realistic setting. In practical applications, it is often necessary to adapt the methodology to the particular situation. Selected recent applications include Dillon, John, and von Winterfeldt (2002), who use a simulation-based combining method to combine expert cost judgments in an analysis of alternative tritium suppliers for the U.S. Department of Energy; Lacke and Clemen (2001), who apply the copula method to colorectal cancer risk estimates; Lipscomb, Parmigiani, and Hasselblad (1998), who use a hierarchical Bayes model in a study of physician staffing for U.S. Department of Veteran Affairs medical centers; and Merrick, van Dorp, and Singh's (2005) risk analysis of the Washington State ferries.

Conclusion

We have reviewed a variety of methods for combining probability distributions in decision and risk analysis. The empirical results reviewed in the previous section suggest that mathematical aggregation outperforms intuitive aggregation and that mathematical and behavioral approaches tend to be similar in performance, with mathematical rules having a slight edge. As for different mathematical combination methods, simple combination rules (e.g., a simple average) tend to perform quite well. More complex rules sometimes outperform the simple rules, but they can be somewhat sensitive, leading to poor performance in some instances. All of these conclusions should be qualified by noting that they represent tendencies over a variety of empirical studies, generally conducted in an experimental setting as opposed to occurring in the context of real-world decision analysis. These studies do not, unfortunately, directly assess the precise issue that needs to be addressed. For the purpose of the typical decision analysis in which probability distributions are to be combined, but limited past data are available, the real question is, "What is the best way to combine the probabilities?" Thus, although we should pay careful attention to available empirical results and learn from them, we should think hard about their generalizability to realistic decision-analysis applications.

Both the mathematical combination of probabilities with some modeling and the use of interaction among the experts have some intuitive appeal. It is somewhat disappointing, therefore, to see that modeling and behavioral approaches often provide results inferior to simple combination rules. We feel a bit like the investor who would like to believe that some careful analysis of the stock market and some tips from the pros should lead to high returns but finds that buying a mutual fund that just represents a stock market index such as the S & P 500 would yield better returns. On the other hand, we should remember that the simple combination rules do perform quite well, indicating that the use of multiple experts (or, more generally, multiple information sources) and the combination of the resulting probabilities can be beneficial. One message that comes from the work on the combination of probabilities is that, at a minimum, it is worthwhile to consult multiple information sources (including experts and other sources) and combine their probabilities.

Another message is that further work is needed on the development and evaluation of combination methods. The challenge is to find modeling procedures or behavioral approaches (or processes involving both modeling aspects and behavioral aspects) that perform well enough to justify the extra cost and effort that is associated with serious modeling or expert interaction. On the behavioral side, Davis (1992) states: "The engineering of increases in decision performance while maintaining [the advantages of group decision making] is a proper challenge for fundamental theory and research in applied psychology." Gigone and Hastie (1997) echo this in their concluding comments: "The quality of group decisions and judgments is an essential ingredient in democratic institutions and societies, but research on group judgment accuracy is stagnant. . . . Better methods and analyses will help behavioral scientists, engineers, and policymakers to design and select group decision-making procedures that will increase efficiency, justice, and social welfare."

Regarding mathematical combining procedures, we believe that simple rules will always play an important role, because of their ease of use, robust performance, and defensibility in public-policy settings where judgments about the quality of different experts are eschewed. However, we also believe that further work on Bayesian models, with careful attention to ease of modeling and assessment, as well as to sensitivity (e.g., avoiding extreme situations such as highly negative weights), can lead to improved performance. In principle, the Bayesian approach allows for careful control in adjusting for the quality of individual expert distributions (including overconfidence) and dependence among experts. One reason that the simple average works well is that it results in a distribution that is broader than any individual distribution, thereby counteracting in part typical expert overconfidence. Our preference would be to use a Bayesian model that permits the explicit modeling and appropriate adjustment for overconfidence as well as dependence. It is also worth noting that the normal and copula models allow the symmetric treatment of the probability distributions, in which case simple combining rules fall out of these models as special cases.

Generally, the process of combining probability distributions in decision and risk analysis may well involve both mathematical and behavioral aspects and should be considered in the context of the overall process for obtaining and utilizing information (including expert judgment) in a given application. For discussions of this process, see the references cited in the introduction. Important issues to consider include the following:

- *Flexibility and Process Design.* We believe that there is no single, all-purpose combining rule or combining process that should be used in all situations. Rather, the design of the combining process (as part of the overall information-gathering process) should depend on the details of each individual situation. This process design should take into account factors such as the nature and importance of the uncertainties, the availability of appropriate experts or other information sources, past evidence available about the information sources and about the quantities of interest, the degree of uncertainty about quantities of interest, the degree of disagreement among the probability distributions, the costs of different information sources (e.g., the cost of consulting an expert or bringing experts together), and a variety of other factors. We believe that a carefully structured and documented process is appropriate.

- *The Role of Modeling versus Rules.* Decision and risk analysis applications involving the combination of probability distributions or other quantities have often used simple combination rules, usually a simple average. Such simple rules are valuable benchmarks, but careful consideration should be given to modeling in order to include, in a formal fashion, factors such as the quality of the information from individual sources and the dependence among different sources. One possible scenario is that the experts or other information sources are judged to be exchangeable and their probabilities should be treated symmetrically, but this should be a conscious choice on the part of the decision analysts or decision makers. The degree of modeling will vary from case to case, ranging from fairly simple modeling (e.g., unequal weights based on judgments of relative precision) to more detailed modeling (e.g., building a full copula-based model).

- *The Role of Interaction.* This aspect of the combination process will also vary from case to case, depending on such factors as the perceived desirability of exchanging information and the ease with which such information can be exchanged. Evidence to date does not provide strong support for benefits of interaction, yet it has considerable intuitive appeal and has been used in risk analysis applications (e.g., EPRI 1986; Hora and Iman 1989; Winkler et al. 1995). We feel that the jury is still out on the impact of interaction on the quality of the resulting combined probabilities and that any benefits are most likely to come from exchanges of information (possibly including individual experts' probability distributions) as opposed to forced consensus through group probability assessments. This implies that mathematical combination will still be needed after interaction and individual probability assessment or reassessment. Also, it is important that the interaction process be carefully structured with extensive facilitation.

- *The Role of Sensitivity Analysis.* It is helpful to conduct a sensitivity analysis to investigate the variation in the combined probabilities as parameters of combining models are varied. This can help in decisions regarding the scope of the modeling effort. A related note is that reporting the individual probabilities, as well as any combined probabilities, provides useful information about the range of opinions in a given case.

- *The Role of the Analyst or the Analysis Team.* As should be clear from the above discussion, the decision analyst, or the team of decision analysts or risk analysts, plays a very important role in the combination of probability distributions as well as in all other aspects of the information-gathering process. With respect to mathematical combination, this includes performing any modeling, making any assessments of information quality that are needed in the modeling process, and choosing the combination rule(s) to be used. On the behavioral side, it includes structuring any interaction and serving as facilitators. In general, the analysts are responsible for the design, elicitation, and analysis aspects of the combination process.

In summary, the combination of probability distributions in decision analysis and risk analysis is valuable for encapsulating the accumulated information for analysts and decision makers and providing the current state of information regarding important uncertainties. Normatively and empirically, combining can lead to improvements in the quality of probabilities. More research is needed on the potential benefits of different modeling approaches and the development of mathematical combination rules.

Acknowledgments

This research was supported in part by the National Science Foundation under Grants SBR-93–20754, SBR-94–22527, SBR-95–96176, and SES-03–17867.

REFERENCES

Armstrong, J. S. (2001a). Combining forecasts. In J. S. Armstrong (Ed.), *Principles of forecasting: A handbook for researchers and practitioners*. Norwell, MA: Kluwer, pp. 417–439.

Armstrong, J. S. (Ed.). (2001b). *Principles of forecasting: A handbook for researchers and practitioners*. Norwell, MA: Kluwer.

Armstrong, J. S., Denniston, W. B., and Gordon, M. M. (1975). The use of the decomposition principle in making judgments. *Organizational Behavior and Human Performance, 14*, 257–263.

Arrow, K. J. (1951). *Social choice and individual values*. New York: Wiley.

Bacharach, M. (1979). Normal Bayesian dialogues. *Journal of the American Statistical Association, 74*, 837–846.

Bates, J. M., and Granger, C. W. J. (1969). The combination of forecasts. *Operational Research Quarterly, 20*, 451–468.

Bernreuter, D. L., Savy, J. B., Mensing, R. W., and Chen, J. C. (1989). *Seismic hazard characterization of 69 nuclear sites east of the Rocky Mountains*. Vol. 1–8, NUREG/CR 5250, UCID-21517.

Bunn, D. W. (1975). A Bayesian approach to the linear combination of forecasts. *Operational Research Quarterly, 26*, 325–329.

Bunn, D. W. (1988). Combining forecasts. *European Journal of Operational Research, 33*, 223–229.

Bunn, D., and Wright, G. (1991). Interaction of judgmental and statistical forecasting methods: Issues and analysis. *Management Science, 37*, 501–518.

Chandrasekharan, R., Moriarty, M. M., and Wright, G. P. (1994). Testing for unreliable estimators and insignificant forecasts in combined forecasts. *Journal of Forecasting, 13*, 611–624.

Chhibber, S., and Apostolakis, G. (1993). Some approximations useful to the use of dependent information sources. *Reliability Engineering and System Safety, 42*, 67–86.

Clemen, R. T. (1989). Combining forecasts: A review and annotated bibliography. *International Journal of Forecasting, 5*, 559–583.

Clemen, R. T., Fischer, G. W., and Winkler, R. L. (2000). Assessing dependence: Some experimental results. *Management Science, 46*, 1100–1115.

Clemen, R. T., Jones, S. K., and Winkler, R. L. (1996). Aggregating forecasts: An empirical evaluation of some Bayesian methods. In D. Berry, K. Chaloner, and J. Geweke (Eds.), *Bayesian statistics and econometrics: Essays in honor of Arnold Zellner.* New York: Wiley, pp. 3–13.

Clemen, R. T., and Reilly, T. (1999). Correlations and copulas for decision and risk analysis. *Management Science, 45*, 208–224.

Clemen, R. T., and Winkler, R. L. (1985). Limits for the precision and value of information from dependent sources. *Operations Research, 33*, 427–442.

Clemen, R. T., and Winkler, R. L. (1987). Calibrating and combining precipitation probability forecasts. In R. Viertl (Ed.), *Probability and Bayesian statistics.* New York: Plenum, pp. 97–110.

Clemen, R. T., and Winkler, R. L. (1990). Unanimity and compromise among probability forecasters. *Management Science, 36*, 767–779.

Clemen, R. T., and Winkler, R. L. (1993). Aggregating point estimates: A flexible modeling approach. *Management Science, 39*, 501–515.

Clemen, R. T., and Winkler, R. L. (1999). Combining probability distributions from experts in risk analysis. *Risk Analysis, 19*, 187–203.

Cooke, R. M. (1991). *Experts in uncertainty: Opinion and subjective probability in science.* New York: Oxford University Press.

Dall'Aglio, G., Kotz, S., and Salinetti, G. (1991). *Advances in probability distributions with given marginals: Beyond the copulas.* Dordrecht, The Netherlands: Kluwer.

Davis, J. (1992). Some compelling intuitions about group consensus decisions, theoretical and empirical research, and interpersonal aggregation phenomena: Selected examples, 1950–1990. *Organizational Behavior and Human Decision Processes, 52*, 3–38.

Dawes, R. M., Faust, D., and Meehl, P. A. (1989). Clinical versus actuarial judgment. *Science, 243*, 1668–1673.

de Finetti, B. (1937). La prévision: Ses lois logiques, ses sources subjectives. *Annales de l'Institut Henri Poincaré, 7*, 1–68. Translated in 1980 by H. E. Kyburg, Jr., Foresight. Its logical laws, its subjective sources. In H. E. Kyburg, Jr. and H. E. Smokler (Eds.), *Studies in subjective probability* (2nd ed.). Huntington, New York: Robert E. Krieger, pp. 53–118.

Dillon, R., John, R., and von Winterfeldt, D. (2002). Assessment of cost uncertainties for large technology projects: A methodology and an application. *Interfaces, 32* (Jul/Aug), 52–66.

EPRI (1986). *Seismic hazard methodology for the central and eastern United States. Vol. 1: Methodology.* NP-4/26. Palo Alto, CA: Electric Power Research Institute.

Flores, B. E., and White, E. M. (1989). Subjective vs. objective combining of forecasts: An experiment. *Journal of Forecasting, 8*, 331–341.

French, S. (1981). Consensus of opinion. *European Journal of Operational Research, 7*, 332–340.

French, S. (1985). Group consensus probability distributions: A critical survey. In J. M. Bernardo, M. H. DeGroot, D. V. Lindley, and A. F. M. Smith (Eds.), *Bayesian statistics 2.* Amsterdam: North-Holland, pp. 183–197.

French, S., and Ríos Insua, D. (2000). *Statistical decision theory.* London: Arnold.

Garthwaite, P. H., Kadane, J. B., and O'Hagan, A. (2005). Statistical methods for eliciting prior distributions. *Journal of the American Statistical Association, 100*, 680–700.

Gelfand, A. E., Mallick, B. K., and Dey, D. K. (1995). Modeling expert opinion rising as a partial probabilistic specification. *Journal of the American Statistical Association, 90*, 598–604.

Genest, C. (1984). Pooling operators with the marginalization property. *Canadian Journal of Statistics, 12*, 153–163.

Genest, C., and McConway, K. J. (1990). Allocating the weights in the linear opinion pool. *Journal of Forecasting, 9*, 53–73.

Genest, C., and Schervish, M. J. (1985). Modeling expert judgments for Bayesian updating. *Annals of Statistics, 13*, 1198–1212.

Genest, C., and Zidek, J. V. (1986). Combining probability distributions: A critique and annotated bibliography. *Statistical Science, 1*, 114–148.

Gigone, D., and Hastie, R. (1997). Proper analysis of the accuracy of group judgments. *Psychological Bulletin, 121*, 149–167.

Gokhale, D. V., and Press, S. J. (1982). Assessment of a prior distribution for the correlation coefficient in a bivariate normal distribution. *Journal of the Royal Statistical Society, Series A, 145*, 237–249.

Goodman, B. (1972). Action selection and likelihood estimation by individuals and groups. *Organizational Behavior and Human Performance, 7*, 121–141.

Hammitt, J. K., and Shlyakhter, A. I. (1999). The expected value of information and the probability of surprise. *Risk Analysis, 19*, 135–152.

Hastie, R. (1986). Experimental evidence on group accuracy. In B. Grofman and G. Owen (Eds.), *Information pooling and group decision making*. Greenwich, CT: JAI Press, pp. 129–157.

Hill, G. W. (1982). Group vs. individual performance: Are $N + 1$ heads better than one? *Psychological Bulletin, 91*, 517–539.

Hogarth, R. M. (1987). *Judgment and choice*. (2nd ed.). Chichester, England: Wiley.

Hora, S. C. (1992). Acquisition of expert judgment: Examples from risk assessment. *Journal of Energy Engineering, 118*, 136–148.

Hora, S. C. (2004). Probability judgments for continuous quantitites: Linear combinations and calibration. *Management Science, 50*, 597–604.

Hora, S. C., Dodd, N. G., and Hora, J. A. (1993). The use of decomposition in probability assessments on continuous variables. *Journal of Behavioral Decision Making, 6*, 133–147.

Hora, S. C., and Iman, R. L. (1989). Expert opinion in risk analysis: The NUREG-1150 methodology. *Nuclear Science and Engineering, 102*, 323–331.

Jouini, M. N., and Clemen, R. T. (1996). Copula models for aggregating expert opinions. *Operations Research, 44*, 444–457.

Kahneman, D., and Tversky, A. (1972). Subjective probability: A judgment of representativeness. *Cognitive Psychology, 3*, 430–454.

Keeney, R. L., and von Winterfeldt, D. (1989). On the uses of expert judgment on complex technical problems. *IEEE Transactions on Engineering Management, 36*, 83–86.

Keeney, R. L., and von Winterfeldt, D. (1991). Eliciting probabilities from experts in complex technical problems. *IEEE Transactions on Engineering Management, 38*, 191–201.

Lacke, C. J., and Clemen, R. T. (2001). Analysis of colorectal cancer screening regimens. *Health Care Management Science, 4*, 257–267.

Larrick, R. P., and Soll, J. B. (2006). Intuitions about combining opinions: Misappreciation of the averaging principle. *Management Science, 52*, 111–127.

Lawrence, M. J., Edmundson, R. H., and O'Connor, M. J. (1986). The accuracy of combining judgmental and statistical forecasts. *Management Science, 32*, 1521–1532.

Lichtendahl, K. C. (2005). *Bayesian nonparametric combination of multivariate expert forecasts*. Ph.D. dissertation, Duke University.

Lindley, D. V. (1983). Reconciliation of probability distributions. *Operations Research, 31*, 866–880.

Lindley, D. V. (1985). Reconciliation of discrete probability distributions. In J. M. Bernardo, M. H. DeGroot, D. V. Lindley, and A. F. M. Smith (Eds.), *Bayesian statistics 2*. Amsterdam: North-Holland, pp. 375–390.

Lipscomb, J., Parmigiani, G., and Hasselblad, V. (1998). Combining expert judgment by hierarchical modeling: An application to physician staffing. *Management Science, 44,* 149–161.

MacGregor, D., Lichtenstein, S., and Slovic, P. (1988). Structuring knowledge retrieval: An analysis of decomposing quantitative judgments. *Organizational Behavior and Human Decision Processes, 42,* 303–323.

Merkhofer, M. W. (1987). Quantifying judgmental uncertainty: Methodology, experience, and insights. *IEEE Transactions on Systems, Man, and Cybernetics, 17,* 741–752.

Merrick, J. R. W., van Dorp, J. R., and Singh, A. (2005). Analysis of correlated expert judgments from extended pairwise comparisons. *Decision Analysis, 2,* 17–29.

Morgan, M. G., and Henrion, M. (1990). *Uncertainty: A guide to dealing with uncertainty in quantitative risk and policy analysis.* Cambridge, MA: Cambridge University Press.

Morgan, M. G., and Keith, D. W. (1995). Subjective judgments by climate experts. *Envirionmental Science and Technology, 29,* 468–476.

Morris, P. A. (1974). Decision analysis expert use. *Management Science, 20,* 1233–1241.

Morris, P. A. (1977). Combining expert judgments: A Bayesian approach. *Management Science, 23,* 679–693.

Morris, P. A. (1983). An axiomatic approach to expert resolution. *Management Science, 29,* 24–32.

Mosleh, A., Bier, V. M., and Apostolakis, G. (1987). A critique of current practice for the use of expert opinions in probabilistic risk assessment. *Reliability Engineering and System Safety, 20,* 63–85.

Newbold, P., and Granger, C. W. J. (1974). Experience with forecasting univariate time series and the combination of forecasts. *Journal of the Royal Statistical Society, Series A, 137,* 131–149.

Otway, H., and von Winterfeldt, D. (1992). Expert judgment in risk analysis and management: Process, context, and pitfalls. *Risk Analysis, 12,* 83–93.

Ravinder, H. V., Kleinmuntz, D. N., and Dyer, J. S. (1988). The reliability of subjective probabilities obtained through decomposition. *Management Science, 34,* 186–199.

Reagan-Cirincione, P. (1994). Improving the accuracy of group judgment; A process intervention combining group facilitation, social judgment analysis, and information technology. *Organizational Behavior and Human Decision Processes, 58,* 246–270.

Rohrbaugh, J. (1979). Improving the quality of group judgment: Social judgment analysis and the Delphi technique. *Organizational Behavior and Human Performance, 24,* 73–92.

Savage, L. J. (1954). *The foundations of statistics.* New York: Wiley.

Schmittlein, D. C., Kim, J., and Morrison, D. G. (1990). Combining forecasts: Operational adjustments to theoretically optimal rules. *Management Science, 36,* 1044–1056.

Seaver, D. A. (1978). *Assessing probability with multiple individuals: Group interaction versus mathematical aggregation.* Report No. 78–3, Social Science Research Institute, University of Southern California.

Shlyakhter, A. I. (1994). Improved framework for uncertainty analysis: Accounting for unsuspected errors. *Risk Analysis, 14,* 441–447.

Shlyakhter, A. I., Kammen, D. M., Brodio, C. L., and Wilson, R. (1994). Quantifying the credibility of energy projections from trends in past data: The U. S. energy sector. *Energy Policy, 22,* 119–130.

Sniezek, J. A. (1989). An examination of group process in judgmental forecasting. *International Journal of Forecasting, 5,* 171–178.

Spetzler, C. S., and Staël von Holstein, C.-A. S. (1975). Probability encoding in decision analysis. *Management Science, 22,* 340–358.

Staël von Holstein, C.-A. S. (1972). Probabilistic forecasting: An experiment related to the stock market. *Organizational Behavior and Human Performance, 8,* 139–158.

Stone, M. (1961). The opinion pool. *Annals of Mathematical Statistics, 32,* 1339–1342.

West, M. (1988). Modelling expert opinion. In J. M. Bernardo, M. H. DeGroot, D. V. Lindley, and A. F. M. Smith (Eds.), *Bayesian statistics, 3*, Amsterdam: New Holland, pp. 493–508.

West, M. (1992). Modelling agent forecast distributions. *Journal of the Royal Statistical Society, Series B, 54*, 553–567.

West, M., and Crosse, J. (1992). Modelling probabilistic agent opinion. *Journal of the Royal Statistical Society, Series B, 54*, 285–299.

Winkler, R. L. (1968). The consensus of subjective probability distributions. *Management Science, 15*, 361–375.

Winkler, R. L. (1981). Combining probability distributions from dependent information sources. *Management Science, 27*, 479–488.

Winkler, R. L. (1986). Expert resolution. *Management Science, 32*, 298–303.

Winkler, R. L., and Clemen, R. T. (1992). Sensitivity of weights in combining forecasts. *Operations Research, 40*, 609–614.

Winkler, R. L., and Clemen, R. T. (2004). Multiple experts vs. multiple methods: Combining correlation assessments. *Decision Analysis, 1*, 167–176.

Winkler, R. L., and Makridakis, S. (1983). The combination of forecasts. *Journal of the Royal Statistical Society, Series A, 146*, 150–157.

Winkler, R. L., and Poses, R. M. (1993). Evaluating and combining physicians' probabilities of survival in an intensive care unit. *Management Science, 39*, 1526–1543.

Winkler, R. L., Wallsten, T. S., Whitfield, R. G., Richmond, H. M., Hayes, S. R., and Rosenbaum, A. S. (1995). An assessment of the risk of chronic lung injury attributable to long-term ozone exposure. *Operations Research, 43*, 19–28.

Wright, G., and Ayton, P. (Eds). (1987). *Judgmental forecasting*. Chichester, UK: Wiley.

Wright, G., Saunders, C., and Ayton, P. (1988). The consistency, coherence, and calibration of holistic, decomposed, and recomposed judgmental probability forecasts. *Journal of Forecasting, 7*, 185–199.

Wu, J. S., Apostolakis, G., and Okrent, D. (1990). Uncertainties in system analysis: Probabilistic versus nonprobabilistic theories. *Reliability Engineering and System Safety, 30*, 163–181.

10 Model Building with Belief Networks and Influence Diagrams

Ross D. Shachter

ABSTRACT. Belief networks and influence diagrams use directed graphs to represent models for probabilistic reasoning and decision making under uncertainty. They have proven to be effective at facilitating communication with decision makers and with computers. Many of the important relationships among uncertainties, decisions, and values can be captured in the structure of these diagrams, explicitly revealing irrelevance and the flow of information. We explore a variety of examples illustrating some of these basic structures, along with an algorithm that efficiently analyzes their model structure. We also show how algorithms based on these structures can be used to resolve inference queries and determine the optimal policies for decisions.

We have all learned how to translate models, as we prefer to think of them, into arcane representations that our computers can understand, or to simplify away key subtleties for the benefit of clients or students. Thus it has been an immense pleasure to work with graphical models where the representation is natural for the novice, convenient for computation, and yet powerful enough to convey difficult concepts among analysts and researchers.

The graphical representations of belief networks and influence diagrams enable us to capture important relationships at the structural level of the graph where it easiest for people to see them and for algorithms to exploit them. Although the diagrams lend themselves to communication, there remains the challenge of synthesis, and building graphical models is still a challenging art. This chapter presents many examples of model structures within these representations and some of their most important properties. It is designed for students and practitioners with a basic understanding of decision analysis.

An example illustrates the value of a clear representation. For many years the accepted model for contract bidding (Friedman, 1956) corresponded to the network shown in Figure 10.1a, where "&" represents background information. Buried in the mathematics was an incorrect assumption that if we know our bid then the bids of our competitors provide us no new information about the value of the contract. It was only after analyzing bidding patterns that had cost oil companies many extra millions of dollars in Gulf Coast leases that Capen, Clapp, & Campbell (1971) discovered the mistake and presented the model corresponding to the network shown in Figure 10.1b. In their model, the value of the contract renders our bid and the bids of our competitors irrelevant to each other, assuming no collusion. As a result we have the "winner's curse," because observing that we

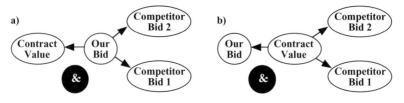

Figure 10.1. Different models for contract bidding.

won the bid makes it more likely that our bid is in error. In hindsight and with the insights from graphical models, it is disturbing that the error went undetected for so many years.

The use of a directed graph factorization of a joint distribution is usually credited to Wright (1921, 1934) and Good (1961a, 1961b), although it was first fully described by Howard & Matheson (1984); Miller, Merkofer, Howard, Matheson, & Rice (1976). It came to computer science and statistics attention through Kim & Pearl (1983); Lauritzen & Spiegelhalter (1988); Pearl (1988). Since then, there have been many significant developments in model building and analysis, particularly with the use of undirected graphs, but our focus here is on the basic models in directed graphs.

In the next section we present examples of probabilistic models represented by belief networks, followed by a section featuring algorithms to explore the belief network structure and use simple directed graphical transformations to analyze inference queries. The final two sections present examples of decision models represented by influence diagrams, and algorithms and directed transformations to analyze them.

Probabilistic Models

In this section we consider examples of probabilistic models represented by *belief networks*. Such networks are known by many names, including Bayesian networks, relevance diagrams, causal probabilistic networks, and recursive causal models. The structure of the graph captures irrelevance information about the underlying probabilistic model through deterministic variables and the arcs that could be present but are missing. The data associated with the nodes in the graph provide a complete probabilistic description of the uncertainties in the model and allow an updating of that description as variables are observed.

The *structure* of a *belief network* $B = (U, A, F \mid \&)$ consists of nodes U, directed arcs A between those nodes, and a subset F of the nodes that are determined (functionally) by other nodes. Corresponding to each node j is an uncertain variable X_j, and X_J refers to the variables corresponding to the set of nodes J. The *background state of information* $\&$ represents the perspective of the *decision maker* (DM) at a point in time. It captures her beliefs, biases, and life experiences in the context of the current situation.

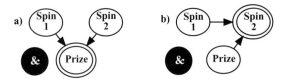

Figure 10.2. Different models for a coin-spinning contest.

Consider the belief network shown in Figure 10.2a, representing a contest in which the prize is determined by two coin spins. *Spin 1* and *Spin 2* are oval *probabilistic nodes* and *Prize* is a double oval *deterministic node*. If both spins are observed then we will know the prize with certainty, but if they are not then we might be uncertain about *Prize*. The background state of information & is represented by a dark oval node, which might be labeled with the date and/or the DM's name. In Figure 10.2a, *Spin 1* and *Spin 2* direct arcs toward *Prize*, so they are its *parents* and it is their *child*. Similarly, in Figure 10.2b if the parents *Spin 1* and *Prize* are known, then their child, *Spin 2*, is also known. We denote the parents of node j by $Pa(j)$ and following the familial analogy, the set of nodes along directed paths from node j are called its *descendants*, $De(j)$.

A belief network B is *completely specified* if data is assigned to each node in the network. For each node j there is a set of *possible values* $x_j \in \Omega_j$, and we denote the possible values for a set of variables J by $x_J \in \Omega_J = \underset{j \in J}{\times} \Omega_j$. If X_j has been observed, then it has only the possible value x_j. We assume in this chapter that Ω_j is finite, but most results can be extended to continuous variables as well. For each X_j there is also a *conditional probability distribution* for X_j given its parents $X_{Pa(j)}$ (and &), $P\{X_j \mid X_{Pa(j)}, \&\}$. If j is a deterministic variable, $j \in F$, then this conditional distribution can be represented by a function, $X_j = f_j(X_{Pa(j)} \mid \&)$. If X_j has been observed then this conditional distribution is a likelihood function, $P\{X_j = x_j \mid X_{Pa(j)}, \&\}$.

It is sometimes tempting to construct a model with a *directed cycle*, that is, a path following directed arcs taking us back to where we started. Although work has been done to analyze such models, any joint probability distribution can be represented without a directed cycle and we will therefore assume here that there is no such cycle in the network. These cycles can arise when we have a dynamic equilibrium process, such as the relationship between prices and quantities shown in Figure 10.3a, which can be represented instead as a sequence of prices and quantities over time as shown in Figure 10.3b. A simultaneous system, such as the one shown in Figure 10.3c, can usually be triangulated into the system shown in Figure 10.3d. The cases where it cannot be triangulated are the same as for deterministic systems, that is, when the system is either inconsistent or indeterminate.

When there is no directed path in the network, there must be at least one *ordered list* of the nodes such that any descendants of a node follow it in the list. Such a list can be constructed in linear time by iteratively selecting a node

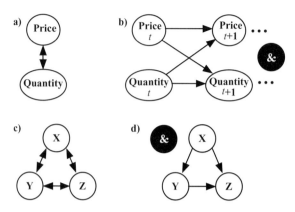

Figure 10.3. Directed cycles are not permitted.

without a parent and deleting the arcs it directs to its children. For example, in the belief network shown in Figure 10.2a there are two ordered lists, (*Spin 1*, *Spin 2*, *Prize*) and (*Spin 2*, *Spin 1*, *Prize*), but there is only one for the network shown in Figure 10.3d, (*X*, *Y*, *Z*).

It is convenient to think in terms of an *assessment order* of the uncertain variables, an ordered list such that the conditional probability of X_j given the variables preceding it in the list is obtained by conditioning X_j on its parents (and the background state of information) alone, $P\{X_j \mid X_1, \ldots, X_{j-1}, \&\} = P\{X_j \mid X_{Pa(j)}, \&\}$, where we have assumed that the assessment order is 1, 2,.... The conditional irrelevance (or independence) embodied in the belief network B is satisfied by a joint probability distribution, and the distribution is said to admit a *directed factorization* with respect to B, if X_j is a deterministic function of $X_{Pa(j)}$ for each j in F and

$$P\{X_U \mid \&\} = \prod_{j \in U} P\{X_j \mid X_{Pa(j)}, \&\}.$$

Given the joint probability distribution $P\{X_U \mid \&\}$ for X_U, X_J and X_L are said to be *probabilistically irrelevant* (or independent) given X_K (and &) if $P\{X_J \mid X_K, X_L, \&\} = P\{X_J \mid X_K, \&\}$.

Given the belief network structure B and any sets of nodes J, K, and L, X_J and X_L are irrelevant in B given X_K if X_J and X_L are probabilistically irrelevant given X_K (and &) for *any* joint probability distribution $P\{X_U \mid \&\}$ that admits a directed factorization with respect to B.

Therefore, if X_J and X_L are irrelevant in B given X_K then, no matter what probability distributions are assigned consistent with the network structure, they are probabilistically irrelevant, and we are assured that, having observed X_K we can learn nothing about either X_J or X_L by observing the other. This condition is equivalent to X_j and X_l are irrelevant in B given X_K for all j in J and l in L, even though such a decomposition is not true in general for probabilistic independence (Pearl, 1988).

Figure 10.4. Markov chain for stock values.

As a result, the belief network makes strong assertions about conditional irrelevance but weak ones about relevance, based on which nodes are deterministic and which arcs are present. Each deterministic node and missing arc implies probabilistic irrelevance, while there might always be additional probabilistic irrelevance not captured in the belief network structure. Thus we can be sure which irrelevance statements *must* be true and what node data is *not* needed to resolve a query, but we can only say which relevance statements *might* be true and what node data *might* be needed. In the next section we will present an algorithm to answer these questions.

To explore this difference between probabilistic irrelevance and irrelevance in B, consider the network for the coin-spinning contest shown in Figure 10.2a. DM believes that the two spins are irrelevant and that the prize is completely determined by the two spins, and will consider only probability distributions consistent those beliefs. If she also believes that the spins are both equally likely to land "heads" or "tails" and that the prize will be determined by whether the two coins match, then the network shown in Figure 10.2b would also be valid, since winning the prize and either coin spin are probabilistically irrelevant in that case. Even in that case, the network shown in Figure 10.2a still seems more informative! Note that probabilistic independence cannot be decomposed in the same way as irrelevance in B, since seeing both coins determines whether we win the prize, even when they each provide no information about the prize.

Now that we have a formal definition of irrelevance in B, we can apply it to the belief network shown in Figure 10.4. This is the simplest example of conditional irrelevance, since the missing arc from *Stock Value Yesterday* to *Stock Value Tomorrow* assures us that, no matter what conditional distributions DM uses consistent with the diagram, yesterday's value and tomorrow's value are irrelevant given today's. This embodies the "Markov property," namely, the present stock value tells us everything we need to know from the present and the past to predict the future. A Markov process, whether it is stationary or not, can be represented by such a "sausage link" belief network, with a node for each stage or time period.

Another fundamental example involves repeated trials as represented by the belief networks shown in Figure 10.5. If DM spins a coin n times and observes each time whether it lands "heads" or "tails" she might be tempted to represent this experiment by the belief network shown in Figure 10.5a, in which all of the different spins are irrelevant (given &). However, many coins are not equally likely to land "heads" or "tails" after being spun because of precession, and there is a real opportunity to learn about *Spin n* from the first $n - 1$ spins. Therefore, she might prefer the belief network shown in Figure 10.5b, in which the spins

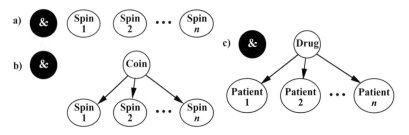

Figure 10.5. Repeated trials that are conditionally irrelevant.

would be irrelevant if she knew some properties of the coin (and &), in this case the probability that it will land "heads" after being spun. This network allows her to learn about the coin from the spins she has observed in order to revise her beliefs about the other spins. Of course, our interest in this model does not arise from a desire to spin coins but because its structure shows up in so many important problems. Consider an experimental drug being tested on some patients, represented by the belief network shown in Figure 10.5c. If DM assumed that the patients' recoveries were irrelevant then there would be no benefit to knowing what happened to the earlier patients before she received (or administered) the treatment.

The belief network facilitates the updating of DM's beliefs about all of the variables when she obtains evidence. Evidence is represented as the observation of one of the variables in the network. Consider the network shown in Figure 10.6a, which represents how the alignment of a production process affects the quality of the product. It is possible to sample some of the product for testing in order to learn whether the process is still in alignment. If DM observes the test results, she can update her beliefs about alignment and make a decision whether to ship the product. We represent the observed variable with shading and recognize that it now only has one possible value – the value observed. (If it had children in the network, then she could also cut those arcs, since the children can condition on the observed value for this variable.)

Treating a variable as observed is absolute. If DM is not sure that it has that value, then she can represent that uncertainty by creating a new node, such as

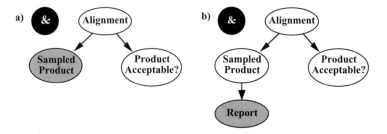

Figure 10.6. Evidence enters through its likelihood of observation.

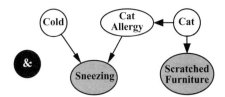

Figure 10.7. Observing a common child can make irrelevant uncertainties relevant.

Report in the network shown in Figure 10.6b, to represent what she has observed. In this case, she would need to specify how likely this report would be for all of the possible values of the sample test results. Many famous paradoxes are avoided by this simple mechanism of observation rather than directly updating DM's beliefs about *Alignment*. In fact, she is using this mechanism whether she observes *Sampled Product* or *Report*. Of course, if she is not sure what is in the report, then she can create still another node, its child, that she has observed instead.

The DM's background state of information & is a special case of an observed variable. There is only one possibility for & in the network and everything is implicitly conditioned on it.

In this example and the ones that follow, the observed node can be considered an "effect" and its parent(s) the "causes." Most updating situations in belief networks involve observing an effect child to learn about a causal parent. This is because it is usually more natural to construct a belief network in the causal direction and because we often obtain evidence about a variable of interest through its effects (Shachter & Heckerman, 1987).

We saw in the coin-spinning contest example that two spins DM considered irrelevant could become relevant if she observed a prize determined by them. This situation can arise whenever she observes a common descendant of uncertainties that she had believed to be irrelevant. Suppose DM is visiting a friend's house and suddenly starts sneezing. She worries she is coming down with a cold until she notices some scratches on the furniture. If her friend has a cat, her sneezing might be due to her allergy to cats rather than a cold (Henrion & Druzdzel, 1990). The belief network shown in Figure 10.7 represents this story.

Before she started sneezing, DM thought that *Cold* and *Cat Allergy* were irrelevant and that observing one would tell her nothing about the other. Once she observes *Sneezing*, however, they become relevant – if she observed that one were absent then the other would become more likely. When she also observes *Scratched Furniture*, *Cat* and *Cat Allergy* become more likely, and *Cold* becomes less likely than it was after she first observed *Sneezing*.

We will see a general algorithm for recognizing irrelevance in the next section, but this example provides some intuition. In some cases, an observation creates irrelevance while in other cases it can eliminate it. Before she observed *Sneezing*, *Cold* and *Scratched Furniture* were irrelevant, but once she sneezed, they became relevant. On the other hand, if she then also observed *Cat* or *Cat Allergy* then

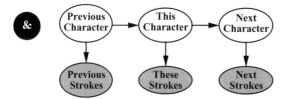

Figure 10.8. Partially observable Markov chain.

Cold and *Scratched Furniture* would again be irrelevant, since the scratches on the furniture are relevant to cold only because they suggest to us the presence of a cat and our cat allergy.

Another common and important model is the partially observable Markov chain, as shown in Figure 10.8, in the context of an optical character recognition system. The system observes pen strokes and tries to infer a sequence of characters, using a Markov model to capture the relevance of adjacent characters. The strokes for each character represent an imperfect observation of the character. Adding more layers of meaning could refine this model, much as people employ in deciphering handwriting, but it would become considerably more complex.

The belief network structure shown in Figure 10.8 also corresponds to Kalman filters and hidden Markov models. The models all feature a Markov process backbone with imperfect observations of the Markov variables. Usually the models are used for processes over time but they can also be applied to other sequences as well.

Many applications involve whether a critical system is functioning. Suppose a security system has two kinds of sensors, one for intrusion and one for motion, both sharing a common power supply. The system can function as long as one of the sensors and the master control are working. There are potential failures of all of these systems in the event of an earthquake or a fire. A belief network for this example is shown in Figure 10.9, where the deterministic nodes have "and" and "or" functions. Note that if the DM could observe *Motion Sensor*, *Power Supply*, *Intrusion Sensor*, and *Master Control*, then she would know the values

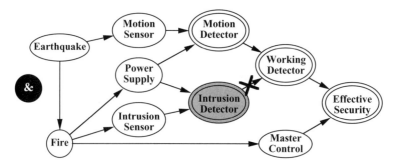

Figure 10.9. Fault belief network.

of all of the deterministic variables. If she observed that the intrusion sensor was not working, she could update her beliefs about all of the other variables, both to know whether the overall system is functioning and how to plan repairs for the parts that have failed. At that point, *Intrusion Detector* would have only one possible value and the arc to its child can be cut. Even though it is a deterministic function of its parents, there are multiple values of the parents that might yield that value, so the diagnostic task is not deterministic in general, even for a system with determinacy.

Traditionally, these systems have been modeled using fault trees, which must be augmented to capture common cause failure, the relevance among components. The belief network makes it easier to represent these relationships. There are three fundamentally different kinds of tasks that one can perform using this type of network. First is prediction – given the observations available (and &), how likely the system is to remain effective until repairs are completed. Second is diagnosis – given those same observations, which components are likely to have failed. Both of these tasks lead to decisions about information collection, such as troubleshooting, and repair strategies. Third is system design – looking prospectively at the response of the system to internal and external failures, such as whether there is sufficient redundancy to deal with the impacts of fires or earthquakes.

In the next section we will see how we can analyze these belief networks to understand the implications of the model structure and how we can update our beliefs.

Analyzing Probabilistic Models

Much of the popularity of belief networks arises from our increasing computational power and the development of efficient algorithms. This section presents some of those algorithms, primarily to determine the implications of our belief network structure for irrelevance and data requirements, but also to show how we could update our beliefs after making observations. There is a large and growing literature on the efficient solution of these inference problems, mostly using undirected graphical structures and beyond the scope of this chapter (Jensen, Lauritzen, & Olesen, 1990; Lauritzen & Spiegelhalter, 1988; Shenoy & Shafer, 1990). Our focus instead will be on how we can explore and modify the belief network structure in order to gain some intuition for modeling and analysis.

A useful and efficient algorithm, Bayes-Ball, identifies for any query $P\{X_J \mid X_K, \&\}$ which variables in a belief network must be irrelevant to X_J given X_K (and &), and which conditional distributions and observation might be needed to resolve the query (Shachter, 1998). We call the information that might be needed the *requisite distributions* and *requisite observations* for J given K. The Bayes-Ball Algorithm runs in time linear in the size of the belief network and is based on the metaphor of a bouncing ball. The ball sometimes bounces off a node, sometimes passes through it, and sometimes gets stuck, depending on the type of node and

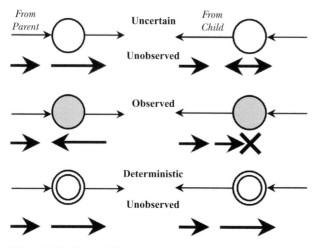

Figure 10.10. Bayes-Ball.

whether the ball is approaching the node from a parent or from a child, as shown in Figure 10.10.

The Bayes-Ball Algorithm explores a structured belief network $B = (N, A, F \mid \&)$ with respect to the expression $P\{X_j \mid X_K, \&\}$ and constructs the sets of irrelevant and requisite nodes.

1. Initialize all nodes as neither visited, nor marked on the top, nor marked on the bottom.
2. Create a schedule of nodes to be visited, initialized with each node in J to be visited as if from one of its children.
3. While there are still nodes scheduled to be visited:
   a. Pick any node j scheduled to be visited, mark it as visited ($\checkmark$) and remove it from the schedule.
   b. If $j \notin K$ and j was scheduled for a visit from a child:
      i. If the top of j is not yet marked, then mark its top and schedule each of its parents to be visited;
      ii. If $j \notin F$ and the bottom of j is not yet marked, then mark its bottom and schedule each of its children to be visited.
   c. If j was scheduled for a visit from a parent:
      i. If $j \in K$ and the top of j is not yet marked, then mark its top and schedule each of its parents to be visited;
      ii. If $j \notin K$ and the bottom of j is not yet marked, then mark its bottom and schedule each of its children to be visited.
4. The irrelevant nodes, $N^I(J \mid K)$, are those nodes *not* marked on the bottom.
   The requisite distribution nodes, $N^P(J \mid K)$, are those nodes marked on the top.
   The requisite observation nodes, $N^E(J \mid K)$, are those nodes in K marked as visited.

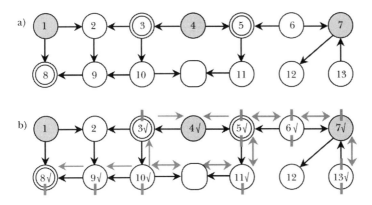

Figure 10.11. Bayes-Ball algorithm example.

An example of the Bayes-Ball Algorithm is shown in Figure 10.11 for the query $P\{X_{10}, X_{11} \mid X_1, X_4, X_7, \&\}$. The algorithm determines irrelevant set $N^I = \{1, 2, 3, 4, 7, 12\}$, requisite distributions $N^P = \{3, 5, 6, 7, 10, 11, 13\}$ and requisite observations $N^E = \{4, 7\}$. The non-requisite nodes $N - (N^P \cup N^E) = \{1, 2, 8, 9, 12\}$ could be deleted from the belief network and we would still be able to resolve the query.

Probabilistic inference can be performed by graphical operations on the belief network that alter the ordered list of the requisite nodes. This allows us to transform from the assessment order ideal for model construction and communication with DM to the ordered list needed to resolve a query, such as $P\{X_J \mid X_K, \&\}$. Once the nodes K (some of which might already be observed) are the only other parents of the nodes J, we have solved the problem (Shachter, 1988).

Consider the belief network shown in Figure 10.12a representing an HIV test. $HIV+$ is an uncertain variable indicating whether DM has been infected with the HIV virus and "$HIV+$" is her test result. Her test result and *Risk Behavior* are irrelevant given her infection status, and the type of *Test* performed is irrelevant to both her risk behavior and her infection status, at least until she observes her test result. Suppose she would prefer the ordered list (*Risk Behavior, Test,* "$HIV+$," HIV). Bayes-Ball can be used to find the requisite observations for $P\{$"$HIV+$" $\mid$ *Risk Behavior, Test,* $\&\}$ and both *Risk Behavior* and *Test* are requisite. All of the variables that precede HIV are also requisite, so we obtain the belief network

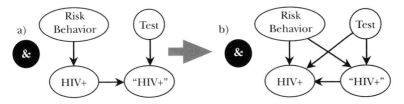

Figure 10.12. HIV Test and arc reversal.

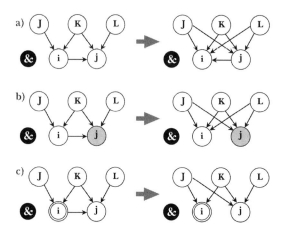

Figure 10.13. The three kinds of arc reversal.

in Figure 10.12b. This is intuitive, since the type of test is now relevant to her infection status, and her risk behavior is relevant to the test results.

This graphical transformation is called arc reversal. The arc from node i to node j is *reversible* if there is no other directed path from i to j; if there were, then an arc from j to i would create a directed cycle. Reversing the direction of the arc so that it goes from j to i is exactly the same operation as flipping a probability tree. In the process, the two nodes inherit each other's parents, so arc reversal can add arcs as shown in Figure 10.13a. The first step is to compute the joint distribution of the two corresponding variables,

$$P\{X_i, X_j \mid X_J, X_K, X_L, \&\} = P\{X_i \mid X_J, X_K, \&\} P\{X_j \mid X_i, X_K, X_L, \&\},$$

where $J = Pa(i) - Pa(j)$, $K = Pa(i) \cap Pa(j)$, and $L = Pa(j) - (\{i\} \cup Pa(i))$.

From that joint distribution we can compute new distributions for X_i and X_j,

$$P\{X_j \mid X_J, X_K, X_L, \&\} = \sum_{x_i \in \Omega_i} P\{X_i, X_j \mid X_J, X_K, X_L, \&\}$$

and

$$P\{X_i \mid X_j, X_J, X_K, X_L, \&\} = \frac{P\{X_i, X_j \mid X_J, X_K, X_L, \&\}}{P\{X_j \mid X_J, X_K, X_L, \&\}}.$$

There are two special cases for arc reversal. The first, *evidence reversal*, arises when X_j has been observed and thus has only one possible value. The only difference is that there is no need for an arc from j to i afterward as shown in Figure 10.13b. The same reversibility condition applies nonetheless, since any other path from i to j would go through the set L of nodes becoming parents of i, thus creating a directed cycle. The other special case, *deterministic propagation*, arises when i is a deterministic node. In this case, there is no uncertainty about X_i given $X_{Pa(i)}$, so there is no need to add additional parents, either j or L, as shown in Figure 10.13c. In this case there is no reversibility condition at all since the only

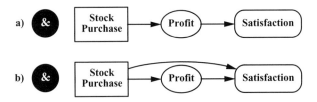

Figure 10.14. Investor's decision opportunity.

arcs being added are from J to j replacing the arc from i to j, and corresponding to the substitution,

$$P\{X_j \mid X_J, X_K, X_L, \&\} = P\{X_j \mid f_i(X_J, X_K), X_K, X_L, \&\}.$$

Given arc reversal, computing $P\{X_J \mid X_K, \&\}$ is then a matter of reordering the graph so that the nodes in K precede the nodes in J and they both precede the other nodes. In fact, once a node outside of $J \cup K$ has no children, it can be removed from the network as a *barren node*. Any node outside of $J \cup K$ can be removed from a model by reversing the arcs to its children in order until it is barren (Shachter, 1988).

Decision Models

In this section we consider examples of decision models represented by *influence diagrams*. Influence diagrams express choices and preferences as well as beliefs and information. They consist of belief networks with two additional node types, representing decisions and criteria for making choices. In addition to the beliefs at the time the network is constructed, the influence diagram represents the prospective observation of variables that are still uncertain.

The *structure* of an *influence diagram* consists of nodes, arcs, and &, as in the belief network but now there are additional types of nodes. Decision nodes D correspond to variables completely under DM's control, and value nodes V represent the criteria she uses to make those choices. Consider the influence diagram shown in Figure 10.14a, representing an investor's decision problem. She has complete control over *Stock Purchase* and she will choose it to obtain *Profit* that will maximize the expected value of her *Satisfaction*. Her decision variable *Stock Purchase* is drawn as a rectangle and her value variable *Satisfaction* is drawn as a rounded rectangle. (In the literature, value variables are drawn in a variety of shapes.)

An influence diagram is *completely specified* if possible values are assigned for each node and conditional probability distributions for all the nodes in U and V. The value variables V are assumed to be deterministic functions of their parents, just like the uncertain variables in F, and we assume that the *total value* is the sum of all of the value functions. (Some results still apply even if the value functions are multiplied instead of added.) Conditional probability distributions are not needed for the decision nodes D – these will be determined so as to maximize the expected total value.

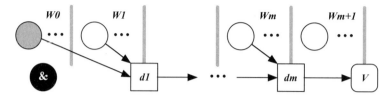

Figure 10.15. Decision windows and the *no forgetting* condition.

We assume that all of the decision variables can be ordered in time, $d_1, d_2, \ldots,$ d_m, and that the parents of each decision variable represent all of the other variables that will have been observed before that choice must be made. We assume the *no forgetting* condition, that the parents of each decision include all earlier decisions and the variables observed before them (Howard & Matheson, 1984). As a result, we can partition the uncertainties into $m + 2$ sets, *decision windows* $W_0, \ldots, W_{m+1}$, where the uncertain variables in W_0 have already been observed, those in W_i will be observed before the choice of d_i but after the choice of d_{i-1}, and those in W_{m+1} will not be observed before any of the decisions, as shown in Figure 10.15. The windows can be thought of as one-way, so future decisions can observe anything from earlier windows but nothing from the future. More formally, $Pa(d_1) = W_0 \cup W_1$ and $Pa(d_i) = Pa(d_{i-1}) \cup \{d_{i-1}\} \cup W_i$ for $i = 2, \ldots, m$. To reduce clutter in the diagram, arcs into decisions will not be drawn when they can be inferred by no forgetting.

Consider again the influence diagram drawn in Figure 10.14a. As stated above, DM completely controls the decision *Stock Purchase* so as to maximize the expected value of her *Satisfaction*. This is a causal notion, because she is convinced that her choice will have some impact or effect on the world, in this case on *Profit*. She anticipates the prospect of satisfaction based on that profit. Therefore, her choice of stocks affects every descendant of her decision, her satisfaction as well as her profit. If she could not affect any of her value variables by making her choice, why would she devote any attention to that choice? Now, suppose that she wants to base her purchase decisions on factors besides profit, that is, she is willing to forgo some potential profit to own companies she prefers for other reasons. The influence diagram shown in Figure 10.14b represents this situation, since *Stock Purchase* and *Satisfaction* are no longer irrelevant given *Profit*.

Now that we have seen the role that cause plays in influence diagrams we can recognize a particular type of belief network called a causal network, in which all of the arcs have a causal interpretation (Heckerman & Shachter, 1994; Pearl, 2000). A belief network is said to be a *causal network* if, were DM able to completely control one (or more) of the uncertain variables, the influence diagram obtained by cutting any incoming arcs from parents, and changing it (them) to decision node(s), is valid. (We should have a meaningful value node, too, although this is not usually mentioned.)

Consider the belief networks shown in Figures 10.16a and 10.16b. A full gas tank is necessary to complete the mission and the gas gauge indicates whether

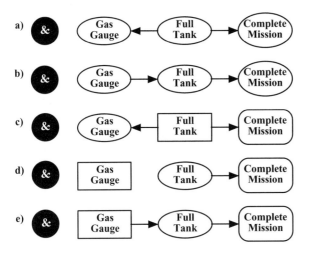

Figure 10.16. Causal networks are special belief networks.

the tank is full. Probabilistically, these two networks are indistinguishable, representing identical irrelevance relationships. However, they have quite different meanings as causal networks. If we could control the tank in the first network we obtain the influence diagram shown in Figure 10.16c. Filling (or emptying) the tank would affect the gauge and the mission. If, instead we control the gas gauge, we get the influence diagram shown in Figure 10.16d. Manipulating the gauge has no effect on either the tank or the mission. On the other hand, if we could control the gauge in the second belief network we get the influence diagram shown in Figure 10.16e. According to this diagram, manipulating the gauge affects both the tank and the mission. Clearly, the belief network shown in Figure 10.16a is a causal network and the one shown in Figure 10.16b is not.

The influence diagram shown in Figure 10.17a represents a prototypical decision opportunity. The DM is choosing a vacation activity but her favorite activity

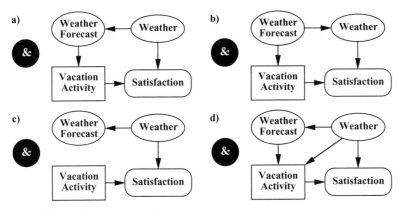

Figure 10.17. Choosing a vacation activity.

if the weather were nice would not be her choice if the weather were bad. She can obtain a long-range weather forecast before she has to put down a deposit on her choice. She has no ability to change the weather, but she does have an opportunity to learn about it before she makes her choice. Her satisfaction is based on the weather and her choice of activity.

The arc from *Weather Forecast* to *Vacation Activity* is an informational arc, indicating that she will observe the forecast before she must commit to an activity. Because the informational arc is explicit rather than implicit, as it is in decision trees, the assessment order does not represent the order in which uncertain variables are observed. Thus, even though *Vacation Activity* is a descendant of *Weather*, there is no claim that *Weather* will be known at the time of *Vacation Activity*. This also means that this problem cannot be represented as a decision tree without reversing the direction of the arc from *Weather* to *Weather Forecast* to obtain the influence diagram shown in Figure 10.17b.

It is common to ask what a decision "depends upon," and on reflection it is clear that all of the elements of the influence diagram contribute to making a good decision. But the arcs do not indicate what the decision "depends upon," any more than they represent a flow chart. The arcs into the decision represent what other variables will have been observed before the choice is made and the arcs into the value node(s) indicate what criteria should be used in making that choice, all based on our background state of information.

Consider now the influence diagram shown in Figure 10.17c. It only differs from the one shown in Figure 10.17a by the deletion of the informational arc from *Weather Forecast* to *Vacation Activity*. If the forecast were available at no cost then DM would be at least as well off in the earlier situation as in this one. Observing *Weather Forecast* cannot make her worse off, since it gives her the opportunity to make a different choice of activity for each possible forecast instead of having to make just one choice. If she chose the same activity regardless of which forecast she observed then she should be indifferent between the two situations and there is no benefit to making the observation. The difference in value between these two diagrams represents the value to DM of observing *Weather Forecast* before making the *Vacation Activity* decision.

Consider instead the influence diagram shown in Figure 10.17d. It only differs from the one shown in Figure 10.17a by the addition of the informational arc from *Weather* to *Vacation Activity*. We saw that this additional information cannot make DM worse off, and in this particular case we would expect her to be much better off, since the weather is the key uncertainty in making her decision. This new diagram represents *perfect information* or *clairvoyance* in her choice and we can measure that change by the difference in the value of the two diagrams. If the value for each diagram represents her willingness to pay to be in that decision situation then the difference represents her willingness to pay a *clairvoyant* to tell her what the weather would be before she makes her choice. Of course, such a clairvoyant does not exist in real life, but the value provides an upper bound on the amount she should pay for any information about the weather. In fact, she might achieve the same benefit by choosing a resort that offers a variety of different activities that

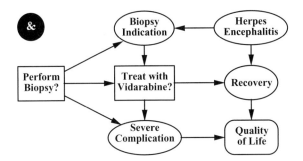

Figure 10.18. Treating suspected herpes encephalitis.

she enjoys, so that she can make her choice each day knowing what the weather will be. In this particular example *the value of clairvoyance* is clearly the benefit of observing *Weather* before choosing *Vacation Activity*, but when there are multiple decisions and uncertain variables, there can be multiple values of clairvoyance, depending on which variables will be observed and when they will be observed.

We can extend these concepts to situations with multiple decisions and, in particular, a decision about collecting information. The influence diagram shown in Figure 10.18 represents a decision by a patient with suspected Herpes encephalitis (Barza & Pauker, 1980). Left untreated, the patient is unlikely to survive, but the standard therapy, treatment with vidarabine, has serious side effects. To test for the presence of the disease, doctors can perform a biopsy, removing some of her brain tissue for examination, a procedure that can also have serious side effects. There are two decisions, *Perform Biopsy?* and *Treat with Vidarabine?*, both posing potential complications. The key uncertainty is *Herpes Encephalitis*, and she cares about her *Quality of Life*. Her treatment decision affects her quality of life both through possible *Recovery* and *Severe Complication*, while her biopsy decision affects it directly through *Severe Complication* and indirectly through the information available about *Herpes Encephalitis* when the treatment decision is made. (If she does not perform the biopsy then *Biopsy Indication* will have the value "not available.") Note that if the arc from *Perform Biopsy?* to *Treat with Vidarabine?* had been omitted, it would have been inferred through *no forgetting*.

In this situation, there is considerable value to clairvoyance on *Herpes Encephalitis?* before *Treat with Vidarabine?*, since otherwise brain cells might be taken from DM to gather information. In medical problems, the cost of testing can be expensive in dollars but also in terms of pain, morbidity, and mortality, both from the test itself and from the delay in treatment. In this influence diagram it is not possible to determine the value of clairvoyance on *Recovery* before *Treat with Vidarabine?*, because an arc from *Recovery* to *Treat with Vidarabine?* would create a directed cycle. Recovery is affected by her treatment choice, so it would not make sense for her to know whether she recovers before making that choice. We resolve this problem by adding more data and structure to the influence diagram until it is in canonical form, as explained below.

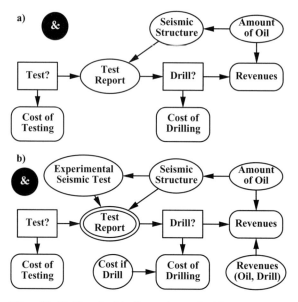

Figure 10.19. The oil wildcatter and canonical form.

Another example of an information gathering decision is faced by an oil wildcatter DM considering a potential drilling location (Raiffa, 1968), represented by
the influence diagram shown in Figure 10.19. The wildcatter must choose whether
to perform a seismic test and then whether to drill, and her key uncertainty is
the amount of oil. There are costs for testing and drilling and there are potential
revenues if she drills and finds oil. Before she chooses whether to drill, she will
know whether she ordered a test and its results. *Test Report* will be "not available"
if she orders no test, equal to *Seismic Structure* if she orders that test, or otherwise
equal to the results of a cheaper experimental seismic test.

The wildcatter can use the influence diagram shown in Figure 10.19a to make
and value her decisions. It would even permit her to compute her value of clairvoyance on the amount of oil or the seismic structure before either of her decisions.
However, there are things that are hidden about the test report, and she is unable
to compute her value of clairvoyance on the revenues or the cost of drilling. We
can address these issues by adding information and structure to the diagram so
that it is in canonical form as shown in Figure 10.19b.

An influence diagram is in *canonical form* if every uncertainty that is affected
by a decision is represented by a deterministic node descendant of that decision in
the influence diagram (Heckerman & Shachter, 1995; Howard, 1990; Matheson,
1990). The cost of drilling depends on whether she chooses to drill and how much
it would cost if she drills. Thus it is both uncertain and somewhat under the control of the decision maker. To make *Cost of Drilling* deterministic, we must the
remove the uncertainty to another node, *Cost if Drill*, unaffected by DM, and
for which she can value clairvoyance. Likewise, to make *Revenues* deterministic,
we must remove the uncertainty to another node, *Revenues(Oil, Drill)*, which is

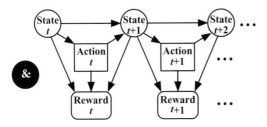

Figure 10.20. Markov decision process.

an uncertain table of values corresponding to all possible values of *Amount of Oil* and *Drill?*. This table is unaffected by DM so she can value clairvoyance for it. Similarly, to make *Test Report* deterministic, we must explicitly represent the results from the different tests as uncertain variables, unaffected by DM and for which she can value clairvoyance. In the process of transforming an influence diagram into canonical form, the causal mechanisms must be explicitly represented for every uncertain variable affected by decisions.

A classic model of decision making over time is the Markov decision process (Howard, 1960) represented by the influence diagram shown in Figure 10.20. There are multiple stages, usually thought of as epochs in time, $t, t + 1, \ldots$, and in each stage there is a state of the process, an action to be chosen, and a (discounted) reward for that period. The state for the next stage is affected by the current action and the reward for each period is based on the current state, the current action, and the next state. It is well known that even though all of the states and decisions in the past are observable now through no forgetting, the current state contains all of the information from the past and present needed to value and make decisions in the present and in the future. In the terminology of the next section, it is the requisite observation for the current action.

There are many situations where DM wants to analyze the decisions of others. Imagine a health care provider deciding whether to offer a screening test. If DM were the patient receiving the test, she might represent the situation using the influence diagram shown in Figure 10.21a, similar to the one in Figure 10.17a. The focus when considering a screening test is typically on the sensitivity and specificity of the test, $P\{Test\ Results | Disorder, \&\}$. However every aspect of the influence diagram matters. What treatment alternatives are available and how effective are they in terms of the health outcomes? What is the prevalence of the disorder, $P\{Disorder | \&\}$? If the DM is not the patient, but rather the health

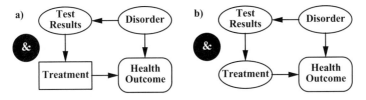

Figure 10.21. Screening for disease.

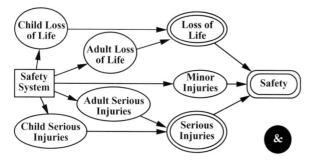

Figure 10.22. Objectives hierarchy for automobile safety.

care provider offering the screening test, then *Treatment* is someone else's choice, not under her control and therefore uncertain, and we get the diagram shown in Figure 10.21b.

The focus in the examples so far has been on the relationships among the uncertain and decision variables, but influence diagrams can be used to capture the structure of preferences as well. Consider the objectives hierarchy for automobile safety (Keeney, 1992) represented by the influence diagram shown in Figure 10.22. This could easily be incorporated into a more complex decision model, harnessing the graphical intuition of the influence diagram for models with multiple attributes and objectives.

Analyzing Decision Models

Although influence diagrams have not yet achieved the popularity of belief networks, they benefit from many of the same improvements in computational power and the development of efficient algorithms (Jensen, Jensen, & Dittmer, 1994; Shachter & Peot, 1992). This section presents some of those algorithms, not in their most efficient implementations, but primarily to gain some intuition for modeling and analysis.

There is a straightforward extension of the Bayes-Ball Algorithm for decisions that explores a structured influence diagram to determine the requisite observations for each decision (Shachter, 1999). Visiting each decision node d_i in reverse chronological order, $i = m, \ldots, 1$, and replacing d_i with a deterministic node with parents $Pa(i) = N^E(V \cap De(d_i) \mid \{d_i\} \cup Pa(d_i)) - \{d_i\}$, the requisite observations for d_i with respect to the values it affects. (Note that if d_i is not in its requisite observation set it can be eliminated, since it has no effect on DM's total value.) At this point, the requisite observations to determine the total value are given by $N^E(V \mid W_0)$. Of course, while gathering the requisite observations, we can also determine the requisite distributions.

As an example of the Bayes-Ball Algorithm for decisions, consider a situation in which both historical data and new experimental evidence about an uncertain state are available to DM in making a decision, and she also chooses which

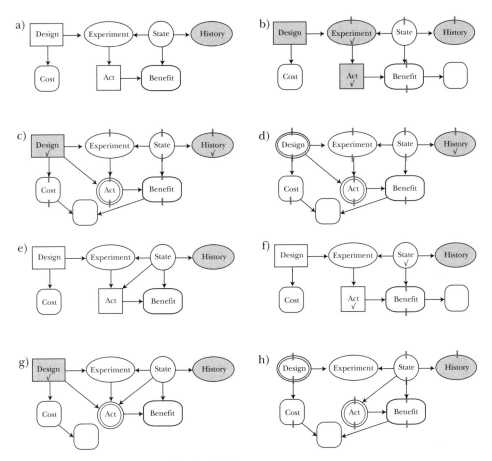

Figure 10.23. Bayes-Ball algorithm for decisions.

evidence to collect. There is a cost of the evidence and a benefit based on her choice and the state. The influence diagram for this situation is shown in Figure 10.23a. Bayes-Ball is run on the *Act* decision, the *Design* decision, and on the situation before the *Design* decision in the diagrams shown in Figures 10.23b, 10.23c, and 10.23d. In this situation all of the variables are requisite.

The same decision situation with clairvoyance on *State* before *Act* is represented by the influence diagram shown in Figure 10.23e and the Bayes-Ball diagrams are shown in Figures 10.23f, 10.23g, and 10.23h. Now the only requisite information to make the optimal choices are the value functions and the *State* observation. Considerably more information is needed to value this decision situation prospectively. In that case the only non-requisite variable is *Experiment*.

The task of analyzing influence diagrams, actually determining the optimal policies, and valuing the decision situation can be accomplished by graphical operations on the diagrams that alter the ordered list and successively remove nodes

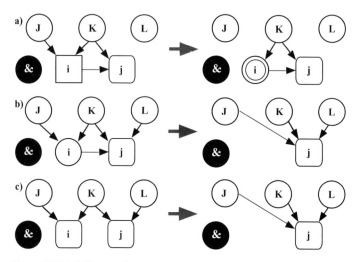

Figure 10.24. Influence diagram operations to remove nodes.

from the diagram. The diagram is reduced until all that remains is a single value node so that we can value the decision situation.

The simplest transformation, barren node removal, can be used at any time that a decision or unobserved uncertain node has no children – at that point, it can be simply removed from the diagram, since it no longer affects the total value. The requisite parent sets for decisions computed by Bayes-Ball can also be used to simplify the problem by eliminating some parents of decisions.

There are three other graphical transformations needed, one to remove decision nodes, one to remove uncertain nodes, and one to remove value variables (when there are multiple value nodes).

When a decision node i has only one child, a value node j, and all of the other parents of the value node are also parents of the decision node, $Pa(i) \supseteq Pa(j) - \{i\}$, then *optimal policy determination* replaces the decision variable with a deterministic variable, as shown in Figure 10.24a. The new deterministic function for node i is given by

$$f_i(x_K \mid \&) = \arg\max_{x_i \in \Omega_i} f_j(x_i, x_K) \text{ for all } x_K \in \Omega_K,$$

where $K = Pa(i) \cap Pa(j) = Pa(j) - \{i\}$. The choice of x_i can be arbitrary when there are ties. This optimal policy should be recorded before it is itself removed. Note that any parents of i that are not parents of j are ignored in choosing the optimal policy and might become barren. (These are all identified by Bayes-Ball.) The other parents of i, given by K, are the requisite observations for i.

When an uncertain node i has only one child, value node j, then *uncertain node removal* removes the node i from the diagram, as shown in Figure 10.24b. The new function for node j is obtained by taking expectation,

$$f_j(X_J, X_K, X_L \mid \&) = \sum_{x_i \in \Omega_i} P\{x_i \mid X_J, X_K, \&\} f_j(x_i, X_K, X_L),$$

where $J = Pa(i) - Pa(j)$, $K = Pa(i) \cap Pa(j)$, and $L = Pa(j) - (\{i\} \cup Pa(i))$. Similarly, when there are multiple value nodes, i and j, *value node removal* removes the node i by replacing the function in node j with their sum, as shown in Figure 10.24c. The new function for node j is given by

$$f_j(X_J, X_K, X_L \mid \&) = f_i(X_J, X_K) + f_j(X_K, X_L).$$

This operation computes the partial sum familiar to dynamic programmers, but it should be delayed as long as possible, so that decisions and uncertain nodes can be removed into smaller value functions, ideally waiting until J or L is the empty set (Tatman & Shachter, 1990).

Given these operations, an influence diagram with no directed cycles and ordered decisions with *no forgetting* can be solved by the following algorithm (Shachter, 1986).

1. If there is a value node with children, turn it into an uncertain node and give it a value node child with value equal to its own.
2. While there are nodes remaining besides those in V or W_0:
   a. If there is a barren node, remove it;
   b. Otherwise, if conditions are satisfied to remove the latest decision then determine its optimal policy;
   c. Otherwise, if there is chance node that is not observed before the latest decision and has at most one value child then remove it, after reversing any arcs to its non-value children in order;
   d. Otherwise, a value node needs to be removed, preferably a descendant of the latest decision.

Many people use influence diagrams to construct their decision models but prefer to solve them using decision trees. The conversion to decision trees is immediate if there are no non-sequential arcs (Howard & Matheson, 1984). An arc is said to be *non-sequential* if it goes from an uncertain node in a later decision window to one in an earlier decision window. Whenever there are such arcs in an influence diagram at least one of them will be reversible (Shachter, 1990). Although it might not be the optimal algorithm, a simple and effective process is to iteratively find reversible non-sequential arcs and reverse them until there are no more non-sequential arcs, and the diagram can be converted to a tree.

Acknowledgments

I am grateful to the many colleagues and students with whom I have learned this subject, the editors and, most especially, Ward Edwards, who was a constant inspiration to all of us working to bring decision analysis "out of the boutique."

REFERENCES

Barza M., and Pauker S. G. (1980). The Decision to Biopsy, Treat, or Wait in Suspected *Herpes encephalitis*. *Annals of Internal Medicine*, 92(5), 641–649.

Capen, E. C., Clapp, R. V., & Campbell, W. M. (1971). Competitive Bidding in High-Risk Situations. *Journal of Petroleum Technology*, *23*(6), 641–653.

Friedman, L. (1956). A Competitive Bidding Strategy. *Operations Research*, *4*(1), 104–112.

Good, I. J. (1961a). A Causal Calculus–I. *British Journal of Philosophy of Science*, *11*, 305–318.

Good, I. J. (1961b). A Causal Calculus–II. *British Journal of Philosophy of Science*, *12*, 43–51.

Heckerman, D., & Shachter, R. (1995). Decision-Theoretic Foundations for Causal Reasoning. *Journal of Artificial Intelligence Research*, *3*, 405–430.

Heckerman, D. E., & Shachter, R. D. (1994). A Decision-Based View of Causality. In R. Lopez de Mantaras & D. Poole (Eds.), *Uncertainty in Artificial Intelligence: Proceedings of the Tenth Conference* (pp. 302–310). San Mateo, CA: Morgan Kaufmann.

Henrion, M., & Druzdzel, M. J. (1990). *Qualitative propagation and scenario-based approaches to explanation of probabiliistic reasoning.* Paper presented at the Sixth Conference on Uncertainty in Artificial Intelligence, Cambridge, MA.

Howard, R. A. (1960). *Dynamic Programming and Markov Processes.* Cambridge, MA: MIT Press.

Howard, R. A. (1990). From Influence to Relevance to Knowledge. In R. M. Oliver & J. Q. Smith (Eds.), *Influence Diagrams, Belief Nets, and Decision Analysis* (pp. 3–23). Chichester: Wiley.

Howard, R. A., & Matheson, J. E. (1984). Influence Diagrams. In R. A. Howard & J. E. Matheson (Eds.), *The Principles and Applications of Decision Analysis* (Vol. II). Menlo Park, CA: Strategic Decisions Group.

Jensen, F., Jensen, F. V., & Dittmer, S. L. (1994). From Influence Diagrams to Junction Trees. In R. Lopez de Mantaras & D. Poole (Eds.), *Uncertainty in Artificial Intelligence: Proceedings of the Tenth Conference* (pp. 367–373). San Mateo, CA: Morgan Kaufmann.

Jensen, F. V., Lauritzen, S. L., & Olesen, K. G. (1990). Bayesian Updating in Causal Probabilistic Networks by Local Computations. *Comp. Stats. Q.*, *4*, 269–282.

Keeney, R. L. (1992). *Value-Focused Thinking.* Cambridge, MA: Harvard University Press.

Kim, J. H., & Pearl, J. (1983). *A computational model for causal and diagnostic reasoning in inference engines.* Paper presented at the 8th International Joint Conference on Artificial Intelligence, Karlsruhe, West Germany.

Lauritzen, S. L., & Spiegelhalter, D. J. (1988). Local Computations with Probabilities on Graphical Structures and Their Application to Expert Systems. *JRSS B*, *50*(2), 157–224.

Matheson, J. E. (1990). Using Influence Diagrams to Value Information and Control. In R. M. Oliver & J. Q. Smith (Eds.), *Influence Diagrams, Belief Nets, and Decision Analysis* (pp. 25–48). Chichester: John Wiley.

Miller, A. C., Merkofer, M. M., Howard, R. A., Matheson, J. E., & Rice, T. R. (1976). *Development of Automated Aids for Decision Analysis*: Stanford Research Institute, Menlo Park, CA.

Pearl, J. (1988). *Probabilistic Reasoning in Intelligent Systems.* San Mateo, CA: Morgan Kaufmann.

Pearl, J. (2000). *Causality: Models, Reasoning, and Inference*: Cambridge University Press.

Raiffa, H. (1968). *Decision Analysis.* Reading, MA: Addison-Wesley.

Shachter, R. D. (1986). Evaluating Influence Diagrams. *Operations Research*, *34*(November–December), 871–882.

Shachter, R. D. (1988). Probabilistic Inference and Influence Diagrams. *Operations Research*, *36*(July–August), 589–605.

Shachter, R. D. (1990). An Ordered Examination of Influence Diagrams. *Networks*, *20*, 535–563.

Shachter, R. D. (1998). Bayes-Ball: The Rational Pastime (for Determining Irrelevance and Requisite Information in Belief Networks and Influence Diagrams). In *Uncertainty in Artificial Intelligence: Proceedings of the Fourteenth Conference* (pp. 480–487). San Francisco, CA: Morgan Kaufmann.

Shachter, R. D. (1999). Efficient Value of Information Computation. In *Uncertainty in Artificial Intelligence: Proceedings of the Fifteenth Conference* (pp. 594–601). San Francisco, CA: Morgan Kaufmann.

Shachter, R. D., & Heckerman, D. E. (1987). Thinking Backwards for Knowledge Acquisition. *AI Magazine, 8*(Fall), 55–61.

Shachter, R. D., & Peot, M. A. (1992). Decision Making Using Probabilistic Inference Methods. In *Uncertainty in Artificial Intelligence: Proceedings of the Eighth Conference* (pp. 276–283). San Mateo, CA: Morgan Kaufmann.

Shenoy, P. P., & Shafer, G. (1990). Axioms for Probability and Belief-Function Propagation. In R. D. Shachter, T. S. Levitt, J. F. Lemmer & L. N. Kanal (Eds.), *Uncertainty in Artificial Intelligence 4* (pp. 169–198). Amsterdam: North-Holland.

Tatman, J. A., & Shachter, R. D. (1990). Dynamic Programming and Influence Diagrams. *IEEE Transactions on Systems, Man, and Cybernetics, 20*(2), 365–379.

Wright, S. (1921). Correlation and Causation. *Journal of Agricultural Research, 20,* 557–585.

Wright, S. (1934). The Method of Path Coefficients. *Annals of Mathematical Statistics, 5,* 161–215.

11 A Bayesian Approach to Learning Causal Networks

David Heckerman

ABSTRACT. Bayesian methods have been developed for learning Bayesian networks from data. Most of this work has concentrated on Bayesian networks interpreted as a representation of probabilistic conditional independence without considering causation. Other researchers have shown that having a causal interpretation can be important because it allows us to predict the effects of interventions in a domain. In this chapter, we extend Bayesian methods for learning acausal Bayesian networks to causal Bayesian networks.

There has been a great deal of recent interest in Bayesian methods for learning Bayesian networks from data (Spiegelhalter and Lauritzen 1990; Cooper and Herskovits 1991, 1992; Buntine 1991, 1994; Spiegelhalter, Dawid, Lauritzen and Cowell 1993; Madigan and Raftery 1994; Heckerman et al. 1994, 1995). These methods take prior knowledge of a domain and statistical data and construct one or more Bayesian-network models of the domain. Most of this work has concentrated on Bayesian networks interpreted as a representation of probabilistic conditional independence. Nonetheless, several researchers have proposed a causal interpretation for Bayesian networks (Pearl and Verma 1991; Spirtes, Glymour, and Scheines 1993; Heckerman and Shachter 1995). These researchers show that having a causal interpretation can be important because it allows us to predict the effects of interventions in a domain – something that cannot be done without a causal interpretation.

In this paper, we extend Bayesian methods for learning acausal Bayesian networks to causal Bayesian-networks learning. We offer two contributions. First, we show that acausal and causal Bayesian networks (or acausal and causal networks, for short) are significantly different in their semantics and that it is inappropriate blindly to apply methods for learning acausal networks to causal networks. Second, despite these differences, we identify circumstances in which methods for learning acausal networks are applicable to learning causal networks.

In the Causal Networks section, we describe a causal interpretation of Bayesian networks developed by Heckerman and Shachter (1995) that is consistent with Pearl's causal-theory interpretation (e.g., Pearl and Verma 1991; Pearl 1995). We show that any causal network can be represented as a special type of influence diagram. In the Learning Acausal Networks section, we review Bayesian methods for learning acausal networks. We emphasize two common assumptions and one property for learning network structure that greatly simplify the learning task. One assumption is *parameter independence*, which says that the parameters associated with each node in an acausal network are independent. The other assumption is *parameter modularity*, which says that if a node has the same parents in two distinct networks, then the probability distributions for the parameters associated with this node are identical in both networks. The property is *hypothesis equivalence*, which says that two network structures that represent the same assertions of conditional independence correspond to the same random-sample assumption.

In the Learning Influence Diagrams section, we show how methods for learning acausal networks can be adapted to learn ordinary influence diagrams. In the Learning Causal-Network Parameters section, we identify problems with this approach when learning influence diagrams that correspond to causal networks. We identify two assumptions, *mechanism independence* and *component independence,* which circumvent these problems. In the Learning Causal-Network Structure section, we argue that the assumption of *parameter modularity* is also reasonable for learning causal networks. Also, we argue that although the assumption of *hypothesis equivalence* is inappropriate for causal networks, we can often assume *likelihood equivalence*, which says that data cannot help to discriminate causal network structures that are equivalent when interpreted as acausal networks. Given the assumptions of parameter independence, parameter modularity, likelihood equivalence, mechanism independence, and component independence, we show that methods for learning acausal networks can be used to learn causal networks.

We assume that the reader is familiar with the concept of a random sample, the distinction between epistemic uncertainty based on lack of knowledge and aleatory uncertainty based on variability in the environment and the distinction between *chance variables* and *decision variables*. We will refer to probabilities characterizing epistemic uncertainty simply as p and we will refer to probabilities characterizing aleatory uncertainty as ap. We sometimes refer to a decision variable simply as a "decision." We consider the problem of modeling relationships in a domain consisting of chance variables U and decision variables D. We use lower-case letters to represent single variables and uppercase letters to represent sets of variables. We write $x = k$ to denote that variable x is in state k. When we observe the state for every variable in set X, we call this set of observations a state of X, and write $X = k$. Sometimes, we leave the state of a variable or a set of variables implicit. We use $p(X = j | Y = k, \xi)$ to denote the (subjective) probability that $X = j$ given $Y = k$ for a person whose state of information is ξ; whereas we use $ap(X = j | Y = k)$ to denote the aleatory probability of this conditional event.

An *influence diagram* for the domain $U \cup D$ is a model for that domain having a structural component and a probabilistic component. The *structure* of an influence diagram is a directed acyclic graph containing (square) decision and (oval) chance nodes corresponding to decision and chance variables, respectively, as well as information and relevance arcs. Information arcs, which point to decision nodes, represent what is known at the time decisions are made. Relevance arcs, which point to chance nodes, represent (by their absence) assertions of conditional independence. Associated with each chance node x in an influence diagram are the probability distributions $p(x | Pa(x), \xi)$, where $Pa(x)$ are the parents of x in

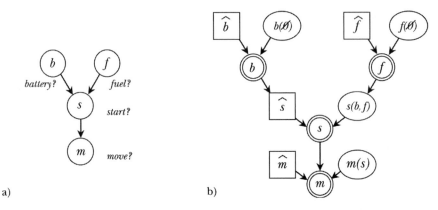

Figure 11.1. (a) A causal network. (b) A corresponding influence diagram. (Double ovals denote deterministic nodes.)

the diagram. These distributions, in combination with the assertions of conditional independence, determine the joint distributions $p(U|D, \xi)$. A special kind of chance node is the deterministic node (depicted as a double oval). A node x is a *deterministic node* if its corresponding variable is a deterministic function of its parents. Also, an influence diagram may contain a single distinguished node, called a *utility node* that encodes the decision maker's utility for each state of the node's parents. A utility node is a deterministic function of its predecessors and can have no children. Finally, for an influence diagram to be well formed, its decisions must be totally ordered by the influence-diagram structure (for more details, see Howard and Matheson 1981).

An *acausal Bayesian network* is an influence diagram that contains no decision nodes (and, therefore, no information arcs). That is, an acausal Bayesian network represents only assertions of conditional independence (for more details, see Pearl 1988).

Causal Networks

In this section, we describe causal Bayesian networks and how we can represent them as influence diagrams. The influence-diagram representation that we describe is identical to Pearl's causal theory, with one exception to be discussed. Rather than present the representation directly, we follow the approach of Heckerman and Shachter (1995) who define cause and effect, and then develop from this definition the influence-diagram representation of causal networks.

Roughly speaking, a causal network for a domain of chance variables U is a directed acyclic graph where nodes correspond to the chance variables in U and each nonroot node is the direct causal effect of its parents (Pearl and Verma 1991). An example of a causal network is shown in Figure 11.1a and the corresponding influence diagram is shown in Figure 11.1b.

The diagram indicates that whether or not a car starts is caused by the condition of its battery and fuel supply, that whether or not a car moves is caused by whether or not it starts, and that (in this model) the condition of the battery and the fuel supply have no causes. In this example, we assume that all variables are binary. Before we develop the influence-diagram representation of a causal network, we need to introduce the concepts of *unresponsiveness*, *set decision*, *mapping variable*, *cause*, *causal mechanism*, and *canonical form*. To understand the notion of unresponsiveness, consider the simple decision d of whether or not to bet heads or tails on the outcome of a coin toss c. Let the variable w represent whether or not we win. Thus, w is a deterministic function of d and c: we win, if and only if, the outcome of the coin matches our bet. Let us assume that the coin is fair (i.e., $p(heads|\xi) = 1/2$), and that the person who tosses the coin does not know how we bet. In this example, we are uncertain whether or not the coin will come up heads, but we are certain that whatever the outcome, it will be the same even if we choose to bet differently. We say that c is unresponsive to d. We cannot make the same claim about the relationship between d and w. Namely, we know that w depends on d in the sense that if we bet differently then w will be different. For example, we know that if we will win by betting heads then we will lose by betting tails. We say that w is responsive to d.

In general, to determine whether or not chance variable x is unresponsive to decision d, we have to answer the query: "will the outcome of x be the same no matter how we choose d?" Queries of this form are a simple type of counterfactual query, discussed in the philosophical literature. It is interesting that, in many cases, it is easy to answer such a query, even though we are uncertain about the outcome of x. Note that when x is unresponsive to d, x and d must be probabilistically independent; whereas, the converse does not hold.

To understand the concept of a set decision, consider the chance variable *battery?* in our automobile example. Let us assume that it has only two states: "good" and "bad." Although *battery?* is a chance variable, we can imagine taking an action that will force the variable into one of its possible states. If this action has no side effects on the other variables in the model other than those required by the causal interactions in the domain, we say that we are setting the variable. For example, we can force the battery to fail by blowing up the car. This action, however, will also force the variable *fuel?* to become empty, and therefore does not qualify as a setting of *battery?* In contrast, if we force the battery to fail by emptying the battery fluid on the ground, the only side effects will be those that follow from the causal interactions in the domain. Therefore, this action qualifies as a setting of *battery?* We can extend the idea of setting a variable to a decision variable. Namely, we set a decision variable simply by choosing one of its alternatives.

A set decision for chance variable x, denoted $\hat{x}$, is a decision variable whose alternatives are "set x to k" for each state k of x and "do nothing." In our example, the set decision corresponding *battery?* has three alternatives: "set the battery to be good," "set the battery to be bad," and "do nothing." Pearl and Verma (1991) introduce the concepts of setting a variable and set decision as primitives. Heckerman and Shachter (1995) formalize these concepts in terms of unresponsiveness.

Table 11.1. The four states of one mapping variable $m(s)$

	State 1		State 2		State 3		State 4	
Start	no	yes	no	yes	no	yes	no	yes
Move	no	yes	no	no	yes	yes	yes	no

To understand the concept of a mapping variable, suppose we have a collection of variables Y (which may include both chance and decision variables) and a chance variable x. We can imagine setting Y to each of its states and observing x – that is, observing how Y maps to x. A *mapping variable* $x(Y)$ is a chance variable whose states correspond to all the possible mappings from Y to x. For example, consider the variables s (start?) and m (move?) in our automobile example. The states of the mapping variable $m(s)$ are shown in Table 11.1.

The first state represents the normal situation. That is, if we make the car start (in the sense of a set action), then it would move; and if we prevent the car from starting, then it would not move. The second state represents the situation where, regardless of whether or not we make the car start, the car not will move. This state would occur, for example, if a parking attendant placed a restraint on one of the car's tires. Note that, by definition, x will always be a deterministic function of the mapping variable $x(Y)$ and the variables Y. For example, if $m(s) = $ "state 4" and $s = $ "yes," then $m = $ "no."

We can observe the mapping variable $m(s)$ directly. Namely, we can see if the car moves before and after we start the car. In general, however, mapping variables cannot be fully observed. For example, consider the decision x of whether to continue or quit smoking and the chance variable y representing whether or not we get lung cancer before we reach 60 years of age. In this case, we cannot fully observe the mapping variable $y(x)$ because we cannot observe whether or not we get lung cancer given both possible choices. In general, a mapping variable represents a counterfactual set of possible outcomes, only one of which we can actually observe. Rubin (1978), Howard (1990), and Matheson (1990) define concepts similar to the mapping variable.

Given these concepts, Heckerman and Shachter (1995) say that a set of variables C are causes for x with respect to decisions D if (1) $x \notin C$ and (2) C is a minimal set of variables such that $x(C)$ is unresponsive to D. Roughly speaking, C is a cause for x with respect to D if the way C affects x is not affected by D. This explication of cause is unusual in that it is conditioned on a set of decisions. Heckerman and Shachter discuss the advantages of this approach. When C are causes of x with respect to D, we call the mapping variable $x(C)$ a causal mechanism or simply a mechanism.

Given chance variables U and decisions D, Heckerman and Shachter show that we can construct an influence diagram that represents causes for each caused variable in U as follows. First, we add a node to the diagram corresponding to each variable in $U \cup D$. Next, we order the variables $x_1, \ldots, x_n$ in U so that the variables unresponsive to D comes first. Then, for each variable x_i in U in order, if x_i is responsive to D we (1) add a causal-mechanism node $x_i(C_i)$ to the diagram, where $C_i \subseteq D \cup \{x_1, \ldots, x_{i-1}\}$, and (2) make x_i a deterministic function of $C_i \cup x_i(C_i)$. Finally, we assess dependencies among the variables that are unresponsive D. They show that the resulting influence diagram has the following two properties: (1) all chance nodes that are responsive to D are descendants of decision nodes; and (2) all nodes that are descendants of decision nodes are deterministic nodes. Influence diagrams that satisfy these conditions are said to be in canonical form. We note that information arcs and a utility node may be added to canonical form influence diagrams, but these constructs are not needed for the representation of cause and are not used in this discussion.

We can use an influence diagram in canonical form to represent the causal relationships depicted in a causal network. Suppose we have a set of chance variables U, a corresponding collection of set decisions $\hat{U}$ for U, and a causal network for U. Let $Pa(x)$ be the parents of x in the causal network. Then, we can interpret the causal network to mean that, for all x, $Pa(x) \cup \{\hat{x}\}$ is a set of causes for x with respect $\hat{U}$. Now, if we construct an influence diagram in canonical form as we have described, using an ordering consistent with the causal network, then we obtain an influence diagram where each variable x is a deterministic function of the set decision $\hat{x}$, $Pa(x)$, and the causal mechanism $x(Pa(x), \hat{x})$. By the definition of a set decision, we can simplify the deterministic relationship by replacing the causal mechanism $x(Pa(x), \hat{x})$ with $x(Pa(x))$, which denotes the mappings from $Pa(x)$ to x when $\hat{x}$ is set to "do nothing." For example, in our automobile domain, if $m(s) =$ state 4, $\hat{s} =$ "do nothing," and $s =$ yes, then $m = no$.

The transformation from causal network to canonical form influence diagram for our automobile domain is illustrated in Figure 11.1. We call the variables in the original causal network domain variables. Each domain variable appears in the influence diagram, and is a function of its set decision $\hat{x}$, its parents in the causal network $Pa(x)$, and the mapping variable $x(Pa(x))$. (Note that $x(\phi) = x$ when $\hat{x} =$ "do nothing.") The mechanisms and set decisions are independent because, as is required by canonical form, the mechanisms are unresponsive to the set decisions. Although not required by the canonical-form representation, the mechanisms are mutually independent in this example.

In general, this influence-diagram representation of a causal network is identical to Pearl's causal theory, with the exception that Pearl requires the mechanisms (which he calls disturbances) to be independent. One desirable consequence of this restriction is that the variables in the causal network will exhibit the conditional independencies that we would obtain by interpreting the causal network as an acausal network (Spirtes et al. 1993; Pearl 1995). For example, the independence of causal mechanisms in our example yields the following conditional independencies:

$$p(f|b, \xi) = p(f|\xi) \qquad p(m|b, f, s, \xi) = p(m|s, \xi).$$

We obtain these same independencies when we interpret the causal network in Figure 11.1a as an acausal network. Nonetheless, as we will illustrate, dependent mechanisms cannot be excluded in general.

Learning Acausal Networks

Given the correspondence in the previous section, we see that learning causal networks is a special case of learning influence diagrams in canonical form. In this section, we review methods for learning acausal Bayesian networks, such as those described by Spiegelhalter and Lauritzen (1990), Cooper and Herskovits (1991, 1992), Buntine (1991, 1994), Spiegelhalter et al. (1993), Madigan and Raftery (1994), and Heckerman et al. (1994, 1995). In the following sections, we show how these methods can be extended to learn arbitrary influence diagrams and influence diagrams in canonical form.

Suppose we have a domain consisting of chance variables $U = \{x_1, \ldots, x_n\}$. Also, suppose we have a database of cases $C = \{C_1, \ldots, C_m\}$ where each case C_l contains observations of one or more variables in U. The basic assumption underlying the Bayesian approach is that the database C is a random sample from U with joint aleatory probability distribution $ap(U)$. As is done traditionally, we can characterize this aleatory probability distribution by a unite set of parameters Θ_U. For example, if U contains only continuous variables, $ap(U)$ may be a multivariate-Gaussian distribution with parameters specifying the distribution's means and covariances. In this paper, we limit our discussion to domains containing only discrete variables. Therefore, the parameters Θ_U correspond exactly to the aleatory probabilities in the distribution $ap(U)$. (We will use the Θ and ap notation interchangeably.)

In the general Bayesian approach to learning about these uncertain parameters, we assess prior distributions for them, and then compute their posterior distributions given the database. In the paradigm of learning acausal Bayesian networks, we add one twist to this general approach: we assume that the aleatory probability distribution $ap(U)$ is constrained such that it can be encoded in some acausal-network structure whose identity is possibly uncertain.

To start with a special case, let us suppose that $ap(U)$ can be encoded in some known acausal-network structure B_s, and that we are uncertain only about the values of the probabilities associated with this network structure. We say that *the database is a random sample from B_s*. Given this situation, it turns out the database C can be separated into a set of random samples, where these random samples are determined by the structure of B_s. For example, consider the domain consisting of two variables x, where each variable has possible states 0 and 1. Then, the assertion that the database is a random sample from the structure $x \rightarrow y$ is equivalent to the assertion that the database can be separated into at most three random samples: (1) the observations of x are a binomial sample with parameter $\Theta_{x=1}$; (2) the observations of y in those cases (if any) where $x = 0$ are a binomial sample with parameter $\Theta_{y=1|x=0}$; and (3) the observations of y in those cases (if any) where $y = 1$ are a binomial sample with parameter $\Theta_{y=1|x=1}$. Figure 11.2a contains an acausal network that illustrates some of the conditional independencies among the database cases and network parameters for this assertion, and Figure 11.2b adds the additional assumption of parameter independence.

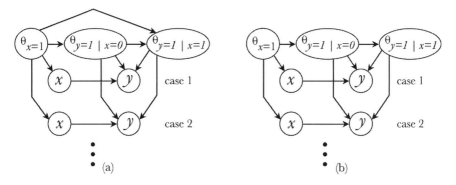

Figure 11.2. (a) Conditional independencies associated with the assertion that the database is a random sample from the structure $x \rightarrow y$, where x and y are binary. (b) The additional assumption of parameter independence.

Given this decomposition into random samples, it is tempting to update each parameter separately. Unfortunately, this approach is not correct when the parameters are dependent as shown in the figure. For example, as we observe instances of x and update our beliefs about $\Theta_{x=1}$, our beliefs about $\Theta_{y=1|x=0}$ and $\Theta_{y=1|x=1}$ may also change. If all of the parameters are independent as shown in Figure 11.2b, however, we can update each parameter separately under certain circumstances. We call this assumption *parameter independence*.

Let us examine this updating for an arbitrary acausal-network structure B_s for domain U. Let r_i be the number of states of variable x_i; and let $q_i = \prod_{x_l \in Pa(x_i)} r_l$ be the number of states of $Pa(x_i)$. Let θ_{ijk} denote the parameter corresponding to the aleatory probability $p(x_i = k \mid Pa(x_i) = j, \xi)(\theta_{ijk} > 0; \sum_{k=1}^{\eta} \theta_{ijk} = 1)$. In addition, we define

$$\Theta_{ij} \equiv \bigcup_{k=1}^{r_i} \{\theta_{ijk}\}, \qquad \Theta_{B_s} \equiv \bigcup_{i=1}^{n} \bigcup_{j=1}^{q_i} \Theta_{ij}.$$

That is, the parameters Θ_{B_s} correspond to the aleatory probabilities of the acausal-network structure B_s.

Under the assumption that the database is *complete,* that is every variable is observed in every case, it is not difficult to show that if parameters are independent a priori, then they remain independent given a database. Consequently, we can update each parameter set Θ_{ij} independently. For example, suppose that each variable set Θ_{ij} has a Dirichlet distribution:

$$p\left(\Theta_{ij} \mid B_s^h, \xi\right) = c \cdot \prod_{k=1}^{r_i} \theta_{ijk}^{N'_{ijk}-1}, \tag{11.1}$$

where B_s^h is the assertion (or "hypothesis") that the database is a random sample from the network structure B_s, and c is some normalization constant. Then, if N_{ijk} is the number of cases in database C in which $x_i = k$ and $Pa(x_i) = j$, we obtain

$$p\left(\Theta_{ij} \mid C, B_s^h, \xi\right) = c \cdot \prod_{k} \theta_{ijk}^{N'_{ijk}+N_{ijk}-1}, \tag{11.2}$$

where c is some other normalization constant. Furthermore, taking the expectation of θ_{ijk} with respect to the distribution for Θ_{ij} for every i and j, we obtain the probability that each $x_i = k$ and $Pa(x_i) = j$ in C_{m+1} (the next case C_{m+1} to be seen after seeing the database):

$$p(C_{m+1}|C, B_s^h, \xi) = \prod_{i=1}^{n} \prod_{j=1}^{q_i} \frac{N'_{ijk} + N_{ijk}}{N'_{ij} + N_{ij}}, \tag{11.3}$$

where $N'_{ij} = \sum_{k=1}^{r_i} N'_{ijk}$ and $N_{ij} = \sum_{k=1}^{r_i} N_{ijk}$. We discuss the situation where the database C contains missing data in the following paragraph.

Now, suppose we are not only uncertain about the probabilities, but also uncertain about the structure that encodes them. We express this uncertainty by assigning a prior probability $p(B_s^h|\xi)$ to each possible hypothesis B_s^h, and update these probabilities as we see cases. In so doing, we learn about the structure of the domain. From Bayes' theorem, we have

$$p(B_s^h|C, \xi) = c \cdot p(B_s^h|\xi) p(C|B_s^h, \xi), \tag{11.4}$$

where c is a normalization constant. Also, from the product rule, we have

$$p(C|B_s^h, \xi) = \prod_{l=1}^{m} p(C_l|C_1, \dots, C_{l-1}, B_s^h, \xi). \tag{11.5}$$

We can evaluate each term on the right-hand-side of this equation using Eq. 11.3, under the assumption that the database C is complete. For the posterior probability of B_s^h given C, we obtain

$$p(B_s^h|C, \xi) = c \cdot p(B_s^h|\xi) \cdot \prod_{i=1}^{n} \prod_{j=1}^{q_i} \frac{\Gamma(N'_{ij})}{\Gamma(N'_{ij} + N_{ij})} \cdot \prod_{k=1}^{r_i} \frac{\Gamma(N'_{ijk} + N_{ijk})}{\Gamma(N'_{ijk})}. \tag{11.6}$$

Using these posterior probabilities and Eq. 11.3, we can compute the probability distribution for the next case to be observed after we have seen a database. From the expansion rule, we obtain

$$p(C_{m+1}|C, \xi) = \sum_{B_s^h} p(C_{m+1}|C, B_s^h, \xi) p(B_s^h|C, \xi). \tag{11.7}$$

When the database contains missing data, we can compute $p(B_s^h|C, \xi)$ exactly, by summing the result of Eq. 11.5 over all possible completions of the database (see the Learning Hidden Variables section). Unfortunately, this approach is intractable when many observations are missing. Consequently, we often use approximate methods such as filling in missing data based on the data that is present (Titterington 1976; Cowell et al. 1995), the EM algorithm (Dempster et al. 1977), and Gibbs sampling (York 1992; Madigan and Raftery 1994).

When we believe that only a few network structures are possible, the approach we have discussed is essentially all there is to learning network structure. Namely, we directly assess the priors for the possible network structures and their parameters, and subsequently use Eqs. 11.3 and 11.6 or their generalizations for continuous variables and missing data. Nonetheless, the number of network structures for a domain containing n variables is more than exponential in n. Consequently, when we cannot exclude almost all of these network structures, there are several issues that must be considered. In particular, computational constraints can prevent us from summing over all the hypotheses in Eq. 11.3. Can we approximate $p(C_{m+1}|D, \xi)$ accurately by retaining only a small fraction of these hypotheses in the sum? If so, which hypotheses should we include? In addition, how can we efficiently assign prior probabilities to the many network structures and their parameters?

Rather remarkably, it has been shown experimentally that if we retain one or a few of the more likely network structures in Eq. 11.3, then we can accurately approximate $p(C_{m+1}|D, \xi)$ (e.g., Cooper and Herskovits 1992; Aliferis and Cooper 1994; and Heckerman et al. 1995). In practice, when many structures are possible, we use heuristic search methods to identify network structures with high relative posterior probabilities (see, e.g., Cooper and Herskovits 1992; Heckerman et al. 1995).

Several researchers have described simple and efficient methods for assigning prior probabilities to network structures (e.g., Buntine 1991; Heckerman et al. 1995). Here, we present an efficient method described by Heckerman et al. 1995 for the more difficult task of assigning priors to the parameters of all possible network structures. In their approach, a user assesses a prior network: an acausal Bayesian network for the first case to be seen in database, under the assumption that there are no constraints on the parameters. More formally, this prior network represents the joint probability distribution $p(C_1|B_{sc}^h, \xi)$, where B_{sc} is any network structure containing no missing arcs. Then, the user assesses an equivalent sample size N' for this prior network. (N' is a measure of the user's confidence in his assessment of the prior network.) Then, for any given network structure B_s, where x_i has parents $Pa(x_i)$, we compute the Dirichlet exponents in Eq. 11.1 using the relation:

$$N'_{ijk} = N' \cdot p(x_i = k, \, Pa(x_i) = j|B_{sc}^h, \xi), \qquad (11.8)$$

where the probability is computed from the prior network.

Heckerman et al. (1995) derive this approach from the assumption of parameter independence, an additional assumption called *parameter modularity*, and a property called *hypothesis equivalence*. The property of hypothesis equivalence stems from the fact that two acausal-network structures can be *equivalent* – that is, represent exactly the same sets of probability distributions (Verma and Pearl 1990). For example, for the three variable domain $\{x, y, z\}$, each of the network structures $x \rightarrow y \rightarrow z, x \leftarrow y \rightarrow z$, and $x \leftarrow y \leftarrow z$ represents the distributions where x and z are conditionally independent of y, and are therefore equivalent. Given the definition of the hypothesis B_s^h, it follows that the hypotheses corresponding to two equivalent structures must be the same, which is the property of hypothesis equivalence.

The assumption of parameter modularity says that, given two network structures B_{s1} and B_{s2}, if x_i has the same parents in B_{s1} and B_{s2}, then

$$p(\Theta_{ij}|B_{s1}^h, \xi) = p(\Theta_{ij}|B_{s2}^h, \xi),$$

for $j = 1, \ldots, q_i$. Heckerman et al. (1995) call this property *parameter modularity* because it says that the distributions for parameters Θ_{ij} depend only on the structure of the network that is local to variable x_i – namely, Θ_{ij} only depends on x_i and its parents. In the Learning Causal-Network Structure section, we examine the appropriateness of hypothesis equivalence and parameter modularity for learning causal networks.

Learning Influence Diagrams

Before we consider the problem of learning influence diagrams that correspond to causal networks, let us examine the task of learning arbitrary influence diagrams.

   This task is straightforward once we make the following observations. One, by the definitions of information arc and utility node, information arcs, and the predecessors of a utility node are known with certainty by the decision maker and, therefore, are not learned. Thus, we need only learn the relevance-arc structure and the aleatory probabilities associated with chance nodes. Two, by definition of a decision, the states of all decision variables are known by the decision maker in every case. Thus, assuming these decisions are recorded, we have complete data for D in every case of the database.

   Given these observations, it follows that the problem of learning influence diagrams for the domain $U \cup D$ reduces to the problem of learning acausal Bayesian networks for $U \cup D$, where we interpret the decision variables D as chance variables. The only caveat is that the learned relevance-arc structures will be constrained by the influence-diagram semantics. In particular, a relevance-arc structure is eligible to be learned (i.e., has a corresponding hypothesis that can have a nonzero prior) if and only if (1) every node in D is a root node, and (2) that structure when combined with the information-arc structure declared by the decision maker contains no directed cycles. (Note that both of these constraints are satisfied by canonical-form representations of causal networks.)

Learning Causal-Network Parameters

In this section, we consider aspects of learning influence diagrams peculiar to influence diagrams in canonical form. In this discussion, we assume that the structure of the influence diagram is known, and that we need to learn only the parameters of the structure.

   One difficulty associated with learning influence diagrams in canonical form occurs in domains where we can set variables only once (or a small number of times) so that the mechanisms are not fully observable. For example, recall our decision to continue or quit smoking where x denotes our decision and y denotes whether or not we get lung cancer before the age of sixty. In this case, we cannot fully observe the mapping variable $y(x)$ because we cannot observe whether or not we get lung cancer for both possible choices. Given any one choice for x and observation of y, we exclude only two of the four states of $y(x)$. Consequently, it would seem that learning about $y(x)$ would be difficult, if not impossible.

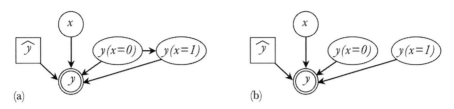

Figure 11.3. (a) A decomposition of the mapping variable $y(x)$. (b) The assumption of component independence.

We can understand this difficulty in another way. Given any mapping variable $y(x)$ where X has q states, we can decompose $y(X)$ into a set of variables $y(X = k_1), \ldots, y(X = k_q)$, where variable $y(X = k)$ represents the variable y when X is set to state k. We call these variables *mechanism components*. For example, Figure 11.3a illustrates the components of the mechanism variable $y(x)$, where x is a binary variable. Note that, by the definition of a mechanism component, we have

$$ap(y(X = k)) = ap(y|X = k). \tag{11.9}$$

An analogous equation holds for (subjective) probabilities.

Given this decomposition, the setting of X and the observation of y is equivalent to the observation of exactly one of the components of $y(X)$. Thus, if we can set X only once, as in the smoking example, we cannot observe multiple mechanism components. Consequently, we cannot learn about the aleatory probabilities that characterize the dependencies among the components. Holland (1986) calls this problem, albeit in a different mathematical formalism, the "fundamental problem with causal inference."

To circumvent this problem, we can assume that mechanism components are independent, an assumption we call *component independence*,[1] illustrated in Figure 11.3b. If this assumption is incorrect, then we will not learn correct counterfactual relationships. Regardless of the assumption's correctness, however, we can correctly quantify the effects of a single setting action.

For example, in the smoking decision, the mechanism components are clearly dependent: Knowing that we quit and got lung cancer $(y(x = 0) = 1)$ makes it more likely that we would have gotten lung cancer had we continued $(y(x = 1) = 1)$. Nonetheless, suppose we assume the components are independent and learn the aleatory probabilities from a database of cases. Then, although we learn incorrect counterfactual relationships – namely, that $y(x = 0)$ and $y(x = 1)$ are independent – we can still learn the correct marginal aleatory probabilities associated with both mechanism components. Thus, by Eq. 11.9, we can learn the correct aleatory probability that that we will get cancer if we continue to smoke as well as the correct aleatory probability of cancer if we quit smoking.

---

[1] We note that, from Eq. 11.9, under the assumption of component independence, we can fill in the probability tables associated with the canonical-form representation of a causal network by copying the probabilities associated with that causal network. Without this assumption, the canonical-form representation requires additional probability assessments.

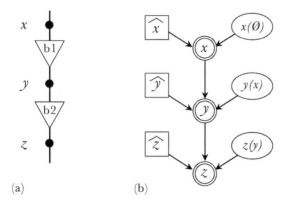

Figure 11.4. (a) A logic circuit containing two buffers in series. (b) A causal network for the circuit, represented as an influence diagram in canonical form.

A second complication with learning influence diagrams in canonical form is the possible dependency among different mechanisms. For example, suppose we model the voltages in a logic circuit containing two buffers in series as shown in Figure 11.4a. Here, x and z represent the input and output voltages of the circuit, respectively, and y represents the voltage between the two buffers. The causal network for this circuit is $x \to y \to z$. The corresponding influence diagram in canonical form is shown in Figure 11.4b. The causal mechanism $y(x)$ represents the possible mappings from the input to the output of the first buffer. The possible states of $y(x)$ are "output normal," "output always zero," "output always one," and "output inverted." That is, this causal mechanism is a representation of the working status of the buffer. Similarly, the mapping variable $z(y)$ represents the working status of the second buffer. Thus, these mechanisms will be dependent whenever buffer function is dependent – for example, when it is possible for the circuit to overheat and cause both buffers to fail.

Dependent mechanisms lead to practical problems. Namely, given the large number of states typically associated with mapping variables, the assessment of priors is difficult, and we require vast amounts of data to learn. Fortunately, we can often introduce additional domain variables in order to render mechanisms independent. In our circuit example, if we add to our domain the variable t representing the temperature of the circuit, then the new mechanisms $y(x, t)$ and $z(y, t)$ will be independent. This solution sometimes creates another problem with learning: we may not be able to observe the variables that we introduce. We address this issue in the Learning Hidden Variables section.

Given mechanism independence and component independence for all mechanisms, the only chance variables that remain in a canonical form influence diagram are mutually independent mechanism components. Consequently, if we also assume parameter independence, then the problem of learning a causal network essentially reduces that of learning an acausal network.

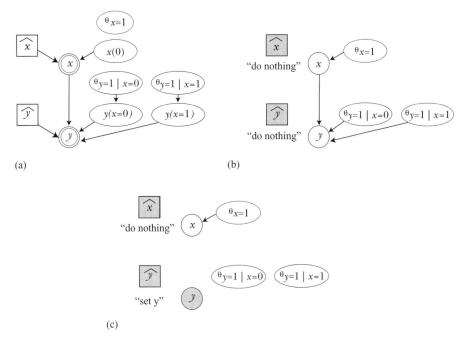

Figure 11.5. (a) Mechanism independence, component independence, and parameter independence associated with the causal network $x \rightarrow y$. (b, c) Corresponding diagrams when (b) $\hat{x}$ and $\hat{y}$ are "do nothing" and (c) $\hat{x} =$ "do nothing" and $\hat{y} \neq$ "do nothing."

To illustrate this equivalence, consider again our two binary-variable domain, and assume that the database is a random sample from an influence diagram corresponding to the causal network $x \rightarrow y$. Given the assumptions of mechanism, component, and parameter independence, we have the influence diagram in Figure 11.5a, where the deterministic functions for x and y are given by

$$x = x(\phi) \text{ if } \hat{x} = \text{"do nothing," or } x = k \text{ if } \hat{x} = \text{"set } x \text{ to } k\text{"}$$

and

$$y = y(x = j), \text{ if } \hat{y} = \text{ "do nothing," and } x = j, \text{ or } y = k \text{ if } \hat{y} = \text{ "set } y \text{ to } k\text{"}$$

by the definitions of set decision and mechanism component.

Now, suppose that all the set decisions are "do nothing." In this situation, if we integrate out the mechanism variables from the diagram (Shachter, 1986), then we obtain the influence diagram shown in Figure 11.5b. This structure is equivalent to the one shown in Figure 11.2b for learning the acausal network $x \rightarrow y$. Thus, we can update the parameters of the causal network $x \rightarrow y$ just as we can update those for the corresponding acausal network.

This result generalizes to arbitrary causal networks. In particular, if all set decisions in a particular case C_l are "do nothing," we say that observations of the domain variables in C_l are *nonexperimental data*. Otherwise, we say that the observations are *experimental data*. Given a case of nonexperimental data, we update the parameters of a causal network just as we would update the parameters of the corresponding acausal network (assuming mechanism, component, and parameter independence).

The updating procedure for experimental data is slightly different from that for nonexperimental data. In our two-variable example, if we set y and observe x (with $\hat{x}$ set to "do nothing"), then we obtain the influence diagram shown in Figure 11.5c. Here, the arcs to y are removed because we have set the variable y. Consequently, neither $\theta_{y=1|x=0}$ nor $\theta_{y=1|x=1}$ are updated given this data. In general, to update the parameters for a canonical form influence diagram given experimental data where we have set x_i, we break all arcs to x_i, and update the parameters as we would for an acausal network.

Learning Causal-Network Structure

In the Learning Acausal Networks section, we saw that, given the assumptions of parameter independence, parameter modularity, and hypothesis equivalence, we can assess priors for the parameters of all possible acausal-network structures by constructing a single prior network for the first case to be seen in the database and assessing an equivalent sample size (confidence) for this prior network. Thus, given the discussion in the previous section, it follows that we can use this prior-network methodology to establish priors for causal-network learning, provided we assume mechanism independence, component independence, parameter independence, parameter modularity, and hypothesis equivalence. In this section, we examine the assumptions of parameter modularity and likelihood equivalence for learning causal networks.

The assumption of parameter modularity has a compelling justification in the context of causal networks. Namely, suppose a domain variable x has the same parents $Pa(x)$ in two possible causal-network structures. Then, it is reasonable to believe that the causal mechanism $x(Pa(x))$ should be the same given either structure. It follows that its parameters $\Theta_{x|Pa(x)}$ for both structures must have the same prior distributions – that is, parameter modularity must hold.

In contrast, the property of hypothesis equivalence cannot be applied to causal networks. For example, in our two-variable domain, the causal network $x \rightarrow y$ represents the assertion that x causes y, whereas the causal network $y \rightarrow x$ represents the assertion that y causes x. Now, it is possible for both x to cause y and vice versa when the two variables are somehow deterministically related (e.g., consider the variables pressure and volume in a closed physical system). Barring such deterministic relationships, however, the hypotheses corresponding to these two network structures are mutually exclusive. Consequently, hypothesis equivalence does not hold.

Nonetheless, when we know little about the structure of a domain, we have often found it reasonable to assume that data cannot help to distinguish between equivalence network structures. To express this assumption formally, let Θ_U

denote the parameters of the joint space, and let C_s^h denote the hypothesis that the database is a random sample from the influence diagram corresponding to the causal-network structure C_s. Then, we have

$$p\left(\Theta_U | C_{s1}^h, \xi\right) = p\left(\Theta_U | C_{s2}^h, \xi\right),$$

whenever the causal-network structures C_{s1}^h and C_{s2}^h are equivalent (when interpreted as acausal networks). We call this assumption *likelihood equivalence*. Heckerman et al. (1995) show that the prior-network methodology is still justified when we replace the assumption of hypothesis equivalence with that of likelihood equivalence.

Under the assumptions of mechanism, component, and parameter independence, the assumption of likelihood equivalence has an interesting characterization. Consider again our two-variable domain. Suppose we know nothing about the domain, having uninformative Dirichlet priors on the parameters of both network structures (all Dirichlet exponents arbitrarily close to -1). Further, suppose we adopt the assumption of likelihood equivalence for the two network structures $x \rightarrow y$ and $y \rightarrow x$. Now, suppose we obtain a single case of experimental data where we set $x = 1$ and observe $y = 1$. According to our updating procedure described in the previous section, for the network structure $x \rightarrow y$, we update the parameter $\theta_{y=1|x=1}$, but not the parameter $\theta_{x=1}$. In contrast, for the network structure $y \rightarrow x$, we update the parameter $\theta_{y=1}$, but not the parameter $\theta_{x=1|y=1}$. As a result, our posterior distributions for $\Theta_U = \{\theta_{x=0,y=0}, \theta_{x=0,y=1}, \theta_{x=1,y=0}, \theta_{x=1,y=1}\}$ will no longer satisfy likelihood equivalence. One can show that, for any domain, if we have an uninformative Dirichlet prior for that domain, and we are given a database containing experimental data, then the resulting posterior distributions for Θ_U will violate likelihood equivalence. Therefore, we can assess whether or not likelihood equivalence holds by asking ourselves whether or not our prior knowledge is equivalent to having seen only nonexperimental data.

We note that the assumption of likelihood equivalence tends to be less reasonable for more familiar domains. For example, a doctor may be uncertain as to whether disease d_1 causes disease d_2 or vice versa, but he may have well-defined hypotheses about why d_1 causes disease d_2 and vice versa. In this case, the assumption of likelihood equivalence would likely be unreasonable.

We emphasize that experimental data can be crucial for learning causal structure. In our two-variable domain, suppose we believe that either x causes y or y causes x. Then, if we set x to different states and learn that the probability of y depends on x, then we learn that x causes y. To verify this relation, we can set y to different states and check that the probability of x remains the same. Conversely, if we set y to different states and learn that the probability of x depends on y, then we learn that y causes x.

Also, we may need experimental data to quantify the effects of intervention–for example, to learn the aleatory probability distribution $ap(y|\hat{x} = 1)$. Given a causal structure, however, there are situations where we can quantify the effects of intervention using observational data only (Pearl and Verma 1991; Pearl 1995).

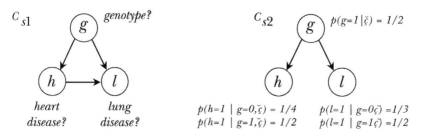

Figure 11.6. Two possible causal networks that explain an observed dependence between heart and lung disease.

Learning Hidden Variables

In the Learning Causal-Network Parameters section, we saw that we could often remove dependencies between causal mechanisms by adding additional domain variables. In many situations, however, we can never observe these variables. We say that these variables are *hidden*.

As we have discussed, methods for learning acausal networks with missing data are known (e.g., exact, EM, Gibbs sampling). These methods can be applied to databases containing hidden variables. Thus, under the assumptions of mechanism independence, component independence, parameter independence, parameter modularity, and likelihood equivalence, we can learn causal networks with hidden variables using these methods in conjunction with the prior-network methodology.

To illustrate this approach, let us consider a simple medical domain containing two observable variables h and l representing the presence or absence of heart disease and lung disease, respectively, and a hidden variable g representing the presence or absence of a gene that predisposes one to both diseases. Two possible causal-network structures for this domain are shown in Figure 11.6. In the network structure labeled C_{s1}, h causes l, and g is a hidden common cause of both diseases. In C_{s2}, the disease variables are related only through the hidden common cause. Suppose that only these two network-structure hypotheses are possible and that they are equally likely a priori. In addition, suppose our prior network for this domain is C_{s2} with the probabilities shown in Figure 11.6, and N' (the equivalent sample size for this network) is 24. Finally suppose we have a database C containing two cases where – in both cases – all set decisions are "do nothing," $h = 1$ (heart disease present), and $l = 1$ (lung disease present).

Because there are only two cases, we can compute the posterior probabilities of both network-structure hypotheses exactly, using Eq. 11.6 (which applies to complete databases), Eq. 11.8, and the relation

$$\begin{aligned}
p(C|C_s^h, \xi) = \ &p(g_1 = 1, h_1 = 1, l_1 = 1, g_2 = 1, h_2 = 1, l_2 = 1|C_s^h, \xi) \\
&+ p(g_1 = 0, h_1 = 1, l_1 = 1, g_2 = 1, h_2 = 1, l_2 = 1|C_s^h, \xi) \\
&+ p(g_1 = 1, h_1 = 1, l_1 = 1, g_2 = 0, h_2 = 1, l_2 = 1|C_s^h, \xi) \\
&+ p(g_1 = 0, h_1 = 1, l_1 = 1, g_2 = 0, h_2 = 1, l_2 = 1|C_s^h, \xi),
\end{aligned}$$

where the subscripts on the variables denote case numbers.

For example, from Eqs. 11.6 and 11.8, the first term in this sum for C_{s1} is given by

$$\frac{\Gamma(24)}{\Gamma(26)} \frac{\Gamma(14)}{\Gamma(12)} \frac{\Gamma(12)}{\Gamma(14)} \frac{\Gamma(8)}{\Gamma(6)} \frac{\Gamma(6)}{\Gamma(8)} \frac{\Gamma(5)}{\Gamma(3)} = 1/50.$$

Performing the sums and applying Bayes' theorem, we obtain $p(C_{s1}^h | C, \xi) = 0.51$, and $p(C_{s2}^h | C, \xi) = 0.49$.

For domains containing hidden variables, Pearl has suggested a generalization of the assumption of likelihood equivalence, which says that if two causal networks are equivalent with respect to the distributions they encode for the *observed* variables, then the parameters for those observed variables should have identical priors. We call this property *strong-likelihood equivalence*. This property does not hold in our simple medical example. Namely, the two network structures C_{s1} and C_{s2} are equivalent with respect to the variables h and l (i.e., both structures can represent any joint distribution over these variables). Nonetheless, as we saw in the previous example, observations can help to discriminate the two network structures. Thus, given the assumptions of mechanism and component independence, strong-likelihood equivalence is not consistent with our prior-network methodology. That is, strong-likelihood equivalence is not consistent with the assumptions of parameter independence and parameter modularity. Consequently, strong-likelihood equivalence may lead to a method for assessing priors on parameters that is an alternative to the prior-network approach.

Learning More General Causal Models

Our presentation has concentrated on domains where all variables (except root nodes) have causes. We emphasize that this restriction is unnecessary, given the definition of cause given by Heckerman and Shachter (1995). In particular, as shown by these researchers, the relationships in domains where only some variables have causes can be encoded in canonical form. Consequently, we can often apply the learning methods we have described to these more general domains.

Acknowledgments

Many thanks to Ross Shachter who helped me understand causality in terms of decision-theoretic concepts. Thanks also to Max Chickering, Greg Cooper, Dan Geiger, and Judea Pearl for useful discussions.

REFERENCES

Aliferis, C., and Cooper, G. (1994). An evaluation of an algorithm for inductive learning of Bayesian belief networks using simulated data sets. In *Proceedings of Tenth Conference on Uncertainty in Artificial Intelligence*. Seattle, WA: Morgan Kaufmann, 8–14.

Buntine, W. (1991). Theory refinement on Bayesian networks. In *Proceedings of Seventh Conference on Uncertainty in Artificial Intelligence*. Los Angeles, CA: Morgan Kaufmann, 52–60.

Buntine, W. (1994). Operations for learning with graphical models. *Journal of Artificial Intelligence Research*, 2, 159–225.

Cooper, G., and Herskovits, E. (1991). A Bayesian method for the induction of probabilistic networks from data. *Technical Report SMI-91-1*. Section on Medical Informatics, Stanford University.

Cooper, G., and Herskovits, E. (1992). A Bayesian method for the induction of probabilistic networks from data. *Machine Learning, 9*, 309–347.

Cowell, R., Dawid, A., and Sebastiani, P. (1995). A comparison of sequential learning methods for incomplete data. *Technical Report 135*, Department of Statistical Science, University College London.

Dempster, A., Laird, N., and Rubin, D. (1977). Maximum likelihood from incomplete data via the EM algorithm. *Journal of the Royal Statistical Society, B39*, 1–38.

Heckerman, D., Geiger, D., and Chickering, D. (1994). Learning Bayesian networks: The combination of knowledge and statistical data. In *Proceedings of Tenth Conference on Uncertainty in Artificial Intelligence*. Seattle, WA: Morgan Kaufmann, 293–301.

Heckerman, D., Geiger, D., and Chickering, D. (1995). Learning Bayesian networks: The combination of knowledge and statistical data. *Machine Learning, 20*, 197–243.

Heckerman, D., and Shachter, R. (1995). Decision-Theoretic Foundations for Causal Reasoning. *Journal of Artificial Intelligence Research, 3*, 405–430.

Holland, P. (1986). Statistics and causal inference. *Journal of the American Statistical Association, 81*, 945–968.

Howard, R., and Matheson, J. (1981). Influence diagrams. In R. Howard, and J. Matheson (Eds.), *Readings on the Principles and Applications of Decision Analysis, Vol. II*. Menlo Park, CA: Strategic Decisions Group, 721–762.

Howard, R. (1990). From influence to relevance to knowledge. In R.M. Oliver and J.Q. Smith (Eds.), *Influence Diagrams, Belief Nets, and Decision Analysis*. New York: Wiley and Sons, 3–23.

Madigan, D., and Raftery, A. (1994). Model selection and accounting for model uncertainty in graphical models using Occam's window. *Journal of the American Statistical Association, 89*, 1535–1546.

Matheson. J. (1990). Using influence diagrams to value information and control. In R.M. Oliver and J.Q. Smith (Eds.), *Influence Diagrams, Belief Nets, and Decision Analysis*. New York: Wiley and Sons, 25–48.

Pearl, J. (1988). *Probabilistic Reasoning in Intelligent Systems: Networks of Plausible Inference*. San Mateo, CA: Morgan Kaufmann.

Pearl, J. (1995). Causal diagrams for empirical research. *Biometrika, 82*, 669–710.

Pearl, J., and Verma, T. (1991). A theory of inferred causation. In J. Allen, R. Fikes, and E. Sandewall, (Eds.), *Knowledge Representation and Reasoning: Proceedings of the Second International Conference*. New York: Morgan Kaufmann, 441–452.

Rubin, D. (1978). Bayesian inference for causal effects: The role of randomization. *Annals of Statistics, 6*, 34–58.

Shachter, R. (1986). Evaluating influence diagrams. *Operations Research, 34*, 871–882.

Spiegelhalter, D., Dawid, A., Lauritzen, S., and Cowell, R. (1993). Bayesian analysis in expert systems. *Statistical Science, 8*, 219–282.

Spiegelhalter, D., and Lauritzen, S. (1990). Sequential updating of conditional probabilities on directed graphical structures. *Networks, 20*, 579–605.

Spirtes, P., Glymour, C., and Scheines, R. (1993). *Causation, Prediction, and Search*. New York: Springer-Verlag.

Titterington, D. (1976). Updating a diagnostic system using unconfirmed cases. *Applied Statistics, 25*, 238–247.

Verma, T., and Pearl, J. (1990). Equivalence and synthesis of causal models. In *Proceedings of Sixth Conference on Uncertainty in Artificial Intelligence*. Boston, MA: Morgan Kaufmann, 220–227.

York, J. (1992). *Bayesian methods for the analysis of misclassified or incomplete multivariate discrete data*. Ph.D. thesis, Department of Statistics, University of Washington, Seattle.

12 Utility and Risk Preferences

David E. Bell

ABSTRACT. Utility theory has been a primary method used for the analysis of decision making under uncertainty for the last 60 years. We describe the rationale and uses of the approach in the case of decisions involving money. Our focus is the question of which particular utility function should be used by a decision maker.

Introduction

Playing games of chance for money is an activity that has diverted people for at least 6 millennia, so it is reasonable to suppose that an interest in how one should think about maximizing wealth under uncertainty has existed at least as long.

The starting point for all students of decision analysis is Expected Monetary Value (EMV) (Raiffa 1968). If there are i possible courses of action under consideration, and n possible outcomes $x_1, \ldots, x_n$, and if p_{ij} is the probability that action i leads to monetary outcome x_j, then EMV suggests that one select the action i that maximizes $\sum_j p_{ij} x_j$. The justification for this criterion – and it's a good one – is that any other criterion, if used repeatedly, will assuredly (almost certainly) leave you less well off at the end. Though few people get to repeat the same gamble over and over again, EMV is still relevant in our lives because we often make decisions involving financial uncertainty, and using EMV to make them will almost certainly be the right criterion for choice.

There are two very notable exceptions when EMV should not be used. The first is when payoffs are multiplicative rather than additive. In decision analysis, as opposed to other fields such as finance, it is usual to think of uncertain payoffs as incremental to existing wealth, $w + \tilde{x}$, as opposed to multiplicative, $w\tilde{x}$. The latter type we will refer to as "investments." Using EMV to select among investments would be a big mistake. The investment offering a 50–50 chance of either 1.50 (a 50 percent return) or 0.6 (a 40 percent loss) has a positive EMV, but if it is accepted repeatedly it will almost certainly lead you to ruin (because $1.50 \times 0.60 < 1$). Only investments for which $E \log \tilde{x} > 0$ have the property that repetitions will lead inexorably to profit. The second notable exception – and our primary focus in this article – is that EMV is not appropriate "when risk is an issue." The caveat refers to situations where repetition is not a realistic option for overcoming an early bad outcome. The argument that a 50–50 bet between +\$50,000 and −\$20,000 will make you rich if repeated often enough is not relevant if a loss at the first iteration makes you financially unable or unwilling to continue.

The problem is *not* necessarily that as you become poorer you become "more risk averse," because even a decision maker with constant risk aversion would not use EMV. Rather it is because gains and losses are not equivalent. Gaining $100,000 is a delight, losing $100,000 is painful. For most people, the downside pain is greater than the upside delight. No scholar, to my knowledge, has managed to argue that there is a precise relationship between the value of gains and monetarily equal losses. It is generally accepted that the relationship varies between individuals, varies for one individual as his or her wealth changes and even, though this is less well studied, as his or her "attitude to life" changes.

In this chapter our focus will be on advising the "rational actor"; a decision maker not buffeted by psychological distractions such as regret (Bell 1982; Loomes and Sugden 1982), disappointment (Bell, 1985; Loomes and Sugden 1986), or anxiety (Wu 1999). Although these can be real concerns to real people, if they are genuine concerns that a decision maker wishes to seriously avoid they can be accommodated by multiattribute theory (Keeney and Raiffa 1976).

Stochastic Dominance

If $\tilde{x}$ and $\tilde{y}$ are resolved by some common uncertainty such that with probability p_i the outcomes are x_i and y_i, respectively, and if $x_i \geq y_i$ then surely no rational person would prefer $\tilde{y}$ over $\tilde{x}$. Clearly $\tilde{x}$ dominates $\tilde{y}$. One alternative is said to *stochastically dominate* another if for all sums of money, $a, P(\tilde{x} \geq a) \geq P(\tilde{y} \geq a)$. But now suppose that the two are resolved independently, though the individual gambles have the same probabilities and outcomes as before. Even though $x_i \geq y_i$ for all i is still true, it could happen that the *actual* outcome of $\tilde{y}$ is superior to that of $\tilde{x}$. A person who suffers regret might think that it was not so obvious that $\tilde{x}$ still dominates $\tilde{y}$. A rational actor should argue that if $\tilde{x}$ is selected, the actual outcome of $\tilde{y}$ is irrelevant and can be ignored.

Strength of Preference

It has been appreciated at least since the eighteenth century (Bernoulli 1738; Luce and Raiffa 1957) that if EMV fails because losing an amount of money is more painful than gaining it is good, then the analytic solution is to create a scale that reflects the real value of money to a person. People seem quite comfortable making judgments of the form "the increment from having $10,000 to having $20,000 is about as attractive as the increment from having $20,000 to $35,000." The problem for scholars has been to validate these statements by connecting them to action. One solution is to use some yardstick like "work expended." If you claim to be indifferent between working 6 weeks for $10,000 and working 10 weeks for $20,000, and also between 6 weeks for $20,000 and 10 weeks for $35,000,

I might conclude that the increments \$10,000→\$20,000 and \$20,000→\$35,000 had equal *strength of preference*.

The problem with the yardstick approach is that money and hours worked might interact; your distaste for working might increase more rapidly when rich because of the more attractive uses you have for leisure time. Nor does it help with decisions under uncertainty unless decisions involving uncertain numbers of hours worked can be solved via expectation.

Utility Theory

It was not until 1947 when John von Neumann and Oskar Morgenstern published the second edition of their book *Theory of Games and Economic Behavior* that a satisfying axiomatization of risky choice was offered to justify the use of value functions – which in this context we refer to as *utility functions*. Consider two axioms:

(i) Independence from Irrelevant Alternatives (IIA): If A is the best alternative from among some set of alternatives, then A is the best alternative from any subset of those alternatives (if the subset includes A).
(ii) Independence from Irrelevant States (IIS): If a particular outcome has the same probability of occurring for all alternatives in a set, then the best alternative in that set is independent of the level of the particular outcome.

IIA implies *transitivity* ($A > B$ and $B > C$ implies $A > C$). For if A is the best from the set of alternatives $\{A, B, C\}$ then IIA implies $A > B$ and $A > C$. If $B > C$ then transitivity holds ($A > B$, $B > C$ and $A > C$) or if $C > B$ then transitivity holds ($A > C$, $C > B$ and $A > B$). Either way IIA $\Rightarrow$ Transitivity. If we further assume that the decision maker is able to select the best alternative for any set of alternatives (*comparability*) then IIA implies that there exists a rank order (simple order) of all alternatives (Krantz et al. 1971; Fishburn 1970).

Let us restrict ourselves for the moment to gambles having n equally likely payoffs. Let $(x_1, \ldots, x_n)$ be the payoffs of such a gamble where the ordering of the xs is irrelevant because they are all equally likely. Let ϕ be the simple order implied by IIA and comparability. In this context the interpretation of IIS is that tradeoffs among, say, the payoffs $x_1, \ldots, x_j$ are independent of the values of the remaining payoffs $x_{j+1}, \ldots, x_n$. This is true for any subset of the attributes. By a well-known result for ordinal value functions (Debreu 1960; Gorman 1968a, 1968b) ϕ is additive; that is, for some functions Ψ, $v_1, \ldots, v_n$ we have

$$\Psi(\phi(x_1, \ldots, x_n)) = \sum_{i=1}^{n} v_i(x_i).$$

By symmetry of the xs (the ordering doesn't matter because they are equally likely) we have $v_i = v_j = u$ for all i and j. Hence, gambles may be ranked according to the quantity $\sum u(x_i)$, where u is the utility function.

Because this argument applies for any n, the quantity $\sum_{i=1}^{n} p_i u(x_i)$ may also be used to compare gambles where p_i are rational numbers. *Continuity* makes this criterion valid for all values of p.

Uses of Utility Theory

There are three kinds of applications for the theory. The first, most obviously, is to enhance the ability of a decision maker to act coherently. If there are many alternatives and many possible outcomes the cognitive load may be greatly simplified by first estimating an appropriate utility function, estimating the relevant probabilities and then applying the expected utility formula. Relative to EMV the only extra step is to estimate the utility function. If multiple decisions are to be made, the utility function need be estimated only once.

A second use of utility is as a means of delegating decisions to an agent. Just as I would not expect someone to acquire artwork on my behalf without a thorough discussion of my tastes, a financial agent should have some sense of my taste for gambles. The utility function is the information the agent needs.

Finally, and this is where the theory has found the most application, utility functions are useful for investigating general rules of behavior (e.g., Grayson 1960).

Assessment of the Utility Function

Nothing in the theory requires that different people have different utility functions. But people do react quite differently to the prospect of risk. Suppose you are given a lottery ticket that gives you a 50–50 chance of winning zero or $100,000. Would you rather accept the risk or trade the opportunity for a guaranteed $40,000? Some people will answer this one way, some people the other way. The answer, of course, tells us how $u(40,000)$ relates to $1/2\, u(0) + 1/2\, u(100,000)$.

By asking the decision maker to answer a carefully selected set of similar stylized questions, it is possible to estimate a person's utility function. Farquhar (1984) gives a review of estimating procedures. The practical problem in assessment is that even if a decision maker agrees that IIA and IIS make sense, he or she may nevertheless give answers that are inconsistent with those axioms. If the answers do conflict then resolution can be obtained only by "fitting" the utility function as closely as possible to the stated preferences, or by confronting the decision maker with his inconsistencies and asking him to reconcile them.

A third way around this dilemma is to find ways to restrict the "degrees of freedom" the decision maker has in selecting a utility function. For example, if we discover that the decision maker's preferences, although perfectly consistent with the theory, nevertheless suggest that $u(20,000) > u(30,000)$ we would feel justified in thinking something was wrong.

One frequent "error" in judgment is that people are very unreliable in their judgment about small gambles (Schlaifer 1962). A person might say that they would exchange a 50–50 gamble between zero and $10 for $4, and say they would exchange a 50–50 gamble between zero and $10,000 for $3,500. No plausible utility function can capture that kind of risk attitude "in the small" and "in the large." Schlaifer warned that it was inadvisable to rely on any assessments that were not in terms of sums of money of the order of the respondent's assets.

Risk Aversion

It is to be expected that rational actors will prefer more money to less (u is increasing), and that risk is bad (u is concave). How does one measure risk aversion? If one's wealth is w then a 50–50 gamble between zero and $100 is really a gamble between w and $w + 100$. If $c(\tilde{x}, w)$ is the *certainty equivalent* of $\tilde{x}$ when you have wealth w, that is, $u(w + c(\tilde{x}, w)) = Eu(w + \tilde{x})$, then risk aversion is equivalent to the statement that $w + c(\tilde{x}, w) < w + E(\tilde{x}) \equiv w + \bar{x}$.

Pratt (1964) and Arrow (1971) discovered that a useful measure of (local) risk aversion (for small gambles) is $-u''/u'$ because approximately,

$$\bar{x} = c(w, \tilde{x}) + \tfrac{1}{2} E(\tilde{x} - \bar{x})^2 \left[-u''(w)/u'(w)\right].$$

In this expression the *risk premium* of $\tilde{x}$ at w, the difference between the EMV, $\tilde{x}$, and the certainty equivalent, $c(\tilde{x}, w)$, is proportional to the variance of the payoffs, $E(\tilde{x} - \bar{x})^2$. The proportion depends on the individual (through u) and on the particular wealth level (through w).

Constant Risk Aversion

Although the degree of risk aversion might vary with wealth, a first approximation (generalizing EMV) might assume that risk aversion is independent of wealth. This has many practical advantages. First it means that in order to make a decision we do not need to know the decision maker's wealth. Many people do not know their own wealth with any precision, and for an agent, the lack of knowledge may be worse. It also means that for repetitive situations (recall the EMV discussion) the same choice among gambles will always have the same answer. Pfanzagl (1959) was an early proponent that constant risk aversion made sense as a *prescription* (how people should behave) as much as it was a *description* (how people really behave). He showed that a person with constant risk aversion had to have a utility function that was either linear (zero risk aversion as a special case) or exponential; $u(w) = -e^{-cw}$ where the constant c varied with the decision maker. Note that $-u''(w)/u'(w) = c$ for the exponential.

If a decision maker believes that constant risk aversion is a good match for her preferences, then in principle, a single assessment is sufficient to nail down the value of c.

Relative Risk Aversion

The von Neumann–Morgenstern axiomatization of decreasing marginal value [money gets incrementally less valuable as wealth increases] through gambles, although elegant, is somewhat dissatisfying. The intuitive idea of strength of preference has nothing (or seemingly nothing) to do with uncertainty. Are these two concepts indeed one and the same?

If $v(w)$ is the strength of preference function for money, then we may write $u(w) = u^*(v(w))$. Sarin (1982) gives axioms that lead to the conclusion that $u(w) = v(w)$. Dyer and Sarin (1982) defined *relative risk aversion* as the degree of risk aversion of u *relative* to that implicit in v. Bell and Raiffa (1988) argued that relative risk aversion should be constant. Their notion is that any residual risk aversion, over and above that expressible by a varying value function must be an "intrinsic" distaste for risk. If a 50–50 gamble between, say, a 10 value-point gain and a 7 value-point loss is just acceptable, then that should be true no matter what the underlying decision problem (whatever wealth level if the uncertainty is about money, or even uncertainty about health issues, so long as the gains and losses have the same value implications). This hypothesis has been supported by Smidts (1997).

Whether constant or not, it is of great interest to understand what factors influence the level of relative risk aversion for a rational actor.

Decreasing Risk Aversion

It is clear that u should be increasing and exhibit risk aversion (u concave, or $c(\tilde{x}, w) < \bar{x}$) for all uncertain gambles and wealth levels w. It also seems reasonable to suppose that risk aversion should decrease as a person gets wealthier, that is, $c(\tilde{x}, w^*) < c(\tilde{x}, w)$ for $w > w^*$.

If a person finds $\tilde{x}$ just equivalent to a sure event c at wealth level w^*, then at wealth level $w > w^*$ a decreasingly risk averse person should be more willing to take a risk, so that now $\tilde{x}$ becomes preferable to c. This is equivalent to requiring that the Pratt–Arrow measure $-u''(w)/u'(w)$ is decreasing in w, or that $u''(w)^2 < u'(w)u'''(w)$. Because $u'(w)$ is positive, and $u''(w)^2$ is positive, this means that $u'''(w)$ has to be positive. A positive third derivative is not a guarantee of decreasing risk aversion however.

How far might risk aversion decrease? Can we assume for example that $\lim_{w \to \infty} -u''(w)/u'(w) = 0$? I think the answer must be yes. For one thing, the relevance of EMV depends on most people being approximately risk neutral for small gambles, or similarly for any given wealth level there comes a point when the stakes are small enough that a person becomes risk neutral, or nearly so. For any gamble there must be some wealth level, no matter if very large, that makes the person with that wealth level regard the gamble as essentially riskless.

Contextual Uncertainty

So far we have examined risk averse behavior assuming that w is known. Anyone owning a car or home, or with job insecurity, knows that wealth is always uncertain. The myriad of financial uncertainties that face us all may be termed *contextual uncertainty*. Surely as contextual uncertainties grow we should become more risk averse, a condition described by Gollier and Pratt (1996) as *risk vulnerability*. Pratt and Zeckhauser (1987) proposed that if $\tilde{w}, \tilde{x}$, and $\tilde{y}$ are probabilistically independent, and if $\tilde{w} + \tilde{x} < \tilde{w}$ and $\tilde{w} + \tilde{y} < \tilde{w}$ then also $\tilde{w} + \tilde{x} + \tilde{y} < \tilde{w} + \tilde{y}$. In the special case where $\tilde{x} = \tilde{y}$, so that one is just an independent repetition of the other, the condition implies that repetition can't turn a bad gamble into a good one. Pratt and Zeckhauser term their condition *proper risk aversion*. It is hard to see why a rational actor would not want to satisfy this condition. Pratt and Zeckhauser show that any utility function that is a mixture of exponentials ($u(w) = \int_0^\infty g(s)e^{-sw}ds$ for any probability distribution g) is proper. This is an extraordinarily broad set of functions that includes, for example, the power and logarithmic functions.

Both risk vulnerability and proper risk aversion are based on the notion that *adding* uncertainty increases risk (Eeckhoudt et al. 1996). Another way to increase risk is by *multiplying* the size of an uncertainty. If $k > 1$ then $k\tilde{x}$ will always be riskier than $\tilde{x}$ for a risk averse person, that is, if $Eu(w + \tilde{x}) < u(w)$ then $Eu(w + k\tilde{x}) < Eu(w + \tilde{x})$. Let us say that if $\tilde{z}_1$ and $\tilde{z}_2$ are independent but related risks in that $\tilde{z}_2 = k\tilde{z}_1$ for $k > 1$, then $\tilde{z}_2$ is a *larger* risk than $\tilde{z}_1$ and $\tilde{z}_1$ is a *smaller* risk than $\tilde{z}_2$.

Suppose there are two contextual uncertainties affecting wealth that complicate a decision maker's choice between two further gambles $\tilde{x}$ and $\tilde{y}$. The contextual uncertainties are due to be resolved *after* the choice between $\tilde{x}$ and $\tilde{y}$ is made. It cannot harm and might be of definite benefit if either or both of the contextual uncertainties were to be resolved *before* the choice is made.

But what if only one of the contextual uncertainties can be resolved early? If one is larger than the other (in the sense described above) surely it would make sense to prefer resolving the larger rather than the smaller contextual uncertainty. Bell (1995b) showed that the only increasing, risk averse and decreasingly risk averse utility function to satisfy this condition is the linear plus exponential form, $u(w) = w - be^{-cw}$ where b and c are positive constants.

This family of functions satisfies all of the properties that I would regard as requirements for a rational actor: in addition to being increasing, risk averse and decreasingly risk averse, it satisfies risk vulnerability, is proper, and in the limit is risk neutral.

Measuring Riskiness

When can it be said that one gamble is riskier than another? There are many studies of how people measure riskiness (e.g., Weber 1988), but for our rational actor any measure of riskiness should be compatible with utility theory. If EMV truly is an appropriate criterion "except when risk is an issue" it should be possible to express $Eu(w + \tilde{x})$ as some equivalent expression involving $w, \tilde{x}$ and some measure of riskiness $R(\tilde{x})$, say $f(\bar{x}, R(\tilde{x}), w)$. We know that for small gambles the certainty equivalent of $\tilde{x}$ is approximately $\bar{x} - \frac{1}{2}\sigma^2(-u''(w)/u'(w))$, so that $R(\tilde{w})$ is approximately equivalent to the variance. Certainly the variance of a distribution, or its relation, the standard deviation, is a widely understood measure of dispersion. Though variance is compatible with risk aversion "in the small," it is rarely so "in the large" (Fishburn 1977). The quadratic utility function $u(w) = aw^2 + bw + c$ has $\mathrm{E}u(w + \tilde{x}) = aw^2 + bw + c + (b + 2aw)\bar{x} + a\bar{x}^2 + a\sigma^2$, which is of the form $f(\bar{x}, \sigma^2, w)$, but this is unsatisfactory not least because the quadratic is never decreasingly risk averse. The exponential may be written as $\mathrm{E}u(w + \tilde{x}) = -\exp(-cw)\exp(-c\bar{x})\mathrm{E}\exp(-c(\tilde{x} - \bar{x}))$, which is in the right format, if we take $\mathrm{E}\exp(-c(\tilde{x} - \bar{x}))$ as a measure of riskiness, but the exponential is not decreasingly risk averse.

Suppose $\tilde{x}$ is preferred to $\tilde{y}$ at wealth level w_1. Suppose that at a higher wealth level, w_2, the preference is now $\tilde{y}$ over $\tilde{x}$. Could it be that at an even higher wealth level, w_3, the decision maker might revert to preferring $\tilde{x}$ to $\tilde{y}$? Most people think not. They reason that the switch in preference as wealth went from w_1 to w_2 implies that $\tilde{y}$ must be riskier than $\tilde{x}$; any further increase in wealth makes you even less risk averse, and this means $\tilde{y}$ remains preferred to $\tilde{x}$. But this presupposes that each decision maker has a (perhaps implicit) ranking of gambles according to riskiness and that this ranking is independent of wealth. As Bell (1988b, 1995a) shows, only a handful of utility functions satisfy this condition, and of those, only the linear plus exponential function is compatible with the other desiderata.

If EMV is the criterion of choice when wealth is high we might expect that any switches in preference between gambles should be in favor of the gamble with the higher EMV. That is, if $\tilde{x} > \tilde{y}$ at w_1 but $\tilde{y} > \tilde{x}$ at $w_2 > w_1$, then $\bar{y} > \bar{x}$. This, too, is true for an increasing, risk averse and decreasingly risk averse utility function *only if* it is linear plus exponential.

In this case $\mathrm{E}u(w + \tilde{x}) = a(w + \bar{x}) - \exp(-c(w + \bar{x}))\mathrm{E}\exp(-c(\tilde{x} - \bar{x}))$, which is of the form $f(\bar{x}, R((\tilde{x}), w)$ if we set $R(\tilde{x}) = \mathrm{E}\exp(-c(\tilde{x} - \bar{x}))$. Thus, this is the only measure of riskiness that is compatible with utility theory (Weber and Milliman 1997).

Utility for Consumption

A closely related concept of utility is for consumption. So far, we have thought of w as an endowment to be used in a beneficial but unspecified manner for the decision maker over time. But now let us be a little more concrete and assume that the quality of life that results from spending x dollars i years from now is $u_i(x)$. Making lots of simplifying assumptions we can connect the two kinds of utility functions by means of the maximization problem:

$$u(w) = \max_{x_1,\ldots,x_{n-1}} \sum_{i=1}^{n-1} u_i(x_i) + u_n\left(w - \sum x_i\right).$$

To simplify still further we can reduce the consumption problem down to the relevant question of how much to spend this year:

$$u(w) = u_1(x) + u_2(w - x),$$

where x is current consumption and $w - x$ is "savings." An interesting question, studied by Kimball (1990, 1993) is how current consumption is influenced by uncertainty in savings. Because of the potential confusion between utility as we have been discussing it, and utility for consumption, I prefer to present Kimball's analysis in terms of *hedging*, the intuition being the same.

Hedging

Suppose you face a 50–50 gamble between zero and $\tilde{x}$. If a coin lands heads, you get $\tilde{x}$, if it lands tails, you get nothing. Suppose you are permitted to *hedge* by modifying the gamble to $\tilde{x} - h$ if heads and $+h$ if tails (h could be a positive or negative amount). Kimball shows that for small risks the optimal h is approximately $1/4\sigma^2 u'''(w)/u''(w)$. If $\bar{x} = 0$ we would expect h to be negative. If $u''(w)$ is negative then u''' needs to be positive. Kimball calls the quantity $-u'''(w)/u''(w)$ the degree of *prudence*. It is interesting to consider how prudence should vary with wealth.

One would certainly suppose that the more risk averse a person is the greater desire there will be to hedge. Similarly, we would expect h to increase as the riskiness of $\tilde{x}$ increases. In the particular case of linear plus exponential we have the hedging problem:

$$\max_{h} \tfrac{1}{2}\left(w - h - be^{c(w-h)}\right) + \tfrac{1}{2}\left(w + \bar{x} + h - be^{-c(w+\bar{x}+h)}R(\tilde{x})\right),$$

where $R(\tilde{x}) = Ee^{-c(\tilde{x}-\bar{x})}$.

The optimal h is found by solving

$$1 + bce^{-c(w-h)} = 1 + bce^{-c(w+\bar{x}+h)}R(\tilde{x}),$$

which implies

$$w - h = w + \bar{x} + h - \tfrac{1}{c}\log R(\tilde{x}), \quad \text{so} \quad h = \bar{x}/2 + \tfrac{1}{2c}\log R(\tilde{x})$$

The optimal hedge is to transfer half the EMV plus a "prudence premium" of $\tfrac{1}{2c}\log R(\tilde{x})$.

Note that although the premium does increase with the riskiness of $\tilde{x}$ it does not decline with w. Should it decline with w? Certainly we would expect the decision maker to feel the urgency to hedge declining as she gets wealthy, but should the *size* of the optimal hedge change? Not necessarily. Because the hedge is EMV neutral, and costless, its only purpose is to reduce risk. The unique aspect of the linear plus exponential is that the relative riskiness of gambles is independent of wealth; so the optimal hedge is also independent of wealth, in this case.

Derived Utility

If one day your utility function is $u(w)$, and the next day you are given an unresolved contextual uncertainty of $\tilde{z}$, then your *de facto* derived utility function is $Eu(w + \tilde{z})$. That is true because you should pick $\tilde{x}$ over $\tilde{y}$ only if $Eu(w + \tilde{z} + \tilde{x}) \geq Eu(w + \tilde{z} + \tilde{y})$. As it happens the linear plus exponential family is consistent with contextual uncertainty, though the "b" parameter changes from b to $bEe^{-c\tilde{z}}$. But suppose the decision maker is to decide between $\tilde{x}$ and $\tilde{y}$ while simultaneously owning an *unresolved* decision between $\tilde{z}_1$ and $\tilde{z}_2$. In this case the *derived utility function* may not even be concave (Bell 1988a). Added to these complexities, a rational actor should anticipate future, uncertain, additions to wealth.

Is there any realistic hope of identifying a suitable utility function? The answer lies with the original concept of EMV. EMV is commonly used as an approximate guide to action, even though it has limitations. Similarly, utility theory should be thought of as a guide to action in cases where "risk is an issue." In this spirit there is a danger in making the theory overly complicated. For most applications an approximate utility function, perhaps even the linear plus exponential function, will be close enough.

REFERENCES

Arrow, K. J. (1971). *Essays in the theory of risk-bearing*. Chicago: Markham Publishing Company.

Bell, D. E. (1982). Regret in decision making under uncertainty. *Operations Research, 30,* 961–981.

Bell, D. E. (1985). Disappointment in decision making under uncertainty. *Operations Research, 33,* 1–27.

Bell, D. E. (1988a). The value of pre-decision sidebets for utility maximizers. *Management Science, 34,* 797–800.

Bell, D. E. (1988b). One-switch utility functions and a measure of risk. *Management Science, 34,* 1416–1424.

Bell, D. E. (1995a). Risk, return, and utility. *Management Science, 41,* 23–30.

Bell, D. E. (1995b). A contextual uncertainty condition for behavior under risk. *Management Science, 41,* 1145–1150.

Bell, D. E., and Raiffa, H. (1988). Marginal value and intrinsic risk aversion. In D.E. Bell, H. Raiffa and A. Tversky (Eds.) *Decision Making.* Cambridge UK: Cambridge University Press, pp. 9–30.

Bernoulli, D. (1738). Specimen theoriae novae di mensura sortis. *Commentarii Academiae Scientiarum Imperialis Petropolitanea, 5,* 175–192. (Translated in 1954 by L. Sommer, Exposition of a new theory on the measurement of risk. *Econometrica, 22,* 23–36.)

Debreu, G. (1960). Topological methods in cardinal utility theory. In K. J. Arrow, S. Karlin, and P. Suppes (Eds.), *Mathematical Methods in the Social Sciences.* Stanford, CA: Stanford University Press.

Dyer, J. S., and Sarin, R. K. (1982). Relative risk aversion. *Management Science, 28,* 875–886.

Eeckhoudt, L., Gollier, C., and Schlesinger, H. (1996). Changes in background risk and risk taking behavior. *Econometrica, 64,* 683–689.

Farquhar, P. H. (1984). Utility assessment methods. *Management Science, 30,* 1283–1300.

Fishburn, P. C. (1970). *Utility Theory for Decision Making.* New York: Wiley.

Fishburn, P. C. (1977). Mean-risk analysis with risk associated with below target returns. *American Economic Review, 67,* 116–126.

Gollier, C., and Pratt, J. W. (1996). Risk vulnerability and the tempering effect of background risk. *Econometrica, 64,* 1109–1123.

Gorman, W. M. (1968a). The structure of utility functions. *Review of Economic Studies, 35,* 367–390.

Gorman, W. M. (1968b). Conditions for additive separability. *Econometrica, 36,* 605–609.

Grayson, C. J. (1960). *Decisions under uncertainty: Drilling decisions by oil and gas operators.* Cambridge, MA: Harvard University, Division of Research, Graduate School of Business Administration.

Keeney, R. L., and Raiffa, H. (1976). *Decisions with multiple objectives: Preferences and value tradeoffs*. New York: Wiley.

Kimball, M. S. (1990). Precautionary saving in the small and in the large. *Econometrica, 58,* 53–73.

Kimball, M. S. (1993). Standard risk aversion. *Econometrica, 61,* 589–611.

Krantz, D. H., Luce, R. D., Suppes, P., and Tversky, A. (1971). *Foundations of measurement.* (Vol. I). New York: Academic Press.

Loomes, G., and Sugden, R. (1982). Regret theory: An alternative theory of rational choice under uncertainty. *Economic Journal, 92,* 805–824.

Loomes, G., and Sugden, R. (1986). Disappointment and dynamic consistency in choice under uncertainty. *Review of Economic Studies, 53,* 271–282.

Luce, R. D., and Raiffa, H. (1957). *Games and decisions: Introduction and critical survey.* New York: Wiley.

Pfanzagl, J. (1959). A general theory of measurement applications to utility. *Naval Research Logistics Quarterly, 6,* 283–294.

Pratt, J. W., and Zeckhauser, R. (1987). Proper risk aversion. *Econometrica, 55,* 143–154.

Pratt, J. W. (1964). Risk aversion in the small and in the large. *Econometrica, 32,* 122–136.

Raiffa, H. (1968). *Decision analysis: Introductory lectures on choices under uncertainty.* Reading, MA: Addison-Wesley.

Sarin, R. K. (1982). Strength of preference and risky choice. *Operations Research 30,* 982–997.

Schlaifer, R. O. (1962). Assessment of the utility of money. Unpublished seminar notes. Harvard University, Graduate School of Business Administration.

Smidts, A. (1997). The relationship between risk attitude and strength of preference: A test of intrinsic risk attitude. *Management Science, 43,* 357–370.

von Neumann, J., and Morgenstern, O. (1947). *Theory of games and economic behavior.* 2nd ed. Princeton, NJ: Princeton University Press.

Weber, E. U. (1988). A descriptive measure of risk. *Acta Psychologica, 69,* 185–203.

Weber, E. U., and Milliman, R. A. (1997). Perceived risk attitudes: Relating risk perception to risky choice. *Management Science, 43,* 123–144.

Wu, G. (1999). Anxiety and decision making with delayed resolution of uncertainty. *Theory and Decision, 46,* 159–198.

13 Practical Value Models

Ralph L. Keeney and Detlof von Winterfeldt

ABSTRACT. Many complex decision problems require value judgments, and it is often useful to build formal models of these value judgments. Several models and assessment procedures exist for this task ranging from simple rating and weighting techniques to sophisticated multiattribute utility models that incorporate trade-offs and risk attitudes. In this chapter, we argue that the choice of a value model and assessment procedure depends on the decision context, the purpose of the model, the quality of available value judgments, time, and other factors. We propose the notion of a *practical value model* that is useful for a given decision context and purpose, using simplifications and approximations, when appropriate. We then discuss practical considerations when choosing a value model, for example, when deciding whether a value model is additive over attributes or not. We also consider practical issues when choosing an assessment procedure, for example, when selecting equivalent-cost procedures versus rating and weighting procedures. We discuss several topics related to interacting with decision makers when constructing value models, and we conclude with the description of two generic practical value models that we have found useful in many past applications.

Two types of models are commonly used in decision analysis: *consequence models* incorporate the facts, judgments, and uncertainties inherent in decision problems to describe or predict possible consequences of alternatives and *value models* incorporate the values or value tradeoffs and risk tolerances to evaluate consequences. This chapter addresses the value modeling aspect of decision analysis. It focuses on the choices that a decision analyst has to make when selecting an appropriate value model and assessment procedure.

Most people are familiar with value models, but they may not realize it, as the term is somewhat new and not in common use (Keeney 1988). In operations research and management science, one term for a value model is an *objective function*, often referring to a single objective, such as maximizing profit or minimizing delays. In decision analysis, value models are sometimes called utility functions, value functions, or preference functions. We prefer to use the general term *value model*, as the process of constructing such a model is the same as the process used to construct any other type of model. The analyst decides on the variables to use in constructing the value model, selects and/or verifies the relationships among those variables to get a mathematical representation of interest (preferences in this case), and then quantifies the parameters for the model using information that is available and/or can be gathered.

A value model is built such that a number, referred to as a value, can be calculated for each of the alternatives considered in a decision. These numbers provide a ranking of the desirability of each alternative, thereby providing the basis for making a choice. In many cases we know of, the value models involve multiple conflicting objectives. In some cases the value model provides a ranking of desirability and in some cases of undesirability, suggesting either to maximize or to minimize the value.

This chapter does not present the mathematical theories for constructing value models. There are many references for these theories (e.g., Krantz et al. 1971; Keeney and Raiffa 1976; and von Winterfeldt and Edwards 1986). This chapter is about the appropriate use of these theories for building a value model. Specifically, we focus on how one should build a value model that is appropriate and practical for a specific decision problem. We call such a model a "practical value model." We also are concerned with the practical assessment procedures that go along with a choice of a practical value model.

We add the word "practical" to suggest that it is not always necessary or useful to construct a state-of-the-art value model that is completely justified on theoretical grounds or to use theoretically justifiable assessment procedures. Approximations may do well both in modeling and assessment. The choice of value models and assessment procedures is a function of the characteristics of the decision being faced, the characteristics of the decision maker or makers, the time available for the process, and the skills of the decision analyst who is facilitating that process. A practical value model needs to balance the theoretical soundness of the model to represent the details of the decision makers' preference, the time and effort needed to construct the model, the quality of insight that can be gained from using the model, and the ability of decision makers to understand the insights from the model. An implication is that a practical value model should be "good enough" so that it is not the weak link in the overall analysis of the decision. If the refinement of the alternatives or the quality of the information about how well the alternatives measure up in terms of the objectives is such that additional legitimate insights could not be gained by an analysis with a more sophisticated or "better" value model, then the value model is good enough in terms of the overall analysis. If the analysis is of a quality such that the main limits to its use are the willingness of the decision makers to use it, or their ability to understand the insights, then the value model is good enough given the process.

Building a Value Model

There are two types of value models: *Utility functions* and *value functions*. The theoretical foundations of utility functions are found in von Neumann and Morgenstern (1947) and Keeney and Raiffa (1976). The theoretical foundation for value functions are found in Krantz et al. (1971) and Dyer and Sarin (1979). Krantz et al. develop value functions based on the notion of "strength of preferences." Dyer and Sarin refer to value functions as "measurable value functions." Constructs used for the existence of utility and value functions in these references are our basis for judging the appropriateness or theoretical correctness of value models. We can simplify these models using assumptions for a specific decision problem that are practical as described above.

In a given decision problem, analysts have to choose among a variety of possible value models. In essence, the question is what value model should be built for this decision? Some notation will be useful. We will assume that a set of alternatives A_j, $j=1,\ldots,J$ has been identified for the decision problem. Also, suppose we have identified a set of fundamental objectives O_i, $i=1,\ldots,n$ using concepts such as those described in Chapter 7 in this volume. Also, assume that an appropriate attribute X_i, $i=1,\ldots,n$ has been defined respectively to measure each of those objectives. For instance, in a public policy decision about highway safety, one fundamental objective would be to "minimize the loss of life in traffic accidents," and a corresponding attribute might be the "number of individuals dying in traffic annually." With this notation, a possible consequence of any chosen alternative can be written as $(x_1,\ldots,x_n)$ or more compactly as x, where x_i is a specific level of X_i.

Once a set of fundamental objectives and associated attributes are defined, the next step in constructing a value model is to obtain a general structure for the preference relationship among the various xs. Building a value model is analogous to building a factual model of, for instance, automobile accidents that might relate driver behavior, vehicle features, weather conditions, and road quality to subsequent accidents and highway fatalities. To combine the attributes in a value model, one uses independence concepts analogous to probabilistic independence or conditional probabilistic independence used in factual models. The main types of independence concepts are *utility independence, preferential independence,* and *additive independence.* Descriptions of these independence concepts and the implications for the functional forms of the resulting value models are described in detail in Keeney and Raiffa (1976) and von Winterfeldt and Edwards (1986).

It is also important in a value model to describe the preferences for consequences that differ in terms of only a single attribute. The common concepts for single-attribute utility functions concerned with uncertainties of consequences are risk aversion, risk neutrality, and risk proneness. For the measurable value functions analogous conditions are marginally decreasing, constant, or increasing value.

Certain sets of assumptions about preferences among consequences imply a specific functional form of the value model. An example is the additive value function

$$v(x_1,\ldots,x_n) = \sum w_i v_i(x_i), \tag{13.1}$$

where v is the overall value model, the v_i are single attribute value functions, and the w_i are scaling constants. The original work for this type of value model was presented in Luce and Tukey (1964) and Krantz (1964), who considered only ordinal judgments when constructing this value function. Fishburn (1970) and Krantz et al. (1971) considered value functions based on strength of preference judgments.

When alternatives involve uncertainty, it is common to begin with a utility function and, depending on appropriate assumptions, develop decompositions over attributes. The most common decompositions are the additive and multiplicative ones (see Keeney and Raiffa 1976):

$$u(x_1, \ldots x_i \ldots, x_n) = \sum k_i u_i(x_i), \qquad (13.2)$$

or

$$1 + ku(x_1, \ldots x_n) = \pi \{1 + k k_i u_i(x_i)\}, \qquad (13.3)$$

where u is the overall value model, the u_i are single-attribute utility functions, and the k_i are scaling constants. The seminal work on assumptions for an additive utility function is Fishburn (1965).

The v_i, w_i, u_i, k_i, and k terms in Eqs. 13.1–13.3 are the necessary ingredients to construct the value model. These must be determined using value judgments from the decision maker or assigned to represent the value judgments of the decision maker. These value judgments are the "data points" that one needs to construct the value model. For such value data, the basic information exists in the minds of the decision makers or individuals knowledgeable about that decision maker's preferences and the given problem. This is different from collecting data to assign parameters in a consequence model of automobile accidents, for instance. For consequence models the data is "out there" in the world and can be observed or inferred by analyzing drivers, vehicles, road surfaces, weather conditions, and accident information.

The value data to assign parameters is typically gathered by finding different consequences that are of equal value to the decision maker. Then, using a value model such as Eq. 13.1, the values of the two different consequences, which we will call y and z, can be equated using Eq. 13.1 to yield:

$$v(y) = \sum w_i v_i(y_i) = \sum w_i v_i(z_i) = v(z), \qquad (13.4)$$

which provides one equation with the $w_i s$ as the n unknown parameters to be specified. By finding n pairs of consequences of equal value, we generate n equations with collectively n unknowns and then solve for those unknowns, which gives us numerical values of the w_i parameters.

Practical Considerations for Choosing a Value Model

A value model must explicitly address the complex and important value judgments that can influence a decision. If fun and excitement are important objectives of a major vacation, then those objectives should be explicitly included in a value model to evaluate alternative vacation destinations. If one of the main impacts of a decision is the potential loss of life, such as decisions involving the setting of national ambient air quality standards, then an objective should explicitly address the potential loss of life. The objective should be "minimize loss of life" with a corresponding attribute such as "number of lives lost annually because of the pollutant." Analyses that use an attribute such as parts per million of the pollutant in the air as a proxy for loss of life are inadequate and miss the substance of the decision. Anybody using such an analysis would have to informally relate the parts per million of the pollutant to the loss of life to make a reasoned decision.

For decisions involving the potential loss of life, value tradeoffs between cost and potential loss of life are typically critical to the choice of an alternative. In those cases, that value tradeoff should be included in the value model. In an investment decision, the risk attitude concerning financial outcomes may be very important and, if that is the case, should be carefully modeled.

In general, whenever a value judgment is important to a decision, it should be explicitly included in the value model. In a personal decision about whether to have amniocentesis or chorionic villus sampling during pregnancy to assess any potential genetic damage of the fetus, a reasoned decision partly depends on the relative desirability to the parents of having a perfectly healthy child, no child, or a child with the various congenital problems caused by gene defects. For this decision, the relative desirabilities of these different situations are sometimes more crucial to making an appropriate choice for a family than are the exact probabilities of the different outcomes.

Utility versus Measurable Value

An analyst can choose whether or not to develop a utility function or a measurable value function. Which of these two functions is appropriate depends on many considerations. Theoretically, the choice mainly depends on the problem characteristics. If uncertainties are large and explicitly incorporated in the consequence model for the decision, then a utility function is the theoretically appropriate value model. If there are no uncertainties or only minor uncertainties about the consequences, then a measurable value function is more appropriate.

Beyond the theory, there are practical considerations that are relevant. If the previously mentioned risk aversion of one of the objectives was important, then it may matter and a utility function would be appropriate. However, if there are only minor uncertainties and if the degree of risk aversion is small, then it probably does not matter whether one chooses a value or a utility function. In such cases, a more important consideration is the relative ability of the decision maker to provide information about values during the assessment of value or utility functions. Generally speaking, the assessment of value functions is easier, involving primarily ordinal or strength-of-preference judgments between pairs of consequences. The theoretically correct assessment of utility functions involves preferences among lotteries or uncertain prospects and some decision makers have difficulty expressing preferences among these often complex options.

One very important result of the research on value and utility functions is that they must be closely related. In all cases, value and utility functions must be related by a strictly monotone increasing function h:

$$u(x) = h\{v(x)\}. \tag{13.5}$$

Further restrictions on the function h obtain when both the value function and the utility functions are additive. In that case the function h must be a linear positive transformation (see Krantz et al. 1971), so

$$u(\boldsymbol{x}) = av(\boldsymbol{x}) + b, a > 0, \tag{13.6}$$

where a and b are constants.

Another example is the case in which the value function is additive, but the utility function is multiplicative. In this case, the value and utility functions must be related by an exponential function (see Dyer and Sarin 1979; Keeney and Raiffa 1976; Barron, von Winterfeldt and Fischer 1984), so

$$u(\boldsymbol{x}) = a \ \exp^{cv(\boldsymbol{x})} + b, a > 0, \tag{13.7}$$

where a, b, and c are constant. As a byproduct of these functional relationships between u and v, the relationships between the single-attribute functions v_i and u_i are also highly constrained to be either linear or exponential. Proofs of these relationships can be found in Keeney and Raiffa (1976), Dyer and Sarin (1979), and von Winterfeldt (1979).

If it can be established that a value function is additive and that the utility function is either additive or multiplicative, a sound way to proceed is to construct an additive value function, followed by an assessment of the parameters of the function h in Eq. 13.5. This function is sometimes called the "relative risk aversion function" because it is the risk aversion expressed relative to a value function.

Some research suggests that utility functions and measurable value functions should be the same (Bell and Raiffa 1988). Other empirical research indicates that people distinguish between these concepts in some situations. For example, Barron, von Winterfeldt, and Fischer (1984) showed that empirically assessed utility functions differ from value functions in the sense of showing relative risk aversion. An exponential relationship between value and utility provided a good fit to their data.

For many decisions, it is reasonable to assume that the measurable value function and the utility function are identical. It is often the case that the quality of the information describing the consequences of the alternatives is such that this assumption about a common function for utility and measurable value is not the weak link in any analysis. In a book written for individuals to help themselves analyze decisions (Hammond et al.1999), the assumption was made that a utility function and a measurable value function are identical.

Additive versus Nonadditive Value Models

An additive value model is simpler to construct and to use than a nonadditive model. The key to determine if an additive value model is appropriate is the set of objectives used for the value model. If these objectives are fundamental objectives for the decision and meet the criteria specified for a good set of fundamental objectives (see Chapter 7 in this volume), then a strong case can be made that an additive value model is appropriate. In most of our own recent applications of decision analysis, we have created a set of fundamental objectives that satisfied these criteria so the resulting value model was additive.

The main cause of nonadditivity is the use of means objectives in the value model (see also Chapter 7 in this volume for the distinction between *means objectives* and *ends objectives*). Suppose one is concerned about the loss of life from automobile accidents. One means objective is to minimize speeding of drivers, and a second means objective is to minimize driving under the influence of alcohol. Any value model that simply added up the two effects related to each of these objectives would not incorporate the natural dependency that speeding while under the influence of alcohol is likely worse than the sum of the consequences of each separately. Another case of nonadditivity occurs, when one objective works as a multiplier on a second objective. For example, when evaluating a new piece of equipment, its reliability and its performance may be objectives. In this case reliability acts like a multiplier, because with zero reliability, one should not care about the degree of performance. If one encounters a case such as this, it is often better to develop another objective such as "expected performance" and to develop a model that combines reliability and performance to measure this new objective.

Formally, Fishburn's (1965) necessary and sufficient condition for the additive utility function (13.2) was that preferences only depend on the marginal probability distributions over consequences. Dyer and Sarin (1979) showed that a measurable utility function is additive, if the strength of preference between two alternatives that vary only on a subset of attributes remains the same, if the consequences in the other attributes that are identical across alternatives are changed.

It is worth mentioning that many value models may have several additive terms and perhaps one or two nonadditive terms. However, even in these situations one might interpret the value model as being additive. To illustrate this, consider a simple decision problem where a decision maker wishes to please two separate individuals A and B. the decision maker's objectives are explicitly stated as "maximize the desirability of the consequences to individual A" and "maximize the desirability of the consequences to individual B." If there are major uncertainties, the value model should be a utility function. In these situations, it is reasonable that utility independence assumptions hold so that the decision maker's utility function u can be written as

$$u(u_A, u_B) = k_A u_A + k_B u_B + k u_A u_B, \qquad (13.8)$$

where u_A and u_B are utility functions representing preferences of individuals A and B and the ks are constants. If k is not 0, then this function is commonly thought of as a nonadditive value model. This thinking is based on a value model with two objectives and three terms, one of which is a product term. On the other hand, Eq. 13.8 is clearly additive with three terms. The first two terms directly measure the degree to which the two stated fundamental objectives are met. But what does the third term measure? As discussed in Keeney (1981), the third term can be considered a measure for the objective of the decision maker "to have an equitable consequence for individuals A and B." If this third objective is added to the other two fundamental objectives, then Eq. 13.8 is clearly an additive utility function for three fundamental objectives.

There are two important points of this simple example. First, it emphasizes that with an appropriate set of fundamental objectives, an additive value model is practical and logically sound. Second, it indicates that one can get most of the benefits of an additive value model, which is simpler than nonadditive models, and, yet, incorporate a term that may not be additive to capture important consequences in the decision. Even if one does not identify an appropriate label to characterize the nonadditive term with a new fundamental objective, the decision maker should understand why it is included in the value model and how it can easily be handled in practice.

Linearity

Three general situations lead to linearity of single-attribute value or utility functions. One situation is when the attribute for a fundamental objective measures something that is of value in itself, as opposed to value for its uses. Suppose one is evaluating several medical programs and one of the objectives is to save as many lives as possible. The attribute for this objective might be the number of lives saved. Clearly each life saved is valuable in and of itself. It is of course valued by the individual whose life is at risk and by their family and friends. It seems reasonable to count each life saved as equal to any other, especially when the medical intervention is typically used for individuals of roughly the same age and the same health state.

How could one justify a value function, which valued the first life saved much more than the hundredth life saved? One reason might be that the first life saved proved the feasibility of the intervention being used. Subsequently, this may lead to more lives being saved in the future. We certainly recognize that proving feasibility of an intervention, and saving more lives in the future are important, but we feel these should be identified as separate objectives for the decision problem. That being the case, these reasons could not be any justification for valuing the first life save more than later lives saved. The point is that if the value of saving lives is basically for those whose lives are saved and those who know them, counting each life saved equally is reasonable and the implication is that a linear value model for that single attribute is reasonable.

A second situation that leads to linearity is the following. Sometimes the consequence estimates are simply estimates thought to be somewhere around the expected consequence. If one could quantify a reasonable standard deviation in this case, it may be 20 percent or more of that expected consequence. By using the expected value, linearity is naturally implicitly assumed. Therefore, it does not make any sense to use a value model other than a linear model in such situations.

The third situation where linearity is a reasonable assumption concerns single decisions when many other decisions also contribute to the same objective. Therefore, the range over which the consequences may fall in that single decision is small relative to the range for all the decisions collectively. A specific case is when a major company that has profits in the billions of dollars per year is making a decision that may at most affect annual profits by plus or minus $20 million. Any reasonable utility function over profits for the company, whether it was risk averse or risk prone, would effectively be equivalent to a linear function over a $40 million range. Any additional benefit of using a nonlinear utility function would likely not be worth the shortcomings of additional effort for such a decision.

In some circumstances, the linearity assumption may be reasonable for 99 percent of the consequences evaluated in a decision problem, but there may be one or two consequences where there should be an adjustment because linearity may not be appropriate. For instance, a recent study involved a major project in the area of a large dam (Keeney and von Winterfeldt, 2005). The project cost was in the neighborhood of $600 million and, as a result of the project, there will be a very small chance that there could be a dam failure induced. Alternatives were available that would reduce that small chance and cost up to $26 million. There were other relatively minor problems that could be caused in the area of the dam such as landslides in local neighborhoods. Considering all the consequences in this decision problem and the cost of the alternatives considered, the range of consequences was about $30 million, except for the dam failure, which was valued at $1.2 billion. In this situation for reasons discussed in the previous paragraph, a linear model was appropriate for all possible consequences except those involving a dam failure. In this case, we tripled the consequences of a dam failure to $3.6 billion, which effectively is the same as utilizing risk aversion for evaluating the consequence of dam failure.

Figure 13.1 illustrates this situation. All of the consequences except the dam failure are in region A and the risk averse utility function over costs shown in the figure is very close to linear in that region. A $1.8 billion consequence, which is $0.6 billion for construction and $1.2 billion due to a dam failure, evaluated at point B with a risk averse utility function, has the same utility as the $4.2 billion consequence, which is $0.6 billion plus a dam failure cost tripled to $3.6 billion, evaluated at point C, using a linear utility function.

Risk Aversion

In some decisions, it is reasonable to assume that the utility function or the measurable value function for single attributes is not linear. If these are utility functions, the main issue is whether they should exhibit risk aversion or risk proneness. It is usually practical in these situations to select utility functions that are appropriately risk prone or risk averse that have one parameter. Specifically, based on the work of Pratt (1964), it is often appropriate to select the constantly risk-averse exponential utility function:

$$u_i(x_i) = a_i + b_i(-e^{-c_i x_i}), b_i, c_i > 0, \tag{13.9}$$

where a_i, b_i, and c_i are constants. With an exponential utility function, it is easy to conduct sensitivity analyses to determine if either the decision or the insight from

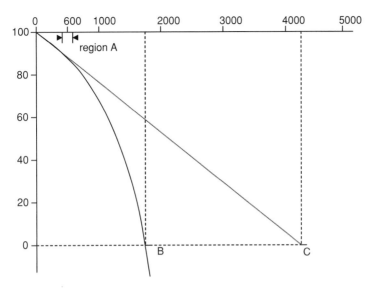

Figure 13.1. Adjustment of consequences to allow use of linearity assumption for preferences.

the analysis changes as a result of varying the risk coefficient over a reasonable range.

As mentioned in the discussion about the relationships between utility and measurable value, one can develop a measurable value function for use in a decision problem and use this as a single attribute in a utility function if uncertainties are significant. One can also use the exponential utility function in this case and conduct sensitivity analyses to examine the relevance of risk aversion to the decision.

There are some situations where it is appropriate to use a risk-averse utility function that may be more sophisticated than assuming constant risk aversion. The main situations where this occurs are in investment decisions where the range of financial consequences extends over significant amounts of money and/or long time periods. For individuals doing financial planning for their lifetime, it may be reasonable to use a decreasing risk averse utility function that automatically accounts for the wealth level of the individual. Meyer (1970) used such utility functions in his analysis of personal investment and consumption strategies. Another circumstance where more sophisticated levels of risk aversion may be appropriate concerns environmental resources. When there are a lot of these resources, one should behave with a relatively risk-neutral attitude, but as these resources become rarer, a more risk-averse attitude may be very appropriate to represent public values.

Practical Considerations for Selecting an Assessment Procedure

In principle, assessing the parameters of a value model (the single-attribute value or utility functions v_i or u_i, and the weights w_i or k_i) is only a matter of asking a series of questions about indifferences and determining from this series of questions a set of n equations with n unknown and then to solve for the unknowns.

In practice, several procedures have emerged as being practical for assessing single-attribute utility and value functions and weights. We have found two types of assessment procedures especially useful: the equivalent-cost assessment procedure and the rating and swing weighting procedure.

Equivalent-Cost Procedure

This procedure is most appropriate, when the consequences can be described by simple numerical scales, when the single-attribute value functions are linear, and when the overall value model is additive. In that case, it is often possible to determine the unit equivalent cost of each attribute (e.g., the cost of an injury or of the loss of an acre of land) and to calculate the overall value of a vector of consequences as the sum of the equivalent costs of each attribute (calculated by the unit cost times the number of unit consequences for each alternative).

This procedure is similar to a benefit–cost model, except for two distinctions. First, the equivalent costs are obtained by asking decision makers for value trade-offs, instead of deriving them from market considerations and observed prices. Markets and prices can inform this dialogue, but other information is often used in this process as well. In many public decisions, there are no market prices for the consequences of some important objectives. Examples include lives lost, habitat destroyed, or jobs created. Second, several assumptions are typically checked to see whether the equivalent-cost model makes sense. These assumptions include the additivity and linearity previously mentioned and whether or not the cost attribute is a significant attribute in the value model. This latter point can be illustrated with a simple example.

In Figure 13.2, assume that the consequences of a decision can be displayed in terms of two attributes. One of these attributes is cost C. The other attribute Y measures an objective that one would like to minimize. For example, Y may be the acres of trees destroyed in building various facilities considered as alternatives for the problem. Suppose all of the consequences are as indicated in Figure 13.2a by dots. Also, suppose that one had assessed a complete value model as illustrated by the indifference curves with an equal value between adjacent curves. As seen from this figure, the range of the Y-consequences covers just the difference between adjacent indifference curves, whereas the range of the cost consequences covers about eight indifference curves illustrated on the C-axis. This implies that the cost implications in the decision, given the range of possible consequences, are about eight times more significant than the Y-consequences for that decision. Given this situation, it is quite reasonable to convert these Y-consequences into equivalent costs for the value model.

There are two ways one could obtain equivalent costs, illustrated respectively in Figures 13.2a and 13.2b. In Figure 13.2a, equivalent-cost values for all the Y-levels are determined and one "costs out" all of these down to the 0 level of the Y-attribute. If one did this for each of the point consequences in the figure (i.e., dots),

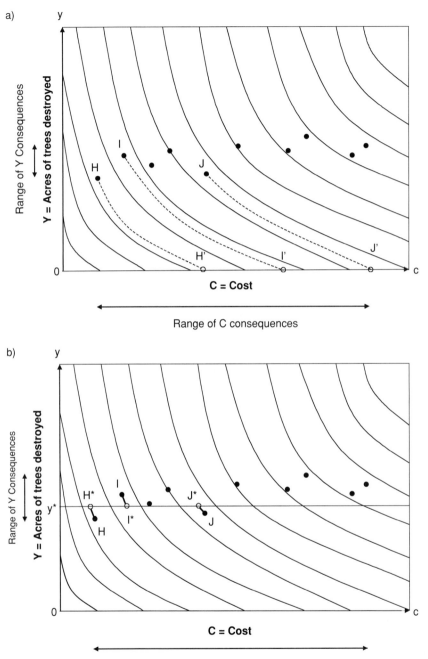

Figure 13.2. Converting two-attribute consequences to one attribute using a reasonable linear value tradeoff. The figure above, (a), represents nonlinear tradeoff over long range, and the figure below, (b), linear tradeoff over short range.

the corresponding equivalent consequence would be found by following the indifference curve down to the Y axis. Thus, for instance, the consequence labeled H would be converted to the consequence labeled consequences H'. Note that the attribute level of Y associated with H' is outside the range of the set of Y-levels for the original consequences.

Now consider Figure 13.2b. Here we draw a horizontal line through the consequences given Y set arbitrarily at a level $y*$ in the original range of the Y-levels. Now we can find the consequence equivalent to H, referred to as $H*$, that is on the $y*$ line of consequences. Note that consequence H is much closer to consequence $H*$ than it is to consequence H' in Figure 13.2a. Thus, it is reasonable to use a linear function to translate consequence H into $H*$. For instance, that transformation may state that an acre of trees has an equivalent value of D dollars. The same unit value tradeoff, meaning equivalent dollars per acre of trees, might be used for consequences I and J, illustrated in Figure 13.2b, to convert them to equivalently valued consequences $I*$ and $J*$.

As a result of conversions such as this, an equivalent valued consequence with a y-level of $y*$ is found for each of the original consequences in the decision and it is naturally differentiated only on the cost attribute. Thus, only the equivalent costs of those consequences are necessary for differentiating the desirability of the alternatives. Also, as a result of the closeness of the equivalent consequences to the corresponding original consequences, the relative impact on the evaluation due to the assessed value tradeoffs to develop the cost-equivalent evaluations is much less than when all of the Y-levels are costed out to a level, where $y = 0$.

Now let us return to the general case where there are n objectives and attributes X_i other than cost C. Let a consequence be described by $(x_1, x_2, \ldots, x_i, \ldots, x_n, c)$, where c is the cost level. If all tradeoffs between X_i and C are linear (or approximately linear as in Figure 13b above), then an equivalent cost model is a practical value model and its construction is particularly simple. In this case, one needs to elicit only the equivalent costs for a unit consequence of each attribute to calculate the equivalent cost v as

$$v(x_1, x_2, \ldots x_i, \ldots x_n, c) = c + \sum w_i x_i, \qquad (13.10)$$

where w_i is the equivalent cost of one unit of attribute X_i.

The assumptions necessary for an equivalent-cost model are often appropriate for major public policy decisions. We have used this simple value model in many recent decision analysis applications, including siting the first nuclear repository in the United States (Merkhofer and Keeney 1987), managing nuclear waste from powerplants (Keeney and von Winterfeldt 1994), retrofitting buildings to reduce earthquake risks (Benthien and von Winterfeldt 2001), managing potential health risks from electric powerlines (von Winterfeldt et al. 2004), and reducing risks of a dam failure (Keeney and von Winterfeldt 2005).

Rating and Weighting Procedure

In problems that involve softer attributes like "aesthetics" or attributes that do not have a cost equivalent, it is often practical to use a rating and weighting method, as described, for example in Edwards and Newman (1982) and von Winterfeldt and Edwards (1986). In this method the consequences of alternatives are rated on a scale (usually from zero to 100) reflecting their relative value on each attribute (100 being best). The attributes are then assigned weights, paying close attention to the relative ranges of the consequences in each attribute.

RATING CONSEQUENCES. Typically, this step starts by defining a low and a high consequence for each attribute and by assigning these two extremes a value of zero and 100. All other consequences are then rated between zero and 100 reflecting the degree of preference of each rated consequence relative to the lowest and highest ranked ones. When the attribute is defined on a continuous numerical scale, other methods such as bisection (dividing the scale into steps of equal changes of preference) can be used as well.

WEIGHTS. Weights can often be assessed for either units of the attributes or for ranges of the attributes. It is very important that weights are not assigned to objectives and attributes themselves as this can lead to significant biases (e.g., von Winterfeldt and Edwards 1986). If the attributes have linear value functions, it is easiest to assess the relative importance of a unit of each attribute. For example, in a recent study evaluating decision science programs at U.S. universities (Keeney, See, and von Winterfeldt 2006), we identified several attributes, including the number of refereed articles published in the past 5 years, the number of scholarly and popular books in prints, and the number of dissertations in the past 5 years. With linear attributes it is then easy to ask, for example: What is more important, one book or one refereed article and how much more important is it? Answers to these questions, provided in the study by eight scholars in decision analysis and behavioral research, proved to be quite consistent.

When attributes have nonlinear value functions, it is more appropriate to assign weights, referred to as "swing weights," to the ranges of the attributes (von Winterfeldt and Edwards 1986). In this method, the decision makers are asked to consider a hypothetical alternative that is described by the worst consequences on all attributes. They are then asked which attribute they would like to change ("swing") most from its worst level to its best level. Once this judgment is made, they are asked which attribute they would like to change next and so on until a complete rank order of these weights is established. With the rank order in place, one can assign an arbitrary weight of 1 to the lowest ranked attribute and ask the decision makers to scale the remaining weights based on the relative importance of those ranges. Alternatively, one can start with assigning an arbitrary weight of 100 to the highest ranked attribute and scale the remaining ones as fractions of 100.

When applying this method, it is important to cross check the results with some tradeoff questions. In particular, when cost is an attribute, it is important to discuss the implications of these range weights for equivalent cost comparisons. For example, if the costs of decision alternatives range from $200 million to $300 million and with a possible loss of productive wetlands ranging from 0 acres to 100 acres, a decision maker may judge the latter range to be more important than the former. In that case it should be pointed out that this implies that it would be worth spending at least $100 million dollars to avoid 100 acres of lost wetlands or $1 million per acre. This may not be an unreasonable judgment, but it clearly depends on the type of wetlands, the existence of similar wetlands, and the number and rareness of species in this environment, etc.

Using Constructed Scales

With some objectives it is not possible to identify an attribute with a natural scale and, as a result, one needs to develop a constructed scale (see Chapter 7 in this volume). With a constructed scale, there are typically two to ten well-defined points on that scale. The basic task in a value model is to assign appropriate relative values to each of those levels. One needs to make sure that the values for these levels cover the range of possible consequences. For instance, if you have six possible levels of consequences defined on a constructed scale and wish to assign relative values from zero to one hundred to those consequences, is it not reasonable to have a value between zero and five assigned for five of those consequences and a value of one hundred assigned to the sixth. Unless there were no possible consequences between five and one hundred, it would be better if consequence levels on the constructed scale were chosen so that their utilities would correspond more closely to the amounts zero, twenty, forty, . . . , one hundred when consequences cover the full range of consequences.

Practical Considerations for Developing Value Models with Decision Makers

When the decision maker or decision makers are identified, their values should be incorporated in the value model. If the decision maker or decision makers have sufficient time and interest, then a complete value assessment could be done. However, sometimes they may have limited available time or they really do not understand why spending a significant amount of time expressing their value judgments is important. In these situations, it is still important to involve them at some level to obtain a few of the key value judgments. This both increases the decision makers' interest in the results of the analysis and their potential willingness to act on them.

Some decision makers consider it worthwhile to spend time expressing values for the analysis. In these cases, it is important to ask the most relevant value questions first. It is also reasonable to ask these value judgments from different perspectives that will facilitate consistency checks. We have found that if you can point out inconsistencies in values that decision makers consider important, they begin to understand why there is substantial value in clarifying their values for the decision. This certainly increases their willingness to participate.

For some decisions, especially those concerned with long-term consequences in governmental or other large organizations, it is not clear who makes the decision or perhaps even how the decision will be made. In these situations, the value model should represent values appropriate for the decision problem for the organization that will eventually make the decision. Input judgments about specific values can come from different individuals in the organization or constructed based on the knowledge of the organization by the analyst.

Generic Objectives

Obtaining an appropriate set of objectives for a decision problem requires effort and creativity. Indeed, Chapters 6 and 7 in this volume suggest procedures that might help people in this task. As a practical suggestion for specific types of problems, there are often generic sets of objectives that will apply to a wide range of decisions. For many public policy decisions, one wants to consider objectives in categories that might be referred to as costs, socioeconomic impacts, impacts on the natural environment, and health and safety. Sometimes this categorization is extended to include political consequences to or within the decision making organization and impacts on its relationship with public groups and other governmental organizations.

On any major decision, it is worthwhile to initially think of objectives from the viewpoint of various stakeholders concerned about a decision. For instance, if a large corporation is making a major decision, it is certainly worthwhile to consider objectives that deal with the impacts on shareholders, customers, employees, and management and then break these objectives into both short-term consequences and long-term consequences.

Constructing Value Models

In many situations, an analyst will begin to understand the values appropriate for the decision better than any one individual in the organization responsible for the decision. Part of this is because the analyst talks to many people throughout the organization and different individuals understand the appropriate values for different objectives, and part of it is because some individuals do not know how to express their values in a clear manner to be used in the value model. Analysts can help by combining values expressed throughout the organization and by improving the communication of values within the organization.

Decision makers will often indicate, in general terms, that they are risk averse with regards to consequences of a certain attribute. However, they do not seem to understand thoroughly the value questions concerning choices between lotteries, either because they do not understand well-defined probabilities or they cannot deal with the hypothetical circumstances that have a few consequences in a simple lottery when the real world has the possibility for numerous consequences. In these situations, it is reasonable for the analyst to translate the basic values of the decision maker in order to define parameters in the value model. This is very consistent with the ideas of Payne and Bettman and their colleagues (Payne et al. 1992; Payne et al. 1999), regarding the constructive nature of building value models.

Focus on Key Values

There are many situations where the time available to interview the key decision makers about their values is limited, or when one is not sure how much time will be available. In both of these situations, it is critical to focus the interview process on the key value judgments that are presumed to strongly influence the results of that analysis. One of the most important aspects of this is to make sure that all the fundamental objectives of concern to the decision maker are included in the analysis. The other two types of critical value judgments typically concern the value tradeoffs between some key attributes and the levels of risk aversion appropriate for certain attributes. The intent is to quickly find out what is going on in the head of the decision maker so that the analyst can spend the appropriate time to construct a model.

Consider an analysis of different alternatives that address potential terrorist activities. Furthermore, assume that the potential loss of life is one of the main objectives. There are circumstances where the decision maker, when being asked about relative values for the life lost, might say that the first loss of life is worth at least a billion dollars, and the next few are worth more than $100 million dollars a piece, but after 100 or so fatalities, the loss of additional life is worth about $5 million in equivalent dollars. If these preferences are meant to reflect a utility function, it would be consistent with a strongly risk prone utility function. The important point here is to inquire about why these are the preferences of the person expressing them. It may be that the first few fatalities indicate failure of a major system, which will induce a large public response that results in major psychological and economic impacts. Once the terrorist acts have caused say 100 fatalities, then the indirect psychological and economic consequences will have been caused, and the additional impact of more fatalities is the additional loss of life. Understanding this as the reason for the preferences allows one to do a much better job of defining the objectives of the problem. Specifically, we recommend separating out objectives to indicate the indirect consequences of the terrorist act from the direct loss of life due to that act. Then the single-attribute value model over the fatalities should be linear if it concerns the loss of life and the impact on families and friends only. The psychological and economic consequences can then be defined more clearly and presumably values for different levels of those consequences can be better understood and assessed.

Bounding Value Parameters

For parameters that deal with value tradeoffs, such as the w_i in Eq. 13.1 and with risk aversion, such as the c in Eq. 13.9, it is often useful to assess a range that the decision maker considers appropriate to bound the parameter level. Then one can easily perform a sensitivity analysis by varying the parameters within this range. In many situations, it turns out that the evaluation of the alternatives and the insights from the analysis do not depend on most of these parameters given their reasonable ranges. This allows one to focus on those parameters that are most important to the problem, which leads to the critical insights that can inform making better choices.

Understanding Values

One of the most practical and powerful of assessment tools is simply to ask the question "why?" Assessing a utility function or a measurable value function involves a series of questions. The intent is to understand what is in the mind of the person being assessed about values appropriate to the decision of concern. It is not hard to get an answer to many questions about values, but one wants to probe deeper to understand the fundamental value judgments that are leading to these responses. Inquiring about the reasoning for each response is very useful. The responses help both to build a better value model and provide a better analysis.

Suppose a decision is being made about placing natural gas pipelines through forested areas to bring natural gas to an urban area. One of the negative consequences might be the acres of forest destroyed in placing those pipelines. When asked a question about what is the value tradeoff between costs and an acre of forest destroyed, the respondents may say $1 million is an equivalent cost to use for an acre destroyed. Asked why, the respondents may state that the price of the lumber for an acre of that forest is worth $1 million. Alternatively, they may respond that the forest is the home to many animal species and the value of the habitat of those species is $1 million. Or they may state that many individuals take a vacation in that area and enjoy the forest, and over the time that the forest is disrupted, the value of the loss of enjoyment by those individuals is $1 million. Any of those responses suggest ways in which the values should be potentially separated out for the decision problem and/or ways in which the values are not complete. Indeed, if each of those three sets of implications were tied to the loss of an acre of forest, and if those stated value judgments were appropriate for evaluating the components of that loss, one might say that $3 million was equivalent to the loss of an acre of that forest. The point is that by routinely asking the question "why," one learns a lot more about the values.

Conclusions

When building value models an analyst has to answer several critical questions and, depending on the answers, has to make decisions about what type of value model to build and how to build it. The most important questions are:

1. Does the problem require a value function or a utility function? If a utility function is needed, should one assess a value function first?

2. Is the value function or the utility function additive? If not, what other aggregation model should be used?
3. Are the single-attribute value or utility functions linear and, if not, how should risk aversion be addressed?
4. Is an equivalent-cost model appropriate for the problem or should a rating and weighting method be used?

The answers to the questions and the implications for building a value model should be driven by the problem that needs to be solved and by the decision makers' needs and preferences. In our experience over the past two decades of building value models, we have found that, depending on the answers to these questions, two classes of models and some minor variants are often appropriate. The first class of value models is an equivalent-cost value function, possibly with a parametric exploration of risk aversion through an exponential transformation into a utility function. The second class of value models is a simple additive value function with unit or range weights and with no particular need to develop a utility function to account for risk attitudes.

The equivalent-cost model has proven valuable in many public policy applications, but it is also applicable in many decisions for private businesses, where the objectives are more limited (e.g., net profit, growth, and market share). It has been our experience that it is almost always useful to first build a value function and that a careful choice of fundamental objectives often justifies a linear or near-linear single- attribute value functions. If this is the case, and cost is a major part of the decision, then using linear value functions and unit costs to determine weights is both easiest to assess and to communicate. An example of this type of value model is used in the analysis of alternative policies to reduce electromagnetic field exposure from electric powerlines (see von Winterfeldt et al. 2004).

Several variants of this approach have been used in the past. For example, when constructed measures are used, it is better to assess weights using the equivalent values for the whole range of the attribute rather than for attribute units (see Keeney and von Winterfeldt 2005). When risk aversion is important, it is often useful to supplement the value function with a parametric analysis of a constantly risk averse utility function (see Merkhofer and Keeney 1987).

Using a simple additive value model without assessing equivalent costs is useful in "softer" problems when costs and uncertainties do not play an important part. Assessing the quality of consumer products is one example. Another example is a recent evaluation of decision science programs at U.S. universities (Keeney et al. 2006). These simple models are similar to the rating and weighting models first proposed by Edwards and his colleagues (see Edwards and Newman 1982; von Winterfeldt and Edwards 1986). However, it is important not to oversimplify the value model in these cases. In particular, we emphasize the importance of using fundamental objectives, natural or constructed measures, checks of additivity, and care in assessing unit or range weights.

As with the equivalent-cost model, it is useful to identify fundamental objectives and attributes that are additive and have linear or near-linear single-attribute value functions. If some objectives appear nonadditive, we suggest redefining the objectives or adding objectives that can capture the reasons for the nonadditivity. Similarly, if some attributes have clearly nonlinear value functions, it is useful to probe the reasons for the nonlinearity and possibly redefine objectives or separate an objective into several parts. Regarding attributes, we encourage the use of natural measures to the extent possible. This helps address the factual part of the problem – the assessment of the degree to which alternatives satisfy objectives – and separates the value model from the factual model. When constructed measures are needed, it is important that these are carefully defined so that independent experts can arrive at similar judgments about how an alternative scores on the constructed measure.

We end with a caveat. This chapter is about using practical value models, meaning models that are good enough to gain all the important insights for a decision that might be expected or hoped for. We believe that often this does not require developing a state-of-the-art value model. It does, however, always require sound logic and judgments to justify the decision not to build a state-of-the-art model. Nothing in this paper is meant to suggest that a quick and dirty listing of poorly defined objectives and rating or weighting of these objectives is reasonable or justifiable.

There are times, especially for very complex and important decisions, when one should develop a state-of-the-art value model. This requires explicit assessments to justify all assumptions, to select the set of fundamental objectives, to choose attributes, to select all utility or value functions (both in single-attribute and multiattribute form), to assess the parameters, and to perform consistency checks for all elements of a value assessment.

REFERENCES

Barron, F. H., von Winterfeldt, D., and Fischer, G. W. (1984). Empirical and theoretical relationships between value and utility functions. *Acta Psychologica, 56,* 233–244.

Bell, D., and Raiffa, H. (1988). Marginal value and intrinsic risk aversion. (1988). In D. Bell, H. Raiffa, and A. Tversky (eds.) *Decision making: Descriptive, normative, and prescriptive interactions.* Cambridge, UK: Cambridge University Press, 384–397.

Benthien, M. and von Winterfeldt, D. (2001). Using decision analysis to improve seismic rehabilitation decisions. Working Paper WP-01–01, Institute for Civic Enterprise, University of Southern California, Los Angeles, CA.

Dyer, J. S. and Sarin, R. (1979). Measurable multiattribute value functions. *Operations Research, 22,* 810–822.

Edwards, W., and Newman, J. R. (1982). *Multiattribute evaluation.* Beverly Hills, CA: Sage.

Fishburn, P. C. (1965). Independence in utility theory with whole product sets. *Operations Research, 13,* 28–45.

Fishburn, P. C. (1970). *Utility theory for decision making.* New York: Wiley.

Hammond, J. S., Keeney, R. L., and Raiffa, H. (1999). *Smart choices: A practical guide to making better decisions.* Boston, MA: Harvard Business School Press.

Keeney, R. L. (1981). Analysis of preference dependencies among objectives. *Operations Research, 29,* 1105–1120.

Keeney, R. L. (1988). Building models of values. *European Journal of Operational Research, 37,* 149–157.

Keeney, R. L. and Raiffa, H. (1976). *Decisions with multiple objectives: Preferences and value tradeoffs*. New York: Wiley. Reprinted in 1993 by Cambridge University Press.

Keeney, R. L., and von Winterfeldt, D. (1994). Managing nuclear waste from power plants. *Risk Analysis, 14*, 107–130.

Keeney, R. L., See, K., and von Winterfeldt, D. (2006). Evaluating interdisciplinary academic programs: With applications to U.S. graduate decision programs. *Operations Research, 25*, 1–16.

Keeney, R. L., and von Winterfeldt, D. (2005). *Evaluation of Capilano-Seymour tunnel project alternatives*. Technical Report, submitted to the Greater Vancouver Regional District, Vancouver, Canada.

Krantz, D. H. (1964). Conjoint measurement: The Luce-Tukey axiomatization and some extensions. *Journal of Mathematical Psychology, 1*, 248–277.

Krantz, D. H., Luce, R. D., Suppes, P., and Tversky, A. (1971). *Foundations of measurement, Volume I*. New York: Academic Press.

Luce, R. D. and Tukey, J. W. (1964). Simultaneous conjoint measurement: A new type of fundamental measurement. *Journal of Mathematical Psychology, 1*, 1–27.

Merkhofer, M. L. and Keeney, R. L. (1987). A multiattribute utility analysis of alternative sites for the disposal of nuclear waste. *Risk Analysis, 7*, 173–194

Meyer, R. F. (1970). On the relationship among the utility of assets, the utility of consumption, and investment strategy in an uncertain, but time invariant world. In J. Lawrence (Ed.). *OR 69: Proceedings of the Fifth International Conference on Operational Research*. London: Tavistock Publications.

Payne, J.W., Bettman, J.R., Coupey, E., and Johnson, E.J. (1992). A constructive process view of decision making: Multiple strategies in judgment and choice. *Acta Psychologica, 80*, 107–141.

Payne, J. W., Bettman, J. R., and Schkade, D. A. (1999). Measuring constructed preferences: Towards a building code. *Journal of Risk and Uncertainty, 19*, 243–270.

Pratt, J. W. (1964). Risk aversion in the small and the large. *Econometrica, 32*, 122–136.

von Neuman, J., and Morgenstern, O. (1947). *Theory of games and economic behavior* (2nd ed.). Princeton, NJ: Princeton University Press.

von Winterfeldt, D. (1979). *Functional relationships between risky and riskless multiattribute utility functions*. Technical Report No. 79–3. Social Science Research Institute, Los Angeles: University of Southern California.

von Winterfeldt, D. and Edwards, W. (1986). *Decision analysis and behavioral research*. Cambridge, UK: Cambridge University Press.

von Winterfeldt, D., Eppel, T., Adams, J., Neutra, R., DelPizzo, V. (2004). Managing potential heath risks from electric powerlines: A decision analysis caught in controversy. *Risk Analysis, 24*, 1487–1502.

14 Extensions of the Subjective Expected Utility Model

Robert F. Nau[1]

ABSTRACT. The subjective expected utility (SEU) model rests on very strong assumptions about the consistency of decision making across a wide range of situations. The descriptive validity of these assumptions has been extensively challenged by behavioral psychologists during the last few decades, and the normative validity of the assumptions has also been reappraised by many statisticians, philosophers, and economists, motivating the development of more general utility theories and decision models. These generalized models are characterized by features such as imprecise probabilities, nonlinearly weighted probabilities, source-dependent risk attitudes, and state-dependent utilities, permitting the pattern of the decision maker's behavior to change with the decision context and to perhaps satisfy the usual SEU assumptions only locally. Recent research in the emerging field of neuroeconomics sheds light on the physiological basis of decision making, the nature of preferences and beliefs, and interpersonal differences in decision competence. These findings do not necessarily invalidate the use of SEU-based decision analysis tools, but they suggest that care needs to be taken to structure preferences and to assess beliefs and risk attitudes in a manner that is appropriate for the decision and also for the decision maker.

The SEU Model and Its Assumptions

The subjective expected utility (SEU) model provides the conceptual and computational framework that is most often used to analyze decisions under uncertainty. In the SEU model, uncertainty about the future is represented by a set of *states of the world*, which are mutually exclusive and exhaustive events. Possible outcomes for the decision maker are represented by a set of *consequences*, which could be amounts of money in the bank or more general "states of the person" such as health, happiness, pleasant or unpleasant experiences, and so on. A decision alternative, known as an *act*, is defined by an assignment of consequences to states of the world. In the case where the set of states is a finite set $(E_1, \ldots, E_n)$, an act can be written as a vector $x = (x_1, \ldots, x_n)$, where x_i is the consequence that is received or experienced in state E_i. The decision maker's beliefs concerning states of the world are represented by a *subjective probability distribution* $p = (p_1, \ldots, p_n)$, where p_i is the probability of E_i, and her values for consequences are represented

[1] I am grateful to Jill Stowe, Jim Smith, and the editors for helpful comments. Any errors or omissions are my own.

by a *utility function* $v(x)$, in terms of which the value she assigns to an act x for decision making purposes is its *subjective expected utility*:

$$SEU(x) = \mathbf{E}p[v(x)] = \sum_{i=1}^{n} p_i v(x_i). \tag{14.1}$$

This recipe for rational decision making has ancient roots: it was first proposed by Daniel Bernoulli (1738) to explain aversion to risk in problems of gambling and insurance as well as to solve the famous St. Petersburg Paradox. Bernoulli recognized that different individuals might display different risk attitudes, especially if they differ in wealth, and he recommended using the logarithmic utility function $v(x) = \log(x)$ because it implies that "the utility resulting from any small increase in wealth will be inversely proportionate to the quantity of goods previously possessed." The idea of seeking to maximize the expected value of a utility function – particularly a logarithmic one – was discarded and even ridiculed by later generations of economists, who doubted that utility could ever be measured on a cardinal numerical scale. (See Stigler 1950 for an excellent historical review.) However, it was revived and rehabilitated in dramatic fashion by von Neumann and Morgenstern (1944/1947) and Savage (1954), who showed that the expected-utility model could be derived from simple and seemingly reasonable axioms of consistent preferences under risk and uncertainty, in which a pivotal role is played by an independence condition known as the *sure-thing principle* (Fishburn and Wakker 1995).

Von Neumann and Morgenstern considered the special case in which states of the world have objectively known probabilities (as in games of chance), and Savage extended the model to include situations where probabilities are subjectively determined by the decision maker. The key axioms of Savage are as follows. (P1) Preferences among acts are weakly ordered, that is, *complete* and *transitive*. (P2) Preferences satisfy the *independence* condition (sure-thing principle) that requires that if two acts "agree" (i.e., yield the same consequence) in some state, it does not matter *how* they agree there. This permits a natural definition of conditional preferences, namely that x is preferred to y conditional on event E if x is preferred to y and they agree in the event not-E. (P3) Preferences among consequences are *state independent* in the sense that conditional preferences between "constant" acts (those which yield the same consequence in all states) do not depend on the conditioning event. (P4) Events can be unambiguously *ordered by probability* in the following way: if x and y are any two consequences such that x is preferred to y (as a constant act), and if the act that yields x if E and y if not-E is preferred to the act that yields x if F and y if not-F, then E is revealed to be at least as probable as F. These four substantive behavioral postulates, together with a few purely technical assumptions, imply the SEU formula. Other systems of axioms also lead to SEU (e.g., Anscombe and Aumann 1963; Wakker 1989).

The SEU model had a revolutionary impact on statistical decision theory and social science in the 1950s and 1960s, providing the mathematical foundation for a broad range of social and economic theories under the general heading of "rational choice," including the development of Bayesian methods of statistical inference, the emergence of decision analysis as an applied science taught in engineering and business schools, the establishment of game theory as a foundation for microeconomics, and the development of expected-utility-based models of portfolio optimization and competitive equilibria in asset markets by finance theorists. The logarithmic utility function originally proposed by Bernoulli even came to be hailed as the "premier" utility model for investors in financial markets (Rubinstein 1976).

The SEU model also had its early detractors, most notably Allais (1953) and Ellsberg (1961) who constructed famous paradoxes consisting of thought-experiments in which most individuals willingly violate the independence axiom (Savage's P2), but for several decades it was widely accepted as both an appropriate normative standard and a useful descriptive model, as if it were self-evident that a thinking person should be an expected-utility maximizer. That consensus began to break down in the late 1970s, however, as an emerging body of behavioral decision research showed that subjects in laboratory experiments display an array of predictable "heuristics and biases" that are inconsistent with SEU theory, even beyond the paradoxical behavior identified by Allais and Ellsberg. The normative status of the SEU model was also questioned, insofar as violations of completeness or independence do not necessarily expose a decision maker to exploitation as long as she respects more fundamental principles such as dominance and transitivity. In response to these developments, decision theorists and economists proceeded to extend the SEU model by weakening various of its axioms, giving rise to a host of theories of "nonexpected utility" (e.g., Kahneman and Tversky 1979; Machina 1982; Fishburn 1982; Quiggin 1982; Loomes and Sugden 1982; Bell 1982, 1985; Chew 1983; Luce and Narens 1985; Yaari 1987; Becker and Sarin 1987; Schmeidler 1989; Gilboa and Schmeidler 1989; Machina and Schmeidler 1992; Tversky and Kahneman 1992; Wakker and Tversky 1993). This chapter provides a nontechnical summary of some extensions of the SEU model which appear most relevant to decision analysis and which can be defended normatively as well as descriptively. For more breadth and technical depth, the recent surveys by Starmer (2000), Sugden (2004), and Schmidt (2004) are highly recommended; a vast online bibliography has been compiled by Wakker (2006).

Incomplete Preferences, Imprecise Probabilities and Robust Decision Analysis

Arguably the strongest and most unrealistic assumption of the SEU model is that the decision maker's preferences are *complete*, meaning that between any two alternatives that might be proposed, no matter how complicated or hypothetical or even counterfactual, the decision maker is always able to say either that she strictly prefers one to the other or else she is exactly indifferent between them: she is never "undecided." This assumption is somewhat antithetical to the spirit of decision analysis, which provides tools for *constructing* preferences where they may not already exist. The completeness assumption also amplifies the effects of all the other axioms, making it relatively easy to generate examples in which they are violated.

Incompleteness of preferences is implicitly acknowledged whenever ad hoc methods of sensitivity analysis are applied to subjectively assessed probabilities and utilities, which are often among the most controversial and hard-to-measure parameters in a decision model, especially where decisions must be taken on behalf of a group whose members may disagree. Incompleteness can also be acknowledged more explicitly by carrying out the entire analysis in terms of *imprecise probabilities and utilities*, which are intervals of numbers rather than point values. Thus, for example, each state of the world might be assigned a distinct *lower and upper probability*, each consequence might be assigned a distinct *lower and upper utility*, and each alternative would then be assigned a lower expected utility and an upper expected utility by computing the minimum and maximum values attained by the SEU formula (1) as the probabilities and utilities are varied between their lower and upper bounds in all possible combinations (e.g., Rios Insua 1990, 1992; Nau 1989, 1992, 2006b; Moskowitz et al. 1993; Rios Insua and Ruggeri 2000). This type of analysis, known as *robust Bayesian analysis*, need not yield a unique optimal decision: there may be several "potentially optimal" decisions whose expected-utility intervals overlap to some extent. Further introspection and analysis may or may not shrink the intervals to the point where a unique optimal decision emerges; hence at the end of the day it may be necessary to acknowledge that the analysis leaves some room for doubt and to base the final decision at least partly on other criteria not explicitly included in the quantitative model.

In financial decisions where the outcomes are measured in monetary terms, the most critical imprecision is that of the *probabilities* rather than the utilities because it often suffices to assume linear utility or else to use a simple parametric utility function such as the exponential function ($v(x) = -\exp(\alpha x)$), which has a single parameter, the risk aversion coefficient (α), that can be manipulated. Axiomatic models of imprecise probability have a long history in the literature of statistics and philosophy, including the work of Koopman (1940), Smith (1961), Hacking (1967), Kyburg (1974), and Levi (1980). Even de Finetti's "fundamental theorem of probability" (1974) is stated in terms of lower and upper bounds that can be inferred for probabilities of events, given knowledge of probabilities of other events. However, the publication of Walley's (1991) book *Statistical Reasoning with Imprecise Probabilities* sparked an upsurge of interest in this subject, and over the last 15 years a large literature on imprecise-probability models has emerged, as well as a related professional society, the Society for Imprecise Probabilities and Their Applications (SIPTA), which has held biannual meetings since 1999.

Allais' Paradox, Transformed Probabilities, and Rank-Dependent Utility

One of the most compelling objections against Savage's SEU model was raised at its inception by Allais (1953), who constructed the following paradox. Suppose there are three states of the world (E_1, E_2, E_3) whose probabilities – whether objective or subjective – are approximately 0.89, 0.10, and 0.01. (The exact values are unimportant: the states could just be regarded as "very likely," "rather unlikely," and "very unlikely," respectively.) Now consider the following two pairs of alternative gambles over these states:

Table 14.1

	E_1 ($p \approx .89$)	E_2 ($p \approx .10$)	E_3 ($p \approx .01$)
x	$1M	$1M	$1M
y	$1M	$5M	$0
x'	$0	$1M	$1M
y'	$0	$5M	$0

Most individuals strictly prefer x over y and also strictly prefer y' over x'. The intuition for this pattern is clear: most would prefer to get $1M for sure rather than accept a very small (1 percent) risk of getting nothing at all in order to obtain a small (10 percent) chance of getting $5M instead of $1M, but if they are most likely going to get nothing anyway, they would prefer to have a small (10 percent) chance at $5M rather than a slightly larger (11 percent) chance at $1M. (The effect is even stronger if the second pair of alternatives is simply presented as "an 11 percent chance of $1M versus a 10 percent chance of $5M" rather than a specific match-up of events and payoffs.) This preference pattern strikes most people as rational, yet it cannot be rationalized by the SEU model because it violates the independence axiom. Here, x and y agree in state E_1, both yielding $1M, so according to the independence axiom it should not matter if some other agreeing payoff is substituted there. But replacing $1M with $0 in state E_1 yields x' and y', reversing the direction of preference for most individuals, a phenomenon known as the "common consequence effect."

The Allais paradox was once regarded as a curiosity, a cognitive illusion that would probably disappear under closer scrutiny. Savage (1954) himself admitted that he was taken in at first, but after further reflection he "corrected an error" and reversed his instinctive preference for y' over x'. However, after the frontier of SEU theory had been well explored in the 1950s and 1960s, and after violations of the independence axiom began to emerge as a very robust finding in behavioral experiments in the 1970s, many decision theorists began to explore the possibilities for a theory that would relax the independence axiom in some way.

The remainder of this section will focus on the general *rank-dependent utility* model, an extension of the SEU model that has emerged as the most widely studied alternative in connection with the Allais paradox and other violations of the independence axiom that occur in situations where probabilities of events are assumed to be known. Variants of this model were developed independently by Quiggin (1982), Schmeidler (1989), Luce and Narens (1985), and Yaari (1987), and were later refined by others (e.g., Chew et al. 1987; Luce and Manders 1988;

Segal 1989; Wakker 1991, 1996; Chew and Wakker 1996); its intuition is nicely discussed by Diecidue and Wakker (2001).

The rank-dependent utility model is motivated by two key observations concerning violations of the independence axiom. One observation is that violations often occur when comparing acts whose relative riskiness is dramatically changed by replacing an agreeing payoff with a different agreeing payoff. In the Allais paradox as shown above, replacing \$1M with \$0 in state E_1 changes a comparison of a safe alternative against a risky alternative to a comparison of two almost-equally-risky alternatives. Perhaps the independence axiom would be easier to obey if it applied only to comparisons among alternatives with qualitatively similar risk profiles.

The second observation is that attitudes toward risk ought to be explained at least in part as a response to risk *per se*, rather than "as if" they are due to diminishing marginal utility for money. Intuitively, the decision maker's perception of risk is rooted in her *beliefs*, which are represented by probabilities in the SEU model, but the independence axiom permits her utility to depend only linearly on those probabilities. If the independence axiom were relaxed in some way, perhaps the decision maker's evaluation of an act could depend *nonlinearly* on her probabilities, analogously to the way it is allowed to depend nonlinearly on payoffs.

In the rank-dependent utility model, the decision maker's utility for an act x is computed according to a formula which, at first glance, looks very much like the SEU formula:

$$RDU(x) = \sum_{i=1}^{n} \pi_i v(x_i).\tag{14.2}$$

The coefficients $\{\pi_i\}$, which are called *decision weights*, are positive and sum to 1, exactly as if they were subjective probabilities of states. The key difference is that the decision weights are *not* necessarily subjective probabilities, and the decision weight attached to a particular state is not necessarily the same for all acts. In particular, the decision weight π_i that is applied to state E_i when evaluating the act x may depend on how that state is *ranked* relative to other states in terms of the goodness or badness of its payoff, as well as on the decision maker's beliefs.

The most general forms of the RDU model include the *Choquet expected utility* model (Schmeidler 1989), the *cumulative prospect theory* model (Tversky and Kahneman 1992; axiomatized by Wakker and Tversky 1993), and the *rank-and-sign-dependent utility* model (Luce and Fishburn 1991, Luce 2000). In Choquet expected utility and cumulative prospect theory the decision maker's beliefs are represented by nonadditive probability measures known as "capacities," and in cumulative prospect theory and rank-and-sign-dependent utility there are also reference-point effects: the utility function may be kinked at the status quo wealth position so that the decision maker is risk averse even for very small gambles, a behavioral phenomenon known as "loss aversion." However, in the simplest version of RDU, beliefs are represented by subjective or objective probabilities, and for decision making purposes the cumulative distribution of payoffs is merely distorted by an increasing function $w(p)$ that satisfies $w(0) = 0$ and $w(1) = 1$, the so-called *probability weighting function*. For a given act x, let the states be labeled in *decreasing* order of payoff, so that $x_1 \geq \cdots \geq x_n$, and let $(p_1, \ldots, p_n)$ denote the corresponding probabilities. Then the decision weights in the RDU formula (14.2) are given by:

$$\pi_1 = w(p_1) \quad \text{and} \quad \pi_i = w(p_1 + \cdots + p_i) - w(p_1 + \cdots + p_{i-1}) \quad \text{for} \quad i = 2, \ldots, n.$$

It follows that $\pi_1 + \cdots + \pi_i = w(p_1 + \cdots + p_i)$, that is, the cumulative decision weight attached to the top i payoffs of x is equal to the transformed cumulative probability of those states.

If the probability weighting function w is linear, then the RDU model reduces to the SEU model with $\pi_i = p_i$ for all i. However, if w is nonlinear, the decision maker may exhibit pessimism or optimism in her attitude toward risk, even though she has probabilistic beliefs and even though she may have linear utility for money. In particular, if w is a *convex* (upward curving) function, then payoffs near the top of the ranking tend to be underweighted relative to their probabilities, whereas those near the bottom of the ranking tend to be overweighted. Thus, an RDU decision maker with a convex probability weighting function will pessimistically behave in a risk averse fashion (provided her utility function $v(x)$ is also either linear or concave) because she gives disproportionate "attention" to the very worst outcomes. For example, in the Allais paradox, an RDU decision maker with convex w would strongly overweight state E_3 (the zero-payoff event that receives the last 1 percent of probability) when evaluating act y in comparison with act x, whereas the effect of probability weighting would be much less pronounced in evaluating x' and y' (where the zero-payoff event receives either the last 10 percent or 11 percent of probability).

The key underlying assumption that distinguishes the RDU model from the SEU model is the replacement of the independence axiom by a weaker axiom of *comonotonic independence* (a.k.a. the "comonotonic sure-thing principle"). Two acts x and y are said to be comonotonic if they order the states in the same way, so that the same state yields the highest payoff under both acts, the same state yields the second-highest payoff, and so on down the line. The comonotonic independence axiom requires (only) that whenever two *comonotonic* acts agree in some states, then it does not matter how they agree there. Because comonotonic pairs of acts have the same qualitative risk profile, any change of an agreeing payoff in a particular state cannot hedge the risk of one of the acts without similarly hedging the other. The Allais paradox does not violate comonotonic independence because the pairs of acts are not comonotonic: all states are equally good under x whereas they are strictly ranked by y in the order $E_2 > E_1 > E_3$.

The idea that decision makers use nonlinearly transformed cumulative probabilities in their evaluations of acts has been very widely studied in the last 20 years, and empirical estimation of the probability weighting function has been an active industry among behavioral decision theorists (e.g., Tversky and Fox 1995; Wu and Gonzalez 1996; Prelec 1998; Bleichrodt and Pinto 2000). A common finding is that many individuals behave as though their probability weighting function is inverse S-shaped, that is, concave for very small cumulative probabilities and convex for moderate or large cumulative probabilities. Such a weighting function potentially explains why otherwise-risk-averse individuals will often gladly pay more than expected value for state lottery tickets offering very small probabilities of very large gains. It is also consistent with the folk wisdom that most people do not discriminate very well among probabilities that are anything other than 0 or 1, tending to treat them as closer to one-half than they really are.

The relevance of this body of work for decision analysis is somewhat ambiguous. The fact that unaided experimental subjects exhibit nonlinear weighting of cumulative probabilities could be interpreted either as proof of the need for SEU-based methods of decision analysis or else as proof that SEU-based methods do not capture the preferences of many decision makers. An interesting synthetic approach has been proposed by Bleichrodt et al. (2001), who argue that nonlinear probability weighting (as well as loss aversion, that is, overweighting of small losses relative to small gains) should be anticipated during preference elicitation and should be corrected in order to estimate the individual's "true" underlying probabilities and utilities. A recent experiment by van de Kuilen and Wakker (2006) also shows that nonlinear probability weighting in Allais-type experiments tends to disappear if subjects are given the opportunity to learn through both experience and thought, although not through thought alone.

Ellsberg's Paradox, Knightian Decision Theory, Maxmin Expected Utility, and Second-Order Utility

In recent years, interest among decision theorists and economic theorists has shifted somewhat away from Allais-type paradoxes and toward Ellsberg-type paradoxes involving "ambiguous" probabilities, which are perceived as a more serious challenge to SEU theory insofar as they raise deep questions about the existence of personal probabilities (not merely the linearity of the decision maker's response to probabilities) and the distinction (if any) between risk and uncertainty. The claim that uncertainty is something different from risk is commonly traced to the following passage by Frank Knight (1921):

> There is a fundamental distinction between the reward for taking a known risk and that for assuming a risk whose value itself is not known. It is so fundamental, indeed, that as we shall see, a known risk will not lead to any reward or special payment.

This was written, however, at a time before expected utility and subjective expected utility had been given their modern form by von Neumann and Morgenstern and Savage (in the 1940s and 1950s) and before the principles of portfolio optimization and the distinction between diversifiable and nondiversifiable risks had been worked out by finance theorists (in the 1950s and 1960s). It is, by now, well understood that an agent (e.g., an individual or firm) should be rewarded for bearing *nondiversifiable* risk according to the market price of risk and that subjective probabilities can, in principle, be used where objective ones are lacking, and that interagent differences in risk aversion and subjective probabilities present opportunities for profit in the face of uncertainty. However, there are situations in which the uncertainty is of a more fundamental nature and the conventional decision-analytic and finance-theoretic models do not seem to apply, which was emphatically demonstrated by Ellsberg (1961).

In one of Ellsberg's paradoxes, a subject is presented with two urns, one of which is said to contain exactly 50 red balls and 50 black balls whereas the other contains 100 balls that are red and black in unknown proportions. (In Ellsberg's own informal experiments, he not only portrays the composition of the second urn as unknown, but even invites the suspicion that it is somehow "rigged.") A single ball is to be drawn randomly from each urn, and the subject is presented with the following pairs of acts whose payoffs are pegged to the four possible results:

Table 14.2

Ball from urn 1 (known 50% red)	red	red	black	black
Ball from urn 2 (unknown % red)	red	black	red	black
x	$100	$100	$0	$0
y	$100	$0	$100	$0
x'	$0	$0	$100	$100
y'	$0	$100	$0	$100

Most subjects strictly prefer x over y and also strictly prefer x' over y', whereas they are indifferent between x and x' and also indifferent between y and y'. In other words, they would prefer to bet on the color of a ball drawn from the "unambiguous" urn rather than the "ambiguous" one, regardless of whether the winning color is red or black. This is another direct violation of the independence axiom because swapping the agreeing payoffs in the first and last column converts x to y' and y to x', and, moreover, it is a violation that cannot be explained by any model such as RDU in which states are distinguished *only* by the probabilities and payoffs assigned to them, even if probabilities are evaluated in a nonlinear way. Even a model of state-dependent utility (to be discussed in the next section) cannot explain this pattern.

Two different interpretations can be placed on this phenomenon. One is that the subject is unable to assign a probability to the event of drawing a red ball from urn 2, and she is averse to betting on an event whose probability is undetermined. (The SEU model of course would require the decision maker to subjectively assign *some* probability and then proceed exactly as if it were objective.) This interpretation suggests the need for a preference model in which beliefs are represented by something more general and "fuzzier" than probabilities, perhaps *sets* of probabilities or *functions* defined on sets of probabilities. The other possible interpretation is that the individual thinks that red and black are equally likely to be drawn from the second urn, exactly as they are from the first urn, but she is nevertheless *more risk averse toward bets on the second urn* in a way that is incompatible with the independence axiom. The independence axiom permits the decision maker's risk attitude to be *state* dependent but does not permit it to be *source* dependent, that is, dependent on how states are grouped together to form events on which a given winning or losing payoff is received. In the two-urn problem, the four states ought to be regarded symmetrically by the decision maker, each being the conjunction of a color from urn 1 and a color from urn 2, hence it should not matter which two states are combined to form the event on which the winning payoff of $100 is received.

Regardless of how Ellsberg's phenomenon is viewed, whether as an aversion to undetermined probabilities or as a source-dependent attitude toward risk, it strikes at the heart of a key principle of applied decision analysis, namely that the decision maker's attitude toward risk can be assessed by contemplating simple reference gambles with objective probabilities, and the same risk attitude can be safely assumed to apply to decisions with respect to events whose probabilities are highly subjective. From a normative perspective it is hard to condemn violations of this principle as irrational because (unlike some examples of nonlinear probability weighting) they cannot be portrayed as misperceptions of an objective reality.

A variety of models have been proposed for explaining the typical pattern of behavior in Ellsberg's paradox. One such model has already been introduced, namely the incomplete-preference model in which beliefs may be represented by imprecise probabilities. Bewley (1986) has used this model as the basis for a "Knightian" decision theory by adding to it a behavioral assumption of *inertia*, namely that when presented with a new alternative, the decision maker will choose it only if its minimum possible expected value or expected utility exceeds that of the status quo. Under this theory, the decision maker's beliefs with respect to the draw of a red ball from urn 2 can be represented by an interval of probabilities, perhaps the entire interval $[0, 1]$. The minimum expectation of acts y and y' is therefore something less than $50 (perhaps as low as $0), and their maximum expectation is greater than $50 (perhaps as great as $100), whereas acts x and x' have precise expectations of $50. Such a decision maker is technically undecided between the two alternatives in each pair, that is, she regards them as noncomparable. However, if a status quo position is specified and inertia is assumed, the decision maker's choice can be predicted. For example, if the status quo is to "do nothing" or perhaps receive some fixed payment of less than $50, then acts x and x' are preferable to the status quo whereas y and y' are not. Bewley's inertia assumption has interesting implications for intertemporal decisions, where it gives rise to hysteresis and path-dependence, but its use of the status quo as a reference point seems arbitrary in some applications and has been criticized as an ad hoc assumption rather than a compelling normative postulate. (Its descriptive validity has also been questioned, for example, by Eisenberger and Weber 1995.) To return to Ellsberg's example, if the status quo is possession of y or y', the inertial decision maker will never wish to trade it for x or x', contrary to intuition.

As an alternative to the inertia assumption, it can be assumed that, no matter what alternatives are offered, the decision maker always chooses the one that *maximizes the minimum possible expected utility* over a set P of probability distributions that represents her imprecise beliefs. This is the implication of Gilboa and Schmeidler's (1989) *maxmin expected-utility* (MEU) *model*, also commonly known as the "multiple priors" model, in which the utility of act x is:

$$MEU(x) = \min_{p \in P} \mathbf{E}_p[v(x)] = \min_{p \in P} \sum_{i=1}^{n} p_i v(x_i).$$

This model rationalizes the typical pattern of responses in Ellsberg's paradox as long as the set P of prior probabilities for drawing a red ball from urn 2 includes values on both sides of 1/2. It is derived from a modification of Anscombe and Aumann's version of the SEU axioms in which the independence condition is replaced by a weaker condition of "certainty independence" and an explicit axiom of uncertainty aversion is adopted. The uncertainty aversion axiom states that whenever a decision maker is indifferent between two acts, she prefers to objectively randomize between them. This axiom jibes nicely with another observation about Ellsberg's two-urn problem, namely that when subjects are presented with a head-to-head choice between the two ambiguous acts y and y', they prefer to randomize between them by flipping a coin, which resolves the ambiguity by rendering the probability of a red ball irrelevant.

The multiple-priors model does not really distinguish between the decision maker's *perception* of ambiguous probabilities and her *attitude* toward the ambiguity: once the set of priors has been specified, the only permissible ambiguity attitude is the maximally pessimistic one that is implicit in the MEU decision rule. A more nuanced approach, which permits a range of attitudes toward ambiguity, is provided by the concept of a *second-order utility function,* which appears in recent papers by Klibanoff et al. (2005), Ergin and Gul (2004), Chew and Sagi (2006), and Nau (2001b, 2006a). The second-order utility function is applied to the expected utilities computed at an intermediate stage of solving the decision tree, while the usual first-order utility function is applied to the terminal payoffs, so that the overall evaluation of an act is based on an expected-utility-of-an-expected-utility. There are two versions of the second-order utility model, one of which involves a unique prior distribution (the "source-dependent risk attitude" model), and one of which involves multiple priors (the "uncertain prior" model).

To illustrate the source-dependent risk-aversion attitude model, suppose that the decision problem involves two distinct sources of uncertainty, represented by logically independent sets of events $(A_1, \ldots, A_J)$ and $(B_1, \ldots, B_K)$, so that the state space is the Cartesian product $(A_1, \ldots, A_J) \times (B_1, \ldots, B_K)$, where the A-events are a priori "more uncertain" (such as the color of the ball from Ellsberg's second urn) and the B-events are a priori "less uncertain" (such as the color of the ball from the first urn). Suppose that the decision maker has probabilistic beliefs in which her unconditional distribution on the A-events is $p = (p_1, \ldots, p_J)$ and given event A_j her conditional distribution on the B-events is $q_j = (q_{j1}, \ldots, q_{jK})$.

Thus, her probability for state $A_j B_k$ is exactly $p_j q_{jk}$. Let acts be represented by doubly subscripted payoff vectors, so that x_{jk} is the payoff of act x in state $A_j B_k$. If the decision maker is an "uncertainty neutral" SEU maximizer, her risk attitudes are described by a first-order utility function $v(x)$, and her evaluation of x is:

$$SEU(x) = \sum_{j=1}^{J} p_j \sum_{k=1}^{K} q_{jk} v(x_{jk}).$$

When the decision tree is solved by dynamic programming (backward induction), the conditional expected utility given event A_j is computed first, and the expected value of the conditional expected utility is computed second, although the order of events is unimportant: the decision tree could be "flipped" by an application of Bayes' rule. If she has no prior stakes in events, such a decision maker will exhibit the same degree of risk aversion toward bets on A-events or B-events, as determined by the concavity of $v(x)$. Suppose, however, that she also has a second-order utility function $u(v)$, which is applied to the conditional expected utility given a particular A-event, so that her evaluation of x is based on the two-stage expected-utility calculation:

$$SOU(x) = \sum_{j=1}^{J} p_j u \left(\sum_{k=1}^{K} q_{jk} v(x_{jk}) \right). \tag{14.3}$$

Under this preference model, if there are no prior stakes, the decision maker will behave toward bets on B-events as if her utility function were $v(x)$, and she will behave toward bets on A-events as if her utility function were $u(v(x))$. If u is a concave function, then despite the fact that she assigns unique probabilities to all events, the decision maker will be uniformly more risk averse toward bets on A-events than toward bets on B-events, as though she is averse to uncertainty. Tree-flipping can no longer be performed in this case: the decision tree is solvable by dynamic programming only if it is drawn so that A-events are resolved first.

To see how this model potentially explains Ellsberg's paradox, suppose that the first-order utility function is simply the linear function $v(x) = x$, that is, the individual is risk neutral, and the second-order utility function is any concave function, such as the exponential utility function $u(v) = -\exp(-\alpha v)$, where the parameter α is now a measure of (constant) uncertainty aversion. For simplicity, assume $\alpha = \ln(4)/100$, so that $u(100) = -0.25$, $u(50) = -0.5$, and $u(0) = -1$. Then the Ellsberg acts x and y are evaluated as follows:

$$SOU(x) = \frac{1}{2}u(\frac{1}{2}(100) + \frac{1}{2}(0)) + \frac{1}{2}u(\frac{1}{2}(100) + \frac{1}{2}(0))$$
$$= \frac{1}{2}u(50) + \frac{1}{2}u(50) = -0.5, \tag{14.4a}$$

$$SOU(y) = \frac{1}{2}u(\frac{1}{2}(100) + \frac{1}{2}(100)) + \frac{1}{2}u(\frac{1}{2}(0) + \frac{1}{2}v(0))$$
$$= \frac{1}{2}u(100) + \frac{1}{2}u(0) = -0.625. \tag{14.4b}$$

The corresponding certainty equivalents for x and y are $u^{-1}(-0.5) = \$50$ and $u^{-1}(-0.625) = \$33.90$, respectively, and exactly the same values would be obtained for x' and y', rationalizing the usual strict preferences for x over y and for x' over y'.

The source-dependent risk attitude model can be derived from a two-stage application of the independence axiom, in which it is first assumed to apply only to acts that agree on entire A-events, which permits conditional preferences to be defined on A-events, and then the A-conditional preferences are assumed to satisfy independence with respect to agreements on B-events. In general, the first- and second-order utility functions may be state dependent (Model I in Nau 2006a), although state-independence can be forced by replacing the nested independence axioms with stronger nested axioms of tradeoff consistency (Model II in Nau, 2006a, analogous to Theorem 3 of Ergin and Gul 2004).

Alternatively, a second-order utility function can be embedded in a model of uncertain priors, which is somewhat more general than the source-dependent risk attitude model (14.3) and is easier to relate to the multiple-priors model as well as to the literature of hierarchical Bayesian models. Suppose that the decision maker's ambiguous beliefs are represented by a *second-order probability distribution* over a set of possible first-order priors, as in a hierarchical Bayesian model, except with the added twist that the decision maker is averse to the uncertainty about which prior is "correct," or more precisely she is *averse to the uncertainty in her first-order expected utility* that is induced by her uncertainty about which prior is correct. The second-order utility function models her attitude toward the second-order uncertainty. Suppose that the set of priors is a finite set with I elements, $(q_1, \ldots, q_I)$, and to maintain continuity with the previous model, assume that the set of payoff-relevant events is the set $(A_1, \ldots, A_J) \times (B_1, \ldots, B_K)$, although this Cartesian product structure is no longer essential. Then q_i is a vector with elements indexed by jk, where q_{ijk} denotes the probability of event $A_j B_k$ under prior i. For simplicity, assume that under every prior the decision maker has the same risk attitude, represented by a first-order utility function $v(x)$, although more generally her first-order risk attitude could also vary with the index i. (For example, the decision maker could be acting on behalf of a group of individuals with different beliefs *and* risk attitudes, and she might be averse to any lack of consensus among them.) Finally, let $p = (p_1, \ldots, p_I)$ denote the decision maker's second-order probability distribution over the first-order priors, and let $u(v)$ denote her second-order utility function that represents aversion to second-order uncertainty, so that her overall evaluation of an act x is given by the two-stage expected-utility calculation:

$$SOU(x) = \sum_{i=1}^{I} p_i u \left(\sum_{j=1}^{J} \sum_{k=1}^{K} q_{ijk} v(x_{jk}) \right). \tag{14.5}$$

This version of the second-order-utility model is discussed by Nau (2001b) and axiomatized for general (possibly infinite) sets of states and consequences by Klibanoff et al. (2005).

The uncertain-prior model is strictly more general than the source-dependent risk attitude model and the MEU model. The source-dependent-risk attitude model can be viewed as the special case in which $I = J$ and the ith prior simply assigns probability 1 to event A_j. Then p is effectively the probability distribution over the A-events and q_{ijk} is the conditional probability of B_j given A_j if $i=j$, and $q_{ijk} = 0$ otherwise, whence (14.5) reduces to (14.3). For example, the specific model (14.4ab) that was used above to explain Ellsberg's two-urn paradox can be reinterpreted to mean that the decision maker thinks urn 2 is rigged, but she does not know which way. Specifically, she thinks that it either contains 100 percent red balls or 100 percent black balls, she regards these possibilities as equally likely, and her aversion to this second-order uncertainty is modeled by the second-order utility function $u(v) = -\exp(-\alpha v)$. The MEU model, meanwhile, is a limiting case of the uncertain-prior model in which the decision maker has a uniform distribution over some set of possible priors but is pathologically averse to second-order uncertainty (i.e., $u(v)$ is a radically concave function, like the exponential function with a large risk-aversion coefficient α), so her second-order expected utility for an act is simply its worst-case first-order expected utility.

To sum up this section, there is fairly compelling evidence that individuals do not – and perhaps should not – treat all risks the same. Thus, a decision maker might display different risk attitudes in betting on the spin of a roulette wheel, betting on the outcome of a football game, purchasing various kinds of insurance, and managing a retirement portfolio. A variety of formal extensions of the SEU model have been developed to model this phenomenon. Whether or not one of these models is adopted, the bottom line is that assessments of the decision maker's risk attitude ideally should be carried out in terms of hypothetical bets on real events that are similar to the ones involved in the decision at hand, not arbitrary, artificial events.

State-Preference Theory, State-Dependent Utility, and Decision Analysis with Risk-Neutral Probabilities

Much of the controversy over SEU theory in the last few decades has focused on the normative or descriptive validity of particular preference axioms such as independence or completeness, taking as given the underlying analytic framework introduced by Savage, in which acts consist of arbitrary mappings from a set of states of the world to a set of consequences, or the more tractable framework of Anscombe and Aumann that also includes objective randomization. However, the primitive concepts of those analytic frameworks are also open to question, particularly the concept of a "consequence" that yields the same value to the decision maker no matter what state of the world it occurs in, and the concept of an "act" in which states are mapped to consequences in arbitrary and often counterfactual ways. Savage introduced these concepts in order to build a theory in which the decision maker's beliefs would turn out to be representable by subjective probabilities, which in turn would be uniquely determined by her preferences. The use of subjective probabilities to represent beliefs was controversial then, and to some extent it is still controversial today, partly because of the persistence of alternative views of probability among many economists and philosophers, but also partly because of an emerging realization that the preferences among

counterfactual acts which are required by Savage's definition of subjective probability are not really observable because they cannot be instantiated by feasible
choices. But more importantly, even if they *were* observable, they *still* would not
enable the decision maker's subjective probabilities to be uniquely separated from
her utilities for consequences.

The problem with trying to define probabilities in terms of preferences is that
no matter how consequences are defined, it is impossible to verify whether their
utilities are really state-independent. The axiom that Savage uses to force state-
independence of preferences for consequences (P3) does not actually imply that
utilities must be state-independent: it requires the decision maker's utility function to rank the consequences in the same order in every state of the world, but
their utilities could still have *state-dependent scale factors* whose effects would
be impossible to separate from the effects of subjective probabilities. Such an
entanglement of probability and utility is quite likely to arise in decisions that
involve life-changing events, such as insurance, health care, savings for retirement, or choosing a career or a spouse. In a famous exchange of letters with
Savage, Aumann (1971) raised the example of a man who must decide whether
his critically ill wife should undergo a risky operation. If the man's enjoyment of
utterly everything would be severely diminished by the event of his wife's death,
then there may be no "consequence" whose utility is state-independent for him,
and the contemplation of bets on her survival may not help him to think more
clearly about the probability of that event.

A related problem is that the decision maker could have *unobservable prior
stakes in events*, which would give rise to the appearance of state-dependent
utilities and/or distorted probabilities in her observed preferences. For example, suppose that the decision maker is an SEU-maximizer with subjective probability distribution p and state-independent exponential utility function $v(x)$
$= -\exp(-\alpha x)$, but meanwhile she has large prior financial stakes in events – that
is, "background risk" – represented by a wealth vector $w = (w_1, \ldots, w_n)$, known
only to herself. Then her expected utility of an act whose observable payoff vector
is x is actually:

$$SEU(w + x) = -\sum_{i=1}^{n} p_i \exp(-\alpha(w_i + x_i))$$

$$= -\sum_{i=1}^{n} p_i \exp(-\alpha(w_i)) \exp(-\alpha x_i),$$

which, up to a scale factor, is also the expected utility of x for someone with
identical risk aversion who has *no* prior stakes but whose probability for state i is
$p_i' \propto p_i \exp(-\alpha w_i)$. Hence, even under the assumptions of the SEU model, it is
impossible for an outside observer to infer the decision maker's true probabilities
from her preferences without independently knowing her prior stakes in events,
and for the same reason it may be hard for a decision maker with large vested
interests to think clearly about her own beliefs by introspectively examining her
own preferences. This is likely to be especially problematic when contemplating

events that strongly affect everyone, such as natural or economic disasters. Many individuals now have their retirement portfolios invested in mutual funds, even if they are not professional investors, and moreover everyone's economic future is likely to be affected in some complex way by a "boom" or "bust" in the market, so it is hard to conceive of a realistic way to model attitudes toward uncertainty in financial markets that does not admit the presence of background risk.

Various authors have studied the difficulties of subjective probability measurement that are raised by state-dependent utility and prior stakes (e.g., Fishburn 1970; Karni et al. 1983; Karni 1985; Shafer 1986; Rubin 1987; Drèze 1987; Kreps 1988; Kadane and Winkler 1988; Schervish et al. 1990; Karni and Schmeidler 1993; Karni 1996; Wakker and Zank 1999; Karni and Mongin 2000; Nau 1995, 2001a), and the results can be described as a mix of good and bad news for decision analysis. The *bad* news is that there does not appear to be any foolproof way to measure "true" subjective probabilities by eliciting preferences among acts that are actually available or even remotely possible. Rather, it generally seems to be necessary to elicit preferences among acts that are by definition impossible, such as acts in which arbitrary objective probabilities are assigned to states of world (as in Karni et al. 1983), or else to abandon the preference-based approach and instead treat subjective probability as an undefined psychological primitive that can be measured verbally without reference to specific acts (as in Degroot 1970). The conspicuous exceptions to this rule are situations where events really do have objective probabilities (or "almost-objective" probabilities as defined by Machina 2005) and/or the decision maker has no intrinsic interest in the events. But the *good* news is that *it does not matter*: it is possible to carry out decision analysis without measuring the "true" subjective probabilities of the decision maker, particularly in problems involving financial markets.

An alternative framework for analyzing choice under uncertainty, which sidesteps the measurement of subjective probabilities, was proposed by Arrow (1951, 1953) at around the same time that Savage unveiled his SEU model and Allais responded with his paradox. In fact, Savage, Allais, and Arrow all gave presentations of their nascent theories at a legendary econometrics colloquium held in Gif-sur-Yvette, near Paris, in May 1952 (CNRS 1953). Arrow's approach, which has come to be known as *state-preference theory*, was refined and extended by Debreu (1959), Hirshleifer (1965), Yaari (1969), and Drèze (1970, 1987), among others. It has been very widely adopted in financial economics, especially in the theories of insurance, general equilibrium under uncertainty, and asset pricing by arbitrage. Economists have been receptive to this approach in part because it is agnostic concerning the existence of subjective probabilities, and in part because it uses old familiar concepts of utility measurement that date back to the work of Walras, Pareto, and Edgeworth in the nineteenth century. State-preference theory is merely a straightforward adaptation of neoclassical consumer theory to an environment in which goods may be distinguished by the times and states in which they are delivered or consumed. Thus, objects of preference are not just apples, bananas, and money, but also *state-contingent* and/or *time-contingent claims* to apples, bananas, and money.

In the simplest case, which resembles the framework of the SEU and non-SEU models discussed earlier, there is a single date, a single consumption good (money), and n states of the world. The states could be possible values for a stock index or an interest rate, or various hazards that might be insured against, or any other verifiable events on which financial contracts can be written. In this setting, an act is a vector x whose ith component is an amount of money x_i to be paid or received in state i. These are not consequences in Savage's sense because receiving a given amount of money need not count as the same experience in all states of the world, and it need not represent the decision maker's entire wealth in that state – she could have prior stakes. If preferences among such acts are merely assumed to be continuous, reflexive, transitive, and monotonic, it follows that there is some continuous utility function $U(x)$, increasing in x_i for each i, that represents the decision maker's preferences under uncertainty.

If no stronger assumptions are imposed, then $U(x)$ represents general nonexpected-utility preferences, and it is merely an *ordinal* utility function in the tradition of neoclassical consumer theory: any monotonic transformation of U represents the same preferences, hence, it is not meaningful to compare utility differences between different pairs of acts. However, if U is a *differentiable* function – which can be assumed if preferences are sufficiently smooth – it is meaningful to compare the *marginal utilities* of different state-contingent commodities, and a great deal of analysis can be done in these terms. Assuming that more money is strictly preferred to less, the partial derivatives of U are positive and can be normalized to yield a local probability distribution associated with act x, which will be denoted here by $\pi(x)$. That is:

$$\pi_i \equiv \frac{\partial U(w)/\partial x_i}{\sum_{j=1}^{n} \partial U(w)/\partial x_j}.$$

The distribution $\pi(x)$ need not represent the decision maker's true probabilities, but it is very useful information because it completely characterizes the decision maker's local gambling behavior in the vicinity of x. In particular, one who already possesses x would strictly prefer to accept a small gamble z (i.e., would strictly prefer $x + z$ over x) if and only if z has positive expected value under $\pi(x)$, that is, $E_\pi(x)[z] > 0$, provided that z is small enough so that $\pi(x + z)$ is not significantly different from $\pi(x)$. Thus, every decision maker with sufficiently smooth preferences behaves locally like a risk-neutral SEU-maximizer, and it is therefore appropriate to refer to the local distribution $\pi(x)$ as her *risk-neutral probability distribution* evaluated at x.

If the independence axiom is also assumed, it follows that the utility function $U(x)$ has the additively separable *cardinal* form:

$$U(x) = \sum_{i=1}^{n} u_i(x_i), \tag{14.6}$$

which is a *state-dependent SEU model without separation of probabilities from utilities*. The state-dependent utility functions $\{u_i\}$ simply lump together the effects of beliefs, risk attitudes, and prior stakes in events, and the decision maker's risk-neutral probabilities are their normalized derivatives: $\pi_i(x) \propto u'(x_i)$. The standard SEU model is obtained if $u_i(x) = p_i v(x)$ for some "true" probability distribution p and state-independent utility function $v(x)$, in which case risk-neutral probabilities are the product of true probabilities and state-dependent marginal utilities: $\pi_i(x) \propto p_i v'(x_i)$. But risk-neutral probabilities exist for decision makers with more general smooth preferences, and they are useful terms of analysis even for decision makers with SEU preferences, especially in multiagent settings such as games and markets.

It is obvious that low-stakes financial decisions can be analyzed in terms of the decision maker's risk-neutral probabilities because the risk-neutral local approximation applies to small transactions by definition. However, it is also possible, in principle, to analyze *any* decision entirely in terms of risk-neutral probabilities, regardless of the stakes, because the decision maker's indifference curves are completely determined by $\pi(x)$ – it is merely necessary to take into account the functional dependence of π on x. Decisions that take place in the context of a *complete market for contingent claims* are especially easy to analyze in these terms. In a complete and arbitrage-free market, the Arrow-Debreu security for each state (which pays \$1 if that state occurs and \$0 otherwise) has a unique market price, and normalization of these state prices yields a probability distribution that is called the *risk-neutral distribution of the market*, which will be denoted here by π^*. Suppose the decision maker faces a choice among some set X of alternative capital-investment projects that can be financed through investments in the market, and suppose that she is a "small player" in the sense that her choices are not expected to influence market prices. In the simplest case, there is single future time period and the projects can be described by vectors representing the net present (or future) value of their cash flows in different states of the world. Therefore, let $x \in X$ denote the vector whose ith element x_i is the NPV of a project in state E_i. Then the decision maker's utility-maximizing strategy is simply to choose the project with the highest market risk-neutral valuation, that is, to choose project x^* where $x^* = \arg \max \{\mathbf{E}_{\pi^*}[x], x \in X\}$, assuming this is positive, and meanwhile execute trades in the market to yield additional cash flows z^* such that $\mathbf{E}_{\pi^*}[z^*] = 0$ (i.e., the trades are self-financing at relative prices π^*) and such that $\pi(x^* + z^*) = \pi^*$ (i.e., her "posterior" risk-neutral probabilities equal those of the market, thus optimally financing the project x^*). Effectively the decision maker reaps an arbitrage profit equal to $\mathbf{E}_{\pi^*}[x^*]$ and then optimally invests the money in the market. The *only* role for her own preferences is to determine the optimal financing scheme z^*, not the optimal project x^*, and the problem of finding z^* can be parameterized in terms of the decision maker's risk-neutral probabilities rather than her true probabilities. The same approach generalizes to multiperiod problems, although it becomes necessary to explicitly model the decision maker's preferences for consumption in different periods as well as different states of the world, and the analysis is greatly simplified (i.e., decision tree can be solved by dynamic programming) if the independence axiom is applied so that utility is additively separable across *both* periods and states of the world.

The presence of a complete market thus allows a financial decision problem to be neatly separated into two parts, one of which is solved by the market and the other of which is solved by the decision maker, and both of which can be solved in terms of risk-neutral probabilities. In the case where X consists of a single project and the only question is how to optimally finance it, this result is known as the "fundamental theorem of risk bearing": at the risk bearing optimum, the individual's relative marginal expected utilities must equal relative market prices. If the market is only "partially complete," then its risk-neutral probabilities for some events will be imprecise and there will be a larger role for the decision maker's own preferences, but under suitable restrictions it is possible to decompose the dynamic-programming solution of the decision tree into an alternation between steps in which the risk-neutral probabilities of the market are used and steps in which the risk-neutral probabilities of the decision maker are used (Smith and Nau 1995). More details and examples of decision analysis in terms of risk-neutral probabilities are given by Nau and McCardle (1991) and Nau (2001a, 2003).

To sum up this section, Savage's analytic framework of states, consequences, and acts is not the only possible framework for modeling choice under uncertainty. The alternative framework of state-preference theory is more appropriate for many applications, particularly those involving financial markets, and it does not unduly emphasize the state-independence of utility or the measurement of "true" subjective probabilities. Using this framework, it is possible to recast many of the tools of decision analysis (risk aversion measures, risk premia, decision tree solution algorithms) in terms of risk-neutral probabilities, which are often the most natural parameters in settings where risks can be hedged by purchasing financial assets.

Neuroeconomics: The Next (and Final?) Frontier

The SEU model and its extensions (including game theory) follow a centuries-old tradition of importing mathematical methods from physics into economics, descending from Bernoulli to von Neumann. Individuals are imagined to rationally pursue a single goal, namely the maximization of some all-inclusive measure of utility, which enables the analytic tools of physical scientists (calculus, probability theory, equilibrium, etc.) to be applied to the study of human behavior. The brain is conceived as a calculating engine that operates on two distinct sources of data, namely *beliefs* (represented by probabilities of events that might occur) and *values* (represented by utilities of outcomes that might be experienced), which it uses to evaluate every new opportunity. The same types of calculations are performed regardless of whether the situation is simple or complicated, familiar or unfamiliar, certain or uncertain, financial or nonfinancial, competitive or noncompetitive. The great innovation of von Neumann and Morgenstern and Savage was to show that this model of rational decision making is implied, in an "as if" sense, by simple axioms of consistency among preferences. Thus, SEU theory is at bottom a theory of *consistency* rather than a theory with any particular empirical content.

The utilitarian, consistency-focused view of decision making has always been to some extent controversial. During the last 50 years, the bulk of the criticism has come from behavioral economists and psychologists in the tradition of Herbert

Simon, Vernon Smith, Richard Thaler, Amos Tversky, and Daniel Kahneman, who have imported experimental methods from psychology into economics. The latest frontier has been opened during the last decade or so by developments in cognitive neuroscience, giving rise to an emerging field of "neuroeconomics," which studies the root causes of economic behavior at a physiological level, yielding empirical insights into decision making that are potentially explanatory rather than merely descriptive. The most distinctive tools of neuroeconomics are real-time measurements of the neural activity of experimental subjects, which have revealed that different brain areas may be activated by different attributes of decisions – for example, certainty versus uncertainty, gains versus losses, immediate versus delayed rewards. Such measurements include functional MRI, positron emission topography, and magnetoencephalography in human-subject experiments; more invasive studies of single-neuron activity in animal experiments; and recordings of other psychophysical variables such as galvanic skin response and pupil dilation. Other research tools include "depletion studies" that explore the effects on mood and emotion of amino acids such as tryptophan and serotonin; administration of hormones such as oxytocin, which raises the level of "trust" among subjects in experimental games; electrical stimulation of different brain regions to determine the sensations or feelings that are processed there; case studies of decision making by patients with who have suffered lesions in specific brain regions; and behavioral experiments designed to test hypotheses about decision processes that are otherwise suggested by evolutionary and/or neuroscientific arguments. Some excellent recent surveys of the field have been given in review articles by Camerer et al. (2004ab) and Glimcher and Rustichini (2004), as well as a book by Glimcher (2003); philosophical and social implications of research in cognitive neuroscience have also been discussed in popular books by Damasio (1994, 2003) and Pinker (1997, 2002).

There is insufficient space here to do justice to this vibrant area, but some of the stylized facts are as follows. First, the human brain turns out not to be a calculating engine with a knowledge base of coherent beliefs and values. Rather, it is composed of distinct modules and layers, which are: (1) responsible for different aspects of cognition and behavior; (2) partly "programmable" by experience but also partly "hard-wired" by evolution; (3) sometimes influenced by transient body chemistry; and (4) not always in perfect harmony with each other. Like other anatomical structures, they have evolved by a series of "exaptations" from structures that may have originally served other purposes in other environments. Some brain activities are under conscious control, but others proceed automatically, and "learning" consists not only of acquiring information but also of shifting repetitive tasks from conscious to automatic control.

An important distinction can be drawn between cognitive processes (reasoning) and affective processes (emotions). Cognitive processes are controlled by areas of the higher brain (in the cerebral cortex), and affective processes are controlled by areas of the lower brain (especially the amygdala, which is closely associated with the sense of smell). Affective responses have an intrinsic positive or negative valence (i.e., they are automatically classified as good or bad), they may be accompanied by physiological reactions in other parts of the body (literally "gut feelings"), and they often occur automatically and unconsciously, so that the higher brain is not always aware of the stimuli that may have provoked a particular emotional response (Bechara et al. 1999). One of the most striking findings is that affective processes appear to be critical for decision making: patients who have suffered brain lesions that disengage their cognitive processes from their emotions are sometimes unable to make effective decisions on their own behalf, despite otherwise being able to reason as logically as before (Bechara et al. 1994; Damasio 1994). Risk and ambiguity normally give rise to emotions of fear or discomfort (although persons who are genetically predisposed to compulsive behavior may get emotional thrills from inappropriate risk-taking), and they appear to activate different brain areas (Hsu et al. 2005; Huettel et al. 2006); patients with lesions in these areas have been shown to be less risk-averse or less ambiguity-averse than normal subjects (Shiv et al. 2005), for better or worse.

The brain, due to its modular structure, is not equally good at solving all kinds of inference and decision problems. Rather, some of its parts are specialized for efficiently solving classes of problems that were especially important for the survival and reproduction of early humans, including the use of language and strategic reasoning about reciprocity and exchange, as well as intuition about the physical and biological environment. For example, there appears to be a built-in cheater-detection system: if a logical inference problem can be framed in terms of detecting an instance of cheating on an obligation, it is much more likely to be correctly solved by an experimental subject than if it is presented in abstract terms. There is also some evidence of a utility-for-money effect, that is, money appears to have a direct utility rather than merely an indirect utility for the consumption that it buys later (Prelec and Loewenstein 1998), whereas von Neumann-Morgenstern and Savage deliberately constructed their theories so that money would play no distinguished role. The human brain also appears to have a module that harbors a "theory of mind" concerning the motivation and reasoning of other human agents, which is necessary for social interactions and game-playing but is absent or damaged in autistic individuals. However, as Camerer et al. (2004b) observe, "the modularity hypothesis should not be taken too far. Most complex behaviors of interest to economics require collaboration among more specialized modules and functions. So the brain is like a large company – branch offices specialize in different functions, but also communicate to one another, and communicate more feverishly when an important decision is being made."

Although much of neuroeconomics has sought to import findings from neuroscience into economics, some of it has aimed the other way, looking for evidence of Bayesian inference or expected-utility maximization at a neuronal level, on the theory that evolutionary pressure for "rational choice" algorithms may be strongest in more primitive areas of the brain where the simplest decisions are made. In single-neuron studies in which animal subjects receive uncertain rewards for either strategic or nonstrategic choices, where both the probabilities and values of the rewards are manipulated, the firing rate of activated neurons in the parietal area appears to be proportional to the "relative subjective desirability" of the chosen alternative, that is, it depends on the probability as well as the value in relative terms, compared to other available alternatives (Platt and Glimcher 1999; Dorris and Glimcher 2004). This finding tentatively suggests that probability may not be separated from utility at a primitive level as learning occurs under risk and uncertainty.

The neuroeconomic view of a modular, internally-collaborative, emotion-driven and not-fully-transparent brain raises new questions about the extent to which individual decisions can be improved by externalizing beliefs and values and forcing them into a single, coherent structure that is supposed to govern preferences across a wide range of situations. Effective decision making under risk and uncertainty appears to also require drawing on the right part of the brain at the right time, harnessing appropriate emotions, and suppressing inappropriate ones. Individuals may differ widely in their innate and acquired abilities to do this, hence the same prescriptive tools may not work equally well for all decisions and decision makers.

REFERENCES

Allais, M. (1953). Le Comportement de l'Homme Rationnel devant le Risque: Critique des Postulats et Axiomes de l'Ecole Américaine. *Econometrica, 21*, 503–546.

Anscombe, F., and Aumann, R. (1963). A Definition of Subjective Probability. *Annals of Mathematical Statistics, 34*, 199–205.

Arrow, K. (1951). An Extension of the Basic Theorems of Classical Welfare Economics. *Proceedings of the Second Berkeley Symposium on Mathematical Statistics and Probability*. Berkeley: University of California Press.

Arrow, K. (1953/1964). The Role of Securities in the Optimal Allocation of Risk-Bearing. *Quarterly Journal of Economics, 31*, 91–96.

Aumann, R. (1971). Letter to L. J. Savage. Reprinted in Drèze, J. (1987). *Essays on Economic Decision Under Uncertainty*. London: Cambridge University Press.

Bechara, A., Damasio, A., Damasio, H., and Anderson, S. (1994). Insensitivity to Future Consequences Following Damage to Human Prefrontal Cortex. *Cognition, 50*, 7–15.

Bechara, A., Damasio, H., Damasio, A., and Lee, G. (1999). Different Contributions of the Human Amygdala and Ventromedial Prefrontal Cortex to Decision-Making. *J. Neuroscience, 19*, 473–481.

Becker, J., and Sarin, R. (1987). Lottery Dependent Utility. *Management Science, 33*, 1367–1382.

Bell, D. (1982). Regret in Decision Making under Uncertainty. *Operations Research, 30*, 961–981.

Bell. D. (1985). Disappointment in Decision Making under Uncertainty. *Operations Research, 33*, 1–27.

Bernoulli, D. (1738). Specimen Theoriae Novae de Mensura Sortis. *Commentarii Academiae Scientiarum Imperialis Petropolitanae, 5*, 175–192. Translation by L. Sommer (1954) Exposition of a New Theory on the Measurement of Risk. *Econometrica, 22*, 23–36.

Bewley, T. (1986). Knightian Decision Theory Part I. Cowles Foundation Discussion Paper No. 807. Reprinted in (2002). *Decisions in Economics and Finance, 25*, 79–110.

Bleichrodt, H., and Pinto, J. (2000). A Parameter-Free Elicitation of the Probability Weighting Function in Medical Decision Analysis. *Management Science, 46*, 1485–1496.

Bleichrodt, H., Pinto, J., and Wakker, P. (2001). Making Descriptive Use of Prospect Theory to Improve the Prescriptive Use of Expected Utility. *Management Science, 47*, 1498–1514.

Camerer, C., Loewenstein, G., and Prelec, D. (2004a). Neuroeconomics: How Neuroscience Can Inform Economics. *Journal of Economic Literature, XLIII*, 9–64.

Camerer, C., Loewenstein, G., and Prelec, D. (2004b). Neuroeconomics: Why Economics Needs Brains. *Scandinavian Journal of Economics, 106*, 555–579.

Chew, S. H. (1983). A Generalization of the Quasilinear Mean with Applications to the Measurement of Income Inequality and Decision Theory Resolving the Allais Paradox. *Econometrica, 51*, 1065–1092.

Chew, S.H. and Sagi, J. (2006). Small Worlds: Modeling Attitudes Toward Sources of Uncertainty. Working paper, University of California at Berkeley.

Chew, S. H., and Wakker, P. (1996). The Comonotonic Sure-Thing Principle. *Journal of Risk and Uncertainty, 12*, 5–27.

Chew, S.H., Karni, E. and Safra, Z. (1987). Risk Aversion in the Theory of Expected Utility with Rank Dependent Probabilities. *Journal of Economic Theory, 42*, 370–381.

CNRS. (1953). *Econometrie, Paris, 12–17 Mai 1952.* Colloques Internationaux, 40, Centre National de la Recherche Scientifique, Paris.

Damasio, A. (1994). *Descartes' Error: Emotion, Reason, and the Human Brain.* New York: Putnam.

Damasio, A. (2003). *Looking For Spinoza: Joy, Sorrow, and the Feeling Brain.* Orlando: Harcourt.

de Finetti, B. (1974). *Theory of Probability, Vol. 1.* New York: Wiley.

Debreu, G. (1959). *Theory of Value.* New Haven: Cowles Foundation.

Degroot, M. (1970). *Optimal Statistical Decisions.* New York: McGraw-Hill.

Diecidue, E., and Wakker, P. (2001). On the Intuition of Rank-Dependent Utility. *Journal of Risk and Uncertainty, 23*, 281–298.

Dorris, M., and Glimcher, P. (2004) Activity in Posterior Parietal Cortex is Correlated with the Subjective Desirability of an Action. *Neuron, 44*, 365–378.

Drèze, J. (1970). Market Allocation Under Uncertainty. *European Economic Review, 2*, 133–165.

Drèze, J. (1987). *Essays on Economic Decision Under Uncertainty.* London: Cambridge University Press.

Eisenberger, R., and Weber, M. (1995). Willingness-to-Pay and Willingness-to-Accept for Risky and Ambiguous Lotteries. *Journal of Risk and Uncertainty, 10*, 223–233.

Ellsberg, D. (1961). Risk, Ambiguity and the Savage Axioms. *Quarterly Journal of Economics, 75*, 643–669.

Ergin, H., and Gul, F. (2004). A Subjective Theory of Compound Lotteries. Working paper, MIT.

Fishburn, P. (1970). *Utility Theory for Decision Making.* New York: Wiley

Fishburn, P. (1982). Nontransitive Measurable Utility. *Journal of Mathematical Psychology, 26*, 31–67.

Fishburn, P. and Wakker, P. (1995). The Invention of the Independence Condition for Preferences. *Management Science, 41*, 1130–1144.

Gilboa, I., and Schmeidler, D. (1989). Maxmin Expected Utility with Nonunique Prior. *Journal of Mathematical Economics, 18*, 141–153.

Glimcher, P. (2002). Decisions, Decisions, Decisions: Choosing a Neurobiological Theory of Choice. *Neuron, 36*, 323–332.

Glimcher, P., and Rustichini, A. (2004). Neuroeconomics: The Concilience of Brain and Decision. *Science, 306*, 447–452.

Glimcher, P. (2003). *Decisions, Uncertainty, and the Brain: The Science of NeuroEconomics.* Cambridge, MA and London: MIT Press.

Hacking, I. (1967). Slightly More Realistic Personal Probability. *Philosophy of Science, 34*, 311–325.

Hirshleifer, J. (1965). Investment Decision under Uncertainty: Choice-Theoretic Approaches. *Quarterly Journal of Economics, 74*, 509–536.

Hsu, M., Bhatt, M., Adolphs, R., Tranel, D., and Camerer, C. (2005). Neural Systems Responding to Degrees of Uncertainty in Human Decision-Making. *Science*, *310*, 1680–1683.

Huettel, S., Stowe, J., Gordon, E., Warner, B., and Platt, M. (2006). Neural Signatures of Economic Preferences for Risk and Ambiguity. *Neuron*, *49*, 765–775.

Kadane, J.B., and Winkler, R. L. (1988). Separating Probability Elicitation from Utilities. *Journal of the American Statistical Association*, *83*, 357–363.

Kahneman, D. and Tversky, A. (1979). Prospect Theory: An Analysis of Decision under Risk. *Econometrica*, *47*, 263–291.

Karni, E. (1985). *Decision-Making under Uncertainty: The Case of State-Dependent Preferences*. Cambridge, MA: Harvard University Press.

Karni, E. (1996). Probabilities and Beliefs. *Journal of Risk and Uncertainty*, *13*, 249–262.

Karni, E. and Mongin, P. (2000) On the Determination of Subjective Probabilities by Choices. *Management Science*, *46*, 233–248.

Karni, E., Schmeidler, D., and Vind, K. (1983). On State Dependent Preferences and Subjective Probabilities. *Econometrica*, *51*, 1021–1031.

Karni, E., and Schmeidler, D. (1993). On the Uniqueness of Subjective Probabilities. *Economic Theory*, *3*, 267–277.

Klibanoff, P., Marinacci, M., and Mukerji, S. (2005). A Smooth Model of Decision Making Under Ambiguity. *Econometrica*, *73*, 1849–1892.

Knight, F. (1921). *Risk, Uncertainty, and Profit*. New York: Houghton Mifflin.

Koopman, B. (1940). Axioms and Algebra of Intuitive Probability. *Annals of Mathematics*, *41*, 269–292.

Kreps, D. (1988). *Notes on the Theory of Choice*. Boulder: Westview Press.

Kyburg, H. (1974). *The Logical Foundations of Statistical Inference*. Dordrecht: Reidel.

Levi, I. (1980). *The Enterprise of Knowledge*. Cambridge, MA: MIT Press.

Loomes, G., and Sugden, R. (1982). Regret Theory: An Alternative Theory of Rational Choice under Uncertainty. *Economic Journal*, *92*, 805–824.

Luce, R. D. (2000). *Utility of Gains and Losses: Measurement-Theoretical and Experimental Approaches*. Mahwah, NJ: Erlbaum.

Luce, R. D., and Fishburn, P. (1991). Rank-and Sign-Dependent Linear Utility Models for Finite First-Order Gambles. *Journal of Risk and Uncertainty*, *4*, 29–59.

Luce, R. D., and Narens, L. (1985). Classification of Concatenation Measurement Structures According to Scale Type. *Journal of Mathematical Psychology*, *29*, 1–72.

Luce, R. D., and Manders, K. (1988). Rank-Dependent Subjective Expected-Utility Representations. *Journal of Risk and Uncertainty*, *1*, 305–332.

Machina, M. (1982). Expected Utility without the Independence Axiom. *Econometrica*, *50*, 227–323.

Machina, M. (2005). 'Expected Utility/Subjective Probability' Analysis without the Sure-Thing Principle or Probabilistic Sophistication. *Economic Theory*, *26*, 1–62.

Machina, M. and Schmeidler, D. (1992). A More Robust Definition of Subjective Probability. *Econometrica*, *60*, 745–780.

Moskowitz, H., Preckel, P. and Yang, A. (1993). Decision Analysis with Incomplete Utility and Probability Information. *Operations Research*, *41*, 864–879.

Nau, R. (1989). Decision Analysis with Indeterminate or Incoherent Probabilities. *Annals of Operations Research*, *19*, 375–403.

Nau, R. (1992). Indeterminate Probabilities on Finite Sets. *Annals of Statistics*, *20*, 1737–1767.

Nau, R. (1995). Coherent Decision Analysis with Inseparable Probabilities and Utilities. *Journal of Risk and Uncertainty*, *10*, 71–91.

Nau, R. (2001a). De Finetti Was Right: Probability Does Not Exist. *Theory and Decision*, *59*, 89–124.

Nau, R. (2001b). Uncertainty Aversion with Second-Order Probabilities and Utilities. *Proceedings of the Second International Symposium on Imprecise Probabilities and Their Applications.* Web site: http://www.sipta.org/isipta01/proceedings/063.html

Nau, R. (2003). A Generalization of Pratt-Arrow Measure to Non-Expected-Utility Preferences and Inseparable Probability and Utility. *Management Science, 49,* 1089–1104.

Nau, R. (2006a). Uncertainty Aversion with Second-Order Utilities and Probabilities. *Management Science, 52,* 136–145.

Nau, R. (2006b). The Shape of Incomplete Preferences. *Annals of Statistics 34, 5,* 155–164.

Nau, R. and McCardle, K. (1991). Arbitrage, Rationality, and Equilibrium. *Theory and Decision, 31,* 199–240.

Pinker, S. (1997). *How the Mind Works.* New York: Norton.

Pinker, S. (2002). *The Blank Slate: the Modern Denial of Human Nature.* New York: Viking.

Platt, M. and Glimcher, P. (1999). Neural Correlates of Decision Variables in Parietal Cortex. *Nature 400,* 233–238.

Prelec, D. (1998). The Probability Weighting Function. *Econometrica, 66,* 497–527.

Prelec, D., and Loewenstein, G. (1998). The Red and the Black: Mental Accounting of Savings and Debt. *Marketing Science, 17,* 4–28.

Quiggin, J. (1982). A Theory of Anticipated Utility. *Journal of Economic Behaviour and Organization, 3,* 323–343.

Rios Insua, D. (1990). *Sensitivity Analysis in Multiobjective Decision Making.* Berlin: Springer-Verlag.

Rios Insua, D. (1992). On the Foundations of Decision Making Under Partial Information. *Theory and Decision, 33,* 83–100.

Rios Insua, D., and Ruggeri, F. (2000). *Robust Decision Analysis.* New York: Springer-Verlag.

Rubin, H. (1987). A Weak System of Axioms for "Rational" Behavior and the Non-Separability of Utility from Prior. *Statistics and Decisions, 5,* 47–58.

Rubinstein, M. (1976). The Strong Case for the Generalized Logarithmic Utility Model as the Premier Model of Financial Markets. *Journal of Finance, 31,* 551–571.

Savage, L. (1954). *The Foundations of Statistics.* New York: Wiley.

Schervish, M., Seidenfeld, T., and Kadane, J. (1990). State-Dependent Utilities. *Journal of the American Statistical Association, 85,* 840–847.

Schmeidler, D. (1989). Subjective Probability and Expected Utility without Additivity. *Econometrica, 57,* 571–587.

Schmidt, U. (2004). Alternatives to Expected Utility: Formal Theories. In S. Barberà, P. Hammond, and C. Seidl, *Handbook of Utility Theory, Vol. 2.* Dordrecht: Kluwer.

Segal, U. (1989). Anticipated Utility: A Measure Representation Approach. *Annals of Operations Research, 19,* 359–373.

Shafer, G. (1986). Savage Revisited (including comments). *Statistical Science, 1,* 463–501.

Shiv, B., Loewenstein, G., Bechara, A., Damasio, H., and Damasio, A. (2005). Investment Behavior and the Negative Side of Emotion. *Psychological Science, 16,* 435–439.

Smith, C. (1961). Consistency in Statistical Inference and Decision. *Journal of the Royal Statistical Society B, 23,* 1–25.

Smith, J., and Nau, R. (1995). Valuing Risky Projects: Option Pricing Theory and Decision Analysis. *Management Science, 41,* 795–816.

Starmer, C. (2000). Developments in Non-Expected Utility Theory: The Hunt for a Descriptive Theory of Choice under Risk. *Journal of Economic Literature, XXXVIII,* 332–82.

Stigler, G. (1950). The Development of Utility Theory: I; II. *Journal of Political Economy, 58,* 307–327; 373–396.

Sugden, R. (2004). Alternatives to Expected Utility: Foundations. In S. Barberà, P. Hammond, and C. Seidl, *Handbook of Utility Theory, Vol. 2.* Dordrecht: Kluwer.

Tversky, A., and Fox, C. (1995). Weighing Risk and Uncertainty. *Psychological Review*, *102*, 269–283.

Tversky, A., and Kahneman, D. (1992). Advances in Prospect Theory: Cumulative Representation of Uncertainty. *Journal of Risk and Uncertainty*, *5*, 297–323.

van de Kuilen, G., and Wakker, P. (2006). Learning in the Allais Paradox. *Journal of Risk and Uncertainty*, *33*, 155–164.

von Neumann, J., and Morgenstern, O. (1947). *Theory of Games and Economic Behavior*. Princeton: Princeton University Press.

Wakker, P. (1989). *Additive Representations of Preferences: A New Foundation for Decision Analysis*. Dordrecht: Kluwer.

Wakker, P. (1991). Additive Representations on Rank-Ordered Sets. I. The Algebraic Approach. *Journal of Mathematical Psychology*, *35*, 501–531.

Wakker, P. (1996) The Sure-Thing Principle and the Comonotonic Sure-Thing Principle: An Axiomatic Analysis. *Journal of Mathematical Economics*, *25*, 213–227.

Wakker, P. (2006). Annotated References on Decisions and Uncertainty. Web site: http://www1.fee.uva.nl/creed/wakker/refs/rfrncs.htm. Accessed 11/14/06.

Wakker, P., and Tversky, A. (1993). An Axiomatization of Cumulative Prospect Theory. *Journal of Risk and Uncertainty*, *7*, 147–176.

Wakker, P., and Zank, H. (1999). State Dependent Expected Utility for Savage's State Space. *Mathematics of Operations Research*, *24*, 8–34.

Walley, P. (1991). *Statistical Reasoning with Imprecise Probabilities*. London: Chapman & Hall.

Wu, G., and Gonzalez, R. (1996). Curvature of the Probability Weighting Function. *Management Science*, *42*, 1676–1690.

Yaari, M. (1969). Some Remarks on Measures of Risk Aversion and Their Uses. *Journal of Economic Theory*, *1*, 315–329.

Yaari, M. (1987). The Dual Theory of Choice under Risk. *Econometrica*, *55*, 95–115.

15 Probabilistic Risk Analysis for Engineered Systems

Vicki M. Bier and Louis Anthony Cox, Jr.

ABSTRACT. Probabilistic risk assessment (PRA) provides practical techniques for predicting and managing risks (i.e., frequencies and severities of adverse consequences) in many complex engineered systems. In this chapter, we survey methods for PRA and decision making in engineered systems, emphasizing progress in methods for dealing with uncertainties (e.g., via Bayesian belief networks, with dependencies among inputs expressed via copulas), communicating results effectively, and using the results to guide improved decision making by multiple parties (e.g., teams of stakeholders). For systems operating under threats from intelligent adversaries, novel methods (e.g., game-theoretic ideas) can help to identify effective risk-reduction strategies and resource allocations. The focus on methodology reflects the belief of the authors that in hard decision problems, where the risks and the best courses of action are unclear (often because of sparse, ambiguous, or conflicting data), state-of-the-art methodology may be critical to good risk management. This chapter discusses some of the most useful current methodologies, and suggests possible directions for extensions and improvements.

Overview of Risk Analysis for Engineered Systems

Application Areas

Probabilistic risk assessment (PRA) provides a body of practical techniques that can help engineers and risk managers to predict and manage risks (i.e., frequencies and severities of adverse consequences) in a variety of complex engineered systems. Examples of the types of systems to which PRA has been successfully applied include: nuclear power plants (beginning with the Reactor Safety Study (USNRC, 1975) and continuing to the present day); the space shuttle (to which risk analysis has been applied both before and especially after the Challenger disaster); dam and reservoir planning; highways and bridges; emergency planning; terminals and storage facilities for liquefied natural gas and other hazardous chemicals; and electric power generation and planning.

The common elements of the above examples are that they all involve: (1) a *designed system* intended to withstand different levels of stress, with the option of incorporating different levels of backup and fail-safe design, etc.; (2) a *system operator/risk manager* faced with decisions about how to use the system (e.g., when to launch, when to shut down, and generally what level of precaution to adopt); and (3) an uncertain *environment* (involving either random events such as equipment failures and acts of nature, or else the unknown actions of intelligent agents such as terrorists) that generate stresses and adverse conditions that the system should ideally be able to withstand. From this perspective, both the designer and the operator/risk manager would like to make decisions that will allow the system to achieve its goals to the extent possible given the uncertain environment (and given any resource constraints). Of course, the decisions and tradeoffs faced by the operator/risk manager will often be affected by the decisions made by the system designer.

PRA is typically applied primarily to rare and/or catastrophic events for which it may be difficult to estimate risks directly because of factors such as the sparseness of empirical data, the possibility of unobserved changes (e.g., deterioration) in the system, and changes in the system's environment and/or use. Risk assessment can also be applied to predict routine (e.g., occupational accident) risks, although in such cases, it may be possible to rely primarily on empirical data, to reduce the need for modeling. In general, PRA is used to estimate, predict, and find ways to reduce the risks to facility or system owners, employees, and the public.

This chapter focuses on methodological advances in engineering risk analysis, with selected applications (including some applications of PRA methods and insights to fields other than engineering) to illustrate the methodology. Chapter 16 emphasizes the application of PRA methods in engineering risk management.

Uses of Risk Analysis to Improve Decisions

Risk analysis can help to inform both design decisions (e.g., trade-offs among safety and performance, cost, etc.), and also operational decisions (e.g., when to shut down a facility). Risk analysis can be useful regardless of whether the decisions are made by facility owners/operators, regulators, or through a participatory risk management and conflict-resolution process (see Part VI: Decision Analysis in a Behavioral and Organizational Context, in this volume).

Overview of Current Challenges in PRA for Risk Management

PRA has been used both by government regulators and by private industry for 30 years, and hence can be considered a reasonably mature discipline. However, because of the complexity of the situations often addressed by PRA and the need for subjective judgments when inputs are uncertain, PRA still has important elements of art as well as science, with plenty of opportunity for methodological enhancements to improve the reliability, applicability, and acceptance of PRA results.

Some remaining challenges include: how to better quantify system behavior and predict probable performance (given a design and the operator's decisions) in the face of inadequate data; how to optimize the joint decisions faced by the system designer and owner operator (which can involve NP-hard combinatorial optimization problems, as well as "softer" problems of coordination and communication between different organizations); how to most effectively model dependencies and uncertainties about the system's current state; more cost-effective "screening"-type methods for addressing the myriad possible risks in "open" systems (such as the risk of terrorist attack); and how to deal with scale-up problems for extremely complex systems (such as infrastructure networks). Also, there is still room to benefit more fully from adaptation of methods developed in other fields, including decision analysis and related fields (such as Bayesian statistics). Finally, this chapter reviews relevant aspects of single-person and multiperson decision making for risk management decisions, and touches on related challenges in risk communication.

Hazard Identification: What Should We Worry About?

Probabilistic risk assessment typically begins by defining the system to be analyzed and identifying undesired outcomes that might occur when it is operated. *Hazard identification* methods have been developed to identify potential adverse consequences of system operation. Structured qualitative techniques include hazard and operability studies, and failure modes and effects analysis (which describes potential failure modes, causes, effects, safeguards, and recommendations for reducing risks).

Fault trees and event trees can also be used in a qualitative mode for hazard identification, but can be quantified in addition, to estimate the likelihood of adverse events. *Fault tree analysis* (Barlow 1998) begins with an undesired outcome, called the "top event," and reasons backward to identify which combinations of more basic events (e.g., component failures) could bring about the top event (e.g., failure of the system). The result is a tree that represents those sets of basic events that would be sufficient to cause the top event using "AND" and "OR" logic (and possibly more complicated logic gates as well). The tree generally goes down to the level of basic events whose probabilities can be reliably estimated from experience, judgment, and/or data. Figure 15.1 shows a simple example of a fault tree for car accidents at an intersection, taken from the Health and Safety Policy Advisory Group (2004) of the Institution of Engineering and Technology.

The second major approach, *event tree analysis*, begins with an "initiating event" and works forward to identify its potential consequences. In essence, an event tree (see Figure 15.2) is a decision tree without decision nodes, which just shows potential sequences of events, with the probability of each branch being conditionally independent of earlier information, given that the branch point has been reached. The probability (or frequency) of a given event sequence is then just the product of the conditional branch probabilities along that path. Both fault trees and event trees can be represented as logically equivalent influence diagrams and be solved by standard influence diagram algorithms (Barlow 1998; Bobbio et al. 2001).

Structuring Risk Quantification: Models for Accident Probabilities and Consequences

A quantitative risk model typically consists of a formal mathematical and/or simulation model of the system of interest, together with one or more consequence

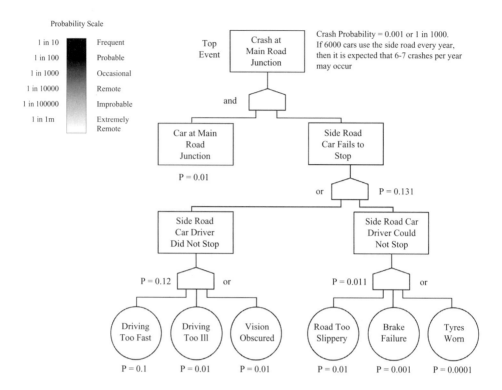

Figure 15.1. A simple fault tree.

attributes of interest, and one or more alternative risk management decisions to be evaluated. The model is used to predict the probable consequences of alternative decisions. Preferred decisions are those that yield preferred probability distributions (or, more generally, preferred stochastic processes) for the consequences of interest.

Some general approaches for risk modeling (not necessarily mutually exclusive) are:

System representation (Barlow 1998; Smith 2005). An engineered system is often represented mathematically in one of the following forms: (a) a "black-box" *statistical model* (e.g., a lifetime hazard function quantifying the conditional failure rate of a system, given that it has not failed until now); (b) component failure rates combined via a *coherent structure function* (such as a fault tree or an event tree) mapping the states of system components to the states of the system (a coherent structure function must be monotonically increasing, going from a system failure probability of zero if all components work to a system failure probability of one if all components fail); (c) a stochastic *state transition* model (e.g., a Markov or semi-Markov model for transitions among working and failed components, representing component failure and repair rates); or (d) a discrete-event *simulation model* (Smith 2005).

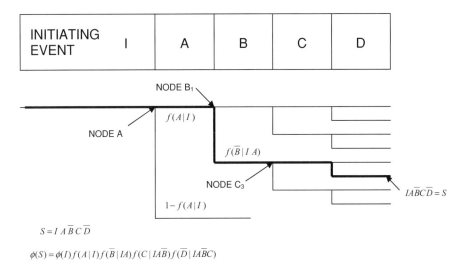

$$S = I\,\overline{A}\,\overline{B}\,C\,\overline{D}$$

$$\phi(S) = \phi(I)f(A\,|\,I)f(\overline{B}\,|\,IA)f(C\,|\,IA\overline{B})f(\overline{D}\,|\,IA\overline{B}C)$$

Figure 15.2. A simple event tree.

Environment representation. Like a system model, a model of the environment may be a statistical black-box model (e.g., a function describing the frequency and intensity of stresses to the system's components), a stochastic process, or a simulation. Plausible worst-case or bounding scenario analyses are sometimes used when probabilistic descriptions of uncertainty are unavailable or difficult to assess. (Note that the model of the environment is often incorporated directly into the system model, as with traffic levels and weather conditions in Figure 15.1.)

Decision-rule representation. A *decision rule* for managing an engineered system maps observed information about the system into a resulting action or intervention. For example, a component may be replaced based on the observed history of failures and repairs. Optimization methods, including recently developed simulation-optimization techniques (see for example Ólafsson and Kim 2002), can help to identify "good" or "best" decision rules, given a system model, an objective function (e.g., a multiattribute utility function), and a model of the environment. Of course, many decisions in the real world (even when informed by PRA) are made without a formal decision rule, either because the PRA results themselves make the best decision clear, or because of the need to address concerns of multiple stakeholders, etc.

Example: Bug-Counting Models of Software Reliability. An example of a simple black-box risk model for software reliability is a "bug-counting" model, in which the (unknown) initial number of bugs in a piece of code is represented by a random variable N with a prior distribution. As the code is tested and debugged, the remaining number of bugs presumably decreases, and the random times between successive bug discoveries stochastically increase. The empirical record of bug discoveries can be used to trigger a decision rule such as "If no bugs have been discovered within M tester-hours, then release the software." Simulation optimization can then be used to numerically optimize the parameter

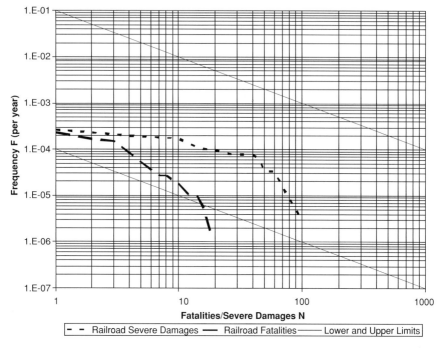

Figure 15.3. Simple *F–N* curves.

M. Alternatively, for analytic approaches, see Singpurwalla and Wilson (1999) and Wilson and Samaniego (2002).

Example: Risk Management for Dams and Reservoirs. Wurbs (2005) describes the use of decision rules to manage water releases for dams and reservoirs as follows:

> Release decisions depend upon whether or not the flood control storage capacity is exceeded ... federal reservoirs are typically sized to contain at least a 50-year recurrence interval ... flood and, for many projects, design floods greater than the 100-year flood ..., perhaps much greater. A specified set of rules, based on downstream flow rates, are followed as long as sufficient storage capacity is available to handle the flood without having to deal with the water surface rising above the top of flood control pool ... For extreme flood events which would exceed the reservoir storage capacity, moderately high damaging discharge rates beginning before the flood control pool is full are considered preferable to waiting until a full reservoir necessitates much higher release rates.

Figure 15.3, taken from Nardini et al. (2003), illustrates one common way of displaying risk variables. The risks of railroad transport of hazardous materials. Risks are summarized as *F–N* curves (or complementary cumulative distributions), showing the expected annual frequencies *F* of fatalities or damages exceeding any given level *N*. (Technically, such diagrams make sense only for compound Poisson processes, not for more general renewal processes. However, *F–N* curves

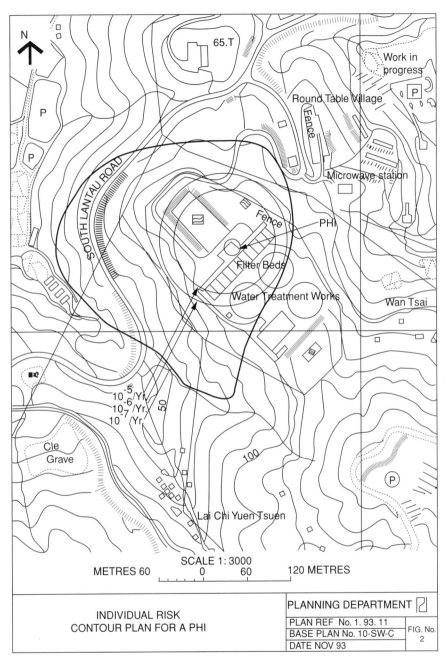

Figure 15.4. Risk contours around a potentially hazardous installation (PHI).

are often used to summarize the results of PRA calculations, which typically use compound-Poisson – that is, steady-state – approximations to risk in any case.) F–N curves are not perfect summaries of the distribution of risk within a population, largely because they do not describe individual risks, which may differ substantially. Other risk displays can give more information; for example, showing how risk varies by location, over time, and with other covariates. For example, Figure 15.4, taken from the Planning Department of Hong Kong (2006), shows "risk contours" for individuals in the vicinity of a potentially hazardous installation (PHI).

Major technical challenges for developing PRA results include:

1. Constructing and validating models of the system and its environment. Statistical analysis of accident precursors provides a promising approach to this task, in which data on "near misses" are used to validate and refine model-based predictions (Yi and Bier 1998; Borgonovo et al. 2000; Phimister et al. 2004).
2. Calculating or estimating probabilities of rare events. Simulation methods for addressing this challenge, such as adaptive importance sampling, have advanced significantly in recent years (e.g., Rubinstein and Kroese 2004).
3. Treatment of dependencies among failure events and system components. Methods for treatment of dependencies presently include: common-cause failure analysis (to show dependence in the failure rates of similar components due to a common underlying cause); dependency matrices and event trees (to show dependence of some systems on "support" systems such as electric power); and external-events analysis (to capture the fact that events such as earthquakes, fires, and floods can affect multiple components).

Quantifying Model Components and Inputs

A model typically expresses risk (e.g., probability of failure by a certain time) as a function of the performance of model components and/or input parameters. These must be quantified from available data, typically using some combination of expert judgment and Bayesian statistics (because of the sparseness of directly relevant data).

In Bayesian statistics, a prior distribution is updated by conditioning on observed data to yield a posterior probability distribution for the quantities of interest (see, for example, Lee 2004). Such methods include hierarchical Bayesian methods (in which partially relevant data are used to help construct the prior distribution), as well as empirical Bayesian methods (in which the actual data for the problem at hand are used to help construct the prior distribution); see Carlin and Louis (2000).

Although this general approach to quantification of risk models is well accepted and frequently applied in practice, there are numerous areas in which advances are still being made. These include more flexible and tractable models for the treatment of probabilistic dependence in risk models, alternatives to the reliance on subjective prior distributions (which can sometimes be problematic), and the treatment of model uncertainty.

Treatment of Dependence

If the state of a system is described by a coherent structure function – for example, $y = F(x_1, x_2, \ldots, x_n)$ – and each x_j independently deteriorates stochastically (e.g., from "working" to "failed") over time, then the probability distribution of observing a particular system state y can be obtained relatively easily (e.g., by stochastic simulation of the behaviors of the components, or through routine application of combinatorial models such as fault trees or event trees). However, if component behaviors are interdependent (e.g., if each component failure increases the stress on those components that have not yet failed), then it becomes more complex to calculate the risk that the system will have failed by any given time.

Dependence can also be a problem for uncertainty analysis, even if the various components in the model are conditionally independent given their failure rates. In particular, the failure rates (or probabilities) of the various components can be uncertain and dependent on each other. For example, learning that one component had a higher failure rate than expected may cause one to increase one's estimates of the failure rates of other similar components. Failure to take such dependence into account can result in substantial underestimation of the uncertainty about the overall system failure rate (or probability), and in some cases also underestimation of the mean failure probability of the system (e.g., if the components whose failure probabilities are dependent are functionally in parallel with each other); see Apostolakis and Kaplan (1981), Burmaster and Anderson (1994), and Kraan and Cooke (1997).

Historically, for reasons of computational tractability (among others), dependencies among random variables have often been either ignored, or else treated using unrealistic and simplistic assumptions such as perfect correlation. Fortunately, substantial progress is being made in the modeling of dependency among components (and/or in the information about the components). First, the use of copulas (functions that link a multivariate cumulative distribution to its one-dimensional cumulative marginal distributions; see for example Nelsen, 1999) has become more common – being applied, for example, to analyses of the correlation between opinions from different experts (Jouini and Clemen 1996; Lacke 1998) or between system failure rates during normal and accident conditions (Yi and Bier 1998).

Of course, copulas are not always the most convenient way to represent dependencies; see Joe (1997) for a compendium of multivariate distributions. Recently, Merrick et al. (2005) used an inverted Wishart distribution to model uncertainty about the dependencies among experts in assessing risks to the Washington State Ferries system. Unlike most past approaches, the method used by Merrick et al. allows the analyst to "learn about the dependencies between the experts from their responses." This is achieved by asking the experts to provide multiple different assessments of maritime risk under differing circumstances.

Cooke and colleagues (Bedford and Cooke 2001; Kurowicka and Cooke 2004) have developed a practical method for specifying a joint distribution over n continuous random variables with specified rank correlations, using only

$n(n-1)/2$ assessments of conditional correlations. Kurowicka and Cooke (2004) point out that use of continuous multivariate distributions as the basis for a Bayesian belief net allows for more tractable Bayesian updating than the commonly used discrete distributions (Lauritzen and Spiegelhalter 1998).

Example: Analysis of Accident Precursors. Consider a risk analyst attempting to estimate the failure probabilities of critical safety systems in a nuclear power plant in the event of an accident. Fortunately, few if any accidents will have been observed on plants of that type, suggesting the analyst may use data regarding failure probabilities of those systems during routine testing. However, these data will clearly be only partially relevant to the probabilities to be assessed; for example, one might expect that many systems will have higher failure probabilities under accident conditions than during routine testing.

Yi and Bier (1998) show how copulas can be used to represent dependency between the system failure probabilities under normal versus accident conditions. This approach makes it possible to perform a Bayesian update showing the effect of data collected under normal conditions on the system failure probabilities under accident conditions. Thus, for example, if routine testing showed a particular system to be much less reliable than was previously believed, this information could be used to update the expected failure probability of the system in the event of an accident. However, Yi and Bier's model is not sufficiently general to account for all relevant prior assumptions about dependencies. Thus, further work to enhance our ability to model dependencies would be desirable.

Example: Flight-Crew Alertness. A challenge in modeling flight-crew alertness (Roelen et al. 2003) is that various predictive variables are correlated not only with crew alertness, but also with each other. For example, the crew's workload on a given flight is likely to be a function of both the length of the flight (with longer flights having higher total workload), and also how much rest the crew members obtain during the flight (more rest being associated with a lower workload). However, assessing the combined impact of these variables on crew alertness may be difficult if longer flights also allow more rest time during flight.

Kurowicka and Cooke (2004) develop a continuous Bayesian belief net for this situation that would allow airline managers to identify ways to compensate for known causes of poor alertness (such as long flights, or insufficient sleep prior to flight time). By allowing the variables in their model to have continuous distributions (rather than discrete distributions, which are more common in applications of Bayesian belief nets), they are able to achieve a highly parsimonious model requiring assessment of only eight conditional rank correlations, compared with the much larger numbers of assessments that would be required for a discrete model – even a simplistic binary model (in which each variable can take on values of only "OK" and "not OK," for example).

Alternatives to Subjective Prior Distributions

Unlike classical statistical procedures, Bayesian analysis can be used in situations of sparse data, because important subjective and other nonstatistical types of evidence can be used in the estimation process. However, with sparse data, the results of Bayesian analyses become sensitive to the analyst's choice of distributions for both the prior and the likelihood (Small and Fischbeck 1999). Hence, Bayesian methods can be more subjective and less readily accepted when data are sparse. Maximum-entropy distributions have sometimes been proposed to help solve this problem. This approach uses whatever information is available about the uncertain quantity of interest (e.g., mean, median, or mean and variance) to constrain the assumed distribution for that quantity, but presupposes as little additional information as possible beyond that, to avoid inadvertently assuming more than is actually known. A maximum-entropy distribution is defined to be the least informative distribution that satisfies the specified constraints (Jaynes 2003). The resulting distribution can then be used either as a prior distribution for Bayesian analysis (if additional data become available), or as a partially informative distribution without updating. For example, Meeuwissen and Bedford (1997) use maximum entropy to identify the minimally informative distribution with a given set of rank correlation coefficients, using a piecewise constant numerical approximation (a so-called chessboard distribution).

However, maximum-entropy and related approaches (such as the use of noninformative prior distributions) lead to significant problems even in some relatively simple examples. For example, if all we know about a random variable X is that it is bounded by 0 and 1, then a maximum-entropy distribution for it would be uniform between these limits. Of course, exactly the same reasoning presumably applies to X^2, but X and X^2 cannot both be uniformly distributed between 0 and 1. Such lack of invariance to transformations of variables (e.g., from half-life to decay rate) means that maximum-entropy distributions may depend on essentially arbitrary choices of scale, or of how to represent the same physical situation. In addition, the maximum-entropy distribution can be difficult to compute in some cases (especially when quite a bit is known about the quantity of interest, so that the maximum-entropy distribution must satisfy numerous constraints).

As a result of such limitations, there has recently been some interest in "robust" Bayesian methods and other bounding approaches. Robust Bayesian methods (Rios Insua and Ruggeri 2000) generally involve updating an entire class, family, or set (usually convex) of prior distributions with observed data, rather than just a single prior distribution. If the class is chosen carefully, the computational effort required to update all distributions in the class need not be substantially greater than for a single distribution. If all (or most) prior distributions in a suitably broad class give similar results, this can lead to greatly improved confidence in the results of the analysis.

In a similar spirit is probability bounds analysis (Ferson and Donald 1998), which is used for propagation of uncertainties (rather than to choose a prior distribution for Bayesian updating). In this approach, the analyst specifies bounds on the cumulative distribution functions of the various input parameters to a model, rather than selecting specific cumulative distributions. These bounds are then propagated through the model. The uncertainty propagation process, which again can be quite computationally efficient, yields valid bounds on the cumulative distribution function for the final result of the model (e.g., a risk level).

Note that this approach can take into account not only uncertainty about the probability distributions of the model inputs, but also uncertainty about their correlations and dependence structure. This is valuable, because correlations will often be more difficult to assess accurately than marginal distributions, and correlations of 1 or −1 among the input variables do not necessarily produce the most extreme possible distributions for the output variable(s) of interest; see, for example, Ferson and Hajagos (2006).

Example: Effects of Exposure to Contaminated Soil. Ecological and environmental risk models frequently involve a high degree of uncertainty, because some important parameters in the model may not be readily measurable. Consider the problem of attempting to estimate the effect of soil contamination on predator species (Hope 1999), which may be exposed to contamination both directly (through ingestion of soil) and indirectly (by ingestion of a variety of prey species). Estimating the exposure to the predator species requires estimating the concentration of the contaminant in the flesh of all prey species, some of which may themselves be predators. This requires estimating overall food and water intake and diet composition for each relevant species, as well as the uptake of the contaminant. Good data or expert opinion may be available for some parameters, but for others (such as the fraction of a particular predator's diet made up of a particular prey species), experts may feel uncomfortable assessing an informative probability distribution, and may prefer simply to state, for example, that the fraction must be between zero and one. Standard practice would either press the experts to provide informative distributions, or simply assume a uniform distribution between zero and one, but this may not always conform to the experts' judgments. Correlations between the fractions of the diet made up of differing foods can also obviously be difficult to estimate reliably.

Regan et al. (2002) compare a traditional two-dimensional Monte Carlo analysis of this problem with the results obtained using probability bounds. Even using bounds of zero and one for some parameters, the qualitative conclusions of the analysis (e.g., that the predator species of interest was "potentially at risk" from exposure to soil contamination) remained essentially unchanged between the two-dimensional Monte Carlo analysis and the probability bounds analysis. Thus, bounding analysis can help support a particular decision, if it shows that the qualitative results and recommendations resulting from the analysis are not highly sensitive to the specific choices of probability distributions used in the simulation.

Model Uncertainty and Bayesian Model Averaging

The approaches discussed above are primarily suited to dealing with uncertainty about the *parameters* of a particular model. However, uncertainty about the most appropriate functional form for a model can be even more important in practice. Some researchers have suggested assessing a probability distribution over multiple plausible models by evaluating the consistency of the various models with the observed data (in much the same way as the likelihood function in Bayesian updating evaluates the consistency of various parameter values with observed data), and determining how much weight to put on each model based on its consistency with the data (Hoeting et al. 1999).

However, it is frequently not reasonable to attempt to estimate the probability that a given model is "correct," because as Box (1979) pointed out, "All models are wrong, some models are useful." For example, it seems highly implausible that any of the current models for estimating the probability of human error on a given task is close to "correct" (because all are presumably gross oversimplifications of the real world), nor can the current models be considered a collectively exhaustive set of possible models of human error.

Bayesian updating of probability distributions over such partial subspaces of possible models may not always work well in practice. Some models may be intentionally conservative (e.g., for regulatory and/or screening purposes), or intentionally simplified (e.g., for computational tractability, or to yield qualitative insights). The fact that such models may be inconsistent with observed data does not necessarily invalidate their use for their intended purposes.

Finally, of course, more complex models with larger numbers of parameters may be more likely to fit the observed data well in many situations (subject to possible limitations of overfitting), but may not always be preferable, if only for reasons of parsimony. Thus, standard approaches for dealing with uncertainty probabilistically are often not well suited for handling model uncertainty.

Bayesian model averaging (see for example Hoeting et al. 1999) was developed to deal with at least some of the above challenges. In particular, this approach (based on "Occam's razor") effectively penalizes models that achieve good fits only by using large numbers of parameters. Thus, Bayesian model averaging avoids the pitfall of giving too much weight to models that are excessively complex, and generally performs reasonably well in practice (Raftery and Zheng 2003). However, this approach still relies on the idea of assigning probabilities to particular models, and uses Bayes' theorem to update those probabilities in light of the observed data. Therefore, for example, Bayesian model averaging will tend to put little weight on conservative models that are inconsistent with the observed data, even if they are reasonably parsimonious.

An alternative approach that avoids assigning probabilities to individual models, "comprehensive uncertainty evaluation" (Brown 1999), involves subjectively adjusting the probability distributions resulting from a particular model in order to take into account known weaknesses of the model (such as conservatisms, or risks that are not adequately modeled). This approach is consistent with subjectivist probability theory, and avoids some of the theoretical conundrums associated with assigning probabilities to models. Brown has applied this method to support regulatory decision making for nuclear power plants, for example, but it has not yet seen widespread application by other analysts in practice.

In many applications of Bayesian analysis to situations involving models, the input parameters are assumed to be known, and the model results are used to update the prior distribution over model outputs (see, for example, Chick 1997).

However, observing the output of a model could also cause one to revise the prior distribution over model inputs, if the true values of the model outputs were known reasonably well (e.g., from empirical data); for example, Bayesian analysis could be used to estimate which values for the rate of disease progression are most consistent with observed data on disease prevalence and severity (Andradóttir and Bier 2000).

In general, however, one will of course be uncertain about both the inputs and the outputs of a model. In this case, one would ideally like to update the prior distributions for both the model inputs and outputs in a consistent manner, with the distribution that initially reflected greater uncertainty presumably being more sensitive to the observed model results. (Of course, observing an inconsistency between the output values computed by the model and the prior distribution for those outputs could also lead one to revise the model.) So far, unfortunately, this sort of joint updating of model inputs and outputs appears to be largely an unsolved problem. Raftery et al. (1995) attempted this using an approach called *Bayesian synthesis* for an ecological model of whale populations, but the approach taken there was shown to be subject to Borel's paradox (Wolpert 1995; Schweder and Hjort 1996). In particular, Bayesian synthesis can involve conditioning on a set of measure zero (because there may be virtually no input/output pairs from the analyst's joint prior over inputs and outputs that are perfectly consistent with the model), and can therefore give differing results depending on (irrelevant) aspects of the model representation.

Scheder and Hjort propose a non-Bayesian approach that is not subject to Borel's paradox. Givens and Roback (1999) and Roback and Givens (2001) address the problem by assuming that the decision maker takes the prior distributions over model inputs and outputs as "data." However, to our knowledge, the question of how to achieve joint updating of model inputs and outputs in a fully coherent Bayesian manner has not yet been solved.

Risk Characterization

The output of a PRA to support risk management decision making is a characterization of the risk caused by each decision option being evaluated. (Occasionally, the decision task is to identify an optimal risk management policy from a large set of possibilities, rather than to explicitly characterize the risks for each of a small number of alternatives. In this case, simulation-optimization algorithms or special-purpose techniques, such as Markov decision processes, can be used. However, explicit comparison of risks from a few options is more usual, and will constitute our main focus in this section.)

"Risk" is usually defined as the frequency and severity of losses arising from operation of the designed system in its uncertain environment, including a specification of losses (i.e., what consequences matter, and to whom?). An effective display of risk shows how it is affected by different actions (e.g., different risk management decisions), and allows "drill-down" to view the risks to particular subpopulations, as well as the contributions of various different causes to the overall level of risk. For example, showing how the risk curves in Figure 15.3 shift leftward when risk-reducing measures are implemented would help managers identify the most effective measures. Uncertainty and sensitivity analysis are also essential to risk characterization, because they support estimates of the value of information.

Challenges in Communicating the Results of PRAs

Risk communication (including both presenting the results of risk analyses to stakeholders, decision makers, and other audiences, and listening to their concerns so that they can be addressed in the risk analyses in the first place) facilitates the effective participation and interaction of technical experts, stakeholders, and decision makers in risk management decisions and deliberations. There is an extensive body of literature on risk communication (including guidelines, survey results, and experiments), including many web resources on risk communication.

Even more than PRA, risk communication is still an art rather than a science, but one that can be usefully informed and improved by theory, experience, and experimental results. Current challenges in risk communication include dealing with framing effects, communicating highly technical results to decision makers who may not be intimately familiar with some of the methods used in the risk analysis, and building trust among affected stakeholders and members of the public more generally. Adding to the difficulty is the fact that communication and presentation styles that are most effective in expressing the technical content of risk-assessment findings may not always be those that invite and elicit public understanding, participation, and interaction.

Cullen and Frey (1999) provide a useful discussion of the distinctions between state-of-knowledge uncertainty and population variability (sometimes referred to simply as uncertainty and variability, respectively). State-of-knowledge uncertainty is generally taken to reflect those uncertainties that affect all of the elements being studied, and could be reduced through further research; for example, uncertainty about the average level of risk faced by members of a population exposed to a particular chemical. Variability refers to variations among the elements being studied (often assumed to be due to randomness); for example, differences in how different individuals in the population would respond to the chemical being studied. Variability is often taken to be essentially irreducible through further study.

With the development and increased popularity of so-called second-order Monte Carlo analysis for quantifying uncertainty about risks, it is now common practice to distinguish between uncertainty and variability. This increases the value of the risk analysis for decision making, because different policy options may be appropriate for dealing with uncertainty rather than variability. For example, in situations of high population variability but low state-of-knowledge uncertainty, such as airbag effectiveness (Thompson 2002), it may make sense to target risk-reduction efforts at those facilities or members of the population with the highest estimated risks (in this case, children and small adults). By contrast, situations of low variability but high uncertainty would tend to suggest that further research may be desirable before undertaking costly risk-reduction actions. However, the widespread use of second-order Monte Carlo simulation does increase the challenges of effectively communicating ever more sophisticated and sometimes abstruse risk-analysis methods and results to decision makers (and members of the public) in a way that clearly supports improved decision making (Bier 2001a).

Of course, technically accurate risk communication by itself is not sufficient to achieve other key goals of risk communication, such as changing people's behavior (Blaine and Powell 2001), gaining their trust in the results of the analysis, or even giving them the information they need to make improved decisions. Rather, effective and persuasive communication about risks generally requires a concerted effort to build trust, gain and maintain credibility and legitimacy, and summarize relevant information simply and clearly (Bier 2001b). Brevity, clarity, focus, candor, the use of cogent examples, and avoiding negative stereotypes of risk communicators may be crucial for communicating technical risks to nonspecialist audiences in a way that ensures the message is heard and absorbed rather than tuned out or dismissed (e.g., Byrd and Cothern 2000). Audience members generally take into account not only technical content, but also message framing, the source of the information, and the emotional style and assumed motives of the presenter in assessing the credibility of risk communication messages (Chartier and Gabler 2001).

Methods for Risk Management Decision Making

In practice, formal decision analysis is seldom applied directly to make important risk management decisions, in part because different participants may have different utility functions (which may be their own private information), different trade-offs among goals (e.g., minimizing average risk versus reducing inequities in the distribution of risks), and different tolerances for risk. In such cases, consensus utilities may not exist, and risk management decision making requires not only analysis and deliberation (Stern and Fineberg 1996), but also negotiation and compromise. Even when decision analysis is not directly applied, however, its conceptual framework is still useful for organizing analysis and deliberation (Apostolakis and Pickett 1998), separating beliefs from preferences, and identifying and resolving relevant conflicts and/or uncertainties about facts and values. Byrd and Cothern (2000) and Cox (2001) further discuss individual and group decision-making processes and frameworks for risk management decision making.

Methods of Risk Management to Avoid

Well-informed and effective risk management (i.e., risk management that is likely to produce the desired consequences) requires considering *all* of the most important impacts – good and bad – that an intervention is likely to create. Unfortunately, some risk assessments ignore the risks that proposed risk management interventions might *create* (Dowell and Hendershot 1997; Bier 1997), focusing instead entirely on the risks that they might reduce or prevent. This represents a breakdown in sound risk assessment and risk management. Rational risk management requires considering and comparing the *total* consequences of the risk management decision options being evaluated. Risk characterization should therefore provide risk managers with a balanced accounting of the adverse effects that a risk management intervention might *cause*, as well as of those that it might *prevent*.

Risk management processes that recommend interventions based primarily on protection of the *status quo* and/or beliefs about what might constitute "precautionary" risk management should also be avoided if they do not explicitly identify and compare probable consequences of alternative decision options. Such procedures violate important principles of decision theory. A more effective approach, according to widely accepted principles of decision analysis, is to use quantitative information about the *probable consequences* of alternative interventions to eliminate dominated options, and to choose the best among those that remain. Heal and Kriström (2002) have argued on theoretical grounds that precautionary measures might make sense in situations where harm is irreversible; their argument is based on utility theory and real options theory.

A Novel Approach: Game-Theoretic Models

Game theory has long been viewed by risk analysts as being of little relevance for practical risk management decision making. Several recent developments have changed that view, in our opinion. These include not only increased interest in terrorism, homeland security, and critical infrastructure protection (which can be viewed as games between an attacker and a defender), but also increased interest in risk-informed regulation (which can be viewed as a game between a regulator and a regulated firm). As a result of such developments, game theory is becoming an increasingly important research tool in a variety of application areas related to risk. Recent work on reliability optimization (e.g., Levitin 2003; Levitin and Lisnianski 2001; and Levitin et al. 2003) attempts to identify cost-effective risk-reduction strategies; for example, by optimizing physical separation of components that are functionally in parallel with each other, or allocation of physical protection to various hierarchies of a system (e.g., whether to harden the system as a whole, or individual components). However, the "threat" against which systems are to be hardened is generally taken to be static in this work.

Hausken (2002) has applied game theory to study allocation of resources to ensuring component (and hence system) reliability in situations where different agents are responsible for the reliability of different components. In this situation, system reliability is viewed as a "public good." For example, agents responsible for the reliability of a component in a parallel system or subsystem might "free ride" on investments in the reliability of other components in that system – e.g., postponing needed reliability enhancements in the hopes that some other agent will implement such improvements instead.

Game-Theoretic Models for Security and Infrastructure Protection. After the events of September 11, 2001, and subsequent terrorist attacks, there has been increasing interest in security, including protection of public and commercial buildings, water supply systems, and computer systems and software. Numerous researchers and practitioners have proposed the use of risk analysis in one form or another for homeland security (e.g., Paté-Cornell and Guikema 2002; Garrick et al. 2004), especially for critical infrastructure (see for example Haimes et al. 1998; Ezell et al. 2001; Apostolakis and Lemon 2005). Most of this work is not formally game-theoretic; for instance, Paté-Cornell and Guikema discuss the need for "periodic updating of the model and its input" to account for the dynamic nature of counterterrorism, but do not attempt to anticipate the effects of defensive investments on attacker strategies. Protection from intentional sabotage or terrorism differs from many other areas of risk management, because sabotage protection involves an intelligent adversary that can adapt in response to protective measures. Thus, reducing the vulnerability of some systems may cause adversaries to shift their attacks to other systems that have not yet been "hardened" to the same degree. Risk management in this context can be modeled as a game against an adversary — or, conversely, as a game between defenders, because security investment by one defender can have either positive or negative externalities on the threats faced by other defenders (Kunreuther and Heal 2003; Keohane and Zeckhauser 2003).

There is a large body of work on applications of game theory to security, much of it by economists (e.g., Frey and Luechinger 2003; Arce and Sandler 2001; Enders and Sandler 2004; Keohane and Zeckhauser 2003; Lakdawalla and Zanjani 2005). Much of this work is intended to inform policy-level decisions such as the relative merits of public versus private funding of defensive investments, or deterrence versus other protective measures. Recently, efforts have begun to focus more on operational risk management decisions, such as deciding how much defensive investment to allocate to particular assets (e.g., O'Hanlon et al. 2002), and have more of a risk-analysis flavor (e.g, taking the success probabilities of potential attacks into account); see for example Bier et al. (2005) and Woo (2002).

Game-Theoretic Models of Risk-Informed Regulation. In safety and environmental regulation, regulated parties generally know more about the risks of their facilities than regulators. As a result, regulators may wish to provide incentives to encourage regulated parties to accurately disclose unfavorable information about their risks. Such situations have often been modeled as games of incomplete information between regulators and regulated parties. More widespread use of risk analysis in regulatory decision making has the potential to both reduce risk and decrease compliance cost, by increasing management flexibility in determining how to achieve acceptable levels of safety (see, for example, Bier and Jang, 1999). However, this approach has been slow to be adopted in practice. This is in part because of the inability of regulators to directly and accurately measure risk (Chinander et al. 1998), and the fact that companies may have incentives not to disclose unfavorable risk information to regulators and/or not to collect such information in the first place (Wagner 1997). Game-theoretic work in environmental economics to date (e.g., Heyes 2000; Livernois and McKenna 1999) has generally emphasized applications such as pollution monitoring, in which a regulator can (with some effort) determine a firm's level of performance essentially with certainty, and in which firm performance can reasonably be modeled as binary (e.g., compliant with pollution-control regulations or not). Lin (2004) recently applied the same general approach in the context of *risk-informed regulation*, in which regulators may not be certain to detect high risk levels even with substantial effort, and continuous risk levels may be more relevant than binary compliance status. Lin shows that it can still be optimal (i.e., better than a traditional direct-monitoring regulatory scheme) for regulators to offer a loosened standard to firms that voluntarily disclose their risk levels, provided that certain conditions are satisfied.

Conclusion

This chapter has surveyed key methods and concepts for PRA and decision making in engineered systems. Although modeling of uncertain systems has been tremendously enabled by recent advances (e.g., in Bayesian belief networks, with dependencies among inputs expressed via copulas), PRA still poses many challenges. In addition to the technical issues involved in constructing valid models of systems and their environments from engineering knowledge and data, and in identifying optimal or near-optimal risk management policies, communicating the results effectively and using them to guide improved decision making by multiple parties (e.g., teams of stakeholders) also poses practical questions that go beyond the framework of single-person decision theory. If the environment in which a system operates includes intelligent adversaries, then insights from novel methods (e.g., game-theoretic principles) may also need to be taken into account in order to ensure that risk-reduction strategies are effective and cost effective. These challenges are likely to stimulate further advances in both the theory and practice of applied decision analysis.

REFERENCES

Andradóttir, S., and Bier, V. M. (2000). Applying Bayesian ideas in simulation. *Simulation Practice and Theory, 8*, 253–280.

Apostolakis, G., and Kaplan, S. (1981). Pitfalls in risk calculations. *Reliability Enineering and System Safety, 2*, 135–145.

Apostolakis, G. E., and Lemon, D. M. (2005). A screening methodology for the identification and ranking of infrastructure vulnerabilities due to terrorism. *Risk Analysis, 25*, 361–376.

Apostolakis G. E., and Pickett, S. E. (1998). Deliberation: Integrating analytical results into environmental decisions involving multiple stakeholders. *Risk Analysis, 18*, 621–634.

Arce M., D. G., and Sandler, T. (2001). Transnational public goods: Strategies and institutions. *European Journal of Political Economy, 17*, 493–516.

Barlow, R. E. (1998). *Engineering reliability*. Philadelphia: Society for Industrial and Applied Mathematics.

Bedford, T., and Cooke, R. M. (2001). Probability density decomposition for conditionally dependent random variables modeled by vines. *Annals of Mathematics and Artificial Intelligence, 32*, 245–268.

Bier, V. M. (1997, April). *Illusions of safety*. Paper presented at the Workshop on Organizational Analysis in High Hazard Production Systems: An Academy/Industry Dialogue, Dedham, MA.

Bier, V. M. (2001a). On the state of the art: Risk communication to decision makers. *Reliability Engineering and System Safety, 71*, 151–157.

Bier, V. M. (2001b). On the state of the art: Risk communication to the public. *Reliability Engineering and System Safety, 71*, 139–150.

Bier, V. M., and Jang, S. C. (1999). Defaults and incentives in risk-informed regulation. *Human and Ecological Risk Assessment, 5*, 635–644.

Bier, V., Nagaraj, A., and Abhichandani, V. (2005). Protection of simple series and parallel systems with components of different values. *Reliability Engineering and System Safety, 87*, 315–323.

Blaine, K., and Powell, D. (2001). Communication of food-related risks. *AgBioForum, 4*, 179–185.

Bobbio, A., Portinale, L., Minichino, M., and Ciancamerla, E. (2001). Improving the analysis of dependable systems by mapping fault trees into Bayesian networks. *Reliability Engineering and System Safety, 71*, 249–260.

Borgonovo, E., Smith, C. L., Apostolakis, G. E., Deriot, S., and Dewailly, J. (2000). Insights from using influence diagrams to analyze precursor events. In S. Kondo and K. Furuta (Eds.), *Proceedings of PSAM 5, Probabilistic Safety Assessment and Management.* Tokyo: Universal Academy Press.

Box, G. E. (1979). Robustness in the strategy of scientific model building. In R. Launer and G. Wilkinson (Eds.), *Robustness in statistics*. New York: Academic Press, pp. 201–236.

Brown, R. (1999). *Using soft data to make "probabilistic risk assessments" realistic.* http://fisher.osu.edu/~butler_267/DAPapers/WP000002.pdf Accessed 7/29/05.

Burmaster, D., and Anderson, P. D. (1994). Principles of good practice for the use of Monte Carlo techniques in human health and ecological risk assessments. *Risk Analysis, 14*, 477–481.

Byrd, D.M., and Cothern, C.R. (2000). *Introduction to risk analysis: A systematic approach to science-based decision making.* Houston: ABS Group, Chapter 12.

Carlin, B. P., and Louis, T. A. (2000). *Bayes and empirical Bayes methods for data analysis.* (2nd ed.). Boca Raton: Chapman and Hall/CRC.

Chartier, J., and Gabler, S. (2001). *Risk communication and government: Theory and application for the Canadian Food Inspection Agency.* Ottawa: Canadian Food Inspection Agency.

Chick, S. E. (1997). Bayesian analysis for simulation input and output. In S. Andradóttir, K. J. Healy, D. H. Withers, and B. L. Nelson (Eds.), *Proceedings of the 1997 Winter Simulation Conference.* Washington: IEEE Press, pp. 253–260.

Chinander, K. R., Kleindorfer, P. R., and Kunreuther, H. C. (1998). Compliance strategies and regulatory effectiveness of performance-based regulation of chemical accident risks. *Risk Analysis, 18*, 135–143.

Cox, L.A. Jr. (2001). *Risk analysis: Foundations, models, and methods.* Boston: Kluwer.

Cullen, A. C., and Frey, H. C. (1999). *Probabilistic techniques in exposure assessment: A handbook for dealing with variability and uncertainty in models and inputs.* New York: Plenum.

Dowell, A. M., and Hendershot, D. C. (1997). No good deed goes unpunished: Case studies of incidents and potential incidents caused by protective systems. *Process Safety Progress, 16*, 132–139.

Enders, W., and Sandler, T. (2004). What do we know about the substitution effect in transnational terrorism? In A. Silke, and G. Ilardi, (Eds.), *Researching terrorism: Trends, achievements, failures.* London: Frank Cass.

Ezell, B. C., Haimes, Y. Y., and Lambert, J. H. (2001). Cyber attack to water utility supervisory control and data acquisition (SCADA) systems. *Military Operations Research, 6*, 23–33.

Ferson, S., and Donald, S. (1998). Probability bounds analysis. In A. Mosleh, and R. A. Bari, (Eds.), *Probabilistic safety assessment and management.* New York: Springer-Verlag, pp. 1203–1208.

Ferson, S., and Hajagos, J. G. (2006). Varying correlation coefficients can underestimate uncertainty in probabilistic models. *Reliability Engineering and System Safety, 91*, 1461–1467.

Frey, B. S., and Luechinger, S. (2003). How to fight terrorism: Alternatives to deterrence. *Defence and Peace Economics, 14*, 237–249.

Garrick, B. J., Hall, J. E., Kilger, M., McDonald, J. C., O'Toole, T., Probst, P. S., Parker, E. R., Rosenthal, R., Trivelpiece, A. W., Van Arsdale, L. A., and Zebroski, E. L. (2004). Confronting the risks of terrorism: Making the right decisions. *Reliability Engineering and System Safety, 86*, 129–176.

Givens, G. H., and Roback, P. J. (1999). Logarithmic pooling of priors linked by a deterministic simulation model. *Journal of Computational and Graphical Statistics, 8*, 452–478.

Haimes, Y. Y., Matalas, N. C., Lambert, J. H., Jackson, B. A., and Fellows, J. F. R. (1998). Reducing vulnerability of water supply systems to attack. *Journal of Infrastructure Systems, 4*, 164–177.

Hausken, K. (2002). Probabilistic risk analysis and game theory. *Risk Analysis, 22*, 17–27.

Heal, G., and Kriström, B. (2002). Uncertainty and climate change. *Environmental and Resource Economics, 22*, 3–39.

Health and Safety Policy Advisory Group. (2004). Quantified risk assessment techniques – Part 3: Fault tree analysis – FTA, *Health and Safety Briefing 26c*, Institution of Engineering and Technology, http://www.theiet.org/publicaffairs/health/hsb26c.pdf. Accessed 10/5/06.

Heyes, A. (2000). Implementing environmental regulation: Enforcement and compliance. *Journal of Regulatory Economics, 17*, 107–129.

Hoeting, J., Madigan, D., Raftery, A., and Volinsky, C. (1999). Bayesian model averaging. *Statistical Science, 14*, 382–401.

Hope, B. K. (1999). Assessment of risk to terrestrial receptors using uncertain analysis – A case study. *Human and Ecological Risk Assessment, 5*, 145–70.

Jaynes, E. T. (2003). *Probability theory: The logic of science*. Cambridge, UK: Cambridge University Press.

Joe, H. (1997). *Multivariate models and dependence concepts*. London: Chapman & Hall.

Jouini, M., and Clemen, R. T. (1996). Copula models for aggregating expert opinions. *Operations Research, 44*, 444–457.

Keohane, N. O., and Zeckhauser, R. J. (2003). The ecology of terror defense. *Journal of Risk and Uncertainty, 26*, 201–229.

Kraan, B., and Cooke, R. (1997). The effect of correlations in uncertainty analysis: Two cases. In R. Cooke (Ed.), *Technical committee uncertainty modeling: Report on the benchmark workshop uncertainty/sensitivity analysis codes*. Delft: European Safety and Reliability Association.

Kunreuther, H., and Heal, G. (2003). Interdependent security. *Journal of Risk and Uncertainty, 26*, 231–249.

Kurowicka, D., and Cooke, R. (2004, June). *Distribution-free continuous Bayesian belief nets*. Paper presented at the Fourth International Conference on Mathematical Methods in Reliability: Methodology and Practice, Santa Fe, NM.

Lacke, C. (1998). *Decision analytic modeling of colorectal cancer screening policies*. Unpublished doctoral dissertation, North Carolina State University.

Lakdawalla, D., and Zanjani, G. (2005). Insurance, self-protection, and the economics of terrorism. *Journal of Public Economics, 89*, 1891–1905.

Lauritzen, S. L., and Spiegelhalter, D. J. (1998). Local computations with probabilities on graphical structures and their application to expert systems. *Journal of the Royal Statistical Society, Series B, 50*, 157–224.

Lee, P. M. (2004). *Bayesian statistics: An introduction*. (3rd ed.). London: Arnold.

Levitin, G. (2003). Optimal multilevel protection in series-parallel systems. *Reliability Engineering and System Safety, 81*, 93–102.

Levitin, G., and Lisnianski, A. (2001). Optimal separation of elements in vulnerable multi-state systems. *Reliability Engineering and System Safety, 73*, 55–66.

Levitin, G., Dai, Y., Xie, M., and Poh, K. L. (2003). Optimizing survivability of multi-state systems with multi-level protection by multi-processor genetic algorithm. *Reliability Engineering and System Safety, 82*, 93–104.

Lin, S.-W. (2004). *Designing incentive systems for risk-informed regulation.* Unpublished doctoral dissertation, University of Wisconsin-Madison.

Livernois, J., and McKenna, C. J. (1999). Truth or consequences: Enforcing pollution standards with self-reporting. *Journal of Public Economics, 71*, 415–440.

Meeuwissen, A. M. H., and Bedford, T. (1997). Minimally informative distributions with given rank correlation for use in uncertainty analysis. *Journal of Statistical Computation and Simulation, 57*, 143–174.

Merrick, J. R. W., van Dorp, J. R., and Singh, A. (2005). Analysis of correlated expert judgments from pairwise comparisons. *Decision Analysis, 2*, 17–29.

Nardini, L., Aparicio, L., Bandoni, J.A., and Tonelli, S. M. (2003). Regional risk associated with the transport of hazardous materials, *Latin American Applied Research, 33*, 213–218.

Nelsen, R. B. (1999). *An introduction to copulas.* New York: Springer-Verlag.

O'Hanlon, M., Orszag, P., Daalder, I., Destler, M., Gunter, D., Litan, R., and Steinberg J. (2002). *Protecting the American homeland.* Washington, DC: Brookings Institution.

Ólafsson, S., and Kim, J. (2002). Simulation optimization. In E. Yücesan, C.-H. Chen, J. L. Snowdon, and J. M. Charnes (Eds.), *Proceedings of the 2002 Winter Simulation Conference*, pp. 79–84.

Paté-Cornell, E., and Guikema, S. (2002). Probabilistic modeling of terrorist threats: A systems analysis approach to setting priorities among countermeasures. *Military Operations Research, 7*, 5–20.

Phimister, J. R., Bier, V. M., and Kunreuther, H. C. (Eds.). (2004). *Accident precursor analysis and management: Reducing technological risk through diligence.* Washington, DC: National Academies Press.

Planning Department of Hong Kong. (2006). *Hong Kong Planning Standards and Guidelines*, August 2006, Government of the Hong Kong Special Administrative Region, http://www.pland.gov.hk/tech_doc/hkpsg/english/ch12/ch12_figure2.htm. Accesssed 10/5/06.

Raftery, A. E., Givens, G. H., and Zeh, J. E. (1995). Inference from a deterministic population dynamics model for bowhead whales. *Journal of the American Statistical Association, 90*, 402–415.

Raftery, A. E., and Zheng, Y. (2003). Discussion: Performance of Bayesian model averaging. *Journal of the American Statistical Association, 98*, 931–938.

Regan, H. M., Hope, B. K., and Ferson, S. (2002). Analysis and portrayal of uncertainty in a food-web exposure model. *Human and Ecological Risk Assessment, 8*, 1757–1777.

Rios Insua, D., and Ruggeri, F. (Eds.). (2000). *Robust Bayesian analysis.* New York: Springer-Verlag.

Roback, P. J., and Givens, G. H. (2001). Supra-Bayesian pooling of priors linked by a deterministic simulation model. *Communications in Statistics-Simulation and Computation, 30*, 447–476.

Roelen, A. L. C., Wever, R., Hale, A. R., Goossens, L. H. J., Cooke, R. M., Lopuhaa, R., Simons, M., and Valk, P. J. L. (2003). Casual modeling for integrated safety at airport. In T. Bedford and P. H. A. J. M. van Gelder (Eds.), *Proceedings of ESREL 2003, The European Conference on Safety and Reliability, 2*, 1321–1327.

Rubinstein, R. Y., and Kroese, D. P. (2004). *The cross-entropy method: A unified approach to combinatorial optimization, Monte-Carlo simulation and machine learning.* New York: Springer-Verlag.

Schweder, T., and Hjort, N. L. (1996). Bayesian synthesis or likelihood synthesis – What does Borel's paradox say? *Forty-Sixth Report of the International Whaling Commission*. Cambridge, UK: International Whaling Commission, pp. 475–479.

Singpurwalla, N. D., and Wilson, S. P. (1999). *Statistical methods in software reliability: Reliability and risk*. New York: Springer-Verlag.

Small, M. J., and Fischbeck, P. S. (1999). False precision in Bayesian updating with incomplete models. *Human and Ecological Risk Assessment, 5*, 291–304.

Smith, D. J. (2005). *Reliability, maintainability and risk: Practical methods for engineers including reliability centered maintenance and safety-related systems* (7th ed.). New York: Elsevier.

Stern, P. C., and Fineberg, H. V. (Eds.). (1996). *Understanding risk: Informing decisions in a democratic society*. Washington, DC: National Academy Press.

Thompson, K. M. (2002). Variability and uncertainty meet risk management and risk communication. *Risk Analysis, 22*, 647–654.

U.S. Nuclear Regulatory Commission (USNRC) (1975). WASH 1400 (NUREG – 75/014), *Reactor Safety Study: Assessment of Accident Risks in U.S. Commercial Nuclear Plants*. Washington, DC: Nuclear Regulatory Commission.

Wagner, W. E. (1997). Choosing ignorance in the manufacture of toxic products. *Cornell Law Review, 82*, 773–855.

Wilson, S., and Samaniego, F. (2002, June). *Nonparameteric methods in software reliability*. Paper presented at the Third International Conference on Mathematical Methods in Reliability: Methodology and Practice, Trondheim, Norway.

Wolpert, R. L. (1995). Comment on "Inference from a deterministic model for bowhead whales." *Journal of the American Statistical Association, 90*, 426–427.

Woo, G. (2002). Quantitative terrorism risk assessment. *Journal of Risk Finance, 4*, 7–14.

Wurbs, R. A. (2005). *Comparative evaluation of generalized river/reservoir system models*. College Station: Texas Water Resources Institute.

Yi, W., and Bier, V. M. (1998). An application of copulas to accident precursor analysis. *Management Science, 44*, S257–S270.

16 The Engineering Risk Analysis Method and Some Applications

M. Elisabeth Paté-Cornell

ABSTRACT. Engineering risk analysis methods, based on systems analysis and probability, are generally designed for cases in which sufficient failure statistics are unavailable. These methods can be applied not only to engineered systems that fail (e.g., new spacecraft or medical devices), but also to systems characterized by performance scenarios including malfunctions or threats. I describe some of the challenges in the use of risk analysis tools, mainly in problem formulation, when technical, human, and organizational factors need to be integrated. This discussion is illustrated by four cases: ship grounding due to loss of propulsion, space shuttle loss caused by tile failure, patient risks in anesthesia, and the risks of terrorist attacks on the US. I show how the analytical challenges can be met by the choice of modeling tools and the search for relevant information, including not only statistics but also a deep understanding of how the system works and can fail, and how failures can be anticipated and prevented. This type of analysis requires both imagination and a logical, rational approach. It is key to proactive risk management and effective ranking of risk reduction measures when statistical data are not directly available and resources are limited.

Engineering Risk Analysis Method: Imagination and Rationality

Risk analysis for well-known, well-documented and steady-state systems (or stable phenomena) can be performed by methods of statistical analysis of available data. These include, for example, maximum likelihood estimations, and analyses of variance and correlations. Generally, these methods require a projection in the future of risk estimates based on a sufficient sample, of preferably independent, identically distributed data, and other experiences from the past. However, when designing or operating a new type of engineered system, one can seldom rely on such a body of evidence, even though there may exist relevant data regarding parts of the system or the problem. The same is true in all new situations in which the risk can only be evaluated from a rigorous and systematic analysis of possible scenarios, and from dependencies among events in a scenario. For instance, assessing the risk of a terrorist attack on the US requires "imagination" as emphasized in the 9/11 Commission Report (NCTA 2004). To do so, one has to rely first on a systems analysis, and second, on Bayesian probability and statistics (e.g., Savage 1954; Press 1989). The engineering method of "Probabilistic Risk Analysis" (PRA or here, simply RA), which was designed in the nuclear power industry and in other fields (USNRC 1975; Henley and Kumamoto 1992; Bedford and Cooke 2001), was presented in the previous chapter.[1] In the next sections, I describe some specific features and applications of the engineering risk analysis method with the objective of finding and fixing system weaknesses, whether technical or organizational[2] (Paté-Cornell 2000, 2002a). The focus is mostly on the formulation phase of a risk analysis, which can present major challenges. I describe and illustrate four specific problems and possible solutions: the explicit inclusion of human and management factors in the assessment of technical failure risks using influence diagrams,[3] with, as an example, the case of *ship grounding* due to loss of propulsion; the characterization of the dynamics of accident sequences illustrated by a model of analysis of *patient risk in anesthesia*; the treatment of spatially distributed risks with a model of the risk of an accident caused by a failure of *the tiles of the NASA space shuttle*; and the challenge of structuring the modeling of a type of threat that is new – at least on the scale that has been recently observed – illustrated by the *risks of different types of terrorist attacks* on the US.

Proactive Risk Management

Early Technology Assessment and Anticipation of "Perfect Storms"

The risk analysis (RA) method used in engineering is based both on systems analysis and probability and allows computation of the risk of system failure under normal or abnormal operating circumstances.[4] More important, it permits addressing and computing the risk of "perfect storms," that is, rare conjunctions of events, some of which may not have happened yet even though some of their elements may have been observed in the past. These events can affect, for instance, the performance of a new space system faced with a combination of challenges (e.g., a long voyage, cosmic rays, or planetary storms). The same method can be used to perform early technology assessment, which is especially critical in the development of systems such as medical devices, which are expensive to engineer and less likely than not to pass the statistical tests required by the U.S. Food and Drug Administration before approval (Pietzsch et al. 2004). In that context, RA can thus be used to anticipate the effectiveness and the safety of a new medical device when the practitioners may not be accustomed to it, when there may be

---

[1] Bier and Cox, 2007.

[2] There exist other forms of risk analysis, for instance those used in environmental/health risk analysis, which often rely on "plausible upper bounds" or other "conservative" measurements to characterize, for example, dose–response relationships (Paté-Cornell 1996). These methods generally do not involve Bayesian probability.

[3] An influence diagram is a directed graph, whose nodes represent random events or variables and the arrows probabilistic dependences among them (Shachter 2006).

[4] In industry, however, the risk of failure of an engineering project is often understood as the risk of missing the project deadline or exceeding its budget. The technical failure risk is often "managed" through insurance. Furthermore, it is often assumed that once the specifications have been met everything will be fine, when in fact the problem may be first, in their definition and second, in ensuring that they have actually been met. In this paper, the focus is on technical failure risk and its management through actual system reinforcement.

some design problems, and/or when the patients happen to be particularly vulnerable (e.g., premature babies). In a different setting, one can also use this type of analysis to assess the risks of combined factors on a firm's bottom line, for example, a competitor's move, a labor strike that affects its supply chain, and/or a dip in demand caused by a major political event. In that perspective, RA can be applied, for instance to the quantification of the risks of bankruptcy in the insurance industry when a company is faced with a decline in market returns, repeated catastrophes, and prosecution of its executives for professional misconduct (Paté-Cornell and Deleris 2005). Also, as shown further, the same RA method can be used to support the choice of counterterrorism measures, given the limited information provided by the intelligence community, in the face of ever-changing situations (Paté-Cornell 2002b).

Remembering the Past While Looking Ahead

Anticipating rare failures, as well as shedding light on mundane but unrecognized problems, can provide effective support for risk management. But there is a clear difference between probabilistic risk analysis and expected-utility decision analysis (e.g., Raiffa 1968), in which the decision makers are known at the onset of the exercise (Paté-Cornell 2007). The risk analysis question is often: what are the risks (as assessed by an analyst and a group of experts), and how can the results be formulated to best represent uncertainties and be useful to the eventual decision maker(s)?

The key issue, in all cases, is to anticipate problems that may or may not have occurred before, and to recognize existing ones in order to devise proactive risk management strategies. The engineering risk analysis method permits ranking risk management options and setting priorities in the use of resources. The quantification of each part of the problem by probability and consequence estimates allows their combination in a structured way, using both Bayes' theorem (to compute the probability of various scenarios) and the total probability theorem (to compute the overall probability of total or partial failures). Effective risk-management options can then be formulated. They include for instance, adding redundancies, but also, the observation of precursors, that is, signals and near-misses, which permit anticipating future problems and implementing proactive measures (Phimister et al. 2004).

A Brief Overview of the Method and Formulation Challenges

The Challenge of Structuring the Model

The first step in a risk analysis is to structure the future possible events into *classes* of scenarios[5] as a set of mutually exclusive and collectively exhaustive elements,

---

[5] The emphasis is on *classes* of scenarios, that is, a partition of the scenario set that is sufficient to capture the different levels of system failures without going into details that would make the formulation almost unmanageable and the collection of data almost impossible.

discrete or continuous. Each of these scenarios is a conjunction of events leading to a particular outcome. The choice of the model structure, level of detail, and depth of analysis is critical: as one adds more details to a scenario description (A and B and C etc.), its probability decreases. In the limit, the exact realization of a scenario in a continuous space would have a zero probability, making the exercise useless. Therefore, one needs first to formulate the model at a level of detail that is manageable, yet sufficient to identify and characterize the most important risk reduction options. This level of detail may vary from one subsystem to the next. Second, one needs to compute the probability of the outcomes that can result from each class of scenarios, adjusting the level of detail, as shown further, to reflect the value of the information of the corresponding variables as support for risk management decisions. Finally, one needs to quantify the outcomes of these scenarios and to aggregate the results, sometimes as a probability distribution for a single attribute (e.g., money), displayed as a single risk curve (e.g., the complementary cumulative distribution of annual amounts of potential damage); or as the joint distribution of several attributes of the outcome space[6] (e.g., human casualties and financial losses). To represent the fundamental uncertainties about the phenomenon of interest, one can display a family of risk curves, which represent a discretization of the distribution of the probability (or future frequency) of exceeding given levels of losses per time unit (Helton 1994; Paté-Cornell 1996, 1999b).

One can thus represent accident scenarios in various ways. The first is simply accident sequences, starting with initiating events followed by a set of intermediate events leading to an outcome described either by a single measure (e.g., monetary) or by a multiattribute vector. The distribution of these outcomes allows representation of the risk at various levels of failure severity. Another analytical structure is to identify "failure modes" or min-cut sets, that is, the conjunctions (without notion of sequencing) of events that lead to system failure described as a Boolean variable (USNRC 1975). These failure modes account for the structure of the system, for example, the fact that the failure of a redundant subsystem requires failure of all its components.

To model the risk using the accident sequence approach, note $p(X)$ the probability of an event per time unit (or operation), $p(X|Y)$ the conditional probability of X given Y, $p(X,Y)$ the joint probability of X and Y, IE_i the possible initiating events of accident sequences indexed in i, and F the (total[7]) technical failure of the system. In its simplest form, one can represent the result of the PRA model as the probability $p(F)$ of a system failure per time unit or operation as:

$$p(F) = \sum_i (p(IE_i)p(F \mid IE_i)) \tag{16.1}$$

where $p(F \mid IE_i)$ can be computed as a function of the conditional probabilities of the (intermediate) events that follow IE_i and lead to F. The accident sequences

---

[6] Alternatively, one can describe for simplicity, the marginal distribution of each of the attributes and a measure of their correlation.
[7] One can rewrite these equations to characterize partial failures using the same concepts.

can be systematically represented, for instance, through event trees and influence diagrams.

Alternatively, one can start from the system's failure modes. Noting M_j these conjunctions of events (min-cut sets), one can write the probability of failure $p(F)$ using the total probability theorem as

$$p(F) = \sum_j p(M_j) - \sum_j \sum_k p(M_j, M_k)$$
$$+ \, p(\text{three failure modes at a time}) - \text{etc.} \tag{16.2}$$

External events that can affect all failure modes (e.g., earthquakes) or the probabilities of specific events in an accident sequence can be introduced in the analysis at that stage. The method is to condition the terms of the equation(s) on the occurrence (or not) of the common cause of failure and its severity level.

The choice of one form or another (sequences versus failure modes) depends on the structure of the available information. In the ship-grounding risk analysis model and the risk analysis of a shuttle accident presented later in this chapter, the accident-sequence structure was chosen because it was the easiest way to think systematically through a collectively exhaustive and mutually exclusive set of failure scenarios. However, faced with a complex system, best described by its functions and by a functional diagram, focusing on the failure modes might be an easier choice.

Dynamic Analysis

The robustness of a system as well as the challenges to which it is subjected may change over time. A structure fails when the loads exceed its capacity. On the one hand, one may want to account for the long-term pattern of occurrences of the loads (e.g., earthquakes), as well as the short-term dynamics of the different ways in which such events can unfold, for example, the time-dependent characteristics of the pre-shocks, main shock, and aftershocks of an earthquake that can hit a structure. On the other hand the system's capacity may vary as well. It can deteriorate independently from the loads (e.g., by corrosion), or it can decrease because of the fatigue caused by repeated load cycles (e.g., the effect of the waves on a structure at sea). Accounting for variations of loads and capacities requires a knowledge base that may come from different domains, for example, from geophysics to structural engineering in the case of seismic risks.

Another form of dynamic analysis may be required to analyze the evolution of accident sequences in which the consequences depend on the time elapsed between the initiating event and the conclusion of an incident. This is the case of an analysis of risks of fires in oil refineries (Paté-Cornell 1985) as well as that of patient risks in anesthesia described further. In both cases, stochastic processes were used to describe the evolution of the system over time, which is needed when the timing of human intervention is essential to effective risk management.

Imagination and Rationality

This RA method has been developed in detail in the past for specific cases such as electrical circuits, civil engineering systems, nuclear reactors, aircraft, and space systems. But in its principles, as shown further, RA has applications to many other problems for which one needs to "imagine" *systematically*, beyond a simple, arbitrary "what-if" exercise, the potential failures in absence of directly relevant experience. In these cases, the choice of *evidence* is critical because available information may be incomplete and imperfect, yet essential to support a rational decision that needs to be made, before the occurrence of an event such as a specified type of terrorist attack or before a medical device is used in a real setting.

Imagination and rationality are thus two main bases of the PRA method. Risk analysis is meant to support risk management decisions, assuming a rational decision maker or a homogenous group of them.[8] Rationality is defined here by the von Neumann axioms of decision making (von Neumann and Morgenstern 1947), and by the definition of probability that they imply.[9] This Bayesian definition differs from the classical frequentist approach in that it relies on a degree of belief based on a decision maker's willingness to make bets and to choose among lotteries given all available evidence. Therefore, by definition, this kind of probability cannot be "validated" in the classical statistical sense, at least not until one has gathered a sufficient body of experimental data, and provided that the system has remained in a steady state. This is rarely the case in innovative engineering or policy making. Instead, one has to seek *justification* of the model through a careful presentation of assumptions, reasoning, data, and conclusions.

Incomplete Evidence Base

The Bayesian RA method is thus at the root of *evidence-based* decisions.[10] but this does not necessarily imply that the evidence involves a complete set of classic statistical data. Again, this is true because one often has to make such decisions in the face of uncertainty (e.g., in medicine or in astronautics) before complete information can be obtained. Therefore, the method uses all the evidence that *exists,* imperfect as it may be when needed, as opposed to the "perfect" one that one would want to have to follow the classic statistics path. In effect, the inputs

---

[8] A risk analysis can support the decision of a "heterogeneous" group of decision makers, but they will have to agree on either a decision process or on analytical methods of aggregation of probabilities and preferences.

[9] There are many other ways of performing a normative or prescriptive "decision analysis." The Analytical Hierarchy process, for example, is designed to guide a decision, and therefore, it can be considered prescriptive even though it does not rely on the norms of the von Neumann axioms.

[10] The notion of evidence-based decisions is currently at the heart of a debate in the medical community. I want to stress here that evidence cannot be restricted to large statistical samples and that one should not wait to save lives until complete statistics are available to make decisions that can be reasonably supported by Bayesian reasoning.

of the RA method, that is, the best information available, may be subjective and imperfect, but the *process* by which the output is generated is a rigorous one.

Because one often needs to use the concept of Bayesian probability based on a degree of belief, the first question is, of course: whose beliefs? At the onset of a risk analysis, the identity of the ultimate decision maker is seldom known, it may vary over time, along with the number of incidents, operations, systems, years of operation. Yet, the results have to be complete enough to provide information relevant to decision support under various levels of uncertainties when the event of interest can repeat itself. This implies, in particular that one needs to separate what has been traditionally referred to as "risk" and "uncertainty" but is better described as two kinds of uncertainties, *aleatory* (i.e., randomness) and *epistemic* (i.e., incomplete information about the fundamental phenomenon of interest (Apostolakis 1990)). At the end of the analysis, the probability of an event, in the face of epistemic uncertainty, is the mean future frequency of that event, a measure that is compatible with the maximization of expected utility.[11] However, one needs to quantify and fully describe uncertainties about probabilities of various outcomes to allow decision makers to use the risk results in the case of repeated "experiments."

Data

The data that are used in risk analysis thus cover a wide range of sources. In the best of all worlds, one has access to operational data that describe a particular system or phenomenon in its actual setting, for example, flight data for a space system, or steady-state operating room statistics for a well-known form of surgery. More often, however, in innovative circumstances, one has, at best, surrogate data regarding performance of subsystems and components in a different but similar environment. Other times, one may have to use test data and lab data (e.g., on human performance on simulators). The problem is that tests may have to be performed in an environment that cannot exactly represent the operational one, for instance microgravity for a spacecraft. When one knows the characteristics of the loads to which the system will be subjected and the factors that influence its capacity, one can also use engineering models as a source of information. Finally, when facing a new situation with no access to such data, in a first iteration of an analysis, or to supplement existing data, one may need to use expert opinions, provided that the questions have been phrased in such a way that the experts can actually respond based on their experience. Biases in these responses have been widely documented and require all the care of the analyst (e.g., Kahneman et al. 1982). Next, one often faces the unavoidable challenge of aggregating expert opinions, which is easier when the decision maker is known and can inject his

---

[11] This is an approximation that applies first, to the case where that frequency is small given the time unit, and second, to a repetitive event or something that can be construed as one, not to unique events or hypotheses. Therefore, this is a shortcut, but one that is useful to bridge gaps in reasoning between two communities of risk analysts: one focused on frequencies and one focused on degrees of belief.

own "weighting" (in effect, the equivalent of likelihood functions) in the exercise and is more complex when the risk analysis has to be performed for unknown decisions and decision makers.[12]

The Tool Kit

The tools of RA thus include all those that allow the description of the problem structure and the computation of failure probabilities, in a context that can be either static or dynamic. They involve event trees, fault trees, influence diagrams, Bayesian probability, and descriptive statistics,[13] but also stochastic processes of various sorts depending on the system's memory, time dependencies etc. They also include characterization of human errors and of the outcomes of the various scenarios based, for example, on economic analysis. When expanded to the analysis of risk-management decisions, the tool kit includes decision trees (and the corresponding version of influence diagrams) and utility functions, single or multiattribute (Keeney and Raiffa 1976).

Simulation is often needed to propagate uncertainties through the model in order to link uncertainties in the input and those in the output. To do so, one can use, for instance, Monte Carlo simulation, or, often better, the Latin Hypercube method, which is based on a similar approach but allows for a more efficient search.

Extension of RA to Include Human and Management Factors: The SAM Model

Most of the classic risk analyses do include human reliability in one form or another. Human errors may be included in failures or accident scenarios as basic events, or as part of the data of component failures. Yet, they are not necessarily an explicit part of a scenario, and often simply weaken a component, for example, through poor maintenance, which increases a component's vulnerability. In addition, human errors are often based on management problems, for example, wrong incentives, lack of knowledge on the part of the technicians, or excessive resource constraints.

To address these problems, a three-level model called SAM was devised (Murphy and Paté-Cornell 1996) based, at the first level, on an analysis of the system's failure risk (S). The second level, involves a systematic identification and

---

[12] The aggregation of expert opinions can be based on analytical procedures such as Bayesian weights representing likelihoods, or on interactive methods such as the Delphi method, or hybrid methods such as the SHAC method used in seismic hazard analysis, which has the advantage of focusing on the basic mechanisms and the supporting data, irrelevant of the field of application (Budnitz et al. 1998). Another approach is empirical calibration of the experts themselves (Cooke 1991) or the use of copula models (Clemen and Winkler 2006).

[13] Many PRA input come from classical statistics. Note, however, that this requires a steady state and a sample of sufficient size, in which case classical and Bayesian statistics (if they are based on weak prior distributions) yield similar results.

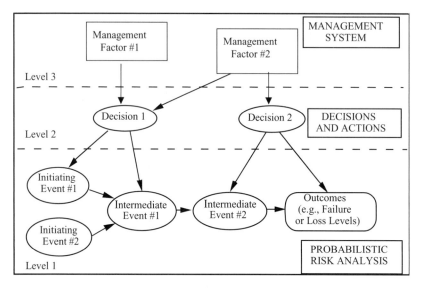

Figure 16.1. Generic influence diagram representing the structure of the SAM model.

probabilistic characterization of the human decisions and actions (A) that influence the probabilities of the basic events of the model. Finally, a third level represents the management factors (M) that in turn, affect the probabilities of the human decisions and actions.[14]

The main characteristic of the SAM model is that it starts with an analysis of the performance of the physical system. This model can be represented by a three-tier influence diagram (see Figure 16.1), in which the influences run from the top to the bottom but the analysis is performed from the bottom to the top. The equations of the SAM model can be described using the notations of Eqs. 16.1 and 16.2, and in addition, noting as $p(L_h)$ the probability of the different loss levels L_h associated with various degrees of technical system failure indexed in h, (DA_m) the probabilities of the decisions and actions of the different actors, and MN_n the relevant management factors that affect peoples decisions and actions.

The SAM equations are:

SAM step 1: probability of system failures characterized by levels of losses

$$p(L_h) = \sum_i (p(IE_i)p(L_h \mid IE_i)) \qquad (16.3)$$

SAM step 2: effects of human decisions and actions on p (losses)

$$p(L_h) = \sum_i \sum_m p(DA_m)p(IE_i \mid DA_m)p(L_h \mid IE_i, DA_m) \qquad (16.4)$$

SAM step 3: effects of management factors on p (losses)

$$p(L_h \mid MN_n) = \sum_i \sum_m p(DA_m \mid MN_n)p(IE_i \mid DA_m)p(L_h \mid IE_i, DA_m) \qquad (16.5)$$

---

[14] Another approach is to start from an analysis of the work process (Davoudian et al. 1994).

Note that the effects of management factors on the probabilities of losses are assessed through their effects on the probabilities of the decisions and actions of the people involved. Also, we assume here, for simplicity, that the different decisions and actions are mutually independent conditional on management factors (which can be modified easily if necessary).

In what follows, we present four examples of risk analyses, some at the formulation stage and some with results that include identification of possible risk management options, to illustrate different features of the RA model and, in three cases, of its SAM extension.

Example 1. Ship-Grounding Risk: Influence Diagram and SAM Model Representation

The Grounding of Oil Tankers or Other Cargo Ships

The experience with the grounding of the Exxon Valdez in Alaska as well as the breaking at sea of several oil tankers and cargo ships, such as the AMOCO-Cadiz, off the coasts of Europe posed some serious risk management problems. Are the best solutions technical, for example, requiring double hulls, or essentially managerial and regulatory in nature, for instance, increased regulation of maritime traffic and Coast Guard surveillance and/or improvements of the training of the crew? In some cases, one could even imagine drastic options such as blowing up rocks that are too close to shipping lanes. Obviously, the risk depends, among other factors, on the nature of the ship and its cargo, on the skills of its crew, and on the location of maritime routes. Some areas such as the Molucca Strait are particularly dangerous because of the density of international traffic and at times, the anarchic or criminal behavior of the crews. Other sites are especially vulnerable because of their configuration, such as Puget Sound, the San Francisco Bay, or Prince William Sound.

Problem Formulation Based on a SAM-Type Influence Diagram

An analysis of the risks of oil spills due to ship grounding following loss of propulsion can be represented by an influence diagram, expanded to include human and management factors in the SAM format. To support a spectrum of risk management decisions, this diagram can be structured as shown in Figure 16.2 to include the elements of Figure 16.1. It represents the sequence of events starting with loss of propulsion that can lead to a breach in the hull and in the case of oil tankers, release of various quantities of oil in the sea, and possibly, sinking of the ship

The lower part of Figure 16.2 represents the system's failure risk analysis model. The accident sequence starts with the *loss of propulsion at sea* (initiating event). Given that this event has happened, the second event is *drift control*: can the crew control the drift? If not, the next event is *grounding of the ship*: does it happen or not given the speed, the location, and the weather? If grounding occurs, the next question is: what is the *size of the breach* in the hull? It depends

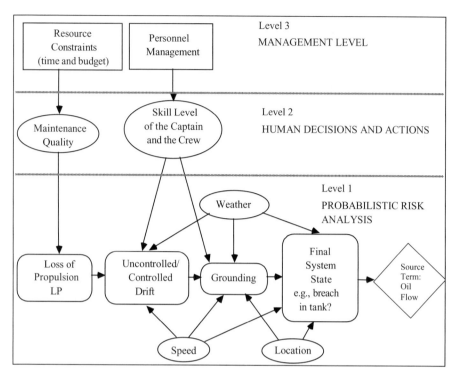

Figure 16.2. Influence diagram for the risk of grounding of an oil tanker.

on the nature of the seabed or the coast (sand, rocks etc.), on the characteristics of the hull, and on the energy of the shock. Finally, given the size of the breach, the next question is: what is the *amount of oil spilled* in the water? This outcome depends on the amount of oil carried in the first place and on the size of the breach as well as the external response to the incident. The final outcome can then be characterized by the financial loss and the environmental damage measured, for instance, in terms of number of animals or length of coastline affected, or in terms of time to full recovery.

The middle and upper parts of Figure 16.2 represent the decisions, actions, and organizational roots of the elements of the accident sequence represented in the lower part of the figure. The failure of a ship's propulsion system starts with its design, but more importantly in operations, with inspection and maintenance procedures. The performance of the crew in an emergency and its ability to prevent grounding depend not only on the skills of its captain but also on the experience of the sailors, and on the ability of the group to work together and to communicate, especially in an emergency. The decisions and actions of the crew may thus depend in turn, on decisions made by the managers of the shipping company who may have restricted maintenance resources, hired a crew without proper training, and forced a demanding schedule that did not allow for inspection and repair when needed. The decisions and actions of crews are treated here as random events and variables conditional on a particular management system. In this example, the evidence base includes mostly statistics of the frequency of loss of propulsion for the kind of ship and propulsion system considered and on expert opinions.

The Overall Risk Analysis Model

Using the influence diagram shown in Figure 16.2, one can construct a simple risk analysis model represented by a few equations. Note LP (or not: NLP) the event *loss of propulsion*, and $p(LP)$ its probability per operation; CD (or not: UD) the *control of the drift*; G (or not: NG) the *grounding of the ship*; B the random variable for the "final system state," that is, the *size of the breach* in the hull characterized by its probability density function given grounding $f_B(b|G)$; and O (random variable) the "source term," here, the *quantity of oil released* characterized by its probability density function $f_O(o)$, and by its conditional probability density function $f_{O|B}(o|b)$ given the size of the breach in the hull. Grounding can occur with or without drift control. Using a simple Bayesian expansion, the PRA model can then be written as one overall equation to represent this particular failure mode:[15]

$$f_O(o) = \int_b p(LP)\{p(UD \mid LP)p(G \mid UD)$$
$$+ p(CD \mid LP)p(G \mid CD)\} f_B(b \mid G) f_{O|B}(o \mid b)db \qquad (16.6)$$

Given a total budget constraint (management decision), the maintenance quality can be represented by the frequency and the duration of maintenance operations (e.g., at three levels). Given the management policy regarding personnel, the experience of the crew can be represented by the number of years of experience of the skipper (on the considered type of ship) and/or by the number of voyages of the crew together.[16] These factors, in turn, can be linked to different probabilities of loss of propulsion and to the probability of drift control given loss of propulsion, using expert opinions or statistical analysis.

Numerical data need to be gathered for a specific site and ship, and the model can then be used to compute the probability distribution of the benefits of different types of risk reduction measures. For instance, improving maintenance procedures would decrease the probability of propulsion failure in the first place. Requiring a double hull would reduce the size of the breach given the energy of the shock. Effective control of the speed of the ship would also reduce the energy of the

---

[15] Note the assumption here that the size of the breach depends only on grounding and not on drift control, and that the amount of oil spilled depends only on the size of the breach when in fact, many other factors could be included, for example, the weather, tides, and especially, damage control measures.

[16] One of the challenges is to ensure that, after the fact, these variables are defined precisely enough to pass the "clarity test" of unambiguity of what the realization was (Howard 2004). This means that, once the uncertainties are resolved, the analyst can point to the realization of that variable that actually occurred.

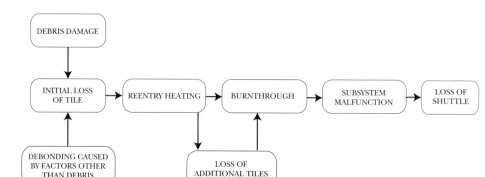

Figure 16.3. Influence diagram for an analysis of the risk of an accident caused by the failure of tiles of the space shuttle. *Source*: Paté-Cornell and Fischbeck 1993a.

shock in case of grounding. Quick and effective response procedures would limit the amount of oil spilled given the size of the breach in the hull. The model can then be used as part of a decision analysis. This next step, however, also requires a decision criterion, for example, what level of probability of grounding or an oil spill can be tolerated in the area, or, for a specified decision maker, his or her disutility for the outcomes, including both financial factors and environmental effects in a single attribute or multi-attribute utility function.

Example 2. A Two-Dimensional Risk Analysis Model: The Heat Shield of the Space Shuttle Orbiters

In a study of the tiles of the space shuttle's heat shield, funded by NASA between 1988 and 1990, the problem was to determine first, what were the most risk-critical tiles, second, what were their contributions to the overall risk of a mission failure, and third, what were the risk management options, both technical and organizational that could be considered (Paté-Cornell and Fischbeck 1993a, 1993b). The challenge was to formulate the problem of the risk of tile debonding and of a "burnthrough" for each tile given its location on the aluminum surface of the orbiter, considering that they are all different, subjected to various loads, and that they cover areas of varying criticality.

The key to the formulation was first to determine the nature of the accident sequences, and the way they could unfold. A first tile could debond either because of poor bonding in installation or during maintenance, or because it is hit by a piece of debris. In turn, adjacent tiles could come off under aerodynamic forces and the heat generated by turbulent flows in the empty cavity. Given the size and the location of the resulting gap in the heat shield, the aluminum could then melt, exposing to hot gases the subsystems under the orbiter's skin. These subsystems, in turn, could fail and, depending on their criticality, cause a loss of the orbiter and the crew. Therefore, faced with about 25,000 different tiles on each orbiter, the challenge was to structure the model to include the most important risk factors,

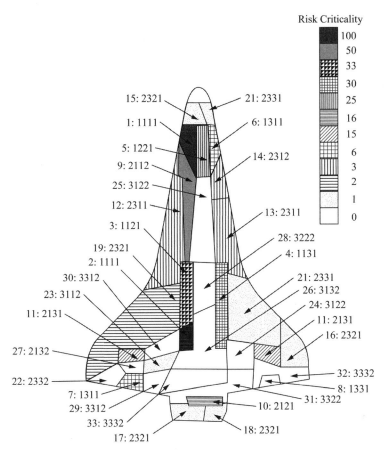

Risk Criticality

	100
	50
	33
	30
	25
	16
	15
	6
	3
	2
	1
	0

15: 2321
21: 2331
1: 1111
6: 1311
5: 1221
14: 2312
9: 2112
25: 3122
12: 2311
13: 2311
3: 1121
19: 2321
28: 3222
2: 1111
4: 1131
30: 3312
21: 2331
23: 3112
26: 3132
11: 2131
24: 3122
11: 2131
16: 2321
27: 2132
22: 2332
32: 3332
7: 1311
8: 1331
29: 3312
31: 3322
33: 3332
10: 2121
17: 2321
18: 2321

Figure 16.4. Map of the risk criticality of the tiles on the space shuttle orbiter as a function of their location. *Source:* Paté-Cornell and Fischbeck 1993a.

whose values vary across the surface: aerodynamic forces, heat loads, density of debris hits, and criticality of the subsystems under the orbiter's skin in different locations. The solution was to divide the orbiter's surface into areas in which the values of these factors were roughly in the same range, and to represent this partition on a two-dimensional map of the orbiter.[17] Figure 16.3 is an influence diagram representing the structure of the model.

Data were gathered from both NASA and its main contractors. Figure 16.4 shows the result of the analysis, that is, the risk criticality of each tile in different zones (represented by various shades of gray) as measured by its contribution to the probability of mission failure. The main results were that tile failures

---

[17] Clearly, the tile system is not literally a plane; but the projection of the orbiter's undersurface on a flat plane allowed its two-dimensional partition for the purposes of the analysis in the same way as one can partition a geographic map into seismic zones to compute earthquake risks.

contributed about 10 percent of the overall probability of a shuttle accident, and that 15 percent of the tiles contributed about 85 percent of the risk.

The recommendations to NASA, at the end of the study, were to decrease the time pressure on the maintenance crews, prioritize inspection, and improve the bonding of the insulation of the external tank. Some of them were adopted (e.g., reduction of the time pressures), others not (e.g., improvements of the external tank). The key to a robust computation of the risk resided in the Bayesian model structure that was adopted as opposed to relying on the small statistical data sets that existed at the time (e.g., the number of tiles lost in flight). Such a statistical analysis led to unstable results that varied drastically later with the loss of a few tiles, when evidence already existed at a deeper level to permit a more stable risk assessment.

Example 3. A Dynamic Analysis of Accident Sequences: Anesthesia Patient Risk

In 1993, a Stanford team was asked to analyze the different components of patient risk in anesthesia, and to identify and estimate changes in procedures that would improve the current situation (Paté-Cornell et al. 1996a, 1996b; Paté-Cornell 1999a). This project was motivated by the occurrence of several publicized accidents that suggested that substance abuse among practitioners (drugs or alcohol) was a major source of the risk. As we showed, it turned out the reality was much closer to mundane problems of lack of training or supervision. One of the changes at the time of the study was the development of simulators that allowed training first, individuals, then operating room teams together. The focus of the study was on "healthy patients" (e.g., undergoing knee surgery) and trained anesthetists in large Western hospitals. The base rate of death or severe brain damage was on the order of 1/10,000 per operation.

Severe accidents, resulting in death or brain damage, occur when the brain is deprived of oxygen for a prolonged duration (e.g., two minutes). The challenge was to structure the model so that the dynamics of accident sequences could be linked to the performance of the anesthesiologists, then to the factors that affect this performance. The data included two types of statistics: base rates of anesthesia accidents, and occurrences of different types of initiating events. The latter were the results of the Australian Incident Monitoring study (Webb et al. 1993). Following an initiating event (e.g., disconnection of the tube that brings oxygen to the lungs), the dynamics of accidents was linked to the occurrence of intermediate events (e.g., observation of a signal) as random variables, and to the time that it takes for these intermediate steps, that is, to observe abnormal signals, diagnose the problem, and take corrective actions, and, hopefully, for the patient to recover. Figure 16.5 shows on a time axis the evolution of both the patient and the anesthesia system in the operating room (incident occurrence, signal detection, problem diagnosis, and correction). The total time elapsed determines the eventual patient state.

One challenge was to quantify the durations of intermediate phases (and of different patient states), which were uncertain and were not documented by

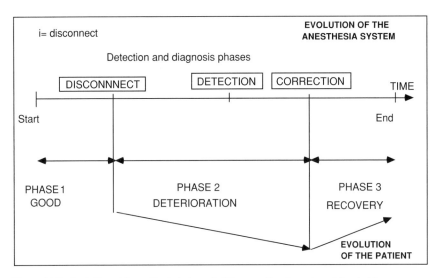

Figure 16.5. Evolution of the patient state and of the anesthesia system following the occurrence of an accident initiator such as a tube disconnect. *Source*: Paté-Cornell et al. 1996a.

statistical data at the time of the study. They were estimated from expert opinions in order to assess their effects on the results. The analysis was then based on a Markov chain representation of the concurrent unfolding of the incident phases (occurrence and detection of the problem by the anesthesia team) and of the evolution of the patient. The combination was represented by "super states," for example, "disconnection of the oxygen tube *and* patient hypoxemia." The contribution of each possible initiating event to the overall patient risk per operation was then computed based on the probability distribution of the duration of the corresponding type of incident (see Table 16.1).

The factors influencing the patient risks (occurrences of initiating events and duration of intermediate phases) were then linked to the performance of

Table 16.1. Incidence rates of initiating events during anesthesia from the AIMS database and effects on patient risk. *Source*: Webb et al. 1993; Paté-Cornell 1999a.

Initiating event	Number of AIMS reports[a]	Report rate	Probability of an initiating event	Relative contribution to patient risk
Breathing circuit disconnect	80	10%	7.2×10^{-4}	34%
Esophageal intubation	29	10%	2.6×10^{-4}	12%
Nonventilation	90	10%	8.1×10^{-4}	38%
Malignant hyperthermia	n/a	–	1.3×10^{-5}	1%
Anesthetic overdose	20	10%	1.8×10^{-4}	8%
Anaphylactic reaction	27	20%	1.2×10^{-4}	6%
Severe hemorrhage	n/a	–	2.5×10^{-4}	1%

[a] Out of 1,000 total reports in initial AIMS data.

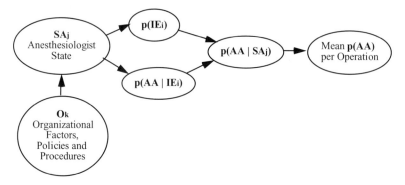

Figure 16.6. Influence diagram showing the analysis of patient risk in anesthesia linked to human and organizational factors. *Source*: Paté-Cornell et al. 1996a, 1996b.

anesthesiologists, based on their level of competence and alertness and on various problems that they can experience. For example, we considered the possibility of "lack of training among experienced anesthesiologists," which may occur when a senior practitioner, who does not operate frequently, forgets what can happen and what should be done in rare incidents that he/she has never had to face. Different possible policies were then identified to address these problems and improve performance, for example, regular training on a simulator, reduction of the length of time on duty, improvement of resident supervision, or testing of the practitioners for substance abuse. The potential benefits of each policy were then computed, based on the changes that the policy could bring in the probability that the anesthesiologist experiences specified problems in a given operation, and on the probabilities of an accident given each problem (see Figure 16.6).

Note that the costs were not computed. Using the notation defined in the legend of Figure 16.6, the equations of the model are shown here.

Step 1

The probability of an anesthesia accident per operation ($p(AA)$) *is* obtained through the dynamic analysis of the different accident types and summed using the total probability theorem.

$$p(AA) = \sum_i p(IE_i)p(AA \mid IE_i). \tag{16.7}$$

Step 2

The probability of an accident is computed first, for each of the potential problems that can be experienced by the anesthesiologist and the corresponding probabilities of the accident occurrence, and parameter values.

$$p(AA \mid SA_j) = \sum_i p(IE_i \mid SA_j)p(AA \mid IE_i, SA_j), \tag{16.8}$$

$$p(AA) = \sum_j p(AA \mid SA_j)p(SA_j). \tag{16.9}$$

Table 16.2. Effects of proposed policy changes on the anesthesia patient's risk. *Source:* Paté-Cornell et al. 1996a, 1996b.

Policy	Effects of policy	Replacement	Risk with policy (x 10^{-5})	Risk reduction (%)
Base case (current policies)		–	7.12	–
Work schedule restriction	Fatigue cut 50%	Problem-free	6.72	6%
Simulator testing for residents	Cognitive problems cut 90% Personality problems cut 50%	New dist'n	7.02	2%
Simulator training for practitioners	Lack of training cut 75%	Problem-free	5.98	16%
Recertification every 3 years	Decreases lack of training, aging, cognitive, personality problems. For 10 recerts: 84% reduction	Problem-free	5.06	29%
Recertification every 5 years	Decreases lack of training, aging, cognitive, personality problems. For 6 recerts: 67% reduction	Problem-free	5.48	23%
Mandatory retirement	Affects 10% of operations: aging, lack of training, alcohol abuse more heavily weighted	New dist'n	6.89	3%
Drug testing	Drug abuse cut 95%	New dist'n	7.03	1%
Alcohol testing	Alcohol abuse cut 90%	New dist'n	6.97	2%
Annual medical examination	Aging/neurol. problems cut 75% Drug, alcohol abuse cut 25% Fatigue cut 10%	New dist'n*	6.92	3%
Supervision of residents	Lack of supervision cut 50%	Problem-free	6.16	14%

* Except "fatigued" replaced by "problem-free." New dist'n: new distribution: new distribution of the probability of problems among practitioners with increase of the probability of "problem-free."

Step 3

Finally, the probability of an anesthesia accident conditional on a particular organizational policy is computed as a function of the effect of that policy on the state (thus the performance) of the anesthesiologist.

$$P(AA \mid O_k) = \sum_j p(SA_j \mid O_k) p(AA \mid SA_j). \qquad (16.10)$$

Different policies were then considered (e.g., reduction of the time on duty), and their benefits were computed as shown in Table 16.2. The results showed that,

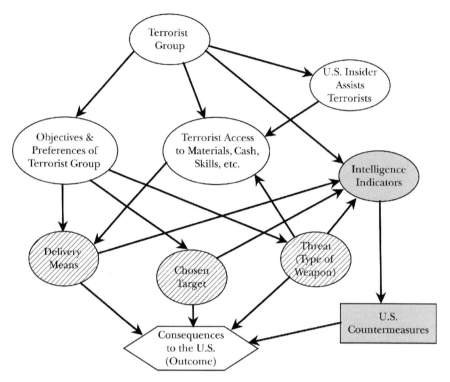

Figure 16.7. Structure of an influence diagram designed to assess the risks from different scenarios of terrorist attack on the United States. *Source*: Paté-Cornell and Guikema 2002.

contrary to previous perceptions, the most beneficial policies concerned improvement of the training of both novice and experienced practitioners, as well as supervision of residents. The benefits of substance abuse control were found to be limited, first because the problem may actually be less frequent than perceived, and second because the tests could be ineffective given anesthesiologists' training.

Example 4. Probabilistic Analysis of Threats of Terrorist Attacks

Shortly after the 9/11 attacks on the United States, this country faced the problem of setting priorities among the possible measures that can be taken to reduce the probabilities of different types of attack, capture signals of a possible attack, and reinforce the potential targets. The question was thus to design a general risk analysis model that allowed combination of threats and vulnerabilities and the end of the uncertainties about them based on all existing information including that gathered by the intelligence community (Paté-Cornell and Guikema 2002).[18] See Figure 16.7.

---

[18] Another risk analysis model, focused on vulnerability to terrorist attacks, was presented by Rowe (2003).

The model included first, the identification of the different terrorist groups known at the time and of their objectives as revealed by their own statements. The key issue was then to assess for each of them their "supply chain," including people and skills, weapons, cash, communications, and transportation based on all information available to the US. The possibility of insider help and its effect on that supply chain was considered. The next step was to describe the different attack scenarios by the choice a weapon, target and mean of delivery. The planning of such an attack could possibly generate signals intercepted by US intelligence and allow for countermeasures. Finally, the probabilities of an attack's effects on the US were assessed as the result of the probabilities of different scenarios and of the effectiveness of US countermeasures.

The probabilities of the scenarios were assessed as a function of their attractiveness to the different terrorist groups based (1) on their ease of execution and probability of success and (2) the desirability of the consequences to the perpetrators. In turn, the desirability of different countermeasures was assessed as a function of the probability of success of the corresponding attack scenarios, their negative values ("disutility") to the US, and the potential of the countermeasures to reduce the probability and/or consequences of different attacks.

The challenge in this type of exercise is to design a global model that captures the first-order factors and allows for further development of the model given the decisions that have to be supported. It provides a "back-of-an-envelope" model structure that permits systematic thinking about the problem and its potential solutions. It also demonstrates the use of the engineering systems analysis application to a different type of problem, of which little is known in terms of global statistics – in part because of nonstationarity – but partial information can be gathered for each of the major factors. This framework can be further developed, as far and deeply as needed, to analyze the benefits of various policies. The results, as usual, are only as good as the information that can be gathered, but the method, if applied well, permits systematic thinking and best use of that information.

At the end of this study, the most likely attack scenarios (in an illustrative application) were found to be repeated conventional attacks on urban targets, followed by "dirty bombs" and biological attacks. But the most destructive to the US remains a possible attack with a nuclear warhead, either fabricated or purchased by a terrorist group.

Conclusions

The engineering risk analysis method can be used in many different settings. The principles of risk analysis based on systems analysis and probability to address problems for which little or no statistics exist, can be applied to many questions involving new technologies, and can be extended to include human and organizational factors. In this chapter, we illustrated the formulation of risk analysis problems for maritime, space, and medical systems as well as for the complex issues of counterterrorism. The key to the success of such an analysis is the formulation of the problem so that the most relevant factors are captured and can be described further if needed in subsequent analytical developments. Bayesian probability is a fundamental concept in such a model. Influence diagrams are useful tools in the formulation phase because they provide both an analytical framework and means of communication. The dynamics of accident sequences is often critical, and can be described through stochastic processes. This method allows anticipation of accidents, failures, or attacks that may not have happened before, even though it requires "imagination" and can be challenged based on the credibility of new failure scenarios and the computation of their probabilities. It can be used to support proactive risk management as an alternative to merely responding to the last event, and to set priorities among risk management options under common constraints of time and money. The keys to its success remain imagination, that is, the willingness and the ability to face events that have not occurred yet) and rationality, that is, the discipline and the systematic thinking that allows structuring the models.

REFERENCES

Apostolakis, G. (1990). The Concept of Probability in Safety Assessments of Technological Systems. *Science*, 1359–1364.

Bedford, T., and Cooke, R. M. (2001). *Probabilistic Risk Analysis: Foundations and Methods*. Cambridge, UK: Cambridge University Press.

Bier, V. M., and Cox, Louis, A. (2007). Probabilistic risk analysis for engineered systems, In *Advances in Decision Analysis*, W. Edwards, R. F. Miles and D. von Winterfeldt (Eds.), New York: Cambridge University Press, 279–301.

Budnitz, R. J., Apostolakis, G., Boore, D. M., Cluff, L. S., Coppersmith, K. G., Cornell, C. A., Morris, P. A. (1998). Use of Technical Expert Panels: Applications to Probabilistic Seismic Hazard Analysis. *Risk Analysis, 18*(4), 463–469.

Clemen, R. T., and. Winkler, R. L. (2007). Aggregation of expert probability judgments. In *Advances in Decision Analysis*, W. Edwards, R. F. Miles, and D. von Winterfeldt (Eds.), Cambridge, UK: Cambridge University Press, pp. 129–153.

Cooke, R. M. (1991). *Experts in uncertainty: opinion and subjective probability in science*. Oxford University Press.

Davoudian, K., Wu, J.-S., and Apostolakis, G. (1994). Incorporating organizational factors into risk assessment through the analysis of work processes. *Reliability Engineering and System Safety, 45*, 85–105.

Helton, J. C. (1994). Treatment of uncertainty in performance assessments for complex systems. *Risk Analysis, 14*, 483–511.

Henley, E., and Kumamoto, H. (1992). *Probabilistic Risk Assessment: Reliability Engineering, Design, and Analysis*. New York: IEEE Press.

Howard, R. (2004). *Speaking of Decisions: Precise Decision Language. Decision Analysis, 1*, 71–78.

Kahneman, D., Slovic, P., and Tversky, A. (Eds.). (1982). *Judgment Under Uncertainty: Heuristics and Biases*. Cambridge, UK: Cambridge University Press.

Keeney, R. L., and Raiffa, H. (1976). *Decision Analysis with Multiple Objectives: Preferences and Value Trade-offs*. New York: John Wiley and Sons.

Murphy, D. M., and Paté-Cornell, M. E. (1996). The SAM Framework: A Systems Analysis Approach to Modeling the Effects of Management on Human Behavior in Risk Analysis, *Risk Analysis, 16*(4), 501–515.

National Commission on Terrorist Attacks upon the United States (NCTA) (2004). *The 9/11 Commission Report*. Washington DC.

Paté-Cornell, M. E. (1985). Reduction of Fire Risks in Oil Refineries: Economic Analysis of Camera Monitoring. *Risk Analysis, 5*(4), 277–288.

Paté-Cornell, M. E. (1996). Uncertainties in risk analysis: six levels of treatment, *Reliability Engineering and System Safety, 54*, 95–111.

Paté-Cornell, M. E. (1999a). Medical application of engineering risk analysis and anesthesia patient risk illustration. *American Journal of Therapeutics, 6*(5), 245–255.

Paté-Cornell, M. E. (1999b). Conditional Uncertainty Analysis and Implications For Decision Making: The Case of the Waste Isolation Pilot Plant, *Risk Analysis, 19*(5), 995–100.

Paté-Cornell, M. E. (2000). "Greed and Ignorance: Motivations and Illustrations of the Quantification of Major Risks", *Proceedings of the study week on Science for Survival and Sustainable Development*: 231–270, Pontificiae Academiae Scientiarum Scripta Varia (Report of the Pontifical Academy of Sciences), The Vatican.

Paté-Cornell, M. E. (2002a). Finding and fixing systems weaknesses: probabilistic methods and applications of engineering risk analysis. *Risk Analysis, 22*(2), 319–334.

Paté-Cornell, M. E. (2002b). Fusion of intelligence information: a Bayesian approach. *Risk Analysis, 22*(3), 445–454. *Erratum* published in *23*(2), 423.

Paté-Cornell, M. E. (2007). "Probabilistic Risk Analysis vs. Decision Analysis: Similarities, Differences, and Illustrations", in *"Uncertainty and Risk: Mental, Formal and Experimental Representations,"* M. Abdellaoui, R. D. Luce, M. Machina and B. Munier, Eds., Springer Pub.

Paté-Cornell, M. E., and Deleris, L. A. (2005). Risks of Bankruptcy in the Insurance Industry. *Research Report to the Risk Foundation*, Department of Management Science and Engineering, Stanford University.

Paté-Cornell, M. E., and Fischbeck, P. S. (1993a). Probabilistic risk analysis and risk-based priority scale for the tiles of the space shuttle. *Reliability Engineering and System Safety, 40*(3), 221–238.

Paté-Cornell, M. E., and Fischbeck, P. S. (1993b). PRA as a management tool: organizational factors and risk-based priorities for the maintenance of the tiles of the space shuttle orbiter. *Reliability Engineering and System Safety, 40*(3), 239–257.

Paté-Cornell, M. E., and Guikema. S. D. (2002). Probabilistic modeling of terrorist threats: a systems analysis approach to setting priorities among countermeasures. *Military Operations Research, 7*(4), 5–23.

Paté-Cornell, M. E., Lakats, L. M., Murphy, D. M., and Gaba, D. M. (1996a). Anesthesia patient risk: A quantitative approach to organizational factors and risk-management options. *Risk Analysis, 17*(4), 511–523.

Paté-Cornell, M. E., Murphy D. M., Lakats, L. M. and Gaba D. M.. (1996b). Patient risk in anesthesia: Probabilistic risk analysis, management effects and improvements. *Annals of Operations Research, 67*(2), 211–233.

Pietzsch, J. B., Paté-Cornell, M. E., and Krummel, T. M. (2004). A Framework for Probabilistic Assessment of New Medical Technologies. In *Proceedings of PSAM7 / ESREL04, Berlin, Germany*. London, UK: Springer-Verlag, pp. 2224–2229.

Phimister, J. R., Bier, V. M., and Kunreuther, H. C. (Eds.). (2004). *Accident Precursor Analysis and Management: Reducing Technological Risk through Diligence*. Washington, DC: National Academies Press.

Press, S. J. (1989). *Bayesian Statistics: Principles, Models, and Applications*. New York: John Wiley and Sons.

Raiffa, H. (1968). *Decision Analysis*. Cambridge, MA: Addison Wesley.

Rowe, W. D. (2003). Vulnerability to Terrorism: Addressing the Human Variables. In Haimes, Moser, Stakhiv, Ivry Zisk, Dirickson, and Zisk, (Eds.), *Risk-Based Decision-making in Water Resources*. ASCE/EWRI/UE, Reston, VA: 155–159.

Savage, L. J. (1954). *The Foundations of Statistics* Wiley: New York.

Shachter, R. (2006). Influence Diagrams. In *Advances in Decision Analysis*, Edwards, W., Miles, R. F., and von Winterfeldt, D. (Eds.). New York: Cambridge University Press, pp. 177–201

U.S. Nuclear Regulatory Commission (USNRC) (1975). WASH 1400(NUREG-75/014), *Reactor Safety Study: Assessment of Accident Risk in U.S. Commercial Nuclear Plants*, Washington, DC: U.S. Nucear Regulatory Commission.

Von Neumann, J., and Morgenstern, O. (1947). *Theory of Games and Economic Behavior.* (2nd ed.). Princeton: Princeton University Press.

Webb, R. K., Currie, M., Morgan, C. A., Williamson, J. A., Mackay, P., Russel, W. J., and Runciman, W. B. (1993). The Australian incident monitoring study: an analysis of 2000 incident reports. *Anaesthesia and Intensive Care, 21,* 520–528.

17 Health Risk Analysis for Risk-Management Decision Making

Louis Anthony (Tony) Cox, Jr.

ABSTRACT. Health risk assessment offers a framework for applying scientific knowledge and data to improve "rational" (consequence-driven) risk-management decision making when the consequences of alternative decisions are uncertain. It does so by clarifying both: (a) The *probable consequences* of alternative decisions (usually represented by conditional probabilities of different consequences occurring, given specified current information and probabilistic risk models); and (b) How *current uncertainties about probable consequences might change* as more information is gathered. This chapter summarizes methods, principles, and high-level procedures for using scientific data (e.g., biological and epidemiological knowledge) (1) to assess and compare the probable human health consequences of different exposures to hazards (i.e., sources of risk); (2) to predict likely changes in exposures and risks caused by alternative risk-management interventions; and (3) to evaluate and choose among interventions based on their probable health consequences. The usual goal of these methods is to identify and select actions or interventions that will cause relatively desirable probability distributions of human health consequences in affected populations. We discuss the steps of hazard identification (including causal analysis of data), exposure assessment, causal dose-response modeling, and risk and uncertainty characterization for improving health risk-management decision making.

Public health risk analysis deals with decisions about which of a set of available risk-management *interventions* (usually including the *status quo* or "do-nothing" option) should be implemented. For example, should cell phone use in cars be banned? Under what conditions, if any, should cattle be imported from countries with low levels of diseases such as BSE? Should antibiotics used in human medicine be prohibited from uses in food animals, even if doing so can cause more sick animals (and, therefore, perhaps more sick people), in order to preserve the effectiveness of the antibiotics in treating human patients? To what extent should industrial emissions of specific compounds be restricted?

Health risk analysis provides a set of methods, principles, and high-level procedures for using scientific data (e.g., biological and epidemiological knowledge) to assess and compare the probable human health consequences of different exposures to hazards (i.e., sources of risk); to assess the likely changes in exposures and risks arising from alternative risk-management interventions; and to evaluate and choose among alternative risk-management interventions based on their probable health consequences. The goal is usually to identify and select actions or interventions that will cause relatively desirable (e.g., stochastically undominated) probability distributions of human health consequences in the affected population. Health risk analysis is often divided into the overlapping stages of *risk assessment, risk management,* and *risk communication,* organized as an iterative process. Table 17.1 summarizes several traditionally defined steps in this process.

Hazard identification deals with how to establish cause-and-effect relations from data. *Exposure assessment* quantifies the changes in exposures caused by alternative interventions. Dose-response modeling (or exposure-response modeling) quantifies the causal relation between changes in exposures and probable resulting changes in adverse consequences. Finally, *risk characterization* integrates the preceding components to predict the probable changes in health that will be caused by a risk-management action that changes exposures.

Health risk assessment uses available facts, data, and models to estimate the health risks to individuals, to an entire population, and to selected subpopulations (e.g., infants, the elderly, immunocompromised patients) caused by hazardous exposures and by the decisions and activities that create them. Health risks of sporadic illnesses due to exposures to chemicals, radiation, bacteria, or other hazards are measured quantitatively by the changes in the *frequencies and severities* of adverse health effects caused by the exposures.

Quantitative Definition of Health Risk

For sporadic illnesses (as opposed to epidemics), individual and population health risks can be defined as follows:

- The *individual risk* of sporadic illnesses (or accidents, injuries, or other adverse outcomes) caused by an exposure can be represented by the *frequency and severity of additional adverse health effects per capita-year caused by that exposure.* It can often be tabulated or plotted as the expected number of cases per capita-year in each severity category – for example, mild, moderate, severe, or fatal, as defined in Buzby, et al. (1996) based on illness-days and mortality. To avoid having to carefully define, describe, and compare the severities of different illnesses, one can simply use days of illness per year for each category of illness (e.g., mild, moderate, or severe) to summarize morbidity impacts, perhaps broken down by different age groups or other population subgroups.

Alternatively, and often more conveniently, the loss due to increased mortality and morbidity can be expressed in terms of quality-adjusted life-years (QALYs), which can serve as a single summary measure of severity if the required preference-independence conditions justifying QALYs are accepted (Hazen 2003; Miyamoto 1999). Individual risk is then given by the joint probability distribution of the number of cases per capita per year and the associated severities (i.e., QALYs lost per case).

- *Population risks* are described by the sum (or, in more detail, by the frequency distribution) of individual risks over all person-years in the population. They can be expressed as *numbers of additional adverse health effects per year* (of

Table 17.1. Traditional steps in health risk analysis

Step	Purpose and description	Relevant information and techniques
Hazard identification	Identify potential sources of harm or loss. These sources are called hazards. Hazard identification identifies possible adverse health effects of activities or exposures and possible causes of observed adverse effects.	Human data: Epidemiology, clinical and public health statistics; surveillance data Animal tests and bioassays In vitro tests Structure-activity patterns, molecular modeling, pattern recognition, and statistical classification techniques
Exposure assessment	Quantify the number of people receiving various levels or intensities of exposure to a hazard over time. Relevant exposure metrics may depend on dose-response relations.	Environmental fate and transport models, possibly summed over multiple media (paths) and sources. Studies of human activity patterns. Biological monitoring of exposed individuals and receptors.
Quantitative exposure-response and dose-response modeling	Quantify the magnitude of risk created by exposure of a target to a hazard. Characterize the probable frequency and severity of adverse health outcomes or losses caused by exposure to the hazard.	A quantitative risk assessment (QRA) runs multiple exposure scenarios through dose-response models to predict likely health impacts. Statistical, simulation, or biomathematical models of biological processes are used to quantify dose-response relations.
Risk characterization and uncertainty analysis	Combine estimated probabilities and severities of health harm (adverse consequences), together with indications of uncertainty or confidence, to create an overall summary and presentation of risk.	Monte Carlo simulation calculates risks by sampling many scenarios. Risk profiles, probability distributions, and trade-off and sensitivity analyses display risk, uncertainty, and variability.
Risk communication	Deals with how to present risk information to stakeholders. Considers how different types of recipients perceive risks and internalize/act on messages about them, in deciding what messages to send via what media.	Psychological theories and models and behavioral/experimental findings on risk perception and effective risk communication
Risk-management decision making	Decide what actions to take to control risks and hazards – that is, accept, ban, abate, monitor, further research, reduce, transfer, share, mitigate, or compensate.	Risk-cost-benefit analysis, formal decision analysis for groups and individuals, risk quantification and comparison

each type or severity category) occurring in the population. Population risks can also be further characterized by identifying subpopulations with especially high individual risks.

TECHNICAL NOTE: USE OF EXPECTED VALUES. Use of the expected number of events per year to quantify risk is justified for sporadic illnesses that occur independently, or with only weak statistical dependence, in large populations, when the Poisson approximation (Janson 1994) or the compound Poisson approximation (Barbour and Mansson 2002) holds. The expected number of cases per year then determines the full probability distribution of the number of illnesses per year, to a close approximation (made precise in the above references). Moreover, the Poisson probability distribution is stochastically increasing in its mean; thus, larger numbers of expected cases correspond to less preferred distributions for *all* decision makers who prefer fewer cases per year to more. The formulae *Individual risk = expected number of additional illnesses per year × expected QALYs lost per illness* and *Population risk = sum of individual risks* are useful for sporadic illnesses, although they must be generalized for other types of risks, for example, to allow for risk aversion (Cox 2001).

The main goals of risk assessment are to produce information to improve risk-management decisions by *identifying and quantifying valid cause-and-effect relations between alternative risk-management decisions and their probable total human health consequences*, and by identifying decisions that make preferred outcomes more likely. Health risk assessments typically use explicit – and, if possible, validated – analytic models (e.g., statistical, biomathematical, or simulation models) of causal relations between actions and their probable health effects. In general, quantitative risk assessment applies specialized models and methods to quantify likely exposures and the frequencies and severities of their resulting health consequences.

Example: Opposite Statistical and Causal Risk Relations

As illustrated by the following (perhaps counterintuitive) example, *there is no necessary relation between statistical exposure-risk associations and the change in risk that would be caused by changing exposure*. As a simple counterexample, consider a hypothetical population in which 100 percent of men and 0 percent of women are exposed (i.e., Exposure = 1 for men, Exposure = 0 for women); and in which Risk = 0 for women, Risk = 100 percent for unexposed men, and Risk = 10 percent for exposed men. In this example, exposure reduces risk, but the statistical association between them is positive. The *statistical* relation between exposure and risk in this population is:

$$\text{Risk} = 0.1 \times \text{Exposure},$$

that is, when Exposure = 1, Risk = 10 percent (for exposed men), and when Exposure = 0, Risk = 0 (for unexposed women). Yet, the *causal* effect of reducing

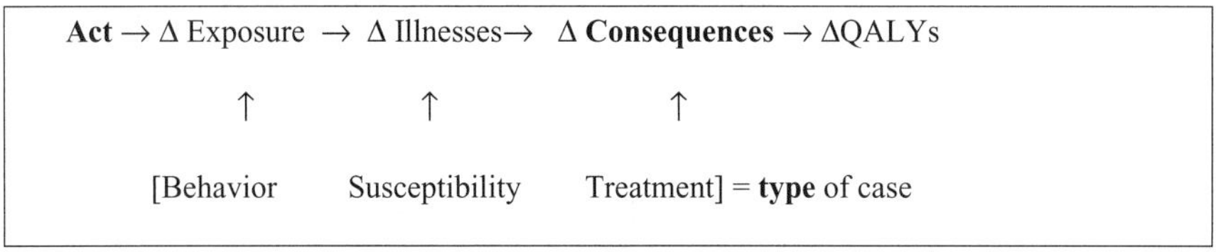

Act → Δ Exposure → Δ Illnesses→   Δ **Consequences** → ΔQALYs

↑   ↑   ↑

[Behavior   Susceptibility   Treatment] = **type** of case

Figure 17.1. A causal graph for health risk analysis.

Exposure is to *increase* risk in the population, by shifting men from the lower-risk exposed group to the higher-risk unexposed group. The causal relation between Exposure and Risk in this population is thus:

$$\text{Risk} = 1 - 0.9 \times \text{ Exposure for men; Risk} = 0 \text{ for women.}$$

In general, fitting a simple reduced-form statistical model to data does *not* allow one to correctly predict the effects of changing the independent variables on resulting changes in the dependent variable (Shipley 2000; Freedman 2004). [This example is motivated by empirical relations found in a real data set collected by CDC (Friedman et al. 2000) for the foodborne bacterial pathogen Campylobacter. Men *do* appear to have greater susceptibility to campylobacteriosis than women; they *do* appear to have greater exposure to risk factors such as eating undercooked meat in restaurants and swimming in untreated water; and exposure to chicken (e.g., buying and handling raw chicken, preparing and eating chicken at home) *does* appear to reduce risk of campylobacteriosis, for both sexes. The above counterexample exaggerates these empirical patterns to extremes to provide a simple illustration of the disconnect between statistical and causal relations.]

A Bayesian Network Framework for Health Risk Assessment

To support effective risk-management decisions, human health risk assessments must characterize known or suspected potential causal relations between risk-management actions (including the *status quo* or "do-nothing" option), on the one hand, and probable resulting human health consequences on the other. Actions typically affect exposures to sources of risk (i.e., hazards), and consequences typically include changes in the frequency or severity of resulting illnesses or deaths in affected populations. *Hazard identification* identifies causal relations (possibly including causal paths) leading from risk-management actions to their human health consequences. Hazard identification often precedes any plan to develop a risk-management strategy, as effective risk management is often impossible if causal relations are not understood.

Figure 17.1 outlines a causal graph (Shipley 2000; Greenland and Brumback 2002) for assessing risks to humans from changes in exposures to hazards. In this template, risk-management *actions* can change *exposures* of individuals to potentially harmful agents (the hazards). Changes in exposures, in turn, change expected *illness rates* and hence adverse *health consequences* (e.g., illness-days or early deaths per capita-year) in susceptible members of the exposed population. If desired, different human health consequences can be aggregated into a single summary measure, such as quality-adjusted life-years (QALYs), if the required preference conditions hold (Hazen 2003), but this is optional. The effects of such changes on the number of QALYs lost per year in the population can be mediated by individual behaviors or attributes (e.g., immune status, age, gender, diet, behaviors, and other covariates that affect susceptibility to infections). These covariates may also influence each other (indicated by the brackets [] around them in Figure 17.1). For example, an AIDS patient may have food consumption and preparation behaviors and medical treatments that differ from those of a non-AIDS patient. Risk assessment helps to identify risk-management options (acts) that decrease adverse health consequences, taking into account the distribution of covariates in the population.

TECHNICAL NOTE: INFLUENCE DIAGRAM INTERPRETATION. Figure 17.1 can be interpreted as a Bayesian belief network or causal graph model (Greenland and Brumback 2002; Chang and Tian 2002). In this framework, each variable to which arrows point is interpreted as a random variable with a conditional probability distribution that is completely determined by the values of the variables that point into it. Because this diagram has a decision node ("act") and a value node ("ΔQALYs"), it is an example of an influence diagram (Owens et al. 1997). Important details are represented only implicitly, by conditional probability distributions. Algorithms to identify possible causal graph structures from data (and hence to test whether hypothesized causal theories are consistent with data) have been developed (e.g., Tsamardinos et al. 2003), but are not yet routinely applied in risk assessment. Such causal graph models are useful because effective algorithms exist to (a) quantify the conditional probability distributions of any subset of their variables, given observed values of the rest; and (b) solve for acts that give maximum expected utility (once a utility function has been defined for outcomes such as ΔQALYs). Each choice of a risk-management act in Figure 17.1 generates a corresponding random number of incremental illness cases ("responses") caused or prevented each year in each severity class of consequences (e.g., mild, moderate, severe, fatal) in the population (and in each subpopulation, if there are several). The expected health consequences of this change can be calculated from the following three submodels, which are common to most risk assessments:

- An *exposure model* (the "act → Δexposure" link in Figure 17.1) that quantifies the amounts of exposure received per unit time by exposed individuals.
- A *dose-response* or *exposure-response* model (the "Δexposure → Δillnesses" link in Figure 17.1) that quantifies the probability of illness, or the expected incremental number of cases at each given severity level, per unit of exposure. In general, this relation may depend on the individual's "type" (i.e., on the combination of covariate values that influence risk for that individual), as well as on the dose (units of exposure) received.

■ A *health consequence model* (the "Δillnesses → Δconsequence" link in Figure 17.1) quantifying the conditional probabilities of different health outcomes (e.g., survival *versus* fatality, or number of QALYs lost) from each case. These outcome probabilities may depend on factors such as physician prescription behavior or hospital infection-control standards.

These three submodels determine the expected illnesses and QALYs lost per year in each severity class for each act. Multiple exposure pathways and at-risk populations (perhaps including groups receiving different medical treatments) can be included to quantify the *total* human health impact of different acts. Summing health impacts over all distinct combinations of hazards, exposure routes, and target populations (each corresponding to an instance of Figure 17.1) gives the total probable change in human health consequences for the act.

TECHNICAL NOTE: MONTE CARLO SIMULATION. If there are too many combinations of hazards, exposure routes, and target populations for explicit summation over all of them to be practical, then Monte Carlo simulation (Thompson et al. 1992) can be used to obtain accurate numerical approximations of the average risk (and the distribution of health effects). For example, suppose that risk is given by $f(x_1, x_2, \ldots, x_n) = f(\boldsymbol{x})$, and that one can sample from the joint probabilitity density function (PDF) of the $x_i, Pr(x_1, x_2, \ldots x_n) = Pr(x_1) Pr(x_2|x_1) \ldots Pr(x_n|x_1, \ldots, x_{n-1})$. Then Markov Chain Monte Carlo (MCMC) simulation techniques such as Gibbs sampling (Andrieu et al. 2003; Lange 2003) can be used to generate random samples from the joint PDF of $\boldsymbol{x}$. Taking a simple arithmetic average of the values of $f(\boldsymbol{x})$ obtained for a sufficiently large random sample of $\boldsymbol{x}$-values will give an accurate estimate of the true average risk $E_{Pr(x)}[f(\boldsymbol{x})]$ implied by $f(\boldsymbol{x})$ and $Pr(\boldsymbol{x})$. Commercial risk analysis software tools such as Analytica™, @RISK™, and Crystal Ball™ include Monte Carlo simulation routines that can generate estimated means, confidence bands, and entire estimated probability distributions for $f(\boldsymbol{x})$. Vose (2000) provides a basic introduction to Monte Carlo simulation in spreadsheet models for microbial risk assessment and Cassin et al. (1998) discusses how to use Monte Carlo simulation for tasks such as priority-setting and risk management. Burmaster and Anderson (1994) provide guidance and principles for using and documenting Monte Carlo uncertainty analysis in risk characterization.

The conceptual framework in Figure 17.1 can be implemented with greater or lesser degrees of sophistication. Perhaps the simplest approach is to generate point estimates for each risk-management act and exposure pathway for each of the following:

■ *Exposure factor* = units of exposure received per capita per year;
■ *Dose-response* factor = expected cases of illness per unit of exposure;
■ *Health consequence factor* = expected QALYs lost (or illness-days created, etc.) per case of illness. (Alternatively, a vector of expected numbers of different health outcomes can be estimated; for example, mild, moderate, severe, and fatal outcomes per case.)

In this approach, each submodel (corresponding to a horizontal arrow in Figure 17.1) is represented by a single number. One can then multiply these numbers together, and multiply by the number of people affected, for each causal path and each risk-management action. (Causal paths may include not only different exposure paths, but may encompass all three links.) Summing the results over all causal paths provides an estimate of the total human health impact per year for each action. A more refined calculation can be made by considering how these factors might change over time, and then summing over time periods (perhaps with discounting).

At the other end of the spectrum, Figure 17.1 can be applied to risk estimation using conditional probability algorithms developed for Bayesian networks and causal graphs (Chang and Tian 2002). In this case, *hazard identification* can be thought of as identifying instances of Figure 17.1 that are consistent with available data. Statistical methods are available to test whether specified causal graph models are indeed consistent with data (Greenland and Brumback 2002; Shipley 2000), and practical algorithms have been developed to identify potential causal graph models from multivariate data (Aliferis et al. 2003; Tsamardinos et al. 2003). The remaining steps in the risk assessment process can then be interpreted as quantifying and applying the resulting Bayesian network. In this framework, the simple approach of multiplying exposure, dose-response, and consequence factors generalizes to allowing arbitrary probability distributions for inputs and conditional probability relations to be combined via Monte Carlo simulation (Andrieu et al. 2003) to derive the joint probability distributions of the outputs.

Bayesian network methods – combined with objective statistical tests for potential causality, such as conditional independence tests (Shipley 2000; Greenland and Brumback 2002) – appear promising for providing more effective, data-driven risk assessments, while also allowing for the use of expert judgment when necessary. There has been a fair amount of preliminary work on Bayesian networks and related methods for risk assessment.

Hazard Identification

Risk assessment begins with *hazard identification*, the process of specifying the scope of the assessment and summarizing the available empirical evidence that exposure to a specific "hazard" causes specified adverse health effects in exposed individuals or populations. Thus, hazard identification can serve to:

1. *Rapidly screen potential hazards* by identifying whether available data support the hypothesis that the hazard might cause specific adverse health effects (possibly using formal statistical methods of causal analysis; see for example, Shipley 2000).
2. *Identify causal relations between specific hazards and specific adverse human health effects.*

Table 17.2. Steps to establish a causal exposure-risk relation

1	*Identify a statistically significant exposure-response association*; for example, using case-control, prospective cohort, or other cross-sectional or longitudinal epidemiological data.
2	*Eliminate confounding* as a possible explanation of the association, by accounting for factors such as lifestyle, age, or exposure to other hazards, for example, using conditional independence tests (Feldman 1998; Greenland and Morgenstern 2001).
3	*Eliminate biases in sampling, information collection, and modeling choices* as possible explanations for the association (Choi and Noseworthy 1992; Deeks et al. 2003).
4	*Test and confirm hypothesized causal and conditional independence relations*, for example, by showing that the response is *not* conditionally independent of the hypothesized exposure that causes it, given other variables (Shipley 2000; Friedman and Goldszmidt 1996; Frey et al. 2003).
5	*Confirm efficacy of interventions*, for example, by experimental manipulations and/or intervention and change point analyses of time-series data (e.g., Swanson et al. 2001; Green 1995).
6	*Identify and elucidate causal mechanism(s)*, identified from experimental data and/or from generally accepted principles.

3. *Identify risk factors, behaviors, and exposure conditions that increase risks to specific exposed populations* (e.g., the old, the young, the immuno-compromised).
4. *Summarize empirical evidence both for and against the hypothesis that exposures to specific hazards cause specific adverse human health effects* (Patton 1993).

In reality, of course, *joint causation* is common; that is, observed adverse consequences are often due to a combination of a hazardous agent, activities resulting in exposures to that agent, failure to undertake protective actions, and possibly other confounding factors, such as decreased immunity in a subpopulation. In general, *any* event or condition that hastens the occurrence of an adverse effect or increases its likelihood can be viewed as a contributing "cause" of the effect. For more on the philosophical definition and ambiguities of "causation," see Williamson (2005). Thus, "the cause" of an adverse health effect is often not uniquely defined. Nonetheless, for purposes of risk management, it often suffices to predict the effects of alternative risk-management interventions on the rates of adverse events of different severities. Hazard identification helps to identify such effects.

Table 17.2 outlines steps for forming and testing causal hypotheses about exposure-response relations using epidemiological data. As more of these steps are completed, the empirical support increases for a causal relation between exposure and risk. Most statistical methods in epidemiological risk analysis focus on steps 1–3; that is, identifying nonrandom associations, and then eliminating potential biases and confounders as likely explanations. These steps can often be carried out using observational data, even without experimental controls, by using the *refutationist approach* (Maclure 1990, 1991). This systematically enumerates possible competing explanations for the observed data, and then eliminates each of those potential noncausal explanations (if possible) using statistical tests on the available data.

Many epidemiologists have recognized that, to draw valid causal inferences, it is necessary to refute competing (noncausal) hypothesized explanations for observed exposure-response associations (Maclure 1990, 1991). Table 17.3 summarizes common competing explanations (mainly, confounding and/or sampling, information, or modeling biases), and some suggested statistical methods to refute them (Cox 2001).

As stated by Savitz et al. (1990), "Biases that challenge a causal interpretation can always be hypothesized . . . It is essential to go beyond enumerating scenarios of bias by clearly distinguishing the improbable from the probable and the important from the unimportant." Fortunately, well-developed statistical methods and algorithms are now available to: (a) identify significant statistical associations from data showing spatial and temporal associations between exposures and health effects (e.g., Mather et al. 2004); and (b) screen them for potential causality based on the above criteria.

TECHNICAL NOTE: STATISTICAL TESTS FOR ASSESSING POTENTIAL CAUSALITY. Over the past 40 years, intuitive criteria for causality used in epidemiology (such as the Bradford Hill criteria, emphasizing strength, consistency, biological gradient, coherence, etc. of an association) have been made more rigorous, general, and quantitative by advances in applied decision sciences. For example, an approach based on information theory proposes that, roughly speaking, a data set provides evidence that exposure variable X is a *potential cause* of response variable Y if and only if X is: (a) INFORMATIVE about Y, that is, the mutual information between X and Y, denoted by $I(X; Y)$ and measured in bits (Cheng et al. 2001), is positive in the data set. (This allows for nonlinear and even nonmonotonic relations.) (b) UNCONFOUNDED: X provides information about Y that cannot be removed by conditioning on other variables, that is, $I(X; Y|Z) > 0$ for all subsets of variables Z disjoint from X and Y. (c) PREDICTIVE: Past values of X are informative about future values of Y, even after conditioning on past values of Y. (This generalizes the concept of Granger causality for time series, see for example, Guatama and Van Hulle (2003.) (d) CAUSALLY ORDERED: Y is conditionally independent of the parents of X, given X, that is, $I(P; Y|X) = 0$, for any parent or ancestor P of X. These principles yield practical algorithms (e.g., BayesiaLab™, Tsamardinos et al. 2003) for detecting potential causation in cohort, case-control, and time series data sets, even if the functional relations involved are nonmonotonic. (Causation may be present even if these conditions are not satisfied, but then the data do not provide evidence of it.) Formal tests for statistically significant associations between the timing of one event (e.g., introduction or cessation of exposures) and subsequent changes in a series of measurements

Table **17.3.** Potential noncausal explanations for exposure-response associations

Potential noncausal explanations	Methods to refute potential explanations
Modeling biases	
Variable selection bias (includes selection of covariates in model)	Bootstrap, Bayesian model averaging (BMA), and cross-validation for variable selection (Wang et al. 2004).
Omitted explanatory variables (including omitted confounders)	Include potential confounders in an explicit causal graph model; test for unobserved latent variables
Variable coding bias (coding may affect apparent risk)	Do not discretize continuous variables. Use automated variable-coding methods (e.g., classification trees).
Aggregation bias/Simpson's paradox	Test hypothesized relations at multiple levels of aggregation, down to individual-level data.
Multiple testing/comparisons bias	Adjust p-values (Romano and Wolf 2005).
Choice of exposure and dose metrics; choice of response effect definitions	Use multiple exposure indicators (e.g., concentration and time). (Do not combine.) Use survival functions and/or transition rates among observed health states.
Model form selection bias; uncertainty about correct model	Use flexible nonparametric models (e.g., smoothers, wavelets) and BMA for multiple models. Report model diagnostics and sensitivities of results to model forms (Greenland 1989).
Missing data	Use data augmentation, expectation maximization (EM) algorithm, MCMC algorithms (Schafer 1997).
Measurement and misclassification errors in explanatory variables	Use Bayesian measurement error models, data augmentation, missing-data techniques (Schafer 1997; Ibrahim et al. 2005).
Unmodeled heterogeneity in individual response parameters	Latent variable and finite mixture distribution models, frailty models of inter-individual variability.
Biases in interpreting and reporting results	Report results (e.g., posterior PDFs) conditioned on data, models, and statistical methods. Show sensitivities.
Sample selection biases	
Sample selection (sample does not represent population)	Randomly sample all cohort members if possible.
Data set selection bias (i.e., selection of studies may affect results)	Meta-analysis of sensitivity of conclusions to studies. Use causal graph models to integrate diverse data sets.
Health status confounding, hospital admission/referral bias	If possible, use prospective cohort design and population-based cases and controls (Choi and Noseworthy 1992).

(continued)

Table 17.3 (*continued*)

Potential noncausal explanations	Methods to refute potential explanations
Selective attrition/survival (e.g., if exposure affects attrition rates) Differential follow-up loss	Use a well-specified cohort. "Include nonsurviving subjects in the study through proxy interviews" (Choi and Noseworthy, 1992). Compare counterfactual survival curves.
Detection/surveillance bias	Match cases to controls (or exposed to unexposed subjects) based on cause of admission.
Membership bias (e.g., lifestyle bias, socioeconomic history)	In cohort studies, use multiple comparison cohorts. Hard to control in case-control studies.
Self-selection bias; response/volunteer bias	Achieve response rate of at least 80% by repeated efforts. Compare respondents with sample of nonrespondents.
Information collection biases	
Intra-interviewer bias	Blind interviewers to study hypotheses, subject classifications.
Inter-interviewer bias	Use same interviewer for study and comparison groups.
Questionnaire bias	Mask study goals with dummy questions; avoid leading questions/response options.
Diagnostic suspicion bias; exposure suspicion bias	Hard to prevent in case-control studies. In cohort studies, make diagnosis and exposure assessments blind to each other.

(e.g., human illness rates in a surveillance program) can be based on *intervention analysis* and *change point analyses* (Green 1995) for time series. These methods for testing for potential causality are entering common biostatistical and risk-analysis practice only slowly, but appear to be very promising (Shipley 2000).

Exposure Assessment

For environmental risk assessment, U.S. EPA experts have stated that "Questions raised in the exposure analysis concern the likely sources of the pollutant...its concentration at the source, its pathways (air, water, food) from the source to target populations, and actual levels impacting target organisms" (Patton 1993). Similarly, for microbial hazards, the U.S. FDA has defined exposure assessment as, "a component of a risk assessment that characterizes the source and magnitude of human exposure to the hazard". Hazard is defined as "Biological, chemical or physical agents with the potential to cause an adverse health effect." The magnitude of human exposure, also called the dose, is defined as "The amount of a toxic component or the number of a pathogen that is ingested or interacts with an organism (host)" (FDA-CFSAN 2002).

Exposure assessment seeks both to identify exposed subpopulations at risk from exposures to hazards and also to identify conditions leading to high-risk exposures. It describes the extent of exposures (frequency and magnitude of individual exposures in the population in relation to susceptibility and covariates) and uses models to predict how risk-management decision options will probably affect them. A successful exposure assessment should describe the frequency distribution of exposures received by members of exposed populations and subpopulations and should show how these distributions change for different risk-management decisions. The descriptions should contain enough detail to discriminate among different exposure distributions that would cause significantly different health outcomes. This information is used, together with dose-response information, to characterize risks.

The shape of the frequency distribution of exposures relative to the dose-response relation (e.g., how frequent are exposures that are likely to cause illness?) drives quantitative risk. It is common for exposures to be very uncertain, especially if they depend on unmeasured and/or highly variable processes. The exposure assessment influence diagram may then look like this:

$$\text{Act} \rightarrow \text{exposures} \rightarrow \text{illnesses} \leftarrow \text{individual covariates}$$
$$\downarrow$$
$$\text{measured exposure surrogates.}$$

For example, available data may consist of surrogate measurements (e.g., contaminant levels in exposure pathways) rather than direct measurements at the point of exposure. True exposures then play the role of *latent variables* in causal modeling, that is, they affect observed outcomes but are not observed themselves. Appropriate statistical techniques for causal diagrams with latent variables (e.g., Shipley 2000 for linear models; Pearl 2002 and Hartemink et al. 2001 for more general Bayesian network models) can be applied to the above diagram with surrogate measurements of exposure for data. Software such as WinBUGS helps to automate the required computations for inference with missing data and unobserved or surrogate variables.

Exposure models describe the transport and distribution of hazardous materials through different media and pathways (e.g., air, foods, drinking water) leading from their source(s) to members of the exposed population. In addition, exposure models may consider the distribution over time of human populations among locations and activities that result in exposures. Simulation models of transport and behavioral processes, often developed using discrete-event simulation software, can be used to estimate frequency distributions of population exposures from assumptions about or submodels of the more detailed microprocesses involved.

Example: Simulation of Exposures to Pathogens in Chicken Meat

The World Health Organization (WHO) has described a process simulation model of human exposures to the foodborne pathogen *Salmonella* as follows:

> The exposure assessment of *Salmonella* in broiler chickens mimics the movement of *Salmonella*-contaminated chickens through the food chain, commencing at the point of completion of the slaughter process. For each iteration of the model, a chicken carcass was randomly allocated an infection status and those carcasses identified as contaminated were randomly assigned a number of *Salmonella* organisms. From this point until consumption, changes in the size of the *Salmonella* population on each contaminated chicken were modeled using equations for growth and death. The growth of *Salmonella* was predicted using random inputs for storage time at retail stores, transport time, storage time in homes, and the temperatures the carcass was exposed to during each of these periods. Death of *Salmonella* during cooking was predicted using random inputs describing: the probability that a carcass was not adequately cooked; the proportion of *Salmonella* organisms attached to areas of the carcass that were protected from heat; the temperature of exposure of protected bacteria; and the time for which such exposure occurs. The number of *Salmonella* consumed were then derived using a random input defining the weight of chicken meat consumed, and the numbers of *Salmonella* cells in meat as defined from the various growth and death processes. Finally, in the risk characterization, the probability of illness was derived by combining the number of organisms ingested (from the exposure assessment) with information on the dose-response relationship (hazard characterization). (WHO/FAO 2002.)

The results of the Monte Carlo simulation exposure modeling are presented as: (a) an estimated 2 percent prevalence of contaminated chicken servings; and (b) the conditional frequency distribution for the dose (CFUs)-per-serving from contaminated servings as shown in Figure 17.2.

This frequency distribution shows how large an exposure a person is likely to receive from a serving of contaminated, undercooked broiler chicken. This is the main output of the exposure assessment and the main input to the dose-response model for calculating illness risk per serving.

Example: Mixture Distributions and Unknown Exposure-Response Models

Unknown or uncertain exposure-response relations in a population can often be estimated by decomposing the risk as follows:

$$Pr(\text{Illness} \mid \text{exposure} = x) = \sum_r Pr\,(\text{Illness} \mid \text{exposure} = x \\ \&\ \text{response type} = r) \times Pr\,(\text{response type} = r).$$

Here, "response type" is an unobserved (latent) variable summarizing all of the missing information needed to predict the probability of illness from a known

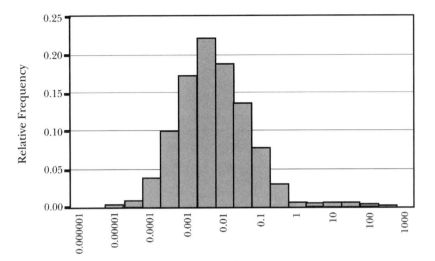

Figure 17.2. Average CFU per cooked chicken serving. *Source:* WHO/FAO 2002.

level of exposure. (For example, if each individual has an unknown threshold number of bacteria that must be ingested in one meal to cause illness, then r would be that threshold number. If there is a continuum of response "types," the above sum is replaced by an integral.) A useful development in mathematical statistics is the recognition that the uncertain quantities Pr(response type $= r$) can be interpreted as *statistical coefficients* to be estimated directly from data on the aggregate number of responses observed in populations for different exposure conditions, and the conditional response probabilities that are paired with these coefficients, Pr(illness | exposure $= x$, type $= r$) can be estimated simultaneously from the same data (provided that technical identifiability conditions are met. These are automatically satisfied by many families of statistical distributions.) The required statistical methodology is that of *finite mixture distribution models* if the number of types is finite; or continuous mixture models if types are continuous. Well-developed computational Bayesian algorithms can be applied to estimate the number of components in the mixture (i.e., the number of statistically significantly different "types") and the corresponding coefficients and conditional response probabilities (e.g., Richardson and Green 1997; Stephens 2000; Miloslavsky and van der Laan 2003). In this construction, the exposure variable x can be any measured quantity that can be paired with corresponding illness rates. All unobserved details are absorbed into the latent "type" variable, r. Missing values and errors in measured values of x can also be handled within the computational Bayesian framework (e.g., using the data augmentation algorithm; Schafer 1997) to allow the conditional distributions of outputs given observed data to be quantified, even when other data are missing. There is thus great flexibility within simulation approaches to use all available data (via conditioning), but without requiring use of unavailable data.

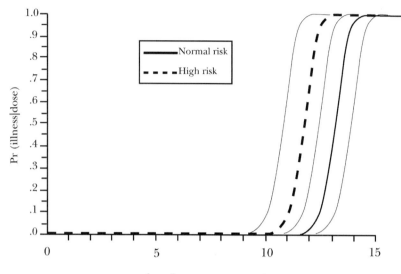

Figure 17.3. Example dose-response function for *Listeria monocytogenes*. *Source:* FAO/WHO, 2001.

Dose-Response Modeling

Dose-response models quantify the conditional probability of illness caused by each level of exposure; thus, the term *exposure-response model* is also appropriate. Figure 17.3 shows an example of a dose-response model developed for *Listeria monocytogenes* in ready-to-eat foods.

A specific parametric dose-response model was assumed (an exponential model) and fit to epidemiological data for immunocompromised ("High risk") and nonimmunocompromised ("Normal") subpopulations. The dark solid curve in Figure 17.3 is the estimated dose-response model for the "Normal risk" subpopulation. The dashed line above and to the left of it is the dose-response model for the "High risk" subpopulation. The lighter gray curves indicate estimated statistical confidence bands around these best-estimate curves – an upper confidence band for each (corresponding to the upper end of the 95 percent confidence interval estimated for the parameter of the exponential dose-response model), and a lower 95 percent confidence band for the right-most (Normal) dose-response model.

As in Figure 17.3, it is often necessary to fit separate dose-response models to "normal" and "susceptible" subpopulations within the general population to account for inter-individual variability in dose-response relations. Although more than two gradations of susceptibility can be modeled using finite mixture distributions, distinguishing between only two levels or response "types" in the population, that is, susceptible and normal, often suffices to explain most of the variability in the data. If different degrees or severities of illness are distinguished, ranging from

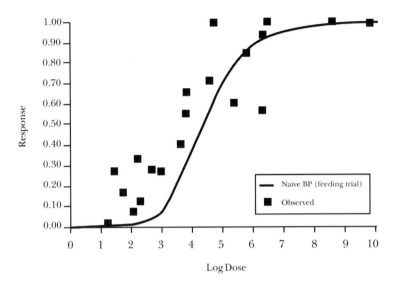

Figure 17.4. The best-fitting beta-poisson model under-predicts low-dose risks. *Source:* WHO/ FAO 2002. (Naïve BP = approximate binomial poisson.)

mild through severe to fatal, then a *health consequence model* describing the con-ditional probabilities of different levels or severities of health outcomes, given that illness occurs, is needed to augment the conditional probability of illness as a func-tion of exposure. In general, risk characterization requires describing the *severities* as well as the *frequencies* of adverse health outcomes caused by exposures.

In practice, biologically motivated parametric dose-response models are the most common, and usually the best justified, models in widespread use. They are typically fit to data by a combination of maximumum likelihood estimation (MLE) for point estimates and computationally intensive resampling techniques (e.g., bootstrapping algorithms) for confidence intervals, simultaneous confidence bands around the dose-response curve, and joint confidence regions for model parameters (e.g., Haas et al. 1999).

Example: Best-Fitting Parametric Models May Not Fit Adequately

Figure 17.4 for *Salmonella* feeding trial data shows that even the best-fitting model in a certain class of parametric models (here, the approximate Beta-Poisson dose-response family, widely used in microbial risk assessment) may not adequately describe the observed data. The parametric family of models is then said to be *misspecified* for the data, that is, it is not appropriate for describing the empirical relation. In this example, the approximate Beta-Poisson model family is inappro-priate for the data because even the best-fitting curve in the family dramatically under-predicts low-dose risks. See Figure 17.4.

If the correct dose-response model is unknown and several models all provide adequate fits to the available data, multiple plausible models may be used to carry out the rest of the assessment. In this case, the analysis can be organized and presented as a *model uncertainty decision tree* in which different modeling choices correspond to different branches in the tree. The results of the risk analysis at the end of each branch are contingent on the assumptions and modeling choices that lead to it. Different branches may be weighted by the relative strength of the evidence supporting them (Kang et al. 2000). Bayesian Model Averaging (BMA) provides a more formal version of this approach (Viallefont et al. 2001; Keiding and Budtz-Jorgensen 2004). Model uncertainty decision trees can also be used to present and analyze uncertainties due to choices of dose metrics, response definitions, and other modeling decisions, as well as choices of particular dose-response models.

Uncertainty about illness probabilities caused by a given dose is often dominated by uncertainty about the most appropriate dose-response model. A decision tree presentation of alternative modeling choices and the resulting predicted risks – or even a simple plot of different plausible dose-response curves – can express much of the relevant uncertainty with a minimal amount of statistical sophistication. Other important computational methods and algorithms for uncertainty analysis include:

- *Monte Carlo uncertainty analysis* using commercial software products such as Analytica™, @RISK™, Crystal Ball™ (Vose 2000). For more on uncertainty and sensitivity analysis software, see the descriptions at product web sites.
- *Bayesian uncertainty analysis* for model parameters and predictions (e.g., based on the WINBUGS software for inference with missing data).
- *Bootstrapping and other resampling techniques* for estimating joint confidence regions for model parameters and predictions.
- *Model cross-validation* techniques for estimating the accuracy and prediction error characteristics of model predictions from performance on multiple subsets of data.

These methods are discussed in general computational statistics texts and, for dose-response modeling, in risk-analysis texts such as Haas et al. 1999, Vose 2000, and Cox 2001.

Risk And Uncertainty Characterization For Risk Management

Risk characterization is the ultimate output of a risk assessment. It integrates hazard identification, exposure assessment, and dose-response information to determine the probable frequency and severity of adverse health effects in a population caused by exposures to a hazard. Characterizing the change in risk for different risk-management interventions helps decision makers choose among them. Risk characterization also includes characterization of current *uncertainty about risk*. This allows the value of gathering additional information to be assessed as part of risk-management deliberation and decision making, based on the potential value

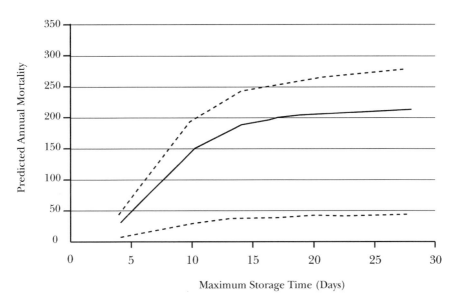

Maximum Storage Time (Days)

Figure 17.5. Predicted annual mortality in the elderly subpopulation attributable to deli meats as a function of maximum storage time. *Source:* FDA-CFSAN 2003.

of such information (VoI) to enable risk managers to make choices that are more likely to result in desired consequences (Yokota and Thompson 2004).

Given the results from:

(a) Exposure assessment (i.e., the conditional probability distribution of exposures, for each act);
(b) Exposure-response/dose-response modeling (i.e., the conditional probability of illness for each exposure pattern); and
(c) Consequence modeling (e.g., the conditional probability distribution of adverse consequences given illness),

the risk characterization step calculates, for each act being assessed, the resulting probability distributions for adverse consequences. (This can be done by literally summing or integrating expressions such as Pr(consequence $= c$ | illness) $\times$ Pr(illness | exposure $= x$) $\times$ Pr(exposure $= x$ | Act) over all exposure levels x, to obtain the probability of each consequence, c.)

Example: Risk Characterization Outputs

Figure 17.5 shows one of the risk characterization outputs from a risk assessment of *Listeria monocytogenes* (FAO/WHO 2001). The solid curve shows the median estimate of the mortalities per year caused among the elderly subpopulation by *L. moncytogenes* in deli meats, for different maximum allowed storage times. The dotted curves represent the fifth and ninety-fifth percentiles of the uncertainty distribution, as assessed by Monte Carlo uncertainty analysis.

This display shows how predicted risks in this subpopulation vary with the effects of different potential interventions that would limit the maximum storage times allowed for deli meats. Similar curves can be shown for the effects of such interventions for other foods or groups of foods (e.g., dairy products, produce, sea food products) and for other subpopulations and the U.S. population as a whole.

Risk management is often viewed as a decision process that takes scientific information obtained from risk assessment as an input, along with value judgments and policy goals and constraints, and that recommends choices of risk-management actions as its output. Alternative risk-management approaches include risk acceptance, prevention or avoidance (e.g., by reducing exposures), mitigation of consequences (e.g., by appropriate clinical screening, diagnosis, and prescription procedures), transfer (e.g., health insurance), and compensation.

A successful risk analysis shows the estimated changes in the frequencies and magnitudes of adverse consequences resulting from different risk-management decision options. (Of course, if hazard identification and risk management reveal that the risk from the *status quo* is so small that no risk-management action is needed, analysis may stop there. A full risk analysis is usually carried out only when a risk-management intervention is being contemplated.) Risk analysis uses probability distributions, confidence intervals, and other displays to show uncertainties about the human health consequences of different decisions. It identifies a subset of one or more decision options leading to preferred (e.g., stochastically undominated) probability distributions of health risks and other outcomes.

The outputs of a health risk analysis should allow a risk manager to answer the following questions for each risk-management decision alternative being evaluated or compared:

- *What probable change in human health risk would result from each risk-management intervention?* If the risk-management decision option or action being assessed is implemented, how will the probable adverse human health effects (e.g., expected numbers of mild, moderate, severe, and fatal illnesses per year; expected numbers of illness-days and, if desired, quality-adjusted life-years (QALYs) lost per year) change, both in the whole population and in subpopulations with distinct risks?
- *How certain is the change in human health risk that would be caused by each risk-management action?* Instead of a single value, that is, a point estimate of risk, uncertain risks are characterized by intervals or probability distributions indicating how closely the change in human health risk caused by a proposed risk-management intervention can be predicted. There are several technical options for expressing uncertainty around point estimates (e.g., plausible upper and lower bounds, confidence limits, coefficients of variation, tolerance intervals, prediction intervals, Bayesian posterior probability intervals and distributions) The essential information to provide about uncertainty in any risk assessment is how large or how small the true risks might be, consistent with the data and with the specified assumptions of the risk assessment. Point estimates that are "best" with respect to various technical statistical criteria will typically fall between these extremes.

TECHNICAL NOTE: STATISTICAL POINT ESTIMATES AND INTERVAL ESTIMATES. Many criteria have been used to define and identify "best" point estimates in risk models, for example, maximum likelihood estimates (MLE), maximum *a posteriori* (MAP) Bayesian estimates, maximum entropy, "minimum description length," least squares, minimum absolute deviation, and minimum expected loss (for various loss functions) (see Cox 2001 for a survey for risk analysts). Although these criteria have led to useful theory and algorithms for estimating the parameters of risk models, *none* of them is satisfactory as the sole output from a risk assessment. *It is essential to provide intervals or probability distributions around any point estimate of risk* to inform the users of a risk assessment about the full range of risks that might be prevented (or caused) by a risk-management intervention. This principle applies to qualitative and fuzzy risk ratings as well. If a point estimate of a risk is "High," then some indication must be given of how certain this value is and of how compatible the frequency and severity components of the risk are with other qualitative labels, such as "Low." A risk assessment that produces a single overall value for risk with no indication of uncertainty should be avoided.

▪ *What are the key drivers of risks and uncertainties for each option?* The analysis should make clear to the user the main reasons *why* the estimated risk from each decision option is as high or low as it is. Are the results driven mainly by predicted exposure levels, by the responses of sensitive subpopulations, by genetic or epidemiological data that establish tight constraints on the plausible values, or by other factors? Sensitivity analyses that plot how estimated risks would change as input assumptions and estimates vary within plausible ranges (e.g., within a few standard deviations of their median values) can help to identify the combinations of input values that drive the main conclusions and the extent to which these could be changed without changing the comparison of different risk-management interventions.

▪ *Which risk-management interventions are undominated?* One risk-management intervention *dominates* another if it produces smaller probabilities of exceeding any specified level of adverse consequences per year. For example, if two different interventions lead to different expected numbers of sporadic illness cases per year (with the actual number being a Poisson random variable), and if the probable health consequences per case (e.g., the distribution of the number of days of illness of given severity) is the same for each intervention, then the one giving the smaller expected number of illnesses per year dominates the other. Scientific risk assessment can, at most, identify undominated risk-management alternatives for risk managers to further assess and prioritize using value trade-off judgments.

CONCLUSIONS

This chapter has briefly described how risk analysis can promote improved risk-management decision making. A successful risk analysis estimates the causal relations between decisions and probable resulting exposures, and between exposures and their probable total human health consequences. To guide rational decision making, a risk analysis should yield evaluations and comparisons of proposed risk-management *actions and interventions*, not simply descriptions of the current situation. It should show the estimated changes in frequencies and magnitudes (and uncertainties) of human heath consequences resulting from different proposed risk-management decisions. It is important to identify an adequate range of risk-management options to ensure that dominant alternatives are not overlooked. For each option, total health consequences are found by summing the impacts of proposed actions on human exposures over all relevant pathways that contribute significantly to the outcome. Applying an exposure-response model to the changed exposures for different decisions then yields the estimated risks associated with them.

A well-conducted risk analysis enables its recipients to participate more effectively in risk-management deliberations and to communicate questions and concerns more clearly and concisely than would otherwise be possible. It does so by providing them with the relevant information needed to determine the probable consequences of proposed actions and by showing how sensitive these predicted consequences are to specific remaining uncertainties.

ACKNOWLEDGMENTS

I thank Professor Vicki Bier of the University of Wisconsin at Madison for comments and suggestions on an early draft of this chapter that substantially improved the final exposition. Parts of this chapter, including several examples, are condensed and adopted from my book *Quantitative Health Risk Analysis Methods: Modeling the Human Health Impacts of Antibiotics Used in Food Animals*, published by Springer in 2005.

DEDICATION

This chapter is dedicated to the memory of Professor Alvin W. Drake of MIT – an outstanding teacher, counselor, and friend and a source of many insights into decision analysis and risk analysis and the interplay between them.

REFERENCES

Aliferis, C., Tsamardinos, I., and Statnikov, A. (2003). Hiton. A novel Markov Blanket algorithm for optimal variable selection. *AMIA Annual Symposium Procedings*, 21–25.

Andrieu, C., de Freitas, N., Doucet, A., and Jordan, M. I. (2003). An introduction to MCMC for machine learning. *Machine Learning, 50*, 5–43. http://citeseer.ist.psu.edu/andrieu03introduction.html. Accessed 10/31/2006.

Barbour, A. D., and Mansson, M. A. (2002) Compound Poisson approximation. *The Annals of Probability, 30*(3), 1492–1537.

Burmaster, D. E., and Anderson, P. D. (1994). Principles of good practice for the use of Monte Carlo techniques in human health and ecological risk assessments. *Risk Analysis, 14*, 77–81.

Buzby, J. C., Roberts, T., Jordan Lin, C. T., and MacDonald, J. M. (1996). Bacterial Food-borne Disease: Medical Costs and Productivity Losses. *USDA, Economic Research Service, Agricultural Economics Report # 741.* http://www.ers.usda.gov/publications/Aer741/. Accessed 10/31/2006.

Cassin, M. H., Paoli, G. M., and Lammerding, A. M. (1998). Simulation modeling for microbial risk assessment. *Journal of Food Protection, 61,* 1560–1566.

Chang, K. C., and Tian, Z., (2002). Efficient inference for mixed Bayesian networks. http://citeseer.ist.psu.edu/570208.html. Accessed 10/31/2006.

Cheng, J., Greiner, R., Kelly, J., Bell, D., and Liu, W. (2001). Learning Bayesian Networks from Data: An Information-Theory Based Approach. http://citeseer.ist.psu.edu/628344.html. Accessed 10/31/2006.

Choi, B. C., and Noseworthy, A. L. (1992). Classification, direction, and prevention of bias in epidemiologic research. *Journal of Occupational Medicine, 34*(3), 265–271.

Cox, L. A. (2001). *Risk Analysis: Foundations, Models, and Methods.* Boston: Kluwer Academic.

Deeks, J. J., Dinnes, J., D'Amico, R., Sowden, A. J., Sakarovitch, C., Song, F., Petticrew, M., and Altman, D. G. (2003). International Stroke Trial Collaborative Group; European Carotid Surgery Trial Collaborative Group. Evaluating nonrandomised intervention studies. *Health Technology Assessment, 7*(27), iii–x, 1–173.

FAO/WHO. (2001). Joint FAO/WHO Expert Consultation on Risk Assessment of Microbiological Hazards in Foods: Risk characterization of Salmonella spp in eggs and broiler chickens and *Listeria monocytogenes* in ready-to-eat foods. FAO Headquarters, Rome, Italy 30 April–4 May. http://www.who.int/foodsafety/publications/micro/en/may2001.pdf Accessed 10/31/2006.

FDA-CFSAN (2002). U.S. Food and Drug Administration Center for Food Safety and Applied Nutrition. Initiation and Conduct of All 'Major' Risk Assessments within a Risk Analysis Framework. http://www.cfsan.fda.gov/~dms/rafw-toc.html. Accessed 11/02/2006.

FDA-CFSAN. (2003). FDA/Center for Food Safety and Applied Nutrition USDA/Food Safety and Inspection Service Centers for Disease Control and Prevention. Quantitative Assessment of Relative Risk to Public Health from Foodborne *Listeria monocytogenes* Among Selected Categories of Ready-to-Eat Foods. Appendix 3. September. http://vm.cfsan.fda.gov/~dms/lmr2-a3.html. Accessed 10/31/2006.

Feldman, R. A. (1998). Confounding factors in observational and intervention studies. *Ital J Gastroenterol. Hepatol., 30*(3), S248–253.

Freedman, D. A. (2004). Graphical models for causation, and the identification problem. *Eva Rev., 28*(4), 267–293.

Frey, L., Fisher, D., Tsamardinos, I., Aliferis, C., and Statnikov, A. (2003). Identifying Markov Blankets with Decision Tree Induction. http://citeseer.ist.psu.edu/frey03identifying.html. Accessed 10/31/2006.

Friedman, N., and Goldszmidt, M. (1996). Learning Bayesian Networks With Local Structure. http://citeseer.ist.psu.edu/friedman96learning.html. Accessed 10/31/2006.

Friedman, C., Reddy, S., Samual, M., Marcus, R., Bender, J., Desai, S., Shiferaw, B., Helfrick, D., Carter, M., Anderson, B., Hoekstra, M., and the EIP Working Group. (2000). Risk Factors for Sporadic *Campylobacter* Infections in the United States: A Case-Control Study on FoodNet Sites. 2nd International Conference on Emerging Infectious Diseases. Atlanta, GA. July.

Green, P. J. (1995). Reversible jump Markov chain Monte Carlo computation and Bayesian model determination. http://citeseer.ist.psu.edu/green95reversible.html Accessed 10/31/2006.

Greenland, S. (1989). Modeling and variable selection in epidemiologic analysis. *American Journal of Public Health, 79*(3), 340–349.

Greenland, S., and Brumback, B. (2002). An overview of relations among causal modeling methods. *International Journal of Epidemiology, 31*(5), 1030–1037.

Greenland, S., and Morgenstern, H. (2001). Confounding in health research. *Annual Review of Public Health, 22,* 189–212.

Guatama, T., and Van Hulle, M. M. (2003). Surrogate-Based Test For Granger – Causality. http://citeseer.ist.psu.edu/588339.html. Accessed 10/31/2006.

Haas, C. N., Rose, J. B., and Gerba, C. P. (1999). *Quantitative Microbial Risk Assessment.* New York: John Wiley & Sons, Chapter 7, cf. p. 293.

Hartemink, A. J., Gifford, D. K., Jaakkola, T. S., and Young, R. A. (2001). Using graphical models and genomic expression data to statistically validate models of genetic regulatory networks. *Pac Symp Biocomput.*, 422–433.

Hazen, G (2003). Multiattribute Structure for QALYS. http://fisher.osu.edu/~butler_267/DAPapers/WP030018.pdf. Accessed 11/02/2006.

Ibrahim, J. G., Chen, M.-H., Lipsitz, S. R., and Herring, A. H. (2005). Missing-data methods for generalized linear models: A comparative review. *Journal of the American Statistical Association, 100*(469), 332–346.

Janson, S. (1994). Coupling and Poisson Approximation. http://citeseer.ist.psu.edu/janson94coupling.html. Accessed 11/2/2006.

Kang, S. H., Kodell, R. L., and Chen, J. J. (2000). Incorporating model uncertainties along with data uncertainties in microbial risk assessment. *Regul Toxicol Pharmacol, 32*(1), 68–72.

Keiding, N., and Budtz-Jorgensen, E. (2004). The Precautionary Principle and statistical approaches to uncertainty. *Int J Occup Med Environ Health, 17*(1), 147–151.

Lange, K. (2003). *Applied Probability.* New York: Springer.

Maclure, M. (1990). Multivariate refutation of aetiological hypotheses in nonexperimental epidemiology. *Int J Epidemiol, 19*(4), 782–787.

Maclure, M. (1991), Taxonomic axes of epidemiologic study designs: a refutationist perspective. *J Clin Epidemiol., 44*(10), 1045–1053.

Mather, F. J., White, L. E., Langlois, E. C., Shorter, C. F., Swalm, C. M., Shaffer, J. G., Hartley, W. R. (2004). Statistical methods for linking health, exposure, and hazards. *Environ Health Perspect., 112*(14), 1440–1445.

Miloslavsky, M., and van der Laan. M. (2003). Fitting of mixtures with unspecified number of components using cross validation distance estimate. *Computational Statistics and Data Analysis, 41*(3–4), 413–428.

Miyamoto, J. M. (1999). Quality-adjusted life years (QALY) utility models under expected utility and rank dependent utility assumptions. *J Math. Psychol., 43*(2), 201–237.

Owens, D. K., Shachter, R. D., and Nease, R. F. Jr. (1997). Representation and analysis of medical decision problems with influence diagrams. *Medical Decision Making.*, Jul–Sep; 17(3):241–62.

Patton, D. E. (1993).The ABCs of risk assessment. *EPA Journal, 19*(1), 10–15. http://www.bethel.edu/~kisrob/hon301k/readings/risk/RiskEPA/riskepa1.html Accessed 11/02/2006.

Pearl, J. (2002). Causal Inference in the Health Sciences: A Conceptual Introduction. *Health Services Outcomes Research Methodology* 2:189–220, http://citeseer.ist.psu.edu/599949.html. Accessed 11/02/2006

Richardson, S., and Green, P. J. (1997). On Bayesian analysis of mixtures with an unknown number of components. http://citeseer.ist.psu.edu/richardson97bayesian.html. Accessed 11/02/2006.

Romano, J. P., and Wolf, M. (2005). Exact and approximate stepdown methods for multiple hypothesis testing. *Journal of the American Statistical Association, 100*(469), 94–108.

Savitz, D. A., Greenland, S., Stolley, P. D., and Kelsey, J. L. (1990). Scientific standards of criticism: A reaction to "Scientific standards in epidemiologic studies of the menace of daily life," by A.R. Feinstein. *Epidemiology, 1*(1), 78–83.

Schafer, J. L. (1997). *Analysis of Incomplete Multivariate Data*. New York: Chapman & Hall.

Shipley, B. (2000). *Cause and Correlation in Biology. A User's Guide to Path Analysis, Structural Equations and Causal Inference.* Cambridge University Press.

Stephens, M. (2000). Bayesian analysis of mixture models with an unknown number of components – an alternative to reversible jump methods. *Ann. Statist., 28*, (1), 40–74.

Swanson, N. R., Ozyildirim, A., and Pisu, M. (2001). A comparison of alternative causality and predictive accuracy tests in the presence of integrated and co-integrated economic variables. http://citeseer.ist.psu.edu/427252.html. Accessed 11/2/2006.

Thompson, K. M., Burmaster, D. E., and Crouch, E. A. (1992). Monte Carlo techniques for quantitative uncertainty analysis in public health risk assessments. *Risk Analysis, 1*, 53–63.

Tsamardinos, I., Aliferis, C., and Statnikov, A. (2003). Time and Sample Efficient Discovery of Markov Blankets and Direct Causal Relations. http://citeseer.ist.psu.edu/tsamardinos03time.html. Accessed 11/02/2006.

Viallefont, V., Raftery, and A. E., Richardson, S. (2001). Variable selection and Bayesian model averaging in case-control studies. *Stat Med., 20*(21), 3215–3230.

Vose, D. J. (2000). *Risk Analysis: A Quantitative Guide* (2nd ed.). New York: John Wiley & Sons.

Wang, D., Zhang, W., and Bakhai, A. (2004). Comparison of Bayesian model averaging and stepwise methods for model selection in logistic regression. *Stat Med., 23*(22), 3451–3467.

WHO/FAO. (2002). Risk assessments of *Salmonella* in eggs and broiler chickens – Interpretative Summary and Full Report. http://www.fao.org/docrep/005/y4393e/y4393e00.htm. Accessed 11/02/2006.

Williamson, J. (2005). *Bayesian Nets and Causality Philosophical and Computational Foundations.* Oxford, UK: Oxford University Press.

Yokota, F., and Thompson, K. M. (2004). Value of information analysis in environmental health risk-management decisions: Past, present, and future. *Risk Analysis, 24*(3), 635–650.

18 What Have We Learned from Our Mistakes?

Barbara Mellers and Connson Locke

ABSTRACT. The authors discuss the steps involved in good decision making and use those steps to organize results from behavioral decision research. Framing effects, self serving biases, and context effects are a few of the many errors and biases that are presented. The authors also discuss techniques for reducing errors. They conclude by providing examples of human cognitive strengths, while emphasizing the importance of learning from our mistakes.

Good Decision Making

To the lucky few, good decisions come naturally. But to most of us, decisions are difficult, grueling, and sometimes quite painful. The process requires us to make delicate tradeoffs, sort through complex scenarios, hunt for good ideas, estimate the odds of future states, and answer a voice inside that keeps asking, "Is this what I *really* want?"

Many scholars describe good decision making as a series of interrelated steps. Although there are many ways to categorize steps, most researchers agree that the process includes the following stages:

Define the Problem and Set the Goals

The best way to get what you want is to know what that is. This step could be extremely easy or extremely difficult depending on the problem. Good decision makers ask, "What do I want to achieve? What are my goals and objectives? How will I know if I am successful?"

Gather Information and Identify Options

Important choices require a careful and unbiased search for evidence. Normative theory says that the search for information should continue until the costs outweigh the benefits. New information leads to the discovery of new options that may mean the gathering of more information and possibly more options. The best way to find a good option is to identify lots of options. Many problems have more than one solution, but the solutions may not be obvious. Creating, finding, devising, and isolating alternatives is a key part of decision making.

Evaluate the Information and the Options

Here, the decision maker should ask, "What really matters to me? Why do I care?" Answers to these questions should lead to the evaluation of outcomes and the measurement of beliefs. Then, the decision maker combines evaluations and beliefs to form overall assessments of the options.

Make a Choice

Criteria for the selection of an option should be based on the decision maker's goals and objectives. There may be a single criterion, such as maximizing pleasure, or multiple criteria, such as maximizing profit, minimizing time, and minimizing risk.

Implement the Choice and Monitor the Results

This step may be the most important of all. All prior steps are useless without a commitment to action. Moreover, choices must be monitored. Because most decisions rarely proceed as planned, a decision maker should keep a watchful eye on the consequences and be prepared to make corrective adjustments as needed. Good decision makers should be committed to their decisions, but flexible in their approaches.

To Error Is Human

Those are the steps. How well can people do them? For the last 5 decades, behavioral decision researchers have been asking that question along with a variety of others, including "What, if anything, do people do instead?" The most well known research program in behavioral decision making was started by Kahneman and Tversky in the early 1970s. Human judgments and decisions were held up to scrutiny and evaluated in light of the standards set by normative theory. Results were surprising, intriguing, and quite perplexing. Kahneman and Tversky proposed that human judgments were not described by normative theory, but could be captured in terms of heuristics and biases.

Initially, there were three heuristics: *availability*, *representativeness*, and *anchoring and adjustment*. The availability heuristic states that people assess the probability of an event based on the degree to which instances come to mind. What comes to mind is based on vividness and recent experience. Ross and Sicoly (1979) illustrated this heuristic when they asked husbands and wives to estimate the extent to which each was responsible for domestic activities, such as cooking, cleaning, and shopping. When individual percentages were summed, the average sum was 130 percent. Each partner could quickly remember instances in which he or she took out the garbage, unloaded the dishwasher, or folded the clothes. The other person's contributions were less accessible. Similar effects were found with a student and faculty member who estimated the percentage of work they did on a joint research project. When individual estimates were summed, the average sum was 130 percent. Because people have vivid memories of their own efforts, they tend to overweight their contributions relative to those of their partners.

The second heuristic is called representativeness. This heuristic states that, when making a judgment, people consider the degree to which the specific information represents a relevant category or population. The Linda problem (Tversky and Kahneman 1983) is a compelling example. In the Linda problem, participants are told:

Linda is 31 years old, single, outspoken, and very bright. She majored in philosophy. As a student, she was deeply concerned with issues of discrimination and social justice, and also participated in antinuclear demonstrations. Rank the following descriptions in terms of the probability they describe Linda.

1. Linda is active in the feminist movement.
2. Linda is a bank teller.
3. Linda is a bank teller and is active in the feminist movement.

The description of Linda is representative of a feminist, not a bank teller. If people make their judgments according to the description of Linda, they will say that the first statement is most likely, followed by the third statement, and finally the second statement. This is exactly what happens, even though this order violates an important rule of probability called the *conjunction rule*. The conjunction rule states that the combination of two events can never be more probable than the chance of either event by itself. In contrast, the representativeness heuristic says we judge probability in terms of the similarity of the target stimulus to a category. The Linda problem shows that the rules of probability differ from the rules of similarity.

Finally, the third heuristic is called anchoring and adjustment. This heuristic asserts that people make probability judgments by starting with a number that easily comes to mind and adjusting for additional information. But adjustments are often insufficient. Anchors may be valid and useful cues, or completely irrelevant. Effects of irrelevant anchors were demonstrated by Russo and Schoemaker (1989) who asked respondents to write down the last three digits in their telephone number. Then respondents were asked whether Attila the Hun was defeated in Europe before or after the year defined by the three-digit number. Finally, respondents estimated the year of Attila's defeat. Telephone numbers are obviously unrelated to Attila the Hun. Nonetheless, the numbers influenced the historical estimates. Estimates of the year of Attila the Hun's defeat were higher among participants with larger three-digit numbers and lower among participants with smaller three-digit numbers. A variety of similar examples are well documented (e.g. Tversky and Kahneman 1974; Strack and Mussweiler 1997; Chapman and Johnson 1994).

Even experts can fall prey to anchoring and adjustment effects. In one study, practicing auditors estimated the incidence of executive fraud. Before providing their estimates, auditors in one condition were asked if the incidence of fraud was more than 10 in 1,000 among companies audited by Big Five accounting firms.

In the second condition, auditors were asked if the incidence was more than 200 in 1,000. Auditors then gave their estimates. In the first condition, the average estimate was 16.52 per 1,000, but in the second, the average estimate was 43.11 per 1,000, over twice as large. (Joyce and Biddle 1981)

Kahneman and Frederick's (2002) more recent view of heuristics and biases is that the first two heuristics – availability and representativeness – can be subsumed under a single heuristic called attribution substitution.[1] If a target attribute is relatively inaccessible, people substitute it with something that more easily comes to mind. Many attributes may be substituted for the relevant attribute, especially those that are vivid and emotional. An example in which people substitute emotional reactions for monetary values comes from the literature on contingent valuation. *Contingent valuation* is a method used by economists to assign a monetary value to a public good that would never be bought or sold in the marketplace, such as clean air, clean beaches, or clean lakes. Economists ask participants to state the maximum amount they would be willing to pay to either maintain a public good or restore it to a previous state. Judged values reported in these surveys are not always consistent with common properties of real economic values.

In one study, Desvouges, Johnson, Dunford, Hudson, Wilson, and Boyle (1993) asked different groups of participants to state the maximum amount they would be willing to pay to clean up oil ponds that had led to the deaths of 2,000, 20,000, or 200,000 migratory birds. Average amounts of $80, $78, and $88, respectively, were relatively insensitive to the number of birds that would be saved. Kahneman, Ritov, and Schkade (1999) argued that the death of birds evokes a feeling of outrage, and that emotional response is mapped onto a monetary scale. Similar degrees of outrage are associated with a wide range of economic consequences (e.g., 200 to 200,000 birds), so unlike real economic values, judged values remain constant.

If people use these heuristics and apply them incorrectly, how well do they make decisions? Behavioral decision researchers have much to say about the types of mistakes that can occur when, where, how, and why. We now present some well-known errors and biases in the context of the five steps of good decision making. Our list is by no means exhaustive; it is purely intended to illustrate how natural behavioral tendencies can interfere with good decisions.

Define the Problem and Set the Goals

When people think about choices, they often accept and use information as it was received. This tendency can lead to systematic differences in preference known as framing effects. Framing is a bit like taking a photograph. One must decide how far away to stand, what to include, and which elements define the figure and the ground. Behavioral decision researchers have found that, when the same

---

[1] Kahneman and Frederick note that anchoring does not fit this model because it does not involve substituting one attribute for another.

choice is presented using different frames, people often reverse their preferences. A classic example is the Asian Disease Problem (Tversky and Kahneman 1981). Both versions of the problem state:

> Imagine that the U.S. is preparing for the outbreak of an unusual Asian disease, which is expected to kill 600 people. Two alternative programs to combat the disease have been proposed. Assume that the exact scientific estimates of the consequences of the programs are as follows:

In the gain frame, participants are told:

> If Program A is adopted, 200 people will be saved.
> If Program B is adopted, there is a 1/3 probability that 600 people will be saved, and a 2/3 probability that no one will be saved.

In the loss frame, participants read:

> If Program A is adopted, 400 people will die.
> If Program B is adopted, there is a 1/3 probability that no one will die, and a 2/3 probability that 600 people will die.

Despite the different descriptions, Program A is the same across both frames, and Program B is the same across both frames. Tversky and Kahneman found that 76 percent preferred Program A in the gain frame, but 71 percent preferred Program B in the loss frame. Participants' preferences were risk averse with gains and risk seeking with losses.

Frames are subtle, yet consequential. Most consumers would agree that ground beef sounds better if the package says 75 percent lean than 25 percent fat (Levin and Gaeth, 1988). A hospital policy sounds more effective if the report indicates that 75 percent of beds were full than 25 percent of beds were empty. Even a change in pricing might seem fair if described as a discount, but unfair if described as a surcharge. Northwest was one of the first airlines to charge passengers $10 more for tickets purchased at the airport than they did for tickets purchased online (New York Times 2004). The headline of the Times article read, "Will This Idea Fly? Charge Some Travelers $10 for Showing Up!" Company executives pointed out that JetBlue had the same $10 fee. JetBlue quickly replied that Northwest executives were wrong. JetBlue charged *standard* fares for tickets purchased at the airport, but offered $10 *discounts* to customers who bought tickets electronically.

Framing effects can have powerful financial consequences. Johnson, Hershey, Meszaros, and Kunreuther (1993) described framing effects in the insurance industry. In 1988, the standard auto policy in New Jersey did not allow drivers the right to sue for pain and suffering from minor injuries, although they could purchase that right with a higher-priced policy. Only 20 percent of New Jersey drivers bought the more expensive policy. In 1990, the standard auto policy in Pennsylvania included the right to sue, and 75 percent of Pennsylvania drivers purchased it. Johnson et al. (1993) estimated that Pennsylvanians spent $200 million more on auto insurance than they would have if the default had been the cheaper option. Unless decision makers are able to think about a problem from different perspectives, they may be "framed" by information as it appears.

Gather Information and Identify Options

Some say that the greatest danger to good intelligence gathering is not insufficient time; it is, rather, the mental biases and distortions that we bring to the search process. Unfortunately, we do not always know what we need to know, and we focus inordinate attention on evidence that confirms our beliefs and hypotheses. This tendency runs directly counter to the scientific method. With the scientific method, we try to disprove – not prove – our hypotheses. But thinking negatively takes considerably more effort.

A classic example of the confirmation bias comes from a study by Wason (1960). He asked subjects to imagine that the sequence of three numbers, such as "2–4–6," follows a rule. The task is to discover the underlying rule by generating sequences and receiving feedback about whether those sequences are consistent or inconsistent with the rule. Suppose the real rule is "any three ascending numbers." When given an initial starting sequence of "2–4–6," subjects often assume the rule is "numbers that go up by two." They test the hypothesis with sequences such as "1–3–5" or "8–10–12." It is fairly unusual for subjects to test the hypothesis with a disconfirming sequence, such as "10–15–20" or "6–4–2."

Another example is the four-card problem. Subjects are shown four cards with a number on one side and a letter on the other. The cards are labeled, "E," "4," "7" and "K." Subjects are asked to identify only those cards that must be checked to test the claim that "If a card has a vowel on one side, it must have an even number on the other side." Most subjects choose "E" (to see if it has an even number on the other side) and "4" (to see if it has a vowel on the other side). But both of these tests confirm the claim. The correct answer is "E" and "7." If the claim is true, "E" should have an even number on the other side, and "7" should have a consonant on the other side. The other two cards are irrelevant to the claim.

The confirmation bias, or the tendency to gather information that supports our hypotheses, has been attributed, at least in part, to self-serving attributions. Psychologists have identified a variety of ways in which people maintain positive views of themselves. Overconfidence is the tendency to be more confident in one's own ability than reality dictates. In a typical overconfidence experiment, participants are given a series of true–false questions, such as "The population of London is greater than that of Paris." They answer "True" or "False" and then judge their confidence that they are correct. If they were completely unsure of their answer, they would say "50 percent." If they were absolutely sure they were correct, they would say "100 percent." Average confidence ratings over questions are significantly greater than the actual percentage of correct items (Fischhoff, Slovic, and Lichtenstein 1986). In fact, when participants say they are 100 percent confident, their accuracy rates for those items are typically around 75 percent.

Overconfidence goes far beyond true–false questions on general knowledge tests. It has been observed in physicians (Lusted 1977), clinical psychologists (Oskamp 1965), lawyers (Wagenaar and Keren 1986), negotiators (Neale and Bazerman 1992), engineers (Kidd 1970), security analysts (Stael von Holstein 1972), and eyewitness testimonies (Sporer, Penrod, Read, and Cutler 1995). Confidence in one's accuracy guarantees very little, even among professionals.

Closely related to overconfidence is the "above average effect." People perceive themselves as being better than others on most desirable attributes, including honesty, cooperativeness, health, intelligence, managerial skill, and even driving ability (Babcock and Loewenstein 1997; Larwood and Whittaker 1977). A survey conducted with 1 million high school students in 1976–1977 by the College Board found that 70 percent of students rated themselves as above average in leadership ability, and only 2 percent rated themselves as below average.

People also seem to have undue optimism about their future. Predictions are systematically better and brighter than reality. For example, MBAs overestimate the number of offers they will receive, the magnitude of their starting salary, and how early they will get their first offer (Hoch 1985). Newlyweds almost uniformly expect their marriages to last a lifetime (Baker and Emery 1993), and financial investors predict that, unlike others, their forecasts will beat the market averages (Barber and Odean 2000).

Self-serving biases can even influence perceptions of fairness in distributions of scarce resources. In an illustrative experiment, Messick and Sentis (1983) told participants to assume they had worked with another person on the same job. Their task was to allocate a sum of money between themselves and the other person as they saw fit. In some conditions, participants learned that they (or the other person) had either worked twice as long or had accomplished twice as much. Most participants gave themselves more than half if they worked longer or harder. But if the other person worked longer or harder, participants thought that an even split was fair. Apparently, it is hard to view one's efforts and accomplishments from a neutral point of view.

Loewenstein, Issacharoff, Camerer, and Babcock (1993) also illustrated self-serving biases in fairness in a negotiation settlement. They randomly assigned participants to the role of the defendant or the plaintiff and gave them identical case materials about a legal dispute. The task was to negotiate a monetary amount that the defendant would pay the plaintiff, and both parties were financially penalized if they failed to reach an agreement. If an agreement was not reached, a judge would determine a fair amount for the defendant to pay the plaintiff. Before negotiating, participants were asked to predict the judge's settlement. Plaintiffs' predictions of the judge's settlement were substantially higher than defendants' predictions. Perceptions of "fair" settlements were self-serving perceptions, despite incentives for accuracy.

If we are overly confident about our abilities, convinced that we are better than others, and excessively optimistic about our futures, we won't need to gather as much information when making decisions. Furthermore, if the information we gather confirms our hunches, we may believe we need even less information. This is a recipe for disaster.

Evaluate the Information and the Options

Unlike physics, where the assessments of length and weight do not depend on the stimuli previously measured, psychological assessments vary with the context. Responses to the same stimulus differ depending on the surrounding stimuli. For example, a 10-pound sack of apples seems light after carrying a 50-pound child, but heavy after carrying a soft drink and potato chips.

Stimulus contexts can be local or global. In the domain of choice, the local context refers to the particular choice set. A classic local contextual effect is called *asymmetric dominance* (Huber, Payne, and Puto 1982). Participants choose between two options, A and B, each of which is described by two attributes, such as price and quality. Later, participants are given the same two options in a choice set that contains a third option, C, which is dominated by B and asymmetrically dominated (on one attribute) by A. With C in the choice set, the relative preference for B increases. According to most theories of choice, preferences should never increase as more options are added to the consideration set. But that is exactly what happens.

The global context, again in the domain of choice, refers to all of the choices being made. Mellers and Cooke (1996) found that preferences for a given choice can reverse when made in different global contexts. They asked students to make choices between pairs of apartments described in terms of monthly rent and distance to campus. In one context, rents went from $100 to $1000, and distances varied from 10 to 26 minutes. In another, rents went from $100 to $400, and distances varied from 10 to 50 minutes. Both contexts included a choice between a $400 apartment that was 10 minutes from campus and a $200 apartment that was 26 minutes away. When the context included more expensive apartments, 60 percent of students preferred the $400 apartment that was 10 minutes away. When the context included greater distances, 64 percent preferred the $200 apartment that was 26 minutes away. The less desirable attribute did not seem as bad when the context included apartments that were worse.

Another global context effect is the order in which questions are asked. Order effects are changes in response due to sequence. Strack, Martin, and Schwarz (1988) demonstrated an amusing order effect by asking college students two questions: "How happy are you with your life in general?" and "How many dates did you have last month?" The correlation between students' responses was negligible when the happiness question came first. But that correlation rose to 0.66 when the dating question came first. The dating question evoked a general feeling of satisfaction or dissatisfaction with one's life, and that feeling was used to answer the happiness question.

Primacy effects and *recency effects* occur when people place disproportionate weight on the initial stimulus or final stimulus, respectively. Lawyers scheduling the appearance of witnesses for court testimony and managers scheduling speakers at meetings take advantage of these effects when they organize the sequences of events. Primacy effects have been found in impression formation. Participants are asked to form an impression of a person who has been described with various traits (Asch 1946). Half of the participants are told the person is envious, stubborn, critical, impulsive, industrious, and intelligent. The other half are told the person is intelligent, industrious, impulsive, critical, stubborn, and envious. Although the two lists contain identical traits, participants describe the person as less likeable when the negative traits come first. Over-reliance on first impressions is a form of primacy. Recency effects occur in debates when the person who gets the "final word" seems to win. The last word is often easier to remember than words uttered earlier.

If we allow contextual effects and order effects to distort our evaluation of the options, we might not make the best decisions. But these are not the only challenges we face.

Make a Choice

Several problems can occur at this step. People may ignore options, outcomes, information, or values. They may engage in wishful thinking and tell themselves that an unfortunate event will not happen to them. They may be lazy and satisfied by selecting the first option that seems to be "good enough," even though a far better option might lie just around the corner (Simon 1956). People also base their choices on immediate emotional reactions that may differ from their true beliefs and values (Slovic, Finucane, Peters, and MacGregor 2004).

During the choice process – especially with difficult choices – people often stick with the status quo, possibly because the perceived costs of a change seem larger than the perceived benefits. Samuelson and Zeckhauser (1988) demonstrated the status quo effect in a study of decisions about health plans made by Harvard employees. In 1980, Harvard employees could choose one of four health plans. By 1986, that number had increased to eight. Old enrollees who had made their choices before 1980 kept the status quo more often than new enrollees who came between 1980 and 1985. The low rate of transfer among those who had been with their plans longer was consistent with the status quo bias.

Status quo biases can develop remarkably fast. In one experiment, Knetsch (1989) gave students a university coffee mug and then asked them to complete a short questionnaire. Students had the mug in their possession while they worked on the questionnaire. When they were finished, students were offered a choice between keeping their mug or exchanging it for a large, Swiss chocolate bar. Only 11 percent wanted to trade. Knetsch (1989) then repeated the experiment but the initial gift was the Swiss chocolate bar. After completing the questionnaire, students could either keep their Swiss chocolate bar or exchange it for a mug. Only 10 percent wanted to trade.

The status quo bias can have serious consequences. Ritov and Baron (1990) asked participants to imagine that their child had a 10 out of 10,000 chance of death from a flu epidemic. A vaccine could prevent the flu, but for some, it was fatal. Participants were asked to indicate the highest risk they would accept for the vaccine, before they would refuse it. Most subjects answered that the chance of death from the vaccine had to be well below 9 out of 10,000. Anyone who insisted the vaccine be safer than 10 out of 10,000 was putting their child at greater risk by refusing the vaccination. In follow up questions, participants confessed that they would feel greater regret if the child died from the vaccine than from the flu. The sense of regret is another driving force behind the status quo bias.

Some people cannot free themselves from the status quo; others cannot help choosing an option into which they already invested time or money, even if it is not the best option. This finding is known as the sunk cost effect. Most people find it hard to leave a meal unfinished at a restaurant or walk out of a bad movie. They want to "get their money's worth." Nonetheless, past costs should not influence choices; only future costs should matter.

An example of sunk-cost effects comes from the health club industry. Gourville and Soman (1998) obtained usage data from members of a club that charged dues twice a year. Attendance at the health club was highest in the months when dues were paid, then declined over the next 5 months, only to jump again when the next dues were paid.

Thaler (1999) says that although sunk costs linger, they do not hang on indefinitely. A thought experiment illustrates the point. Suppose you buy a pair of shoes. They feel very comfortable in the store, but the first day you wear them, they hurt badly. A few days later you try them again, but they hurt even worse than they did the first time. What happens next? The more you paid for the shoes, the more times you will try to wear them. This may be rational, especially if you need to replace the shoes with another pair. Eventually you stop wearing the shoes, but you do not throw (or give) them away. The more you paid for the shoes, the longer they sit in the back of your closet. Finally, you throw away (or give away) the shoes. This is when the payment has been fully depreciated.

Status quo biases and sunk cost effects are potential pitfalls whenever we make choices. These mistakes suggest that we are more likely to select options with which we are familiar or into which we have already invested time or money.

Implement the Choice and Monitor the Results

Escalation of commitment and the hindsight bias are two important errors that can occur in this step. Recall that the sunk cost effect occurs when decision makers choose an option because of a prior investment, even when it is not the best option (e.g., Arkes and Blumer 1985). Escalation of commitment (Staw 1976) is the tendency to continue investing in that suboptimal option. Decision makers are more likely to throw good money after bad when (1) they are personally responsible for the initial investment, (2) the initial investment is failing, and (3) they have publicly announced their position.

In organizational settings, it is not easy to decide when to fire a slow employee, drop a disappointing new product, or loan more money to a company that lost the initial loan. Deescalation might only happen when and if the person who made the initial decision leaves the organization. In a longitudinal study of California banks, Staw, Barsade, and Koput (1997) found that turnover rates among managers was associated with deescalation of commitment to bad loans, whereas turnover rates among the board of directors was not. Managers appeared to be justifying their decisions by escalating their commitments, and de-escalation was possible only after a change in management.

The hindsight bias is the tendency to misremember the degree to which one accurately forecasted an outcome. We remember being more accurate than we actually were. When looking back and thinking about an initial forecast, we find it difficult to ignore the outcome that occurred. In addition, we are better able to recall information that was consistent rather than inconsistent with the outcome (Dellarosa and Bourne 1984). Some call the hindsight bias the "knew-it-all-along" effect because it leads people to view whatever occurred as relatively inevitable (Fischhoff, 1975). In an early study of the hindsight bias, Fischhoff and Beyth (1975) asked students to predict what would happen in 1972 when Nixon visited China and the former Soviet Union. Would Nixon meet with Mao? Would the US and the former Soviet Union form a joint space program? Two weeks later, the experimenters asked the students to recall their earlier probability estimates. 67 percent of students remembered themselves as being more accurate than they actually were. As time went on, the bias increased, with 84 percent showing the hindsight bias after 3 to 6 months. Recalled probabilities incorporated the knowledge of outcomes.

Hindsight biases have been documented in elections (Leary 1982; Synodinos 1986), medical diagnoses (Arkes, Saville, Wortmann, and Harkness 1981), business ventures (Bukszar and Connolly 1988), and historical records (Fischhoff 1975). To evaluate past decisions, and thereby improve future decisions, we must put ourselves into the mindset of the decision maker prior to outcome feedback. But research shows it is not easy to make that cognitive leap.

Minimizing Mistakes

Each step in the process of good decision making is vulnerable to biases and errors. Researchers have explored a variety of ways to reduce or eliminate these mistakes. One approach targets the information used by the decision maker. Combining frames, using frequency formats, or disclosing conflicts of interest change the information with which a decision maker is presented. Another approach targets the decision maker's thought processes. Increasing accountability, providing incentives, and training people to reduce overconfidence change decision makers' motivation and ability to calibrate. In this section, we discuss the strengths and weaknesses of these methods.

Combining Frames

It makes intuitive sense that framing effects could be reduced if decision makers approached a problem from multiple perspectives. But there are different ways to consider multiple perspectives. For example, multiple frames could be presented sequentially with the same choice nested in different frames. If preferences reversed, those shifts could be explored and resolved. Research that has examined this form of multiple frames typically gives subjects a choice using one frame. After some unrelated tasks, subjects are given the same choice in another frame (LeBoeuf and Shafir 2003; Frisch 1993; Levin et al. 2002; Stanovich and West 1998). Although some people have consistent preferences across frames, many others change their preferences. Decision analysts would need to discuss the frames in more detail with these people.

Another way to present multiple frames is to combine them into a single choice. For example, the Asian Disease problem could be expressed as:

If Program A is adopted, 200 people will be saved and 400 people will die.
If Program B is adopted, there is a 1/3 probability that 600 people will be saved, and a 2/3 probability that 600 people will die.

This combined format does not permit decision makers the "luxury" of preference reversals. They must confront any conflicting goals or competing desires directly in order to make their choice.

To examine the combined format, we administered different versions of a questionnaire to three different groups of undergraduates at the University of California Berkeley, with between 162 and 187 participants in each group. Each version included three framing problems: the Asian Disease problem from Tversky and Kahneman (1981), a simplified version of the Layoff problem from Messick and Bazerman (1996), and the Medical problem from McNeil et al. (1982).

The gain and loss frames of the Asian Disease problem replicated Tversky and Kahneman's earlier results. The majority of participants preferred Program A, the safer option, in the gain frame (76 percent), and Program B, the riskier option, in the loss frame (71 percent). That is, preferences were risk averse in the gain domain and risk seeking in the loss domain. In our examination of the combined frame, where gains and losses are both vivid, the majority of respondents preferred Program A (58 percent), the risk averse option. The combined frame more closely resembled the gain frame than the loss frame.

Next we examined the Layoff problem. All three versions said,

A large car manufacturer has recently been hit with a number of economic difficulties, and it appears as if 9,000 employees must be laid off. The vice president of production has been exploring alternative ways to avoid the crisis. She has developed two plans.

In the gain frame, participants were told:

Plan A will result in the saving of 3,000 jobs.
Plan B has a 1/3 chance of saving 9,000 jobs and a 2/3 chance of saving no jobs.

In the loss frame, participants read:

Plan A will result in the loss of 6,000 jobs.
Plan B has a 1/3 chance of losing no jobs and a 2/3 chance of losing 9,000 jobs.

Finally, the combined frame stated that:

> Plan A will result in the saving of 3,000 jobs and the loss of 6,000 jobs.
> Plan B has a 1/3 chance of saving 9,000 jobs and a 2/3 chance of losing 9,000 jobs.

The majority of respondents preferred Plan A in the gain frame (71 percent) and Plan B in the loss frame (63 percent). Once again, the combined frame revealed a tendency toward risk aversion with most participants choosing Plan A, the safer option (73 percent).

Then we examined the Medical problem from McNeil et al. (1982) in which subjects chose between two types of treatment for lung cancer: surgery or radiation. Data given to subjects were presented in terms of survival rates or mortality rates. Surgery offers a better long-term life expectancy, but a 10 percent chance of immediate death on the operating table. For this reason, surgery appears more desirable in the survival frame than the mortality frame. Both versions of the problem stated:

Surgery for lung cancer involves an operation on the lungs. Most patients are in the hospital for 2 or 3 weeks and have some pain around their incisions; they spend a month or so recuperating at home. After that, they generally feel fine. Radiation therapy for lung cancer involves the use of radiation to kill the tumor and requires coming to the hospital about four times a week for 6 weeks. Each treatment takes a few minutes and during the treatment, patients lie on a table as if they were having an x-ray. During the course of the treatments, some patients develop nausea and vomiting, but by the end of the 6 weeks they also generally feel fine. Thus, after the initial 6 or so weeks, patients treated with either surgery or radiation therapy felt the same. Now imagine you are a patient given the choice between these two types of treatments. You are given the following statistics regarding the consequences of each treatment:
In the survival frame, participants were told:

> Of 100 people having surgery, 90 will live through the surgery, 68 will be alive at the end of the first year, and 34 will be alive at the end of 5 years.

> Of 100 people having radiation therapy, all live through the treatment, 77 will be alive at the end of the first year, and 22 will be alive at the end of 5 years.

In the mortality frame, they were told:

> Of 100 people having surgery, 10 will die during the treatment, 32 will have died by 1 year, and 66 will have died by 5 years.

> Of 100 people having radiation therapy, none will die during treatment, 23 will die by 1 year, and 78 will die by 5 years.

McNeil et al. (1982) found an overall preference for surgery in both frames. But the relative preference for surgery was stronger in the survival frame (82 percent) than in the mortality frame (53 percent). McNeil et al. also explored preferences in a combined frame that read:

> Of 100 people having surgery, 10 will die during treatment and 90 will live through the treatment. A total of 32 people will have died by the end of the first year and 68 people will be alive at the end of the first year. A total of 66 people will have died by the end of 5 years and 34 people will be alive at the end of 5 years.

> Of 100 people having radiation therapy, none will die during the treatment (i.e., all will live through the treatment). A total of 23 will have died by the end of the first year and 77 will be alive at the end of the first year. A total of 78 people will have died by the end of 5 years and 22 people will be alive at the end of 5 years.

They found that 60 percent preferred surgery. The combined frame resembled the mortality frame more than the survival frame.

Our results showed an overall reduction in the preference for surgery, but the same relative preference shift. More participants chose surgery in the survival frame (54 percent) than in the mortality frame (32 percent). In our combined frame, 57 percent of participants preferred surgery. Preferences in the combined frame mimicked the survival frame more than the mortality frame.

In a similar study that also examined separate and combined frames for the Medical problem, Armstrong, Schwartz, Fitzgerald, Putt, and Ubel (2002) obtained results that resembled ours. Preferences for surgery were reduced relative to those found by McNeil et al. (1982) and preferences in the combined frame resembled those in the survival frame. Furthermore, Armstrong et al. showed that participants understood the information better in the combined frame and the survival frame than in the mortality frame. Their data provide further evidence that the combined frame better reflects preferences.

We do not mean to imply that all combined frames will lead to risk averse preferences, although the regularity of the results is intriguing. We do, however, wish to point out that combined frames are a useful way of presenting multiple reference points and possibly assessing more stable and robust preferences.

Frequency Formats

Probabilistic inferences are often hard to make, even for those with statistical training. Some scholars have asked whether understanding and accuracy of inferences could be improved if the information were presented in another format. Frequencies seem to be easier to work with than probabilities. Hoffrage and Gigerenzer (1998) asked a group of physicians to make inferences about the presence of a disease given a positive test result on a mammogram. Half of the physicians were given the following question in a probability format that read:

The probability of breast cancer is 1 percent. The probability of a positive test given breast cancer is 80 percent, and the probability of a positive test given no breast cancer is 10 percent. What is the probability that a woman who tests positive for breast cancer actually has breast cancer?

The other physicians were given the same question using a frequency format as follows:

> 10 of every 1,000 women have breast cancer. 8 of those 10 women with breast cancer will test positive, and 99 of the 990 women without breast cancer will also test positive. How many of those women who test positive actually have breast cancer?

The correct answer is 7.5 percent (or 8 out of 107 women). Hoffrage and Gigerenzer found that only 8 percent of physicians made the correct inference in the probability format, but almost half (46 percent) made the correct inference in the frequency format. Frequency formats improve Bayesian reasoning in both laypersons (Gigerenzer and Hoffrage 1995) and experts (Hoffrage and Gigerenzer 1998). Frequency formats can also reduce conjunction errors. Tversky and Kahneman (1983) presented participants with the following question in a probability format:

> A health survey was conducted in a sample of adult males in British Columbia, of all ages and occupations. Please give your best estimate of the following values:
> What percentage of the men surveyed have had one or more heart attacks?
> What percentage of the men surveyed are both over 55-years old and have had one or more heart attacks?

Only 35 percent of participants avoided the conjunction fallacy by assigning a higher percentage to the first question than to the second. Participants given the question in a frequency format read:

> A health survey was conducted in a sample of 100 adult males in British Columbia, of all ages and occupations. Please give your best estimate of the following values:
> How many of the 100 participants have had one or more heart attacks?
> How many of the 100 participants are both more than 55-years old and have had one or more heart attacks?

This time, 75 percent of participants avoided the conjunction fallacy by assigning a higher frequency to the first question than to the second.

Evolutionary psychologists have argued that success in our ancestral environment required an understanding of frequencies, but not probabilities. Therefore, according to these psychologists, it should not be surprising that inferences are more accurate when information is provided with frequencies than with probabilities. Frequency formats do not fix all probability errors (Mellers, Hertwig, and Kahneman 2001), but they do fix some. For an overview of when frequency formats help and when they do not, see Sloman, Over, Slovak, and Stibel (2003).

Disclosure

Conflicts of interest occur when personal interests clash with professional interests in financial, medical, legal, or scientific domains. A common procedure for
constraining self-interest is disclosure. Medical journals require researchers to disclose the sources of their research funding. Stock analysts are required to disclose
their financial conflicts of interest when they make public stock recommendations.
The McCain–Feingold Act mandates public disclosure of political contributions.
Even warning labels on products, such as cigarettes and alcohol, are designed to
give consumers full information about the consequences of consumption.

The widespread use of disclosure is based on the assumption that revealing
a conflict of interest will either result in the advisor providing less biased advice
or the decision maker discounting the advisor's advice, or both, thus allowing
an unbiased decision, despite the conflict of interest. A recent study by Cain,
Loewenstein, and Moore (2005) suggests that disclosure might not only fail to
solve the problems created by conflict of interest but may sometimes make matters
worse. In their experiment, subjects were randomly assigned the role of an advisor
or an estimator. The estimators' task was to guess the total value of a jar filled with
coins; they were given 10 seconds to view the jar from a distance of 3 feet. Advisors
were allowed more time and better viewing. Advisors gave their recommendations
to estimators before estimators made their guesses. Estimators were always paid
based on their accuracy, but advisor payments varied across conditions. In the
control condition with no conflict of interest, advisors were paid if estimators
guessed correctly. In the condition with conflict of interest and no disclosure,
advisors were paid if estimators overvalued the jar, and estimators were not aware
of the advisors' incentives. In the condition with conflict of interest and disclosure,
advisors were paid if estimators overvalued the jar, and estimators *were* aware of
the advisors' incentives.

Estimates were made of several jars, and the average value was $18.16. With
no conflict of interest, the average advisor estimate was $16.48. With conflict of
interest and no disclosure, the average advisor estimate was $20.16. Did disclo-
sure make the advisors give more accurate estimates? No, the average advisor
estimate was $24.16, even higher with disclosure. Disclosure increased advisor
bias, but it also increased estimators' discounting. With disclosure, estimators discounted the recommendations by an average of $2.50 more compared with the
nondisclosure condition. This discounting did not correct for the increased bias in
advisor recommendations of $4. Estimators earned the least amount of money in
this condition.

Advisors may feel that, if they disclose their self-interests, they are less liable
to recipients. Decision makers who learn that an advisor has a conflict of interest
should rely more heavily on their private information, but it is difficult to know
how much the conflict of interest has affected the advisor. And, in a real life
situation, if decision makers are naturally trusting of their advisors and unsure of
their own information, they may interpret the advisor's disclosure as a reason to
believe the advisor's information is even more credible.

Accountability

Common sense suggests that people will be more careful in their judgments and decisions if they expect to be called on to justify their choices or actions to others. Research shows that accountability can be helpful in some circumstances (Lerner and Tetlock 1999). Decision makers are often able to view a problem from different perspectives when anticipating the objections of an audience with unknown views (Ashton 1992; Weldon and Gargano 1988; Tetlock et al. 1989). Accountability can also be helpful when decision makers realize they will be accountable to an audience before, rather than after, they examine the evidence (Tetlock 1983). Predecisional accountability to an unknown audience can reduce cognitive biases.

What, exactly, does accountability do? Predecisional accountability to an unknown audience makes people less sensitive to the order of information (i.e., primacy and recency effects) (Kruglanski and Freund 1983; Tetlock 1983), less overconfident (Tetlock and Kim 1987; Seigel-Jacobs and Yates 1996), and less susceptible to conjunction errors (Simonson and Nye 1992). Accountability also makes people less likely to draw inferences from incomplete evidence, more willing to revise their opinions in response to unexpected feedback, and less likely to be swayed by vivid, but irrelevant, information (Lerner and Tetlock 1999).

Unfortunately, that's not all. With predecisional accountability to an unknown audience, people are more sensitive to status quo effects (Samuelson and Zeckhauser 1988), compromise effects or the tendency to prefer the "middle" option (Simonson and Nye 1992), asymmetric dominance or the tendency to choose the option that dominates another option on one dimension (Simonson 1989), and dilution effects or the tendency to use nondiagnostic information (Tetlock and Boettger 1989).

Predecisional accountability to an unknown audience can reduce some biases, especially those that result from too little effort or a lack of understanding of one's judgmental processes. But it can also have no effect or even detrimental effects if decision makers hedge their choices by sticking with the status quo, picking the "middle" option, or trying to use all possible information, regardless of its diagnosticity.

Incentives

Many scholars have asked whether biases and errors would vanish if the stakes were high enough. Camerer and Hogarth (1999) reviewed seventy-four studies comparing behavior of experimental subjects who were paid zero, low, or high financial incentives based on their performance. Some tasks show performance improvement with higher incentives, such as the recall of items (Libby and Lipe 1992), the effects of anchoring on judgment, the solving of easy problems, and clerical tasks.

People often work harder with incentives, but if the task is too complicated, incentives can hurt rather than help. Without the relevant cognitive training, participants may succumb to the "lost pilot effect" – I do not know where I am going, but I'm sure making good time (Larrick 2004). Incentives hurt performance when extra effort is used inappropriately. In one study, Arkes, Dawes, and Christensen (1986) asked subjects to predict whether twenty students would or would not win honors given their grades. Participants were given a simple formula that gave the correct answer 70 percent of the time. Without incentives, subjects used the formula and got 66 percent correct. With incentives, subjects tried more complex rules and did slightly worse (63 percent correct).

Most of the studies showed that incentives had no effect on performance. Camerer and Hogarth (1999) concluded that "incentives can reduce self-presentation effects, increase attention and effort, and reduce thoughtless responding," but "no replicated study has made rationality violations disappear purely by raising incentives."

Calibration Training

As discussed earlier, most people are overconfident, even when it is in their best interests to be well calibrated. Outcome feedback may be unclear, delayed, or even nonexistent. Only two groups of professionals studied so far have accurate assessments of their own knowledge: meteorologists (Murphy and Winkler 1977) and racetrack handicappers (Ceci and Liker 1986). Their ability may stem from the fact that they face similar problems every day, make precise probability estimates, and receive quick and clear feedback.

Firms can suffer severe financial consequences from overconfidence. Some years ago, Royal Dutch/Shell noticed that their newly hired geologists were wrong much more often than their level of confidence implied, costing Shell millions of dollars with their overconfidence. For instance, junior geologists would estimate a 40 percent chance of finding oil in a particular location, but when ten wells were drilled, only one or two would produce oil.

The geologists needed better feedback. Shell designed a training program that used feedback to help its geologists become better calibrated. Using past cases of drilled wells, geologists were presented with many factors affecting oil deposits. For each case they had to provide their best guesses for the probability of striking oil as well as ranges for how much a successful well might yield. Then they received feedback. The training worked, and Shell geologists are now better calibrated (Russo and Schoemaker 1992). Similar procedures could be used in medicine, the stock market, legal settings, and other domains where miscalibration could have serious consequences.

Conclusion

If our judgments are really this bad and methods of debiasing only help some of the people some of the time, how in the world do we manage to make reasonably good decisions most of the time? The psychological literature is filled with controversy about the heuristics and biases framework. According to one type of critique, the alleged biases are not really biases at all. Errors are defined relative to normative theories, and normative theories rest on assumptions about decision makers' goals, such as maximizing expected utility or minimizing squared errors. If people care about other things, such as obeying social norms, maintaining good impressions, or sticking to their principles, their behavior is obviously not erroneous (Gigerenzer and Murray 1987). Dsyfunctional errors in one framework may be perfectly reasonable in another (Tetlock 2002).

Other critiques of the heuristics and biases framework focus on the generality of errors across people and situations. Biases may occur in laboratory studies, but real world competitive markets should reduce their occurrence. Furthermore, not everyone is equally vulnerable to errors. It helps to be smart. Cognitive ability is correlated with fewer biases in judgment, including the ability to overcome framing effects and the conjunction fallacy (Stanovich and West 1998). It also helps to be knowledgeable. Statistical training reduces some biases (Nisbett, Fong, Lehman, and Cheng 1987).

Still other critiques of the heuristics and biases approach focus on inadequate theory. Heuristics help us organize and understand effects, but what good are they if the findings can be explained by multiple heuristics? Take base-rate neglect, the tendency for people who make probabilistic inferences to discount base rates in favor of individuating information. Base-rate neglect was initially illustrated with the cab problem (Tversky and Kahneman 1982) that read:

A cab was involved in a hit-and-run accident at night. Two cab companies, the Green and the Blue, operate in the city. Eighty-five percent of the cabs in the city are Green and 15 percent are Blue. A witness identified the cab as "Blue." The court tested the reliability of the witness under the same circumstances that existed on the night of the accident and concluded that the witness could correctly identify the color of cab 80 percent of the time and failed to identify the correct color 20 percent of the time. What is the probability that the cab involved in the accident was Blue rather than Green?

The Bayesian solution to this problem is 41 percent, although most people say the probability that a Blue cab was involved in the accident is closer to 80 percent (the individuating information). Kahneman and Tversky attributed this finding to the representativeness heuristic according to which probability is substituted for similarity. Yet, the tendency to say 80 percent might also be attributed to the availability heuristic if the witness's statement was more vivid and salient than the base rate. Or the tendency to say 80 percent might be due to the anchoring and adjustment heuristic if people anchor on the individuating information and insufficiently adjust for base-rate information.

Finally, other critiques say the pendulum has swung too far. With exclusive focus on biases and errors, this research agenda has skewed our perception of human behavior. People have amazing powers, such as the ability to learn patterns, chunk information, store it, and retrieve it as needed. In an ingenious study, Chase and Simon (1973) presented a master chess player and a novice with a half-finished game of chess for five seconds. The chess board contained approximately twenty-five pieces. The master and the novice were then asked to reconstruct the board. The master was able to correctly locate an average of sixteen pieces, while the

novice located only four pieces correctly. These master chess players do not perceive *all* patterns better. Chase and Simon briefly presented the master and the
novice with another chess board containing twenty-five randomly placed pieces.
Both the expert and novice were able to locate only three or four pieces correctly.
The chunking, storing, and retrieving that experts have mastered applies only to
meaningful patterns.

Another form of pattern matching is facial recognition. Human faces are
composed of identical components, and yet peoples' memory for specific faces
is remarkable. In one study, Bahrick, Bahrick, and Wittlinger (1975) tested the
memory of people for their high school classmates. They obtained the high school
yearbooks of approximately 400 people who ranged in age from 18 to 74. Ten pictures were randomly selected from each yearbook and photocopied. Each picture
was placed on a card with four other pictures randomly taken from other yearbooks. Participants were shown the cards and asked to identify the photo of their
classmate. Choices were correct 90 percent of the time, even among participants
who had graduated 35 years earlier. Those who had graduated 48 years ago were
still correct 71 percent of the time. It is easy to imagine evolutionary reasons for
our remarkable talent to recognize faces.

Individuals may have some well-tuned cognitive skills such as pattern matching, but what about groups? Are they capable of any amazing feats? Surowiecki
(2004) describes conditions under which groups of individuals outperform the
elite few. He tells a story of Francis Galton, who came across a weight-judging
contest at a country fair. Individuals entered their guess of the weight of an ox, and
the best guesses received prizes. Approximately 800 people entered the contest.
When it was over, Galton borrowed the tickets from the organizers and plotted the
estimates to see if they formed a bell curve. In the process, he calculated the mean,
and to his surprise, the average guess of the ox's weight was 1,197 pounds – only
one pound away from the actual weight of 1,198 pounds. Even when members of
a group are not particularly well informed, the group can reach a collectively wise
decision, provided the individual opinions are independent, diverse, and decen-
tralized (i.e., no one is at the top dictating the right answer). In addition, there
must be a reasonable method for aggregating judgments and determining the
group decision.

Both experts and novices are susceptible to a host of biases, and debiasing
does not always help. Nonetheless, we can learn from our own mistakes and from
those of others. As Sam Levenson, a twentieth-century U.S. humorist, once said,
"You must learn from the mistakes of others. You can't possibly live long enough
to make them all yourself."

REFERENCES

Arkes, H. R., and Blumer, C. (1985). The psychology of sunk cost. *Organizational Behavior
and Human Decision Processes, 35*, 125–140.
Arkes, H. R., Dawes, R. M., and Christensen, C. (1986). Factors influencing the use of
a decision rule in a probabilistic task. *Organizational Behavior and Human Decision
Processes, 27*, 148–180.

Arkes, H. R., Saville, P. D., Wortmann, R. L., and Harkness, A. R. (1981). Hindsight bias among physicians weighing the likelihood of diagnoses. *Journal of Applied Psychology, 66,* 252–254.

Armstrong, K., Schwartz, J. S., Fitzgerald, G., Putt, M., and Ubel, P. A. (2002). Effect of framing as gain versus loss on understanding and hypothetical treatment choices: Survival and mortality curves. *Medical Decision Making, 22,* 76–83.

Asch, S. E. (1946). Forming impressions of personality. *Journal of Abnormal Psychology, 41,* 258–290.

Ashton, R. H. (1992). Effects of justification and a mechanical aid on judgment performance. *Organizational Behavior and Human Decision Processes, 52,* 292–306.

Babcock, L., and Loewenstein, G. (1997). Explaining bargaining impasse: The role of self-serving biases. *Journal of Economic Perspectives, 11,* 109–125.

Bahrick, H. P., Bahrick, P. O., and Wittlinger, R. P. (1975). Fifty years of memory for names and faces: A cross-sectional approach. *Journal of Experimental Psychology: General, 104,* 54–75.

Baker, L. A., and Emery, R. E. (1993). When every relationship is above average: Perceptions and expectations of divorce at the time of marriage. *Law and Human Behavior, 17,* 439–450.

Barber, B., and Odean, T. (2000). Trading is hazardous to your wealth: The common stock investment performance of individual investors. *Journal of Finance, 55,* 773–806.

Bukszar, E., and Connolly, T. (1988). Hindsight bias and strategic choice – Some problems in learning from experience. *Academy of Management Journal, 31,* 628–641.

Cain, D. N., Loewenstein, G., and Moore, D. A. (2005). The dirt on coming clean: Perverse effects of disclosing conflicts of interest. *Journal of Legal Studies, 34,* 1–25.

Camerer, C. F., and Hogarth, R. M. (1999). The effects of financial incentives in experiments: A review and capital-labor-production framework. *Journal of Risk and Uncertainty, 19,* 7–42.

Ceci, S. J., and Liker, J. K. (1986). A day at the races: A study of IQ, expertise, and cognitive complexity. *Journal of Experimental Psychology: General, 115,* 255–266.

Chase, W. G., and Simon, H. A. (1973). The mind's eye in chess. In W. G. Chase (Ed.), *Visual information processing.* New York: Academic Press, pp. 215–281.

Chapman, G. B., and Johnson, E. J. (1994). The limits of anchoring. *Journal of Behavioral Decision Making, 7,* 223–242.

Dellarosa, D., and Bourne, L. E. (1984). Decisions and memory: Differential retrievability of consistent and contradictory evidence. *Journal of Verbal Learning and Verbal Behavior, 23,* 669–682.

Desvouges, W. H., Johnson, F., Dunford, R., Hudson, S., Wilson, K., and Boyle, K. (1993). Measuring resource damages with contingent valuation: Tests of validity and reliability. In *Contingent valuation: A critical assessment.* Amsterdam: North Holland.

Fischhoff, B. (1975). Hindsight ≠ Foresight: The effect of outcome knowledge on judgment under uncertainty. *Journal of Experimental Psychology: Human Perception and Performance, 1,* 288–299.

Fischhoff, B., and Beyth, R. (1975). "I knew it would happen": Remembered probabilities of once-future things. *Organizational Behavior and Human Decision Processes, 13,* 1–16.

Fischhoff, B., Slovic, P., and Lichtenstein, S. (1986). Knowing with certainty: The appropriateness of extreme confidence. In H. R. Arkes and K. R. Hammond (Eds.), *Judgment and decision making: An interdisciplinary reader.* New York: Cambridge University Press, pp. 397–416.

Frisch, D. (1993). Reasons for framing effects. *Organizational Behavior and Human Decision Processes, 54,* 399–429.

Gigerenzer, G., and Hoffrage, U. (1995). How to improve Bayesian reasoning without instruction: Frequency formats. *Psychological Review, 102,* 684–704.

Gigerenzer, G., and Murray, D. J. (1987). *Cognition as intuitive statistics.* Hillsdale, NJ: Erlbaum.

Gourville, J. T., and Soman, D. (1998). Payment depreciation: The behavioral effects of temporally separating payments from consumption. *Journal of Consumer Research, 25,* 160–174.

Hoch, S. J. (1985). Counterfactual reasoning and accuracy in predictive judgment. *Journal of Experimental Psychology: Learning, Memory, and Cognition, 11,* 719–731.

Hoffrage, U., and Gigerenzer, G. (1998). Using natural frequencies to improve diagnostic inferences. *Academic Medicine, 73,* 538–540.

Huber, J., Payne, J. W., and Puto, C. (1982). Adding asymmetrically dominated alternatives: Violations of regularity and the similarity hypothesis. *Journal of Consumer Research, 9,* 90–98.

Johnson, E. J., Hershey, J., Meszaros, J., and Kunreuther, H. (1993). Framing, probability distortions, and insurance decisions. *Journal of Risk and Uncertainty, 7,* 35–51.

Joyce, E. J., and Biddle, G. C. (1981). Anchoring and adjustment in probabilistic inference in auditing. *Journal of Accounting Research, 19,* 120–145.

Kahneman, D., and Frederick, S. (2002). Representativeness revisited: Attribution substitution in intuitive judgment. In T. Gilovich, D. Griffin, and D. Kahneman (Eds.), *Heuristics and biases: The psychology of intuitive judgment.* New York: Cambridge University Press, pp. 49–81.

Kahneman, D., Ritov, I., and Schkade, D. (1999). Economic preferences or attitude expressions? An analysis of dollar responses to public issues. *Journal of Risk and Uncertainty, 19,* 203–235.

Kidd, J. B. (1970). The utilization of subjective probabilities in production planning. *Acta Psychologica, 34,* 338–347.

Knetsch, J. L. (1989). The endowment effect and evidence of nonreversible indifference curves. *American Economic Review, 79,* 1277–1284.

Kruglanski, A.W., and Freund, T. (1983). The freezing and unfreezing of lay-inferences: Effects on impressional primacy, ethnic stereotyping, and numerical anchoring. *Journal of Experimental Social Psychology, 32,* 437–459.

Larrick, R. (2004). Debiasing. In D. J. Koehler and N. Harvey (Eds.), *Blackwell handbook of judgment and decision making.* Malden, MA: Blackwell Publishing, pp. 316–377.

Larwood, L., and Whittaker, W. (1977). Managerial myopia: Self-serving biases in organizational planning. *Journal of Applied Psychology, 62,* 194–198.

Leary, M. R. (1982). Hindsight distortion and the 1980 presidential election. *Personality and Social Psychology Bulletin, 8,* 257–263.

LeBoeuf, R.A., and Shafir, E. (2003). Deep thoughts and shallow frames: On the susceptibility to framing effects. *Journal of Behavioral Decision Making, 16,* 77–92.

Lerner, J. S., and Tetlock, P. E. (1999). Accounting for the effects of accountability. *Psychological Bulletin, 125,* 255–275.

Levin, I. P., and Gaeth, G. J. (1988). Framing of attribute information before and after consuming the product. *Journal of Consumer Research, 15,* 374–378.

Levin, I. P., Gaeth, G. J., Schreiber, J., and Lauriola, M. (2002). A new look at framing effects: distribution of effect sizes, individual differences, and independence of types of effects. *Organizational Behavior and Human Decision Processes, 88,* 411–429.

Libby, R., and Lipe, M. G. (1992). Incentives, effort, and the cognitive processes involved in accounting-related judgments. *Journal of Accounting Research, 30,* 249–273.

Loewenstein, G., Issacharoff, S., Camerer, C., and Babcock, L. (1993). Self-serving assessments of fairness and pretrial bargaining. *Journal of Legal Studies, XXII,* 135–159.

Lusted, L. B. (1977). *A study of the efficacy of diagnostic radiologic procedures: Final report on diagnostic efficacy.* Chicago: Efficacy Study Committee of the American College of Radiology.

McNeil, B. J., Pauker, S. G., Sox, H. C., and Tversky, A. (1982). On the elicitation of preferences for alternative therapies. *New England Journal of Medicine, 306*, 1259–1262.

Mellers, B. A., and Cooke, A. D. J. (1996). The role of task and context in preference measurement. *Psychological Science, 7*, 76–82.

Mellers, B. A., Hertwig, R., and Kahneman, D. (2001). Do frequency representations eliminate conjunction effects? An exercise in adversarial collaboration. *Psychological Science, 12*, 269–275.

Messick, D. M., and Bazerman, M. H. (1996). Ethical leadership and the psychology of decision making. *Sloan Management Review, 37*, 9–23.

Messick, D., and Sentis, K. (1983). Fairness, preference, and fairness biases. In D. M.Messick and K. S.Cooke (Eds.), *Equity Theory: Psychological and Sociological Perspectives*. New York: Praeger.

Murphy, A. H., and Winkler, R. L. (1977). Can weather forecasters formulate reliable probability forecasts of precipitation and temperature?*National Weather Digest, 2*, 2–9.

Neale, M. A., and Bazerman, M. (1992). Negotiating rationally: The power and impact of the negotiator's frame. *Academy of Management Executive, 6*, 42–51.

New York Times. (2004). Will This Idea Fly? Charge Some Travelers $10 for Showing Up. *Technology News*, August 25.

Nisbett, R. E., Fong, G. T., Lehman, D. R., and Cheng, P. W. (1987). Teaching reasoning. *Science, 238*, 625–631.

Oskamp, S. (1965). Overconfidence in case-study judgments. *Journal of Consulting Psychology, 29*, 261–265.

Ritov, I., and Baron, J. (1990). Reluctance to vaccinate: Commission bias and ambiguity. *Journal of Behavioral Decision Making, 3*, 263–277.

Ross, M., and Sicoly, F. (1979). Egocentric biases in availability and attribution. *Journal of Personality and Social Psychology, 37*, 332–337.

Russo, J. E., and Schoemaker, P. J. H. (1989). *Decision traps*. New York: Simon and Schuster.

Russo, J. E., and Schoemaker, P. J. H. (1992). Managing overconfidence. *Sloan Management Review, 33*, 7–17.

Samuelson, W., and Zeckhauser, R. (1988). Status quo bias in decision making. *Journal of Risk and Uncertainty, 1*, 7–59.

Siegel-Jacobs, K., and Yates, J. F. (1996). Effects of procedural and outcome accountability on judgmental quality. *Organizational Behavior and Human Decision Processes, 65*, 1–17.

Simon, H. A. (1956). Rational choice and the structure of the environment. *Psychological Review, 63*, 129–138.

Simonson, I. (1989). Choice based on reasons: The case of attraction and compromise effects. *Journal of Consumer Research, 16*, 158–174.

Simonson, I., and Nye, P. (1992). The effect of accountability on susceptibility to decision errors. *Organizational Behavior and Human Decision Processes, 51*, 416–429.

Sloman, S. A., Over, D., Slovak, L., and Stibel, J. M. (2003). Frequency illusions and other fallacies. *Organizational Behavior and Human Decision Processes, 91*, 296–309.

Slovic, P., Finucane, M., Peters, E., and MacGregor, D. G. (2004). Risk as analysis and risk as feelings: Some thoughts about affect, reason, risk, and rationality. *Risk Analysis, 24*, 1–12.

Sporer, S. L., Penrod, S. D., Read, J. D., and Cutler, B. L. (1995). Choosing, confidence, and accuracy: A meta-analysis of the confidence-accuracy relation in eyewitness identification studies. *Psychological Bulletin, 118*, 315–327.

Stael von Holstein, C.-A.S. (1972). Probabilistic forecasting: An experiment related to the stock market. *Organizational Behavior and Human Performance, 8*, 139–158.

Stanovich, K. E., and West, R. F. (1998). Individual differences in framing and conjunction effects. *Thinking and Reasoning, 4*, 289–317.

Staw, B. M. (1976). Knee-deep in big muddy: Study of escalating commitment to a chosen course of action. *Organizational Behavior and Human Performance, 16*, 27–44.

Staw, B. M., Barsade, S. G., and Koput, K. W. (1997) Escalation at the credit window: A longitudinal study of bank executives' recognition and write-off of problem loans. *Journal of Applied Psychology, 82*, 130–142.

Strack, F., Martin, L. L., and Schwarz, N. (1988). Priming and communication: The social determinants of information use in judgments of life satisfaction. *European Journal of Social Psychology, 18*, 429–442.

Strack, F., and Mussweiler, T. (1997). Explaining the enigmatic anchoring effect: mechanisms of selective accessibility. *Journal of Personality and Social Psychology, 73*, 437–446.

Suroweicki, J. (2004). *The wisdom of crowds*. New York: Doubleday.

Synodinos, N. E. (1986). Hindsight distortion: I knew it all along and I was sure about it. *Journal of Applied Social Psychology, 16*, 107–117.

Tetlock, P. E. (1983). Accountability and complexity of thought. *Journal of Personality and Social Psychology, 45*, 74–83.

Tetlock, P. E. (2002). Social-functionalist frameworks for judgment and choice: Intuitive politicians, theologians, and prosecutors. *Psychological Review, 109*, 451–471.

Tetlock, P. E., and Boettger, R. (1989). Accountability amplifies the status quo effect when change creates victims. *Journal of Behavioral Decision Making, 7*, 1–23.

Tetlock, P. E., and Kim, J. I. (1987). Accountability and judgment processes in a personality prediction task. *Journal of Personality and Social Psychology, 52*, 700–709.

Tetlock. P. E., Skitka, L., and Boettger, R. (1989). Social and cognitive strategies for coping with accountability: Conformity, complexity, and bolstering. *Journal of Personality and Social Psychology, 57*, 632–640.

Thaler, R. (1999). Mental accounting matters. *Journal of Behavioral Decision Making, 12*, 183–206.

Tversky, A, and Kahneman, D. (1974). Judgment under uncertainty: Heuristics and biases. *Science, 185*, 1124–1131.

Tversky, A., and Kahneman, D. (1981). The framing of decisions and the psychology of choice. *Science, 211*, 453–458.

Tversky, A., and Kahneman, D. (1982). Evidential impact of base rates. In D. Kahneman, P. Slovic, and A. Tversky (Eds.), *Judgment under uncertainty: Heuristics and biases*. Cambridge, UK: Cambridge University Press, pp. 153–160.

Tversky, A., and Kahneman, D. (1983). Extensional versus intuitive reasoning: The conjunction fallacy in probability judgment. *Psychological Review, 90*, 293–315.

Wagenaar, W. A., and Keren, G. B. (1986). Calibration of probability assessments by professional blackjack dealers, statistical experts, and lay people. *Organizational Behavior and Human Decision Processes, 36*, 406–416.

Wason, P. C. (1960). On the failure to eliminate hypotheses in a conceptual task. *Quarterly Journal of Experimental Psychology, 12*, 129–140.

Weldon, E., and Gargano, G. M. (1988). Cognitive loafing: The effects of accountability and shared responsibility on cognitive effort. *Personality and Social Psychology Bulletin, 8*, 226–232.

19 Decision Conferencing

Lawrence D. Phillips

ABSTRACT. This chapter presents the current status of the decision conference process, a way of helping a group of key players to resolve important issues in their organization by working together, under the guidance of an impartial facilitator, with the aid of a decision analysis model of participants' perspectives on the issues, developed on-the-spot over a period of two days. The facilitator serves as a process consultant, guiding the group through the stages of discussing the issues, developing a model, and exploring the results, without contributing to the content of discussions. The model serves as a "tool for thinking," not as providing an optimal solution or "the right answer." Participants are encouraged to express their sense of unease at any stage in the process, for it is the discrepancy between model results and intuitive judgment that drives the dialectic in the group. Exploration generates new insights and stimulates creative thinking, resulting in changes to the model and to intuitions. As this process settles down, participants develop a shared understanding of the issues, generate a sense of common purpose, and gain commitment to the way forward. Two case studies illustrate a typical individual decision conference and how sustained engagement with a client, decision conferencing, can lead to committed alignment in a group. Research on decision conferences provides insights into why decision conferences work.

Introduction

An unexpected event led to the development of decision conferences. The managing director of the Westinghouse Elevator Company brought twenty of his staff, rather than only the few key players expected, to a two-day "contact meeting" at Decisions and Designs, Inc., in May 1979 to deal with issues about the design of a new factory. Cam Peterson, then the Technical Director of DDI, wanted to break away from the standard consultancy model, the "doctor–patient" model described by Schein (1999), in which the consultant gathers information from the client, goes back to the office to analyze the problem and develops some answers, then returns to the client to sell the solution. Instead, the contact meeting brought together the few key people who knew about the problem, and after much discussion and exchange of views, they provided relevant data and judgments, which were input to a computer-based decision model, on the spot, displayed on large monitors. The central idea of the contact meeting was that good information and data are best obtained directly from the decision maker and that perspectives shift and change as information is exchanged. However, this time a large group of key players showed up, which Peterson felt at the time was overkill. Still, in the role of an impartial facilitator and specialist in decision analysis, he led the group through many sensitivity analyses and changes to the model as participants deepened their understanding of the issues. At the end of two days, the group agreed on a decision, which was implemented quickly.

Later follow-through revealed that the success of this contact meeting owed much to the alignment of the twenty participants created during the two days, though DDI remained skeptical that substantial issues could be handled satisfactorily in just two days. But subsequent experience showed it was indeed possible, largely because the information needed to resolve the issues already resided in the heads of the key players, not necessarily in printed papers and reports. In addition, bringing the key players together, encouraging them to participate in the problem-solving process, led everyone to understand how results were obtained, even if not everyone was pleased with the outcome. The buy-in of the team to the results of the modeling was, according to the managing director, the key. And so, the "decision conference" was born, with aligned commitment considered as important as a quality decision.

When I heard about this development early in 1981, I realized that my two major interests, decision analysis and group processes, could be merged. Within weeks, the first decision conference in Europe, facilitated by Clint Kelly, a director of DDI, was held for the UK's Post Office. I could see the great advantage of getting all the key players around the table, talking to each other, exchanging information, debating from different perspectives, arguing their value positions, and using the model as a neutral repository for all the information and value judgments. As the model fed back to the group the collective results of their inputs, it didn't argue or take a position. "Here are the logical results of what you have been telling me," it seemed to say, "and if you don't like them, then feel free to change whatever seems wrong to you, and I will give you the new results." I could see that attempting to play the model did not work; a change that would make one part better often resulted in unexpected consequences elsewhere.

By the end of the decision conference, I knew this was the direction for my future work. Over the years that followed, my colleagues and I at Brunel University, later at the London School of Economics, developed decision conferences. Facilitating decision conferences, training new facilitators and meeting annually with colleagues in the International Decision Conferencing Forum provided research data for my colleagues, particularly Stuart Wooler, Patrick Humphreys, and Mary Ann Phillips, and we collaborated in developing both theory and practice. This paper brings together those many strands.

The Decision Conference

Decision conferences work best when they are about "hot" issues – real concerns of an organization that require resolution. They can be strategic issues that require work over months or years, or operational ones, including immediate crises. Decision conferences don't work very well for issues that are merely "interesting," or "nice to consider," but lacking any sense of urgency for their resolution.

Sometimes the problem has been studied for several months, providing information and data that can be brought to the table. Inevitably, the actual information needed to resolve the issues is substantially less than has been provided by the studies, and typically important information has been missed, so some decision conferences are organized at the very start of further exploration, with sensitivity analyses used to reveal areas that could benefit from additional data. This initial decision conference often helps to provide a new frame for the issues, helping to highlight what information is relevant and what is not. The outputs of such an initial decision conference guide the subsequent data gathering, making the process more efficient than the unguided search for information that may or may not be helpful.

More than 25 years and thousands of decision conferences later, conducted by many facilitators in more than fifteen countries, the elements common to all decision conferences are clear: attendance by key players, impartial facilitation, on-the-spot modeling with continuous display of the developing model, and an interactive and iterative group process.

The key players are chosen to represent all the main perspectives on the issues. Although it is helpful if the decision makers are present, that is not always possible, particularly for decision conferences in the public sector where it is elected representatives who hold the authority for final decisions. In these cases, the task of the decision conference is to make recommendations to the decision makers, so it is important that the perspectives of the decision makers are represented in the conference even if they can't attend.

At the start of the decision conference, the facilitator establishes the neutrality of information, encouraging participants to speak openly and freely, and asks the group to respect the privileged nature of the discussion. The Chatham House rule applies (RIIA 1927):

> When a meeting, or part thereof, is held under the Chatham house rule, participants are free to use the information received, but neither the identity nor the affiliation of the speaker(s), nor that of any other participant, may be revealed.

In decision conferences the output is a group product shaped by participants, so individual attributions are inappropriate.

Impartial facilitation, the second element of a decision conference, refers to the separation of the subject-matter content from the group process. The facilitator attends to content, but does not contribute to it, for to do so compromises the facilitator's impartiality, making it more difficult to function properly as a process guide. Most leaders of groups recognize the difficulty of attending and contributing to content and process. In a decision conference, the appointed leader remains in that role, but is relieved from guiding the process. Thus, all participants contribute actively to content, although the facilitator intervenes as appropriate in the group process to ensure that the group remains task oriented and achieves its objectives.

Special training in facilitation helps budding facilitators to achieve a reasonable level of impartiality. It is very tempting for the facilitator to take on a leadership role, especially if the appointed leader is weak, or if the facilitator is a specialist in the topic under discussion. But over and over again, facilitators tempted to "help the group out" by contributing their expertise at some point in the decision conference, report that at the end of the discussion they find it very difficult to return to a stance of impartiality, mainly because the group now sees the facilitator as trying to steer the group in directions that are not those desired by participants. With training, facilitators can learn to use their expertise as the source of questions to the group, not as providing answers.

On-the-spot modeling with continuous display of the developing model, the third element of a decision conference, ensures that every word and number input into the software is seen by participants, who are free to discuss, modify, and edit the inputs. In this way, the model is built in small, digestible steps, with explanations given only when they are needed, ensuring that the transparency of the model is maintained throughout the whole process of creating it. A sense of ownership develops. If successive decision conferences are scheduled for complex problems, changes to the model in the days between decision conferences should wait until the start of the next decision conference, so participants can then approve them or not, continuing the model-building process from where it left off at the last decision conference.

Another contributor to the sense of ownership is the room in which the decision conference is held. Two basic principles apply, whatever the size or configuration of the room: (1) everyone should be capable of direct eye-to-eye contact, and (2) all displays, flip charts and white boards should be readable by everyone. This means that participants should not be arranged in straight lines behind end-to-end rectangular tables, and visual aids equipment must not obscure lines of sight. For groups of six to fifteen participants, chairs arranged in ∩-shape, work better than ∏-shape. Groups larger than fifteen are better arranged around round tables, cabaret style, for with only slight shifts of position, anyone talking can be seen by everyone else. A good discussion of possible arrangements is found in Hickling (1990). Drinks, not just coffee and tea, and other refreshments should be continuously available at the back of the room so the facilitator can call breaks as milestones are reached, without being constrained by the timetables of the organization providing the room.

The final element, *interactive and iterative group process*, means that as the modeling process proceeds, requiring participants to be clear about each model element, thinking is clarified, particularly as information is exchanged in the group. As new ideas emerge they are captured in the model. Then, as the model combines the information given to it, results may stimulate new perspectives, which may require modification and revision of the model. Thus, there is a reflexive interplay between the participants and the model, as if the model is another participant, but a neutral one, merely reflecting back to the group the collective results of the information that has been fed in.

Dissatisfaction on the part of the participants with elements of the model, or its results, drives the dialectic in the group, resulting in further changes to the model. Unexpected results typically emerge as the group struggles to create a model that both informs and is informed by their experience and understanding

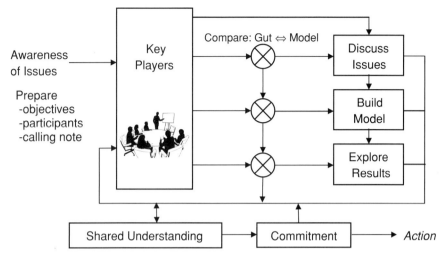

Figure 19.1. Schematic of the decision conference process.

of the data. Eventually, the process settles down as participants' understanding of the issues deepens and grows, and as the model becomes increasingly consistent and realistic. Finally, the model becomes "requisite," just good enough for the group to agree the way forward.

This point is not always reached in a decision conference. It may be necessary for a short period of reflection on the results to take place, for participants to work through the implications of their new understanding of the issues. A follow-through meeting, often with only the decision maker and a few key players, is sufficient to explore any remaining issues, and for the decision maker to take final decisions.

Stages in a Typical Decision Conference

The decision conference process begins with an inquiry from someone in the sponsoring organization who recognizes a need: possibly a gap between desired and actual performance, or a recognition that changes in the environment call for new ways of operating, or that current strategies or policies are losing their relevance to new conditions. Whatever the source, it is helpful to establish if there is a motivation for change, for without it, decision conferences are not likely to lead to commitments that people will implement. If it can be established that a hot issue really exists, and that a decision conference could deal with the issue, then the facilitator engages the client in the next stage, preparation, as shown in Figure 19.1.

At a short meeting, typically less than two hours, usually held with the decision maker, perhaps supplemented by key members of his or her staff, the facilitator explores the nature of the issues to ensure that decision conferencing can help, and works with the team to establish the objectives of the decision conference. Next, the key players who will attend are identified: people whose perspectives can make a useful contribution to the resolution of the issues. This may include people from other parts of the organization who are not necessarily stakeholders, and possibly outside experts if specialist information is lacking within the organization. The outlines of a calling note, to be sent by the decision maker or lead person, are established. These include the purpose of the meeting; administrative details of when and where; a paragraph explaining that the meeting will be conducted as a decision conference, with an attachment providing an introduction to decision conferencing; preparation asked of participants, usually little more than to think about possible options for the way forward; and a request to arrange diaries for uninterrupted attendance throughout the full two days.

The decision conference starts with a reiteration of the objectives, which participants are encouraged to discuss and possibly modify. Agreement to the objectives establishes the primary task of the meeting, grounds the group in a shared social reality, and provides the facilitator with a goal that legitimizes future interventions. The facilitator explains that information is to be shared freely, and treated as a neutral commodity. The three generic purposes of decision conferences, shared understanding, sense of common purpose, and commitment to the way forward, are explained. To achieve these objectives, the facilitator explains, the group will create a model that captures the key elements we must address to resolve the issues. To do this, we will first discuss the issues, then build a model of the issues, and then explore the results. Participants are encouraged to compare the outputs of the stages with their holistic judgment, their gut feelings, and to report any sense of unease, even if they don't know the reason. Exploring the discrepancy may generate new insights, requiring changes to the model or to people's judgments, which help to build the group's shared understanding of the issues. Many sensitivity analyses will show the extent to which results are affected by imprecision in the input data and differences of opinion. As our understanding deepens, we will circle back to previous steps to make changes and revisions that reflect our new perspectives. As this process settles down, a sense of common purpose develops, and agreement about the way forward will most likely emerge. Then the work begins.

After the decision conference is over, the facilitator prepares a report of the meeting, and may hold a short follow-through meeting with the senior staff to resolve any remaining issues.

The Purposes of a Decision Conference

In the early years, I thought that improving decisions was the goal of decision analysis, and this is how we positioned decision conferences in the UK. However, follow-through studies of decision conferences showed that recommendations from the decision conference were not always followed, yet participants valued the experience, particularly as compared to conventional meetings (Chun 1992). Further questioning revealed three underlying reasons why decision conferences were valued: (1) they helped the group to generate a shared understanding of the issues, without requiring consensus about all issues, (2) they developed a sense of common purpose, while allowing individual differences in perspective, and (3) they gained commitment to the way forward, yet preserving individual paths. Senior managers often said their biggest problem was getting everyone to pull in the same direction, and that decision conferences helped to achieve agreement about the way forward, even if not everyone was agreed about the best decisions.

We found that the problem was not so much making poor decisions as it was making wrong decisions. For example, one group of sales managers from six Eastern European countries reported that the decision conference showed that the wrong strategy was being followed in each country. The strategies recommended by the end of the decision conference were not subsequently implemented because the realignment of the country managers' perspectives led them to grasp new opportunities when they returned to their countries. All the managers agreed that the decision conference had been worthwhile (Phillips 1990). Indeed, profits and revenues that had been static for four years more than doubled 18 months after the decision conference, and continued to rise steadily for many years afterwards. The managers attributed this improvement in performance to the new strategies.

Of the eighty organizations for whom I have engaged in consultancy work, only one came to me asking for help to improve decision-making in the organization. Perhaps this is not surprising, for as François de La Rochefoucauld observed, "Everyone complains of his memory, and nobody complains of his judgment." By the six standards of quality decisions (Matheson and Matheson 1998), decision conferences lead to better decisions, but this is rarely mentioned by participants in debriefing. Of the six decision-quality dimensions, only "commitment to action" comes close, but even then it is not so much "action" that is mentioned by decision conference participants as "commitment to the way forward." This is a general orientation that can fall short of specific actions, more like the alignment of iron filings created by a magnet held below the paper on which they are scattered. Furthermore, a case can be made that because it is only individual managers who are held accountable for their decisions, not groups, allowing groups in organizations that are managerial accountability hierarchies to make decisions would undermine the authority of managers (Jaques 1998).

Decision conferences are now positioned as helping managers to achieve committed alignment to the way forward. In managerial accountability hierarchies decision conferences make recommendations, not decisions. This distinguishes them from ordinary workshops, whose only purpose is to achieve a particular technical objective, such as the best design of a system, or an improved allocation of resources, or to choose the best of several alternatives. Decision conferences accomplish both technical and social objectives, so that is why they are positioned as a sociotechnical approach to resolving issues of concern to an organization.

Evolution to Decision Conferencing

Although we often deal with large problems involving substantial resources within the two-day period, some problems, particularly those involving many separate groups of people with specialized knowledge from different parts of the organization, can't be handled adequately with just one decision conference. Then, a succession of interviews, workshops and decision conferences may be held, with the final decision conference bringing together all of the previous work.

We call this overall process of sustained working with a client *decision conferencing*, whose purposes are, again, both technical and social. The second case study in the next section provides an example, and issues concerning the design of an appropriate social process are discussed in the next section on process.

Case Studies

To illustrate a decision conference and the decision conferencing process, two case studies are presented in this section. The first took place over just one day, an unusual application, and not recommended because it fails to take advantage of an overnight reflection that typically brings fresh perspectives to the table at the beginning of the second day. The second case study required my involvement intensively over about two weeks, and periodically over three months. This second example is typical of sustained engagement with a client.

New Business Appraisal

A financial services company in the UK, part of a global organization, wanted to transform and evolve the worldwide Group's business by engaging in a new e-commerce activity. Uncertain about what business to pursue, they hired outside consultants to develop alternatives. The consultants narrowed down a list of thirty possibilities through a process of evaluation on several key criteria to a short list of three, here identified as SMB, Bank, and Benefits. Each showed promise on many criteria, but none was overall best in every respect. The managing director of the financial services company decided to call a one-day decision conference attended by his senior staff and the consultants, altogether sixteen participants, to choose one of the three.

The meeting began with a presentation from the director of IT of the background to the project, followed by brief presentations from the consultants of the key features of the business alternatives. Each presentation provoked discussion as the group sought to clarify the issues. Participants then privately scored the three options on a scale of overall preference, with the most preferred option assigned a score of 100, the least preferred a zero, and the third option a score somewhere in between so that the differences between it and the least and most preferred options reflected their own differences in strength of preference. The majority, ten participants including the four consultants, chose Benefits, but six chose SMB. Nobody chose Bank. Clearly, the group was not agreed about the best way forward.

The group then developed a multicriteria decision analysis (MCDA) model in which the three options were appraised against two monetary cost criteria, five risk criteria and eleven benefit criteria. Direct relative scaling was used for each criterion, including the cost criteria, though many of the scores were based on data provided by the consultants in a briefing pack provided to participants. The value tree took about two hours to develop, with the scoring another two hours. Many criteria were means objectives rather than fundamental objectives. It was necessary to include them because detailed financial models had not yet been built about any of the options. At this stage, the managing director felt that the group could make good relative judgments about the options, and if the MCDA showed one to be a clear winner, it would then be subject to closer financial scrutiny. Of course, most of the criteria in the value tree would be considered in creating the financial model; the MCDA model was simply considered another approach to obtaining an overall result. Some care was taken to ensure that the criteria were defined to be mutually preference independent.

Note that Risk was considered as one aspect of Cost; this is the way the group felt about risk, so each risk criterion was expressed as a 0-to-100 preference scale, with the option judged to be least risky on a criterion assigned a 100, and the most risky a zero. Participants were reminded that all criterion scales were relative scales, like Celsius or Fahrenheit temperature, and that zero represented least value, not no value.

Swing weighting provided the scaling constants used to combine the scales. Lively discussions attended the scoring and weighting. On the few occasions when consensus could not be reached, the majority view was input to the model, with the disagreed figure the subject of later sensitivity analyses. The value tree in Figure 19.2 shows the structure of the model.

Overall results are shown in Figure 19.3 in two ways, as stacked bar graphs, and as overall benefits versus overall costs. (Note that the lower the Costs, the longer the upper portions of the stacked bar graphs, and the further to the right on the plot, because less cost was more preferred.) The left stacked bar graph giving the overall results shows that although SMB is overall most preferred, Bank and Benefits are very close to each other and considerably less attractive than SMB. Several of the ten people whose holistic judgment had led them to choose Benefits challenged some of the scores and weights.

A period of intense sensitivity analyses followed, mainly on the weights assigned to monetary costs and to risks. These were displayed graphically, in the usual way for MCDA, as overall benefits versus the weight on the criterion, resulting in three straight lines, one for each option. Further sensitivity analyses on the Financial, Leadership, and Doability nodes confirmed the attractiveness of SMB. Overall, the dominance of SMB proved remarkably robust over large ranges of difference of opinion about weights, enabling the group to agree that SMB was the way forward. Additional comparisons showing those criteria that account for the advantages and disadvantages of each option showed why SMB was best, and so helped participants to understand why, contrary to the initial opinions of some, SMB emerged as the winner.

It is worth observing that the four consultants initially preferred the Benefits option. Their criteria were less complete than those shown in Figure 19.2. This illustrates a major difficulty with the "doctor–patient model" of consultancy: the

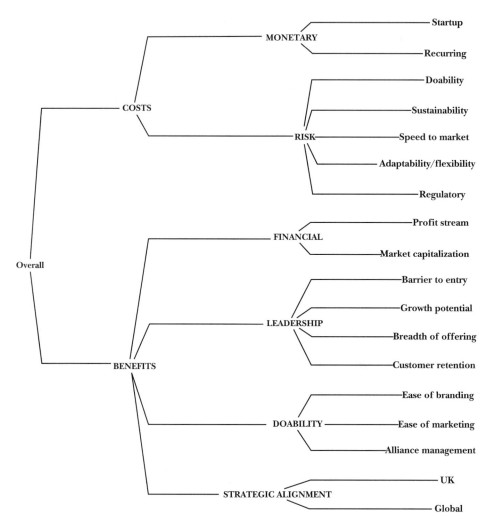

Figure 19.2. Value tree for a financial services company.

consultant's reality does not necessarily correspond to the client's. It is easy for "doctor–patient" consultants to become overly prescriptive, failing to understand fully the client's history, culture and preferences. Decision conferences work with the client's beliefs and values, both understanding and developing them, a constructive approach (Gergen 1993) that allows the client to keep in touch with the problem, its formulation and results.

Prioritization of Projects

The next case study concerns a major pharmaceutical company in the US that used the decision conferencing process to prioritize projects in its late development

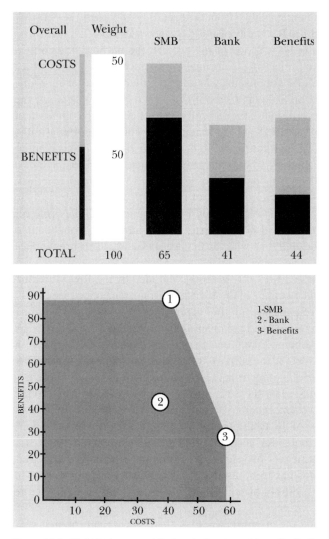

Figure 19.3. Weighted scores at the level of costs and benefits for the e-commerce new venture, and a plot of the benefits vs. preferences for costs for the three options.

portfolio. Decisions in many R&D organizations are made on an individual project basis, which inevitably results in an overall use of the available resource that is not collectively optimal, a condition akin to the well-known Commons Dilemma (Hardin 1968). A better approach is to model the trade-offs between projects, which is effectively done by applying MCDA. It is then possible to find the best combinations of options for a given level of resource, creating a genuine portfolio that will realize more overall benefit as compared with the sum of individual "silo" decisions (Phillips and Bana e Costa 2007). An overview of the approach is given in chapter 13 of Goodwin and Wright (2003).

This type of assignment benefits from a three-tier approach. A Strategy Committee consisting of the R&D director and a few senior staff first meet with the facilitator(s) to establish the scope of the project: the purpose and context for the prioritization, the projects to be included, and the criteria against which the project activities will be appraised. A Working Group, whose chair is one of the senior people on the Strategy Committee, is established to organize the entire process. Among other things, they identify who will be involved in each of the team meetings – not just the team working on each compound, but also the many other key players who can contribute to the prioritization workshops; internal staff representing regulatory affairs, marketing, finance, clinical, etc, and possibly an outside expert. They also identify those staff who will attend all meetings, usually the chair of the Working Group, one or two people from finance, and the analyst who is familiar with the software and builds the model. A key role for these people is to ensure the realism and consistency of inputs from one team to the next. I often work ahead of time with the finance specialists to ensure that just the right level of financial modeling is carried out to support the teams.

The process began with a Kick-Off Meeting, attended by the R&D director, some of his senior staff, all members of the Working Group, the finance specialists, and two senior people from each team, the current Project Leader and Program Manager. The R&D director started the meeting by explaining why this *decision conferencing* approach is being taken, encouraging participants to think afresh and creatively, and he explained the current overall strategy of the R&D Division. This was followed by an explanation from the facilitator of the modeling approach. The benefit criteria suggested by the Strategy Committee were explained to the group, followed by discussion, modification and clarification of the criteria. At this stage, the experience of the facilitator can be helpful, for most organizations are unaware of the attributes for good criteria (Keeney and Raiffa 1976), nor are they aware of the principles of value-focused thinking (Keeney 1992). This expertise of the facilitator has to be used carefully, questioning, not telling, to ensure that the criteria are fully owned by the group, and not imposed by the facilitator.

The facilitator warned the group that getting the criteria right the first year was unlikely. Criteria reflect the underlying core values and strategic intent of the organization, and even if prior thought has been given to them, using them in an MCDA always prompts changes to them. Getting them roughly right the first year is all that can be expected, and is sufficient for the three purposes of decision conferencing. The meeting ended with a question and answer session on how the subsequent team meetings will be conducted. The Kick-Off Meeting lasted about two hours.

It will be helpful at this point to show the structure of the model developed for this case; see Figure 19.4.

Each of the twelve towers represents a different compound, here referred to as a project. The building blocks correspond to strategies associated with the compound. The term "strategy" is used in the sense of "what and why," that is, what the

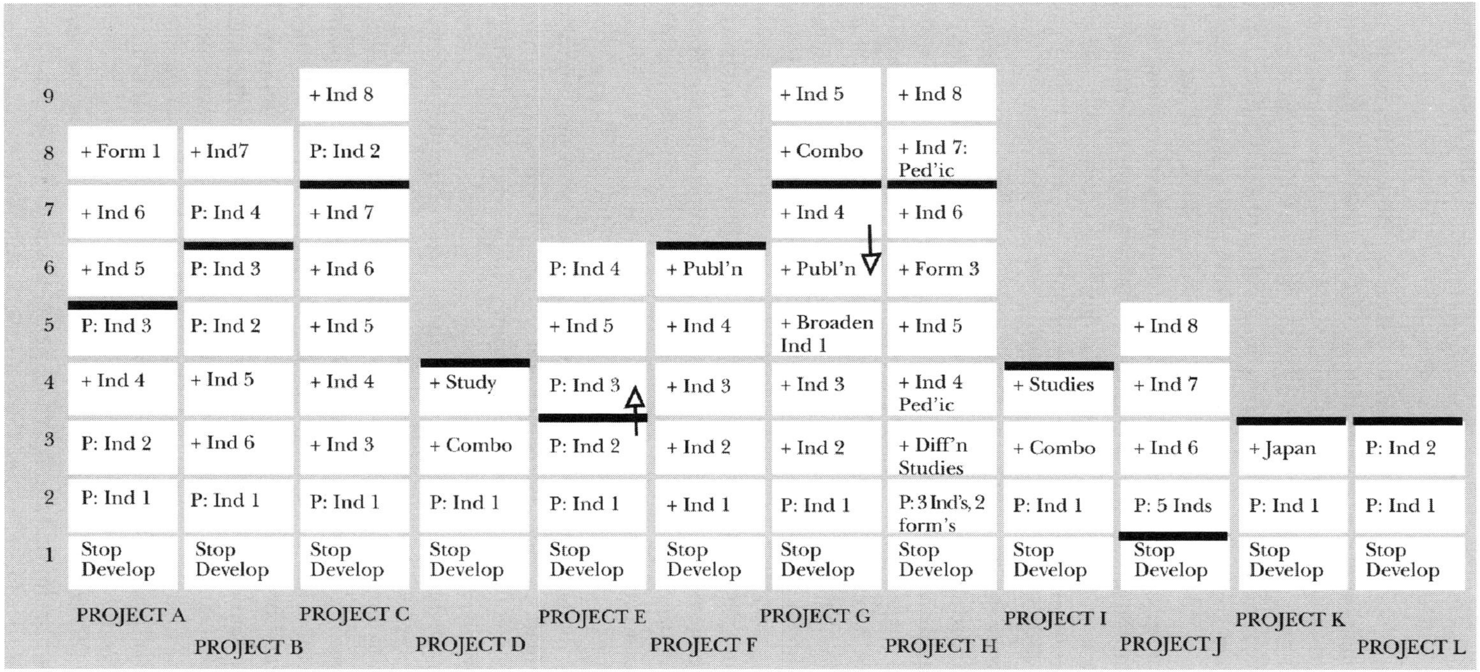

	PROJECT A	PROJECT B	PROJECT C	PROJECT D	PROJECT E	PROJECT F	PROJECT G	PROJECT H	PROJECT I	PROJECT J	PROJECT K	PROJECT L
9			+ Ind 8				+ Ind 5	+ Ind 8		+ Ind 8		
8	+ Form 1	+ Ind7	P: Ind 2				+ Combo	+ Ind 7: Ped'ic		+ Ind 7		P: Ind 2
7	+ Ind 6	P: Ind 4	+ Ind 7				+ Ind 4	+ Ind 6		+ Ind 6	+Japan	
6	+ Ind 5	P: Ind 3	+ Ind 6		P: Ind 4	+ Publ'n	+ Publ'n	+ Form 3				
5	P: Ind 3	P: Ind 2	+ Ind 5		+ Ind 5	+ Ind 4	+ Broaden Ind 1	+ Ind 5	+ Studies			
4	+ Ind 4	+ Ind 5	+ Ind 4	+ Study	P: Ind 3	+ Ind 3	+ Ind 3	+ Ind 4 Ped'ic	+ Combo			
3	P: Ind 2	+ Ind 6	+ Ind 3	+ Combo	P: Ind 2	+ Ind 2	+ Ind 2	+ Diff'n Studies				
2	P: Ind 1	P: Ind 1	P: Ind 1	P: Ind 1	P: Ind 1	+ Ind 1	P: Ind 1	P: 3 Inds, 2 form's	P: Ind 1	P: 5 Inds	P: Ind 1	P: Ind 1
1	Stop Develop	Stop Develop	Stop Develop	Stop Develop	Stop Develop	Stop Develop	Stop Develop	Stop Develop	Stop Develop	Stop Develop	Stop Develop	Stop Develop

Figure 19.4. Structure of the portfolio model, with each tower a different compound, and the white boxes showing current plan (P) and new (+) options. All strategies up to the bold line define the affordable frontier portfolio. The up arrow identifies the next option beyond the affordable frontier and the down arrow the previous option.

387

allocated resource is used for, and why. At this stage, the "how and by when" is not considered, though for every strategy there must, of course, be a "how." Strategies that are currently underway are indicated by a "P," whereas new strategies proposed to join the portfolio are shown by a "+." Many strategies are to develop drugs for specific indications (Ind), which require testing in humans. Some strategies are to conduct studies, to create combinations of compounds, to develop new formulations, even to open new markets. A complete statement of the strategy also includes an explanation of why it is attractive, such as "to develop a new oral formulation that would be more convenient for patients because it would be taken once a day instead of the current three times a day."

Each project team met with the facilitator in a one-day or half-day workshop to develop the model. The group defined the project and explained the current overall strategy for the compound, if there was one, along with a description of the currently funded strategies. The facilitator next engaged the group in a SWOT (Strengths Weaknesses, Opportunities, and Threats) analysis (Ascher and Nare 1990), listing on flipcharts the internal strengths and weaknesses of the compound, the team and the organizational infrastructure, and the external opportunities and threats posed by the extent and seriousness of unmet medical need, untapped markets, developing technology, regulatory restrictions and market competition. The group then used the SWOT analysis to suggest new strategies that would build on the strengths, fix the weaknesses, grasp the opportunities, and stave off the threats. Voting on the resulting list left a shorter list of new strategic options to be included in the prioritization model.

Next, the team scored all the current and new strategies, now referred to as options, against a set of cost and benefit criteria suggested by the Strategy Group and accepted at the Kick-Off meeting. These included the following, which were defined for the teams in more detail: total cost, net present value, extent to which the option will meet unmet medical need, business impact, future potential, and probability of technical success.

All input probabilities assessed by the teams were converted to subtractive penalty scores by a logarithmic mapping, resulting in a proper scoring rule (Bernardo and Smith 1994). This somewhat unconventional procedure for turning an uncertainty into a risk criterion captures the intuitions of people in the pharmaceutical industry that improving the probability of success from, say, 0.10 to 0.20 is more valued than from 0.80 to 0.90. In addition, treating risk as a criterion makes it possible to do sensitivity analyses on the weight of this criterion, allowing risk to be more or less influential on the final result, another desired feature expressed by participants. Of course, an entirely additive model enhances transparency of the results, and as an added bonus makes possible the use of software that only accommodates additive modeling.

Financial staff assisted in assessing total costs and net present values. Linear value functions transformed the NPVs into preference values. Preference values for unmet medical need, business impact and future potential were directly assessed by the group using ratio scaling techniques with balance-beam (Watson and Buede 1987) consistency checks.

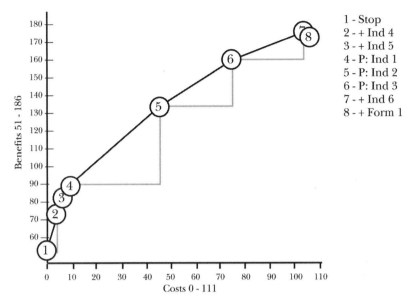

Figure 19.5. Cumulative risk-adjusted benefits versus total costs for project A (weighted preference values).

The group turned next to assessing swing weights on the five benefit criteria scales, thereby equating the units of value across the criteria (Clemen and Reilly 2001; Goodwin and Wright 2003). This important step circumvented judgments of "absolute importance" for the criteria by posing questions that elicited value trade-offs.

With scoring and weighting completed, the computer program calculated a single risk-adjusted benefit and single forward cost for each strategy. Dividing the risk-adjusted benefit by the cost resulted in the priority index for each strategy, the recommended basis for resource allocation in cost-benefit analysis (HM Treasury 2003) and corporate finance (Brealey, Myers, and Marcus 1995). As I have noted elsewhere (Phillips and Bana e Costa 2007), this simple criterion is rarely used by organizations, yet it is easy to demonstrate that any other basis for prioritization will not identify the best value-for-money portfolio.

The computer reordered the team's strategies for each project in value-for-money order; that is the order shown in Figure 19.5, with value-for-money after level 1 declining up the tower. A plot of the cumulative risk-adjusted benefit versus cumulative total cost is shown in Figure 19.5. Note that two new strategies, Ind 4 and Ind 5 fall in highest-priority position, ahead of indications 1, 2, and 3, the current plan. This is a typical result when a team prioritizes for the first time on the basis of value-for-money; current strategies are lower priority than things they are not now doing, a finding which usually leads the team to pause and rethink their current strategies.

When the teams were satisfied with their work, it was submitted to a review panel of vice presidents who checked the scores for realism and consistency. Any

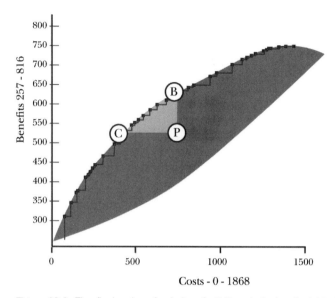

Figure 19.6. The final order of priority of all the strategies (weighted preference values). P represents the overall risk-adjusted benefit and cost of the current portfolio, B is a better portfolio at the same cost, and C is a less costly portfolio at the same benefit.

discrepancies were referred back to the team leader for revision. Final versions were collected into a briefing pack that was sent to all participants in the final Merge Meeting.

The main technical task for the Merge Meeting was to bring together all the work of the individual teams to form a single Order of Priority, or efficient frontier. To do this, participants engaged in a process of assessing swing weights, whose value trade-offs established scale constants between the projects and across the criteria, a double-weighting system that overrode the across-criteria weights assessed by each team. The result is an efficient frontier, shown in Figure 19.6 with each point representing another strategy.

The shaded area shows the locus of all possible portfolios, formed by all combinations of the strategies, in this case, more than 1 billion possibilities. Point P shows the current portfolio, although B and C are better and less costly portfolios, respectively. The lighter shaded area defines the locus of all portfolios that are better than the current one. Participants were keen to see the composition of point B, which is shown in Figure 19.4 as all strategies up to the bold line for each Project. Note that closing down Project J was recommended. This led the team to rethink their approach of wrapping up five indications into one strategy. It would have been better to disaggregate this strategy and let the prioritization process select the best indications to take forward, as most of the other project teams had done. Some modifications to their approach were later agreed.

Another finding that surprised the group was the apparent imbalance in the portfolio: five current strategies fell outside the Better portfolio, and 27 new projects were included within it, a result that is not uncommon in larger organizations whose decisions are taken on a project-by-project basis rather than at the portfolio level, which requires trade-offs to be judged between projects. Trade-off analysis on the completed MCDA model brought this point home. Indication 4 for Project E was considered by many participants to be essential, that it could not be dropped. A trade-off analysis brought Indication 4 into the Better portfolio, but then showed what strategies in the portfolio would have to be forgone in order to pay for Indication 4. Because that strategy was expensive, many other projects would have to be dropped, and this, too, was considered unacceptable by the group. Clearly, this result was such a substantial deviation from the current position that it could not be adopted; too many commitments would have to be broken to stop current low-priority strategies to enable resources to be transferred to new high-priority strategies.

Other organizations, when confronted with such discrepancies, recognize that the model provides a strategic direction for them to move toward over a period of time. It may take several years for the higher value-for-money strategies to be adopted as the lower-values ones are dropped or allowed to perish. This evolutionary approach to change can be very successful, as has been demonstrated by Allergan in the movement over several years of their current portfolio toward the efficient frontier (Phillips and Bana e Costa 2007).

The reader may wonder why these two case studies show MCDA models and no decision trees or influence diagrams. The reason is that my clients over the past 25 years have brought issues that are more about the conflict of objectives than they were about risk and uncertainty. Perhaps this echoes, realistically or not, the finding of MacCrimmon and Wehrung (1986) in their study of more than 500 American and Canadian managers:

> Rather than taking the chances of potential loss, magnitude of loss, and exposure as fixed, the managers tended to adjust the risky situations to make them more attractive. Choices tend to be made only when further adjustment cannot be made.

Echoing this finding, Beach (1990) observed that

> ... probabilities mean little to decision makers and have surprisingly little impact on their decisions. Probability is of little concern because decision makers assume that their efforts to implement their decisions will be aimed, in large part, at *making* things happen. Controlling the future is what decision making really is about.

Often I find it necessary to explain to clients what we decision analysts assume: that expected utility is the only reliable guide to making coherent decisions, so if the future is uncertain, then some representation of uncertainty is necessary. Too often I find clients making decisions on the basis of judging the overall benefits of projects, ordering the projects from best to worst, then allocating resources down the list until the budget is consumed, an approach that is guaranteed to fail the value-for-money test. So, although the vast majority of my clients' models are based on MCDA, most of them also provide means for risk-adjusting the benefits.

The Foundations

Is all the above simply a collection of ad hoc methods, or is there some theoretical foundation on which decision conferencing is built? My belief is the latter, and this section presents the theories that inform decision conferencing practice.

Requisite Decision Models

Years ago, when clients told me how valuable the decision conference was even though they implemented something different, I recognized the need for a new class of models. The model whose recommendations were not followed did not prescribe optimal behavior or describe actual subsequent behavior, nor could the model be considered as satisficing, in the sense of identifying an option that meets aspiration levels (Simon 1955). Immersing myself in the literature on modeling, I came to the conclusion that the models developed in decision conferences are "good enough" models, which I called "requisite" (Phillips 1982, 1984). They differ from operations research models in their definition, generation, process of construction, criterion for "good enough," and what they represent.

First, I define a requisite model as one that is sufficient in form and content to resolve the issues at hand. The key issue may not be a decision. More typically, it is the failure to agree, a conflict of objectives, which moves the modeling in the direction of MCDA. Second, the generation of a requisite model is through the iterative and consultative interaction among key players and specialists, facilitated by an impartial decision analyst, with all the main perspectives on the issues represented by participants in the decision conference. Third, the process of creating a requisite model uses participants' sense of unease about model results. The facilitator can encourage participants to express their discomfort or unease, even if they don't know why they feel it. Exploration of the discrepancy between holistic judgment and the model's results links people's emotional and deliberative systems (Kahneman 2002), helping them to access their experience and knowledge, make it explicit and work on it with the help of the group.

Fourth, at what point is a model requisite? After considerable work on this issue, with the help of Elliott Jaques, I realized that it is when no new intuitions arise in the group. At that point the sense of unease has largely disappeared and the dialectic in the group has ceased. It is then usually possible to summarize the shared understanding of the group, and gain commitment to the next steps. But this doesn't always happen. In working for one organization, three two-day decision conferences over three years on top-level strategy threw up recommendations that the Chief Executive Officer found unpalatable. Only after the third meeting did he finally understand why; it was a fundamental error in the initial framing of the problem that he felt would become invalid within just a few years. He then said he now felt comfortable with a new way forward for the organization, which within a few years proved to be absolutely right.

Finally, what does a requisite model represent? Unlike models in the physical and natural sciences, this model represents the shared understanding of the participants in the decision conference. Interestingly, the model participates in the reality it creates, a feature that gave me some trouble until I found that it is justified from a philosophical perspective because the source of the model, decision theory, is different from the source of its content.

A requisite model is at best conditionally prescriptive; it suggests what could be done given the frame, assumptions, data, and judgments. Its purpose is to help decision makers to construct a new reality, one that more effectively achieves their objectives. Given the temptation for decision analysts to construct beautiful, all-encompassing models, requisite modeling imposes a discipline that clients appreciate. All these issues are elaborated elsewhere (e.g., Phillips 1984).

Process Consultancy

The dual role of academic and practicing decision analyst imposed on me a stance to my clients that I soon found was not at all helpful: I knew what was best for them. Decision theory can easily be seen as a prescriptive science: if you believe this, this, and that, then you are obliged to accept the course of action associated with the highest expected utility. If you don't, then the model is incomplete, so we must go back and fix it. This is the "doctor–patient" model of consultancy, once again. In the concluding personal note in his book on process consultation, Schein (1999) eschews the selling of products, programs, diagnoses and recommendations in favor of a helping relationship with the client. He says:

> ... help will not happen until the right kind of relationship has been built with the various levels of clients we may have to deal with, and ... the building of such a relationship takes time and requires a certain kind of attitude from the helper.

Although the "doctor–patient model" is appropriate in some instances, I have found greater success with the process consultancy approach. Schein has said it all better than I can, so I recommend in particular his ten principles of process consultation, well described in the first three chapters of his book – which is essential reading for my students.

Group Processes

Before turning to the topic of facilitating decision conferences, a few words about my views on group processes are required. I have been fortunate to study group processes at the Tavistock Institute of Human Relations whose research on group processes extends back to World War II. At that time, many returning service men and women were in need of psychological help with the traumas they had experienced. As there were insufficient numbers of trained clinicians, the Tavistock adopted group therapy instead of one-on-one help. It soon became evident that quite apart from the healing effect, group processes themselves were being revealed. This led to the study of group processes in experiential courses, where temporary learning communities form and reform, conducted in the "here-and-now" with people drawn from all walks of organizational life, helped by consultants who are specialists in group processes. Much of this work has now been summarized in an anthology of readings, *The Social Engagement of Social Science* (Trist and Murray 1990).

From this work, and my experience in decision conferences, I take the view of groups as similar to individuals in that the group has a personality, a character and an emotional life. It does not, of course, have a memory. But as individuals in the group take on roles, they find that they shape the group's personality, which then has an impact on the group. In other words, there is a reflexive interplay, not a cause-and-effect one, between the individual and the group. A common experience of individuals in a group is a disjunction between individual feelings and the group life, which can lead to anxiety.

Mature, productive groups acknowledge the anxiety, tolerate it, and hold it, enabling them to get on with the primary task of the group. But often the anxiety remains hidden, and then, just below the surface, the group shifts its emphasis away from working on the task and instead attempts to deal with the anxiety, a covert "basic assumption" that diverts the group from the overt task as they work on dealing with the anxiety. So far, research has identified five common diversions: fighting with each other or the facilitator, pairing of two people who the group expects will protect the group's security, becoming dependent on an individual in the group or on the facilitator to "save" the group, developing an intense sense of belongingness, and acting as if the individual is the only reality (Bion 1961; Lawrence 1996). This wholly inadequate summary belies the power of these basic assumptions, which take hold of a group as it attempts to deal with the anxiety created by the complexity, uncertainty, and conflicting objectives of the primary task.

Facilitation Skills

What can the facilitator do to keep the group task focused when such powerful forces under the surface are diverting the group? The key is to focus on the group, not on individuals, and understand the group life (Phillips and Phillips 1993). This can be done in four ways. First, by observing verbal and nonverbal behavior, particularly the latter, for it contains clues to what is happening in the group beneath the surface. Second, by observing roles and role relationships. Participants often speak from their roles, and relate to each other not so much as individuals, but in their roles. The scientist argues with the marketer, thus bringing to the table perspectives derived from their roles. Third, by making inferences based on overt and symbolic content of group discussion. "What is this group really talking about when it constantly refers to the inadequacy of its absent leader?" Perhaps it is their own inability to work on strategy, the topic assigned them by the leader, because they don't know what strategy is. Fourth, and most important, by monitoring one's own feelings, the only route to becoming a self-aware, impartial observer. Attempting to become the scientific, detached facilitator is doomed to fail, for we are empathic creatures, and turning off our feelings while facilitating a group is bound to impose them on the group. This will be sensed by the group, and the facilitator's impartiality will be compromised along with his or her effectiveness in this role.

Only when facilitators feel they have a reasonable grasp of the group life, is it possible to intervene to help the group. Content interventions must be carefully judged, for contributing to content can interfere with effective work if the group feels the facilitator is attempting to impose his or her views. Contributing content can leave the group feeling de-skilled, or encourage it to become dependent on the facilitator, who may have been tempted into contributing content if the group is working on the basis assumption of dependency. Content delivered by the facilitator can hinder the group's ownership of results and impede implementation, as so often happens in "doctor–patient" consultancy. Interpretations of group or individual behavior are very inadvisable; they anger participants and can exacerbate basic assumption behavior.

When it is appropriate, several forms of intervention are available to the facilitator. *Pacing the task* helps the group to achieve their objectives within the two days of the decision conference. *Directing* the group down paths that the facilitator's experience suggest will be more productive avoids dead end discussions, though any resistance from the group must be faced, with the facilitator ready to work with the group to choose a different path. *Handing back in changed form* is one of the most powerful interventions. It consists of taking in information and drawing a logical conclusion that is presented to the group, who now see the situation in a different light. In one sense, that is what the decision model does; it reassembles the pieces and shows the results, allowing new properties to emerge. *Reflecting back* to the group, perhaps in different words, "You seem to be saying such-and-such," is less powerful, but particularly effective in the early stages of a decision conference. Finally, *questioning* and *summarizing* are both interventions that help a group to conceptualize their work in useful ways.

Although numerous books have been written on the topic of facilitation, many are little more than a collection of techniques. For mature adults, these techniques can often seem childish, and distracting of the real work. I have found it more helpful to deepen my understanding of group processes, a never-ending task, and to find ways of helping that feel comfortable for me. By spending time developing self-awareness, using one's feelings as data while working with a group, and reflecting later on the group experience, consultants can find their own ways of becoming effective facilitators. One size does not fit all. *The Skilled Facilitator* is one of the better guides to good facilitation (Schwarz 2002).

Do Decision Conferences Work?

Evidence for the effectiveness and limitations of decision conferences exists in two sources: case studies and systematic research. As examples of the many published case studies, decision conferencing has been used in many public sector cases: to help the Bank of England relocate its Registrar's Department outside London to reduce operational costs (Butterworth 1989), to help the UK's National Radiological Protection Board develop guidance on relocating the public in the event of a release of radioactivity (Aumônier and French 1992), to various issues faced by the US Department of Defense (Bresnick, Buede, Pisani, Smith, and Wood 1997; Buede and Bresnick 1992), to manage cuts in the budget of the Bedford-shire Police Force in the late 1990s (Holbourn 1998), and to assist water resource planning in South Africa (Stewart 2003). Carlos Bana e Costa is a prolific user of decision conferences in the public sector, where he has tackled problems such as the resolution of conflicts (Bana e Costa, Silva, and Vansnick 2001), bid eval-uation (Bana e Costa, Correa, De Corte, and Vansnick 2002) and evaluation of flood control measures (Bana e Costa, Da Silva, and Correia 2004).

Private sector applications include the use of decision conferences to evaluate alternative ways of replacing or upgrading ageing production facilities (Phillips 1986), to help participants develop more effective strategies for dealing with a strike-prone factory (Wooler and Barclay 1988), to develop better advertising, promotion, and distribution strategies (Phillips 1989), to allocate resources across different sales outlets (Phillips 1990), and for evaluating and prioritizing projects and creating portfolios in the pharmaceutical industry (Charlish and Phillips 1995).

Sustained working with clients using decision conferences characterized the development of long-term environmental planning in Hungary (Vari and Rohr-baugh 1996), and to assist the Social Services Department of Dudley Metropolitan Borough Council to produce a range of budgets that officers felt they could deliver (Morgan 1993). Although these studies convey the flavor and scope of applications of decision conferences, they are a small sample of the thousands of real-world applications. Apparently, decision conference facilitators are too engaged in their work to write it up for publication.

On the research side, McCartt and Rohrbaugh (1995) studied twenty-six deci-sion conferences held mainly in the public sector. Those rated more beneficial were smaller, hosted by organizations more open to change, and agreed on more decisions. In a study of twenty-two decision conferences in the US and UK, Chun (1992) found that decision conferences were consistently rated higher than ordi-nary meetings on all of the twelve criteria measuring the effectiveness of deci-sion processes, overall attitudes toward the system, and decision qualities. He also showed systematic differences between the three facilitators in the study on those twelve criteria, though the effects are not strong, and are compounded with other variables. The perceived effectiveness of decision conferences was greater at senior executive level, than at lower levels in the organizations. Effectiveness was greater for smaller groups (four to eight participants) than for medium-sized (nine to eleven participants) or large groups (fifteen to eighteen participants), but an interaction with the facilitator was also observed.

An important insight into why decision conferences work so well is seen in the work of Regan-Cirincione (1994). She found that small, interacting, facili-tated groups performed significantly better than even the most capable members in the groups, contrary to the findings of much research in social psychology that indicated that groups rarely outperform their best members. She traced the improved performance to the integration of three factors: group facilitation, decision modeling, and information technology. The improved performance of the group appears to be the result of participating in the discussion and receiving feedback from others and from the projected model, and from the help of the facilitator in providing structure to the discussion without contributing to the content. It is reassuring to see systematic research providing support for processes developed through observation and experience on decision conferences.

The Big Picture

Since its birth in 1979, the decision conference has become a well-proven approach to engaging a client in a helping relationship. It combines social processes with technical modeling, creating a sociotechnical approach to problem solving that benefits from skilled and impartial facilitation of the group, on-the-spot modeling and application of information technology. The social process provides an implicit agenda: state and agree the meeting's objectives, discuss the issues, build a model, explore the results, and agree on the way forward, with considerable iteration of those stages. Modeling provides a tool to aid thinking, not to give an optimal solution or "the right answer." The model provides a language, which identifies the key elements, and a grammar, which shows how the elements combine. Creating the model provokes thoughtful discourse from participants as they formulate the inputs and interpret the results. The model also polices coherence, revealing inconsistencies in data or judgments, which are then dealt with in the social process as participants explore discrepancies. Overall, the decision conference provides a forum for participants to engage constructively with each other, structuring and focusing the conversation without constraining it. It improves communication across disparate parts of the organization, stimulates creative thinking and improves team-working. Overall, it generates smarter, defensible decisions. Just what the Westinghouse team found, though now we understand why this process-consultancy, helping approach works where more prescriptive approaches have been less successful: *decision conferencing* ensures that the client continues to own the problem and the solution.

REFERENCES

Ascher, K., and Nare, B. (1990). Strategic planning in the public sector. In D. E. Hussey (Ed.), *International Review of Strategic Management, Vol. 1.* Chichester: John Wiley & Sons.

Aumônier, S., and French, S. (1992). Decision conference on emergency reference levels for relocation. *Radiological Protection Bulletin, 133.*

Bana e Costa, C. A., Correa, E. C., De Corte, J.-M., and Vansnick, J.-C. (2002). Facilitating bid evaluation in public call for tenders: A socio-technical approach. *Omega,* 30, 227–242.

Bana e Costa, C. A., Da Silva, P. A., and Correia, F. N. (2004). Multicriteria evaluation of flood control measures: The case of Ribeira do Livramento. *Water Resources Management, 18,* 263–283.

Bana e Costa, C. A., Silva, F. N. d., and Vansnick, J.-C. (2001). Conflict dissolution in the public sector: A case-study. *European Journal of Operational Research, 130*(2), 388–401.

Beach, L. R. (1990). *Image Theory: Decision Making in Personal and Organizational Contexts*. Chichester, UK: John Wiley & Sons.

Bernardo, J. M., and Smith, A. F. M. (1994). *Bayesian Theory*. Chichester, UK: John Wiley & Sons.

Bion, W. R. (1961). *Experiences in Groups*. London: Tavistock Publications.

Brealey, R. A., Myers, S. C., and Marcus, A. J. (1995). *Fundamentals of Corporate Finance*. New York: McGraw Hill.

Bresnick, T. A., Buede, D. M., Pisani, A. A., Smith, L. L., and Wood, B. B. (1997). Airborne and space-borne reconnaissance force mixes: A decision analysis approach. *Military Operations Research, 3*(4), 65–78.

Buede, D. M., and Bresnick, T. A. (1992). Applications of decision analysis to the military systems acquisition process. *Interfaces, 22*(6), 110–125.

Butterworth, N. J. (1989). Giving up 'The Smoke': A major institution investigates alternatives to being sited in the city. *Journal of the Operational Research Society, 40*(8), 711–717.

Charlish, P., and Phillips, L. D. (1995). Prioritizing projects and creating portfolios. *Executive Briefing, 16*, 33–36.

Chun, K.-J. (1992). *Analysis of Decision Conferencing: A UK/USA Comparison*. London: London School of Economics and Political Science.

Clemen, R. T., and Reilly, T. (2001). *Making Hard Decisions with Decision Tools*. Duxbury Thompson Learning.

Gergen, K. J. (1993). *Toward Transformation in Social Knowledge,* 2nd ed. London: Sage.

Goodwin, P., and Wright, G. (2003). *Decision Analysis for Management Judgment*, 3rd ed. Chichester: John Wiley & Sons.

Hardin, G. (1968). The tragedy of the commons. *Science, 162*, 1243–1248.

Hickling, A. (1990). Decision spaces: A scenario about designing appropriate rooms for 'activity-based' decision management. In C. Eden and J. Radford (Eds.), *Tackling Strategic Problems: The Role of Group Decision Support*. London: Sage, pp. 167–177.

HM Treasury. (2003). *The Green Book: Appraisal and Evaluation in Central Government*. London: The Stationery Office.

Holbourn, M. (1998). Decision conferencing – a tool for budget allocation. *Focus on Police Research and Development, May 1998*(10), 22–23.

Jaques, E. (1998). *Requisite Organisation: A Total System for Effective Managerial Organization and Managerial Leadership for the 21st Century*. Arlington, VA: Cason Hall.

Kahneman, D. (2002). *Maps of bounded rationality: A perspective on intuitive judgment and choice*. The Nobel Foundation. Retrieved December 8, 2002, from the World Wide Web.

Keeney, R. L. (1992). *Value-Focused Thinking: A Path to Creative Decisionmaking*. Cambridge, MA: Harvard University Press.

Keeney, R. L., and Raiffa, H. (1976). *Decisions with Multiple Objectives: Preferences and Value Tradeoffs*. New York: John Wiley.

Lawrence, G. (1996). The fifth basic assumption. *Free Associations, 6*(1), No. 37, 28–55.

MacCrimmon, K., and Wehrung, D. (1986). *Taking Risks: The Management of Uncertainty*. London: Collier Macmillan.

Matheson, D., and Matheson, J. (1998). *The Smart Organization: Creating Value through Strategic R&D*. Boston, MA: Harvard Business School Press.

McCartt, A. T., and Rohrbaugh, J. (1995). Managerial openness to change and the introduction of GDSS: Explaining initial success and failure in decision conferencing. *Organization Science, 6*(5), 569–584.

Morgan, T. (1993). Phased decision conferencing. *OR Insight, 6*, 3–12.

Phillips, L. D. (1982). Requisite decision modelling: A case study. *Journal of the Operational Research Society, 33*, 303–311.

Phillips, L. D. (1984). A theory of requisite decision models. *Acta Psychologica, 56*, 29–48.

Phillips, L. D. (1986). Decision analysis and its applications in industry. In G. Mitra (Ed.), *Computer Assisted Decision Making*. Amsterdam: Elsevier Science Publishers.

Phillips, L. D. (1989). People-centred group decision support. In G. Doukidis, F. Land, and G. Miller (Eds.), *Knowledge-Based Management Support Systems*. Chichester, UK: Ellis Horwood.

Phillips, L. D. (1990). Requisite decision modelling for technological projects. In C. Vlek and G. Cvetkovich (Eds.), *Social Decision Methodology for Technological Projects*. Dordrecht, Netherlands: Kluwer Academic Publishers, pp. 95–110.

Phillips, L. D., and Bana e Costa, C. (2007). Transparent prioritisation, budgeting and resource allocation with multi-criteria decision analysis and decision conferencing. *Annals of Operations Research*, in press.

Phillips, L. D., and Phillips, M. C. (1993). Facilitated work groups: Theory and practice. *Journal of the Operational Research Society, 44*(6), 533–549.

Regan-Cirincione, P. (1994). Improving the accuracy of group judgment: A process intervention combining group facilitation, social judgment analysis, and information technology. *Organizational Behavior and Human Decision Processes, 58*, 246–270.

RIIA. (1927). Royal Institute of International Affairs. Retrieved, from the World Wide Web, on February 3, 2007: http://www.chathamhouse.org.uk/

Schein, E. H. (1999). *Process Consultation Revisited: Building the Helping Relationship*. Reading, MA: Addison-Wesley.

Schwarz, R. (2002). *The Skilled Facilitator: A Comprehensive Resource for Consultants, Facilitators, Managers, Trainers and Coaches*. San Francisco: Jossey-Bass.

Simon, H. A. (1955). A behavioral model of rational choice. *Quarterly Journal of Economics, 69*, 99–118.

Stewart, T. J. (2003). Thirsting for consensus: Multicriteria decision analysis helps clarify water resources planning in South Africa. *OR/MS Today, 30*(2), 30–34.

Trist, E., and Murray, H. (Eds.). (1990). *The Social Engagement of Social Science: A Tavistock Anthology* (Vol. I: The Socio-Psychological Perspective). London: Free Association Books.

Vari, A., and Rorhbaugh, J. (1996). Decision conferencing GDSS in environmental policy making: developing a long-term environmental plan in Hungary. *Risk Decision and Policy, 1*(1), 71–89.

Watson, S. R., and Buede, D. M. (1987). *Decision Synthesis*. Chichester, UK: John Wiley & Sons.

Wooler, S., and Barclay, S. (1988). Strategy for reducing dependence on a strike-prone production facility. In P. Humphreys and A. Vari and J. Vecsenyi and O. Larichev (Eds.), *Strategic Decision Support*, Amsterdam: North Holland.

20 Resource Allocation Decisions

Don N. Kleinmuntz

ABSTRACT. Organizations typically have more good ideas for projects than they have resources available to pursue those ideas. Decision analysis can provide practical guidance to the organization on how to get the maximum benefit from those limited resources. This chapter reviews methods for prioritizing projects using mathematical optimization or benefit-cost ratios in concert with standard decision-analysis and risk-analysis tools. These tools include multiattribute utility and value models, decision trees, influence diagrams, and Monte Carlo simulation. To illustrate issues that arise in implementing these approaches in organizations, the use of resource allocation models in hospital capital budgeting is described at length. The chapter concludes with a call for more research on the use of decision analysis in organizational settings.

The Challenge of Organizational Resource Allocation

What universal dilemma is confronted by organizations of every size, type, and purpose? Stated simply, they have more good ideas for projects, programs, and investments than they have resources available to pursue those ideas. These ideas include facilities expansion or construction, new equipment, innovative manufacturing or service delivery technologies, and information technology upgrades. In addition, many organizations engage in research and development efforts that require identifying the most promising new products, technologies, or process improvements.

Often, the limiting resource is financial because an organization's capacity to borrow funds or raise equity capital has practical limits. There also may be insufficient facility capacity, or not enough time to pursue every idea. In other instances, specialized skills or expertise are the limiting factor. An important example of limited expertise occurs when executives lack the time to oversee the implementation of too many projects. Whatever the resource limitations, the implication is that projects cannot be considered in isolation. Choosing one project implies that fewer resources will remain for the rest. As a consequence, poor choices lead to high opportunity costs as the organization squanders scarce resources.

Most organizations engage in some type of regular capital budgeting or project portfolio selection process. Plans are evaluated and decisions made about which projects to pursue and which to either reject or postpone. Although these processes are as varied as the organizations that pursue them, there are common elements shared across many settings: First, the lists of plans and proposals are dauntingly long, measured in the dozens, hundreds, or even thousands, depending on organization size. Second, no one person can possibly have a complete under-standing of each and every project, with relevant information spread across many individuals. Finally, there is the ever-present temptation for organizational stake-holders to scramble to exert influence to secure resources for favorite projects. In part, this reflects the narrow pursuit of self-interest. All too often, however, not even top-level decision makers have a clear picture of which projects are in their organization's best interest, and this confusion leads to uncertainty and conflict.

Given these challenges, there is a clear role for analytical tools and processes to improve organizational resource allocation. The purpose of this chapter is to provide an overview of decision analysis approaches to resource allocation and an extended description of the use of resource allocation methods in a particular setting, capital budgeting in U.S. not-for-profit hospitals. Rather than attempting a comprehensive review of resource allocation applications, I have tried to provide representative examples. Additional applications are reviewed by Corner and Kirkwood (1991) and by Keefer, Kirkwood, and Corner (2002, 2004).

The remainder of the chapter is organized as follows: First, a mathematical optimization framework for resource allocation is introduced. This is followed by a description of two categories of decision analysis models that are used in concert with the optimization framework: Multiattribute utility and value models are used in situations where project benefits are defined over multiple objectives, and deci-sion trees, influence diagrams, and Monte Carlo simulations are used where there are significant uncertainties regarding project benefits and costs. Next, I describe implementation of resource allocation models in hospital capital budgeting and discuss some issues that arise in practice. I conclude with a call for more research on the organizational implementation of decision analysis models and methods.

Capital Allocation Using Mathematical Optimization

Financially oriented capital budgeting approaches are well developed and have been described in many texts and references (see, for example, Bierman and Smidt 1993; Brealey and Myers 1996; Canada, Sullivan, and White 1996; Lang and Merino 1993; Luenberger 1998). The classic financial approach uses dis-counted cash flows to evaluate projects, based on forecasts of incremental cash flows required to acquire, operate, and then dispose of each plan or project. The cash-flow forecasts are almost always presented as point estimates, although they may be based on extremely detailed deterministic financial models.

Because financial benefits accrue over some period of time, they are almost always measured using a net present value calculation. In most business settings, the discount rate used in this calculation represents the average amount that the organization must pay to obtain funds (i.e., the opportunity cost associated with making the investment). If an organization has no limit on its ability to obtain capital and is concerned only with financial return, then it should accept any project with a positive net present value. However, with limited access to capital, there is a problem of capital rationing: the organization wishes to obtain as much benefit as possible while spending no more than the available amount of capital. This is readily modeled with a binary integer programming formulation (for an early discussion, see Weingartner 1963).

The formulation is not complicated: suppose an organization is considering a set of m proposed capital expenditures, and the only decisions to be made are with regards to funding ("yes" or "no") for each project. Let c_i denote the cost to develop the project ($c_i > 0$ for $i = 1$ to m).[1] Let b_i denote the net present value of project benefits ($b_i > 0$ for $i = 1$ to m). Let x_i represent a binary decision variable for each project ($x_i = 0$ or 1 for all i). Finally, let C denote the budgeted amount available to fund project costs. The objective is to maximize aggregate benefits while staying within the budget constraint:

$$\text{maximize} \sum_{i=1}^{m} b_i x_i$$

subject to

$$\sum_{i=1}^{m} c_i x_i \leq C$$
$$x_i = (0 \text{ or } 1), i = 1, \ldots, m.$$

This model assumes that neither benefits nor costs of a project depend on which other projects are selected, with the implication that both benefits and costs are additive. Solution techniques and optimization software for solving these models are readily available, and are described in most operations research textbooks (e.g., Hillier and Lieberman 2005).

An intuitively appealing alternative to optimization is to rank projects using *benefit-cost ratios* (b_i/c_i) or the closely related *profitability index* ($(b_i - c_i)/c_i$). Projects are prioritized by selecting the highest-ratio projects until funds are exhausted. This approach produces the highest value for the amount spent, but may not spend all available funds. If there are less costly projects with nearly the same ratio values as the last projects funded, then substituting these may produce higher aggregate benefit. However, in practical settings, sorting on benefit–cost ratios often produces a reasonable heuristic solution with only a small deviation from the aggregate benefit achievable through optimization.

One advantage to mathematical programming formulations are that they can be readily extended to allow for additional resource limitations or project dependencies that arise with large, complex projects. For instance, the organization might consider projects requiring funds over multiple time periods, with limited funds available for each period. Extending the formulation requires an additional budget constraint for each time period. Similarly, accounting for other limited resources (e.g., human resources or suitable facilities) is accomplished by adding constraints to enforce those limitations.

A form of project dependency that arises in many settings is mutual exclusivity of project choices. For instance, when considering alternative versions of the same

---

[1] For simplicity of exposition, assume that all project expenditures take place in one year, and that the organization only considers capital allocation one fiscal year at a time.

project, choice is restricted to at most one version of the project. Suppose the set S represents a subset of projects that are mutually exclusive ($S \subset \{1, \ldots, m\}$). A constraint of the form $\sum_{i \in S} x_i \leq 1$ permits selection of no more than one project from the set of mutually exclusive projects, with the possibility that none would be selected. A constraint of the form $\sum_{i \in S} x_i = 1$ requires selection of exactly one project from the set.

In other instances, projects are contingent, meaning that one project can be chosen only when a second project is also selected. An example is a computer software purchase that is only feasible if necessary computer hardware components are acquired simultaneously. If project i is contingent on project k, then the constraint would be $x_i - x_k \leq 0$. If projects are mutually contingent, then one can be chosen if and only if the other is chosen, requiring a strict equality constraint: $x_i - x_k = 0$.

Sometimes, it is convenient to treat contingent projects as a single project with combined costs and benefits. However, unless there is mutual contingency, this requires introducing mutual exclusivity, to allow for scenarios where one wishes to acquire one project but not the other. For instance, when considering constructing a new office building, one might consider a new parking garage as contingent on the construction of the offices, if the garage would have no useful purpose without the new offices. Alternatively, one could consider "office building" versus "office building plus garage" as mutually exclusive projects if this will make the assessment of benefits and costs more convenient.

Almost any of these extensions to the basic model renders the use of benefit–cost ratios problematic. For instance, with multiple resource constraints, it is not clear which resource to use as the denominator in the benefit–cost ratio because one cannot know in advance which will be the limiting resource. Further, as dependency constraints become more numerous, sorting on ratios is unlikely to produce a solution consistent with all the constraints. Under these circumstances, mathematical optimization is the only practical approach.

One context where mathematical optimization has been used extensively is the analysis of U.S. military procurement decisions, such as the acquisition of military weapons systems. Brown, Dell, and Newman (2004) provide an excellent overview and key references. These decisions routinely involve allocating billions or trillions of dollars over years or decades. According to Brown and colleagues, a number of modeling "embellishments" are essential to capture the realities of the setting: (1) Decision variables involve both whether to acquire a particular weapons system, and, if the system is acquired, the number of units required. (2) Both benefits and costs may be nonlinear in the number of units procured, usually modeled using piecewise linear functions. (3) Certain funds may be restricted as to when they may be spent and what they may be spent on, requiring constraints for different "flavors" of money. (4) Project benefits from multiple systems are greater (or less) than the sum of the parts, requiring multiplicative interaction terms in the benefit functions. (5) Budgets must allow for many years between acquisition, development, and deployment of a system, requiring a series of constraints to reflect these dynamics. (6) Other dynamic consideration include both year-by-year and cumulative resource limitations, overhaul and retirement decisions for older equipment, and mission-related requirements for either sequential or concurrent availability of specific weapon systems. One consequence of these complications is that models may have thousands of decision variables and constraints. Solutions, therefore, require a combination of serious computing power and ingenuity in both model formulation and computational methods.

Measuring Project Benefits Using Multiattribute Value Models

One of the most obvious differences between military procurement and business settings is the way in which project benefits are measured. In for-profit business entities, discounted net present value is generally considered the "gold standard" metric. Because the organization's fundamental objective is generally regarded as maximizing the value of the owners' investment, in the world of corporate finance, this metric has both a clear theoretical rationale and practical relevance. However, in government and not-for-profit entities, the organization's objectives are not exclusively focused on financial value.

Multiattribute utility and value models provide a methodology for evaluating project and program benefits in light of multiple conflicting objectives (Keeney 1992; Keeney and Raiffa 1976). An early application of multiattribute value models to resource allocation is reported by Golabi, Kirkwood, and Sicherman (1981). They propose an optimization framework identical to the one described above, except that project benefits are assessed using multiple evaluation criteria. Golabi and colleagues propose the application of this methodology to government procurement, and describe using it to assist the U.S. Department of Energy in selecting a portfolio of solar energy application experiments.

In particular, they propose using a linear-additive multiattribute value function. Suppose there are n *evaluation attributes* (denoted y_{ij} for project $i = 1$ to m and evaluation attribute $j = 1$ to n). The benefit measure is a *weighted value score* (denoted b_i^* for project i), a weighted average of the benefit assessed on each attribute:

$$b_i^* = \sum_{j=1}^{n} w_j v_j(y_{ij}).$$

Each function $v_j(\cdot)$ is a single-dimensional *measurable value function* (also known as an ordinal utility function) that represents a decision maker's preference for performance differences on a single attribute, scaled to a standard range (e.g., from 0 to 1). The w_j parameters are weights that capture a decision maker's assessment of the relative importance of the evaluation attributes over the range of values observed for the particular set of candidate projects, typically scaled to sum to 1.

Applying this approach to project portfolios requires the usual preference independence assumption for the linear-additive form of the value function (see also Keeney and Raiffa 1976), and additional assumptions to obtain additivity of project values across the portfolio. The latter assumptions permit project benefits to be measured one project at a time, which simplifies the application of the method significantly. Although Golabi and colleagues carefully tested and examined the validity of the independence and additivity assumptions, most applications simply apply linear additive project scoring methods without rigorous testing. These can be ad hoc scoring systems or simplified multiattribute value models familiar to many decision analysts, such as SMARTS, the Simple Multiattribute Rating Technique using Swings (see Edwards and Barron 1994; see also Clemen 1996, chapter 15; or Kirkwood 1997, chapter 4). The project scores are then used to prioritize and select projects, either using integer programming or benefit-cost ratios. The optimization formulation is the one described above, except that weighted value scores (b_i^*) replace financial benefit measures (b_i). Net present value (or some other financial metric) is not neglected, but rather, is often included as an attribute.

This approach has been widely applied to public programs and policy issues (e.g., analyzing alternative technologies for military programs, Burk and Parnell 1997; Parnell, Conley, Jackson, Lehmkuhl and Andrew 1998). However, these methods are not only for public sector applications. A case can be made for applying them in for-profit organizations, where exclusive reliance on financial metrics for enterprise performance can lead to neglect of other relevant strategic considerations (Kaplan and Norton 1996; Keeney 1999; Keeney and McDaniels 1999). In these settings, resource allocation models can help to connect strategic issues with decisions about specific portfolios of projects and plans. Multiattribute value models provide a template for a sound and efficient resource allocation process that considers the full range of organizational objectives, including objectives that are not suitably evaluated using standard financial metrics.

The use of multiattribute approaches is particularly appropriate for resource allocation in private, not-for-profit enterprises, where there are clearly multiple objectives at work. These not-for-profit organizations combine the need for financial discipline typical of for-profit enterprises with the rich set of mission-related objectives found in government and military settings. A multiattribute value model provides a direct means for the organization to consider trade-offs between financial and nonfinancial objectives, often a crucial concern. For instance, Kleinmuntz and Kleinmuntz (1999) describe the use of multiattribute value models to allocate capital resources in not-for-profit hospitals. The method closely follows the multiattribute value modeling approach discussed above, using integer linear programming to identify the best portfolio of projects subject to resource limitations and other constraints. Practical considerations in using these models in hospital settings will be discussed at some length in the next-to-the-last section.

Resource Allocation with Uncertain Benefits and Costs

A significant concern in many settings is that projections of both project benefits and project costs are uncertain. In businesses, organizations often cope with this problem by "risk adjusting" the valuation of projects. They do this by calculating net present values using a discount rate that is higher for riskier projects and lower for less risky projects. Methods for selecting project-specific discount rates are discussed in corporate finance textbooks, but in practice, these risk adjustments usually amount to little more than subjective judgments about each project's perceived risk. This is potentially defensible as a heuristic approach when compared with the use of point estimates with no consideration of uncertainty. However, these perceived risk judgments are problematic from a normative decision perspective because they reflect an unsystematic assessment influenced by both the relevant probability distributions over outcomes as well as the organization's risk tolerance.

Most decision analysts avoid project-specific discount rates by implementing systematic models of project uncertainties using standard approaches (decision trees, influence diagrams, or Monte Carlo simulations) and applying a uniform discount rate for all projects. The remaining challenge, then, is to incorporate the resulting project risk profiles into the portfolio optimization. The most common approach is to assume that the organization is risk neutral over the relevant range of portfolio outcomes. Risk neutrality implies that only expected values of project benefits and costs are relevant, and that the objective is to maximize expected benefits subject to resource and other constraints. Therefore, expected values replace deterministic forecasts when using either benefit-cost ratios or mathematical optimization for prioritization.

A complicating issue arises if project resource expenditures are uncertain because portfolio solutions are no longer guaranteed to be within resource constraints. Solving for optimal portfolios with stochastic constraints is a rapidly developing research area, but the analytical and computational burdens can be considerable (see, for instance, Birge and Louveaux 1997). A widely used pragmatic alternative is to reserve a contingency allocation of the scarce resource sufficient to provide for potential overruns.

One area where decision analysis tools have been frequently applied is selection of research and development (R&D) projects, such as the development of new products, processes, or technologies. R&D project portfolios have been addressed using a wide variety of tools and methods (see review by Henrikson and Traynor 1999). Decision and risk analysis have been particularly successful because the uncertainties associated with an R&D project typically loom quite large. In the initial stages, there is considerable uncertainty regarding both the time and resources required to pursue the project, and technical success is a major risk factor. Conditional on meeting technical objectives at various stages, there are also significant uncertainties regarding the size and duration of realized benefits. Published examples of applications are provided by Bodily and Allen (1999), Matheson and Matheson (1998, 1999), Poland (1999), and Sharpe and Keelin (1998).

Another area where decision analysis has been fruitfully applied is in selection and management of portfolios of petroleum and natural gas producing assets. The uncertainty associated with oil exploration is quite familiar to decision analysts (Raiffa 1968). Walls (2004) reviews portfolio management issues that arise when considering a large number of exploration options. Skaf (1999) describes a comprehensive portfolio system that was implemented at a major oil and gas company to support management of both exploration activities and existing producing assets.

An active area for research and application in recent years has been combining financial options pricing tools with standard decision analysis tools (Perdue, McAllister, King and Berkey, 1999; Smith and McCardle 1998; Smith and Nau 1995). Most risky projects are not simply "go versus no-go" decisions because managers have flexibility to adapt and make subsequent decisions as a project develops over time (e.g., abandon if anticipated benefits do not materialize or expand if prospects improve). Both decision analysis and options pricing methods are capable of accounting for uncertainty and managerial flexibility when valuing projects. However, options pricing methods are based on the no-arbitrage theory of financial markets, whereas standard decision analysis methods do not distinguish between uncertainties associated with market-traded assets versus uncertainties unrelated to financial market prices. Although these methods have sometimes been positioned as competitors (Copeland and Antikarov 2005), the argument that they should be viewed as complements is compelling because projects often have uncertainties both with and without financial market equivalents (Borison 2005a, 2005b). Methods and tools for synthesizing the two approaches are not yet widely disseminated. This may be because they are unfamiliar to decision analysts or may be because they are challenging to implement in a fashion that is both rigorous and accessible (Brandão, Dyer and Hahn 2005a, 2005b; Smith 2005). The convergence of methods from decision analysis and financial engineering is an important and promising area for further research.

Another promising area for research is optimal resource allocation in the presence of risk aversion. Relaxing the assumption of risk neutrality greatly increases the complexity of resource allocation for two reasons: First, as a general rule, nonlinear preference functions imply that project benefits are no longer strictly additive because the incremental benefit of any single project depends on the aggregate benefits achieved by the rest of the portfolio. This requires shifting from linear to nonlinear programming formulations for optimization, which can be conceptually straight-forward but computationally challenging for larger portfolios. An exception applies if an assumption of constant risk aversion is plausible, in which case an exponential utility function can be used to compute certainty equivalents that account for risk tolerance without violating additivity. As a case in point, Walls, Morahan, and Dyer (1995) describe a decision support system that Phillips Petroleum Company implemented to analyze oil and gas exploration projects. The system gave the user the ability to model uncertainties for individual projects and compute certainty equivalents based on an exponential utility function. It was used successfully for both project selection and to evaluate risk-sharing opportunities. Walls and colleagues report that this system gave managers the ability to rank projects and stay within budgets while enforcing a consistent level of risk tolerance across the company.

The second and more serious issue with deviations from risk neutrality is that computing the risk profile of aggregate benefits over an entire portfolio requires assessment of joint distributions over outcomes of multiple projects. Because projects are often probabilistically dependent, this requires assessing the nature and degree of dependence. One method for doing this is to use copula functions, which require marginal probability assessments and pairwise correlations (Clemen and Reilly 1999; Yi and Bier 1998). An alternative approach is based on information theoretic entropy methods that require both marginal and pairwise probability assessments (Abbas 2003, 2006; Jaynes 1968; Lowell 1994; MacKenzie 1994; Smith 1995). One implication of probabilistic dependence is that learning about the outcome of one project may lead to revision of assessed probabilities for another project. This can be particularly important in situations where projects are selected sequentially. Bickel and Smith (2006) have developed an approach that combines entropy methods with dynamic programming to determine an optimal sequence of projects, and have applied the approach to the sequential exploration of oil and gas projects.

Recently, Gustafsson and Salo (2005) have proposed a general modeling framework and methodology called Contingent Portfolio Programming to support the selection of a portfolio of projects or investments where the outcomes of the projects are uncertain and there are dynamic considerations in the evolution of both project uncertainties and project values. Their approach also includes a method for taking into account risk attitudes using a risk-value model or a multiattribute value function. The approach combines various elements of other approaches within a comprehensive modeling approach, and appears to be computational feasible for many R&D portfolio problems. Gustafsson (2005) discusses extensions and proposes some promising applications, particularly for analyzing investments that have both financial market and other uncertainties.

The applications discussed so far in this section all involve only a single financial objective. When multiattribute utility models were a relatively recent discovery, there were a number of reported applications that explicitly analyzed both uncertainty and multiple objectives when selecting project portfolios and allocating scarce resources (Crawford, Huntzinger, and Kirkwood 1978; Keefer 1978; Keefer and Kirkwood 1978; Sarin, Sicherman and Nair 1978). These applications appear to have been successful, but more recent reports of this type are nonexistent. Although it is possible that these methods are being used but have not been published, I believe that it is more likely that the implementation is too burdensome for most organizations. Instead, they focus on either uncertainty or multiple objectives, depending on what is more relevant to their situation. One promising recent development that may help is a robust modeling approach that permits analysis of project portfolios with incomplete information on project performance or decision maker preferences (Liesiö, Mild, and Salo, in press).

As models get more complex, there is a danger that they will be treated as a mysterious "black box" by decision makers, who will be reluctant to rely on them. One analytic strategy that is frequently implemented in practice but rarely discussed in the literature is to approximate complex models with relatively simple linear models. For example, Dyer, Lund, Larsen, Kumar, and Leone (1990) describe a decision support system developed to prioritize oil and gas exploration activities subject to limits on the available teams of geologists and geophysicists. They develop a linear multiattribute value model designed to closely replicate a more complex nonlinear model derived from conventional calculations of value of information. Dyer and colleagues note that the simplicity and transparency of the linear model eased both implementation and acceptance of the model by the decision makers. More research on the performance of all sorts of simplified approaches would help to promote informed decisions about model sophistication when deploying systems for resource allocation.

Hospital Capital Budgeting: Lessons from Practice

This last point suggests that there can be a delicate balance between conceptual and methodological rigor on the one hand and the pragmatic requirements of resource-constrained organizations. In order to illustrate, I will focus at length on the application of these methods to a particular domain, capital budgeting in not-for-profit hospitals and multihospital healthcare systems. This context provides an excellent case study of the realities of model implementation in large, complex organizations.

Capital budgeting is an ongoing challenge for hospitals in the United States. Rapid technology advances, an aging population, and a shifting competitive environment create constant needs to acquire or replace equipment, maintain and expand physical infrastructure, improve quality of care, and offer new service lines. At the same time, financial pressures sharply limit what they can afford but increase certain needs, particularly for investments that generate revenues or improve operational efficiency. As a consequence, hospitals often enter their annual budgeting cycle with requests for funds that exceed capital available by a factor of three or more to one. Because only a small fraction of requests can be approved, the process is difficult, as executives struggle to identify the best projects.

To support this process, Strata Decision Technology (Strata), a company that I cofounded with Catherine Kleinmuntz in 1996, has developed a software system called StrataCap$^{®}$ that includes analytical capabilities based on the multiattribute value modeling and optimization approach discussed earlier. The software is designed to combine financial forecasts and assessment of other evaluation criteria within a consistent, logical framework for capital project evaluation. Although the project evaluation and portfolio optimization capabilities can be duplicated with "off-the-shelf" analytical software (or even with spreadsheets), there is also considerable integrated functionality to support other parts of the capital budgeting process. This includes standardized project proposal forms, an interactive proposal review and approval process, integration with email systems to support collaboration and workflow, and the ability to effectively integrate the system with other information systems internal and external to the organization.

Strata has implemented this software and the associated capital budgeting process hundreds of times in not-for-profit hospitals and multihospital healthcare systems across the United States. These organizations range in size from seventy-five-bed community hospitals to major academic medical centers and multihospital healthcare systems comprising anywhere from two to more than forty hospitals each. Including the affiliates of multihospital systems, the approach

Table 20.1. Implementation process for hospital capital budgeting

---

1. **Advance preparation and communication: [1 week]**
   - Review existing capital process
   - Define goals and objectives for budget process
   - Establish project timeline, milestone dates, team members, and roles
   - Define standardized capital request form
   - Define structured organizational review process
   - Present finalized recommendations to senior management for approval

2. **Software configuration and training: [1 week]**
   - Configure software to organization's specifications
   - Train hospital budget coordinator on software administrative functions
   - Train hospital managers and program directors on writing high-quality capital requests
   - Train senior managers with proposal review responsibility on how to qualify proposals
   - Familiarize senior management with relevant steps of the capital request and evaluation processes

3. **Capital requests entered into system: [4 weeks]**
   - Create business plans that justify needs and address anticipated questions
   - Analyze incremental financial impact of capital request on existing operations
   - Import external medical technology assessment data to support equipment selection and pricing analyses

4. **Discussion and review of proposals by senior managers and functional experts: [4 weeks]**
   - Examine requests for accuracy and completeness
   - Assess functional feasibility and necessity of request.
   - Provide management sign-off prior to evaluation
   - Reviewers communicate with proposal writers through online discussion forum

5. **Senior leadership team prioritizes capital requests: [1 day]**
   - Team composed of executive-level managers, including clinical/physician leadership
   - Focused discussion of proposals based on identified financial and qualitative criteria
   - Score proposals on qualitative criteria
   - Establish trade-off weights based on strategic considerations
   - Prioritize capital requests using optimization tool and benefit-cost ratios

---

has been used in more than 750 hospitals and healthcare provider organizations, in some instances for many years.

In tandem with the software implementation, Strata provides consulting services to facilitate the capital budgeting process. A team of two or three consultants guide the organization through a process that starts with a review of existing budgeting practices and culminates in a meeting where the senior leadership team prioritizes requests and arrives at a portfolio recommendation. Over time, Strata consultants have identified best practices for the implementation process (summarized in Table 20.1). In a typical hospital, the entire process will take approximately ten weeks.

The process is designed to emphasize the evaluation criteria that will ultimately guide the decisions. Five evaluation attributes usually cover the major issues of concern to most hospitals (summarized in Table 20.2). These include an attribute related to financial performance (net present value), three related to

Table 20.2. Standard attributes for capital evaluation

Objective	Attribute	Definition
Financial	NPV	Net present value of projected future cash flows (dollars)
Quality	Clinical impact	Improves clinical experience in terms of outcomes, patient safety, waiting times, throughput times, and general comfort (rating from 0 to 100)
	Infrastructure	Improves or maintains quality of hospital and outside facilities and equipment, including expenditures to comply with safety, code, and accreditation standards (rating from 0 to 100)
	Staff/physician relationships	Improves ability of employees and medical staff to work effectively and productively (rating from 0 to 100)
Strategy	Market share	Enhances market share by increasing the number of patients seen and/or increasing ability to attract new patients (rating from 0 to 100)

quality concerns (clinical outcomes, facility quality, and impact on staff and physicians), and one addressing strategic concerns (market share). Although the consultants encourage modifications or additions based on an organization's unique objectives, they also discourage letting the attribute list grow too long because this tends to make the evaluation process more difficult.

The capital evaluation session represents the culmination of the entire process. In a typical hospital, there might be 250 proposals submitted, but only 40 to 50 of the most costly are evaluated by the senior executives, representing 70–80 percent of the requested funds. For the remaining proposals, funding decisions are made by reserving allocation pools for groups of functionally related proposals and letting the relevant functional managers assign those funds as they see fit. Sometimes, these managers also use the software to prioritize the smaller projects. In large multihospital organizations, a similar size-based partition of projects occurs, with the largest projects evaluated by corporate executives and the remaining projects evaluated by local hospital executives.

The senior executive evaluation team usually comprises six to twelve members, including the Chief Operating Officer, Chief Financial Officer, Director of Patient Care, Director of Materials Management, Chief Information Officer, Director of Facilities, and physician representatives. The Chief Executive Officer only sometimes elects to participate. The ideal team represents a cross section of expertise and interests from across the organization.

The evaluation session generally lasts between 4 and 6 hours, with a senior consultant from Strata acting as facilitator. The entire analysis occurs in real time with the evaluation team present. The session is usually held in a location where each evaluator has access to a networked computer. The facilitator starts with a brief review of the evaluation process and guidelines for proposal discussions. Many organizations have managers or directors (the project champions) present each proposal and answer questions. Evaluators then immediately score each request on each evaluation criterion using a 0 to 100 judgment scale.[2] Three to five minutes are allocated to discussion and scoring of each proposal. Once presentations are done, evaluators review their ratings and make any necessary adjustments.

Next, the facilitator helps the team determine the relative weights to be assigned to the evaluation criteria and uses the software to calculate aggregate scores and determine the optimal allocation of the available capital dollars. The budget constraint is usually provided by the Chief Financial Officer in advance of the meeting. The facilitator then explains the results and conducts sensitivity analyses based on questions and comments from the evaluation team. The goal of this discussion is to provide the evaluation team with a clear understanding of the modeling process and why the results turn out as they do. The session concludes after the team has converged on a final list of approved capital requests.

Because the system uses optimization, benefit-cost ratios are not an explicit part of the solution process. However, they are still useful because sorting the list of projects using the ratio provides insight into why some projects are or are not included in the optimal portfolio – the projects at the top of the list are clear winners, providing high benefit per dollar expended. Projects at the bottom of the list provide benefits at too high a cost. The discussion naturally focuses on projects in the middle, where slight changes in either benefit or cost estimates could easily alter recommendations.

A particularly useful form of sensitivity analysis is to "force" a proposal into or out of the accepted set and rerun the optimization. In the absence of additional funds, forcing a proposal into the solution set always requires removing one or more of the others. This analysis explicitly identifies the proposals that will be sacrificed to accommodate the new project, emphasizing the zero-sum nature of the budgeting process and making the consequences of funding the lower-rated project salient.

Another issue well suited to sensitivity analysis is the budget constraint. In most organizations, this is a "soft" constraint because the Chief Financial Officer has some degree of discretion to increase or decrease capital spending. Running the optimization with different budget constraints and examining which projects enter or leave the recommended set gives concrete meaning to the consequences of incremental funding shifts.

Because the analysis relies heavily on subjective assessments, it is important to consider systematic judgment biases that may affect the results. One problem often occurs when the evaluated projects differ greatly in size and scope: In early implementations, Strata consultants observed a tendency to neglect scope differences. Consider, for example, an organization comparing a multimillion dollar renovation of a major facility with spending $75 thousand to replace waiting room chairs. A major facility project is generally going to have a huge impact,

---

[2] An exception is that net present value is usually calculated in advance by hospital finance staff based on deterministic assumptions of incremental effects on patient volumes, revenues, and expenses. The software includes financial modeling templates to support this calculation.

so executives are likely to award it high scores on attributes related to patient comfort or facility quality (e.g., 100 on a 0 to 100 scale). However, they might look at the waiting room furniture, conclude that it is in horrible condition, and assign scores that are nearly as high (e.g., 90). This overemphasizes the impact of a relatively modest improvement and makes it more difficult to justify funding larger projects. Similar insensitivity to scope is well known in studies of the economic valuation of environmental public goods (Kahneman, Ritov, and Schkade 1999).

When this problem was first identified, our initial response was to expand the rating scale to extend from 0 to 1000, and to instruct evaluators to anchor on values of 0, 1, 10, 100, and 1000. The hope was that inducing a log response scale would encourage recognition of project scope. When this was not effective, our response was to return to a 0 to 100 rating scale, but then instruct evaluators to rate each attribute on benefit per dollar expended rather than total benefit realized. Multiplying each rating by the project's proposed cost produced the attribute scores used in the value models. Although I am not aware of any rigorous research that validates this method, evaluators perceive it to be intuitively appealing, and we observe fewer obvious problems with scope neglect.

Another serious problem arose because many of the investments evaluated by hospitals each year are projected to realize little or no financial return, presumably because they are focused on other objectives. The optimization process would sometimes generate a portfolio of projects with a negative aggregate net present value, indicating that the portfolio as a whole was failing to earn more than the cost of the capital invested in that portfolio. When considered in light of a typical hospital's thin profit margin and precarious financial position, most executives would view this negative investment return as unacceptable.

One interpretation is that executives simply were not assigning sufficient weight to financial return. However, healthcare executives were often uncomfortable with increasing this weight enough to make a difference, perhaps because it would constitute an explicit statement that financial return far outweighs the importance of the other objectives. Their concern is that this would effectively undermine their vision of the organization as a mission-focused enterprise primarily concerned with quality and quantity of care delivered rather than financial profit.

In fact, this problem is ultimately related to the additivity and preference independence assumptions required when using linear additive value functions in the optimization objective. Our discussions with healthcare executives suggested that their preferences violated the assumptions. Specifically, when the portfolio's aggregate financial return is negative, improvements in financial return are extremely important to them, but as aggregate financial return increases, their preferences for improvements in financial return become less important relative to improvements in other attributes.

Modeling approaches that account for violations of additivity and preference independence are available, although the required assessments and the associated nonlinear optimizations are more challenging to implement. Our concern was that this added complexity would undermine the practical value of the approach because organizations would be less likely to implement the models or accept the results. Instead, our solution was to modify the optimization model by introducing a financial performance constraint. This constraint required that the aggregate net present value meet or exceed a minimum acceptable level. With this constraint in place, portfolios with poor financial performance become infeasible, essentially narrowing the set of possible portfolios to those where it was reasonable to give financial return a relatively low weight. Typically, introducing this constraint forces a few money-losing projects out and replaces them with a few cash-generating projects. This helps the organization achieve an acceptable financial return without ignoring mission-related objectives.

The approach described here makes no attempt to explicitly address uncertainty, except through the use of sensitivity analysis on project benefits and costs. For projects that require significant financial commitments, healthcare organizations can and should use tools like decision trees, influence diagrams, and probabilistic risk analysis (Kleinmuntz, Kleinmuntz, Stephen, and Nordlund 1999). Recently, one of Strata's larger clients, a multistate healthcare system with nearly thirty hospitals, has started to require a quantitative risk analysis for any new project requesting more than $5 million in capital. Their review process places particular emphasis on whether there are adequate risk management plans in place.

However, this organization is the exception rather than the rule. Most hospitals are hard-pressed to develop deterministic financial analyses for their projects. A full-fledged analysis of both uncertainty and multiple objectives is almost certainly beyond their grasp. The approach described here affords a balance between analytical sophistication and implementation effort, while providing a foundation for implementing more advanced models in the future.

Conclusion: Benefits and Costs of Decision Analysis for Resource Allocation

The ultimate test of any decision analysis approach is the impact on the organization and its decision makers. In the hospital setting, executives clearly perceive an improvement relative to the relatively unsystematic and undisciplined process that they previously used. The process is also accessible and relatively easy to implement with the support provided by the software system. Although Strata provides initial support and facilitation, after several years, most hospitals learn to implement the process with minimal involvement from outside consultants.

The open, collaborative nature of the decision process is also a positive. Because the reasoning behind these resource allocation decisions is transparent, there is a sense that everyone is on a level playing field. This promotes consensus around the recommendations that emerge. In the best spirit of decision analysis, it is the sound and logical nature of the process that gives the participants confidence that scarce resources are being put to the best use.

The presumed advantage of any approach for incorporating decision analysis into resource allocation is that decisions are based on reflective, systematic analysis. On the other hand, the effort required can be considerable when a portfolio contains dozens or hundreds of candidate projects. Many organizations lack either the resources or the resolve to do rigorous decision analysis on this scale. Where organizations often need the most help is in accurately estimating the true benefits and costs of decision analytic approaches relative to other resource allocation processes.

This is a problem that has received remarkably little research attention. In one of the few investigations of its kind, Kiesler (2004) models the portfolio analysis process and compares different analytical strategies. In particular, he compares systematic prioritization strategies both with and without rigorous project analyses. His conclusion is that systematic prioritization without rigorous project analysis (or using heuristic approaches) merits serious consideration in many organizations because prioritization based on informal project evaluation yields a large fraction of the value realized from prioritization based on rigorous evaluation. Care should be taken in interpreting this result, however, because there is at least some field-based evidence to suggest that the value realized from rigorous analysis far outweighs the resources required to implement it (Clemen and Kwit 2001). One way to shed light on this issue would be to conduct more in-depth evaluations of these models at work in real organizations.

Acknowledgments

The author acknowledges the support of the Department of Homeland Security under grant N0014-05-0630 (ONR) to the Center for Risk and Economic Analysis of Terrorism Events at the University of Southern California. However, any opinions, findings, and conclusions or recommendations in this document are those of the author and do not necessarily reflect views of the United States Department of Homeland Security. The author thanks Catherine Kleinmuntz for numerous discussions and creative insights on best practices for implementation of decision analysis methods for resource allocation. He also thanks Jess Block, Greg Shufelt, and the professional staff and clients of Strata Decision Technology for their numerous suggestions, ideas, and pointed questions.

REFERENCES

Abbas, A. E. (2003). Entropy methods in decision analysis. Unpublished Ph.D. dissertation, Stanford University.

Abbas, A. E. (2006). Entropy methods for joint distributions in decision analysis. *IEEE Transactions on Engineering Management, 53*, 146–159.

Bickel, J. E., and Smith, J. E. (2006). Optimal sequential exploration: A binary learning model. *Decision Analysis, 3*, 16–32.

Bierman, H., and Smidt, S. (1993). *The capital budgeting decision.* (8th ed.). Upper Saddle River, NJ: Prentice-Hall.

Birge, J. R., and Louveaux, F. (1997). *Introduction to stochastic programming.* New York: Springer.

Bodily, S. E., and Allen, M. S. (1999). A dialogue process for choosing value-creating strategies. *Interfaces, 29*, 16–28.

Borison, A. (2005a). Real options: Where are the emperor's clothes. *Journal of Applied Corporate Finance*, *17*, 17–31.

Borison, A. (2005b). A response to "Real options: Meeting the Georgetown challenge." *Journal of Applied Corporate Finance*, *17*, 52–54.

Brandão, L. E., Dyer, J. S., and Hahn, W. J. (2005a). Using binomial decision trees to solve real-option valuation problems. *Decision Analysis*, *2*, 69–88.

Brandão, L. E., Dyer, J. S., and Hahn, W. J. (2005b). Response to comments on Brandão et al. (2005). *Decision Analysis*, 2, 103–109.

Brealey, R. A., and Meyers, S. C. (1996). *Principles of corporate finance*. (5th ed.). New York: McGraw-Hill.

Brown, G. G., Dell, R. F., and Newman, A. M. (2004). Optimizing military capital planning. *Interfaces*, *34*, 415–425.

Burk, R. C., and Parnell, G. S. (1997). Evaluating future military space technologies. *Interfaces*, *27*, 60–73.

Canada, J. R., Sullivan, W. G., and White, J. A. (1996). *Capital investment analysis for engineering and management*. (2nd ed.). Upper Saddle River, NJ: Prentice-Hall.

Clemen, R. T. (1996). *Making hard decisions: An introduction to decision analysis*. (2nd ed.). Pacific Grove, CA: Duxbury Press.

Clemen, R. T., and Kwit, R. C. (2001). The value of decision analysis at Eastman Kodak Company, 1990–1999. *Interfaces*, *31*, 74–92.

Clemen, R. T., and Reilly, T. (1999). Correlations and copulas for decision and risk analysis. *Management Science*, *45*, 208–224.

Copeland, T., and Antikarov, V. (2005). Real options: Meeting the Georgetown challenge. *Journal of Applied Corporate Finance*, *17*, 32–51.

Corner, J. L., and Kirkwood, C. W. (1991). Decision analysis applications in the operations research literature, 1970–1989. *Operations Research*, *39*, 206–219.

Crawford, D. M., Huntzinger, B. C., and Kirkwood, C. W. (1978). Multiobjective decision analysis for transmission conductor selection. *Management Science*, *24*, 1700–1709,

Dyer, J. S., Lund, R. N., Larsen, J. B., Kumar, V., and Leone, R. P. (1990). A decision support system for prioritizing oil and gas exploration activities. *Operations Research*, *38*, 386–396.

Edwards, W., and Barron, F. H. (1994). SMARTS and SMARTER: Improved simple methods for multiattribute utility measurement. *Organizational Behavior and Human Decision Processes*, *60*, 306–325.

Golabi, K., Kirkwood, C. W., and Sicherman, A. (1981). Selecting a portfolio of solar energy projects using multiattribute preference theory. *Management Science*, *27*, 174–189.

Gustafsson, J. (2005). Portfolio optimization models for project valuation, Research Report A92. Helsinki: Helsinki University of Technology, Systems Analysis Laboratory. Available from Helsinki University of Technology website http://lib.tkk.fi/Diss/2005/isbn9512277980/.

Gustafsson, J., and Salo, A. (2005). Contingent portfolio programming for the management of risky projects. *Operations Research*, *53*, 946–956.

Henriksen, A. D., and Traynor, A. J. (1999). A practical R&D project-selection scoring tool. *IEEE Transactions on Engineering Management*, *46*, 158–170.

Hillier, F. S., and Lieberman, G. J. (2005). *Introduction to operations research*. (8th ed.). New York: McGraw-Hill, Chapter 11, 478–546.

Jaynes, E. T. (1968). Prior probabilities. *IEEE Transactions on Systems Science and Cybernetics*, *SSC-4*, 227–241.

Kahneman, D., Ritov, I., and Schkade, D. (1999). Economic preferences or attitude expressions? An analysis of dollar responses to public issues. *Journal of Risk and Uncertainty*, *19*, 203–235.

Kaplan, R. S., and Norton, D. P. (1996). *The balanced scorecard: Translating strategy into action.* Boston: Harvard Business School Press.

Keefer, D. L. (1978). Allocation planning for R&D with uncertainty and multiple objectives. *IEEE Transactions on Engineering Management, EM-25,* 8–14.

Keefer, D. L., and Kirkwood, C. W. (1978). A multiobjective decision analysis: Budget planning for product engineering. *Journal of the Operational Research Society, 29,* 435–442.

Keefer, D. L., Kirkwood, C. W., and Corner, J. L. (2002). Summary of decision analysis applications in the operations research literature, 1990–2001. Tempe, AZ: Arizona State University, Department of Supply Chain Management. Available from *Decision Analysis* journal website http://da.pubs.informs.org/supplements.

Keefer, D. L., Kirkwood, C. W., and Corner, J. L. (2004). Perspectives on decision analysis applications, 1990–2001. *Decision Analysis, 1,* 5–24.

Keeney, R. L. (1992). *Value-focused thinking: A path to creative decisionmaking.* Cambridge, MA: Harvard University Press.

Keeney, R. L. (1999). Developing a foundation for strategy at Seagate Software. *Interfaces, 29,* 5–15.

Keeney, R. L., and McDaniels, T. L. (1999). Identifying and structuring values to guide integrated resource planning at BC Gas. *Operations Research, 47,* 651–662.

Keeney, R. L., and Raiffa, H. (1976). *Decisions with multiple objectives.* New York: Wiley. Reprinted in 1993 by Cambridge University Press, Cambridge, UK.

Kiesler, J. (2004). Value of information in portfolio decision analysis. *Decision Analysis, 1,* 177–189.

Kirkwood, C. W. (1997). *Strategic decision making: Multiobjective decision analysis with spreadsheets.* Belmont, CA: Duxbury Press.

Kleinmuntz, C. E., and Kleinmuntz, D. N. (1999). Strategic approaches for capital allocation in healthcare organizations. *Healthcare Financial Management, 53*(4), 52–58.

Kleinmuntz, D. N., Kleinmuntz, C. E., Stephen, R. G., and Nordlund, D. S. (1999). Measuring and managing risk improves strategic financial planning. *Healthcare Financial Management, 53*(6), 50–58.

Lang, H. J., and Merino, D. N. (1993). *The selection process for capital projects.* New York: Wiley.

Liesiö, J., Mild, P., and Salo, A. (in press). Preference programming for robust portfolio modeling and project selection. *European Journal of Operational Research.* Corrected proof available online 24 May 2006, http://www.sciencedirect.com/science/article/B6VCT-4K1HDSF-3/2/caa23ac4997aae0d0759587eb8508969.

Lowell, D. G. (1994). Sensitivity to relevance in decision analysis. Unpublished Ph.D. dissertation, Stanford University.

Luenberger, D. G. (1998). *Investment science.* New York: Oxford University Press.

Matheson, D., and Matheson, J. E. (1998). *The smart organization.* Boston: Harvard Business School Press.

Matheson, D., and Matheson, J. E. (1999). Outside-in strategic modeling. *Interfaces, 29,* 29–41.

MacKenzie, G. R. (1994). Approximately maximum-entropy multivariate distributions with specified marginals and pairwise correlations. Unpublished Ph.D. dissertation, University of Oregon, Eugene, OR.

Parnell, G., Conley, H., Jackson, J., Lehmkuhl, L., and Andrew, J. (1998). Foundations 2025: A value model for evaluating future air and space forces. *Management Science, 44,* 1336–1350.

Perdue, R. K., McAllister, W. J., King, P. V., and Berkey, B. G. (1999). Valuation of R and D projects using options pricing and decision analysis models. *Interfaces, 29,* 57–74.

Poland, W. B. (1999). Simple probabilistic evaluation of portfolio strategies. *Interfaces*, *29*, 75–83.

Raiffa, H. (1968). *Decision analysis: Introductory lectures on choices under uncertainty*. Reading, MA: Addison-Wesley

Sarin, R. K., Sicherman, A., and Nair, K. (1978). Evaluating proposals using decision analysis. *IEEE Transactions on Systems Man and Cybernetics, SMC-8*, 128–131.

Sharpe, P., and Keelin, T. (1998). How SmithKline Beecham makes better resource allocation decisions. *Harvard Business Review*, *76*, 45–57.

Skaf, M. A. (1999). Portfolio management in an upstream oil and gas organization. *Interfaces*, *29*, 84–104.

Smith, J. E. (1995). Generalized Chebychev inequalities: Theory and applications in decision analysis. *Operations Research*, *43*, 807–825.

Smith, J. E. (2005). Alternative approaches for solving real-options problems (Comment on Brandão et al. 2005). *Decision Analysis*, *2*, 89–102.

Smith, J. E., and McCardle, K. F. (1998). Valuing oil properties: Integrating option pricing and decision analysis approaches. *Operations Research*, *46*, 198–217.

Smith, J. E., and Nau, R. F. (1995). Valuing risky projects: Options pricing theory and decision analysis. *Management Science*, *41*, 795–816.

Walls, M. R. (2004). Combining decision analysis and portfolio management to improve project selection in the exploration and production firm. *Journal of Petroleum Science and Engineering*, *44*, 55–65.

Walls, M. R., Morahan, G. T., and Dyer, J. S. (1995). Decision analysis of exploration opportunities in the onshore US at Phillips Petroleum Company. *Interfaces*, *25*, 39–56.

Weingartner, H. M. (1963). *Mathematical programming and the analysis of capital budgeting problems*. Englewood Cliffs, NJ: Prentice-Hall.

Yi, W., and Bier, V. M. (1998). An application of copulas to accident precursor analysis. *Management Science*, *44*, 257–270.

21 From Decision Analysis to the Decision Organization

David Matheson and James E. Matheson

ABSTRACT. Decision analysis has been successfully cast as an intervention to pull together the right team of people to formulate and solve the decision maker's problem by building economic models of the situation, assessing the crucial uncertainties, and determining the risk and return of each alternative. For large one-of-kind problems this method works well. Many organizations claim that they have made millions using it. Yet, in spite of its accomplishments, this model has had limited sustained success. Decision analysts often find themselves relegated to disempowered staff, delighted when the executive occasionally calls on them. With a few important exceptions, internal Decision Analysis groups have generally failed to withstand the test of time. We document and explore the ongoing shift from interventional decision analysis to the decision organization, an embedded ecology of actors and patterns of behavior that needs to be guided to produce a sustainable pattern of good decisions. Enabled by the stunning increase in computing power and connectivity, organizational decision analysts need to use the old tools in new and more productive ways and to guide the organizational decision ecology toward sustainable profitability and growth. What will it mean to be a professional decision analyst in the twenty-first century?

Decision Analysis was originally framed as an intervention to assist major organizations in making large, one-of-a-kind decisions (Howard 1966; Raiffa 1968; Howard and Matheson 1983). In its earliest form, it focused on decision makers who already realized they were facing difficult choices and wanted a more rational way to reach them. Decision analysis was successfully cast as a way to pull together the right team of people to formulate and solve the decision maker's problem by building economic models of the situation, assessing the crucial uncertainties, and determining the risk and return of each alternative. Later, as applications began to treat more ill-defined "strategic" problems, formulating good alternatives for analysis was added to this role. The most time-consuming task of the early decision analyst was building and evaluating decision models, which required special equipment (i.e., computers) and skills.

Because the equipment and skills to do decision analysis resided mostly outside the decision maker's organization, early decision analysis was carried out primarily by outside consultants. This reinforced the intervention model as the consultants focused on big projects. Once the need for a decision was recognized, a decision was "declared," initiating a major intervention in the organization – consultants were hired, internal staff were temporarily pulled off their regular jobs, and a team was assembled. This team typically worked 1–3 months (or more) to come up with recommendations for the decision maker. It was a very big deal, but it was worth it. Over time internal staffs were built up to follow this same intervention model using an organization's own resources. And for large one-of-kind problems this method continues to work well. Many organizations claim that they have made millions using it.

Yet in spite of its accomplishments, this model has had limited sustained success. Decision Analysts often find themselves relegated to disempowered staff, delighted when the executive occasionally calls on them. With a few important exceptions, internal Decision Analysis groups have generally failed to withstand the test of time. Why can't decision analysis be as routine and widespread as accounting?

The decline follows a general pattern. In most cases, an organization commissions a few such interventions, and then grows tired of the process of intervention itself. People are exhausted from their demanding roles in DA projects, while trying to do their "day jobs" as well. When they finish with their DA project roles, they are behind on their ordinary work. The Decision Analysis professionals often find that their role does not have a clear career path, and sometimes executives feel too disempowered by the long and complex process.

The intervention process is a highly disruptive one, which is fine (or even desirable) once in a while to shake an organization out of complacency and force them to face new problems or opportunities, but a steady diet is unsustainable. Retreating to back room studies doesn't work either, as the analysis becomes disconnected from the vital decision-making processes in an organization. Organizational forces often seem to drive decision analysis into irrelevance or decline. We are led to inquire if there is another, more sustainable, way to make good decisions.

Since the 1990s, we have been exploring why some organizations seem to be able to develop good decision-making habits and processes, while others have extreme difficulty. We began by exploring the best practices for decision making in the field of R&D. In doing so we found an underlying prerequisite – organizational readiness for good decision making – characterized by "The Nine Principles of the Smart Organization" (Matheson and Matheson 1998).

These principles represent underlying beliefs or philosophies as well as patterns of behavior that support best practices. Without these kinds of principles, an organization would typically fail to adopt or properly deploy best practices, and with these principles they might even spontaneously invent best practices. So, although best practices are important, the underlying principles and patterns of behavior of the organization are even more important. Through survey research, we are able to show that these principles are correlated with profitable growth of the organization (Matheson and Matheson 2001).

Patterns of behavior do not always support good decision making. We have identified negative patterns of behavior that we call Rogues, which dumb-down many organizations. These rogues are very powerful and difficult to escape – well-meaning individuals often find themselves trapped, unable to break out and do the right thing.

So what is the promise for organizational decision analysis? We are beginning to see the glimmers of where it is headed. Interventional-style decision analysis is being supplemented and replaced by simpler faster processes, and good processes and habits are being embedded into the structure of organizations. Computer power is so much greater than those early days of time sharing that it now supports rapid model building and computation as well as global connectivity. We will conclude by exploring the paradigm shift being brought about by these forces, and the way it changes the face of decision analysis in the twenty-first century.

Our Research on Decision Making in Organizations

In developing our book, *The Smart Organization: Creating Value through Strategic R&D*, we conducted cross-industry benchmarking studies on decision-making practices in R&D (Matheson, Matheson and Menke, 1995). These studies created survey instruments, identified forty-five best practices, demonstrated that they were usually helpful in organizations, and motivated many executives to attempt implementation. Yet, in the end, many executives were unsuccessful at implementation, suggesting that we were missing an important key to success.

Best Practices for Decision Making

The extensive multipart study started with a nomination phase to identify companies worth learning from. Then we interviewed these companies to gather information about what practices they used. This resulted in the blueprint of best practices. The forty-five best practices are logically organized into eight components under three major headings as shown in Figure 21.1. The first group of these components addresses making quality decisions, the second addresses how to organize for decision quality, and the third addresses the issue of improving decision quality.

We used this blueprint to construct a diagnostic instrument for best practices and applied it to approximately a thousand companies to demonstrate that they were in fact best practices. We also used this instrument in a practical way, to help executives develop plans for improving their organizations.

Finally, we conducted a validation phase in which we repeated the study with different groups, most notably with companies represented by the Quality Director's Network of the Industrial Research Institute and companies located in Western Europe (Matheson et al. 1994; Lander et al. 1995). These additional studies confirmed our original results and conclusions. Chapters 4 and 5 of our book *The Smart Organization* detail the development of these forty-five practices experiences in implementing them.

After a few years, it became clear that although the best practices were helpful, they were insufficient to drive lasting change. Highly motivated executives were having difficulty implementing them: they spoke in terms of organizational

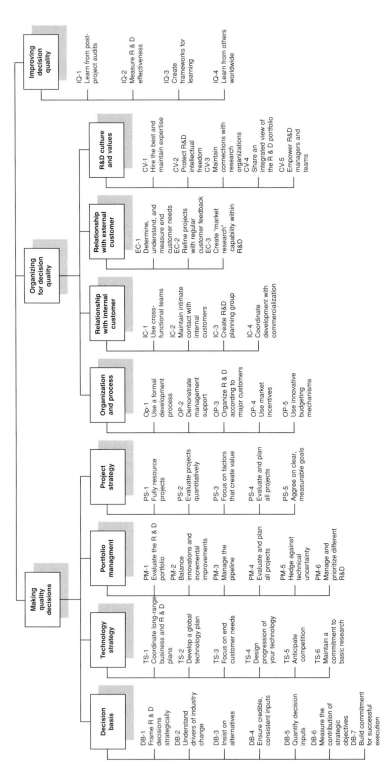

Figure 21.1. The forty-five best practices.

Table **21.1.** Common barriers to adopting best practices

• Short-term focus	• Lack of resources
• Perceived difficulties in measurement	• Lack of discipline
• Organization boundaries	• Lack of strategy
• Internal focus	• Misused metrics
• Lack of credibility	• Tendency to oversimplify
• Secrecy	• People reluctant to change
• Lack of proper skills	• Power and politics

barriers, such as those listed in Table 21.1. Strangely, pushing harder to overcome barriers – the most common strategy – seemed to not produce results very often. Further studies with the Quality Director's Network provided some important clues as to why implementing best practices is difficult, under what circumstances the barriers arise, and how best practice companies successfully implement. These clues lead us to this conclusion: *Cultural and organizational elements are at the root of implementation success or failure.* In other words, the issue is not so much that the practices are intrinsically either difficult or easy to implement; the issue is the context that companies set for or against successful implementation.

The Nine Principles of the Smart Organization

The context is determined by the patterns of behavior and belief – organizational routines (which we call principles) that operate in decision situations. These principles are subtle and work at many levels, influencing the way people think and act. For example, they determine whether people are excited or cynical about adopting a new best practice. In effect, they are enablers of best practice implementation and, thus, the foundation of good decision making. These principles provide the organizational readiness that every company must have if it wants to be a top performer in R&D decision making (or in any other decision domain).

These principles are difficult to see in an organization because principles are intangible and operate beneath the surface. They are bound up in the philosophy, people, culture, and support systems of the organization. Nevertheless, they exert a powerful and undeniable influence on peoples' behavior. Ultimately it is the accumulation of many best practices, all done in the right spirit, that produces the business results.

We have summarized our research in this area in "The Nine Principles of a Smart Organization" (Figure 21.2). Together, the nine principles comprise the worldview required for routinely achieving high-quality strategic decisions. Each principle represents a coherent theory or norm that organizes a particular set of beliefs and, therefore, pattern of behavior. When smart principles are in place, behaviors reinforce best practices and good decision making; when they are absent, behaviors undermine the impact of best practices or even the organization's ability to adopt them. The nine principles are grouped below into three crucial functions: those that help the organization understand its environment,

Figure 21.2. Nine principles of the smart organization.

those that make it possible to mobilize resources, and those that help it achieve its purpose.

Having defined these nine principles, we then devised an "Organizational IQ" test that measures an organization's conformance to these principles. The unit of analysis for our survey instrument is the not the corporation, but its organizational units. Corporations are typically composed of many heterogeneous parts, and some of those parts are usually "smarter" than others. Thus, if we aim to identify points of strength and weakness, we need to measure the intelligence and performance of the organizational units directly. In addition, different people may have different perspectives on the organizational intelligence.

We used various versions of this instrument for two purposes. First, we conducted in-depth assessments of individual organizations to develop improvement plans and to drive learning. Second, we conducted rapid assessments of many organizations for use in statistical analysis. As of this writing, we have more than 1,500 responses from organizations around the world in our database.

Our survey shows that Smart Organizations perform better. High IQ companies are more likely to perform in the top quartile of performance in their industry than Low IQ companies. Figure 21.3 shows the result. We divided organizational IQ into three categories – low (bottom quartile), medium (middle two quartiles),

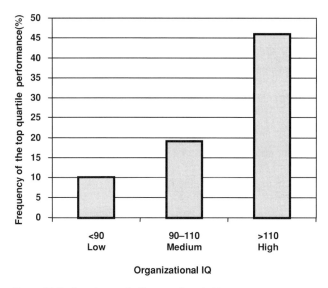

Figure 21.3. Smart organizations perform better.

and high (top quartile). Similarly we divided performance into three categories. High IQ organizations approach a 50 percent chance of also being in the top quartile of performance. In contrast, Low IQ organizations have only a 10 percent chance of being in the top quartile of performance (Matheson and Matheson 2001). *The "High IQ" organization has about 5 times the chance of being a top performer than its "Low IQ" counterpart.* The positive behaviors represented by the nine principles do really matter to the bottom line.

Rogues

Naturally these results and insights led us to work on helping companies actualize the principles. Although we had some success, overall this effort proved extremely difficult. Over time we came to recognize that other patterns of behavior very relevant to decision making were living inside organizations. Although the nine principles describe behaviors that make organizations smarter, in our workshops we encountered and documented negative "rogue" behaviors that dumb organizations down. These have been identified and collected in case studies from experiences in actual engagements and then validated with hundreds of executives in the US and Europe.

Common rogue behaviors are shown in Table 21.2. Often the people involved in these rogue patterns are well aware of these behaviors and their destructive consequences, yet they feel trapped and unable to do anything about them. Rogues seem to represent stable "equilibrium" patterns in that self-perpetuate – no one can unilaterally change them, and anyone trying usually faces nasty consequences. As an example, the corporate liar's game is one of the negative

Table 21.2. Common rogue behaviors

Corporate liar's contest
Managers submit overstated budget requirements anticipating that top management will cut them back to the amount they really need. Management second-guesses proposals knowing that they are overstated. In addition to the waste created by this process, this contest also produces a breakdown in communication about the actual decisions and turns more into a negotiation of a budget number. Both sides regard the others as liars or unreasonable.

Operational incentives
Strategic objectives are in conflict with the realities of operational goals/rewards or processes. For example:

The budget cycle is detached from strategy development.
Strategic goals are turned into operational commitments.

Project champion process
Project champions are expected to advocate their proposals and make the business cases but management is expected to critique and ultimately approve or reject the proposals. (Nobody discusses the real risks and rewards.)

Decision triage
The organization ranks competing funding opportunities, rejecting the worst, approving the "no-brainers," and focusing management attention on the marginal opportunities. (Focusing attention on the best has the highest value potential.)

"Something more important came up"
Commitments and process obligations are routinely broken or given short shrift because "something more important came up" in the eyes of the person who made the commitment or had the obligation. Common excuses are "strategic considerations," "urgent customer requirement," and "the boss wants it." These changes are not communicated back so obligations can be renegotiated and coordination can be maintained.

Cult of the CEO/outsourcing intelligence
A belief that the CEO (or other leadership group or a consulting firm) will set the strategy and the rest of managements' job is simply to implement it. Blame the CEO when the strategy fails to work. (People take little personal responsibility for strategy.)

Perseverance
The organization demands pervasive tendency to loyally continue with a course of action, no matter what the obstacles and without questioning the direction. Naysayers are regarded as disloyal or confused and are pressured to return to the vision.

Wolf in sheep's clothing
Apparent agreements are not carried out. These inactions are not confronted and people are not held accountable. The norms of "tolerance," "diversity," "independence," "professionalism," "empowerment," and "individual initiative" prevent confrontation.

Flight to mediocrity
Because of a miscommunication about the uncertainty about upside potential of an opportunity, a powerful player is left disappointed and with a shortfall. He holds the persons creating the opportunities accountable, and consequently they lower their aspirations to achieve results more consistently. This increases the need for an opportunity with real upside potential, which results in further shortfall.

The comfort zone principle
People substitute their emotional feeling of discomfort with an uncertainty as a measure for the importance of resolving that uncertainty. Because people tend to focus on their areas of comfort or expertise, the result is over-emphasis and overworking of issues that are not major sources of risk. Sources of uncertainty too far from the comfort zone are

overlooked or ignored because they are unfathomable or beyond influence. For example, engineers may overwork the capital cost of a plant but omit discussion of the market demand for the plant's output.

Superficial values or feel-good prioritization
A pattern in which many value metrics are created and legitimized, resulting in confusion over what is really important. Arguing about weights or importance of attributes dominates the discussion, reducing substantive discussion about the actual merits of opportunities. Often particular metrics will gain "power," which results in a relatively blind pursuit of a narrow objective (e.g., cost reduction) and a loss of visibility of the real objectives (e.g., make money). Value metrics become so cluttered that picking the right metrics to support the case becomes an important way to make one's case. In the name of "fairness" or "seeing all sides," it is very difficult to objectively compare opportunities and decision making becomes highly political.

---

patterns you may have experienced firsthand. It occurs around budget time and is observable in many industries. Here's how it works:

> Budget requesters submit proposals to a committee or person who stands in judgment over many such requests. Each person requests more money than he or she will actually need, knowing that cutbacks are likely. The judges know that people are playing this game, so carefully scrutinize each budget – either asking their staffs to second guess requests or challenging requesters to achieve arbitrary budget reduction targets: "Just do that with 20 percent less funding."

In this game, the biggest liar wins, but those who tell the truth about what they need find their funding cut back, along with everyone else, and end up the biggest losers.

One interesting feature of this game is how explicit it can be, even while being acknowledged as destructive. Many an executive and manager we have encountered can recall the first time they entered the budget game and naively proposed the budget they actually needed. Often an old-timer would take them aside and give them coaching how to play the game!

This rogue can be destructive to the intelligence of the organization and result in poor decision making. It is more that just a somewhat inefficient process for budget decisions. The liar's game changes the nature of communication between the senior and junior parties.

It drives out open discussion of uncertainty and alternatives. For example, if you say that you are not sure what your budget requirements will be and provide a range, chances are very high your budget will be set at the low end of your range. So it is best not to explicitly talk about ranges of uncertainty – best to leave things vague or qualitative.

It also reduces analysis to a kind of second-guessing process. Decision Analysts like to produce value-adding analysis that really moves a discussion forward. In the context of the liar's game, analysis becomes an instrument of making a case. The authors have been in more than one situation in which we were asked in to provide a patina of credibility on a fundamentally biased justification.

Some rogues are downright malicious, such as the "Wolf in Sheep's Clothing" rogue. It is a fact of human nature and organizational behavior that sometimes people will agree to a decision or course of action in a meeting, and then do the opposite when they leave. The rogue occurs when this becomes an acceptable pattern of behavior. Usually it is justified through appeals to the "independence" of decision makers; for example, when several heads of business units are coming together to agree on a strategy. If their word is not their intention, then good decision making across the business units is impossible.

The authors have encountered especially nasty cases of this rogue at AT&T and GM. Here the pattern of behavior is so prevalent that the culture has a special word for it. At GM, it is called "The GM Nod"; at AT&T it is called "Grining." It is no surprise to us that these organizations are in serious trouble (indeed, the original AT&T no longer exists – the remnants were bought by SBC who took over the brand). Our advice to any decision analyst: If you come into an organization where this rogue is so prevalent that they have a word for it, run to the exit. Do not walk. Life is too short to waste time in these poisonous environments.

Other rogues result from the unintended consequences of otherwise excellent practices, or the interaction of such practices. Consider the interaction among strategy development, goal setting, and budgeting.

In strategy development one generally wants expansive and visionary thinking. This can produce alternatives that have high upside but significant uncertainty, for example a 50% chance of 100% growth in three years and a 50% chance of 10% growth in three years.

Next comes operational goal setting. A common practice is to set stretch goals. If the strategy process has shown it is possible to achieve 100% growth, why not set that as a goal? So the manager who comes up with an expansive strategy finds himself with a big hill to climb and excessive personal risk. In some organizations, failing to meet a major goal results in termination (called "holding people accountable," another "best practice"), so the interaction between good strategy and good goal setting can result in a situation where the participant has 50% chance of being fired.

Finally, budgeting provides the coup de grâce. A standard practice is to pressurize budgets, being frugal with resources and trying to locate pockets of waste. So the budget needed to achieve the 50% change of the 100% growth target is cut by a third. This cut reduces the probability of achieving the goal to nearly zero. But since the processes are distinct, the loop back to strategy and goal setting is rarely closed.

The interaction among these three otherwise good processes creates a situation where a manager who is doing the right thing for decision making – creating expansive strategies with significant upside – triggers a series of events that results in nearly 100% chance of failure (and possibly being fired). So the intelligent manager will never create the expansive strategy or talk about the upside in the first place. This results in a paucity of alternatives for the organization, and worse, mediocre performance for the company. For example, today the American automotive industry seems to be caught up this sort of cycle.

A key way to fight rogues seems to be to create special rules or situations where these rogues don't apply or their effects are minimized. In intervention-style decision analysis, the consultants and an empowered project team can usually overpower the rogues long enough to get through the engagement. But the modern organization wants to empower its own people to make good decisions routinely. This not only requires the positive patterns of behavior we have been discussing, but also new tools that help keep the organization on track.

We believe that one cause of decline of internal decision analysis groups is that they are crushed by these rogue behaviors. Although these groups can make important contributions, lasting impact is hard to sustain. A powerful champion may prevent destruction, but when patrons lose power, these rogues can crush the group, leaving the participants feeling helpless and unappreciated. Contrast this scenario to the experience of the accounting function. Somehow the accountants seem to be part of a long-term sustainable pattern among executives, shareholders, auditors, etc., that keeps this profession going over the long haul.

In all of this work, we have found that the organizational setting is critical for sustaining the kind of good decision making that ultimately generates profitability and growth. There is a continual battle between maintaining the nine principles (the heroes), and letting the rogues take over. How do we create situations where the rogues are minimized? How do we set up patterns where good decisions are sustained?

A useful analogy is to see an organization as a kind of ecology of patterns of behavior. These patterns control what the organization actually does. They compete for the organizational resources of attention and resources, which bring them to life, and have strategies for sustaining themselves over time.

The Evolution of Decision Analysis

Today's organizational environment is radically different from the one decision analysis grew up in. To create and sustain positive patterns, we need to look at how organizations are operating now. Decisions seem to be moving faster to keep up with competition and the speed at which business moves. Although this may seem to be bad news for the deliberative-minded decision analysis profession, it creates real opportunity if we are willing to shift how we view our work. Several successful approaches have been applied in our practice.

The New Era of the Hyper-World

One word that seems to characterize this modern business environment is "Hyper." Today's Hyper-Competitive organization is a busy place. Everyone is

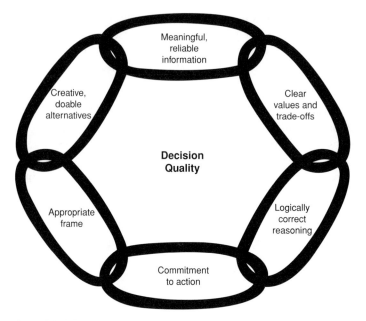

Figure 21.4. The decision quality chain.

Hyper-Connected to everyone else on the whole planet, which leads to Hyper-Distractions and Hyper-Interruptions. Meanwhile the organization is demanding Hyper-Productivity that leads to a Hyper-Operational focus. This Hyped-Up, Hyper-Active environment is giving everyone attention deficit problems. People only get snippets of time before their thoughts are disrupted and they turn their attention to something else. (Should you respond to the Instant Message you just received, or continue reading this article?) Some fight back with Hyper-Scheduling, programming every chunk of their time. People have little time to stop and think about decisions they should be making, and they find it difficult to engage others in the process of exploring and evaluating alternatives.

Decision analysis needs new process and tools for the new era. The decision analysis profession was conceived and grew up during the last half of the twentieth century when large-scale strategic planning was in vogue. The scientific method, which had been so successful in winning World War II, was now redirected at business. The hallmark of the strategy process was a long series of large meetings culminating in strategic decisions and strategic plans that were then rolled out to the organization. On the top of this process sat the decision makers, ratifying the conclusions of the process and authorizing the execution activities and expenditures to carry out the plans.

Decision Analysis arose and thrived in this context. It started with recommending, based on norms (or axioms), good choices from a reasonably well-defined decision basis. The profession responded to various organizational realities, such

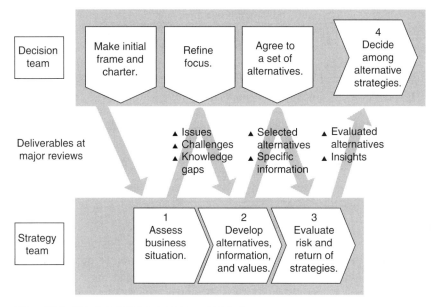

Figure 21.5. The dialog decision process: deciding.

as alternatives not being defined or decision makers being committees, and broadened the tool set.

The "Decision Analysis Cycle" (Howard 1966) was used extensively early in this evolution. But it proved too focused on the analysis and did not provide enough guidance in an organizational setting. Expanding the scope of the analyst's contribution resulted in innovations such as the Decision Quality Chain (Figure 21.4), which moves beyond axioms and iterative analysis to include the quality of alternatives, information, etc. that provide the decision bases.

Further refinements addressed the organizational realities of project management and organized teams for developing strategy and good decisions in the Dialog Decision Process (DDP). (See, for example, *The Meeting of the Minds*, Barabba 1995.) It breaks down the process into six key steps that are typically accomplished through many consultant-led meetings over a period of 2–4 months (Figure 21.5). It also makes a sharp distinction between two teams, the deciders and the doers. The process "snakes" up and down between these two teams, involving the deciders in the substance and guidance of the process, rather than having them sit in judgment at the end, when it is difficult for them to contribute any real value.

The DDP has produced terrific results in the past, but organizations are developing increasing resistance to its meeting-intensive style. The participants must be extracted from their Hyper-Environments, where they are needed to maintain Hyper-Productivity, to spend extensive time in a manually driven process. This heavy participation in process meetings goes against the grain of new era business style with its constant multitasking. Even though this kind of intervention typically produces huge values, clients don't seem overly eager to do it again and again. It is just too heavy and disruptive, and it requires outside consultants or specialized internal staffs to be effective – and as such it is not an easily sustainable solution. So we need a new process paradigm to serve the twenty-first century Hyper-Style business organization.

Making decisions quickly has academic support as well; for example, Kathleen Eisenhardt has conducted case studies showing that decisions made quickly are better (Eisenhardt 1989). The challenge is to design a method to arrive at great decision rapidly, in the sense of decision quality, without being too meeting-intensive. We review a few of the most promising methods in the next section.

Turbo Decision Analysis

One solution is using one or a few intensive meetings where the right people with the right preparation reach decisions quickly – "Turbo Decision Analysis." This approach has been part of the consultant's repertory for perhaps a decade, and includes some special varieties such as Decision Conferencing. Typically this approach has been accomplished by intensifying the resources by bringing ample consulting resources and possibly special equipment to the session. Sometimes this equipment is so specialized that the decision team goes to a special facility.

The same technology driving the hyper world has also reduced the requirements for successful turbo decision analysis. With software running on a laptop, such as SmartOrg's Decision Advisor®, these sessions can be conducted in virtually any conference room with a trained facilitator and analyst. The authors have participated in very short workshops (1 day) in which a team comes together, frames the problem, develops alternatives, creates an influence diagram model, assesses the uncertainties and reviews the analytical results. When they leave, the team has achieved consensus on their decision and a common understanding of the decision basis, contingencies, and other important issues.

This real-time decision analysis is made possible by flexible analytical software designed with group process in mind. The real-time analysis transforms the way people interact with the analysis – it goes from "back room" to "front room." The real-time analysis transforms the way a decision analysis professional has to look at his or her work to be successful – from careful modeling to rapid analysis of only key factors. The insights, shared mental models (Senge 1990), and decisions reached are much more important than an elegant reusable analytical model. Models are either replaced or overhauled to deal with the next situation

The critical success factors are: 1. excellent facilitation and group process skills, 2. rapid real-time modeling tools, and 3. KISS (keep it simple, stupid) – a relentless focus on the real issues of contention and doing the minimum analysis to resolve those issues. Traditional decision analysts risk being sidetracked into exploring interesting model features that are not critical to completing the task at hand.

Compared with the old style, we are able to get the results of a two-month process in a well-prepared one- or two-day meeting. Ironically, in today's hyper world, some executives view a Turbo Decision Analysis as a "deep dive." The time out to do a Turbo Decision Analysis is a short pause in the world of Hyperactivity that mobilizes new activities toward a better future. With its low overhead and rapid turnaround, we see Turbo Decision Analysis as one of the essential elements in sustaining improved decisions.

A shortcoming with this approach is that it is still an event. It is difficult to bring the right people together, so even this approach is used perhaps less than it should be. To meet the total needs of the modern organization, application of Decision Analysis must become part of the way the company does business.

Embedded Decision Analysis

When decision analysis is intimately integrated with the way a company does business, it disappears as an "event." Sound analysis and the building of decision quality can be accomplished by building up the decision basis in snippets through several small incremental tasks in the context of getting work done. This requires sophisticated software and networking to coordinate the process and pull the analysis together.

For example, consider portfolio prioritization. Currently many companies have project leaders submit spreadsheet-based justifications, usually called "business cases." These business cases are then used as an important input to the prioritization process. Because managers know these cases are incomplete and biased, they add various subjective factors, such as "strategic fit" and "risk" to make adjustments. Sometimes these adjustments get very sophisticated, involving multiattribute studies – usually performed very badly. Lots of staff energy goes into preparing the analysis, wrangling version control, etc.

How can we make this whole process more in line with Decision Analysis principles and insights? One approach is to use the intervention style of Decision Analysis to help an organization get through this massive job. The consultant can standardize the models, assess uncertainties using probabilities, and conduct the appropriate portfolio analysis. Probably the best known example of this is the SmithKline Beecham case that was reported in the *Harvard Business Review* (Keelin and Sharpe 1998).

The pharmaceutical industry has taken the lead in this area. Over time, they have moved away from consultant-driven interventions to staff-based processes. If the company can maintain momentum, they typically evolve further into software-based processes, in which the extreme is deployment of a web-based system to help gather the assessments, conduct the analysis, etc. The decision analysis process becomes routine and embedded in the organization.

This approach can shift an organization from one process (staff-intensive business-case based prioritization) to another (embedded decision analysis prioritization). Interestingly, the Decision Analysis largely disappears, becoming part of the background. These organizations support embedded decision analysis by reinforcing positive patterns of behavior to incorporate uncertainty, consider

Table 21.3. Acceleration of the R&D pipeline.

	2003	2004	Improvement
New ideas screened	22	35	60%
Projects initiated	6	9	50%
Projects deployed	1	2	100%
Projects terminated	3	6	100%

alternatives, and stay value focused. The new process produces better results, often more efficiently that the original ones.

However, this path is expensive and fraught with difficulty, as the organization has to maintain the momentum to go through several major process changes, from the original to consultant-driven to staff-driven to software-leveraged processes. There are many points where the whole thing can come unglued and the organization returns to its old patterns.

The authors have had significant success with shortcutting this path and jumping straight to a software-leveraged system, with the process design incorporating the advantages offered by software. This is much less expensive than the more familiar path and has a higher probability of success because there are fewer shifts required.

For example, one manufacturing company converted its process in 3 months – evaluating sixty projects in the portfolio. It started with the development of decision-analytic evaluation templates (i.e., influence diagrams), which were installed in our Portfolio Navigator™ software. Then, in workshops, project leaders were trained to use these templates and in expressing their information using probabilities. By spending a few hours here and there, these leaders used the system as part of their work to plan their projects – with very low incremental cost, as they had to do the planning anyway.

The payoff to project leaders was better understanding of how to create value from their projects. Amazingly, several of them withdrew their own projects as they found low-value prospects! The system then rolled up all of these mini-analyses into a portfolio. The executives reviewed and developed the understanding of the portfolio by reviewing the analyses, which were stored on-line in system, on their own schedules. The process culminated in a portfolio prioritization meeting that was short, high impact, and resolved issues that really needed a meeting. Finally, they used the project models to track changes in information as the projects evolved, so it became a continuous process.

In another case, a similar approach was embedded into the management of a major upstream oil and gas research portfolio. The dramatic improvement in accelerating the whole pipeline from screening of new ideas to deploying projects is shown by their own measurements in Table 21.3. They continue to use this system enthusiastically because their behavior is reinforced by the highly-visible improvements in bottom-line results.

This approach fights fire with fire – that is, to use network-based tools and distributed teams to carry out sound analysis and reach good decisions by harnessing snippets of attention from participants along with a few shorter meetings to reach mutual understanding and agreements. It fits better into the hyper workflow of today's organization because by embedding the decision analysis it becomes more resistant to rogues. But it requires that we rethink our roles as decision analysts a bit.

Yet this approach can still be vulnerable because it requires a company to have process-discipline and is often driven by a management event; for example, the portfolio prioritization meeting.

Plan-of-Record Decision Analysis

One of the characteristics of the hyper-world is an emphasis on learning by doing. Executives and managers try something out, work a plan, and then adjust as they learn. This everyday routine activity of planning, observing, and adjusting can be greatly enhanced by introducing decision analytic ideas into routine work.

In this method of deploying decision analysis, only one alternative – the "plan of record" – is evaluated explicitly. Other alternatives are either completely implicit or described at a high level, such as on a rough strategy table. Nobody believes the current plan is the "right" one; rather the analysis is viewed as a planning and learning exercise.

The authors have had considerable experience with this approach (usually working at turbo-style speed) to help companies with new product development and R&D decisions. In these cases, the organization is trying to learn how to make their project plans, and new product designs, better. The purpose of the analysis is to give guidance on how to change the present plan to one that creates more potential value. It depends on the ability of value-based analysis to uncover the drivers of value, from both technical and market viewpoints. These insights allow the teams to reshape the project plans (including execution and commercialization phases) to make them more valuable.

The tornado diagram (Figure 21.6) is often the most important deliverable, as it provides a kind of importance map of the uncertain future. Teams often discover new insights into what is valuable and learn the relatively low importance of some of the team concerns, resulting in greater alignment and understanding. Usually, the team spontaneously revises its strategy and plans, incorporating elements of the implicit alternatives or conducting very focused alternative generation to exploit the areas of high value.

For example, companies with engineering cultures often overwork capital cost issues in new product development projects – often at the expense of market issues. Usually these teams feel overworked, unable to incorporate everything they know is important. A close look at their project plan will show that 70–80 percent of their effort is going into capital cost issues, which is emotionally perceived as at an unacceptable level of uncertainty. They may be doing relatively little on market issues because these are viewed as unfathomable or beyond influence (another rogue – "the comfort zone principle").

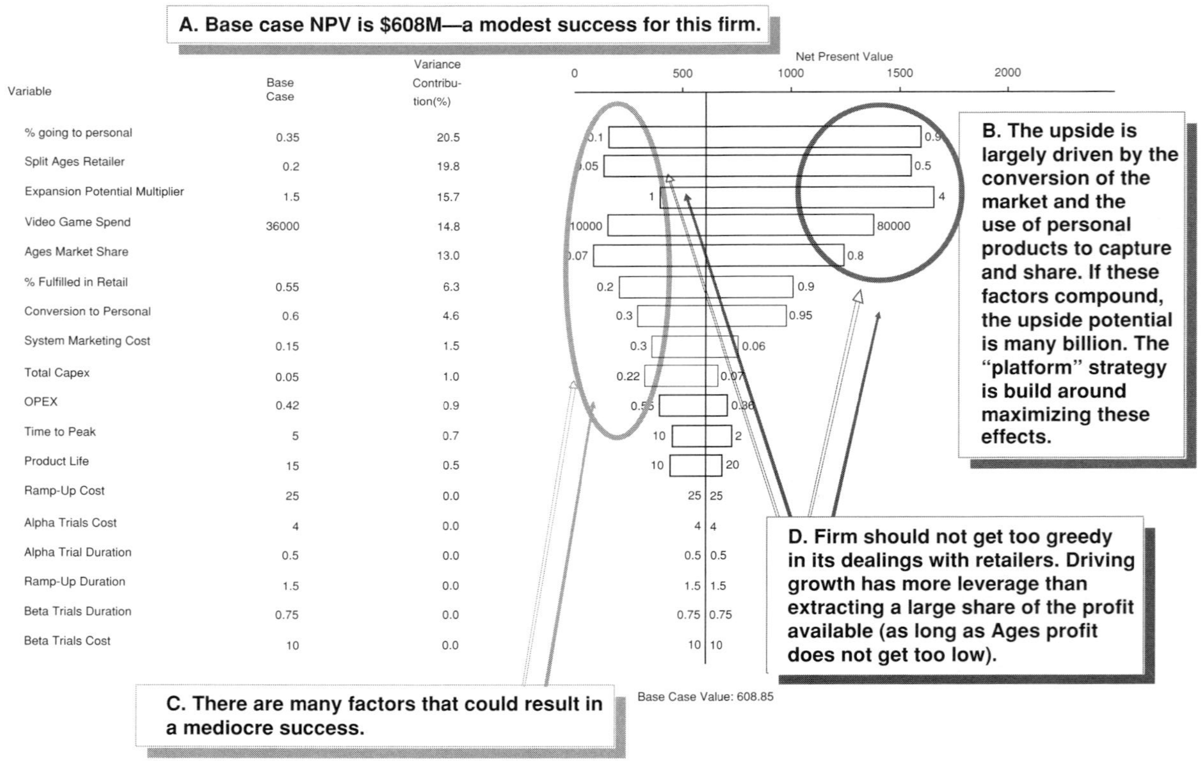
A. Base case NPV is $608M—a modest success for this firm.
Variable
Base Case
Variance Contribu-tion(%)
Net Present Value
0
500
1000
1500
2000
% going to personal 0.35 20.5
Split Ages Retailer 0.2 19.8
Expansion Potential Multiplier 1.5 15.7
Video Game Spend 36000 14.8
Ages Market Share 13.0
% Fulfilled in Retail 0.55 6.3
Conversion to Personal 0.6 4.6
System Marketing Cost 0.15 1.5
Total Capex 0.05 1.0
OPEX 0.42 0.9
Time to Peak 5 0.7
Product Life 15 0.5
Ramp-Up Cost 25 0.0
Alpha Trials Cost 4 0.0
Alpha Trial Duration 0.5 0.0
Ramp-Up Duration 1.5 0.0
Beta Trials Duration 0.75 0.0
Beta Trials Cost 10 0.0
10000
80000
0.8
0.2
0.9
0.3
0.95
0.06
0.22
10
2
20
25 25
4 4
0.5 0.5
1.5 1.5
0.75 0.75
10 10
Base Case Value: 608.85
B. The upside is largely driven by the conversion of the market and the use of personal products to capture and share. If these factors compound, the upside potential is many billion. The "platform" strategy is build around maximizing these effects.
C. There are many factors that could result in a mediocre success.
D. Firm should not get too greedy in its dealings with retailers. Driving growth has more leverage than extracting a large share of the profit available (as long as Ages profit does not get too low).

Figure 21.6. The tornado diagram interpreted for learning.

Upon seeing a tornado diagram based on the team's own inputs in real time, they might find that capital cost falls at the bottom and market share goes to the top. It is not uncommon in engineering cultures for the market share uncertainties to have 50–100 times the impact of the capital cost uncertainties. This perspective changes people's internal models of what is important – suddenly they realize that their emotional assessment of uncertainty has perhaps led them to overlook something absolutely essential.

The team will usually spontaneously change the project plan. In a few cases, we have experienced project teams simply canceling their entire project! This is almost unheard of in many corporate situations, where most project teams are working to perpetuate their projects. More commonly, the team takes a significant turn.

The team will usually invent new alternatives in response to the insights about where value is really coming from. They combine elements of the implicit alternatives or invent new options they had not contemplated in advance. For example, a team may reduce the effort going into capital cost and create major tasks around intellectual property protection. Once faced with a clear value-focused challenge, people can be very inventive. The decision analysis of their plan of record can provide them with this focus.

In this approach, decisions are always viewed as hypotheses to be worked. There is no "ultimate" decision or decision maker. Rather, a team is using decision analysis to guide its planning and direction. This planning in turn guides a number of smaller decisions that add up to the project going in a certain direction. The shared mental model of what creates economic value provided by the decision analysis is as important as – if not more important than – the recommendations regarding any particular alternative.

The team then does its regular work for a while (say 3–6 months) and returns to do another analysis when they have enough new information or circumstances have changed enough to warrant another session. In a sense this method is a hill-climbing way to explore the path to more value. It can work only if the analysis is easy, rapid and value-focused. It fits the hyper-world. It is an emergent, dynamic use of decision analysis, rather than a static, comprehensive one.

Bringing It All Together

One project leader at a major forest products company assembled her team for a day to conduct such an analysis of her project in turbo-style. It revitalized her project and helped her take it from the bottom of the company's priority list to the top. After a year, a lot had changed – they had proven out various technical issues, learned about competitive moves, and so on. So she commissioned another turbo-style plan-of-record analysis. Again, it was very productive, and it helped her take the team in the direction it now needed to go.

We asked her why she had taken a full year to do another analysis – significant new information was available after about six months. She replied "it was too much of a hassle to assemble the team for a day." We were stunned. To our consulting background a day seemed like nothing, but in her hyper environment a day was a major commitment.

So we asked, "If it was not such a hassle, how often would you like to do such updates?" Her surprising reply was, "*every week*, in my staff meeting." Her vision was to update information in the staff meeting, review the relevant uncertainties, and update the probability assessments if necessary. An instantaneous refinement to the analysis would tell her the strategic impact of the new information – does it simply narrow the tornado a bit? Does it provide an opportunity to reduce downside risk or drive toward upside possibility? Does it undermine or cause her to reconsider a key element of her plan of record?

What she is visioning is a new kind of hyper decision analysis that works seamlessly within the realities of her organization. She wants Turbo Decision Analysis that is really fast, streamlined and focused on her immediate issues. She wants Embedded Decision Analysis that is simply part of how she does her work and extended over time. She wants Plan-of-Record Decision analysis that lets her learn rapidly as the situation evolves.

In short, she is calling upon us to reinvent our profession. This vision requires new tools, not geared toward the consultant but geared toward the routine non-expert user. This vision requires new approaches to deploying the Principles of a Smart Organization. This vision requires a new viewpoint for how we think about our contribution to organizational decision making. It is not about us – it is about them! These changes are just beginning.

A New Viewpoint: The Decision Organization

We have enough experience to sketch some of the major elements of this new viewpoint. All three of the above methods support a world where process control shifts from the consultant (internal or external) to the customer or end user. These methods rely on the productivity of modern computer technology to conduct analysis more rapidly and to coordinate decision analysis across people and geographies. They are all very quick, by old era standards. Collectively, they add up to a shift from interventions that make the "best decision" at the moment to creating frameworks for navigating the undiscovered country of the future.

We are sorry to report that this new viewpoint may require goring some sacred cows. Let's start with the idea of a decision maker. Organizational thinking naturally leads to a framework of viewing decisions as the outcomes of organizational processes and routines, rather than the independent actions of optimizing (or satisficing) individuals. This way of looking at organizations is well established in the organizational behavior literature for example see Chris Argyris' latest book (Argyris 2004) or a recent literature review article (Becker 2004). These insights are relatively new to the Decision Analysis community. We would like to briefly discuss some of their implications.

In the traditional Decision Analysis worldview, decisions are seen as explicit choices of an individual based on optimizing behavior. In the Organizational

Decision worldview, decisions are emergent results based on the distributed behavior of strong coalitions as they seek to resolve issues. The decision here is defined as the result that emerges from the actual behavior of many people in the organization – their behaviors add up to something at a higher level. For example, closing a major plant means that the board has to approve closure, plans have to be developed (and refined over time), executives give orders, contracts have to be changed, assets have to be salvaged, people have to be reassigned or let go, etc. This occurs over an extended period of time, and many people have to make individual allocations of resources (time, money, attention). This is the sense in which a decision based on distributed behavior adds up to something. The question is how to design organizational processes and patterns of behavior so that the something they add up to is a series of good decisions.

To understand the idea of decisions as emergent results, let's look at an example. Intel famously got out of the memory business to get into the processor business. This was viewed at the time as a brilliant strategic move, and much credit was given to Andy Grove for his gutsy move. This view is very consistent with the traditional worldview. Work by Brown and Eisenhardt suggests a radically different interpretation (Brown and Eisenhardt 1998). Intel was following a simple rule or procedure that permeates its decision making: allocate capital to the areas of highest return. This led to a whole sequence of individual activities that culminated in creating the choice for Mr. Grove – forcing him to lead the organization in the new direction. This choice would not have been possible if scads of people were not already preparing the way.

Finally, let's consider how strong coalitions resolve issues. In our decades of experience in many organizations, we have seen very few large organizations with a single "organizational decision maker" as measured by the power to make the call and get things done, although plenty of executives have this self-image. Rather, powerful players have roles and responsibilities. Although some executives may be willing to go out on a limb and push an idea, they ultimately need the backing of other powerful players to make something happen. Sometimes it is easy to obtain this backing: often it is not. For example, launching a new product takes the cooperation of marketing, R&D, and manufacturing. Although they have important objectives in common, they also have somewhat different agendas and understandings.

Mobilizing an organization to make good decisions usually requires the recognition or declaration of a problem, such as not enough growth or what to do with a plant or a conflict over possible courses of action. Until such an issue arises, standard operating procedure of the organization just carries along implementing "routine" actions (paying vendors, conducting marketing studies, conducting design work, and so on). When an issue is recognized, it creates a kind of organizational force that perturbs the system and creates a decision opportunity. Like cognitive dissonance, this force moves people to take actions that resolve the issue and achieve normal stability. This is accomplished when a strong coalition aligns on the course of action.

Decision Processes and Organizational Routines

Many organizations anticipate the types of issues that commonly arise and have processes for forming these strong coalitions. Take budgeting for example. Here the issue is the allocation of resources – the requested budget from various players often adds up to more investment than the organization can afford. The budgeting process anticipates this, and a complex negotiation ensues with various players making requests for funding levels, defending and justifying proposals. The finance department is called in to be a sort of referee. Ultimately one or more of the top executives recommends a budget and everyone agrees to live with it. This budget then influences a whole set of downstream activities. The budget is both an emergent decision and a framework that guides other emergent decisions – hopefully to "add up to something." If the Liar's Game rogue is in place, this process produces an inferior result. On the other hand, if the tools and communication process encourage an open deliberative process leading to a high-value portfolio of investments, the process has succeeded.

Or consider product development. These decisions are usually made in the context of a stage-gate system, in which projects go through a series of go/no-go decisions (the "gates"). Between gates ("the phases"), projects develop information (typically technical, market, and business) that matures the ideas. Ideally the result is better control of uncertainty and control of investment through staged commitments. Gate committees are typically cross-functional. Investments are usually relatively small until the final phase of development (e.g. large-scale testing or scale-up) or launch, at which point authority goes to a much higher level for formal decision making and approval of the sometimes massive capital expenditures, advertising costs, or supply chain commitments.

In the Organizational Decision worldview, the products actually launched are the emergent decisions. The decisions revolve around how to respond to various ideas, opportunities, and results coming out of the substantive work during the phases. The strong coalitions are organized by the gate reviews. But if the value of the commercial phase is not taken into account at the beginning, there are no assurances that profitable products will emerge. The Organizational Decision Analysts' challenge is to design a process and set of positive behaviors and then to find ways to get the organization to implement them.

In terms of traditional Decision Quality, notice how every item (information, alternatives, etc.) is generated by the processes and patterns of behavior that control product development. What alternatives do the executives have? It depends on what has been explored and developed. What is uncertain? It depends on the choices for information gathering made at earlier phases. In this light, traditional decision analysis simply pulls together the decision basis in a particularly helpful way – but it does not really control or even strongly contribute to the decision making of the organization. The many individual actions along the way are the preparation for a good decision

As an example of how a decision analyst with this new worldview might improve an organization, let's look at a rogue called "the flight to mediocrity."

It occurs in any situation involving uncertain investments, and it is particularly easy to see in the context of product development. This rogue renders attempts at good decision making in product development like rearranging deck chairs on the *Titanic*, and thereby emasculates traditional decision analysis. It works like this:

> Business executives (finance, general managers) see declining margins and market share in important products. They turn to New Product Development and R&D and request something great. R&D executives explain what might be possible, but fail to convey uncertainty in a meaningful way. This sets high expectations. Because the results of R&D are uncertain, the R&D executives seem to promise too much and then under-deliver relative to expectations. Business executives come to the conclusion that R&D cannot deliver and take two courses of action:

> First, they hold R&D executives accountable to their promises. This results in R&D making less ambitious promises so they can meet them. This focuses the organization on immediate and incremental projects and drives out any longer-term or riskier projects that have real potential to fix the underlying problem.

> Second, they cut the R&D budget. This puts the nail in the coffin for medium-term or high-potential projects.

> As a consequence, shares and margin continue to decline. Executives put further pressure on R&D. Aspirations continue to lower and the company drifts into the long list of mediocre businesses struggling to stay alive.

As companies rush down this slippery slope, their choices become more and more limited. Decision analysis becomes less and less interesting or helpful. Who cares about decisions on deck chair locations when the ship is sinking? Yet paradoxically, bad decisions are at the heart of the matter.

There is hope. Notice how this cycle hinges on a miscommunication about uncertainty and the resulting missed expectations. A decision analyst with the organizational decision worldview could be more helpful to companies by modifying these organizational routines so communication about uncertainty is more effective. They could encourage judging results over a series of opportunities or portfolio of projects rather than on each project. They could ask: What is the risk and return for the portfolio as a whole? Preparation would include the obvious training and less obvious process changes, such as adjusting goal-setting procedures, so that people can talk about upside potential without fear of losing their bonus for failing to meet a stretch goal. These changes include implementing and combining the various new styles of decision analysis discussed above. This transformation requires a shift in perspective from individual decisions to the organizational procedures that create the decisions.

The Organizational Decision Worldview

There are many implications of the Organizational Decision Worldview. Let's use elements of Decision Quality as a point of departure to get a framework for the full implications (Table 21.4). This figure goes through each of the elements of decision quality (plus a few context dimensions) and contrasts the definitions, assumptions, and focus of each. We already discussed some important differences around the definition of a decision, the unit of interaction the analyst focuses upon, and how decisions are framed, as well as the logic driving a decision and commitment. This section fills in with a few additional examples to flesh out the picture.

Start with uncertainty. In the traditional worldview, uncertainty is a property of one's state of knowledge, presumably that of the "decision maker" (or delegate expert). From the organizational point of view, uncertainty also includes difference of opinions about facts or forecasts. In our experience, it is usually difference of opinion that actually drives confusion and conflict about uncertainty, less often individual lack of knowledge

For example, suppose two participants are arguing about the market opportunity for a new product. One believes it is high and therefore the project should be funded; the other believes it is low and therefore the project should be cancelled. This disagreement gets expressed in organizational procedures and results in either a political battle (the more powerful person gets his or her way), or with a recognition of "uncertainty" about the project. As assessment of each expert's individual range of uncertainty would undoubtedly strengthen the second possibility and lead to better decision making.

Incorporating disagreement into our concept of uncertainty might at first seem to complicate things considerably. However, we have found quite the opposite in practice. This expanded concept provides a foundation for dealing with the thorny problem of which experts to use in the assessments. For example, when assessing a 10–90 range of an uncertainty select the maximum credible position. Take the lowest (credible) value for the tenth percentile and the highest (credible) value for the ninetieth percentile. Why? Because, this is the range of disagreement. If you can resolve the issue within this range, for example by showing that it is low on a tornado diagram, then the coalitions represented by the disagreeing experts will align and improve your ability to achieve a decision.

In the narrow view of uncertainty as individual, the experts must be chosen based on the authority and dictates of the decision maker. In the organizational worldview the decision maker does not exist as traditionally conceived. Instead there are multiple coalitions that must be aligned to resolve issues. Therefore, the criterion for expert selection is credibility – how do the coalitions view the experts? Our experience in business settings is that expert credibility is usually not problematic. Once you shift the frame from political battle (we must cancel project versus we must fund it) to discussion of uncertainty and limits of knowledge, coalitions usually agree on which experts are most credible and defer to them.

Table 21.4. Old versus new worldview

	Traditional worldview	Organizational decision worldview
Decision definition	Irrevocable allocation of resources	Emergent pattern of behavior distributed across organization
Unit of interaction	Individual decision maker and delegates	Organizational system
Frame	Explicitly declared decision	Strategic context, pattern of issues, explicit areas of interest with nascent or latent decisions
	Unique decision-specific considerations	
	Intervention, event or project	Continual process with choice episodes
Alternatives	Clear and formally defined alternatives	Dynamically constructed alternatives formed from latent alternative fragments that provide a mechanism for learning, refinement, and increasing commitment across coalitions
Information	Designated experts having uncertain (possibly biased) knowledge	Mix of expertise and perspectives with overlapping judgment and conflict
Values	Tradeoffs can be clearly specified	Aligned on overall objective or mental model in the face of often confused or conflicting goals – defines True North for various coalitions
Logic	Optimize explicit decision basis using SEU	Resolve issues to create a strong coalition around a winning mental model
Commitment	Single decision maker can allocate resources by giving orders.	Strong coalition carries the day
		Key players behind it
		Top-down and bottom-up support
		Shape downstream incremental decisions
		Translation and rollout
		Modification of organizational routines
Result	Good decision	Common vocabulary for perceiving, interpreting, sharing and responding to issues.

We have found that this simple shift can have a profound impact on an organization. Rather than going down a relatively unproductive discussion of who is
right and the arguing about the details of the probability distribution, just move
on using the above rule. Most of the uncertainties will not make it to the top of the
tornado diagram anyway. For those that do, the resolution procedure is defined in
the context of the downstream organizational routines. For example, in a phased
R&D project, an uncertainty at the top of a tornado diagram becomes the focus
of further efforts at the next phase – the decision actually taken is to give the
project resources to take another step, not decide "forever." Experts will tend to
converge in the face of new primary evidence. This gives people a framework for
learning and conflict resolution, rather than the traditional approach which would
advocate refining the decision analysis (often to implausible levels of precision)
and calling the question.

Next, alternatives. Traditional decision analysis calls for the development of
many alternatives. This is often good. However, it is often unnecessary. As discussed above under Plan-of-Record Analysis, good discussion and uncertainty
analysis of a momentum plan or plan or record often has 80 percent of the impact
at far lower effort. People use the analysis to develop better ideas that they could
never have developed beforehand either as an immediate result of the analysis or
during their routine (and refocused) work afterwards. These new alternatives are
tested and refined through real work. Again, the principle is to provide a common
value-focused mental model to build strong coalitions.

Many alternatives are nascent and can get constructed quickly when the need
arises. Consider this dialog from a turbo-DA session of a plan-of-record analysis:

THE BOSS: If we don't go for it, with a mass market launch of a really great
   product, it is not worth our time and attention.
PARTICIPANT: We don't have the experience to pull something off at that
   scale. We need to focus on a higher-end, smaller market so we can start
   with a higher cost product and learn.
THE BOSS: I don't think that is going to cut it. The product has got to be cheap.
PARTICIPANT: It has to be cheap enough to get us traction.
THE BOSS: Then we are agreed. A mass market launch of a great and cheap
   product.
PARTICIPANT: Whatever you say . . . I still think we should stage the launch to
   get experience.

Clearly these two are talking past each other, and you probably recognize that
they are implicitly pursuing different alternatives. But the fact is neither alternative is actually complete – they are more like alternative fragments, organized
around key insights or points of view. In the workshop, we did what many Decision Analysts would do, and clarified and defined the alternatives. Then we went
on evaluating the boss' preferred alternative (rather than both).

The workshop resulted in insights that significantly modified the boss' strategy.
We created a "hybrid" strategy without evaluating multiple alternatives. So far,

this might be seen as a traditional decision analysis, but the differences become clear when we consider what happened next.

A few months later, the boss's plan had failed. It became clear that the product would be too expensive for the market. The team took the brave step of declaring failure of their strategy. (In many cases, a team would not declare failure and continue to work a dead idea for a few years and a few million dollars in expenditures before someone put the project out of its misery). Because the alternatives had been laid out in the workshop, the team was able to rapidly construct a new alternative that combined insights in the previous two plus the lessons learned about the cost structure. They proceeded with this revised plan, and eventually launched (after two more failures), a fantastic new product.

The key to the organizational view of this story is the revision and reinvention of the alternative structure. Alternatives are not being constructed just to support the optimizing behavior suggested by decision analysis, they are being constructed to learn and adjusted dynamically.

Many organizational dysfunctions, such as conflict, confusion, and lost opportunity, can be attributed (in part) to poor alternatives. Yet there is often a rich pool of latent alternatives or alternative fragments that can be assembled into a new alternative given the right context and insight. These latent alternatives are often implicit, poorly articulated, incomplete, not thought through, or not vetted.

Trying to enumerate all alternatives for a decision analysis can be a bit like trying to boil the ocean. Yet the conversations from a good decision analytic process and the insights that result help motivate good thinking about alternatives.

From the new worldview, the decision analyst thinks about alternatives as dynamic entities used to explore hypotheses and learn what works, not static inputs to an analysis. The choice of an alternative is rarely decisive as we might traditionally think, but rather organizations increasingly commit to an increasingly refined definition of the alternative over time.

Finally, value. The organizational view emphasizes the definition and measurement of "True North." Trade-offs are derived naturally as alternatives are brought forth to pursue True North. That is, the analysis shows the implications of each alternative for what is actually in powerful participants' best interest, rather than a subjective judgment of preference. This guides ongoing decisions carried out through organizational routines.

It is the ability to promote leaning and organize powerful players into coalitions that drives this shift of view. Keeney, in *Value-Focused Thinking*, emphasizes the power of knowing what your values are for generating alternatives, which is very consistent with the new worldview (Keeney 1992). However, when groups are in conflict, we find that subjective preferences often become politicized assessments and too often lack the objective force to drive convergence. Often the decision analysis provides the most insight by replacing subjective judgment of preference with a model of the system the group members are supporting against a few shared metrics of system performance (ideally one). Tradeoffs are a means of elaborating what pursuing True North means in the context of the actual situation being examined.

For most business situations, this True North metric is expected net present value of cash flow (the subtleness of risk preference almost never matters.) Participants can rally around this metric and learn from it. The purity of the True North metric provides a real context for having the discussion about other considerations in terms of willingness to pay. Our experience is that in face of the economic value, most of these other considerations vaporize – they were often wish lists and not worth very much. Some considerations, such as the potential inability to actually finance a particular high-value investment, shape the understanding of the ability to pursue True North. This leads to real conversations among the players that help them generate new alternatives, converge to form coalitions, and understand their real tradeoffs in a constructive way.

For example, in the R&D community it is popular for well-meaning committees to judge value with some sort of scoring system (inspired by multi-attribute utility (MAU), but often conducted to less than professional standards), often with each committee member voting or dividing up points on various factors such as probability of success, commercial potential, strategic fit, etc. These methods have serious technical and organizational defects. Technically these systems often subsume the model by applying direct "judgment" of the committee members, when there good reasons to believe that the members are not equipped to make this visceral calculation. Then scores are added when logically they should be combined in other ways; for example, probability of success should be multiplied by the value given success. Finally the scoring systems often cover up a political process of "I'll vote for your project if you'll vote for mine."

Our experience is that the scoring approach usually evolves into an exercise in manipulating the weights to get your favorite projects funded, rather than providing real insight into which course of action should be taken. It does seem to work reasonably well when nobody cares very much about the outcome as in early-stage screening of ideas. However, the more controversy in a situation, the more pressure there is for manipulation and the less it works. One client put it this way: "these methods add sophistication without adding knowledge." These scores too often do not have the objective power to change people's minds about what is in their best interest.

There is a rogue at work here, which we call *superficial values* or *feel-good prioritization*. We have seen the most egregious version of this rogue in the public policy arena. For example, on a project to develop treatments for the tanks full of nuclear waste at the Hanford site, one of the authors worked with an engineering team to develop a remediation plan and conduct a decision analysis. From a decision analysis perspective, it was a winning plan and great public policy.

Our plan took hold and started to gain momentum in the organization. But when it reached a certain level in the organization, we learned that the plan was running into trouble. Apparently it was losing out to another plan called "CLEAN." It was very difficult to find out what this "CLEAN" plan really was, except that it involved zero emissions. After a lot of legwork, our engineering team discovered that THERE WAS NO PLAN. The DOE was debating two alternatives, one of which did not exist!

Westinghouse, the site contractor at the time, had bulldozers poised to break ground on the first plant. The DOE had to break ground on a certain date or break contracts with the EPA and the State of Washington, and was instructing its contractor to move ahead. Clarifying values had become an impediment to making good decisions.

Working to stave off $50B+ of taxpayer money being spent on plants with no engineering basis, we renamed our plan with the one value that trumps "CLEAN". We called our plan "SAFE" and resubmitted it. This restarted the debate and our plan again gained support – a soft of fighting fire with fire approach. (There were committees debating which was more important – "CLEAN" or "SAFE").

This rogue, of manipulating values or using them to obscure what is important, ironically often results in part from the very decision analytic tools designed to improve decision making.

The authors have had considerable success with emphasizing fewer metrics rather than many, which we call the "True North" approach. In business organizations, the overriding measure of value is money (e.g., NPV of cash flow), with supporting metrics that describe the economic shape of the alternative (e.g., timing, probability of success). This metric can be used to help people learn what is in their own best interest. Using objective definitions (e.g., how many dollars) rather than subjective ones (e.g., what is the weight of this attribute) creates a shared framework for understanding the implications by testing alternatives and mental models.

Often this requires building a model of the situation that projects bottom line results (for multiple uncertain scenarios). This permits sensitivity analysis to show the value of the underlying factors (uncertainties, alternatives) and refocus efforts on the most valuable activities. It also creates a level playing field for interproject or portfolio comparisons and reframes the cultural routines to promote discussion of how to create more value.

In R&D, most companies have great difficulty canceling projects because the project leaders continue to perpetuate them even when "decision makers" say no. The True North approach has achieved the very rare result of project teams canceling their own projects. When project teams see that their projects have very poor prospects of producing the kinds of business results they want, and when they see colleagues' projects with great success potential struggling for talent, many project leaders will jump to the colleague's projects. Stimulating this sort of behavior is not the focus of the traditional worldview, but is at the heart of the new worldview.

The True North approach also often works in the public policy setting. For example, the Tennessee Valley Authority has many explicitly stated objectives, among these flood control, navigation, power production, and recreation. Conflict arises when rainfall is low: should reservoirs be lowered drastically in the summer to produce power when it is needed for electricity, at the cost of making the lakes of limited recreational use?

One dry year, this problem reached a political crisis and much effort was expended to "make a decision." Attempts had been made to do a subjective MAU of the various objectives, but it had not stuck nor resulted in a real mechanism for resolving the situation. Focusing on the conflict – recreation versus power production, we developed objective metrics of these two issues, quality recreation days and electric rates.

Rating alternatives on these smoked out an intractable group – the reservoir system modelers – whose models took weeks to run and thus prevented meaningful discussion. We built simpler models focused on our metrics and found a new policy that improved both metrics! Then by giving away the simple model to both the recreational and power constituencies, we helped recreational interests realize that they should not push too far because it was not in their own interest to do so. The intractable modeling group realized this was not a threat, but rather it enhanced the appreciation of their detailed understanding. This approach both resolved the apparent conflict AND helped adversaries learn how to address ongoing decisions about reservoir operations.

The authors have had success in organizations like TVA that are clearly accountable to produce actual results. However, governmental organizations that are not held accountable for results in this sense, relying instead on public voting, presidential appointment or other highly indirect methods for feedback are difficult to help. They have no sense of True North. The reader can decide whether this is a failing of the analysis or of the accountability structure of these organizations.

In these examples, the value metric is being selected to maximize learning and to help people change their own mental models, and less as a measure to be used in an optimization (although optimization calculations are made). This helps resolve conflict in a lasting way, aligning mental models of participating constituencies and expanding the organization's capability for making good decisions regularly.

Conclusions

We have organized our experience in the field into a framework for understanding the evolving decision organization and being effective practitioners in it – a sort of clinical guide. Each element of traditional decision analysis needs to be reviewed and recast in light of the demands of modern realities of organizational decision making.

Many of the old examples and metaphors (e.g. decision makers and clear decisions) have reached the limits of their usefulness, and need to be supplemented by new ones. Although we cannot yet offer a complete new set, we conclude with a couple at the heart of the new worldview.

The first is like a pilots' navigational instrument panel used for flying through bad weather and interacting with navigational aids. The pilot flies the plane generally by looking out the window and manipulating the controls, continually referring to the instruments to make sure he is on course, avoiding storms and oriented correctly. In bad weather, pilots who do not rely on their instruments can unknowingly fly upside-down and crash!

Our vision is a corporate navigational instrument panel for continually guiding ongoing decisions at all levels in organizations. It is a panel for the unseen future that shows True North and the obstacles to getting there. It has two major displays: One is a value-meter defining True North for the organization; for example showing the expected NPV resulting from the current momentum direction of all decisions. The other is mapping the major uncertainties affecting that meter and determining their relative importance to value (such as in a tornado diagram).

Within this metaphor, the role of the decision analyst is to maintain the navigational panel, add new displays as needed, and make it visible to the powerful people who need it.

Second is thinking of an organization as an ecology of patterns of behavior. These patterns of behavior are what actually generate "decisions" and gather the relevant elements of the decision basis (among other things). Like organisms in an ecology, these patterns are sometimes in competition and sometimes in alliance as they struggle to survive.

Within this metaphor, the role of the decision analyst is twofold: (1) to participate in productive patterns so as to produce quality results (much like an accountant participates in patterns of financial accountability), and (2) to perturb the patterns so that ecology supports good decision making – making the principles of a Smart Organization more prevalent and competitive.

Generally speaking, our experience with these metaphors and the worldview they represent has consistently led to simpler, faster and more frequent analyses. Said another way, decision analysis is made more accessible so that it becomes part of the organizational routines.

We believe this process is just getting started and have offered a few initial hypotheses. We invite discussion and input, and sincerely hope that others will pick up on these threads and provide a more solid foundation. If we can step up to the challenge, Decision Analysis may one day become as widespread and as firmly embedded as accounting, and organizations will be able to sustain good decision making.

NOTE

Decision Advisor® and Portfolio Navigator™ are trademarks of SmartOrg, Inc.

REFERENCES

Argyris, C. (2004). Reasons and rationalizations: The limits to organizational knowledge. Oxford: Oxford University Press.

Barabba, Vincent, P. (1995). *Meeting of the minds: Creating the market-based enterprise.* Boston: Harvard Business School Press.

Becker, Markus, C. (2004): Organizational routines: A review of the literature. *Industrial and Corporate Change,* 13(4), 643–678.

Brown, S. L., and Eisenhardt, K. M. (1998). *Competing on the edge: Strategy as structured chaos.* Boston: Harvard Business School Press.

Eisenhardt, K. M. (1989). Making fast decision in high-velocity environments. *The Academy of Management Journal, 32*(3), 543–576.

Howard, R. A. (1966). Decision analysis: Applied decision theory. In D. B. Hertz and J. Melese (Eds.), *Proceedings of the fourth international conference on operational research*, pp. 55–71. (Reprinted in 1983 by Howard.)

Howard, R. A., and Matheson, J. E. (Eds.). (1983). *Readings on the principles and applications of decision analysis*. Menlo Park: Strategic Decisions Group.

Keelin, T., and Sharpe, P. (1998). How SmithKline Beecham makes better resource-allocation decisions. *Harvard Business Review, March*, 45–57.

Keeney, R. (1992). *Value-Focused Thinking*. Cambridge, MA: Harvard University Press.

Lander, L., Matheson, D., Menke, M., and Ransley, D. (1995). Improving the R&D decision process. *Research-Technology Management, January-February*, 40–43.

Matheson, D., and Matheson, J. (1998). *The smart organization: creating value through strategic R&D*. Boston: Harvard Business School Press.

Matheson, D., and Matheson, J. (2001). Smart Organizations Perform Better. *Research-Technology Management, July-August*, 49–54.

Matheson, D., Matheson, J., and Menke, M. (1994). Making excellent R&D decisions. *Research-Technology Management, November–December*, 21–24.

Matheson, D., Matheson, J., and Menke, M. (1995). *R&D decision quality benchmarking*. Menlo Park: Strategic Decision Group.

Raiffa, Howard (1968). *Decision analysis: Introductory lectures on choices under uncertainty*. Boston: Addison-Wesley.

Senge, Peter (1990). *The Fifth Discipline*. New York: Doubleday/Currency.

22 Building Decision Competency in Organizations

Carl S. Spetzler

ABSTRACT. Decision analysis was introduced about 40 years ago. Since that time the practice of decision consultants, whether internal or external to organizations, has expanded from analytical support in difficult decisions to designing governance and decision systems and transforming enterprise capabilities. Organizations realize a significant positive impact when they develop true decision competency – that is, when high-quality decision making becomes part of their organizational DNA. In this chapter, the author first defines organizational decision competency and then describes how to achieve this competency. He describes two cases of two large corporations that have achieved a high level of decision competency. He concludes with a perspective on the first 40 years of corporate adoption of decision competencies that still has a long way to go.

Background

In the mid-1960s, Ronald Howard and James Matheson formed the Decision Analysis Group at Stanford Research Institute[1] with the vision of creating a "teaching hospital" for decision analysis, a then-emerging discipline. Their goal was to advance the practice of decision analysis and build professional competency in the discipline among SRI's clients. Initially, decision analysis practitioners used a systems engineering approach based on normative decision science to identify the optimal choice among a set of alternatives in the light of real-world uncertainty, dynamics, and complexity. As the discipline evolved, it incorporated various methods from the behavioral decision sciences to deal with biases and to obtain organizational alignment with commitment to effective action.

Today, the role of a professional decision consultant, whether internal or external to the organization, includes helping to solve important and complex decision problems, designing governance and decision systems, and transforming enterprise capabilities. Organizations realize a significant positive impact when they develop true decision competency – that is, when sound, high-quality decision making becomes part of their organization's DNA.

---

[1] Now SRI International.

What Is Organizational Decision Competency?

An enterprise possesses decision competency when it meets the following criteria:

1. It routinely makes high-quality decisions. It correctly recognizes and declares decisions, issues, and challenges; it understands the behavioral traps inherent in natural decision making and knows how to compensate for them; it frames decisions appropriately; and it addresses decision making with the balance of content, analytic rigor, and facilitation necessary to pursue the actions most likely to deliver optimal value.
2. It has a broad array of tools, techniques, and processes in place, and decision makers and staff are skilled in using them appropriately.
3. Its decision makers understand their roles and have thoroughly developed the knowledge and skills their roles demand.
4. The organization is well aligned internally. It has a common language for and a solid understanding of what constitutes decision quality; it has a strong common desire to achieve it on a regular basis, and it "walks the talk."
5. The organization continually endeavors to learn and improve its decision competency.

Defining a Standard for High-Quality Decisions

In its search for value creation, an enterprise with true decision competency relishes coping with difficult and complex questions. It confronts high-conflict issues whenever they arise rather than hoping they'll fade away. Such organizations hate opportunity losses as much as they hate out-of-pocket losses. They are motivated to declare the right decisions and actively manage a rolling decision agenda. What seem like courageous acts in most enterprises become habit and an integral part of their organizational culture. They view decisions as a critical step toward effective action rather than as a bureaucratic process.

When skilled decision makers confront important choices, they keep in mind the natural decision behaviors[2] that tend to undermine all human effort and lead us unwittingly into often-deadly traps. For discussion purposes, we categorize such pitfalls in five broad groups: comfort zone bias, motivational bias, cognitive bias, fallacies in reasoning, and groupthink.

In building organizational decision competency, it is of particular importance to overcome comfort zone bias. It is human nature to prefer doing what we already know how to do, whether or not it leads to a good decision. In contrast, good decision-making processes help us to first identify what is most important about the decision and its outcome and then to address those particular issues – even if doing so forces us out of our comfort zone. As we declare a decision, we must recognize

---

[2] See SDG eBriefing (January 15, 2003). "Garbage In, Garbage Out: Reducing Biases in Decision Making." SDG eBriefings are available on SDG's website www.sdg.com.

that each decision situation has its own true nature and that we therefore need to address each one on its own unique terms. Astute decision makers ascertain the needs of most decision situations in each of three metadimensions: organizational complexity, analytical complexity, and content difficulty. Here is how we view each dimension.

ORGANIZATIONAL COMPLEXITY. This dimension embraces all the psychosocial aspects of a decision situation that might arise if various parties are in conflict because of individual and organizational differences. These may be differences in values, desires, and motivation; or in initial convictions and frames; or in personalities and competencies; or in degrees of power and resource availability. Also included in this dimension are the cognitive and motivational biases, as well as group dynamics. Decisions with a high degree of organizational complexity require extra attention to reducing biases and the use of facilitative approaches for achieving organizational alignment and commitment.

ANALYTICAL COMPLEXITY. Here, we include such decision aspects as high uncertainty, decision dynamics (e.g., downstream decisions, learning opportunities, and competitor reactions), many variables that may be closely interrelated, as well as a multitude of decision alternatives and multiple decision criteria. This dimension includes all aspects that make the decision technically difficult to specify and solve.

CONTENT DIFFICULTY. Decision content consists of the key inputs to the decision problem. Typically, these include data about the past, judgments about the future, alternative courses of action, and the values and trade-offs we bring to the respective decision. Adequate reliable content may be readily available, or, if not, the organization may need to engage in research and data analysis and seek the knowledge of experts.

Decision competency enables decision participants to address the true nature of the problem at hand with appropriate skills, tools, and processes. The processes involve the right people contributing in ways that will most help the organization achieve clarity, alignment, and commitment to action.

The specific form of a decision effort differs greatly from one to the next. In some cases, the need will be for a largely facilitative role to help reach agreement and identify the optimal choice. In other cases, the need may be predominantly for a creative effort to help generate better alternatives or research key inputs such as customer response probabilities. Or the need may best be met by a simulation model with many interrelated variables. Whatever one's role in the decision process, it is crucial that everyone involved remain focused on the real need of the decision and not permit the participants to simply address the problem from their comfort zone. Of course, this is much easier said than done because everyone's perspectives and skills are limited.

To have a shared understanding of decision quality means everyone involved in the process is familiar with the key elements of high-quality decisions. This common understanding of the elements that comprise decision quality and how

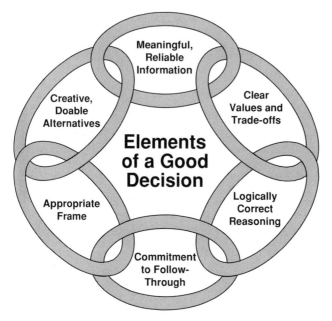

Figure 22.1. The six elements of decision quality.

the quality of each element will be assessed is fundamental to decision competency. Figure 22.1 depicts the six elements of a decision linked as a chain. To make high-quality decisions, each of the six elements must be of the highest standard, and as in an actual chain the weakest link will define the overall quality of decisions.

Having a clearly defined decision process is also critical to achieving decision competency and to making decisions that meet the six requirements of a quality decision. Several variants of the decision process can help build decision quality. Figure 22.2 illustrates a process flow that moves decision makers toward a quality decision through a dialog with the decision team around specific staged deliverables. SDG introduced this process in the early 1980s.[3] Since then, thousands of applications have demonstrated it to be a best practice for achieving clarity and alignment in making significant organizational decisions.

The shared understanding of decision quality and an effective decision-making process are two vital elements that, combined with a diverse tool set, empower decision makers and their staffs to solve most types of decision problems. There are a myriad of analytical and other sophisticated tools available to decision makers and support teams. Among these are tools that facilitate decision framing and assessment, influence diagrams, debiasing and calibration techniques, dynamic structuring, tornado charts, models and templates, value metrics, Monte Carlo simulation, and decision trees. The list is long and continues to grow as new tools and techniques are introduced. Decision professionals with access to an extensive

---

[3] Keelin, T., and Spetzler, C. (1992). "Decision Quality: Opportunity for Leadership in Total Quality Management." SDG white paper (out of print).

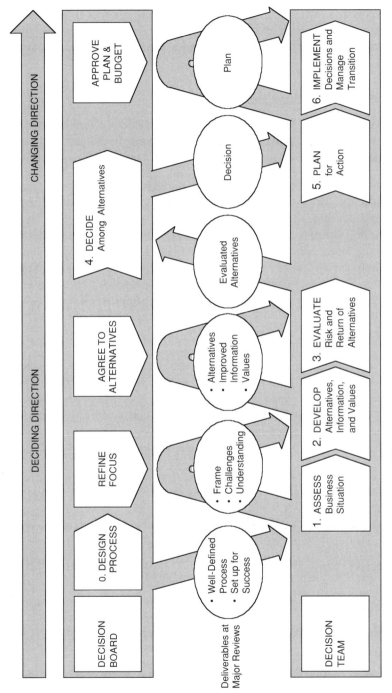

Figure 22.2. The SDG dialog decision process – DPP.

array of tools and extensive experience in using them are free to focus on the nature of the problem itself and to reach for the appropriate tool as needed. By contrast, those with few tools and limited experience in using them are strongly inclined to become tool focused.

Identifying Decision Team Roles

As we've seen, effective decision making flows from a clearly defined process that involves the right people in the right ways to reach the right choices. Participants in strategic decision making generally serve in one of three distinct roles: decision maker, decision staff, or content expert/implementer.

DECISION MAKER. This individual, or decision body, is responsible for making the decision and allocating the resources needed to pursue the chosen course. By definition, the decision maker has the responsibility for overall decision quality. This responsibility for decision quality is distinct from approval authority. Frequently, approval authority is specified – sometimes by law. For example, boards of directors are legally required to approve mergers and acquisitions. This distinction is critical because when serving in the approval role, the approver is being "sold" a recommendation that may or may not reflect decision quality. It is not possible to "inspect quality into the decision" at that late stage.[4]

DECISION STAFF. These individuals, typically operating as a cross-functional team, enable decision makers to make well-informed choices more efficiently. They assist in framing the situation, gathering information, generating alternatives, and analyzing the value of potential outcomes. They facilitate the process by achieving commitment to action from the decision makers and by providing clear direction to those designated to subsequently implement the decision.

CONTENT EXPERTS AND IMPLEMENTERS. These domain experts provide valuable facts and judgments about the consequences of different alternatives. Involving implementers early in the process can avoid the barriers that inevitably arise when people must implement decisions made by others. Implementers' involvement and contributions usually translate to less recycling through the decision process and improved execution. During the decision process, implementers serve as domain experts. They bring practical knowledge – generally acquired firsthand – of what it takes to execute the decision successfully.

Five Means for Achieving Organizational Decision Competency

In the preceding sections, we discussed what decision quality actually means, identified the six elements of a quality decision, how to recognize organizations that

---

[4] Arnold, R., Lang, J., and Spetzler, C. (January/February 2005). "Bringing Quality to Board Decisions." *The Corporate Board.*

possess high levels of decision competency, the importance of having a clearly defined decision process, and the roles of participants in that process. Now, let us explore the means by which organizations develop and sustain decision competency. We identify five primary means for achieving this goal:

1. *Alignment of Organization and Culture.* Continuously strive to make the motivation and skills required for decision competency an integral part of the organization's fabric. This includes making a deliberate effort to develop a common language and understanding for addressing decision-making issues and processes to minimize the potential for misunderstandings. The whole approach to thinking and talking about decisions should become part of "the way we do things here."

2. *Decision Processes and Tools.* Ensure that the processes and tools needed to attain decision quality are at hand. It is equally important to train users thoroughly not only in use of the tools, but also in the advantages and shortcomings of each. Applying the wrong tool can produce misleading results. As with all tools, obtaining quality results depends on the knowledge and skill of their users.

3. *Training and Experience.* Thoroughly train decision makers and their staffs for the roles they are expected to play in the organization's decision processes. For decision makers, SDG finds this typically means about two half-days of training followed by counseling in addressing real-world decisions. About two days of training are appropriate for experts and implementers who serve on decision teams. Usually, part of this training involves working on some aspect of a real decision; for example, in a decision-framing workshop. The professional decision staff requires more extensive training, similar to SDG's decision consultants who receive about five weeks of classroom training and a two-year apprenticeship that prepares them to lead teams under the supervision of an experienced SDG partner.

4. *Dedication to Learning and Improvement.* Ensure that participants remain committed to retaining and extending their competencies. Without such ongoing improvement, decision competency will atrophy because of turnover and other factors. Turnover among decision staff members is generally high and for good reason: they are typically high-potential individuals who rapidly develop broad business perspective and experience and who therefore are presented with many opportunities for advancement, both internally and externally. The positive side of this is that, over time, the organization's cadre of top decision makers grows to include former members of its decision support staff. However, such turnover requires the enterprise's ongoing commitment and investment in developing professional decision support staff. The dedication to learning also includes periodic "look-backs" to earlier decision efforts to see what can be improved. In addition, professional decision staff should be encouraged to continually seek new ideas and concepts and to participate in the learning networks of their respective professions.

5. *Organizational Congruence*[5]: By incorporating the roles and means into the framework shown in Figure 22.3a, organizations can achieve organizational congruence, a state in which decision competency is self-reinforcing. Here, it is important not to confuse the term "congruence" with harmony. In congruent organizations, leaders raise and address important conflicts with intensity in the search for truth and the highest opportunity to create value. In any system, congruence requires alignment of many parts, and a single "broken" part can spell failure. To achieve a high-performance state of organizational decision competency requires bringing all the elements into position and then continuing to learn and strengthen the weakest links in the system.

Although the above framework is easy to explain, implementing it effectively and on a sustained basis is indeed a tall order. Nonetheless, our experience shows organizations that make a concerted ongoing effort to do it can achieve congruence and thereby reap significant benefits. In sections to follow, we describe the journey of two large enterprise-wide implementations to building organizational decision competency – General Motors and Chevron.

The Journey to Organizational Decision Competency

Most organizations see themselves on a path to decision competency. In an SDG e-Briefing attended by more than 50 organizations, most attendees judged their organizations to have partial (or "islands") of competency. Only 5 percent viewed their firms as having achieved excellence in this regard, and 9 percent did not see their organizations as even being on the path to decision competency. See Figure 22.3b.

When SDG assists organizations in building decision competency, it is usually at the behest of a client champion – someone within the organization who provides sponsorship. Once the journey begins, successful clients proceed to advance through the following stages:

ASSESSMENT OF THE SITUATION. This provides a baseline understanding of how the enterprise approaches decision making and the gaps that need to be filled to achieve competency.

DESIGN OF A TRANSFORMATION PROGRAM. Generally, the program is a staged effort tailored to specific organizational needs. It may need to grow slowly to convince organizational leaders of its efficacy early on, or rapid implementation may be necessary to address critical decision failures. The framework shown in Figure 22.3a helps in the design of the program by showing how roles and means are combined to achieve organizational competency.

---

[5] We use the concept of organizational congruence as presented in Nadler, David A., and Tushman, Michael L. (1997). *Competing by Design.* Oxford: Oxford University Press.

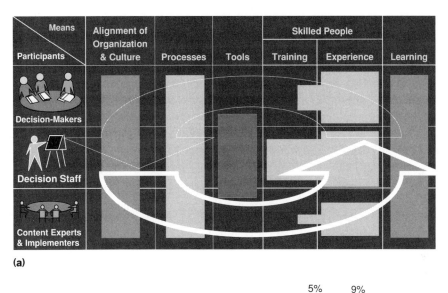

(a)

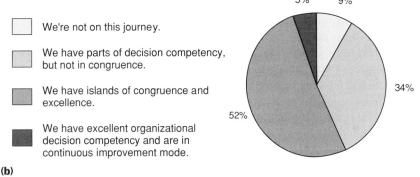

We're not on this journey.

We have parts of decision competency, but not in congruence.

We have islands of congruence and excellence.

We have excellent organizational decision competency and are in continuous improvement mode.

5%   9%

34%

52%

(b)

Figure 22.3. Polling results: where is your organization on this journey?

DEMONSTRATION OF THE PROCESS AND ITS VALUE. Most organizations want to demonstrate the value of decision competency by applying it to a handful of critical decision situations. Participants in the demonstration often become champions of the process who subsequently support its broader adoption and development.

STAGED IMPLEMENTATION. Many decision makers are inclined to adopt the new process quickly. However, the professional staff that will support them will need to be developed in stages. In a poll of more than 50 organizations attending the SDG eBriefing "GM's Decision-Making Transformation," most attendees felt that it would take several years for their organizations to achieve high levels of organizational decision competency – see Figure 22.4.

REINFORCEMENT, LEARNING, AND IMPROVEMENT. As mentioned earlier, management must remain committed to building and improving the organization's decision competency or else watch it atrophy over time.

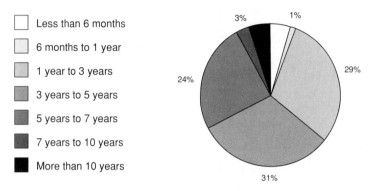

Figure 22.4. Polling results: how long would it take your organization to achieve decision competency? *Source:* SDG Executive eBriefing, "GM's Decision-Making Transformation – A Conversation with Vince Barabba, Nick Pudar and Dan Roesch, September 2004." Responses represent about 50 organizations.

The Current State of Adoption

Today, few organizations have attained high organizational decision competency on an enterprise-wide basis. The cases of GM and Chevron, which follow, are clearly exceptions. High levels of decision competency do exist in a handful of industries where high uncertainty tends to prevail, such as those involving upstream oil and gas investment or drug development. In domains that must routinely confront high uncertainty, a lack of decision competency is now a competitive *disadvantage*. It should be noted that although enterprise-wide decision competency is missing in most organizations, many larger corporations have "islands" within them that do function at high levels of decision competency.

Since the quest for building decision competency began some 40 years ago, practitioners have met many successes, but not without many failures as well. We have learned from those failures and applied their lessons to help enterprises further strengthen their decision competency. Here, for example, are some practices we have learned *do not* help build decision competency:

- Focusing training of decision support staff primarily on analytical tools rather than the essence of the decision problem;
- Concentrating on analytical complexity at the expense of organization and decision content;
- Facilitating organizational agreement while ignoring analytical and content complexities;
- Building competency piecemeal – often with inadequate resources – and not creating organizational congruence;
- Inadequate training and mentoring for process leaders;
- Creating a bureaucratic decision process – a "process monster."

When decision makers focus too intently on analytics and discount organizational issues in the process, the result may still be the "right answer," but nobody will care. And building competency piecemeal is like setting out to buy a car even though you're broke, so you decide to buy the wheels and windshield now and the rest later. We also found some clients actually created a process monster. They do extremely well at building decision competency for 2 or 3 years but then allow themselves to be captivated by the process. They gradually standardize and bureaucratize it, which eventually leads to a backlash. The important lesson here is to stay focused on maximizing value; that is, finding the appropriate balance of analytics, facilitation, and content. And, of course, to succeed in winning the right sponsorship is of great importance.

GM's Road to Decision Competency

General Motors Corporation, the world's largest automobile manufacturer, provides a good example of how a venerable global institution can undergo a transformation that significantly improves decision competency. In 1992, GM was on the verge of bankruptcy because of an inadequate competitive response to the superior quality and manufacturing methods of Japanese rivals and because of long-term promises to stakeholders made during GM's heyday. By 2003, little more than a decade later, GM had rebounded strongly.[6] GM leaders credit the rebound, in part, to improved organizational decision competency.[7]

In 1985, GM hired Vincent Barabba as general manager of corporate strategy and knowledge development. Barabba, who earlier had grown interested in decision analysis while at Kodak, soon recognized that GM's strategic decision-making processes were seriously flawed, and in 1988 he began an initiative to set them right – an initiative that would require several years to implement.[8] Barabba engaged Strategic Decisions Group and other consultants to assist GM in the effort by: (1) identifying the shortcomings in GM's primary decision processes,

---

[6] There is a common perception of General Motors as a company struggling to survive. However, it is a misunderstood enterprise because only a small fraction of its financial value rests in the hands of shareholders. GM's current cost disadvantage (relative to Toyota) of $1500/car was bargained away to the United Auto Workers' Union more than 30 years ago. Toyota earns about $1,700/car whereas GM earns less than $200. GM may not survive under its present financial structure, but as an enterprise, it is performing very competitively. I see in GM a talent-rich organization that embraced organizational decision competency to build immense value for its many stakeholders – including those with legacy entitlements.

[7] This example was presented in the SDG eBriefing on September 15, 2004, "GM's Decision-Making Transformation – A Conversation with Vince Barabba, Nick Pudar and Dan Roesch." Vince Barabba, General Manager, GM Corporate Strategy and Knowledge Development (retired), was the primary change agent who brought Organizational Decision Competency to GM. Nick Pudar, currently Director, GM Global Planning and Strategic Initiatives, led the decision staff and further developed the competency. Dan Roesch, Director, GM Strategic Initiatives (GMSI), currently heads the GM decision staff. Carl Spetzler, Chairman, SDG, served as moderator. An archive of SDG eBriefings is available on the SDG website: www.sdg.com.

[8] Barabba, V. (1995). *Meeting of the Minds: Creating the Market-Based Enterprise*. Harvard Business School Press, pp. 186–205.

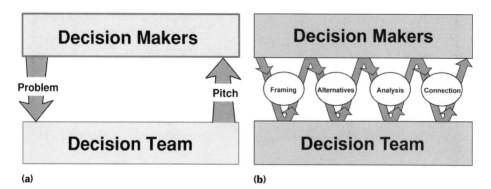

Figure 22.5. Comparison of (a) GM traditional decision process versus (b) GM dialog decision process.

(2) helping it overcome those shortcomings, and (3) increasing the company's overall level of decision competency.

Longstanding Practices and Culture

Initial scrutiny of how GM approached strategic decision making proved telling. Over a period of years, the automaker, like most corporations, had developed a culture in which decisions were typically made on an advocacy and approval basis. Middle management developed and presented *business cases* to senior management who then accepted or rejected them. Because the objective was usually to win senior-management approval, business cases increasingly minimized whatever downside that existed. To win senior-management approval, the task was simple: advocate the most powerful business case possible. Every case therefore tended to present an extremely strong upside with a minimal downside. Finding the weaknesses in a project proposal was perceived to be the job of senior management.

In this advocacy and approval mode, presenting alternative courses of action to approvers was counterproductive because it would provide them ammunition to interrogate the advocate. In fact, advocates quickly dismissed alternatives that the approver might propose during the "pitch" as having already been considered and rejected. Barabba also says, "The adversarial approach to decision making provides little incentive for dealing openly with uncertainty and risk. If your role is that of advocate, bringing these to the surface is tantamount to handing ammunition to your adversaries who will simply use it to point out your proposal's shortcomings."[9]

In Figure 22.5a, you can see how traditional decision making contrasts with the dialog decision process.

In the traditional approach, executives and managers with strategic decision-making responsibility refer problems to a decision support team. These teams are charged with researching and analyzing the problem and recommending a solution

[9] Ibid., p. 195.

to the decision makers. At GM, it gradually became the practice of support teams to present only the recommended solution and to do it in the best possible light. If the decision makers questioned any part of the case being presented, only then would the support team address those issues. This decision process effectively omitted communication between decision makers and the decision support team during the critical phase of identifying, researching, and evaluating potential solutions. The decision makers were, in reality, excluded from the process until the team returned and presented its recommendation. This exclusion had several negative effects:

- Prior to making recommendations, decision makers were usually unaware of the alternatives and variations developed and evaluated by the support teams. Consequently, GM was losing whatever potential value such concepts held.
- There was little opportunity for decision makers to provide guidance to the support team's efforts or to otherwise contribute once they referred a problem to a team.
- Support teams risked proposing flawed solutions or solutions that were unacceptable for some other reason that the decision maker could have identified for them early in the process.

Moreover, support teams were destined to repeat the cycle when decision makers rejected a proposed solution. If management was unwilling to make an up-or-down decision on what support teams presented, they sent the teams back to the drawing board – a recycling process that typically consumes significant time. This advocacy and approval process was effectively diverting a significant measure of responsibility for GM's strategic decision making to the support teams, essentially leaving decision makers to make only up-or-down decisions on the solutions pitched to them.

Introducing the Dialog Decision Process

To remedy the problems arising from the traditional advocacy and approval process, GM introduced the Dialog Decision Process (DDP). DDP involves instituting communication flows between decision makers and the support team at several critical points in the decision process.

The version adopted by GM and illustrated in Figure 22.5b consisted of the following steps:

1. *Framing.* Developing a clear problem statement agreed to by both the decision makers and support team.
2. *Alternatives.* Identifying alternative courses of action that are significantly different from one another, creative, and realistic.
3. *Analysis.* A comprehensive side-by-side comparison of the consequences of each alternative in terms of risk and return.
4. *Connection.* Generating a *hybrid* solution that combines the best aspects of the alternatives considered and articulating the rationale to facilitate decision implementation.

Requiring formal communications at these key points enabled GM to significantly improve both the quality and cost of making complex strategic decisions involving many people in diverse parts of the organization.

Many decision variables are continuous, yet for practical reasons it is necessary to tackle just a handful of significantly different strategies. A metaphor was introduced at GM that likened the initial strategies to test wells (as in exploring for oil) and then creating a hybrid strategy (the production well) that combined the best attributes of all alternatives. The metaphor resonated well with managers, and today test wells are part of the GM vocabulary.

GM initially applied DDP in a small number of select cases and also offered it as an optional tool for others. At first, managers struggled with this dramatically different approach but soon saw its advantages and spread the word to colleagues who, in turn, adopted it. By 1995, more than 2,500 GM managers had participated in training and more than 100 DDPs had been conducted. GM used DDPs to address a broad range of topics, including product planning and development, marketing, globalization, technology choices, information systems, business unit strategy, portfolio resource allocation, and finance issues.

Management also tracked the benefits of improved decision making by comparing the net present value of momentum strategies – what it would have done without DDP – versus the chosen strategies. Their analysis demonstrated that the additional value potential being created was in the billions of dollars. "The business value of these win–win hybrid courses of action is difficult to overstate." wrote Vince Barabba.[10]

Three other unexpected benefits of building organizational decision competency came as a surprise to GM. First, the total time from initiating a DDP to completed implementation of a decision was significantly shorter than under the traditional decision process. Although the DDP itself took longer, the need to recycle through the process because of unacceptable solutions was virtually eliminated. This created an alignment between problem and solution that cut implementation time in half. It was truly a case of "going slow to go fast."

The second benefit was its impact on GM's culture. In his book *Meeting of the Minds*, Barabba writes, "One by-product of the repeated application of DDP at GM has been a noticeable change in the management culture. There has been an observable shift away from a culture of advocative and adversarial interactions toward one that is more open and cooperative. This effect was unexpected. Our objective was to change the way that decisions were made, not to change the culture. But we have come to understand how intimately the two are linked."[11]

The third benefit of GM's transformation was improved learning and knowledge sharing. For many years, the company was, like most companies, tightly organized around major functional areas – an approach that had served it well because of the deep knowledge it was able to acquire in critical areas. However,

---

[10] Ibid., p. 198.
[11] Ibid., pp. 204–205.

dialog between functional areas was minimal, so an area such as engineering, for example, had only a limited understanding of what marketing was trying to accomplish and vice versa. The traditional decision process long used at GM clearly contributed to this problem. Since the inception of DDP, managers throughout the corporation have developed a strong appreciation for the substantial value derived from sharing knowledge and information. Barabba says, "The increase in shared knowledge at GM . . . is the true source of the value increases we have witnessed. It is . . . breaking down the informational barriers that exist between our silos."[12]

Decision Competency Climbs Steadily

During the last decade, under the leadership of Nick Pudar and more recently Dan Roesch, GM broadly adopted decision competency and significantly reshaped those parts of the organization involved in strategic decision making. Decision boards – commonly called leadership or strategy boards – became a way of doing business that is now pervasive at GM. The company has several standing boards that are cross-functional, cross-organizational groups of senior managers who concentrate on such areas as GM's OnStar business, advanced propulsion systems, healthcare benefits, and various regional issues. The company also creates ad hoc decision boards when major issues arise that are not seen as suitable for one of the firm's standing decision boards to address.

GM also maintains about a half dozen decision support teams and a central staff of some twenty-five professionals who constitute the GM Strategic Initiatives (GMSI) Center and provide expertise in decision analytics and facilitation. Among GMSI members are senior technical professionals and skilled experts – most with Ph.D.s. The center has significantly extended the analytical tools available to decision teams and has introduced dynamic modeling applications. Its members are viewed as leaders both within GM and in the field of applied decision making. GMSI also includes managers with significant GM experience that enables them to readily engage others in various functional and practice areas throughout the organization – an ability that is vital to the services GSMI provides.

GMSI uses its analyst positions to train newly recruited MBAs, rotating them through on an 18- to 24-month basis. Today, many recipients of GSMI training have achieved senior leadership positions in the company. Such career development helps maintain and reinforce the organization's decision competency. Roesch, who currently leads GMSI as GM's director of strategic initiatives, says the group has steadily built its credibility throughout the worldwide GM enterprise, and today senior and middle management broadly recognize its value. The group now handles 35 to 40 major decision projects annually. The value of the projects it undertakes is in the billions of dollars. In addition to the services it provides to decision boards, GMSI also provides senior leadership with strategic synthesis of emerging business ideas and trends, as well as management consulting oversight.

---

[12] Ibid., p. 202.

Chevron – Decision Making in a High-Uncertainty Business

The power of organizational decision competency is greatest in decision-intensive industries. We view an industry as decision intensive when decision competency is more important to success than execution. To determine this, we ask which of two organizations in a given industry would be more profitable: one that is average at making the right bets but ranks in the top 2 percent in execution or one that ranks in the top 2 percent in making the right bets but only average in execution. For the oil and gas industry, the latter is the more profitable business, qualifying this industry as decision intensive. Other decision-intensive industries are capital-intensive industries like commodity chemicals or R&D-intensive industries like pharmaceuticals. Of course, being outstanding at both decision making and execution is far superior in any industry. However, in decision-intensive industries, excellence in decision making provides greater advantage. Chevron recognized this at the beginning of the 1990s and engaged SDG to help it build decision competency. After a few projects to demonstrate decision quality principles and the dialog process, Chevron adopted the approach broadly. The company introduced more than 1,000 decision makers to the subject of decision quality in two-day workshops. Dozens of decision staff members attended two-week "boot camps" and then were subsequently coached while assisting in making important real-world decisions. During the early stages, adoption of the practices was optional for individual business units.

As the program matured in the mid-1990s, Chevron's internal consulting organization developed deep competencies and became largely independent in training and developing its staff. When David O'Reilly became Chevron's CEO and reviewed some of its recent decisions that had fallen far short of expectations, he required that the Dialog Decision Process become standard procedure and that decision makers throughout the company be certified in its use. Since then, Chevron has certified thousands of its decision makers and developed hundreds of decision staff members. It also developed a two-day decision simulation exercise that more than 2,000 of its executives have now completed. The company's internal decision consulting group has a staff of more than 100 spread among business units. Of these, 40 to 50 engage full-time in decision analysis and facilitation. Frank Koch, decision analysis practice leader at Chevron, observed that their commitment is high and broadly based. He reports that, by improving its decision competency, Chevron gained significant benefits, including a common language, a set of common expectations, an understanding of what a good decision effort is, and effective behaviors by decision makers who are now much better prepared for decision review board meetings and able to engage in effective dialog.

In looking forward, Koch is turning his attention to maintaining and further refining Chevron's organizational decision competency. The company is introducing value tracking in an effort to better compare the value promise at the time of decision to the value that is actually realized and how the value promise changes over time. Chevron has also introduced dynamic analysis of multiple stakeholder positions and advanced analytical techniques. Although decision competence is now deeply embedded at Chevron, Koch recognizes that without vigilance competence may not survive the transitions in management that every company experiences. Nonetheless, the approach now has many champions among its primary decision makers and a passionate decision staff.

Conclusion

In looking back over 40 years, I am struck by how much and how little we have accomplished in developing true decision competency across entire enterprises. In one way, we accomplished a lot. We now know what true organizational decision competency looks like. We have a limited number of enterprise-wide examples to which we can point. And the benefits of decision competency are now convincing to almost everyone.

Forty years ago, we conceived of decision competency mainly as an analytical skill that was applied to subjective judgments from experts. Thirty years ago, by the mid-1970s, we had broadened our perspective to incorporate powerful lessons from the pioneers of behavioral decision science.[13] We also had numerous successes in corporate consulting and were training internal decision consulting staffs and decision makers in industry-leading organizations.

Among these early successes was Xerox, then one of the world's most successful companies. I recall one Xerox president deciding to have his entire organization adopt decision analysis methods. When I suggested this might be difficult, he responded that would not be the case because he would use *the clapping method*. He said, "Carl, you will lead a one-week seminar. We will bring in all the right people, and I will sit in the front row and clap a lot. You'll see how fast the organization will adopt decision analysis." He was right. We delivered the seminar, and it appeared to be a great success. Within weeks, the office walls of financial staff and product planners were adorned with decision trees. On closer inspection, however, the diagrams were not of new proposals, but existing ones that had decision trees drawn around them. Clearly, it is easier to adopt the form than the substance of decision quality. At Xerox, which then had an adversarial culture, decision analysis evolved into a powerful weapon for winning intramural wars. Indeed, we still had much to learn about organizational behavior before we could build sustainable organizational decision competency.

Twenty years ago, we had mastered using the Dialog Decision Process as a powerful tool for achieving organizational alignment and learning. However, we were still addressing mostly single decisions, frequently the choice of corporate strategy. However, our tools had grown to the point where we were able to address entire decision portfolios. We could do rapid decision analyses on individual initiatives, assets, or R&D programs and then combine the outcomes to optimize entire business portfolios. These applications offered immense value, often enabling

---

[13] See, for example, Spetzler, Carl, and Stael van Holstein, Carl-Axel (1975). "Probability Encoding in Decision Analysis," *Management Science, 22*, 340–358.

companies to grow portfolio value as much as 30 percent without additional resources. This new capability resulted in waves of new applications and subsequent adoption by organizations during the next 15 years, particularly in the oil and gas and pharmaceutical industries where these methods have become standard.

Ten years ago, we saw the early adopters of organizational decision competency as we define it today, including GM and Chevron. The economic bubble of the late 1990s confused the picture somewhat, because disciplined decision making seemed less important than speed in capturing the overwhelming value potential of the dot-com revolution and participating in the economics of "irrational exuberance." We have seen companies during the last five years gradually recovering from the devastation wreaked when that bubble finally burst. Burned by the experience, most avoided taking significant investment risks and amassed cash instead.

Where will we go from here, and what role will decision competency play? Allow me to venture a prediction. Corporate leaders and their boards will be more disciplined as corporations return to growth strategies. Their emphasis on discipline will continue for at least a decade because current leaders have painful lessons still deeply etched in their minds. This will make the development of organizational decision competence a renewed priority, so I foresee wider adoption in the coming years, especially in decision-intensive industries.

Why hasn't that adoption occurred more rapidly? First, we did not see the entire picture until some 15 years ago. Second, the professional community that does comprehend the whole picture is relatively small and includes few academics. Third, as discussed earlier, developing organizational decision competence requires doing a lot of things right and then having them all work well together. It is a major transformational challenge, and there are many ways to fail. Fourth, the notion remains popular that decision making is a matter of *having the feel and making the call* that some people have an innate ability to do this well and all we need do is find them. Finally, many proponents place too much importance on the decisions and denigrate the importance of execution, thereby alienating many line executives. A good decision is only the first step in value creation: it creates value *potential* that cannot become real value until executed effectively. Competent decision making must assume its appropriate place in the overall value creation chain.

Acknowledgments

The author expresses his appreciation to the many professional colleagues who have been part of developing the paradigm of Decision Quality and helping transfer this competence to decision makers, decision staffs, and whole organizations. This includes many colleagues from SDG and Stanford. It started with Ron Howard and Jim Matheson, but it evolved into a professional community that numbers in the hundreds.

23 Negotiation Analysis: Between Decisions and Games[1]

James K. Sebenius

ABSTRACT. Conceptually located between decision analysis and game theory, the emergent field of *negotiation analysis* seeks to develop prescriptive theory and useful advice for negotiators and third parties. It generally emphasizes assessment of the parties' underlying interests, alternatives to negotiated agreement, approaches to productively manage the inherent tension between competitive actions to "claim" value individually and cooperative ones to "create" value jointly, as well as efforts to change perceptions of the negotiation itself. Because advice to one side does not necessarily presume the full (game-theoretic) rationality of the other side(s), negotiation analysts often draw on the findings of behavioral scientists and experimental economists. Further, this approach does not generally assume that all the elements of the negotiation or "game" are common knowledge. It tends to deemphasize the application of game-theoretic solution concepts or efforts to find unique equilibrium outcomes. Instead, to evaluate possible strategies and tactics, negotiation analysts generally focus on changes in perceptions of the "zone of possible agreement" and the (subjective) distribution of possible negotiated outcomes conditional on various actions. It has been used to develop prescriptive advice for the simplest bilateral negotiations between monolithic parties, for negotiations through agents or with linked "internal" and "external" aspects, for negotiations in hierarchies and networks, for more complex coalitional interactions, as well as for moves "away from the table" to change the perceived negotiation itself, including the challenge of "negotiation design" to enhance the likelihood of desirable outcomes.

Beyond the popular bargaining manuals that populate airport bookshelves, to what bodies of theory and empirical work might one turn for informed negotiation advice to sell a car, acquire a business, or forge a global warming treaty?[2] Decades of psychological studies of people negotiating offer many powerful insights, but generally lack a prescriptive theory of action.[3] Instead, this behavioral approach has largely sought accurate descriptions and analytic explanations of how negotiators *do* act. What they *should* do often remains an implicit or *ad hoc* implication of this careful work.

---

[1] This chapter owes a considerable debt to David Lax and Howard Raiffa, longtime colleagues in the development of the theory and practice of negotiation analysis. It represents an evolution of my earlier syntheses of the emerging field of negotiation analysis, including Sebenius (1991, 2001, 2002), and draws extensively on those works.

[2] For genuinely useful popular works on negotiation, see, e.g., Fisher, Ury, and Patton (1991), Ury (1991), and Freund (1992).

[3] See, e.g., Rubin and Brown (1975) or Pruitt (1981).

Decision analysis, the practically oriented cousin of decision theory, would seem a logical candidate to fill this prescriptive void. It suggests a systematic decomposition of the problem: structuring and sequencing the parties' choices and chance events, then separating and subjectively assessing probabilities, values, risk and time preferences. A von Neumann–Morgenstern expected utility criterion typically aggregates these elements in ranking possible actions to determine the optimal choice. This approach is well-suited to decisions "against nature," in which the uncertainties – such as the probability that an earthquake will strike San Francisco in August – are not affected by the choices of other involved parties that themselves anticipate one's own actions.

Yet when decision making is *interactive* – as is true in negotiation, where each party's anticipated choices affects the other's and vice versa – assessment of what the other side will do qualitatively differs from assessment of "natural" uncertainties. Of course, the theory of games was developed to provide a logically consistent framework for analyzing such interdependent decision making. Full descriptions of the courses of action open to each involved party are encapsulated into "strategies." Rigorous analysis of the interaction of strategies leads to a search for "equilibria," or plans of action such that each party, given the choices of the other parties, has no incentive to change its plans. A great deal of analysis by game theorists seeks conditions for unique equilibria among such strategies.[4]

Game theory has been especially useful for understanding repeated negotiations in well-structured financial situations. It has offered useful guidance for the design of auction and bidding mechanisms, has uncovered powerful competitive dynamics, has usefully analyzed many "fairness" principles, and now flourishes both on its own and in applications such as microeconomic theory and the economics of business strategy and industrial organization. Despite signal successes, however, the dominant game-theoretic quest to predict equilibrium outcomes resulting from the strategic interactions of fully rational players often lacks prescriptive power in negotiations.

Three major aspects of mainstream game theory, discussed at length in Sebenius (1992, 2002), contribute to this "prescriptive gap." First, on standard assumptions, there are often numerous plausible equilibrium concepts, each with many associated equilibria – and no a priori compelling way to choose among them. Second, even where one party wishes to act rationally, the other side may not behave as a strategically sophisticated, expected utility-maximizer – thus rendering conventional equilibrium analyses less applicable. A large and growing body of evidence – especially in "behavioral game theory" and experimental economics – suggests that people systematically and significantly violate the canons of rationality. Third, the elements, structures, and "rules" of many negotiating situations are not completely known to all the players, and even the character of what is known by one player may not be known by another. The frequent lack of such "common knowledge" limits – from a prescriptive standpoint – much

---

[4] See the classic discussions of von Neumann and Morgenstern (1944) and Luce and Raiffa (1957); for a more recent, very insightful assessment, see Aumann (1989).

equilibrium-oriented game analysis.[5] Even where it is possible to shoehorn such a situation into the form of a well-posed game, and gain insights from it, the result may lose considerable prescriptive relevance.

The Negotiation Analytic Approach

If descriptive psychological approaches to negotiation lack a prescriptive framework; if decision analysis isn't directly suited to interactive problems; and if traditional game theory generally presupposes too stringent a form of rationality and strict common knowledge, then "negotiation analysis" represents a response that yokes the prescriptive and descriptive research traditions under less exacting assumptions. Using Howard Raiffa's (1982) terms, unlike the "symmetrically prescriptive" approach of game theory – wherein fully rational players are analyzed in terms of what each should optimally do given the other's optimal choices – the "asymmetrically prescriptive/descriptive" approach typically seeks to generate prescriptive advice to one party conditional on a (probabilistic) description of how others will behave. This need not mean tactical naiveté; as appropriate, the assessments can incorporate none, a few, or many rounds of "interactive reasoning."

Works that embody the spirit of this approach can be found as early as the late 1950s. Although Luce and Raiffa's (1957) *Games and Decisions* was primarily an incisive synthesis and exposition of game theory's development since von Neumann and Morgenstern's (1944) classic work, Luce and Raiffa began to raise serious questions about the inherent limits of this approach in analyzing actual interactive situations. Perhaps the first work that could be said to be "in the spirit of negotiation analysis" was *The Strategy of Conflict* by Thomas Schelling (1960). Its point of departure was explicitly game-theoretic but it proceeded with less formal argument and the analysis had far broader direct scope. Though nominally in the behavioral realm, Walton and McKersie's (1965) *A Behavioral Theory of Labor Negotiations* drew on Schelling's work as well as rudimentary decision and game theories.

The first overall synthesis of this emerging field appeared with Raiffa's (1982) *The Art and Science of Negotiation*, elaborated in Raiffa (1997), and greatly extended in Raiffa, Richardson, and Metcalfe's (2002) *Negotiation Analysis: The Science and Art of Collaborative Decision Making*. Building on Sebenius (1984), this approach was systematized into an overall method in Lax and Sebenius' (1986) *The Manager as Negotiator* and extended in their (2006) *3-D Negotiation*. *Negotiation Analysis* (1991), edited by Young, furthered this evolving tradition, which was characterized, summarized, and reviewed in Sebenius (1992, 2001, 2002). Further contributions to the field, in the same rationalist vein, were included in Zeckhauser, Keeney, and Sebenius (1996), Arrow, Wilson, Ross, Tversky, and

---

[5] Work by, e.g., Aumann and Brandenburger (1995) has begun to relax the widespread understanding that common knowledge of the situation was essential to game models.

Mnookin (1995), and, adding insights from organizational and information economics, in Mnookin, Peppet, and Tulumello (2000).

Meanwhile, another group of researchers was coming to a negotiation analytic view from a behavioral point of departure. With roots in the cognitive studies of behavioral decision theorists, for example, Bell, Raiffa, and Tversky (1988), behavioral scholars began in the early 1990s to explicitly link their work to that of Raiffa and his colleagues. In particular, Neale and Bazerman's (1991) *Cognition and Rationality in Negotiation*, Bazerman and Neale (1992), and Thompson (2001) pulled together and developed great deal of psychological work on negotiation in an asymmetrically prescriptive/descriptive framework. These efforts began to systematically build up more structure on what had been, in the works of Raiffa et al., a largely *ad hoc* descriptive side of the ledger.

Elements of a Negotiation Analytic Approach[6]

Full negotiation analytic accounts (e.g., Sebenius 1992, 2000) generally consider the following basic elements: the actual and potential parties, their perceived interests, alternatives to negotiated agreement, the linked processes of "creating" and "claiming" value, and the potential to "change the game" itself.

Parties

In the simplest negotiation, two principals negotiate with each other and enumerating the parties is a trivial exercise. Yet, potentially complicating parties, such as lawyers, bankers, and other agents, may be present, as may multiple internal factions with very different interests. Potentially influential parties, who themselves may not be principals or even involved at all in the nominal negotiation, may be able to block or enable a deal. Multiple parties, some of whom may not be immediately obvious, are thus involved. The crucial first step for an effective negotiation analysis is to map the full set of potentially relevant parties and their relationships in the context of the decision processes. Lax and Sebenius (2006) offer a framework for assessing the full set of parties that are and should or should not be involved.

Interests

The next step is to probe deeply for each relevant party's or faction's underlying interests and to carefully assess its tradeoffs among interests. In principle, this assessment is radically subjective in the sense that less tangible concerns for self-image, fairness, process, precedents, or relationships can have the same analytic standing as the "harder" or "objective" interests such as cost, time, and quality that are common to traditional economic approaches.

---

[6] Much in the following sections is directly from Sebenius (1992).

It is often useful to distinguish the full set of parties' underlying *interests* from the *issues* under negotiation, on which *positions* or stands are taken.[7] To illustrate, suppose you're negotiating a job offer; the base salary will usually be an *issue*. Perhaps your *position* on that issue is that you need to earn $100,000. The *interests* underlying that position certainly include your need for a good income but may also include status, security, new opportunities, and needs that can be met in ways other than salary. Rather than a $15,000 higher base at the start of a new job, your real interests may be better served by a more direct reporting relationship, a wider set of responsibilities, and an expedited compensation review – as well as a later start date that permits you to take that long-postponed vacation with your family. And, of course, an assessment of the full set of the *other* sides' interests is a vital complement to assessing one's own. (Raiffa (1997) and Lax and Sebenius (1986) illustrate this kind of assessment in the context of employment negotiations.)

In conflict situations, emphasizing positions can drive the parties even further from advancing their real interests; in other cases, emphasizing interests will only generate hopeless conflict when mutually beneficial agreement on certain overt positions could be reached. To take the more common case in which an interest-based focus is preferable to a positional one, consider a dispute over a dam project. Environmentalists and farmers opposed a power company's plans to build a dam in the midwestern United States. On the surface, the parties had deeply felt, irreconcilable positions: "absolutely yes" versus "no way." Yet, as in many bargaining situations, these incompatible positions masked compatible interests. In reality, the farmers were worried about reduced water flow below the dam, the environmentalists were focused on the downstream habitat of the endangered whooping crane, and the power company needed new capacity and a greener image. After a costly legal stalemate, the three groups devised an interest-driven agreement that all of them considered preferable to continued court warfare. The agreement included a smaller dam built on a fast track, water flow guarantees, downstream habitat protection, and a trust fund to enhance whooping crane habitats elsewhere. Rather than a convergence of *positions*, this agreement entailed efforts to reconcile each side's deeper *interests*.

In virtually all cases, however, an important first analytic step is to probe deeply for interests, distinguish them from issues and positions, and to carefully assess tradeoffs. Raiffa *et al.* (2002) offers an extended discussion of assessing tradeoffs in negotiation, building on extensive work by Keeny and Raiffa (1976). (See also Keeney 1996; Keeney and Raiffa 1991; Hammond, Keeney, and Raiffa 1998.) Lax and Sebenius (1986, 2006) offer a simplified discussion of the principles behind such tradeoffs and systematic suggestions for "getting interests right," while Wierzbicki (1983) critically surveys the methodologies of multiobjective analysis.

When individuals or groups with different concerns constitute a negotiating "side," it is no longer in general possible to specify overall tradeoffs; however,

---

[7] "Interest-based bargaining" is a centerpiece of Fisher, Ury, and Patton (1991).

carefully tracing which set of interests is ascendant according to the internal bargaining process of given factions may continue to provide insights. (Wilson's (1968) work on "syndicates" suggests the formal conditions under which a "group utility function" exists.) One result of such analysis of interests may be the disaggregation of a side into factions whose interests are shared enough to justify treating the faction as another distinct party. For cases in which such disaggregation is not sensible, Keeney, Renn and von Winterfeldt (1983) discuss "value tree" analysis, whereby effective preferences of larger groups can be assessed for decision-making purposes, including international and broader policy negotiations.

Alternatives to Negotiated Agreement

People negotiate in order to satisfy the totality of their interests better through some jointly decided action than they could otherwise. Thus, for each side the basic test of a proposed joint agreement is whether it offers higher subjective worth than that side's best course of action absent agreement. In examining a negotiation, therefore, one should analyze each party's perceptions of its own – and the others' – valuations of their alternatives to negotiated agreement.

Alternatives to agreement may be certain, with a single attribute: an ironclad competing price quote for an identical new car. They may be contingent and multiattributed: going to court rather than accepting a negotiated settlement can involve uncertainties, trial anxieties, costs, time, and precedents that contrast with the certain, solely monetary nature of a pretrial accord. No-agreement alternatives may also involve potentially competing coalitions, threats and counter-threats, or the necessity to keep negotiating indefinitely.

Evidently, decision analysis (including multiattribute value and utility theory) can often help assess alternatives to agreement. When there are many possible alternatives – or example, many potential purchasers, each with associated uncertainties and costs of discovery for the seller –optimal search theory can provide strategies for searching efficiently and valuing the expected findings from the search (Lax 1985). When the parties' alternatives to agreement are interdependent, concepts from game theory – including the dynamics of threats and counter-threats as well as the many variants of coalitional analysis – can help bargainers understand and assess their no-agreement alternatives (Luce and Raiffa 1957; Raiffa 1982).

Although this evaluation provides a strict lower bound for the minimum worth (the "reservation price") required of any acceptable settlement, alternatives to agreement also play tactical roles. The more favorably that negotiators portray their best alternative course of action and willingness to "walk away," the smaller is the ostensible need for the negotiation and the higher the standard of value that any proposed accord must reach. Moves "away from the table" that shape the parties' alternatives to agreement can strongly affect negotiated outcomes.

For example, faced with a two-party negotiation, the importance of moves to enhance competition – and thereby improve their no-agreement alternatives in the initial negotiation – is virtually an article of faith among top negotiators. A senior AOL executive remarked about the importance of such moves to favorably change the setup: "You would never do a deal without talking to anyone else. Never."[8] Martin Lipton, virtual dean of the New York takeover bar, compared the effects of adding another interested party "at the front end" of corporate acquisition negotiations with simply negotiating more effectively with your initial counterpart "at the back end" of the process. Lipton even roughly quantified the added value of adding competing negotiator with greater negotiating skill in the initial two-party deal: "The ability to bring somebody into a situation is far more important than the extra dollar a share at the back end. At the front end, you're probably talking about 50 percent. At the back end you're talking about 1 or 2 percent."[9] Indeed, as Bulow and Klemperer (1996) analytically demonstrate, moves to transform a two-party negotiation into an active auction with many bidders vying for your deal can be a potent strategy in general.[10]

Converting a two-party setup into more of an auction can change the psychology of a negotiation as well as the competitive pressures. After leading a string of alliances and acquisition negotiations that vaulted Millennium Pharmaceuticals from a 1993 startup to a multibillion-dollar firm less than a decade later, then-chief business officer Steve Holtzman explained the rationale for adding parties:

> Whenever we feel there's a possibility of a deal with someone, we immediately call six other people. It drives you nuts, trying to juggle them all, but it will change the perception on the other side of the table, number one. Number two, it will change your self-perception. If you believe that there are other people who are interested, your bluff is no longer a bluff, it's real. It will come across with a whole other level of conviction.[11]

Representing the Structure

Imagine that two negotiators have thought hard about their underlying interests in different possible settlements of the apparent issues. Further, suppose that they have a relatively clear, if possibly changing, assessment of their tradeoffs and have compared them to the value of their best no-agreement alternatives. Each has a sense of any "rules of engagement" that structure their interaction. From the viewpoint of each party a set of possible agreements has been envisioned. Assume that an analyst were privy to the results of these evaluations by each side, along with the (likely asymmetric) distribution of information about interests, beliefs, no-agreement options, and possible actions; these evaluations need not be common knowledge of the parties. The situation might be familiarly represented as in Figure 23.1.

---

[8] See (Rivlin, 2000).
[9] This quote and an extended discussion of related bargaining implications can be found in Subramanian (2003: 1).
[10] See Bulow and Klemperer (1996).
[11] See "Strategic Deal-making at Millennium Pharmaceuticals," (Watkins, 1999).

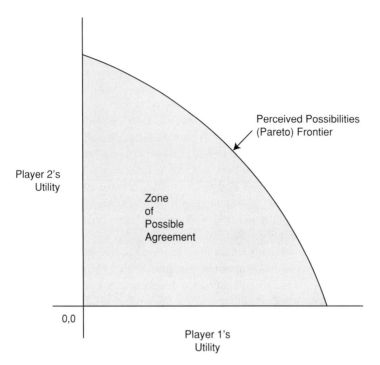

Figure 23.1. Pareto frontier for two players.

The origin represents the value of failing to reach agreement; each side's best alternative to agreement implies the location of this point. The "Pareto frontier" in the northeast part of the graph represents the evaluations of the set of those possible agreements on the issues that could not be improved on from the standpoint of either party without harming the other. In general, neither side knows the location of the frontier, only theoretically that it is there. The entire shaded region – bounded by the two axes and the frontier – is the "zone of possible agreement." In general, each party has its own perceptions of it. (In a purely distributive bargain, with no room for joint gains beyond the fact of agreement, the shaded region would collapse to a diagonal frontier.) Because this representation is quite general, it can in principle encompass the whole range of possible interests, alternatives, and agreements.

From Structure to Outcome: Favorable Changes in the Perceived Zone of Possible Agreement

This is the point at which game-theoretic and negotiation-analytic approaches tend to diverge. A game theorist would typically tighten the above specification of the situation, presume common knowledge of the situation and strategic rationality of the parties, and, by invoking a rigorous concept of equilibrium (such as a Nash equilibrium or Bayesian Nash equilibrium), and investigate the predicted outcome(s) of the interaction. Indeed, as Rubenstein's (1991) insightful commentary noted, "For 40 years, game theory has searched for the grand solution" that would achieve a "prediction regarding the outcome of interaction among human beings using only data on the order of events, combined with a description of the players' preferences over the feasible outcomes of the situation." (p. 923).

Even with as powerful and ubiquitous a concept as that of the Nash equilibrium in noncooperative games, however, it is often impossible, even with the imposition of increasingly stringent requirements or refinements to limit a game's equilibrium outcomes to a unique or even small number of points. Often there is an infinitude of such outcomes. As Tirole (1988) noted when explaining why "we are now endowed with nearly a dozen refinements of perfect Bayesian equilibrium," the "leeway in specifying off-the-equilibrium-path beliefs usually creates some leeway in the choices of equilibrium actions; by ruling out some potential equilibrium actions, one transforms other actions into equilibrium actions." (p. 446). Frequently this implies an infinite number of perfect Bayesian equilibria.

Despite insights into how rational players might select from among multiple Nash equilibria (Harsanyi and Selten 1988), the rationale for a particular choice may ultimately seem arbitrary. As Kadane and Larkey (1982) incisively remark, "we do not understand the search for solution concepts that do not depend on the beliefs of each player about the others' likely actions, and yet are so compelling that they become the obvious standard of play for all those who encounter them." This seems especially apt in light of their observation that "solution concepts are a basis for particular prior distributions" and hence "the difficulty in non-zero sum, N-person game theory of finding an adequate solution concept: no single prior distribution is likely to be adequate to all players and all situations in such games" (pp. 115–116).

Because each party should accept any settlement in the zone of possible agreement rather than no agreement, Schelling (1960) made the potent observation that the outcome of such a situation could only be unraveled by the "logic of indeterminate situations." Yet, without an explicit model or formal theory (equilibrium-based or other) adequate to confidently map structure and tactics onto bargaining outcomes, how can an individual negotiator or interested third party decide what to do? In the (often implicit) view of many negotiation analysts, the negotiator's subjective distribution of beliefs about the negotiated outcome conditional on using the proposed tactics must be compared with his subjective distribution of beliefs about the outcome conditional on not using them. The tactic is attractive if the former distribution gives him higher expected utility than the latter.

Such "improvement" has a subjective basis analogous to the Rothschild–Stiglitz (1970) characterization of a subjectively perceived "increase" in risk. Specifying these distributions may require an internalized and subjective model of the bargaining process because no such general model exists; where there is a well-developed and applicable game-theoretic model, of course, it should be used. Of course, the "better" the empirical and theoretical basis for the assessment, the "better" the subjective distributions of outcomes.

Much negotiation analytic work consists in improving the basis for assessing such outcome distributions. To do this, analysts pay attention to the special structure and dynamics that derive from the *joint decision making* among parties, some of whom may be "boundedly rational."

Improving the Basis for Assessing Outcome Distributions I: Fundamental Processes of Negotiation

At bottom, negotiation processes involve both (1) actions to enhance what is jointly possible through agreement ("creating value"), and (2) actions to allocate the value of agreement ("claiming value").

Creating Value

In most negotiations, the potential value of joint action is *not* fully obvious at the outset. "Creating value" – that is, reaching mutually beneficial agreements, improving them jointly, and preventing conflict escalation – requires an approach often associated with "win-win," "integrative," or "variable sum" encounters: to share information, communicate clearly, be creative, and productively channel hostilities. Yet, regardless of whether one adopts a cooperative *style* or not, it is useful to have an analytic guide as to the underlying substantive bases for joint gains and how to realize them by effective deal design.

First, apart from pure shared interests, negotiators may simply want the same settlement on some issues. Furthering their relationship, or acting in accord with an identical interest, such as a shared vision, ideology, or norm of equity, may create value in an agreement. Interests, such as "good relationships," are analogous to the economist's "public goods" in that all sides can simultaneously "consume" them without diminution.

Second, where economies of scale, collective goods, alliances, or requirements for a minimum number of parties exist, agreement among similar bargainers can create value.

Third – and most interestingly – although many people instinctively seek "common ground" and believe that "differences divide us," it is often precisely the differences among negotiators that constitute the raw material for creating value. Each class of difference has a characteristic type of agreement that makes possible its conversion into mutual benefit. For example, differences in relative valuation suggest joint gain from trades or from "unbundling" differently valued attributes. Differences in tax status, liquidity, or market access suggest arbitrage. Complementary technical capacities can be profitably combined. Probability and risk aversion differences suggest contingent agreements or bets. Differences in time preference suggest altering schedules of payments and other actions. Sebenius (1984) formally characterizes such optimal betting, risk sharing, and temporal reallocations; a general discussion of differences in probabilities and attitudes toward risk can be found in Pratt and Zeckhauser (1989). These observations point up value of a "differences orientation" with knowledge of the characteristic "technologies" for converting differences into mutual benefit. More broadly, much work on optimal contracting (e.g., Hart 1995), as well as classical economic study of gains from trade and comparative advantage, directly bear on the kinds of agreements that create value on a sustainable basis.

Beyond creating value via pure shared interests, scale economies, and differences in multiple dimensions are other classes of situations that can give rise to mutually beneficial agreements. For instance, "insecure contracts" are potentially value-creating deals – such as digging a mine in a developing country under appropriate terms – in which one party has an inherent, structural incentive to defect from the original terms once the agreement has been signed and the other party has made an irrevocable move. In the face of this structure, parties often do not contract, even where substantial benefits are at stake for all. Classes of agreements and devices to "secure" such contracts in situations of considerable importance have been (unsystematically) explored (Lax and Sebenius 1981; Raiffa 1982, especially Chapter 13; Raiffa, Richardson and Metcalfe 2002); beyond contractual flexibility, these approaches involve the equivalent of performance bonds, insurance, and linkages.

In a second class of examples that remains relatively undeveloped in a negotiation context, financial and "real" options have been extensively analyzed, especially in situations where action and information revelation are sequenced (with respect to financial options, see Hull 2002; with respect to "real" options, Mun 2002). In related analysis, Sahlman (1987) has explored the character of staged arrangements between entrepreneurs and investors that generate appropriate incentives, share risk efficiently, and respond to updated information. Hall (1999; 2002) has explored this question more broadly in seeking the principles behind optimal design of multiyear option programs and other forms of executive compensation. In a narrower setting involving option design, different kinds of exit and termination agreements, from reciprocal buy-sell provisions (Raiffa, Richardson and Metcalfe, 2002) to "Texas shoot-outs" (Brandenburger and Nalebuff, 1996) can create value, or, if badly structured, destroy it.

In short, negotiated agreements may systematically improve on the alternatives by: (1) cultivating shared interests, (2) exploiting scale economies, (3) dovetailing differences. Other avenues to value creation include agreements designed to secure potentially insecure contracts and to exploit options. A number of studies have taken situations and analyzed the joint gains latent in them. Barclay and Peterson (1976) carry out this analysis in the context of base rights negotiations; similarly, Brown, Peterson, and Ulvila (1975) analyze alternative Middle Eastern oil agreements. Ulvila and Snider (1980) show how negotiation of international tanker standards followed this methodology. Raiffa (1982) explains this analysis in the context of the Panama Canal negotiations and the talks over Philippine bases. Sebenius (1984) unpacks the sophisticated joint gains embedded in a multiparty deep seabed mining agreement. Bueno de Mesquita and his colleagues (1985) carry out an elaborate analysis of the British negotiations with the

Chinese over the fate of Hong Kong. Chen and Underwood (1988) describe and apply a closely related methodology. Lax and Sebenius (2002, 2006) offer extensive illustrations of these "deal design" principles in practice.

Claiming Value

Crucial aspects of most negotiations, however, are primarily "distributive," "win-lose," or constant-sum; that is, at some points in the process, increased value claimed by one party implies less for others. Several broad classes of tactics used for "claiming value" in these kinds of bargains have been explored. (See Schelling (1960), Walton and McKersie (1965), Raiffa (1982), Thompson (2001), and Lax and Sebenius (1986).) Such tactics include: shaping perceptions of alternatives to agreement, making commitments, influencing aspirations, taking strong positions, manipulating patterns of concessions, holding valued issues "hostage," linking issues and interests for leverage, misleading other parties, as well as exploiting cultural and other expectations. By means of these tactics, one party seeks advantage by influencing another's perceptions of the zone of possible agreement.

Managing the Tension between Creating and Claiming Value: The Negotiators' Dilemma

In general, the potential benefits of cooperation are not fully known at the outset of a negotiation. Colloquially, the parties often do not know how large a "value pie" they can create. The way in which they attempt to expand the pie often affects its final division, while each side's efforts to get a larger share of the pie often prevents its expansion in the first place – and may lead to no pie at all, or even to a fight. Conclusion: Creating and claiming value are not in general *separable* processes in negotiation. This fact undermines much otherwise useful advice (that, for example, presumes "win-win" situations to have no "win-lose" aspects, or "integrative" bargains to be unrelated to "distributive" ones).

Each negotiating party tends to reason as follows: if the other parties are open and forthcoming, I can take advantage of them and claim a great deal of value; thus I should adopt a value-claiming stance. By contrast, if the other parties are tough and adopt value-claiming stances, I must also adopt such a stance in order to protect myself. Either way, a strong tendency operating on all parties drives them toward hardball. Because mutual hardball generally impedes value creation, competitive moves to claim value individually often drive out cooperative moves to create it jointly. Outcomes of this dynamic include poor agreements, deadlocks, and conflict spirals. This tendency, closely related in structure to the famous prisoner's dilemma, was dubbed the "Negotiator's Dilemma." Much negotiation advice is aimed at productively managing the inherent tension between creating and claiming value, especially doing so on a sustainable basis.[12]

---

[12] See Lax and Sebenius (1986), especially Chapters Two and Seven, and Raiffa (1982).

Improving the Basis for Assessing Outcome Distributions II: Behavioral Insight

A fully rational "baseline" analysis helps one to understand the possible responses of a rational other side. Urging consistent, if not fully rational, behavior on the subject of one's advice is often wise. After all, well-structured, repeated negotiations may penalize departures from rational behavior. Yet many negotiating situations are neither well-structured, repeated, nor embedded in a market context. And although negotiators normally exhibit intelligent, purposive behavior, there are important departures from the "imaginary, idealized, super-rational people without psyches" (Bell, Raiffa, and Tversky 1988) needed by many game-theoretic analyses.

Considerable empirical work – such as that cited above by Bazerman, Neale, Thompson, and their colleagues – offers considerable insight into how people actually behave in negotiations. Excellent reviews of the psychological side of negotiation can be found in Bazerman, Curhan, and Moore (2000). Reviews focusing especially on developments on the social psychological side can be found in in Bazerman, Curhan, Moore, and Valley (2000). Complementing this work is the burgeoning research in experimental economics (Kagel and Roth 1995) and what Camerer (1997) described as a "behavioral game theory." This work blends game-theoretic and psychological considerations in rigorous experimental settings. Two related levels are consistently important, the individual and the social.

INDIVIDUAL NEGOTIATING BEHAVIOR. As negotiators, people have different histories, personalities, motivations, and styles. Systematic characteristics of individual cognitive processes can both help and hinder the process of reaching agreement. For example, negotiators may be anchored by irrelevant information, subject to inconsistencies in the way they deal with uncertainty, hampered by selective perception, obsessed by sunk costs and past actions, prone to stereotyping and labeling, susceptible to influence tactics and manipulation by the way in which equivalent situations are framed, liable to see incompatible interests when joint gains are possible, and use a variety of potentially misleading heuristics to deal with complexity, ambiguity, and conflict.

Social Behavior in Negotiation

In groups of two or more, especially where there is some perceived conflict, a variety of social psychological dynamics come into play that may enable or block negotiated outcomes. For example, a powerful norm toward reciprocity operates in most groups and cultures. Tentative cooperative actions by one side can engender positive reactions by the others in a cycle that builds trust over time. By contrast, social barriers can involve aspects of the interactive process that often lead to bad communication, misattribution, polarization, and escalation of conflict, as well as group dynamics that work against constructive agreements. Such dynamics may be especially pronounced when negotiations involve players of different genders, races, or cultures. Group dynamics can involve pressures for conformity, a hardening of approach by a representative before an "audience" of constituents, bandwagon effects, and the individual taking cues from the behavior of others to decide on appropriate actions in the negotiation.

This experimentally-based work is developing an empirical grounding for the behavioral basis of much *a priori* theorizing in economics and game theory. For negotiation analysis, these experimental approaches to actual behavior help to remedy a key defect of prior game theoretic work. Although for the most part not prescriptively framed, this body of work also provides rigorous evidence and theory on how people in fact are likely to behave – to inform assessments of outcome distributions and against which to optimize as appropriate.

CHANGING THE GAME. Much existing theory proceeds from the assumption of a well-specified and fixed situation within which negotiation actions are taken. Yet purposive action on behalf of the parties can *change* the very structure of the situation and, therefore, the outcomes. Often actions can be understood as a tacit or explicit negotiation over what the game itself will be.[13] This means that a perfectly legitimate and potentially valuable form of analysis may involve a search for ways to change the perceived game – even though the menu of possibilities may not be common knowledge.

Issues can be linked or separated from the negotiation to create joint gains or enhance leverage. Parties may be "added" to a negotiation to improve one side's no-agreement alternatives as well as to generate joint gains or to extract value from others. Though perhaps less commonly, parties can also be "subtracted" – meaning separated, ejected, or excluded – from larger potential coalitions. For example, the Soviets were excluded from an active Middle East negotiating role in the process leading up to the Camp David Accords that involved only Israel, Egypt, and the United States. The process of choosing, then approaching and persuading, others to go along may best be studied without the common assumption that the game is fully specified at the outset of analysis; Sebenius (1996) dissects and offers many examples of the process sequencing to build or break coalitions. Walton and McKersie (1965) focus on how negotiators seek to change perceptions of the game by what they called "attitudinal restructuring." In the context of competitive strategy and thinking, Brandenburger and Nalebuff (1996) develop a powerful, analogous logic for "changing the game" that provides an overall approach and many ingenious examples of this phenomenon.

Refer back to Figure 23.1: an improvement in Party One's no-agreement alternative shifts the vertical axis to the right, leaving the bargaining set generally more favorable to that side. If Party Two's no-agreement alternative worsens, the horizontal axis shifts down, worsening its prospects. A successful commitment to a bargaining position cuts off an undesired part of the zone of possible agreement for the party who makes it. A new, mutually beneficial option (e.g., suggestion of

---

[13] Sebenius (1983, 1984) began to investigate this phenomenon, dubbing it "negotiation arithmetic," or "adding" and "subtracting" issues and parties.

a contingent, rather than an unconditional, contract) causes the frontier to bulge upward and to the right, reducing the parties' "conflict of interest." When issues change or other basic aspects of the game vary, each side's perceptions of the basic picture in Figure 23.1, the zone of possible agreement, will be transformed. These possibilities add evolutionary elements to the analysis.

In line with this focus on the potential to change the negotiating game itself, there is often considerable scope for creative "negotiation design" to enhance the chances and value of agreement. Articulated case examples include Singapore's Tommy Koh and the Law of the Sea (Antrim and Sebenius 1991), George Mitchell's efforts in Northern Ireland (Curran and Sebenius 2003), and, in contrast, Richard Holbrooke's work leading to the Dayton Accords ending the war in Bosnia (Curran, Sebenius, and Watkins 2004), and Charlene Barshefsky's choices with respect to negotiating a U.S.–Chinese Intellectual Property Regime (Hulse and Sebenius 2003).

Consider an example illustrating the broader problem of "negotiation design," or how best to (re-)structure ongoing or prospective negotiations. In the late 1980s and early 1990s, various governments sought to decide on how best to structure upcoming negotiations to deal with global warming. For example, would the negotiations best be carried out in separate bilateral encounters, in small groups of like-minded or geographically proximate countries, in large blocs, or on a global basis? Who should be included and excluded? Should a sequential process be constructed? And should the issues be limited to targets for carbon emissions, for example, or should chlorofluorocarbons and acid rain be linked? Should the negotiations also concern debt, financial transfers, population policy, and the like? Should a comprehensive agreement be sought or should a "framework" be negotiated first with subsequent "protocols" hammered out on specific subjects? To sort out these questions, a variety of negotiation analyses proved useful. For example, for various possible configurations of the negotiations, which blocking coalitions were likely to arise and how might they best be dealt with? How could the negotiations be organized such that there are sufficient potential joint gains to attract the key players? Which rules of procedure should be avoided because they are most likely to keep the most painful conflicts salient and to impede effective joint problem-solving? Analyses of such negotiation design issues for the climate change talks, the diplomacy of chlorofluorocarbon control, and the Law of the Sea negotiations can be found in Sebenius (1991, 1995).

These questions exemplify the problem of negotiation design, or how best to configure a specific game in order to improve the chances of a desired outcome. In some cases, this may involve the choice of discrete processes such as optimally matching various alternative dispute resolution mechanisms to different classes of disputes: "matching the forum to the fuss" (Sander and Goldberg 1994). Closely related is the question of influencing a *stream* of negotiated outcomes to improve the odds of mutually beneficial agreements; examples include the design of organizational dispute resolution systems (Ury, Brett and Goldberg 1988; Costantino and Merchant 1996). Finally, the institutional and regulatory context may be consciously shaped to influence the frequency and quality of negotiations carried out within that setting. For example, Wheeler and his colleagues (Wheeler 1994; Wheeler, Gilbert and Field 1997) have evaluated the design characteristics chosen to stimulate productive negotiations in Massachusetts over hazardous waste treatment facilities as well as a New Jersey system designed to foster socially desirable intermunicipal trading of affordable housing obligations.

In short, conscious actions to change the scope and sequence of a negotiation can be used to create and claim value in several distinct ways from complementing the existing players and issues, to reducing transactions costs, removing deal-breakers, invoking dispute resolution mechanisms, as well as broader concepts of negotiation design and systems. Using the term "setup" to refer to a negotiation's parties, interests, no-deal options, sequence, and basic process choices, Lax and Sebenius (2006) offer an extensive prescriptive framework, illustrated by numerous examples from practice, for ensuring the most promising possible situation for achieving a desired agreement.

The Approach as a Whole

Figure 23.1 can now be seen to visually summarize the extended negotiation analytic "model" of possible joint action. Parties determine the axes; interests provide the raw material and the measure; alternatives to agreement imply the limits; agreements hold out the potential; within this configuration, the process consists of creating and claiming value, which gives rise to characteristic dynamics; yet, the elements of the interaction may themselves evolve or be intentionally changed. In this sense, the elements of the approach form a logically consistent, complete whole oriented around perceptions of the zone of possible agreement.

In the skeptical view of Harsanyi (1982), this negotiation analytic approach might boil down to "the uninformative statement that every player should maximize expected utility in terms of his subjective probabilities without giving him the slightest hint of how to choose these subjective probabilities in a rational manner." Yet, as described above, distinct classes of factors have been isolated that appear to improve subjective distributions of negotiated outcomes. Understanding the dynamics of creating and claiming value can improve prescriptive confidence. Psychological considerations can help as can cultural observations, organizational constraints and patterns, historical similarity, knowledge of systematic decision-making biases, and contextual features. Less than full-blown game-theoretic reasoning can offer insight into strategic dynamics as can blends of psychological and game-theoretic analysis. When one relaxes the assumptions of strict, mutually expected, strategic sophistication in a fixed game, Raiffa's (1982) conclusion is appealing: that some "analysis – mostly simple analysis – can help."

Conclusions and Further Directions

Naturally, there are many other related topics ranging from game-theoretic concepts of fairness for purposes of mediation and arbitration to various voting schemes. More elaborate structures are under study. For example, where negotiation takes place through agents, whether lawyers or diplomats, or where a result must survive legislative ratification, the underlying structure of a "two-level game" is present.[14] Negotiations also take place in more complex multilevel and coalitional structures.[15] Perhaps most important, scientific study will continue to strengthen the empirical bases for improving assessments of outcome distributions.

Although game theorists and behavioral scientists will continue to make valuable progress in understanding negotiation from the standpoint of scientific explanation and prediction, a complementary prescriptive approach has been developing that conditions its prescriptions on the likely behavior of the other side, fully "rational" or not, and regardless of whether the "game" is fixed and entirely common knowledge. In describing the logic of negotiation analysis and the concepts and tools that can facilitate it, this discussion has not stressed the many useful ideas that arise from focusing on interpersonal and cultural styles, on atmosphere and logistics, on psychoanalytic motivation, on communication, or on other aspects. Yet because the logic is general, it can profitably accommodate insights from other approaches as well as from experience. The basic elements of this logic – parties' perceptions of interests, alternatives, agreements, the processes of creating and claiming value, and changing the game or "setup" – become the essential filters through which other factors must be interpreted for a meaningful assessment of the zone of possible agreement and its implications for the outcome.

REFERENCES

Antrim, L., and Sebenius J. K. (1991). Multilateral Conference Mediation: Tommy Koh and the Law of the Sea. In J. Bercovitch and J. Z. Rubin (Eds.), *Mediation in International Relations: Multilateral Approaches to Conflict Management*. London: Macmillan.

Arrow, K. J., Wilson, R., Ross, L., Tversky, A., and Mnookin, R. H. (1995). *Barriers to Conflict Resolution*. New York: W. W. Norton.

Aumann, R. J. (1989). Game Theory. In J. Eatwell, M. Milgate, and P. Newman (Eds.), *Game Theory*. New York: Norton, pp. 1–53.

Aumann, R. J., and Brandenburger, A. (1995). Epistemic Conditions for Nash Equilibrium. *Econometrica, 63*, 1161–1180.

Barclay, S., and Peterson, C. (1976). *Multiattribute Utility Models for Negotiations*. McLean, VA: Decisions and Designs, Inc.

Bazerman, M. H., and Neale, M. A. (1992). *Negotiating Rationally*. New York: Free Press.

Bazerman, M. H., Curhan, J., and Moore, D. (2000). In G. Fletcher and M. Clark, (Eds.), The Death and Rebirth of the Social Psychology of Negotiations. *Blackwell Handbook of Social Psychology: Interpersonal Processes*. Malden, Mass.: Blackwell Publishers, 2000, pp. 196–228.

Bazerman, M. H., Curhan, J., Moore, D., and Valley, K. L. (2000). Negotiations. *Annual Review of Psychology, 51*, 279–314.

Bell, D. E., Raiffa, H., and Tversky, A. (1988). *Decision Making: Descriptive, Normative, and Prescriptive Interactions*. Cambridge, UK: Cambridge University Press, p. 9.

Brandenburger, A. M., and Nalebuff, B. J. (1996). *Co-opetition*. New York: Currency Doubleday, pp. 52–55.

---

[14] These have been studied in a number of settings, notably by Putnam (1988).

[15] For analyses, see Raiffa (1982), Lax and Sebenius (1986, 1991), and Sebenius (1996).

Brown, R., Peterson, C., and Ulvila, J. (1975). *An Analysis of Alternative Mideastern Oil Agreements*. Decisions and Designs, Inc.

Bueno de Mesquita, B.D., Newman, and Rabushka, A. (1985). *Forecasting Political Events: The Future of Hong Kong*. New Haven, CT: Yale University Press.

Bulow, J., and Klemperer, P. (1996). Auctions versus Negotiations. *American Economic Review, 86*, 180–194.

Camerer, C. F. (1997). Progress in Behavioral Game Theory. *Journal of Economic Perspectives, 11*, 167–188.

Chen, K., and Underwood, S. E. (1988). Integrative Analytical Assessment: A Hybrid Method for Facilitating Negotiation. *Negotiation Journal, 4*, 183–198.

Costantino, C. A., and Merchant, C. S. (1996). *Designing Conflict Management Systems*. San Francisco: Jossey-Bass.

Curran, D. F., and Sebenius, J. K. (2003). The Mediator as Coalition-Builder: George Mitchell in Northern Ireland. *International Negotiation: A Journal of Theory and Practice, 8*, 111–147.

Curran, D. F., Sebenius, J. K., and Watkins, M. (2004). Two Paths to Peace: Contrasting George Mitchell in Northern Ireland with Richard Holbrooke in Bosnia-Herzegovina. *Negotiation Journal, 20*, 513–537.

Fisher, R., Ury, W., and Patton, B. (1991). *Getting to Yes*. New York: Penguin.

Freund, J. C. (1992). *Smart Negotiating: How to Make Good Deals in the Real World*. New York: Fireside/Simon & Schuster.

Hall, B. J. (1999). The Design of Multi-Year Option Plans. *Journal of Applied Corporate Finance (Summer)*, 97–106.

Hall, B. J. (2002). Incentive Strategy II: Executive Compensation and Ownership Structure. *Case No. 902-134*, Boston: Harvard Business School Press.

Hammond, J. S., Keeney, R. L., and Raiffa, H. (1998). *Smart Choices*. Boston: Harvard Business School Press.

Harsanyi, J. C. (1982). Subjective Probability and the Theory of Games: Comments on Kadane and Larkey's Paper. *Management Science, 28*, 120–124.

Harsanyi, J. C., and Selten, R. (1988). *A General Theory of Equilibrium Selection in Games*. Cambridge, MA: MIT Press.

Hart, O. (1995). *Firms, Contracts, and Financial Structure* (Clarendon Lectures in Economics). Oxford: Oxford University Press.

Hull, J. C. (2002). *Options, Futures, and Other Derivatives*. Upper Saddle River, NJ: Prentice-Hall.

Hulse, R. G., and Sebenius, J. K. (2003). Sequencing, Acoustic Separation, and 3-D Negotiation of Complex Barriers: Charlene Barshefsky and I. P. Rights in China. *Journal of International Negotiation, 8*, 311–338.

Kadane, J. B., and Larkey, P. D. (1982). Subjective Probability and the Theory of Games. *Management Science, 28*, 113–120.

Kagel, J., and Roth, A. E. (1995). *The Handbook of Experimental Economics*. Princeton, NJ: Princeton University Press.

Keeney, Ralph L. (1996). *Value-Focused Thinking: A Path to Creative Decisionmaking*. Cambridge, MA: Harvard University Press.

Keeney, R., and Raiffa, H. (1976). *Decisions with Multiple Objectives: Preferences and Value Tradeoffs*. New York: John Wiley.

Keeney, R. and Raiffa, H. (1991). "Assessing Tradeoffs: Structuring and Analyzing Values for Multiple-Issue Negotiations." In H. P. Young (Ed.), *Negotiation Analysis*. Ann Arbor, MI: University of Michigan Press, pp. 131–151.

Keeney, R. L., Renn, O., and von Winterfeldt, D. (1983). *Structuring Germany's Energy Objectives*. Social Science Research Institute, University of Southern California.

Lax, D. A. (1985). Optimal Search in Negotiation Analysis. *Journal of Conflict Resolution, 29*, 456–472.

Lax, D. A., and Sebenius, J. K. (1981). Insecure Contracts and Resource Development. *Public Policy, 29*, 417–436.

Lax, D. A., and Sebenius, J. K. (1986). *The Manager as Negotiator: Bargaining for Cooperation and Competitive Gain.* New York: The Free Press.

Lax, D. A., and Sebenius, J. K. (1991). Thinking Coalitionally: Party Arithmetic, Process Opportunism, and Strategic Sequencing. In H. P. Young (Ed.), *Negotiation Analysis.* Ann Arbor MI: University of Michigan Press, pp. 153–193.

Lax, D. A. and Sebenius, J. K. (2002). Dealcrafting: The Substance of Three-Dimensional Negotiations. *Negotiation Journal, 18*, 5–28.

Lax, D. A., and Sebenius, J. K. (2003). 3-D Negotiation: Are You Playing the Whole Game? *Harvard Business Review, 81*, 64–74.

Lax, D. A., and Sebenius, J. K. (2006). *3-D Negotiation: Powerful Tools to Change the Game in Your Most Important Deals.* Boston: Harvard Business School Press.

Luce, R. D., and Raiffa, H. (1957). *Games and Decisions.* New York: Wiley.

Mnookin, R. H., Peppet, S. R., and Tulumello, A. S. (2000). *Beyond Winning: Negotiating to Create Value in Deals and Disputes.* Cambridge, MA: Harvard University Press.

Mun, J. (2002). *Real Options Analysis.* New York: John Wiley & Sons.

Neale, M. A., and Bazerman, M. H. (1991). *Cognition and Rationality in Negotiation.* New York: Free Press.

Pratt, J. W., and Zeckhauser, R. J. (1989). The Impact of Risk-Sharing on Efficient Division. *Journal of Risk and Uncertainty, 2*, 219–234.

Pruitt, D. G. (1981). *Negotiation Behavior.* New York, Academic Press.

Putnam, R. D. (1988). Diplomacy and Domestic Politics: The Logic of Two-Level Games. *International Organization, 42*, 427–460.

Raiffa, H. (1982). *The Art and Science of Negotiation.* Cambridge, MA: Harvard University Press, Belknap Press, p. 359.

Raiffa, H. (1997). *Lectures on Negotiation Analysis.* Cambridge, MA: PON Books.

Raiffa, H., Richardson, J., and Metcalfe, D. (2002). *Negotiation Analysis: The Science and Art of Collaborative Decision Making.* Cambridge, MA: Belknap Press of Harvard University Press, pp. 185–186, 374–375.

Rivlin, G. (2000). AOL's Rough Riders. *The Standard*, October 30. http://www.thestandard.com/article/0,1902,19461,00.html. Accessed 10/8/06.

Rothschild, M., and Stiglitz, J. E. (1970). Increasing Risk, I: A Definition. *Journal of Economic Theory, 2*, 225–243.

Rubin, J. and Brown, B. (1975). *The Social Psychology of Bargaining and Negotiation.* New York, Academic Press.

Rubinstein, A. (1991). Comments on the Interpretation of Game Theory. *Econometrica, 59*, 909–924.

Sahlman, W. A. (1987). Note on Financial Contracting: Deals. *Case No. 9–288–014*, Boston, MA: Harvard Business School Press.

Sander, F. A. E. and Goldberg, S. (1994). Fitting the Forum to the Fuss. *Negotiation Journal, 10*, 49–67.

Schelling, T. C. (1960). *The Strategy of Conflict.* Cambridge, MA: Harvard University Press.

Sebenius, J. K. (1983). Negotiation Arithmetic: Adding and Subtracting Issues and Parties. *International Organization, 37*, 281–316.

Sebenius, J. K. (1984). *Negotiating the Law of the Sea: Lessons in the Art and Science of Reaching Agreement.* Cambridge, MA: Harvard University Press.

Sebenius, J. K. (1991). Designing Negotiations Toward a New Regime: The Case of Global Warming. *International Security, 15*, 110–148.

Sebenius, J. K. (1992). Negotiation Analysis: A Characterization and Review. *Management Science, 38*, 18–38.

Sebenius, J. K. (1995). Dealing with Blocking Coalitions and Related Barriers to Agreement: Lessons from Negotiations on the Oceans, the Ozone, and the Climate. In K. Arrow, R. H. Mnookin, L. Ross, A. Tversky and R. Wilson. (Eds.) *Barriers to Conflict Resolution*. New York: W.W. Norton, pp. 150–182.

Sebenius, J. K. (1996) Sequencing to Build Coalitions: With Whom I Should I Talk First? In R. Zeckhauser, R. Keeney, and J. K. Sebenius. (Eds.), *Wise Decisions*. Cambridge, MA.: Harvard Business School Press, pp. 324–348.

Sebenius, J. K. (2000). Dealmaking Essentials: Creating and Claiming Value for the Long Term. *Item 2–800–443*, Boston: Harvard Business School Press.

Sebenius, J. K. (2001). Negotiation: Statistical Aspects. *International Encyclopedia of the Social and Behavioral Sciences, 15*, 10483–10490, Oxford, Pergamon Press PLC.

Sebenius, J. K. (2002). International Negotiation Analysis. In V. Kremenyuk (Ed.), *International Negotiation: Analysis, Approaches, Issues*. San Francisco: Jossey-Bass, pp. 229–252.

Subramanian, G. (2003). The Drivers of Market Efficiency in Revlon Transactions. *Journal of Corporate Law, 28*, 691.

Thompson, L. (2001). *The Mind and Heart of the Negotiator*. Upper Saddle River, NJ: Prentice-Hall.

Tirole, J. (1988). *The Theory of Industrial Organization*. Cambridge, MA: MIT Press, p. 446.

Ulvila, J., and Snider, W. (1980). Negotiation of Tanker Standards: Application of Multiattribute Value Theory. *Operations Research, 28*, 81–95.

Ury, W. (1991). *Getting Past No*. New York: Bantam.

Ury, W., Brett, J., and Goldberg, S. (1988). *Getting Disputes Resolved: Defining Systems to Cut the Costs of Conflict*. San Francisco: Jossey-Bass.

von Neumann, J., and Morgenstern, O. (1944). *Theory of Games and Economic Behavior*. Princeton, NJ: Princeton University Press.

Walton, R., and McKersie, R. (1965). *A Behavioral Theory of Labor Negotiations*. New York: McGraw-Hill.

Watkins, M. D. (1999). Strategic Deal-making at Millennium Pharmaceuticals. *Case No. 899–242*. Boston: Harvard Business School Publishing.

Wheeler, M. A. (1994). *Negotiating NIMBYs: Learning from the Failure of the Massachusetts Siting Law. Yale Journal on Regulation, 11*, 241–291.

Wheeler, M. A., Gilbert, J., and Field, P. (1997). Trading the Poor: Intermunicipal Affordable Housing Negotiation in New Jersey. *Harvard Journal of Law and Negotiation, 2*, 1–33.

Wierzbicki, A. P. (1983). Critical Essay on the Methodology of Multiobjective Analysis. *Regional Science and Urban Economics, 13*, 5–29.

Wilson, R. (1968). The Theory of Syndicates. *Econometrica, 36*, 119–132.

Young, H. P. (Ed) (1991). *Negotiation Analysis*. Ann Arbor, MI: University of Michigan Press.

Zeckhauser, R., Keeney, R., and Sebenius, J. K. (Eds.). (1996). *Wise Decisions*. Cambridge, MA: Harvard Business School Press.

24 The Adoption of Multiattribute Utility Theory for the Evaluation of Plutonium Disposition Options in the United States and Russia

John C. Butler, Alexander N. Chebeskov, James S. Dyer, Thomas A. Edmunds, Jianmin Jia, and Vladimir I. Oussanov

ABSTRACT. At the end of the Cold War, the United States and Russia entered into agreements that reduced the numbers of nuclear weapons in their arsenals. The possibility that excess plutonium recovered from dismantled weapons could fall into the hands of terrorists has been characterized as a "clear and present danger" by the National Academy of Sciences. Other disposition considerations include plutonium's potential for use as an energy source and its environmental impacts. A team of U.S. decision analysts was commissioned by the Department of Energy's Office of Fissile Materials Disposition to develop a multiattribute utility model to help evaluate alternatives for the disposition of the excess-weapons plutonium. Subsequent to the U.S. study, Russian scientists modified the model with the aid of the U.S. team, and used it to evaluate Russian disposition alternatives.

At the end of the Cold War, the United States and Russia entered into arms limitations and reduction agreements that reduced the numbers of nuclear weapons that would be in the arsenals of each nation. When these nuclear weapons are dismantled, plutonium pits – the triggers for modern nuclear weapons – are stored in anticipation of their ultimate disposal. Estimates of the numbers of weapons to be dismantled vary, but may be on the order of 15,000 in the United States and perhaps twice that many in Russia [NAS 95].

Excess-weapons plutonium is highly radioactive and extremely toxic. A greater concern, however, is the fact that excess-weapons plutonium could be used to build a nuclear weapon if it fell into the hands of terrorists. A National Academy of Sciences panel (NAS) termed the situation a "clear and present danger" [NAS 94].

In September 1993, the Office of Fissile Materials Disposition (OFMD) was formed within the U.S. Department of Energy (DOE) to oversee the important task of selecting a technology for the disposition of excess-weapons plutonium in the United States. A variety of approaches for the disposition of plutonium were considered by the OFMD, but only three of these were ultimately judged to be practical and capable of achieving the standards for proliferation resistance set forth by the National Academy of Sciences: irradiation in nuclear reactors by converting the plutonium into mixed-oxide (MOX) nuclear fuel, immobilization in borosilicate glass, ceramics or metal alloy castings, or placement in deep boreholes. Thirteen specific alternatives based on these three general approaches were selected for a detailed evaluation by OFMD.

The Amarillo National Research Center (ANRC) was established in 1994 under a cooperative agreement between the DOE and the state of Texas. Its goals included conducting scientific and technical research, advising decision makers, and providing information on nuclear weapons materials and related environmental, safety, health, and nonproliferation issues. The ANRC was asked to assemble a team of decision analysts to conduct an independent evaluation that might be used to support DOE's final recommendation. As outlined in Dyer et al. (1997, 1998) the team implemented a multiattribute utility (MAU) model to aggregate various performance measures into a single performance measure based on explicit tradeoffs. The ANRC team worked closely with DOE and experts from the National Laboratories (Lawrence Livermore, Los Alamos, Oak Ridge, and Sandia) over the period from May 1995 to August 1996 to determine the objective hierarchy, values and tradeoffs required for a detailed MAU evaluation of the alternatives.

During this same period, Russian scientists and policy makers were also considering alternatives for the disposition of their excess-weapons plutonium. Although a number of individual studies were completed or under way regarding various aspects of the Russian strategy, there was no overall evaluation framework to guide a systematic analysis and evaluation of their options. The European Commission recognized the value of the MAU analysis that was used in the US for this purpose, and supported the adoption of this methodology by Russian scientists in the analysis of their own disposition alternatives (Dyer et al. 2005).

The U.S. MAU analysis was modified by Russian scientists to accommodate Russian policies and alternatives. As a result, these studies have engaged leading Russian scientists involved with policy making regarding both excess-weapons and civil plutonium, and they have been influential in determining Russian policies regarding these issues. Further work on improving and refining these methodologies is continuing in Russia.

After evaluation of the thirteen disposition alternatives with the multiattribute utility model, DOE announced a dual track implementation strategy in January 1997 [DOE ROD 97] that would simultaneously develop an alternative based on using MOX fuel in existing nuclear reactors and an immobilization alternative. One of the major reasons for adopting this hybrid approach was uncertainty regarding the Russian reaction to the U.S. policy and the need for flexibility. There was also concern about opposition to the MOX fuel technologies by nongovernment organizations who would attempt to delay its deployment. Each alternative was favored by some stakeholders and opposed by others. The MAU analysis demonstrated that the dual-track strategy was a low-cost form of insurance for the ultimate success of this mission in a timely manner.

In October 1997, the Russian Federation announced that it would commence a gradual withdrawal of up to 50 metric tons of plutonium from its nuclear defense programs. On September 2, 1998, the presidents of Russia and the United States affirmed the intention of each country to remove by stages approximately 50 metric tons of plutonium from their respective nuclear weapons programs and to convert this material so that it could never be used in nuclear weapons.

In this chapter, we summarize the study performed by the ANRC team, and highlight its impacts on the decision making process that led to the United States policy regarding the disposition of excess-weapons plutonium. In addition, we describe the sequence of events that led to the adoption of MAU by the Russian scientists, and discuss the issues associated with excess-weapons plutonium disposition from their perspective.

The MAU Analysis in the United States

Previous recommendations by DOE, including the selection of Yucca Mountain as the national repository for nuclear waste, had been criticized by the National Academy of Sciences and others for the lack of a formal analysis that would justify the choice. The OFMD anticipated that their recommendation might be controversial, and requested an analysis by a team of decision analysts from the ANRC to provide a transparent and defensible record of the decision process that could withstand the scrutiny of external review by various interest groups. The role of the ANRC team was to support and to inform the OFMD's decision-making process but not to choose the best alternative. All parties understood that the OFMD would base its final recommendation on considerations of this analysis and other factors.

The Objectives and the Measures

The potential objectives for the evaluation of alternatives for the disposition of surplus plutonium were initially developed based on the objectives articulated in Presidential policies and in international agreements, as well as the recommendations of the National Academy of Sciences study on this topic [NAS 94, NAS 95]. These statements of objectives were made public and interested parties were invited to comment on the validity and importance of these objectives, and to suggest additional measures that should be considered. The objectives were organized into a traditional MAU hierarchy, illustrated in Figure 24.1, with three objectives at the highest level: Non-proliferation; Operational Effectiveness; and Environment, Safety, and Health (ES&H). Intuitively, these three objectives reflected the policy of OFMD to achieve proliferation-resistant disposition as efficiently as possible with minimum risk to the public and to the natural environment.

The Non-proliferation objective consists of five subobjectives:

(1) *Theft* (minimize the opportunities for theft of the materials by unauthorized parties, not including the country disposing of the plutonium); (2) *Diversion* (minimize the ability of the country disposing of the plutonium to secretly divert materials during processing, and to provide an internationally verifiable and acceptable process); (3) *Irreversibility* (maximize the difficulty of recovering the material after disposition is complete); (4) *International Cooperation* (foster international cooperation with U.S. disarmament and nuclear non-proliferation objectives); and (5) *Timeliness* (minimize the time required for the disposition effort to begin, and the time to complete the disposition mission).

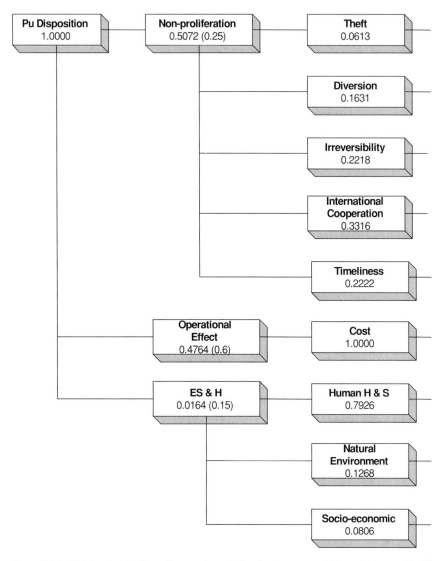

Figure 24.1. High-level objectives. The numbers in the figure represent the weights used in the U.S. (Russian) analysis.

Operational Effectiveness includes the investment and life-cycle costs associated with an alternative. The third high-level objective, *Environment, Safety and Health* (ES&H), is made up of three subobjectives: (1) *Human Health and Safety* (minimize the incremental health impacts to the public and workers); (2) *Natural Environment* (minimize the incremental impact on the environment); and (3) *Socio-economic* (minimize the incremental adverse impacts on the local economy).

The ANRC team worked with OFMD personnel, and met with scientists from National Laboratories (Lawrence Livermore, Los Alamos, Oak Ridge, and

Sandia) and TRW Corp. who were organized in teams to analyze the three major types of alternatives under consideration: reactors, immobilization, and boreholes.

The OFMD also arranged interviews for ANRC personnel with representatives of the Department of State, National Security Council, and the White House Office of Science and Technology Policy. Meetings were also held with representatives of TetraTech Corp., a private consulting firm responsible for the Programmatic Environmental Impact Statement [DOE-PEIS 96].

The objective of these meetings was to define the thirty-seven measures listed in the appendix that were used to determine how well a particular alternative satisfied the disposition objectives. As a result, these measures identified the information required for the evaluation of the thirteen plutonium disposition alternatives considered by OFMD and structured the data collection and analysis effort for the project. A complete 13 × 37 matrix of data was developed as the basis for the evaluation of the alternatives, including both objective data and subjective assessments obtained by the decision team from scientists and policy analysts.

The Alternatives

Table 24.1 provides a list of the thirteen disposition alternatives considered in the U.S. analysis. Five alternatives were identified that would use surplus plutonium to fabricate MOX fuel for nuclear reactors that generate electric power. The spent fuel from these reactors would ultimately be placed in a geologic repository. Reactors introduce highly radioactive fission products into the fuel matrix and physically change the isotopic properties of the plutonium, thereby decreasing its attractiveness for reuse in a weapons program and making it less attractive to potential thieves. The Russians were known to favor reactor options for the disposition of their surplus excess-weapons plutonium, and active cooperation with them could be enhanced if the United States adopted a similar strategy. Finally, the reactor disposition option is the only technology that unambiguously met the NAS "spent-fuel standard" of proliferation resistance [NAS 94, NAS 95].

Six other alternatives would require the immobilization of the surplus plutonium materials in borosilicate glass, ceramics, or metal alloy castings. Additional radionuclides would be added to provide a radiation barrier similar to that present in spent reactor fuel to inhibit recovery and reuse. The immobilized material would be transferred to the federal waste management system. Some of the immobilization alternatives were estimated to have time and cost advantages over the reactor alternatives.

Finally, two disposal alternatives involving the placement of plutonium in a borehole were considered. Each borehole would be between four and six kilometers deep, sealed, and heavily guarded. These alternatives were only moderately expensive and fairly efficient in terms of time to complete the mission. However, at the time of the decision, no borehole facility had been licensed and no specific site had been selected. As a result, there was some concern about the feasibility of this option. For additional details regarding these alternatives, see the DOE technical summary report [DOE-TSR 96].

Table 24.1. U.S. plutonium disposition options

Reactor alternatives

Existing light water reactors (LWRs), existing facilities

   MOX fuel fabrication plant to be built in an existing building at a DOE site, MOX irradiated in existing privately-owned commercial reactors.

Existing light water reactors, greenfield facilities

   A new co-located pit disassembly/conversion and MOX fabrication facility to be built at a DOE site, MOX irradiated in existing privately owned commercial reactors.

Partially completed light water reactors

   Commercial LWRs on which construction had been halted would be completed and operated by DOE. A co-located MOX facility would be built at the site.

Evolutionary light water reactors

   New LWRs would be built and operated by DOE along with a new co-located MOX facility.

CANDU reactors

   MOX fuel fabricated at a U.S. facility would be transported to one or more Canadian commercial heavy water reactors and irradiated.

Immobilization alternatives

Vitrification greenfield

   Surplus plutonium would be mixed with glass and radioactive materials at a new facility to form homogeneous borosilicate glass logs.

Vitrification can-in-canister

   Surplus plutonium would be mixed with nonradioactive glass and poured into small cans. These small cans would be placed in larger canisters, which are then filled with radioactive waste glass.

Vitrification adjunct melter

   Surplus plutonium would be mixed with glass and radioactive materials in a supplemental melter facility to form homogeneous borosilicate glass logs.

Ceramic greenfield

   Surplus plutonium would be mixed with ceramic and radioactive materials at a new facility to form homogeneous ceramic disks. These disks would be placed in a canister.

Ceramic can-in-canister

   Surplus plutonium would be mixed with nonradioactive ceramic materials to form sintered ceramic pellets. These pellets would be placed in larger canisters filled with radioactive waste glass.

Electrometallurgical treatment

   Surplus plutonium would be immobilized with radioactive glass-bonded zeolite.

Direct disposal alternatives

Deep borehole (immobilization)

   Surplus plutonium would be immobilized with ceramic pellets and placed in a borehole.

Deep borehole (direct emplacement)

   Surplus plutonium would be converted to a suitable form and placed in a deep borehole.

The MAU Model

If a decision maker's preferences are consistent with some special independence conditions, then a multiattribute utility model $u(x_1, x_2, \ldots, x_n)$, where x_i represents the level of performance on measure i, can be decomposed into an additive, multiplicative, or other well-structured form that simplifies assessment. An additive multiattribute utility model can be represented as follows:

$$u(x_1, x_2, \ldots, x_n) = \sum_{i=1}^{n} w_i u_i(x_i), \tag{24.1}$$

where $u_i(\cdot)$ is a single-attribute utility function over measure i that is scaled from 0 to 1, w_i is the weight for measure i and $\sum_{i=1}^{n} w_i = 1$. If the decision maker's preference structure is not consistent with the additive model (24.1), then a multiplicative model based on a weaker independence condition may be appropriate.

In this analysis of the thirteen alternatives for the disposition of plutonium, the additive model (24.1) was used to aggregate the results of the evaluation effort. This model was chosen because the independence assumptions that justify the use of the additive model are reasonable for this analysis because of the relationships among the objectives and measures and because the results of the analysis are easier to interpret when the additive model is used. A sensitivity analysis was performed to test the assumption of the additive model.

The ANRC decision team assessed single-attribute utility functions from the experts identified by OFMD and from OFMD personnel. In each case, these utility functions were scaled by identifying the range of feasible values for the corresponding measure, with one endpoint being defined as the worst possible value for the measure and the other endpoint as the best possible value. After some detailed discussions, many of these utility functions were determined to be linear. For example, all of the measures in the ES&H objective were linear because each additional unit of environmental impact was viewed as equally detrimental. However, there were other measures that did require a detailed assessment of the utility function, including some with nonlinear functions, others with piecewise linear functions, and others based on categorical information. For more detail, see Dyer et al. (1997).

Each objective, subobjective, and measure in the objectives hierarchy is given a weight. These weights reflect the value tradeoffs among objectives (or subobjectives and measures within objectives), and are dependent on the ranges of the outcomes considered in the analysis. The ANRC team of decision analysts assessed the weights from experts identified by OFMD using a trade off procedure (Keeney and Raiffa 1976). These tradeoffs considered measures related to the theft and diversion of excess-weapons plutonium, for example, or policy issues related to Russian cooperation and U.S. nonproliferation policies. As a result, value judgments were required to provide the baseline estimates of tradeoffs that give the information necessary to determine the weights on these measures.

Rather than asking for new expert judgments regarding ES&H tradeoffs, however, existing information from other DOE and government programs was used to determine the weights used in the baseline analysis via a pricing procedure. Many different government programs have been subject to evaluations that have involved measures of environmental and safety impacts, and information from these studies was used to estimate reasonable tradeoffs within this category of measures.

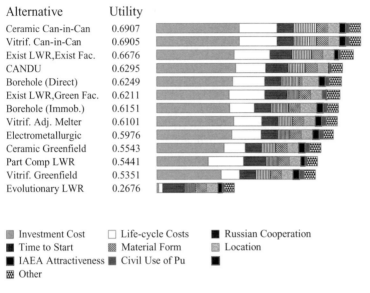

Alternative	Utility
Ceramic Can-in-Can	0.6907
Vitrif. Can-in-Can	0.6905
Exist LWR,Exist Fac.	0.6676
CANDU	0.6295
Borehole (Direct)	0.6249
Exist LWR,Green Fac.	0.6211
Borehole (Immob.)	0.6151
Vitrif. Adj. Melter	0.6101
Electrometallurgic	0.5976
Ceramic Greenfield	0.5543
Part Comp LWR	0.5441
Vitrif. Greenfield	0.5351
Evolutionary LWR	0.2676

Investment Cost ☐ Life-cycle Costs ■ Russian Cooperation
■ Time to Start ▨ Material Form ▧ Location
■ IAEA Attractiveness ■ Civil Use of Pu ■
▦ Other

Figure 24.2. Overall ranking of alternatives.

The weights used to aggregate the three primary objectives were assessed from OFMD personnel. Obviously, these "policy" weights are subject to debate, as will be discussed in the section describing the sensitivity analyses.

Evaluation of the Alternatives

The component utility function scores were aggregated, using the additive MAU function (24.1), within each of the three major objectives, and within each of the categories of objectives identified in Figure 24.1. These results are often presented in the form of *stacked bar graphs,* which provide a visual representation of the aggregated performance of each alternative as illustrated in Figure 24.2. Each segment represents the value of the performance of each alternative on each measure, weighted by its relative importance as captured through the tradeoff responses using the additive MAU model.

The U.S. decision analysis team presented the preliminary results of the MAU analysis to the OFMD on two occasions: early in the project effort and at a second meeting near the project's conclusion. During the first presentation, inconsistencies in the data-collection processes were identified, and deficiencies in some of the alternatives were highlighted. As a result, the OFMD audited and standardized the measures of attribute performance, and modified some of the alternatives to improve their performance measures on key attributes. The alternatives the final MAU analysis ranked highest, which were summarized in the second presentation, were consistent with the final OFMD recommendation. The overall ranking of the alternatives using the base-case data is shown in Figure 24.2.

Table 24.2. Alternatives by measures matrix for alternative selection.
Life-cycle costs are measured in thousands of dollars

Original decision problem				Rescaled decision problem		
Alternative	Life-cycle costs	Start year		Alternative	Life-cycle costs	Start year
Alternative 1	$1,000	8	⇒	Alternative 1′	$1,375	5
Alternative 2	$1,300	6	⇒	Alternative 2′	$1,425	5
Alternative 3	$950	10	⇒	Alternative 3′	$1,575	5
Alternative 4	$1,800	5	⇒	Alternative 4′	$1,800	5

Inspection of Figure 24.2 points out that while some alternatives score better than others, it may be unclear why these differences occur. For example, the Vitrification Can-in-Can alternative receives an overall utility score of 0.6905 while the Existing Reactor, Existing Facilities alternative scores 0.6676. What does this difference imply about the relative superiority of the vitrification alternative? To provide the decision makers with some intuition regarding the difference between alternatives, we rescaled the alternatives' scores based on the concept of even swaps (Hammond et al. 1998).

The overall utility score of each alternative is just a normalized combination of the scores on each measure. The choice of normalizing the overall utility score to a range of [0,1] is arbitrary and done for mathematical convenience. This implies that one could select a measure as the standard of measurement, and exchange utility on the other performance measures for utility in the standard measure. For example, suppose that a decision maker is considering comparing four plutonium disposition alternatives based on only two performance measures: Life-cycle cost and Start year.[1] The decision maker's choice problem for four hypothetical alternatives is presented in the left panel of Table 24.2.

As demonstrated in Hammond et al. (1998), the use of even swaps allows an exchange of utility for Life-Cycle Costs for utility in Start Year. Suppose we artificially set the Start year of each alternative to a common level, say the best possible level of five years, and ask the decision maker to adjust each alternative's Life-cycle cost so that the "new" alternative is equally preferred to the original one. For example, assume Alternative 1 has a Life-cycle cost of $1,000,000 and a Start year of 8. If we were to decrease the start year to five that would clearly be a superior alternative and the decision maker would expect to pay more in Life-cycle costs in order to be indifferent between this hypothetical alternative and the original Alternative 1. Perhaps decreasing the Start year from eight to five would cause the decision maker to be willing to pay $375,000 more, or $1,375,000. DOE

[1] Start year measures the time, in years, between the decision to go forward and the disposition of the first kilogram (kg) of plutonium. An early start in the process was considered to be an important signal to the international community that the United States was serious about disposition, and would reduce the threat window from rogue nations.

Table 24.3. Renormalized utility scores in equivalent life-cycle costs and in equivalent starting date years

	Overall MAU score	Life-cycle costs ($M)	Equivalent life-cycle costs ($M)	Differential life-cycle costs ($M)	Start year	Equivalent start year	Differential start year
Ceramic can-in-can	0.6907	$1,050	$7,140	$0	7.0	55.76	0.00
Vitrif. can-in-can	0.6905	$1,050	$7,145	$5	7.0	55.79	0.03
Exist LWR, Exist Fac.	0.6676	$1,220	$7,674	$534	9.0	59.56	3.80
CANDU	0.6295	$1,660	$8,554	$1,414	10.0	65.81	10.05
Borehole (direct)	0.6249	$1,510	$8,661	$1,521	10.0	66.57	10.81
Exist LWR, green fac.	0.6211	$1,240	$8,749	$1,608	13.0	67.19	11.43
Borehole (immob.)	0.6151	$2,050	$8,886	$1,746	10.0	68.17	12.41
Vitrif. adj. melter	0.6101	$1,830	$9,002	$1,862	12.0	68.99	13.23
Electrometallurgical	0.5976	$1,710	$9,291	$2,151	13.0	71.05	15.29
Ceramic greenfield	0.5543	$2,330	$10,289	$3,149	12.0	78.15	22.39
Part. comp. LWR	0.5441	$1,210	$10,526	$3,386	13.0	79.83	24.07
Vitrif. greenfield	0.5351	$2,550	$10,733	$3,593	12.0	81.30	25.54
Evolutionary LWR	0.2676	$3,660	$16,909	$9,768	14.0	125.20	69.44
Range of values	0.4231	$2,610	$9,768		7.0	69.44	

decision makers indicated that the utility function for Life-cycle costs was linear, so for this example each year change in Start Year would be offset by $125,000 in Life-cycle Costs. For nonlinear utility functions, the starting value of the measure that is varied would matter when estimating the required change to the original alternative. Proceeding in a similar fashion, the decision maker is faced with a choice among the "new" alternatives in the right panel of Table 24.2.

Now the decision maker's task has been simplified. Because all of the alternatives under consideration have the same Start Year, that measure can be ignored when making the decision; it is no longer a discriminator among the alternatives. Therefore, we would choose Alternative 1, whose transformed equivalent alternative, Alternative 1′, has the lowest life-cycle cost.

We can use the assessed weights and utility functions to formalize this intuitive procedure. As shown in Butler et al. (2001), for an additive MAU,

$$x'_s = u_s^{-1}\left(u_s(x_s) + \sum_{i \neq s} \frac{w_i}{w_s}[u_i(x_i) - u_i(x'_i)]\right), \tag{24.2}$$

where x_s is the standard measure used in the exchange and the quantity x'_s is analogous to the rescaled Life-Cycle Costs presented in the right panel of Table 24.2.

Table 24.3 presents a renormalization based on (24.2) for two measures: Life-cycle Costs, and Start Year. Column 3 shows the actual Life-cycle Costs and column

4 shows the rescaled Life-cycle Costs. The difference between columns 4 and 3 can be interpreted as the amount of Life-cycle Costs the decision maker is willing to exchange to shift performance on the other measures from their current to their best levels of performance. The most preferred alternative, Ceramic Can-in-Can, requires the least amount of Life-cycle Costs to move its performance on all other measures from current to best. Finally, column 5 shows the difference in rescaled Life-cycle Costs between each alternative and the most preferred alternative. Columns 6, 7, and 8 display the analogous values for the measure Start Year.

Table 24.3 provides the decision makers with some intuition about how much more or less one alternative is preferred relative to another. For example, Table 24.3 indicates that the 0.0229 utility difference between Vitrification Can-in-Can and Existing LWR, Existing Facilities is equivalent to $529 million of Life-cycle Cost or a 3.80-year delay in Start Time.

Sensitivity Analysis

After the base-case analysis was completed, the robustness of the alternative rankings was tested by varying the weights, the form of the multiattribute utility function, and the assumptions used in the base-case analysis. The first step was to consider the impact of varying the weights on the individual measures and objectives in the MAU model. For example, as the weight on the Russian Cooperation measure increases, the reactor alternatives will be preferred to the nonreactor alternatives.

Of particular importance were the weights at the highest level of the objectives hierarchy on the Non-proliferation, Operational Effectiveness, and ES&H objectives. Many of the weights at lower levels in the hierarchy involved technical factors that limit the ability of non-experts to make the required judgments. These high-level weights represent policy judgments, and it is likely that these weights could be very different for different stakeholders or decision makers.

A sensitivity analysis indicated that for all possible policy weight combinations, only three alternatives could be the most preferred. When the weight on ES&H is relatively low, Ceramic Can-in-Can is preferred; when the weight on Non-proliferation is very high, the Borehole (Immobilized) alternative is preferred; otherwise the Existing LWR, Existing Facility alternative is preferred. See Dyer et al. (1998) for details regarding these sensitivity analyses.

The ANRC team also investigated the sensitivity of the MAU model to changes in the assumptions in the base-case data and the evaluation model. The unique properties of the borehole alternatives' material form, the means of aggregating Theft and Diversion measures across plant facilities, the assumed sensitivity of Congress to alternatives with high investment costs, and the dollar value assigned to statistical fatalities were all investigated in these analyses. These sensitivity analysis studies demonstrated that the base-case recommendations were robust with regard to these issues, and were carried out to identify issues and assumptions that might be criticized, but that had little impact on the recommended disposition alternative.

Hybrid Deployment Strategies

The base-case analysis based on the revised data and alternatives indicated that the four most desirable alternatives were, in order, Ceramic Can-in-Can, Vitrification Can-in-Can, Existing LWR in Existing Facility, and CANDU. The sensitivity analyses showed that these four alternatives are ranked at the top of the list for a wide range of possible weights that could be assigned to the measures. However, two important considerations were not fully captured by the analysis: the risk of failure should a single technology be pursued and the ability to influence Russia to pursue a reciprocal disposition path. In this section, we discuss how parallel development of several technologies can better address these two concerns.

DOE could pursue a joint development approach featuring one reactor technology and one immobilization technology. This would lead to higher initial investment costs, but intuitively, such a "hybrid" should provide additional flexibility in light of the uncertainty about Russian policies and other considerations.

Several factors suggested the need for a hybrid strategy for plutonium disposition. For example, domestic and international concerns about the fabrication and use of MOX fuel in commercial reactors might delay the deployment schedule for the reactor alternative. Similarly, the R&D necessary to qualify the immobilized plutonium for disposal in a geologic repository might identify problems that require more time and budget to resolve than initially anticipated. Thus, the institutional and technical uncertainties associated with each alternative suggest the need for a hybrid approach in order to avoid delays in deployment of a disposition alternative.

A key difference between the reactor and immobilization disposition alternatives is that irradiation of MOX fuel in reactors converts the material from a weapons-grade to a reactor-grade isotopic form of plutonium. It is more difficult to fabricate weapons from reactor-grade plutonium. The importance that Russia and other countries would place on this isotopic degradation was not known at the time of the original MAU analysis.

To evaluate the hybrid strategy, the measure Russian Cooperation was replaced with a probability distribution over the likelihood that that Russians would require isotopic degradation of fissile material. The weights on the other measures were rescaled so that the original ratios among the weights were maintained and the sum of the rescaled weights was one.

This analysis is illustrated by the decision tree shown in Figure 24.3. The logic represented by this tree is as follows: first, the US must select a disposition strategy without knowing the future Russian stand on isotopic degradation; second, at some point after the US announces its decision, the official Russian policy will become known; finally, the US will have the opportunity to react to the Russian announcement. In Figure 24.3, the probability that Russia requires isotopic degradation is shown as 0.50 for illustrative purposes only. No attempt was made to elicit an estimate of this probability from relevant experts. Instead, the objective of this analysis was to identify the best development strategy for different values of the probability. This analysis demonstrated that each of the three disposition

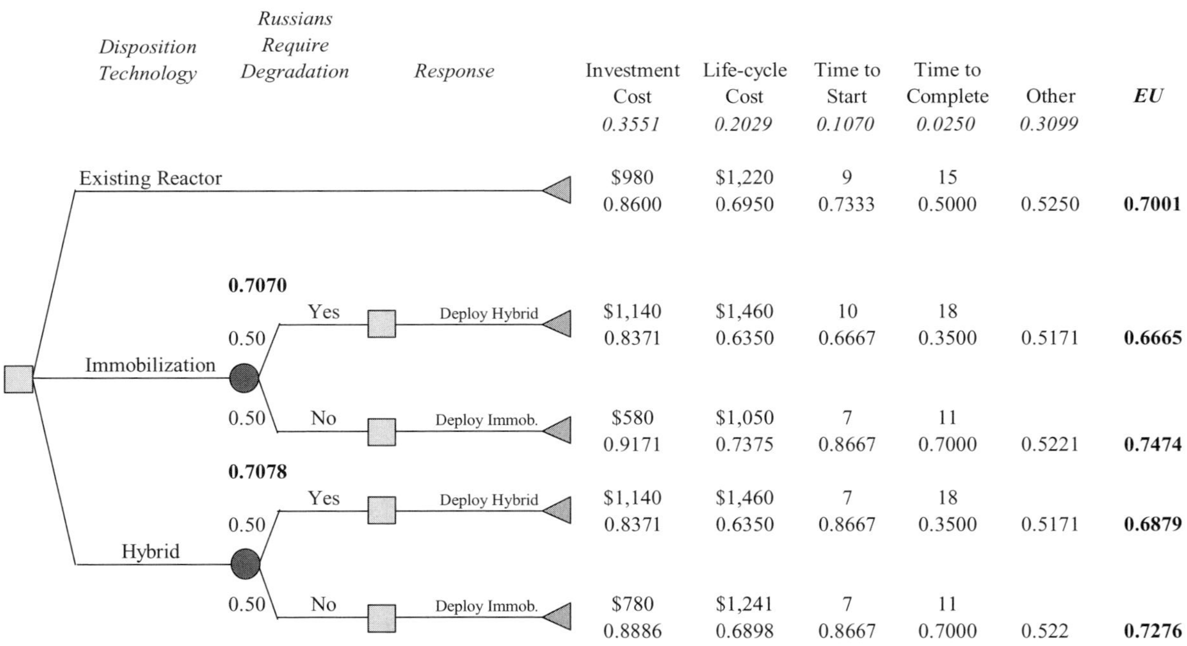

Disposition Technology	Russians Require Degradation	Response	Investment Cost 0.3551	Life-cycle Cost 0.2029	Time to Start 0.1070	Time to Complete 0.0250	Other 0.3099	EU
Existing Reactor			$980 / 0.8600	$1,220 / 0.6950	9 / 0.7333	15 / 0.5000	0.5250	**0.7001**
Immobilization **0.7070**	Yes (0.50)	Deploy Hybrid	$1,140 / 0.8371	$1,460 / 0.6350	10 / 0.6667	18 / 0.3500	0.5171	**0.6665**
	No (0.50)	Deploy Immob.	$580 / 0.9171	$1,050 / 0.7375	7 / 0.8667	11 / 0.7000	0.5221	**0.7474**
Hybrid **0.7078**	Yes (0.50)	Deploy Hybrid	$1,140 / 0.8371	$1,460 / 0.6350	7 / 0.8667	18 / 0.3500	0.5171	**0.6879**
	No (0.50)	Deploy Immob.	$780 / 0.8886	$1,241 / 0.6898	7 / 0.8667	11 / 0.7000	0.522	**0.7276**

Figure 24.3. Decision tree for existing reactor in existing facility, immobilization, and hybrid disposition alternatives.

technology alternatives could be the best choice depending on the estimate of this probability. For a detailed discussion of this analysis, see Dyer et al. (1998).

Therefore, it was logical that the OFMD recommended proceeding with the parallel development of two of the highest-ranked alternatives from this analysis, the Ceramic Can-in-Can immobilization alternative (or possibly the Vitrification Can-in-Can variant) and the Existing LWR, Existing Facilities reactor alternative.

This analysis provided the only quantification of the benefit of simultaneously deploying two technologies to provide flexibility to respond to Russian policy. This "hybrid" approach was eventually adopted by DOE [DOE – ROD 97], and allowed the United States to react quickly to subsequent Russian policy decisions by selecting the reactor alternative for further development.

The MAU Analysis in Russia

The MAU methodology supporting the ANRC study was presented at several scientific forums in parallel with the efforts to complete the analysis. On March 20, 1996, this methodology and some preliminary recommendations were presented at The International Meeting on Military Conversion and Science in Como, Italy (Dyer et al. 1996). This meeting was attended by a number of scientists, including representatives from Russia and from the European Commission of the European Union. The MAU approach was generally well received, and scientists from the European Commission inquired whether it might be used to organize the efforts of Russia's scientists as well.

The International Science and Technology Center (ISTC) is an intergovernmental organization established in 1992 by agreement among the European Union, Japan, the Russian Federation, and the United States. From its headquarters in Moscow, the Center provides weapons scientists from the Commonwealth of Independent States (CIS) countries with opportunities for redirecting their scientific talents to peaceful science through the financial support of selected projects.

After the meeting in Como, Italy, representatives of the Directorate-General XVII on Nuclear Energy of the European Commission reached an agreement with Russian scientists to fund ISTC Project 369. This Project supported the evaluation of Russian alternatives for the disposition of excess-weapons plutonium using the MAU methodology developed by the ANRC team for the DOE. The success of this initial study led to the decision by the European Commission to fund ISTC Project 1443, which enhanced and extended this work.

The Russian scientists accomplished the initial steps in Project 369 based on the descriptions of this methodology that were available on the ANRC website. Later, the Russian scientists made contact with the ANRC team members, and a dialogue was started. Since the first contact between members of the ANRC team and their Russian counterparts, there have been numerous exchanges of information by email and by personal contact. One of the members of the ANRC team was invited by representatives of the European Commission to attend meetings of the Joint Steering Committee on ISTC Project 1443 as an observer, and to provide advice to the project members regarding their work. This cooperation between scientists from Russia and the United States under the sponsorship of a project funded by the European Commission may be unique.

Russian versus U.S. Views on Plutonium Disposition

The main discrepancy between U.S. and Russian views on plutonium disposition can be summarized as follows: The US viewed surplus plutonium as a security liability that must be destroyed, while Russia viewed it as an asset to be exploited as an energy source. The National Academy of Sciences summarized the position of the United States as follows, "In short, in strictly economic terms, excess-weapons plutonium is more a liability than an asset. No matter what approach is taken to long-term disposition, the process is likely to involve a net economic cost, rather than a net benefit" [NAS 94, p. 25]. This point of view explains the rationale behind the evaluation of alternatives for long-term disposition in the United States based on immobilization in other materials, or placement in a deep borehole. These latter approaches emphasize that the plutonium would be considered a waste product, and be treated as such.

In contrast, the Russian position viewed the energy available from the use of excess-weapons plutonium to be a national resource. "In general Russian authorities have objected to weapons plutonium disposition options that would 'throw away' the plutonium without generating electricity" [NAS 94, p. 194]. This attitude was confirmed in the Strategy of Nuclear Power Development of Russia that was approved by the Russian Federation Government in the year 2000: "Utilization of weapons plutonium should be considered as initial part of the closed nuclear fuel cycle creation in the future" [MIN-RF-AE 00, p. 22].

Further, Russian nuclear policy had always favored the use of liquid-metal fast reactors that would actually operate with fissionable plutonium, and their nuclear program included projections to build new nuclear power plants with reactors of this type that would be justified, at least in part, by their contribution to the disposition of the excess-weapons plutonium as fuel. According to the Russian concept, the plutonium generated by thermal and fast reactors would ultimately be reprocessed and reused to balance its production and consumption in the whole nuclear power system, so only a relatively small amount of plutonium would be available for operational needs during any one point in time. Ironically, the Russians viewed the immobilization alternatives as sophisticated storage procedures that could ultimately be mined for the plutonium they contained. Therefore, the alternatives that were considered for evaluation by the Russians were limited to variations involving different combinations of nuclear power plants and operating strategies.

ISTC Project 369

The work on ISTC Project 369 "Study on the Feasibility and Economics of the Use of Ex-Weapons and Civil Plutonium as Fuel for both Fast and Thermal Reactors," was started in 1996, and the initial work was carried out independently by the Russian scientists without benefit of interaction with the ANRC decision team from the United States. Subsequently, a member of the ANRC team visited Moscow for discussions with Russian scientists regarding another project under consideration related to plutonium disposition, and was approached by a member of the ISTC Project 369 team. This contact led to an exchange of ideas and software, and to efforts to clarify the concepts underlying the MAU methodology.

For example, the Russian scientists expressed concern regarding the relatively small weight in the U.S. MAU model for the ES & H objective. This led to a discussion of the impact of the ranges associated with attribute measures on the sizes of the weights assigned to these measures. In the United States, for example, the decision was made that all of the alternatives for the disposition of excess-weapons plutonium would have to comply with existing laws and regulations regarding the environment, all OSHA regulations, and all related statutes, so the differences in the environmental measures among the alternatives was relatively small. In Russia, however, the circumstances were different, and it was recognized that the alternatives could have larger differential impacts on these measures, so a larger weight could easily be justified.

Nevertheless, Russian scientists preferred using a model that was similar to the MAU approach developed in the United States effort to ensure comparability. In fact, the Russian scientists' early models featured the identical hierarchy *and* weights for the evaluation of Russian alternatives. The argument was that this would allow alternatives from Russia and the United States to be compared in the same manner, and provide additional credibility for the results. Subsequent analyses were carried out with the weights shown in parentheses in Figure 24.1 that reflect the unique circumstances in Russia.

This first study involved about 250 Russian scientists from seven research institutes and design organizations associated with MINATOM, the Ministry of Russian Federation for Atomic Power, which is the Russian organization combining the policy making responsibilities in nuclear areas of the Departments of Energy (nuclear power) and Defense (nuclear weapons). The preliminary results of this effort were reported in April 1998 (Chebeskov et al. 1998).

The Russian scientists' analysis considered twelve alternatives composed of different combinations of VVER-1000, BN-600, and BN-800 reactors to burn fuel produced from 50 tons of surplus excess-weapons plutonium. The VVER-1000 reactors are conventional LWRs similar to Western PWR designs, and are considered to be adequately safe and to have adequate capacity to carry out the mission. At the time of the analysis, there were eight VVER-1000 reactors operating in Russia. The BN-600 reactor is an existing fast reactor that may be capable of being used for the disposition of excess-weapons plutonium. However, the BN-800 reactor is a fast reactor of a newer vintage, and is under construction, but its completion has been delayed. MINATOM would prefer to complete this reactor and to build two others of the type by the year 2020.

Complete alternatives by measures matrices based on the same measures used in the ANRC study were calculated for each of these twelve alternatives. The Russian scientists modified some assumptions and single-attribute utility functions for a few of the measures, however, to reflect some unique aspects of the Russian alternatives. For example, the alternatives involving the fast reactors would create and use plutonium in the process of the operations, and some adjustment in the scoring was made for these cases using expert opinions. The Russians did not have the advantage of an independent Programmatic Environmental Impact Statement required in the United States, but used available studies in the literature and past experiences to estimate values for the measures related to environmental safety and health measures.

All twelve of the Russian alternatives were compared under two scenarios. The first scenario assumed that Russia would have the financial means to adhere to the United States standards in the non-proliferation area, and the irreversibility of the nuclear disarmament process was the main goal of the plutonium utilization strategy. The second scenario uses a different set of weights to consider a more "economical" strategy where there is less emphasis on the objectives of timeliness and irreversibility of the process, and less concern about the political, as opposed to commercial, aspects of the International Cooperation objective.

The results of the analyses identified two alternatives as having a distinct advantage over the others relative to the non-proliferation objective. One alternative used twelve VVER-1000 reactors, including some in operation and more to be built, and the second alternative used a BN-800 fast reactor with four existing VVER-1000 light water reactors to process the excess-weapons plutonium. This preliminary study also highlighted the sensitivity of the preferred solution to some critical uncertainties, especially regarding the completion of the BN-800 reactor. The analysis indicated that a five-year delay in its start would change the ranking of the alternative involving the BN-800 and four VVER-1000 reactors to twelfth, however starting the operations five years earlier would change its ranking to first.

When the "economical" strategy was considered, the alternatives involving the existing reactors were rated more highly. Namely, the two alternatives with the highest ranking were the eight existing VVER-1000 reactors and the existing fast reactor BN-600 plus four new VVER-1000 reactors. The Project 369 was the first system study that predicted the increase of the role of the LWR technology in the excess-weapons plutonium disposition strategy in Russia.

The course of events has confirmed this principle finding of Project 369. "In conclusion it should be noted that the results gained within the framework on the Project [369] have been used in elaboration of 'The concept of the Russian Federation on disposition of weapons plutonium being released in the course of nuclear disarmament,' which has recently been approved as an official document of Ministry of Atomic Energy of Russian Federation." (Chebeskov et al. 1999). The base-case scenario recently developed in Russia for the disposition of 34 metric tons of excess-weapons plutonium included four VVER-1000 units and the BN-600 unit.

ISTC Project 369 was a notable success for reasons that go beyond the results of the MAU analysis. As stated in the Project report, "It should be mentioned that system analysis in the nuclear power of Russia is not an everyday, stale procedure.... Actually, the work is the first attempt in the frames of Project #369 to consolidate economic analysis with ecological and non-proliferative ones to give an integrated system outlook on the plutonium utilization options in Russia." (Chebeskov et al. 1998)

ISTC Project 1443

ISTC Project 1443, also funded by the European Commission, continued the efforts started under Project 369. There were several improvements made in the analysis and database supporting the effort, and changes were also made to the MAU model as the Russian scientists learned how to tailor the approach to incorporate their unique concerns. A major focus of this effort was on the refinement of the cost estimates of the various alternatives that were evaluated. Process flow charts were developed for each alternative to carefully evaluate the nuclear fuel cycle and identify the steps necessary to convert the excess-weapons plutonium into nuclear fuel elements, and to utilize them in the appropriate nuclear reactors. In addition, the focus of the evaluation was expanded to include issues related to the civil use of plutonium in the nuclear strategy of the country. Cost estimates for some of the Russian alternatives were in the $2–3 billion range.

These efforts to refine the cost estimates also highlighted several "risks" associated with the alternatives that were difficult to eliminate, and a decision was made to incorporate some of these risks directly into the MAU model. In the United States study, the Operational Effectiveness of an alternative was measured by the investment and life-cycle costs of an alternative. The Russians chose to break the discounted cash flows into components to be evaluated individually. Value functions were developed for each of these measures, and their definitions incorporated estimates of such factors as lending rates in Russia and the International Monetary Fund, and estimates of inflation rates.

There were a number of other changes the Russian team made to the ANRC template. Perhaps the more significant examples of these changes were made in order to distinguish between weapons and civil plutonium. The objective of this modification was to allow the MAU model to be used to evaluate policies related to the disposition of both excess-weapons and civil plutonium. Although plutonium created from the operation of a conventional reactor could be used in a weapon, the required chemistry makes civil plutonium less attractive for theft and diversion by terrorists or the host country. In particular, it would be necessary to change the basic design of the weapon and to make the process much more complicated and costly compared with using excess-weapons plutonium.

Each measure in the Theft and Diversion categories was split into two parts, one for excess-weapons and one for civil plutonium, as illustrated in Figure 24.4. Notice that different weights are assigned to the corresponding measures. This splitting of the measures also was applied to the Timeliness objective because the use of civil plutonium would follow the disposition of the more dangerous weapons plutonium. As a result, the weight on the time to start measure would be lower for the civil plutonium. The time to complete measure for the civil plutonium was discarded.

These distinctions are consistent with Russian policy concerning the continued use of plutonium as a commercial fuel source. Because the policy of the United States forbids reprocessing spent nuclear fuel to obtain plutonium, this feature was not incorporated into the ANRC analysis. The Russians anticipated a lack of

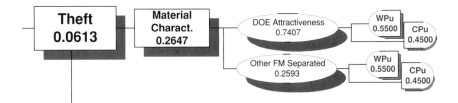

Figure 24.4. Modifying the MAU analysis to accommodate weapons (WPu) and civil (CPu) forms of plutonium (Chebeskov et al. 2001).

international support for an alternative that included an emphasis on disposition of civil plutonium in a manner that delayed the disposition of excess-weapons plutonium, and scored these alternatives lower on the International Cooperation objective as well.

Because all of the Russian options use nuclear reactors and result in spent fuel, the scientists correctly lowered the weight on the Irreversibility objective. The range of performance on this objective was very similar across alternatives, so it received less weight than in the analysis of the alternatives considered by OFMD in the United States. The Russian scientists also developed more detailed models of how the plutonium stockpiles, civil and excess-weapons, would change over time. These models were consistent with the theme of the OFMD evaluation model.

The success of ISTC Project 1443 was dependent on the development of contacts and efficient co-operation with the representatives of Directorate-General XVII on the Nuclear Energy of the European Commission and representatives of companies; collaborators on the ISTC-1443 Project included BELGONUCLEAIRE, COGEMA, BNFL, and SIEMENS. In addition, the structure for the analysis provided by the MAU model was important as well. "The concept of adaptation of multi-factor analysis model, developed in the US as applied to the management of excess-weapons grade plutonium, was presented to the European partners. This approach has caused vast interest of both specialists and management, especially with respect to 'Fissile materials non-proliferation' section" (Chebeskov 2001).

Conclusion

The U.S. team's analysis based on MAU (Dyer et al. 1997, 1998) provided valuable insights regarding alternatives for the disposition of excess-weapons plutonium in the United States. The ranking of alternatives was consistent with the DOE's formal recommendation, and the MAU process helped them to refine the alternatives and to communicate the results to all stakeholders.

Specifically, the U.S. decision analysis effort had the following impacts:

- The MAU model identified the information the OFMD required to evaluate the thirteen plutonium disposition alternatives, and structured the data collection and analysis effort.

- The use of thirty-seven performance measures in the MAU model ensured that the discussions did not focus only on the strengths of some alternatives or only on their weaknesses. The OFMD team managed to avoid an emotional dispute over the alternatives and to maintain a reasoned discussion with different points of view revealed clearly and with a balanced perspective on the alternatives.

- The presentation of the preliminary results of the MAU analysis led to the identification of inconsistencies in data collection and caused the OFMD team to audit and standardize the measures of attribute performance. In addition, the analysis highlighted deficiencies in some of the alternatives, which helped the science teams to modify some of the alternatives to improve their performance measures on key attributes.

- The OFMD recommended two of the alternatives ranked highest by the final MAU analysis for parallel development. The MAU analysis provided the only quantification of the benefit of parallel development. The DOE adopted this hybrid approach [DOE ROD 97], and the US then reacted to subsequent Russian policy decisions by selecting one of these options for further development.

The selected option calls for disposal of plutonium by fabricating it into mixed-oxide (MOX) fuel for irradiation in existing, commercial nuclear reactors.

In addition, the ANRC analysis served as a basis for the Russian analysis of the same problem. The Russian team made some changes to the original hierarchy of objectives and measures but maintained the core of the MAU model. The ANRC analysis served as a template for the Russian analysis, ensuring that the Russian analysis considered disparate performance measures, and it also provided a basis for comparing the alternatives the countries evaluated.

The study by the Russian scientists had the following impacts:

- Prior to implementing the Russian MAU model, the predominant view in Russia was to use their excess-weapons plutonium as a fuel source in fast nuclear reactors of an advanced design planned for future construction. The Russian MAU analysis based on consideration of financial and technical support from the rest of the world favored alternatives in which the plutonium would be fabricated into MOX fuel and irradiated in existing Russian nuclear reactors with a shorter time schedule and an estimated cost on the order of $2 billion to $3 billion.

- The Russian scientists presented the recommendations of the Russian version of the MAU model to MINATOM, which took these results into account in its major policy statements.

- The MAU analysis also highlighted the desirability of parallelism between U.S. and Russian plutonium disposition technologies. The Russians have decided to replicate the design of the U.S. MOX facility in Russia, contributing to the synergy in the disposition policies.

The Russian Federation and the United States signed an agreement on September 1, 2000. According to this agreement, each side will dispose of no less than 34 metric tons of plutonium being withdrawn from nuclear weapons programs, enough plutonium to build thousands of weapons of mass destruction. The scope of the disposition effort was reduced from 50 to 34 metric tons in part because of the reluctance to rely on immobilization technology. Some of the original 50 metric tons of excess materials is not suitable for use in reactor fuel; for example, some impure plutonium that would need to be processed and therefore was not considered for disposition at this time.

Both countries will dispose of surplus plutonium by fabricating it into MOX fuel for irradiation in existing, commercial nuclear reactors. This approach will convert the surplus plutonium to a form that cannot readily be used to make nuclear weapons. The United States is building two facilities to fabricate MOX fuel at the Savannah River Site in South Carolina to carry out the U.S strategy, and Russia is duplicating the design of these facilities to implement a parallel strategy. These policies followed from the recommendations originally supported by the ANRC and Russian MAU studies.

The Russians continue to use the framework of the MAU model to evaluate policies related to plutonium disposition and other non-proliferation issues. The Russians are currently studying non-proliferation issues regarding the possibility of importing spent nuclear fuel from foreign nuclear reactors for long-term storage or reprocessing. The Russian team continues to work on improving and disseminating the MAU model as well with the expectation that this effort will encourage Russian policy makers to adopt MAU and other operations research tools.

Appendix

The thirty-seven measures used in the analysis are defined below. IAEA is an abbreviation for International Atomic Energy Agency.

Non-Proliferation

Resistance to theft by unauthorized parties

DOE attractiveness	Attractiveness of the material	Constructed scale based on DOE order 5633.3B
Other FM separated?	Inventory of other, fissile materials	Presence of other fissile material (yes/no)
Bulk throughput	Throughput of disposition process	Metric tons of bulk throughput per year
No. processing step	Security of the disposition environment concerning process accessibility	Number of processing steps
MAX Pu inventory	Maximum plutonium inventory of the material in process	Maximum Pu inventory
No. of trips	Risk due to transportation exposure	Number of safe and secure transports (per kg Pu)

(continued)

(Continued)

SST trans. miles	Risk due to transportation exposure	Safe and secure transport miles per alternative
Measurement uncertainty	Accounting accuracy of material process	Percentage material difference
Type of NAS	Type of nuclear accounting system	Exponential scale biased toward "Item" (percentage of time "Item")
Accessibility	Accessibility of material in process	Constructed scale based on accessibility of Pu, accessibility of container, and special handling requirements
U.S. classification	Classification of material in process	Constructed scale based on security classification of material (Yes or No)

Resistance to diversion by host nation

IAEA attractiveness	Attractiveness of the material	Constructed scale based on expert opinion of IAEA classification
Bulk throughput	Appeal to IAEA of the throughput of disposition process	Metric tons of bulk throughput per year
No. processing step	Appeal to IAEA of the disposition environment concerning process accessibility	Number of processing steps
MAX Inventory	Appeal to IAEA of the maximum amount of plutonium material in process	Maximum Pu inventory
Measurement uncertainty	Appeal to IAEA of the accounting methods in place	Percentage material difference
Type of NAS	Appeal to IAEA of the type of nuclear accounting system	Exponential scale biased toward "Item" (percentage of time "Item")
Accessibility	Appeal to IAEA of the accessibility of material in process	Constructed scale based on accessibility of Pu, accessibility of container, and special handling requirements
Int'l classification	Appeal to IAEA of the security classification of material in process	Constructed scale based on security classification of material (Yes or No)

Irreversibility of final form

Material form	Irreversibility relative to NAS attractiveness rating	Constructed scale based on attractiveness – A, B, C, D, E per DOE order 5633.3B or IAEA eligible for termination
Material location	Irreversibility relative to the location of the plutonium	Constructed scale based on location – borehole, geologic repository or in process

International cooperation and compliance

Russian cooperation	Impact a U.S. alternative would have in influencing Russian disposition activities	Constructed scale based on factors considered desirable by Russia and the influence of U.S. choices
Civil use of Pu	Do not encourage the civil use of plutonium	Constructed scale based on expert opinion

Timeliness

Time to start	Time to start disposition activities	Years between record of decision and the start of disposition activities
Time to complete	Time to complete disposition activities	Years between start of disposition and completion of disposition mission

Operational effectiveness objectives

Cost

Investment cost	Investment cost	Investment costs in millions of dollars
Life-cycle costs	Life-cycle costs	Discounted life-cycle costs in millions of dollars (R&D, startup, O&dM, decontamination and decommissioning)

Environment, safety and health objectives

Protect human health and safety

Pub. rad. deaths	Public health and safety risks from operations and radiological exposure	Expected number of public fatalities from exposure to radionuclides during operations
Pub. chem. deaths	Public health and safety risks from operations and chemical exposure	Expected number of public fatalities from exposure to chemicals during operations
Wrkr. rad. deaths	Worker health and safety risks from operations and radiological exposure	Expected number of worker fatalities resulting from exposure to radionuclides during operations
Wrkr. chem. deaths	Worker health and safety risks from operations and chemical exposure	Expected number of worker fatalities from exposure to chemicals during operations
Transport deaths	Health and safety risks from transportation	Expected number of fatalities from inter-site transportation
Accident risk	Accident risks	Expected number of fatalities in a severe accident

(continued)

(*Continued*)

Protect the natural environment		
Secondary waste generation	Impacts on secondary waste management	Equivalent cubic yards of incremental waste generated
Impact on species	Impacts on biological species (terrestrial and aquatic)	Number of endangered or threatened species that could be affected

Socio-economic benefits		
Boom/bust	Boom/bust employment losses	Percent decrease in local employment relative to peak employment
New long-term jobs	Sustained increase in employment	Number of permanent new jobs created in the local area

Acknowledgments

Figure 24.1, Table 24.1 and Figure 24.3 reprinted by permission, Butler, J. C., A. N. Chebeskov, J. S. Dyer, T. Edmunds, J. Jia, and V. I. Oussanov, "The United States and Russia Evaluate Plutonium Disposition Options with Multiattribute Utility Theory," *Interfaces*, Volume 35, No. 1., January–February 2005, pp. 88–101. Copyright 2005, the Institute for Operations Research and the Management Sciences, 7240 Parkway Drive, Suite 310, Hanover, MD 21076 USA.

REFERENCES

Butler, J. C., Morrice, D., and Mullarkey, P. (2001). A multiple attribute utility theory approach to ranking and selection. *Management Science, 47*, 800–816.

Chebeskov, A. N., Korobeinikov, V. V., Oussanov, V. I., Zavadsky, M. I., Tikhomirov, B. B., and Iougai, S. V (2001). *Methodology of the multi-attribute system analysis of the selected scenarios for plutonium utilization.* Brussels May 14–16, 2001.

Chebeskov, A. N., Oussanov, V. I., Tikhomirov, B. B., Nevinitsa, V. A., and Pshakin, G. M. (1998). *Preliminary results of systems analysis on plutonium utilization options in Russia.* Paper presented at the workshop on the ISTC Project No 369, Brussels, Belgium, April 6–7, 1998.

Chebeskov, A. N., Zavadski, M. I., and Ousssanov, V. I. (1999). *Multi-attribute analysis of Plutonium use in nuclear reactors.* Paper presented at the Third Meeting of the Contract Expert Group, Dimitrovgrad, Russia, June 7–9, 1999.

[DOE-PEIS 96]. U.S. Department of Energy. (1996). *Storage and Disposition of Weapons-Usable Fissile Materials Final Programmatic Environmental Impact Statement, DOE/EIS-0229.* Office of Fissile Materials Disposition.

[DOE-ROD 97]. U.S. Department of Energy. (1997). *Record of Decision for the Storage and Disposition of Weapons-Usable Fissile Materials Final Programmatic Environmental Impact Statement.* United States Department of Energy; Office of Fissile Materials Disposition.

[DOE-TSR 96]. U.S. Department of Energy. (1996). Technical Summary Report for Surplus Weapons-Usable Plutonium Disposition, *DOE/MD-0003 Rev. 1.* Office of Fissile Materials Disposition.

Dyer, J. S., Edmunds, T. A., Butler, J. C., and Jia, J. (1996). *A proposed methodology for the analysis and selection of alternatives for the disposition of surplus plutonium.* Paper presented at the International Meeting on Military Conversion and Science "Utilization of the Excess-Weapon Plutonium: Scientific, Technological and Socio-Economic Aspects." Villa Olmo, Como, Italy, March 20, 1996.

Dyer, J. S., Edmunds, T. A., Butler, J. C., and Jia, J. (1997). Evaluation of alternatives for the disposition of Surplus weapons-usable plutonium. *Technical Paper 1997–1.* Amarillo National Research Center.

Dyer, J. S., Edmunds, T. A., Butler, J. C., and Jia, J. (1998). A multiattribute utility analysis of alternatives for the disposition of surplus weapons-grade plutonium. *Operations Research, 46,* 749–762.

Dyer, J. S., Edmunds, T. A., Chebeskov, A. N., Oussanov, V. I., Butler, J. C. and Jia, J. (2005). The Adoption of Multi-attribute Utility Theory for the Evaluation of Plutonium Disposition Options in the United States and Russia, *Interfaces vol. 35, no. 1.*

Hammond, J. S., Keeney, R. L., and Raiffa, H. (1998). Even swaps: A rational method for making trade-offs. *Harvard Business Review, 76,* 137–149.

Keeney, R. L., and Raiffa, H. (1976). *Decisions with Multiple Objectives.* New York: John Wiley and Sons.

[MIN-RF-AE 00]. Ministry of Russian Federation for Atomic Energy. (2000). *Strategy of nuclear power development of Russia in the first part of XXI century: The main principles.* Moscow: Ministry of the Russian Federation for Atomic Energy.

[NAS 94]. National Academy of Sciences. (1994). *Management and Disposition of Excess Weapons Plutonium.* Washington, DC: National Academy Press.

[NAS 95]. National Academy of Sciences. (1995). *Management and Disposition of Excess Weapons Plutonium – Reactor Related Options.* Washington, DC: National Academy Press.

25 Choosing a Tritium Supply Technology for Nuclear Weapons: Reflections on a Controversial Decision Analysis

Detlof von Winterfeldt

ABSTRACT. Nuclear weapons require the periodic replacement of tritium, a radioactive gas that decays at approximately 5.5 percent per year. Since 1989 the United States had no tritium supply facility, and, because of the decay of tritium, its inventory was expected to fall below the required reserve level in 2011. To decide how to fill this projected gap, the Department of Energy assessed several tritium supply alternatives, including several types of new reactors, an accelerator, and the use of commercial reactors. This paper describes the decision analysis process, conducted in the mid-1990s, to support the decision by the Secretary of Energy to choose among the options. This process involved two rounds of analysis, several surprises and many adjustments. In the end the decision analysis was successful in shaping both the intermediate decision by then-Secretary O'Leary and the final decision by Secretary Richardson.

The Problem

Tritium is a necessary component of all nuclear weapons. Because tritium decays at a rate of approximately 5.5 percent per year, it must be replaced periodically. Over the past 40 years, the Department of Energy (DOE) has built and operated fourteen reactors to produce tritium and other nuclear materials for weapons purposes. In 1988, then-President Bush shut down the last remaining tritium production facility, a heavy-water reactor in Savannah River, GA. Since that time, no tritium has been produced and the DOE had to rely on recycled tritium from existing weapons to replenish decaying tritium sources.

The strategic arms reduction treaties known as START I and START II resulted in reducing the number of weapons in the stockpile of the US and Russia and made it possible for the US to rely on a tritium recycling program for a limited time. However, when this analysis was conducted in the mid-1990s, it was clear that a new tritium production source would eventually be required. Under the START I treaty a new tritium source would be required by 2005 and under the START II agreement a new source would be needed by 2011 (Figure 25.1).

The main issue was what technology to use for producing tritium. Several new reactor types were considered as well as a large linear accelerator. Purchase of tritium from foreign sources (Canada and Russia have an oversupply of tritium) was considered not acceptable for national security reasons. Using an existing commercial reactor was originally thought to be in violation of national policy

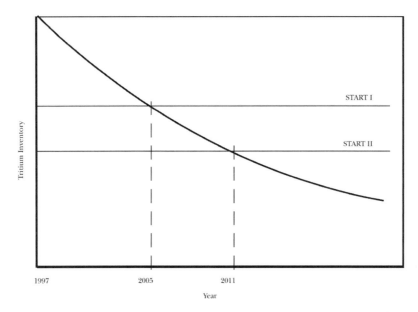

Figure 25.1. The U.S. tritium inventory without new production capabilities and levels to support START I and START II requirements.

and international agreements. Other issues concerned the siting of the tritium production facility and a choice of upgrading the existing tritium recycling facility at Savannah River versus building a new recycling facility co-located with the new production facility.

The stakes in this decision were high. First, the lack of a steady and reliable source of tritium was considered a threat to national security. Although most alternatives appeared to be able to meet the production requirements, significant uncertainties were associated with some. Second, the costs of the alternatives were very high. For example, building a new reactor or an accelerator can cost between $3 billion and $6 billion, and operating them can cost an additional $100 million to $250 million per year. Third, there were environmental concerns with most alternatives, including the production and disposal of radioactive waste and the risk of major accidents resulting in the release of radioactive material.

The Secretary of Energy at the time of this analysis was Hazel O'Leary. She had the ultimate responsibility of choosing among the tritium supply alternatives, sites and recycling facilities. Key participants in the decision-making process were the DOE Assistant Secretary of Defense Programs and the Under Secretary. Major stakeholders were the Department of Defense, Congress, public interest groups, and the private vendors of tritium production. The main concern of the Department of Defense and its Nuclear Weapons Council was to ensure timely tritium production in the required amounts. Congress and its appropriations committees were concerned with cost. Several public interest groups expressed strong opposition to building new nuclear reactors and concern about environmental impacts and employment. The private vendors lobbied for their own designs for tritium production.

Getting Started

In 1993, I was asked by the staff of Fluor Daniel, Inc., a major subcontractor to the DOE, to give several one-week short courses on using decision analysis as a tool to improve the key decisions that had to be made in DOE's Office of Reconfiguration. This office, which was part of DOE's defense program, was created to manage the major transitions of the weapons complex following the demise of the Soviet Union.

The short courses were received well and the director of the Office of Reconfiguration, Fluor Daniel and other subcontractors appeared to be committed to use decision analysis ideas and tools to address a variety of problems. However, in early 1994, the Office of Reconfiguration was split into three parts: a tritium production office, a plutonium disposition office, and a nuclear stockpile steward-ship office. Both the tritium production office and the plutonium disposition office continued to use decision analysis in their major decisions (for the plutonium dis-positions study, see Chapter 24 in this volume). I am not aware of any decision analysis activities regarding stockpile stewardship.

When the Office of Tritium Production was created, I was asked to lead a decision analysis of the choice of a tritium production technology, site, and recy-cling facility. I realized that this was a substantial job and would require help from several decision analysts as well as significant portion of my own time. I therefore asked for a leave of absence from the University of Southern California and recruited Ralph Keeney, Richard John, Robin Dillon (who worked at Fluor Daniel, Inc. at the time), and Robin Keller to work on this project. In the process, I also launched Decision Insights, Inc., which was incorporated on July 1, 1994, serving primarily this effort and several activities to support DOE's environmental management program.

One of the most important tasks in getting a decision analysis started is to iden-tify the decision maker or decision makers involved in the problem and to establish appropriate reporting mechanisms. It was clear to me that the key decision mak-ers were (in order from lower to higher): the deputy director and the director of the tritium production office, the assistant secretary for defense programs, and Secretary O'Leary. Reporting to a subcontractor, and possibly through an ill-understood chain-of-command, seemed to invite problems. I therefore requested to report directly to the director and deputy director of the Office of Tritium Production, thus bypassing the staff of Fluor Daniel, Inc., who were formally my contractors. This decision was absolutely crucial, as it turned out later, because it gave me open and continuous access to the decision makers, without filtering our analyses through layers of management.

Another important part of this analysis was to divide the work between different contractors. Fluor Daniel, Inc. was the main technical contractor and TetraTech, Inc. was the main environmental consulting company. Once my own reporting mechanism was established, I became, in effect, the lead decision analyst working with the directors of the office to oversee and guide the activities of the two major subcontractors. This also was an extremely important development as decisions made later about the direction of the decision analysis had substantial implications for the two contractors.

Physical proximity to the decision makers also turned out to be important. I set up an office in the Fluor Daniel complex in Alexandria, Virginia, with open access to office space in DOE's headquarters. As a result I was in virtually constant and direct personal contact with the key decision makers over the next eighteen months. This was important because many key decisions about the analysis occurred during casual meetings at the offices of Fluor Daniel or at DOE's headquarters.

When the analysis started in April, 1994, about seventy engineers, cost specialists, and environmental analysts worked on various aspects of the tritium project. Fluor Daniel, Inc. was charged with developing the engineering and cost data and estimates for the tritium supply alternatives. TetraTech, Inc., was charged with conducting the environmental analyses and developing the programmatic environmental impact statement (PEIS). A guideline to the contractors was that all estimates were to be based on existing reports and data. As a result, a major part of the early effort was to collect and catalogue several hundred boxes of existing information on the tritium supply alternatives. One of the major challenges was to organize the collection and assessment of information to support the decision by the Secretary of Energy and to draft a record of decision, the legal document presenting the Secretary's decision.

The project lasted for about eighteen months with an overall cost of approximately $20 million. The decision analysis effort cost about $1 million, not counting the work contributed by Fluor Daniel and TetraTech staff to this effort. Figure 25.2 shows a timeline of the project.

The Multiattribute Utility Analysis

The initial formulation of this decision problem included six tritium supply alternatives (a heavy-water reactor, two advanced light-water reactor designs, a modular high-temperature, gas-cooled reactor, and two version of a linear accelerator). The DOE wanted to evaluate these alternatives against numerous conflicting objectives, related to production assurance, cost, and environmental impacts. This concern with multiple objectives suggested the use of a multiattribute utility analysis (Keeney and Raiffa 1976; von Winterfeldt and Edwards 1986). This analysis, conducted in the second half of 1994, consisted of defining the objectives, collecting data to estimate how well the alternatives met them, and obtaining trade-off judgments from DOE officials to evaluate the alternatives in terms of production assurance, cost, and environmental impacts. In addition, we held several expert workshops to quantify the uncertainty in the data and estimates.

The analysis started in a fairly conventional way. Because it was not clear whether production technologies, site alternatives, and recycling options had some

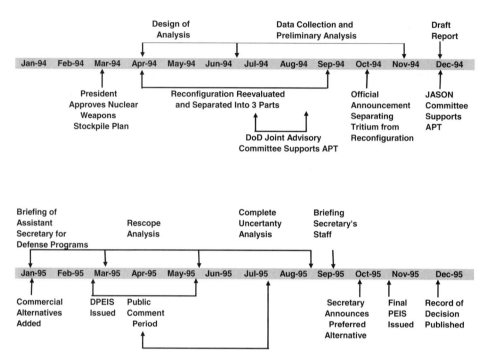

Figure 25.2. Timeline of the tritium decision analysis process.

interactions with respect to the objectives, we decided to analyze all possible combinations – fifty-four altogether:

1. Six production technologies
   a. Large advanced light-water reactor (LAWR)
   b. Small advanced light-water reactor (SALWR)
   c. Heavy-water reactor (HWR)
   d. Modular high-temperature gas-cooled reactor (MHTGR)
   e. Small accelerator (SAPT – designed to meet START II requirements)
   f. Large accelerator (LAPT – designed to meet START I requirements)
2. Five sites
   a. Idaho National Engineering Laboratory (INEL)
   b. Nevada Test Site (NTS)
   c. Oak Ridge Reservation (ORR)
   d. Pantex Plan (PANTEX)
   e. Savannah River Site (SRS)
3. Two recycling alternatives
   a. New recycling facility at any of the five sites
   b. Upgrade existing recycling facility at SRS

Although this generated sixty possible combinations, at Savannah River only upgrading the recycling facility made sense, reducing the set of alternatives to fifty-four.

There were many discussions about whether we could separate the technology choice from the site evaluation and either or both from the decision about recycling. At the early stage of this analysis, the argument prevailed that there could be significant interactions leading to this exhaustive list of combinations.

The objectives for the multiattribute utility analysis were obtained from reviewing the content of a previous programmatic environmental impact statement, previous studies of both technology choice and facility siting decisions and interviews with environmental and technical specialists of the DOE and its contractors. The three major objectives were:

1. Ensure production of tritium.
2. Protect the environment, health, and safety.
3. Reduce costs.

These were broken down as follows: Production assurance had three subobjectives: meet schedule; provide sufficient capacity; Ensure availability. The schedule objective came from the concern that some of the alternatives may not meet the 2011 deadline for producing tritium. The capacity objective was to address concerns, primarily with the accelerator, about the annual amount of tritium that could be produced with the technology. The availability concern addressed issues about the continuity of production throughout the many years of the planned life cycle of the facility.

The environmental objectives were broken down into seventeen objectives ranging from worker risks due to normal operations, to public risks due to major disasters, to pollution and socioeconomic impacts. Costs were broken down into the total life-cycle cost of designing, constructing and operating the tritium supply facility, the cost of the recycling facility, and the possible revenues from electricity production.

Measures were defined for each of the twenty-three objectives. For example, the schedule objective was measured in terms of the year and month at which tritium from the production facility would become available. Worker risks were measured in terms of the expected number of worker cancers and other fatalities due to the operation of the facility over 40 years. Cost was expressed as total life-cycle costs, measured in discounted 1995 dollars.

At this point, the analysis was set up to provide consequence estimates of fifty-four alternatives on twenty-three objectives – a daunting task. Fortunately, many of the cells in this table of alternatives by objectives had identical or similar consequences. For example, the production assurance assessments did not depend on the site chosen. In addition, we had many experienced assessment teams and could build on a draft environmental impact statement to pull together the requisite estimates. The technical, cost, and schedule estimates were provided by the staff of Fluor Daniel, Inc. The environmental estimates were provided by the staff of TetraTech, Inc. In all cases, we organized the elicitation in small group workshops. In some cases (schedule, capacity, availability, and cost), we obtained probabilistic estimates from the experts.

Table 25.1. Aggregate comparisons of six tritium production alternatives

	Production assurance	Environment, health and safety	Total life-cycle cost ($M)
HWR	99.98%	71	$5,551
Large ALWR	99.99%	58	$5,940
Small ALWR	99.97%	65	$4,444
MHTGR	99.89%	72	$6,529
Nominal APT	97.29%	82	$5,943
Full APT	97.39%	82	$6,907

Note: Production assurance assumes no technical or institutional problems; the production assurance for the nominal APT is for START II requirements.

To aggregate the three subobjectives of production assurance into one measure, we developed a model that simulated the production cycle of each technology over 40 years (see below for more detail). This production simulation model gave us an estimate of the expected percentage of tritium production at or above the required amount over the entire 40-year life cycle of production. This percentage ranged from 99.99 percent for the light-water reactors to 97.29 percent for the nominal accelerator.

We aggregated the other sets of subobjectives using standard multiattribute weighting techniques (swing weights and pricing out) involving interviews with four DOE officials. For the environment, health, and safety objectives we used an aggregate utility measure ranging from 0 (worst) to 100 (best). For the aggregate cost we used discounted (at 3.8 percent) total life-cycle cost. We decided early on to assign weights only to the subobjectives under the three main objectives (production assurance; cost; and environment, health and safety), instead of weighting these three subobjectives as well. This was done primarily to leave the decision makers some room for discussion and for deliberating possible tradeoffs among the three major objectives.

As the multiattribute utility analysis progressed, it became clear that only some minor interactions occurred between sites and technologies. As a result, we were able to report the results separately for technologies, sites, and recycling alternatives. The results are shown in Tables 25.1 and 25.2.

Regarding technologies, all alternatives show a high degree of production assurance with the large ALWR being best and the accelerator being worst. From an environmental point of view, the accelerator is the best alternative because it has no severe accident risks and produces no or little waste. The large ALWR is worst for exactly the opposite reasons. Regarding cost, the small ALWR is best, the accelerator is worst. As a result, the decision comes down to a tradeoff among the three main objectives. If a large weight is placed in environmental concerns (60 percent or more), the accelerator is the preferred alternative.

Regarding sites and recycling options (Table 25.2), the best environmental site was the Nevada Test Site; the worst was the Savannah River Site. A new recycling plant co-located with the new production facility was always better from

Table 25.2. Aggregate comparisons of site and recycling alternatives (for the small ALWR)

	Environment, health, and safety	Life-cycle cost ($M)
Nevada Test Site		
New recycling	69	$5,178
Upgrade at SRS	65	$4,444
Idaho National Eng. Lab		
New recycling	59	$5,198
Upgrade at SRS	56	$4,184
Savannah River Site		
New recycling	n/a	n/a
Upgrade at SRS	47	$4,158
Oak Ridge Reservation		
New recycling	53	$4,688
Upgrade at SRS	50	$4,098
PANTEX Site		
New recycling	58	$4,940
Upgrade at SRS	54	$4,250

an environmental perspective. In terms of costs, the Oak Ridge Site was least expensive; the INEL Site was most expensive. Recycling at Savannah River was always cheaper than building a new recycling plant at a different site. These results are shown in Table 25.2 for the small ALWR, but the results are similar for all other technologies. Overall, the finding was that the choice of a site or recycling facility made less difference in terms on environmental impacts or costs than the choice of a production technology.

With this material in hand, we briefed the assistant secretary for defense programs in January 1995. The results were noted by the assistant secretary and his staff, but many issues were raised about the risks and uncertainties surrounding cost and production assurance. As a result, we were asked to start a second phase of analysis, which focused on these risks. Before describing the findings of this analysis, a short interlude about the politics of this decision process is needed.

Interlude about the Politics of Decision Making

While we were conducting the multiattribute utility analysis, two events occurred that indicated a strong support for the accelerator by key decision makers. In the summer of 1994, the Joint Advisory Committee of the DOE and the Department of Defense issued a statement supporting the use of the accelerator for tritium production and in November of 1994 the JASON committee, a scientific advisory committee to the DOE, also supported the accelerator. Both committees considered the accelerator to be a sound technology for producing tritium that was environmentally clean and enjoyed public support. Our analysis team received several messages from DOE staff suggesting that the accelerator may be the pre-ferred alternative, even though our analysis was not completed yet.

This created a potential dilemma. On one hand, I could see how the acceler-ator could be defended using a very high weight on environmental objectives. At the same time, I questioned whether the relatively minor environmental benefits of the accelerator could outweigh the moderate concerns about production assur-ance and the significantly higher costs. In the briefing with the assistant secretary I therefore pushed the issue of this tradeoff, asking, in essence, why the accelerator was so strongly preferred. His arguments were that the accelerator was environ-mentally friendly, would face little opposition or delays, and, although costly, the costs could be reduced through alternative designs and research and development. The analysis left room for this argument, but I pointed out that these benefits came at a significantly increased costs.

Meanwhile, there were other – implied or unspoken – concerns. No nuclear reactor had been built in the United States for 20 years and it seemed unlikely that the Clinton administration wanted to do anything to revive a nuclear power program. In addition, the accelerator was a potential research and development bonanza for the national laboratories, because many technical issues needed to be resolved prior to building it. In contrast, all the reactor options would be developed and constructed by the private sector with little laboratory assistance.

None of these political agenda items were made explicit in the course of this analysis, but it is hard to believe that they did not have an influence on the decision making process. Our briefing on the relative advantages of the accelerator versus a reactor was clearly not a strong endorsement of the accelerator. We also had identified many uncertainties and risks of all technologies, including risks of some of the reactors not receiving licenses and risks of schedule and cost overruns. Whatever the reasons, the result of the briefing with the assistant secretary was to continue our work and conduct a more-detailed risk analysis on production assurance and cost.

As we began to rescope the analysis to include a more thorough risk analysis, five new alternatives were proposed, three that made use of commercial reactors and two that represented advanced designs of the heavy-water reactor and the modular high-temperature gas-cooled reactor. The commercial reactors had been considered in the early analysis stage, but they had been eliminated because it was unclear whether a utility would want to sell a commercial reactor to the DOE or provide tritium production services. With the emerging deregulation of the utility industry, the commercial options appeared more attractive in 1995 and, with their lower costs, had support in the DOE. However, there were significant policy and international treaty issues that needed to be resolved before a commercial option could be viable.

In March 1995, the DOE issued the draft programmatic environmental impact statement (DPEIS) with an analysis of some thirty environmental impacts. The DPEIS results made it clear that there were only three environmental discrimina-tors among the tritium production alternatives: spent fuel production, low-level waste production, and severe accident risks. About the same time, the cost and the uncertainties associated with it became a major issue. To resolve this issue, the secretary issued an independent study by Putnam, Hayes, and Bartlett (1995) that provided cost ranges for all alternatives, but no best estimate or probability distribution. These ranges were substantial, covering, in some cases, $5–10 billion.

In mid-1995, it was clear that the unresolved issues were the uncertainties associated with the schedule aspects of production assurance and with cost. In addition, issues remained about the political viability of the commercial option. In the remainder of the analysis, we therefore focused on quantifying these uncertainties and documenting the results from the environmental impact study. Thus, what began as a fairly standard multiattribute utility analysis turned into three related efforts: A risk assessment of production assurance, a risk assessment of costs, and a simple environmental analysis. In the end, there was no need for making tough trade-offs. The results spoke for themselves.

The Risk Analysis

We began the risk analyses in early 1995, shortly after briefing the assistant secretary. At this point, we were asked to consider ten tritium production alternatives:

1. Large HWR.
2. Small AHWR.
3. Steam-cycle MHTGR.
4. Direct-cycle MHTGR.
5. Large ALWR.
6. Small ALWR.
7. Accelerator production of tritium (full APT).
8. Purchase an operating commercial light-water reactor (CLWR).
9. Purchase a partially completed CLWR.
10. Purchase irradiation services from an operating CLWR.

Production Assurance Analysis

The three production assurance subobjectives contribute to the major objective of providing enough tritium in time to maintain the tritium inventory at the START II level. To analyze how well the ten tritium supply alternatives met this overall objective, we developed a dynamic model that simulated production patterns over 40 years. This model had three uncertain inputs: the schedule, the production capacity, and the annual availability (see Figure 25.3). To quantify the uncertainties about these inputs, we conducted several formal expert elicitation processes (Hora and Iman 1989; Keeney and von Winterfeldt 1991). These expert elicitations included explicit considerations of possible technical and institutional problems with the implementation of the technologies.

SCHEDULE RISK ANALYSIS. For each alternative, Fluor Daniel, Inc. (1995a) developed a base-case schedule divided into the several components ranging from

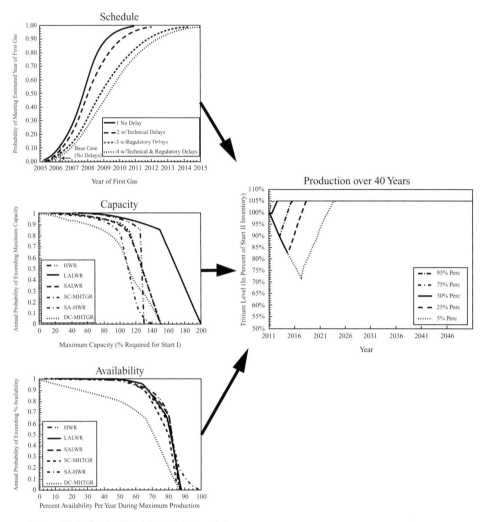

Figure 25.3. Production risk analysis model.

conceptual design to pouring first concrete, to start up and operations. The total length of the schedule was determined with consideration of the critical path relationships between the schedule components.

To assess the schedule uncertainties, we convened three panels of schedule specialists, with 10 technical staff members of the DOE office of reconfiguration, its contractors and consultants in each panel. Participants first made their three probability estimates independently, and, subsequently, we presented all estimates for discussion. During the discussion, participants could revise their initial estimates, but they were not required to reach consensus. After calculating each expert's overall schedule distribution we averaged the distributions across experts, giving each expert equal weight.

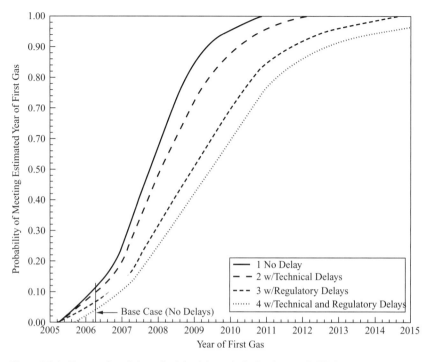

Figure 25.4. The results of the schedule risk analysis for the small ALWR.

In addition to this assessment, we asked the experts to identify technical and institutional problems that could cause delays of greater than one year. We also asked them to provide probabilities for these problems and estimate their schedule impacts. We folded these assessments of technical and regulatory delays into the simulation.

Figure 25.4 shows the resulting cumulative probability distributions over the year of delivering the first tritium gas for the small ALWR. The schedule provides for a high probability of meeting the 2011 start date (0.98 without delays and 0.78 with both technical and regulatory delays). The technical delays were due primarily to the possible failure of the new passive safety system of this reactor. The regulatory delays resulted from possible complication in the licensing process. Table 25.3 provides a summary of the schedule risk analysis, with the first column showing the base-case schedule estimate by Fluor Daniel, Inc, and the other columns showing the probabilities of meeting the 2011 start-up date with and without considering delays.

Two observations about this table are important. All base-case schedule estimates are within the 2011 date. However, the schedule risk analysis shows that these estimates may be highly optimistic in some cases. For example, the heavy-water reactors and the gas-cooled reactors have a fairly low probability of meeting the 2011 start date, when considering technical and institutional delays. The light-water reactors and the accelerator provide the highest assurance of meeting

Table **25.3.** Summary of the schedule uncertainty analysis

Tritium supply alternative	First tritium (Base case)	Probability of Without delays	Meeting 2011 With delays
Large HWR	2009	0.82	0.4
Small advanced HWR	2006	0.84	<0.40
Steam-cycle MHTGR	2009	0.60	0.22
Direct-cycle MHTGR	2010	0.14	0.14
Large advanced LWR	2007	0.92	0.78
Small advanced ALWR	2006	0.98	0.78
Accelerator	2008	0.92	0.76
Purchase operating LWR	2005	>0.99	see note
Purchase partially complete LWR	2006	>0.99	see note
Purchase irradiation services	2004	>0.99	see note

Note: Commercial production requires congressional approval.

the 2011 date. The commercial options can be ready in a few years and provide the highest assurance of meeting the schedule. However, there is the possibility of institutional delays or even a chance that these options are institutionally infeasible.

CAPACITY ANALYSIS. We defined production capacity as the maximum amount of tritium that could be produced in one year, assuming 75 percent availability for tritium production. The results were expressed as percentages of the START I requirement. Most tritium alternatives had no problems with meeting or exceeding the availability requirement, but there were substantial uncertainties.

Fluor Daniel, Inc. (1995b) prepared a summary of the available information on production uncertainties. This summary listed the factors that were likely to increase or reduce the capacity of the ten alternatives. From this information, eleven DOE and contractor staff members provided estimates of the probability that the production capacity would exceed 50, 75, 100, 125, or 150 percent of the START I goal. Participants first wrote down their initial responses for each alternative. Subsequently, they compared and discussed all responses for that alternative and revised their estimates, if they wished to do so. Much of the discussion focused on the plausible upper bounds of the production capacities, and the group came to a consensus on these bounds.

We fit probability distributions to the averages of the individual probability estimates (Figure 25.5). All reactors have a very high probability of meeting the capacity required by START I. Only the direct-cycle MHTGR and the small AHWR have probabilities of meeting the START I goal below 0.90.

AVAILABILITY ANALYSIS. All ten tritium supply alternatives were designed to operate 75 percent of the time. To assess whether they could meet or exceed this goal, we defined availability as the percentage of time that the production facility would be capable of producing tritium during any one year of maximum production.

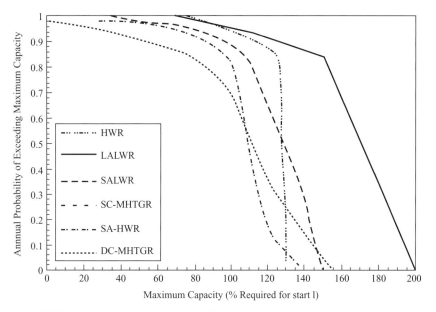

Figure 25.5. Results of the capacity risk analysis.

This availability is referred to as "maximum availability" as opposed to the actual availabilities that one may see during the course of a 40-year history of production.

Fluor Daniel, Inc., provided a summary of qualitative factors that influence the availability of each alternative. We elicited availability estimates for the new reactor options using a process that was similar to that used for capacity estimates. Nine DOE and contractor staff members provided probability estimates that a tritium supply alternative could exceed 50, 65, 75, 85, and 95 percent availability. After discussion and revision, we averaged the probability estimates across individuals and fit a probability distribution (Figure 25.6).

PRODUCTION ASSURANCE SIMULATION. To determine the production behavior of each of the ten alternatives, we conducted a dynamic simulation using the following steps:

1. We sampled the start year of tritium production once from the schedule distribution.
2. We sampled the maximum capacity once from the capacity distribution.
3. We sampled the maximum availability once every 40 years after the start date.
4. From steps 1–3 we calculated the amount of tritium produced in any given year.
5. We added this amount to the amount remaining in the tritium inventory after 1 year of decay.

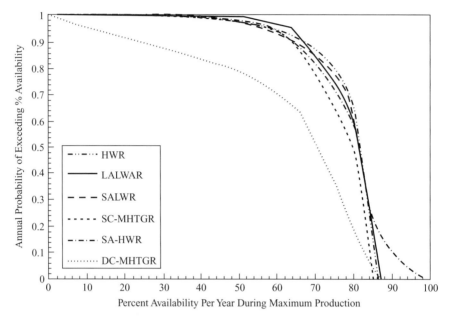

Figure 25.6. Results of the availability risk analysis.

Each iteration of steps 1 through 5 of the simulation provides an output that shows the tritium inventory over time. Repeating the process several thousand times provided a probability distribution over the available tritium inventory at any given point in time. This distribution can be compared with the required inventory levels. For example, the production simulations for the small ALWR shows that it is very likely that production starts on time and that shortfalls are rare (Figure 25.7). In contrast, most production simulations of the steam-cycle MHTGR start with a delay, creating shortfalls (Figure 25.8). However, once production starts, the required tritium inventory level is reached in a few years.

The production simulations showed that the MHTGRs and the HWRs had significant production problems because of start-up delays. All the other alternatives achieved START II production levels close to the required start date and easily maintained or exceeded this level throughout the 40 years of production. In addition, we ran several simulations that assumed a five-year shutdown of tritium production, for example, because of a major accident. Our purpose in these simulations was to determine how long it would take to make up for the five-year decay and return to the START II inventory level. These simulations showed that all alternatives were able to replenish the five-year decay in less than five years.

Cost Risk Analysis

Once the production assurance issues had been settled, cost became a major issue in this analysis (for a more detailed discussion of the cost analysis, see Dillon et al. 2002). First, the costs of all tritium supply alternatives were substantial, ranging from about $1 billion to $10 billion. Second, several alternatives could create

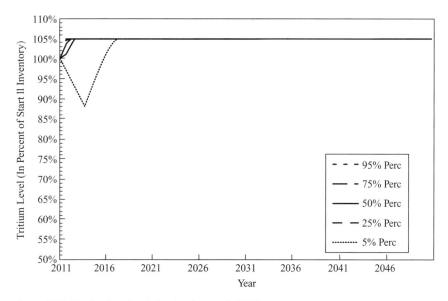

Figure 25.7. Production simulation for the small ALWR.

revenue through electricity generation, and the experts did not agree on how to account for revenues in the analysis. Third, there was substantial uncertainty in cost and revenue estimates, and some cost specialists estimated that the original engineering estimates could be exceeded several times over. Fourth, the discount rate became an issue, with arguments ranging from not discounting at all to using a discount rate as high as seven percent per year.

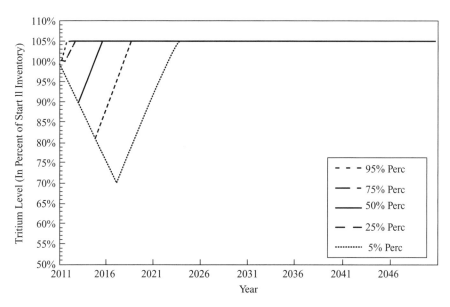

Figure 25.8. Production simulation for the steam-cycle MHTGR.

Table 25.4. The base-case cost estimates for ten
tritium supply alternatives (costs were discounted at
4.9% annually)

Tritium supply alternative	Total life-cycle cost (1995 $m)
Large HWR	$4,354
Small advanced HWR	$2,703
Steam-cycle MHTGR	$4,113
Direct-cycle MHTGR	$2,364
Large advanced LWR	$1,678
Small advanced LWR	$1,212
Accelerator	$3,603
Purchase operating LWR	$30
Purchase partially complete LWR	$675
Purchase irradiation services	$959

Partly because of these issues, we developed the cost analysis in several steps. Fluor Daniel, Inc. (1995a) developed base-case costs using data from previous DOE and commercial studies. It divided the costs for each alternative into several cost categories (e.g., construction, operations and maintenance, fuel and electricity cost) and estimated base-case costs for each category. In addition, Fluor Daniel, Inc., estimated base-case revenue estimates and cost and revenue profiles over time. They used cost and revenue profiles to calculate the net present value in 1995 dollars using a discount rate of 4.9 based on guidance by the Office of Management and Budget. The base-case costs for the new facilities range from a low of $1,212 million for the small ALWR to a high of $4,354 million for the large HWR (Table 25.4). The commercial options are the least expensive, and, because of the revenues, the option to purchase an operating reactor is close to a financial break-even point ($30 million).

Recognizing the uncertainties in these cost estimates, DOE issued a cost study by Putnam, Hayes, and Bartlett (1995) that provided a range of high and low cost estimates for each alternative. These ranges covered in some cases $5–10 billion for a single alternative. However, Putnam, Hayes, and Bartlett did not provide any guidance about the likelihood of the costs within these ranges. Oak Ridge National Laboratory (1995) conducted an additional study to quantify the cost uncertainties, which provided base-case cost estimates plus a contingency cost that depended on the degree of experience with the technologies.

In general, the three cost studies were fairly consistent in that the base-case estimate was usually close to the low end of the cost range of Putnam, Hayes, and Bartlett's study. Oak Ridge National Laboratories' estimate fell in the lower third of the Putnam, Hayes and Bartlett study. However, there also were inconsistencies between studies, and it therefore became important to provide an integration of the results. In particular, DOE considered it useful to obtain probability distributions over the range of costs developed by Putnam, Hayes, and Bartlett.

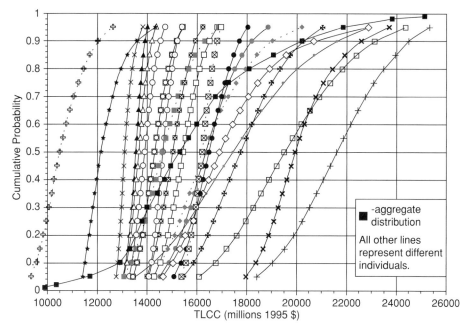

Figure 25.9. Individual and aggregate probability distributions for the total undiscounted life-cycle cost for the accelerator.

To resolve the differences in cost estimates and to assess these probability distributions, we conducted a major expert judgment exercise involving twenty-two cost and technical specialists from within and outside of DOE who met during two two-day meetings. During the first meeting, we introduced the specialists to the base-case cost estimates and presented them with the results of the previous studies on cost uncertainty. In addition, we trained the participants in probability assessment and they practiced cost probability assessment with two of the ten tritium supply alternatives.

Between the first and the second meeting, participants made independent cost estimates for each of the cost categories for each alternative. For each category, they provided a low (5th fractile), median (50th fractile) and high (95th fractile) of their probability distributions. They also provided comments or data sources and logic to justify their estimates and showed the calculations they used to generate estimates.

For major cost categories (construction, operation and maintenance, fuel cost, electricity cost) and for electricity revenues, they provided plausible minimum and maximum estimates in addition to the three fractiles.

Prior to the second meeting we calculated the overall cost distribution for each expert separately. The results of the individual elicitations are shown in Figure 25.9. These distributions of twenty-two experts are nothing short of astonishing. First, almost all experts show a great deal of overconfidence (indicated by very tight distributions). Second, the medians cover an extremely wide range from around $10 billion to $22 billion.

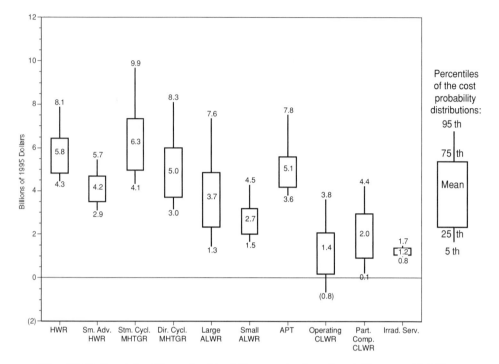

Figure 25.10. Box plots of the costs of ten tritium supply alternatives (with revenue) in billions of 1995 dollars, using a discount rate of 4.9 percent.

We started the second meeting by showing the experts the distributions in Figure 25.9. Each expert was given an envelope that included his or her symbol identifying his or her probability distributions without revealing it to other experts. Interestingly, the experts did not seem to be disturbed by the large variability of their judgments. In most cases, they attributed the variability to making different assumptions about cost growth phenomena. We discussed some of the more contentious estimates and subsequently encouraged participants to revise their estimates, but few did. We then calculated the revised cost distributions for each individual and averaged the distributions. The results are shown in the form of box plots in Figure 25.10.

Although the box plots show a large overlap in the cost estimates, there also are some important insights:

1. The commercial options have the lowest costs and the lower uncertainty. This is especially true for purchasing irradiation services.
2. Of the new construction options, the small ALWR has the lowest cost and lowest uncertainty. In fact, its cost distribution is dominated (higher cumulative probabilities for higher costs) by all other new construction alternatives.
3. The accelerator is one of the highest-cost options. Only the gas-cooled reactor options have higher costs.

Table 25.5. The results of the environmental analysis

Tritium supply alternative	Spent fuel per year (cubic yards)	Solid low-level waste per year (cubic yards)	Annual cancer risk from accidents
Large HWR	7	5,200	5.10E-05
Small advanced HWR	<7	<5,200	<5.10E-05
Steam-cycle MHTGR	80	1,300	1.00E-05
Direct-cycle MHTGR	82	~1,300	<1.00E-05
Large advanced LWR	55	710	2.60E-07
Small advanced LWR	36	660	2.30E-06
Accelerator	0	57	2.80E-11
Purchase operating LWR	40	160	no add. risk
Purchase partially complete LWR	~55	~710	~2.60E-07
Purchase irradiation services	<40	160	no add. risk

Environmental Analysis

In the initial round of analysis we evaluated seventeen environmental impacts, but we soon realized that only three impacts truly make a difference when choosing a tritium production technology: spent fuel production, low-level radioactive waste production, and risks from severe accident. The results are summarized in Table 25.5.

Spent fuel was measured by the cubic yards of radioactive spent fuel rods produced during reactor operations in one year. The new reactors generate spent fuel amounts ranging from 7 cubic yards to 80 cubic yards. The options to purchase an operating reactor or to purchase irradiation services would create up to 40 cubic yards of additional spent fuel (if only one reactor were used) because of shorter refueling cycles. If there were no change to the refueling cycles, no additional spent fuel would be generated. The option to purchase an incomplete reactor would create amounts of spent fuel comparable to those of the large ALWR. The APT does not generate any spent fuel.

For the new facility alternatives, the HWR creates by far the most low-level radioactive waste (5,200 cubic yards), followed by the other new reactors. The APT generates the least amount of low-level radioactive waste. The options to purchase an operating commercial reactor or to purchase irradiation services would create 160 cubic yards of additional low-level radioactive waste due to the use of additional fuel rods and due to handling additional radioactive materials. The option of purchasing an incomplete reactor would produce amounts of low-level radioactive wastes that are similar to those produced by the large ALWR, the small HWR, and the direct-cycle MHTGR. The low-level waste estimate for the APT applies to its helium target only and it is larger for the lithium target. The environmental impacts for purchasing a partially complete CLWR are similar to those of the large ALWR. The amount of additional spent fuel for the option to purchase irradiation services can be as high as 40 cubic yards per year, depending on the number of reactors used and their fuel cycle.

Cancer risks due to severe accidents can affect a population living within a 50-mile radius of a facility. For purposes of comparison, we used the DOE's Savannah River Site (SRS) in South Carolina because it has a relatively large population within 50 miles. The annual cancer risks from a severe accident of the new reactor technologies are very low, ranging from 1.0×10^{-5} to 2.6×10^{-7}. The APT has the lowest annual cancer risk (2.8×10^{-11}). The options to purchase an operating reactor or to purchase irradiation services would pose no significant additional severe accident risks because of adding tritium production. The option to purchase an incomplete commercial reactor would have severe accident risks that are comparable to those of a large ALWR.

In summary, the APT and the commercial options to purchase an operating reactor or to purchase irradiation services generate no additional spent fuel, have the lowest amounts of additional low-level radioactive waste, and have the lowest cancer risks from severe accidents. The new reactor alternatives and the completion of a partially complete commercial reactor produce spent fuel and low level radioactive waste, and they present a very small additional cancer risk from a severe accident.

The Decision

The analysis provided several key insights: First, the HWRs and the MHTGRs have significant problems with meeting the schedule and no cost or environmental advantages. The remaining reactor alternatives (ALWRs and commercial options) have similar production assurance and environmental impacts, but the commercial options are clearly less expensive. Although the commercial options look like a clear winner, they face several institutional issues. These include whether a U.S. utility would be willing to sell a reactor to the DOE and whether production in commercial reactors is compatible with international law and national policy. The accelerator provides a reasonable (though not very high) degree of production assurance and, although it is more expensive than the commercial options and some of the new facilities, it is also environmentally sound and it does not present unresolved institutional issues.

At this point, we faced two tasks: How to present these findings to the Secretary of Energy and how to use these findings in writing a formal "Record of Decision," once the Secretary had made her decision. After several briefings with close associates of Secretary O'Leary, we created the diagram shown in Figure 25.11, which is a qualitative summary of a consequence table representation. This diagram went through many discussions and wording changes, but in the end it conveyed the key messages of the analysis.

First, regarding the heavy water reactors and the gas-cooled reactors, it shows that they have schedule problems, which are not compensated by lower cost or environmental impacts. Therefore, the conclusion was not to go forward without these options.

Second, when looking at the choice between either building a new advanced light water reactor or using an existing one, the diagram illustrates a clear

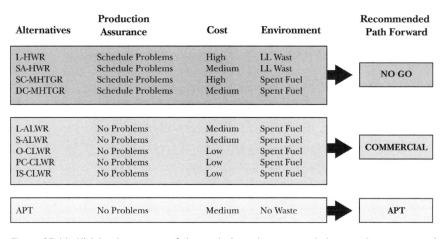

Figure 25.11. High-level summary of the analysis and recommendations to the secretary of energy.

dominance relationship. All reactors have equally high production assurance and produce additional spent fuel, but the commercial options are much cheaper. Thus, when restricting the choice to these five options, it is clear that the commercial options are should be preferred.

Third, the accelerator has a clear advantage in terms on environmental issues. Although the diagram suggests that there are no production assurance problems, some DOE staff members and contractors thought that it had not as high a production assurance as the ALWRs or the commercial options. In addition, although the costs were labeled medium in the diagram, they really were among the highest of the ten options. Thus, the accelerator would make sense only if one places a very high weight on the environmental issues.

When these briefings occurred, two factions had developed within the DOE, one favoring the accelerator and one favoring the commercial option. Although the analysis informed the debate between these two factions, the ultimate decision appeared to be left to political considerations. The Secretary of Energy, faced with the debate about the pros and cons of the two options, decided to pursue both for some time. The diagram shown in Figure 25.12 represents this decision.

The idea of the dual-track decision was to pursue the commercial options to determine whether the institutional issues can be resolved; simultaneously, DOE would pursue the accelerator to make sure that it can meet production goals and time tables. If the DOE can resolve the institutional issues of the commercial options and if it eventually chooses one of the commercial reactor options, the cost savings to the government would be several billions of dollars. If the institutional problems cannot be overcome, the accelerator will provide an environmentally clean alternative.

The DOE published the results of the production assurance and cost analysis described in this article in a technical reference report for tritium supply and recycling (DOE 1995c). It published the environmental analysis, as required by the

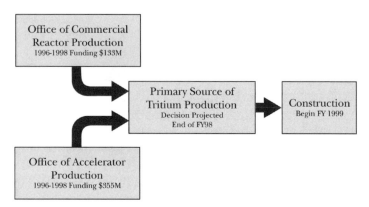

Figure 25.12. The dual-track implementation decision.

National Environmental Policy Act, in the programmatic environmental impact statement (DOE, 1995b). Meanwhile the deputy director of the tritium production office and I drafted the document which became the basis of the formal justification of the Secretary's decision. On December 5, 1995, the Secretary of Energy published the "Record of Decision: Tritium Supply and Recycling Programmatic Environmental Impact Statement" in the Federal Register (DOE 1995a). This decision confirmed and justified the dual-track strategy.

As a result of the Secretary's decision, the DOE discontinued the office of reconfiguration and created two new offices: The Office of Commercial Reactor Production (1996–1998 funding: $133 million) and the Office of Accelerator Production (1996–1998 funding: $355 million), which operated from the end of 1996 to the end of 1998.

The Aftermath and Some Thoughts about the Role of the Decision Analysis

Secretary O'Leary was followed by Secretary Pena to lead the Department of Energy. During Secretary Pena's tenure, Congress affirmed that the commercial option was an acceptable option for producing tritium. As a result, the major obstacle to this option was removed. Shortly after being appointed as Secretary of Energy in 1998, Secretary Richardson decided to cancel the accelerator program and to move ahead with the option to purchase irradiation services from a nuclear power plant. The designated facility for this purpose is the Hartsville nuclear plant owned and operated by the Tennessee Valley Authority.

There is no record that the decision by Secretary Richardson was informed by the decision analysis, though the analysis results are obviously consistent with this decision. Throughout the decision analysis, the justification of the accelerator as a viable option had caused some stress. Although clearly a viable option, it made sense only if DOE was willing to spend additional billions of dollars for what some perceived as relatively minor benefits.

This analysis, after many ups and downs, ended well. But it was not an easy process. The main problems that occurred during the eighteen months of analysis can be summarized as follows:

1. The first round of analysis involved a rather complex representation of many alternatives and many objectives and it did not get to the key issues.
2. Some key decision makers announced their preference for the accelerator early in the analysis.
3. The decision frame, especially the alternatives, was frequently shifting, with new alternatives entering and others being redesigned.
4. In the final stages of the process, decisions were made on a political basis and it is unclear to what extent the analysis informed the political discussions.

The first problem will be familiar to many decision analysts. Almost all analysts go through an early phase, in which the structure of the analysis gets overly complicated. It takes significant skill to include only the important features of the problem and build simple models that capture the essence of the problem, while not ignoring other important features. In hindsight, it is clear that the real issue of the tritium analysis was the choice of the production technology and that the key concerns were the production risks and costs associated with each alternative. Going through an elaborate multiattribute utility analysis was useful because it led to identifying these issues. However, we could have focused on the risk analysis much earlier than we did, had we not committed to a complete analysis of all alternatives early on.

The announcement by key decision makers of a preference for the accelerator came as a bit of a shock to me and the other decision analysts. Quite frankly, I seriously thought about resigning from this analysis because it seemed inappropriate to spend a significant amount of effort simply to justify a decision that may already have been made. However, I was reassured by several considerations and statements by the decision makers. First, the accelerator could indeed be a possible "winner," if a large weight was placed on environmental issues. Therefore, the accelerator would not be a clear "loser." Second, the advocates of the accelerator assured me that they would not interfere with the analysis process and that they would be open to any presentations of the "facts" about all options. Third, and perhaps most importantly, there were advocates of other options, especially of the small ALWR and of the commercial option, in the DOE. Ultimately, I could see how the analysis would inform the debate among these different factions.

The shifting decision frame was more of a nuisance than a serious problem. Decisions about which alternative to include and which to exclude sometimes happened in fairly casual conversations in the hallway. Often, these decisions had significant consequences for the analysis process, and, more importantly, for the subcontractors working on this project. It was useful to work in very close contact with the decision makers and to be able to influence some of these decisions to assure that the new frames were manageable.

It was somewhat disappointing that the analysis was not represented more vigorously in the final stages of decision making. Nevertheless, the eventual decision was consistent with the analysis. Clearly, the analysis showed that the heavy-water reactors and the gas-cooled reactors were nonstarters. It also favored the commercial option over the new light-water reactors. DOE would later be called to task for the rejection of the new light-water reactors by some of the vendors of these reactors, but the analysis was used to successfully defend the decision.

The only point of contention between the analysis and the decision to pursue the dual-track strategy was the wisdom of pursuing the accelerator and spending, as it turned out, another $355 million on that option. Accelerator advocates argued for its value by pointing to the potential for producing medical isotopes and other uses. They also continued to revise the cost estimates downward. But in the end, the investment in the accelerator seemed like a very large investment for relatively minor benefits.

Acknowledgment

This chapter was adapted from von Winterfeldt and Schweitzer (1998) with permission by the Institute for Operations Research and the Management Sciences (INFORMS).

REFERENCES

Department of Energy. (1995a). Record of decision: Tritium supply and recycling programmatic environmental impact statement. *Federal Register*, December 12, 1995.

Department of Energy. (1995b). Final Programmatic Environmental Impact Statement for Tritium Supply and Recycling, DOE/EIS-0161 .Washington, DC: Office of Reconfiguration, United States Department of Energy.

Department of Energy. (1995c). Technical Reference Report for Tritium Supply and Recycling, DOE/DP-0134. Washington, DC: Office of Reconfiguration, United States Department of Energy.

Dillon, R. Dillon, R., John, R., and Winterfeldt, D. (2002). Assessment of cost uncertainties for large technology projects: A methodology and an application. *Interfaces, 32*, 52–66.

Fluor Daniel, Inc. (1995a). Schedule Data Package for Tritium Supply and Recycling. Irvine, CA: Fluor Daniel, Inc.

Fluor Daniel, Inc. (1995b). Technical Data Package for Tritium Supply and Recycling. Irvine, CA: Fluor Daniel, Inc.

Fluor Daniel, Inc. (1995c). Cost Data Package for Tritium Supply and Recycling. Irvine, CA: Fluor Daniel, Inc.

Hora, S. C., and Iman, R. L. (1989). Expert opinion in risk analysis: The NUREG 1150 methodology. *Nuclear Science and Engineering, 102*, 323–331.

Keeney, R. L., and Raiffa, H. (1976). *Decisions with Multiple Objectives*. New York: John Wiley and Sons.

Keeney, R.L., and von Winterfeldt, D. (1991). Eliciting probabilities from experts in complex technical problems. *IEEE Transactions in Engineering Management, 38*, 191–201.

Oak Ridge National Laboratory. (1995). Cost Analysis of Multipurpose Reactor Options. Oak Ridge, TN: Oak Ridge National Laboratory.

Putnam, Hayes, and Bartlett, Inc. (1995). DOE Tritium Production Options: PHB Final Report on Cost Analysis. Washington, DC: Putnam, Hayes, and Bartlett.

von Winterfeldt, D., and Edwards, W. (1986). *Decision Analysis and Behavioral Research*. New York: Cambridge University Press.

von Winterfeldt, D., and Schweitzer, E. (1998). An assessment of tritium supply alternatives in support of the U.S. nuclear weapons stockpile. *Interfaces, 28*, 92–112.

26 Applications of Decision Analysis to the Military Systems Acquisition Process

Dennis M. Buede and Terry A. Bresnick

ABSTRACT. We used decision analysis to define requirements for the U.S. Marine Corps (USMC) mobile protected weapons system during the concept selection phase of the systems acquisition process; to analyze the mix of air defense weapons for the forward area air defense of the U.S. Army during the demonstration and validation phase; to assist in the evaluation by the U.S. Army and the USMC of competing proposals for the light armored vehicle in the full-scale development phase; to determine which service (Army or Air Force) should be the proponent for the PATRIOT missile system in the production and fielding phase; and to provide cost–benefit priorities of projects to the USMC in the program objectives memorandum process, which allocates resources throughout the systems acquisition cycle.

We have supported various systems acquisition decisions for major weapons systems of the U.S. Department of Defense (DoD) since 1977. Over the course of this 29-year period, there have been at least ten official changes to the acquisition process, the most recent occurring in May 2003. The goal is to have a process that produces defensible decisions supported with sound analyses and clear rationale. Decision analysis can provide that capability. Although we focus on systems acquisition, it is hard to separate the acquisition process from the planning, programming, and budgeting system (PPBS). Since Secretary of Defense Robert McNamara created it in 1961, PPBS has been the primary mechanism for determining fiscal needs and funding programs. The two must be coordinated because acquisition cannot take place without adequate resources.

The current acquisition process has five major phases (DODI 2003): new concept refinement, technology development, system development and demonstration, production and deployment, and operations and support. Of the five phases, the first two are described as being preacquisition and the last one is postacquisition. Nonetheless all five are part of the acquisition process. An earlier phase, concept selection, is not precluded but just not part of the current process. We will include concept selection as Phase 0.

The concept selection phase includes the analysis of changing threats and the related impacts on missions, the examination of technological opportunities, and the notation of deficiencies in existing systems. By analyzing the mission area, military officers in charge of developing doctrine and establishing training procedures (or "users") determine mission-oriented needs and required operating characteristics of equipment. Technology personnel (or "developers") explore various concepts for satisfying the needs, evaluate competing proposals submitted by contractors, and prepare an Initial Capabilities Document. Once the appropriate authorities have chosen a concept or architecture, authorities decide whether to sanction a concept refinement effort as a next phase. Applications of decision analyses to this phase have included requirements analyses, mission area analyses, concept definition, and systems architecture definition.

The first phase is concept refinement. The developers and the users refine the needed capabilities of the concept and create a Technology Development Strategy based on the evaluation of costs, concepts, schedules, and affordability. The developers refine the major characteristics of the concepts and analyze program risks in depth. They perform trade-off studies to define the program strategy (including definition of increments in terms of cost, performance, and schedule goals), develop exit criteria for the various phases, and develop test plans. The contractors develop and test prototypes. If the estimated probability of success is high enough, the appropriate authority permits the project to move to the next phase. In this phase, decision analysis can be used for trade-off analyses, weapons-mix studies, design-to-cost analyses, and affordability studies.

Technology Development is the second phase, the primary purpose being to reduce the technology risk of the concept by determining when specific technologies should be incorporated in the system's design. This phase involves substantial risk analysis of competing technologies relevant to the system and the needs of the users throughout the life cycle of the system. Technology demonstrations may be undertaken as needed. As part of this process, a Capability Development Document is written and approved.

During the third phase, system development and demonstration, the contractor(s) design, fabricate, test, and evaluate the weapon system and associated support equipment. The two major elements of this phase are integration, which addresses interfaces, detailed designing and reduction of system-level risk, and system demonstration, which proves the system meets its key performance parameters. Problems are identified, and trade-offs are made to achieve an appropriate cost-performance balance. During this phase, the program manager conducts reviews of the acquisition strategy, its affordability, the manpower requirements, training issues, and logistics support. At the end of this phase, the Milestone Decision Authority decides whether to produce the system. In this phase, decision analysis can be used to continue the refinement of trade offs and the definition of key performance parameters, track trades and select risk mitigation actions, select sources, and organize the test and evaluation of the system.

In the fourth phase, production and deployment, the contractors produce and deliver the system and its associated equipment for deployment. The developers must reexamine life-cycle support issues, such as training, maintenance and support, and upgrades. They test the system extensively and do quality assurance evaluation. In this phase the weapons system is transferred from the developers to the users. Decision analysis can be used to evaluate systems, to study weapons mix, and to analyze organizational issues.

The fifth phase addresses operations and support. Key decisions that are made during this phase address the affordability of mixes of systems as predictions about

Table 26.1. Decision analyses discussed by phase

Phase	Name of analysis
Concept selection	USMC mobile protected weapons system
Concept refinement phase	Air defense weapons-mix analysis
Technology development phase	None
System development and demonstration phase	Source selection of the light armored vehicle
Production and deployment phase	Joint services weapon proponency analysis
Operations and support phase	Airborne and space-borne reconnaissance force mixes
Planning, programming, budgeting	USMC program objectives memorandum

costs become reality. Also as threats change, it is possible that users will move to retire certain systems and procure additional numbers of other existing systems.

Throughout all five current phases (and phase 0), the systems acquisition planners interact with the PPBS. The PPBS must allocate funds for the procurement of the systems, for research and development, for manpower, and for construction and so forth. Decision analysis can be used to allocate resources as part of the program objectives memorandum (POM).

Table 26.1 identifies the selected decision analyses that we are presenting for each of the above defined phases. We are not describing any analyses in the Technology Development Phase because this is a relatively new idea and our analyses in this area are not centered on the focus of the phase. The appendix identifies many of the analyses in which we have participated.

Concept Selection Phase: USMC Mobile Protected Weapons System

In 1980, we used decision analysis to define the requirements for a proposed new program called the mobile protected weapons system (MPWS), which the USMC was considering. The MPWS concept called for a helicopter-transportable, armored vehicle with either a gun or missile system to provide direct fire support during defensive operations, during a beach landing, and during subsequent movements ashore toward their objective. At this time, the Department of Defense emphasized requirements that were tailored to high-level performance capabilities needed to complete missions in specific scenarios rather than the detailed specification of particular system hardware. For example, rather than a requirement asking for six inches of rolled homogeneous armor, the requirement would demand that the armor stop the penetration of a 14.5 mm shell at 2,000 meters. The USMC personnel were wrestling with strongly conflicting requirements that the vehicle be transportable by large helicopters and be mobile on the ground, yet survivable (that is, protected by armor) and lethal. The firepower envisioned for MPWS was an antitank gun or missile system.

During a 3-month period, we developed a multiattribute value analysis to define MPWS minimum capabilities and the weighted trade-offs (Bresnick, Annis, and Buede 1981, 1982). Twenty-three marines and government civilian engineers contributed their specialized expertise to develop an attribute hierarchy, value curves, and value weights for this multiattribute analysis. We first developed a draft structure, value curves, and weights with about ten principal experts from the USMC Headquarters and the Development and Education Center. Then we invited subsets of the rest of participants to working meetings to critique specific portions of the analysis. Finally, from existing MPWS designs developed by contractors, we evaluated these designs with the multiattribute value structure; then we compared these evaluations with the intuitive valuations of the principal experts. There were several discrepancies between the analysis and the intuitive valuation. We resolved these discrepancies in conference sessions and adjusted selected value weights and curves. We then documented this analysis and it was distributed to industry as part of the government's request for proposal (RFP).

Figure 26.1 shows the final multiattribute value structure for MPWS operational effectiveness. The highest level of the hierarchy describes three scenarios which reflect the spectrum of USMC's actions during combat: support in assaulting forces during an amphibious landing, establishing positions to block oncoming forces during defensive stages, and conducting offensive operations to achieve objectives subsequent to the successful completion of an amphibious landing. Different geographic regions were chosen as representative of each of these scenarios to reflect the highest payoff environments for the MPWS. The weights for the scenarios reflected both the relative likelihood of occurrence and the relative contribution of the MPWS to each scenario. Weights everywhere else in the hierarchy are "swing weights"; that is, the weights capture the importance of an attribute, and the importance of the swing from lowest to highest capability represented by the value curves. We elicited and refined a total of thirty-four value curves for the scenarios, one for each performance parameter. Typically the weights of the attributes varied across the scenarios. We defined most of the value curves on continuous performance parameters; however, we had to define a few parameters, such as mobility in water, discretely (e.g., ford, swim [aided], swim [unaided], and surf). Most of the value curves exhibited decreasing returns to scale, but there were a few S-shaped curves as well (see Watson and Buede 1987 for definitions of these properties of value curves). A particular MPWS design would be evaluated on each performance parameter in terms of its most likely capability; these evaluations would be done either subjectively or with the use of simulation models. For each curve, the parameter estimate would be entered on the x-axis and the resulting value for that performance attribute would be found on the y-axis by finding the appropriate (x, y) point on the value curve. These attribute values were then combined using an additive, weighted value function.

Table 26.2 illustrates how the high-level attribute weights varied as a function of the three scenarios. We developed similar tables for each node in the multiattribute tree.

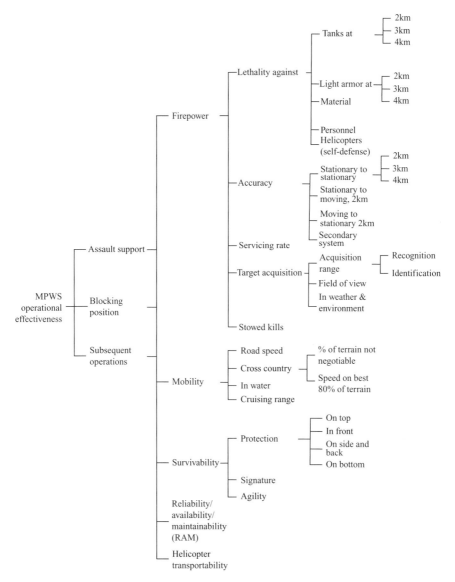

Figure 26.1. The mobile protected weapon system multiattribute value system includes three scenarios within an amphibious landing and a wide range of performance criteria that apply to each scenario.

One of the most unique aspects of this effort was that the analysis hierarchy, value curves, and weights were distributed to potential contractors for their use in designing an MPWS in response to the government's RFP. We sought feedback from the industrial engineering teams that eventually submitted proposals for MPWS. These teams found the multiattribute value analysis in the RFP to be helpful. The engineers felt that the analysis provided them with firm guidance

Table 26.2. The relative importance of the five major elements of operational effectiveness for the mobile protected weapon system (MPWS) varies as a function of the scenario. The most noticeable variation is that of helicopter transportability

	Scenarios		
Operational effectiveness	Assault support	Blocking position	Subsequent operations
Firepower	0.34	0.29	0.29
Mobility	0.20	0.17	0.24
Survivability	0.19	0.20	0.24
RAM	0.10	0.13	0.17
Helicopter transportability	0.17	0.20	0.06

for design decisions. For once, they did not have to speculate about what the government really wanted. The teams varied in their use of the multiattribute value analysis; some used it only as a qualitative reminder while others used it as an analytical tool to compute scores for competing design options. Feedback from the USMC indicated that as a result of providing industry with the output of the above requirements definition process, every one of the ten conceptual designs submitted was outstanding.

The USMC capitalized on the strengths of decision analysis to bring together the best mix of users, developers, engineers, and tacticians to resolve the complex trade-offs inherent in defining weapons systems requirements.

Concept Refinement Phase: Air Defense Weapons-Mix Analysis

In 1988, the U.S. Army air defense community was wrestling with the problem of developing the most cost-effective mix of low-altitude air defense weapons. We were asked to compare and rank order alternate weapons mixes for the forward area air defense system (FAADS). In a two-phased approach, we convened (1) a panel of experts to develop a hierarchy of evaluation criteria, define forward area air defense system weapons mixes, score the alternatives on the evaluation criteria, prioritize the evaluation criteria, and analyze the results; and (2) a larger, more senior panel of officers to review and modify the results. A quantitative framework (multiattribute value analysis) captured qualitative judgments, and to the extent possible, incorporated previous simulations and studies.

The 1988 focus of this analysis was on the predicted 1996 threat in central Europe, during the first few days of a war with the Warsaw Pact (Bresnick, O'Connor, Marvin, and Rausch 1989). The emphasis was on a forward area air defense system battalion that is organic to mechanized or armored Army divisions. We evaluated six alternate mixes, ranging from the current short-range air defense systems (the product improved Vulcan air defense system (PIVADS), Chaparral, and the Stinger man-portable air defense system (MANPADS) to a mix of thirty-six line-of-sight, forward heavy (LOS-F-H), eighteen nonline-of-sight

Table 26.3. For the forward area air defense system there were five alternative weapons mixes defined with new systems. The sixth option is the current set of systems.

	Number of fire units per battalion		
Alternative	LOS-F-H (ADATS)	NLOS (FOG-M)	LOS-R (PMS)
1	36	18	36
2	24	18	36
3	24	12	42
4	18	18	36
5	12	24	42
6 (Current)	24 PIVADS	24 Chaparral	72 MANPADS

(NLOS), and thirty-six line-of-sight, rear (LOS-R) weapons. The LOS-F-H was to be the air defense antitank system (ADATS), the NLOS was the fiber-optic guided missile (FOG-M), and the LOS-R was the pedestal mounted Stinger (PMS). Table 26.3 lists the alternatives, with the number of fire units per battalion. The current option is the sixth in the list.

We developed an evaluation hierarchy (Figure 26.2) and scored each alternative on a relative basis on each criterion at the lowest level of the hierarchy. We assigned weights to the criteria that reflected both the importance of the criteria and the difference in capability among the alternatives ("swing" weights). Only rough estimates were available for costs.

Of the criteria at the bottom level of the hierarchy, those that provided the most significant discrimination among alternatives are shown with an asterisk (*) in Figure 26.2. These eight criteria out of the twenty-seven for operational effectiveness accounted for almost 80 percent of the evaluation differences.

Figure 26.3 shows the results of the analysis using the aggregated scores for operational effectiveness and the rough estimates of costs. On the cost scale, a score of 100 reflects the cheapest (or best cost) alternative and a score of zero reflects the most expensive mix. Alternative 2 (24 – 18 – 26) is less desirable than alternative 3 (24 – 12 – 42), which is both cheaper and more effective. Similarly, alternative 4 (18 – 18 – 36) is less desirable than alternative 5 (12 – 24 – 42), which is cheaper and equally effective. Alternatives 2 and 4 are known as dominated alternatives. Of the remaining alternatives, the expert panel unanimously agreed that alternatives 5 (12 – 24 – 42) and 6 (current short-range air defense) are well below an acceptable threshold of effectiveness; alternative 1 (36–18–36) is clearly the best but may not be affordable; and alternative 3 (24 – 12 – 42) falls just below the acceptable level of effectiveness when operational availability is considered. Although alternative 3 gets good scores in many areas, its ability to support the maneuver concept of Air-Land Battle poses a serious risk because having 24 LOS-F-H leaves some maneuver battalions without adequate coverage. These results were robust on the basis of sensitivity analysis performed on the major criteria.

From an analysis perspective, this effort was unique in that a typical air defense study uses only air defense experts. In this effort, we used decision

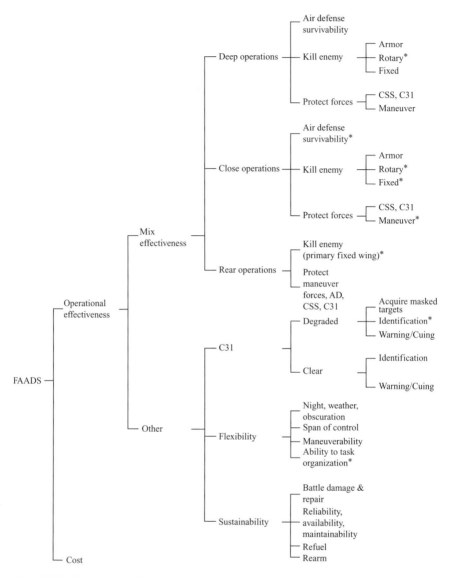

Figure 26.2. The evaluation hierarchy for the forward area air defense system (FAADS) includes both operational effectiveness and cost. Operational effectiveness includes both traditional effectiveness and other issues that relate to command and control, flexibility, and sustainability.

conferencing, a process described in Watson and Buede (1987), to enable the appropriate combat arms (that is, infantry and armor battalion commanders and staffs) to participate. The group finally selected alternative 3 (24 – 12 – 42) as the preferred forward area air defense system mix based on effectiveness and cost considerations.

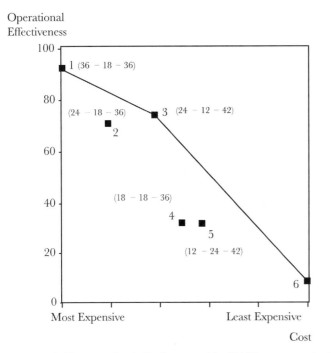

Figure 26.3. The operational effectiveness of the FAADS weapons mix alternatives varies signif-icantly with the cost of the alternatives. Options 2 and 4 are dominated by 3 and 5, respectively. Option 3 was chosen on the basis of this graph and the meaning of the operational effectiveness and cost scales.

System Development and Demonstration Phase: Source Selection of the Light Armored Vehicle

In 1981, as part of the fielding of the Rapid Deployment Force (RDF), Congress dictated that the USMC terminate the development of the MPWS and field a light armored vehicle (LAV) based on existing systems by 1983. The USMC, later joined by the U.S. Army, prepared a new RFP for a gun-carrying, off-the-shelf system and future variants. (The missile alternative was not considered "off-the-shelf.") We convened many of the same USMC and civilian experts that participated in the MPWS study over a 2-month period to revise the MPWS evaluation structure, value curves, and weights; see Figure 26.4 for the revised structure (Bresnick, Annis, and Buede 1982). The light armored vehicle program was to select a win-ner after extensive testing of several off-the-shelf systems from contractors that passed an initial "paper" proposal evaluation, based on a larger population of contractors.

Note the change in emphasis in Figure 26.4 from the MPWS. In this new struc-ture, we defined attributes for performance characteristics that can be measured in tests. In developing a new system, the initial choice of contractor is usually based

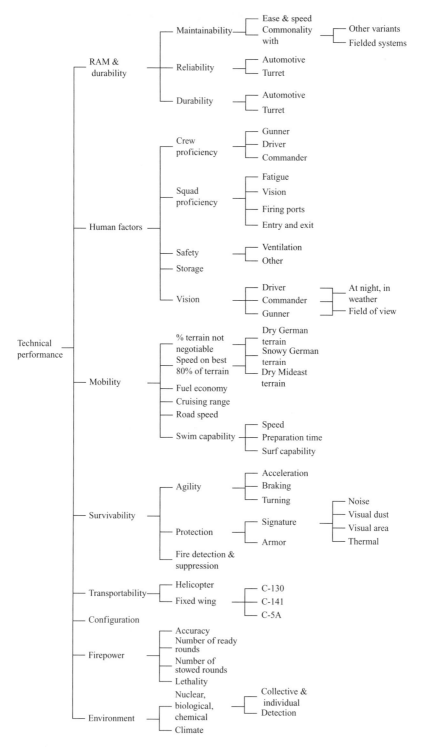

Figure 26.4. The technical performance criteria for the LAV changed dramatically from those of the MPWS as the decision changed from buying a new vehicle to one of buying an existing vehicle.

on paper analyses and limited prototype testing, so the attributes have to be less specific. Because the gun system was going to be furnished by the government to the winning contractor, emphasis on the importance of firepower decreased to reflect small differences among alternatives.

In addition to the criteria shown in Figure 26.4, we developed two other sets of evaluation factors: a similar hierarchy for a variant of the LAV that would carry an assault gun and a hierarchy for the production capability of the contractor. This second hierarchy included such items as the ability to maintain schedule, the adequacy of the quality assurance program, the quality of existing designs and the availability of several variants (command and control, logistics, mortar, engineer, ambulance, and so forth), the adequacy of logistics support, and the quality of their project management. The production hierarchy was important because it includes factors that indicate the ability of a contractor to produce the required systems.

Ten contractors submitted proposals, and the government selected four based on the scores of the analysis. Analytically, there was a clear discrimination in scoring between these top four winners and the remaining six. In this evaluation, the source selection evaluation board used the computer-based analysis to brief the source selection authority on its recommendations. The four winners were then asked to make improvements to their systems and to submit prototypes for a final source selection that was performed by the U.S. Army Tank and Automotive Command based on test results using the prototypes.

Production and Fielding Phase: Joint Services Weapon Proponency Analysis

In 1985, the U.S. Office of the Secretary of Defense asked the U.S. Army and the U.S. Air Force to participate in a joint-service initiative and decide which service should be the proponent for the PATRIOT missile system. The PATRIOT is a mobile, conventional surface-to-air missile designed to protect military forces from attack by medium-to-high altitude aircraft. It is part of the air defense umbrella that includes, among other things, low-altitude air defense missiles and guns and fighter aircraft. At the time of the study, the U.S. Army was the service designated to field, operate, and maintain the PATRIOT systems. The question was whether the U.S. Air Force might accomplish the PATRIOT portion of the air defense mission more efficiently and effectively than the U.S. Army. The purpose of the decision analysis was to determine the feasibility and the desirability of transferring proponency of the PATRIOT missile system from the U.S. Army to the U.S. Air Force.

Joint decision making involving multiple Services is always difficult. Not only must decisions be supported by sound analysis, but political, bureaucratic, and Service rivalries must be resolved. As a result, many analytic models that are technically correct still fail. In this application, both technical and organizational problems were considered to produce a multiattribute value analysis that was used to support a decision at the highest level of the two Services.

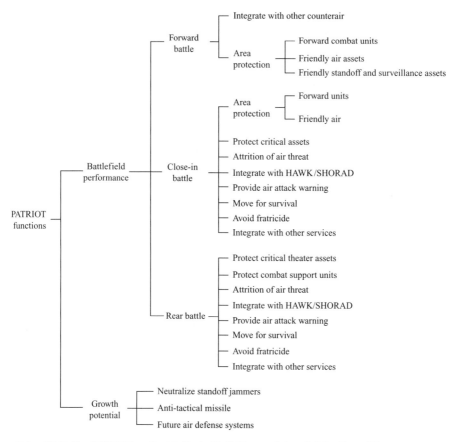

Figure 26.5. The PATRIOT functions in the battlefield as envisioned at the time of the proponency study and into the future show a wide range of activity.

The multiattribute value analysis included issues about the transfer of PATRIOT and the functions that PATRIOT must perform in the combat environment, called the Air–Land Battle at the time. The issues included which Service could best establish future air defense systems requirements, perform positive hostile aircraft identification, conduct air battle management, maintain effective communications, ensure air-based as well as ground-based air defense survivability, sustain the system, and train staff to use the system. The PATRIOT functions are shown in the multiattribute structure in Figure 26.5. We elicited scores and weights, as well as the structure, from a group of a dozen representatives of the U.S. Army and U.S. Air Force during a two-day decision conference. A separate cost analysis estimated direct costs of the transfer as well as intangible costs.

Although the analysis was not especially complex, it was complicated by several factors. First was the time constraint. The entire process, including the analysis and its approval, had to be completed within one month. Second was the approval process itself. Each part of the analysis had to be approved by numerous layers of bureaucracy, and the final result required consensus between the U.S. Army and the U.S. Air Force. Third were the limited resources available for the study. Some specific complications were the following:

First, for the study to be successful, a Memorandum of Understanding had to be agreed on by a joint-service working group that represented at least eight U.S. Army and U.S. Air Force constituencies. These included the communities that operate the system, develop tactics and doctrine, provide training, and perform studies and analyses. In addition, many other communities had to concur with the decision as it moved toward the decision-making levels of the organization (Vice Chief of Staff of the U.S. Army and Vice Chief of Staff of the U.S. Air Force, both four-star generals).

The decision analysts were responsible for building this consensus. Part of our approach was to use "decision conferences" to bring together staff experts, field officers, and decision analysts.

Second, in most studies, the decision analyst and the client can agree on a methodology early in the study and then proceed. In this effort the methodology was subjected to the "wicket test." That is, the methodology had to pass through a nested set of wickets as it was briefed throughout the hierarchy of the organization, with each level imposing its own modifications and special concerns. The pathway to acceptance included: the joint working group level, the lieutenant colonels, who would organize the effort for each service; the air defense senior officers, major generals for each Service; the General Officer steering committee, composed of twelve brigadier, major, and lieutenant generals from both Services; and the Vice Chief of Staff of the U.S. Army and the Vice Chief of Staff of the U.S. Air Force, who were the decision makers.

Third, the "old school," large-scale simulation advocates were very critical. They were uncomfortable with subjective value assessments and what they considered "touchy–feely" problem solving.

We used two methods to overcome these difficulties. First, for a related part of the study, another group ran a large-scale combat simulation in parallel with the decision conference. It was clear to the working group that (1) the conclusions of both efforts were similar, (2) the decision-conferencing analysis was easier to understand and defend, and (3) the simulation was more time-consuming and cost an order of magnitude more. Second, as a cross-check on the analysis, a panel of retired military air defense experts examined the decision-analytic approach and provided input, advice, and feedback each step of the way.

The study determined that it was feasible to transfer proponency of the PATRIOT from the U.S. Army to the U.S. Air Force, but that it was not advisable. No significant gains in operational effectiveness would be realized, and it would cost more than $1 billion. Based on the study, the decision that the U.S. Army retain responsibility for PATRIOT was implemented via a memorandum signed by the Chiefs of Staff of the U.S. Army and U.S. Air Force.

The unique feature of this analysis centered on breaking down the Service parochialism and getting the group to think in terms of the good of the joint effort rather than the individual services. Clearly the U.S. Army participants came into the session "wearing their green hats," while the U.S. Air Force "wore their blue hats." By the close of the session, participants were "wearing purple (joint-service) hats" and operating as a unified team. Another challenging facet was the need to build ownership of the study among a very large spectrum of sometimes competing advocates. The decision-conferencing approach worked well to solve this problem.

Operations and Support Phase: Airborne and Space-Borne Reconnaissance Force Mixes

We conducted an analysis (as part of a large team of contractors that included analysts and subject matter experts) initiated by the Joint Requirements Oversight Council (JROC) of the Joint Chiefs of Staff (JCS). Decision analysis techniques, to include *multiattribute value analysis* and *cost–benefit* analysis, were used to develop a methodology for the evaluation of alternate reconnaissance force mixes (TASC 1996; Bresnick et al. 1997).

Given the importance of joint reconnaissance to today's operational commanders and increasing reliance on reconnaissance for the future, the JROC recognized in 1995 that it had inadequate means to make force mix decisions in terms of end-to-end platform capability and cost across all components: manned aircraft, unmanned aircraft, and overhead systems (satellites). To fulfill this need, the JROC created the Reconnaissance Study Group (RSG) and tasked it to develop and implement a process for making timely and informed reconnaissance force mix decisions.

This analysis was an innovative methodology for determining the composition of promising reconnaissance architectures at various levels of investment for the 2010 time frame. The unique aspects of the approach are its *broad scope and scalability* in addressing the multiple components of the architecture, the use of *value assessments* based on simulations as well as subjective expert judgment to provide *traceability and repeatability*, and its treatment of *cost as an independent variable* (Rush 1997) in the cost–benefit analysis of future force mix options.

The JROC requested that the Reconnaissance Study Group focus on future requirements and capabilities in a time frame beginning in 2005. The JROC was particularly interested in the effort to define criteria and metrics for force structure discrimination and evaluation. In accordance with the JROC's guidance, the following parameters were agreed on:

- The scope of the analysis would include unmanned, manned, and overhead reconnaissance collection platforms as well as exploitation and dissemination systems.
- *All military tasks* to which reconnaissance systems contribute would be considered, not just two major regional conflicts (MRCs).
- The 2010 time frame would be used for both requirements and available capabilities and technologies.
- A set of possible reconnaissance force mixes would be developed with sufficient breadth to enable robust insight into possible budget cuts.

- Unlike most reconnaissance studies, this analysis would be *scenario-independent.*
- The analysis would have an operational focus with reconnaissance requirements being generated by users (Unified Commands, Services, and Joint Staff representatives)
- Cost and benefit to the user would both be independent variables in the analysis; lower cost solutions for reconnaissance force mixes would be of particular interest.

The three major objectives of the analysis were:

- *Establish an initial capability* to assess force mix trades.
- Develop a decision support method that provided *benefit and cost comparisons* of reconnaissance systems in terms of the *overall satisfaction of requirements.*
- *Provide promising, candidate force mixes* that could be subjected to further analysis of different types, including detailed modeling and simulation in specific scenarios.

Finally, there were four critical issues in the design of the analysis that had to be resolved. First, how should the architecture building blocks for reconnaissance force mixes be designed so that both creative and exhaustive sets of force mixes could be defined and analyzed in a reasonable amount of time? Second, how should modeling be used to aggregate concepts in appropriate places in order to achieve 80 percent of the desired effect (e.g., precision, accuracy) with only 20 percent of the mathematical detail? Third, how, and from whom, should the judgmental inputs be obtained so that they were considered valid? Fourth, how should the results be presented so that they are meaningful to the decision makers?

This study developed an analytic process and preliminary analysis recommendations. This summary focuses on the analysis process because the results are classified and were not ends in themselves but have been fed into other decision making processes. The detailed results are contained in a classified report.

The analysis process, consisting of the six steps as shown in Figure 26.6, was briefed to the JROC prior to the study and approved by them for implementation. The Reconnaissance Study Group monitored the study and approved the study's activities at every step. The six steps in Figure 26.6 were:

1. Develop and prioritize the mission-driven tasks and intelligence functions (requirements criteria tree in Figure 26.6);
2. Develop "metrics" for evaluating architectures on the tasks;
3. Identify reasonable and innovative "architectural packages";
4. Evaluate the alternate architectures on the metrics (assess capabilities);
5. Develop a cost model and evaluate costs of the architectures (cost data);
6. Perform a "cost–benefit analysis" of the alternate architectures.

The requirements criteria are shown in Figure 26.7. The numbers reflect the relative importance of improving the reconnaissance performance from minimum

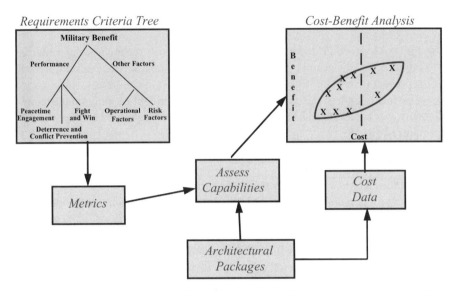

Figure 26.6. Overall decision methodology that was agreed to by all participants before the analysis began.

acceptable to desired in each task; all of the relative swings in importance at the task level sum to 100. For example, performance was given 80 percent of the weight; the 80 percent was allocated as almost 10 percent to peacetime engagement, almost 31 percent to deterrence and conflict prevention, and slightly more than 39 percent to fight and win the joint conflict. The decimal points are an artifact of the normalization process and are not intended to show undue precision in the weighting process, which was the consensus judgment of representatives from each U.S. Commander-in-Chief (CINC) during a three-day decision conference.

The next step, called Metrics, involved selecting intelligence functions and associated measures for each of the lowest level criteria in Figure 26.7 and developing value curves for each measure. This involved the standard elicitation of value curves during decision conferences. One of the key analytical challenges was "how much modeling is enough?" Clearly, we could have evaluated every architecture, on many metrics of every reconnaissance function for every task and intelligence function – a massive task. By recognizing that some tasks were much more heavily weighted than others, we developed an "economy of modeling" rule of thumb that reduced the modeling load with little or no impact on results. For highly weighted tasks such as countering weapons of mass destruction, the analysis included all relevant intelligence functions and all relevant metrics for each; for moderately weighted tasks such as wartime power projection, the analysis included only the single most relevant intelligence function and all relevant metrics for the function; and for the lowest weighted tasks such as force generation, the analysis restricted attention to the single most relevant intelligence function and the single, most pertinent metric for that function. Figure 26.8 shows the resulting hierarchy for the "Fight and Win" part of Figure 26.7.

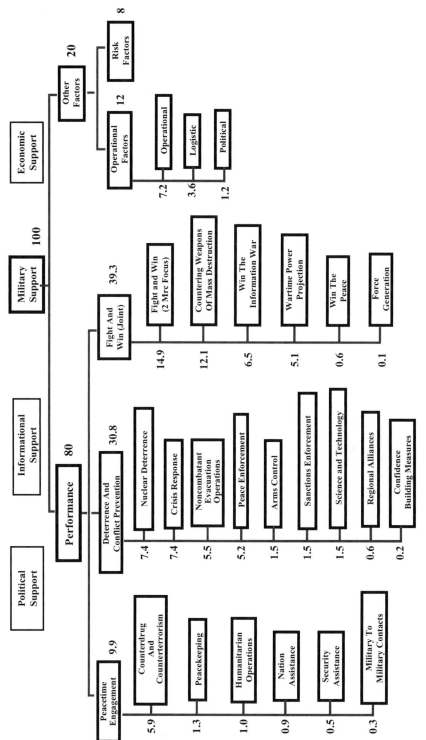

Figure 26.7. Requirements criteria for evaluating alternative force mixes of reconnaissance assets.

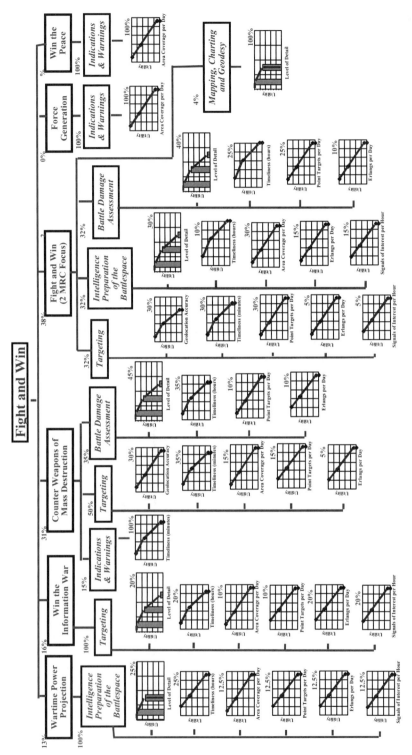

Figure 26.8. A portion of the criteria hierarchy with value curves for specific intelligence functions and associated metrics.

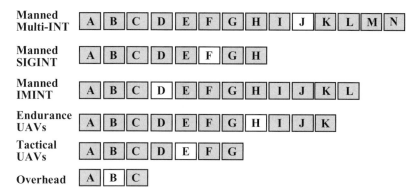

Figure 26.9. The architecture space is shown here for six categories of aerial platforms and one category of overhead satellites. An architecture = one package from each component (e.g., J+F+D+H+E+B).

For this effort, an architecture refers to a system of systems; in this particular case, to a system of airborne and space-borne reconnaissance platforms, each platform comprising one or more systems. Figure 26.9 illustrates how the reconnaissance components were configured for this analysis to represent an overall system-of-systems architecture. For each component (row), the lettered blocks represent alternate packages (referred to as levels) for the row. Architecture is defined by selecting one package (level) for each row. Each component package depicted in Figure 26.9 included "end-to-end" systems (including processing, exploitation, and dissemination systems) as well as the front-end system required to task reconnaissance systems and deliver "products" to users. Each of the packages, i.e., each cell in Figure 26.9, is itself a *combination* of specific reconnaissance platforms in varying configurations and quantities; each of which was evaluated in terms of costs and value (using the value curves and hierarchies shown in Figures 26.7 and 26.8). Each platform contains the requisite systems needed to complete its missions.

The cost and benefit analyses were complex. The cost analysis addressed a twenty-year period of the life of each of the systems, including retirement costs for ending systems. The benefit (or value) analysis was also complex, involving some probabilistic assessments and rules of thumbs for how each platform might be used on average in combination with other platforms.

Once a cost and a benefit measure was determined for each level of each architectural component, a benefit/cost analysis using a Pareto-optimal, efficient frontier approach was completed to determine the best allocation of resources across all components. Commercial off-the-shelf software called EQUITY was used to develop a "1" to "n" list that achieves the most bang-for-the-buck at increasing Life Cycle Cost (LCC) points. See Watson and Buede (1987) for a discussion of this approach and Kirkwood (1997) for a more general discussion of this topic. The major assumption made here is that both the cost and benefits

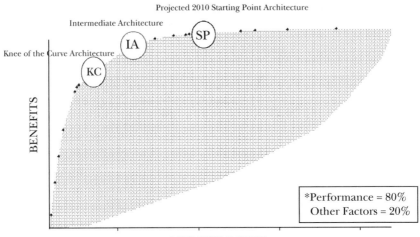

Figure 26.10. The convex hull of the efficient frontier, with three key stopping points that were addressed by the decision maker.

associated with a given component were independent of the packages chosen on other components.

This analytical approach focuses on finding the architectures along the top of the "football"; the convex hull of the "efficient frontier" (Figure 26.10). This establishes the best order-of-buy of packages in the architectural components. There were fifty-four different optimal increments out of the more than 288,000 possible architectures. On the basis of this optimal order we plotted the total LCC and benefit of each of the fifty-four optimal architectures on the convex hull of the Pareto-optimal, or efficient, frontier. Decision makers refer to it as the top of the football. Note that this analysis process did not compute all of the Pareto-optimal architectures that fell between each pair of points on the convex hull. The purpose of this analysis was not to determine the optimal way to spend a predefined amount of money, but rather to provide insight into the sets of packages that were near the optimal allocation of life cycle cost during the timeframe of the study.

The analysis process integrates subject matter experts (system operators and information users), quantitative data, qualitative judgments, and tools into a structured and orderly process to provide timely and meaningful insight and trends to senior decision makers on the relative costs and benefits of reconnaissance alternate architectures.

Linking Systems Acquisition to PPBS: Resourcing the Systems

Throughout all phases of the systems acquisition process, funds must be programmed for the complete procurement of each approved system. Programming for fiscal resources is done in different ways within the U.S. DoD, as part of the program objectives memorandum or a five-year resource allocation process.

The U.S. DoD, the U.S. Navy, the U.S. Army, the U.S. Air Force and the USMC all use somewhat different approaches. As of 1990 the U.S. DoD and the U.S. Navy both divide the pot and tell each subelement how much money they are likely to receive and then ask for a detailed list of what will be funded within that budget, and two small lists of what might be funded with a little more or unfunded with a little less. The U.S. Army, U.S. Air Force, and USMC ask their subelements to create prioritized lists of projects after allocating some predefined amount of money to what are called "core programs"; that is, those programs and segments of programs that will not be questioned during the final decision-making process. Then the prioritized lists from each subelement are merged, yielding an organizational priority list. Then a budget line is drawn to match the available resources to the cumulative resource requirements of the list. Funding for each subelement is determined by the number of its projects that can be funded within the total funding available, that is, the number of projects above the funding line.

In early 1977, the USMC requested some analytic support in this area from the U.S. DOD's Advanced Research Project Agency (DARPA). That support, funded by the USMC after the second year, continues today, more than 28 years later. The problem posed by the USMC in 1977 was that they had to produce a merged priority list of about 100 projects to support decision makers. However, two- and three-star General Officers made the actual decisions in high-level sessions without always using this list or even having it available. Usually, these decisions had to be revised many times over a two-month period because the amount of money allocated to the USMC fluctuated frequently as the POM deadline neared in April of each year. These constant revisions within the USMC led to much frustration among the participants. There was also legitimate concern that projects were often cut in inconsistent ways, typically with inefficient across-the-board cuts.

The approach implemented by the first author and used and improved by others since (Kuskey, Waslov, and Buede 1981) involved meeting with each subelement (called sponsors in the USMC) to develop a ratio benefit scale for all the projects and segments of projects that were being considered for funding in the POM process and were within the purview of that sponsor. The analytical concept, which has proven successful, is to use a ratio scale for each sponsor to merge the project priorities across sponsors. Because the meaning of a ratio scale is that multiplication or division by a constant is the only change to the scale that keeps its meaning intact, the sponsors' scales could be merged simply by finding a ratio scale across a subset of the projects, one from each sponsor. Then a cost–benefit priority list is created by dividing the five-year cost estimates available for each project into its final benefit and then sorting the projects from highest to lowest benefit divided by cost.

The USMC had a process in place for determining what conditions had to be met for a project (or segment of a project) to be considered for funding. Each sponsor was responsible for gathering descriptions and documentation for these projects from program managers within the USMC. We worked with them to ensure that the projects were independent of each other. We developed the ratio scale for each sponsor during several meetings with representatives from the sponsor's office. Section 7.5.4 of Watson and Buede (1987) describes the process for eliciting this ratio scale of benefits.

To merge scales across sponsors, we obtained three ratio-scale judgments rather than the one that is required; this introduced redundancies in the judgment process. These redundancies are critical for several reasons. First, comparisons across sponsor projects are much more difficult than those within a sponsor's projects; the group of "honest-brokers" that was convened for these judgments had to compare the relative needs of the USMC for combat-related systems such as radios, trucks, air-defense radars, howitzers, tanks, and water purification equipment with quality-of-life expenditures such as family housing and child care centers. Second, the redundancies could be used to check for agreement or disagreementbetween the judgments of the sponsors and "honest-brokers." Experience suggested that the sponsors had to be motivated to give truthful judgments. This process comes as close to providing that motivation as any known (Brown et al. 1992).

After the first analysis, the sponsors strongly supported the resulting benefit scale across the projects of all sponsors. However, several sponsors rejected the cost–benefit priority order on the basis that the cost estimates unfairly penalized some important projects. First, the five-year time horizon did not adequately reflect the true cost for many of the projects. Also, not all sponsors used the same procedures for developing the cost estimates. During the next several years of POM preparation, improvements were made in the cost-estimating procedures, until finally the cost–benefit priorities were generally accepted. By the tenth year of this support, the cost–benefit priority list was accepted with few ad hoc modifications.

A major impact of this analysis process was the formalization of the "honest-brokers" into an organizational element called the program evaluation group (PEG). The PEG assumed organizational responsibilities for some cross-sponsor issues besides the resource allocation problem. For most organizations this is an area of general weakness, because upper-level management rarely has the time to deal with all the organizational issues. Although the group's name and location have since changed as the process evolved, its basic function of "honest brokering" remains.

The acceptance of the process and the cost–benefit list noticeably improved the efficiency of the USMC expenditures. The cost–benefit list represents the convex hull of the set of optimal allocations, as can be demonstrated with H. Everett's (1963) method of the generalized Lagrange multiplier.

The process has been continuously improved since its initiation in 1977. The USMC has institutionalized the process, and it has evolved to become a highly effective part of the PPBS process.

Conclusion

These applications of decision analysis are representative of its extensive use over the past 29 years to support U.S. DOD acquisition. (See the appendix for a partial list of other projects.) These analyses have proven to be insightful to the decision makers involved, both in terms of how critical concepts affect decisions and how military organizations can make maximum use of their expertise. Multiattribute value analysis and resource allocation techniques have been the most useful techniques in these applications.

The studies we conducted make some special contributions:

- An explicit format for capturing and representing the trade-off requirements of users for system development;
- Incorporation of the quantitative judgments of all relevant users;
- Computerized analysis in real time to support high-level and complex decisions;
- A model to depoliticize issues involving multiple organizations; and
- Benefit and cost factors to institutionalize an analytic process to integrate and prioritize projects.

Despite these successes, significant barriers still must be overcome before the use of decision analysis in systems acquisition becomes even more widespread. These barriers include a distrust of analysts outside the military community and a "not-invented-here" syndrome for new analytical approaches. As successful applications of decision analysis become more numerous, these barriers should fall.

APPENDIX: Successful Decision Analysis Applications to the Acquisition of Major Defense Systems

Note that there have been changes made to the acquisition phases within the U.S. Department of Defense every two to five years since 1971. Some of these changes have had major impacts; others relatively minor impacts. The phases that were used in this chapter were the latest phases as of August 2005. The phases we are using in this appendix are more similar to those being used in the 1980s when most of these applications occurred.

Concept Selection Phase

- Requirements definition for USMC Mobile Protected Weapons System
- Requirements analysis for U.S. Army Advanced Heavy Antitank Missile System
- Requirements analysis for U.S. Army Division Support Weapons System
- Mission area analysis for USMC small arms weapons
- Mission area analysis for USMC medium assault transport
- System architecture definition for the World-Wide Digital Communications System
- Concept selection for U.S. Army Advanced Scout Helicopter
- Requirements analysis for U.S. Army small arms weapons
- Concept definition for U.S. Navy Seafire system
- Concept evaluations for the U.S. Army light helicopter family

■ Mission area analysis for joint U.S. Army and U.S. Air Force reconnaissance and surveillance

New Concept Refinement Phase

■ Weapons-mix analysis for U.S. Army Forward Area Air Defense System
■ Design-to-cost analysis for U.S. Navy electronic warfare system
■ Trade-off analysis for U.S. Army Single Channel Ground and Airborne Radio System
■ Trade-off analysis and source selection for U.S. Navy Integrated Communications System
■ Trade-off analysis for USMC Tactical Air Command and Control System
■ Avionics system concept design for a Vertical and Short Take-off and Landing Aircraft

Technology Development Phase

■ Strategic planning analysis of mine countermeasures research and development
■ Affordability and capability trade-offs for USMC medium assault transport
■ Affordability and capability trade-offs for U.S. Air Force night and all-weather systems
■ Affordability and capability trade-offs for U.S. Air Force airfield attack weapons

System Development and Demonstration

■ Evaluation of the Duplex U.S. Army Radio/Radar Targeting Aid
■ Source selection evaluation (Phase 1)for U.S. Army and USMC Light Armored Vehicle
■ Source selection for the U.S. Army Single Channel Ground and Airborne Radio System,
■ Test and evaluation of pilot-aiding systems for the F-18 aircraft

Production and Deployment

■ Joint-service proponency study for the PATRIOT missile system,
■ Joint-service weapons mix study for PATRIOT missiles and fighter aircraft.

Operations and Support Phase

■ Analysis of Airborne and Spaceborne Reconnaissance Assets

Ongoing in All Phases (Resource Allocation)

■ Resource allocation for USMC Program Objectives Memorandum (1977–2005)

- Resource allocation for U.S. Army Program Objectives Memorandum (1978, 1980)
- Resource allocation for U.S. Army, U.S. Navy, U.S. Air Force and national intelligence agencies
- Resource allocation of R&D projects for the U.S. Defense Nuclear Agency
- Resource allocation of R&D projects for the U.S. Naval Air Test Center
- Resource allocation of night and in-weather tactical air systems
- Resource allocation of airfield attack weapons
- Resource allocation of U.S. Navy command and control R&D projects

REFERENCES

Bresnick, T. A., Annis, C. P., and Buede, D .M. (1981). Concept Definition and Evaluation Criteria for the Mobile Protected Weapons System (MPWS) and the Light Armored Vehicle (LAV). *Final Report No. PR 81–14-154*. McLean, VA: Decisions and Designs, Inc.

Bresnick, T. A., Annis, C. P., and Buede, D. M. (1982). A multiattribute utility approach to communicating acquisition requirements to industry: USMC mobile protected weapons system. *Phalanx, 15*, 11–14.

Bresnick, T. A., Buede, D. M., Pisani, A. A., Smith, L. L., and Wood. B. B. (1997). Airborne and space-borne reconnaissance force mixes: A decision analytic approach. *Military Operations Research, 3*, 65–78.

Bresnick, T. A., O'Connor, M. F., Marvin, F. F., and Rausch, M. M. (1989). Forward Area Air Defense System Weapons Mix Analysis. *Final Report*. El Paso, TX: COLSA, Inc.

Brown, P. C., Buede, D. M., Miller, J. B., and Thornton, J. R. (1992). A revelation scheme for allocating organizational resources. *Journal of Economic Behavior and Organization, 18*, 201–214.

DODI. (2003). Operation of the Defense Acquisition Process.

Everett, H. (1963). Generalized Lagrange multiplier method for solving problems of optimum allocation of resources. *Operations Research, 11*, 399–417.

Kirkwood, C. (1997). *Strategic Decision Making: Multiobjective Decision Analysis with Spreadsheets*. Belmont, CA: Duxbury.

Kuskey, K. P., Waslov, K. A., and Buede, D. M. (1981). Decision analytic support of the United States Marine Corps' POM development: A guide to the methodology. *Final Report PR 81–158*, McLean, VA: Decisions and Designs, Inc.

Rush, B. C. (1997). Cost as an independent variable: Concepts and risks. *Acquisition Quarterly Review, 4*, 161–172.

TASC. (1996). Final Report on the Reconnaissance Study Group Cost–Benefit Analysis of Airborne and Space-Borne Reconnaissance Force Mixes. TASC Final Report.

Watson, S. R., and Buede, D. M. (1987). *Decision Synthesis*. Cambridge, UK: Cambridge University Press.

27 Balancing Environmental and Operational Objectives in Nuclear Refueling Strategies

Phillip C. Beccue and Jeffrey S. Stonebraker

ABSTRACT. The New York Power Authority (NYPA) wanted to develop a ten-year schedule for refueling its Indian Point 3 Nuclear Power Plant (IP3) that balanced fish protection, which occurs when IP3 is shut down for nuclear refueling, with the costs of buying and loading fuel. We developed a decision analysis model to compare alternative strategies for refueling. In the model, we explicitly considered key uncertainties associated with future operation: how well IP3 operates, how long it takes to refuel, and when New York State is likely to deregulate the electric utility industry. The NYPA decision makers used the model to reinforce their choice of a refueling strategy. They were not surprised that more fish protection occurred with strategies that restricted the starting date for refueling to the last full week in May, rather than allowing the starting date to float throughout the period from May through August. However, the NYPA decision makers were surprised that the more restrictive strategies also resulted in lower costs.

The NYPA is the nation's largest nonfederal public power organization, providing about one-fourth of the electricity used in New York State. The NYPA owns twelve power projects. The Indian Point 3 Nuclear Power Plant (IP3), located on the Hudson River, generates approximately one-fifth of its electrical power. Since 1975, IP3 has saved electric power users in Westchester County and New York City more than $1 billion.

IP3 withdraws 840,000 gallons of water per minute from the Hudson River for cooling steam and then returns it to the river. When water is withdrawn from the river between February and September so are fish eggs and small fish. Some of the fish do not survive as they pass through the cooling water system of IP3 (entrainment) because of temperature increases, pressure changes, and shear forces. The effect of entrainment on fish populations in the Hudson River has been the subject of both extensive litigation and scientific research (Barnthouse et al. 1988). The NYPA can reduce the effect of entrainment by scheduling plant shutdowns to refuel IP3 when fish eggs and small fish are most abundant in the Hudson River and taking those outages as scheduled.

In the past, the NYPA prepared its nuclear refueling outage schedules for IP3 using a ten-year planning horizon, assuming the operation and refueling of IP3 went exactly as planned. However, unforeseen events often altered operation and refueling, causing refueling outage schedules to deviate from what was planned. In the future, there is uncertainty about when New York State will deregulate its electric utility industry and the effect on the cost of replacement power that the

NYPA will have to buy during refueling outages. NYPA must systematically consider these uncertainties to ensure that it can continue to provide low-cost power and can reduce the environmental effects of operating IP3. For these reasons, the NYPA decided to use decision analysis rather than other approaches, such as mixed-integer programming (Fourcade et al. 1997), to help it to schedule nuclear refueling outages at IP3.

In this chapter, we describe the decision analysis process and tools that we brought to the environmental and operational dilemma faced by the NYPA. We will describe the model structure and highlight the key inputs and how we collected those inputs from experts within the NYPA. We conclude with insights and results and comment on our own challenges as well as the reactions from the stakeholders.

Problem Structuring – Designing the Project for Success

The decision analysis project started on October 23, 1997, and the NYPA required that it be finished by December 4, 1997. Our decision analysis approach consisted of four phases: framing, modeling, data collection, and evaluation.

During the framing phase, we determined who would be involved in the project, the scope of the analysis, and the important factors (alternatives, uncertainties, and objectives) of the refueling outage plan. The project team consisted of a core group (NYPA senior managers and decision analysts – the authors), subject-matter experts, and decision makers. Our role was to conduct a decision analysis that was responsive to the needs of decision makers. We used various decision analysis tools to organize and record the results of the framing phase. These included a decision-quality spider diagram, a decision pyramid, an objectives hierarchy, a strategy table, a decision tree, and an influence diagram.

Mission Statement

We determined the scope of the project by (1) developing a mission statement and (2) clearly defining the decisions and their boundaries. We constructed the mission statement by considering four questions: what are we going to do, why are we doing this, how will we know we are successful, and how can we fail? The resulting mission statement was as follows:

1. Identify strategies for scheduling refueling outages at IP3 over the period 1999 through 2008 that range from unrestricted operation, in which outages can begin at any time and protection of fish eggs and small fish is not a concern, to restricted operation, in which outages must begin during a specified week and the primary concern is maximizing protection of fish eggs and small fish,
2. Develop a decision analysis model for comparing the cost and amount of fish protection associated with the refueling strategies based on information provided by the experts at the NYPA and the level of confidence they have in that information,

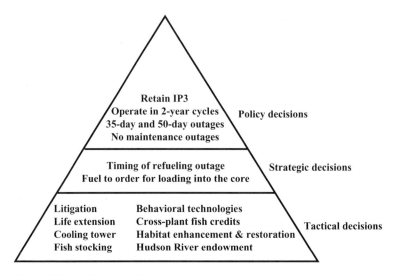

Figure 27.1. Decision pyramid.

3. Compare the refueling strategies in terms of cost and fish protection, and Provide, by December 4, 1997, the results of the decision analysis model to the NYPA decision makers.

Decision Pyramid

During the first week of the project, we listed decisions that could affect the mission. We then categorized each decision as policy, strategic, or tactical to help bound the NYPA's problem and focus our attention at the right level. A decision pyramid (Matheson and Matheson 1998) helped us to organize the three categories of decisions (Figure 27.1). This decision pyramid defines the scope of the analysis for the NYPA by focusing attention on the key strategic choices. We assume that policy decisions are given. Tactical decisions are to be made in the future.

The strategic decisions were the focus of our project. The two key decisions were the time of year that refueling outages should occur and the amount of fuel that should be ordered for loading into the nuclear reactor core of IP3 at the start of an operating cycle to allow operation for a target number of days. Refueling outages for cycles 10–14 were scheduled to occur in the years 1999, 2001, 2003, 2005, and 2007. The time of year that the outages occur affects the level of fish protection, and the amount of fuel loaded affects the cost of operation.

Policy decisions represented corporate philosophy at the NYPA. They provided guidance for the decision analysis but were not to be evaluated in our study. The four policy decisions were as follows: (1) the NYPA would continue to retain the operation of IP3 for at least ten years; (2) it would refuel IP3 once during every two-year operating cycle; (3) it would schedule refueling outages to last 50 days during the three consecutive two-year operating cycles starting in 1999

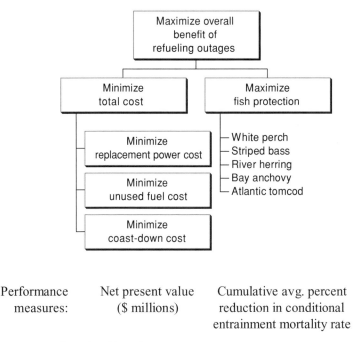

Performance   Net present value   Cumulative avg. percent
measures: ($ millions)   reduction in conditional
                                                            entrainment mortality rate

Figure 27.2. Objectives hierarchy.

(cycles 10–12) and 35 days (in cycles 13 and 14) to allow for anticipated refueling efficiency improvements; (4) and it would not schedule maintenance outages at IP3 in addition to the refueling outages.

The tactical decisions were beyond the scope of our project. They represented alternatives that may have to be considered subsequent to the strategic decisions. By organizing the set of decisions into a decision pyramid, we benefited from a simple tool that focused our attention on the two important strategic decisions: *timing of outage* and *amount of fuel loaded in each cycle*. This prevented us from creating a large, overly complex, unmanageable decision model that we could not finish on time. It also prevented us from solving the wrong problem.

Objectives Hierarchy

We identified the important issues related to scheduling of refueling outages and categorized them as objectives, strategies, or uncertainties. We organized our objectives into a hierarchy (Keeney 1992). The objectives hierarchy shows the objectives and performance measures we used to compare strategies for scheduling refueling outages at IP3 (Figure 27.2). The fundamental objective was to maximize the overall benefit from planned refueling outages. This objective was composed of two subobjectives: to minimize the total cost of the outages and to maximize the fish protection that the outages provided. Although we could have included factors other than cost and fish protection in our analysis, these two were most important to the NYPA decision makers. Also, we thought adding further factors might prevent our completing the project by December 4.

Objective: Minimize Total Cost

The cost objective was itself composed of three objectives: to minimize the cost of buying replacement electricity when IP3 was shut down for refueling, to minimize the amount of unused fuel in the nuclear reactor at the end of each operating cycle, and to minimize the amount of time that IP3 would operate at less than full power (i.e., coasting down) before the next refueling outage. The performance measure we used for the cost objective was net present value (NPV) of future costs for ten years, using an annual discount rate of 6.5 percent.

The NYPA has contracts to provide electricity to its customers. When IP3 is shut down for refueling, the NYPA must buy electricity to replace the electricity it is not producing. The NYPA operates IP3 so as to minimize the purchase of replacement electricity. Therefore, we included the cost of replacing electricity during refueling outages in our analysis. We did not include the cost of replacing electricity during unscheduled outages because we assumed that it would be the same for any refueling strategy.

Before each cycle, fuel is loaded into the nuclear reactor core of IP3 to allow operation for a target number of full power days (FPDs). If a refueling outage occurs before all of the fuel is used, some of the remaining fuel cannot be used for future operation. The NYPA strives to minimize the amount of unused fuel and thus the cost of buying fuel that is not used for producing electricity. The unused-fuel cost is the expense of not using all of the FPDs.

If IP3 operates at full power for a greater number of days than expected, the fuel will not last until the next scheduled refueling outage. Starting a refueling outage before it is scheduled creates problems that the NYPA does not consider acceptable. Rather than start a refueling outage earlier than scheduled, the NYPA can extend the operation of IP3 to the scheduled starting date by reducing power generation from 100 percent to 70 percent in the 20 days before the outage, a process known as coast down. The cost of coast down is the penalty associated with running IP3 at less than full power, measured by the cost of replacement power needed to compensate for reduced power production.

Objective: Maximize Fish Protection

The performance measure for fish protection is the sum of the average percent reduction (APR) in the conditional entrainment mortality rate (CEMR) at IP3 across five taxa (types) of fish over the ten-year period from 1999 through 2008. CEMR is the fractional reduction in abundance of a fish taxon in the Hudson River due to entrainment of fish eggs and small fish, assuming other sources of mortality are density independent, that is, there is no compensatory increase in survival or growth that would offset entrainment mortality.

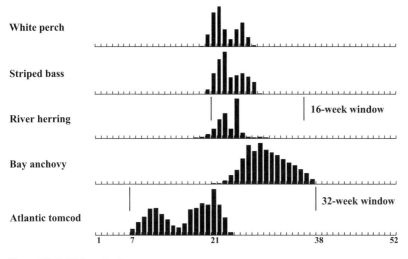

Figure 27.3. Fish protection.

We considered five taxa of fish in this project: white perch, striped bass, river herring, bay anchovy, and Atlantic tomcod. Prior to the start of our study, the stakeholders (the NYPA, state and federal regulators, and environmental advocacy groups) jointly selected these five taxa of fish to evaluate the effects of operating power plants on the Hudson River (Coastal Environmental Services, Inc. 1996). Eggs and small fish of these five taxa are found in the Hudson River near IP3.

We defined the APR in CEMR as the simple average of the annual percent reductions for the five taxa of fish. The APR in CEMR for each taxon is the annual CEMR at IP3 resulting from plant shutdown during an outage divided by the maximum annual CEMR assuming no outage occurred. Using this definition, each fish taxon contributes equally to the annual average, regardless of the number of fish of that taxon in the Hudson River, that is, fish taxa are inversely weighted by their abundance. This inverse weighting was selected by default after the stakeholders were unable to agree on a system for prioritizing fish taxa based on their relative abundance or other criteria. However, our analysis was intended to address the perceived need for fish protection agreed to by the stakeholders, not to debate the merits of their decisions.

We summed the APR in CEMR at IP3 across the ten-year period of a refueling strategy to estimate the cumulative APR (CAPR) in CEMR. We did not discount the APR in CEMR as we did with the total cost because we assumed that fish would have the same value in future years.

The maximum annual CEMR at IP3 differs among fish taxa, as do the weekly contributions to the annual CEMR (Figure 27.3). The percent reduction in CEMR for a fish taxon will be highest if an outage occurs during the weeks that contribute most to the maximum annual CEMR. However, those weeks differ among fish taxa. The weekly contributions for all fish taxa occur within a 32-week period (window) from week 7 (the second week in February) to week 38 (the second week

Table 27.1. Nuclear refueling strategies

Nuclear refueling strategy	Refueling outage schedule
Unrestricted operation (current strategy)	Cycles 10–14: start end of full-power operation
32-week	Cycles 10–12: start weeks 7–29
	Cycles 13–14: start weeks 7–33
16-week	Cycles 10–12: start weeks 21–29
	Cycles 13–14: start weeks 21–31
Fixed 2001	Cycles 10: start in early September
	Cycles 11–14: start last full week in May
Fixed 1999	Cycles 10–14 start last full week in May

Refueling outages scheduled to occur in 1999 (cycle 10), 2001 (cycle 11), 2003 (cycle 12), 2005 (cycle 13), and 2007 (cycle 14).

in September). Thus, a 32-week outage from week 7 to week 38 would result in an APR in CEMR of 100 percent (i.e., maximum fish protection); all other outages would result in a value less than 100 percent. If no outages occurred during that 32-week period, the APR in CEMR would be zero percent. For short-duration outages, moving the starting week of the outage to late spring will produce a relatively higher APR in CEMR. The highest percent reduction in APR of CEMR for a 35-day or a 50-day outage occurs if the outage begins during the last full week in May.

Strategies

We used strategy tables (Clemen 1996) to develop and organize the refueling strategies and selected five for further analysis that represent a range of operating restrictions: unrestricted operation, 32-week, 16-week, fixed 2001, and fixed 1999 (Table 27.1).

In the unrestricted-operation strategy, refueling outages are scheduled every two years, but actually occur at the end of full-power operation, whenever that happens. Thus, the starting date of the outage does not necessarily adhere to the schedule. This strategy represents how IP3 has operated in the past and serves as a baseline for comparison with the other strategies.

In the 32-week strategy, NYPA schedules refueling outages within the 32-week period when fish eggs and small fish of all five taxa would be entrained, that is, a window of weeks 7 to 38. A refueling outage for the 32-week strategy starts at the end of full-power operation or as close to the end as possible with the constraint that the entire outage occurs within the window. That is, refueling outages start from week 7 through week 31 for a planned 50-day outage and from week 7 through week 33 for a planned 35-day outage. This is the second least restrictive strategy and is intended to provide more fish protection than the unrestricted-operation strategy.

In the 16-week strategy, NYPA schedules refueling outages within a 16-week period beginning with week 21. Refueling outages scheduled to last 50 days can start in weeks 21 through 29 and those scheduled to last 35 days can start in weeks

21 through 31. During this 16-week period more fish eggs and small fish would be entrained than in the remaining 16 weeks of the 32-week period. This strategy is more restrictive because the window is half the size of the 32-week strategy and is intended to provide greater fish protection.

In the fixed 2001 strategy, the 1999 refueling outage was expected to start near the beginning of September 1999 (depending on how well IP3 operated). Subsequent refueling outages are constrained to start during the last full week of May, beginning with the 2001 refueling outage and then in odd years thereafter. The fixed 2001 strategy is more restrictive than the 16-week strategy and is intended to provide greater fish protection. This strategy allows IP3 to operate until the end of FPDs in 1999, starting a refueling outage then, and imposing a strict outage window for future outages.

The fixed 1999 strategy differs from the fixed 2001 strategy only in that the 1999 refueling outage was expected to start during the last full week of May 1999 rather than in September 1999. This strategy is more restrictive than the fixed 2001 strategy and is intended to provide maximum fish protection for the 10-year planning horizon with the planned outages. The fixed 1999 strategy stops operation of IP3 before the end of FPDs in 1999, but it also provides maximum fish protection immediately.

Uncertainties

We identified three uncertainties that were likely to have the largest effect on total NPV cost for the five refueling strategies: how well IP3 operates (operating factor), how long it takes to refuel IP3 (outage length), and when New York State is likely to deregulate the electric utility industry. In the influence diagram (Figure 27.4) we show the important factors and their relationships in the NYPA's problem. The rounded rectangular nodes represent objectives, the rectangular node represents refueling strategies, the oval nodes represent uncertainties, and the arrows show the relationships between the parameters. We used the NPV of future costs as a measure of total cost and cumulative average percent reduction in conditional entrainment mortality rate (CAPR in CEMR) as a measure of fish protection. We considered five refueling strategies: unrestricted operation, 32-week, 16-week, fixed 2001, and fixed 1999. Uncertainties include two operating factors for each refueling cycle (before and after the refueling quantity decision is made), outage lengths for each refueling cycle, and deregulation year.

The operating factor is the amount of power IP3 generates divided by the maximum possible power it could generate. The maximum is based on the assumption that IP3 operates at full power during the entire cycle except during the refueling outage. *Actual Operating Factor (i) Before Refuel Decision* (OF_ia1 in the Appendix) is the actual operating factor for cycle i from the time IP3 starts producing electricity until the NYPA determines how much fuel to order for the next cycle. *Actual Operating Factor (i) After Refuel Decision* (OF_ia2 in the Appendix) is the actual operating factor for cycle i after the fuel is ordered and until the

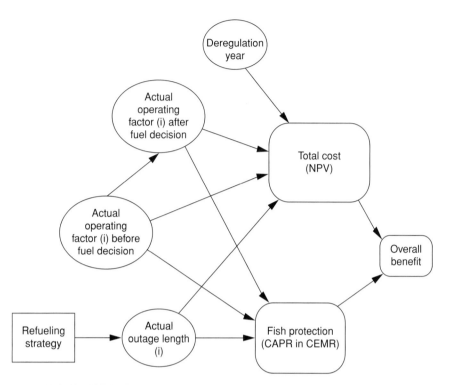

Figure 27.4. The NYPA influence diagram. The (i) represents periods 10, 11, 12, 13, and 14.

next refueling outage. Although IP3 operators plan for high operating factors, the actual operating factor is uncertain.

Outage length is the number of days IP3 is shut down for replacing fuel rods in the nuclear reactor core. *Actual Outage Length (i)* is the actual outage length for cycle *i*, as opposed to the planned outage length of 50 or 35 days (*OutLen$_i$t* in the Appendix).

The U.S. electric utility industry is deregulating, but the pace of change varies by region. Timing for deregulation of the electricity market in New York is uncertain. The deregulation uncertainty is captured by identifying the year that deregulation will be complete in New York.

Modeling – Linking Choices to Outcomes

The two key strategic decisions concern the timing of the refueling outages and how much fuel to order for the next cycle (Figure 27.1). We constructed a decision tree to examine the impact of the five timing strategies on the two key objectives: total cost and fish protection (Figure 27.5). This schematic decision tree representing more than 200 million endpoints shows the scenarios to be evaluated for each of the NYPA's refueling strategies for the IP3 nuclear power plant. Uncertainties include two operating factors: outage lengths and deregulation year. We

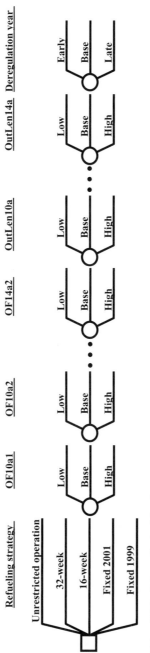

Figure 27.5. Schematic decision tree.

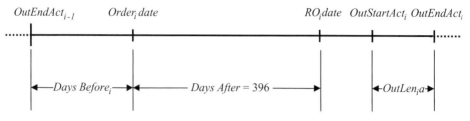

Figure 27.6. Refueling timeline.

modeled the amount of fuel loaded at the beginning of each cycle as a calculated value in the cost model, assuming that IP3 operated at full power in that cycle except during the refueling outage.

For each refueling strategy, we computed total cost (NPV) and fish protection (CAPR in CEMR) for all combinations of uncertainty states. We then weighted each scenario through the tree by its probability, resulting in a distribution of total cost and fish protection for each refueling strategy. We used the expected values of the resulting probability distributions to compare refueling strategies. We computed these scenarios with DPL decision tree/influence diagram software (Manzella and Dalton 2004) linked to an Excel spreadsheet. Incorporating the simulation and code conversion features of DPL allowed efficient approximation of millions of endpoints in less than two minutes.

The cost model contains additional model variables (constants and calculated values) that define the timing of the NYPA's 730-day cycle (Figure 27.6). We captured the logic of the timing in a spreadsheet that computes both cost and fish protection for each scenario of the decision tree for any setting of model variables. Figure 27.6 defines the timing logic of the 730-day cycle at the NYPA's IP3 nuclear power plant. Cycle i begins when IP3 starts producing electricity ($OutEndAct_{i-1}$) and ends when refueling is complete ($OutEndAct_i$). The cycle includes the days IP3 is producing electricity and the days IP3 is shut down for refueling ($OutLen_i a$). The NYPA determines how much fuel to order for loading into IP3's nuclear reactor core for the next cycle 396 days prior to the scheduled refueling outage for the current cycle. The date when the fuel is ordered is the $Order_i date$. For the 730-day cycle, we chose the Monday of week 21 (the last full week in May) as a fixed reference of each cycle ($RO_i date$). We also fixed the $Order_i date$ because it is 396 days before the scheduled refueling outage date ($RO_i date$). We divided the cycle into two periods, one before the $Order_i date$ ($DaysBefore_i$) and one after that date but before the $RO_i date$ ($Days After$). IP3 can actually shut down for refueling ($OutStartAct_i$) before, after, or on the $RO_i date$, depending on how well it operates relative to its target. If the actual operating factor falls below the target operating factor for a cycle, IP3 will continue to operate beyond the scheduled refueling date until it must shut down to stay within the window of a refueling strategy. If the actual operating factor exceeds the target operating factor, it will have to shut down before the scheduled refueling date if it maintains full power throughout the cycle. In this case, IP3 operated more efficiently than expected and can continue to operate only at a reduced power level (derated). If IP3 does not coast into the refueling strategy's window, then it must shut down early and wait until the planned outage begins. The Appendix contains additional details on the model variables and logic.

Data Collection – Developing Reliable Inputs

We collected data on the operating factor, the outage length, the expected year for deregulation, and replacement power cost from subject-matter experts, including the senior managers in the core group. For most of the uncertainties, we used a six-step probability assessment process (Merkhofer 1987; Spetzler and Staël von Holstein 1975) to encode probability distributions from experts. The process consisted of the following steps:

(I) *Motivating*, in which we described the assessment task and its importance to the subject-matter experts, and counteracted motivational biases;

(II) *Structuring*, in which we clearly defined the variables, assumptions, and measurement scales;

(III) *Conditioning*, in which we drew out the subject-matter expert's knowledge concerning the variable and counteracted cognitive biases (Russo and Schoemaker 1990; Kahneman, Slovic, and Tversky 1982);

(IV) *Encoding*, in which we quantified the variable's uncertainty as a cumulative probability distribution by assessing extreme values (first and ninety-ninth percentiles) and five to ten values in between the extreme values;

(V) *Verifying*, in which we confirmed that the distribution accurately reflected the beliefs of the expert; and

(VI) *Discretizing*, in which we selected the tenth, fiftieth, and ninetieth percentiles of the encoded cumulative probability distribution.

The NYPA establishes target operating factors and target outage lengths for each cycle as part of its business plan. However, it cannot forecast actual operating factors and actual outage lengths for each cycle with complete certainty. To reflect this uncertainty, we encoded values for the actual operating factor and outage length that the operators of IP3 and other NYPA experts expected, and their confidence in those values. From the resulting cumulative probability distribution, we selected the tenth, fiftieth, and ninetieth percentiles for use in the decision tree. We conducted each probability assessment in approximately three hours using the six-step process.

For all cycles, the likelihood of operating at an operating factor lower than the target is greater than that of operating at or above the target. As a result, to maintain a predetermined schedule, the NYPA has a higher probability of discarding unused fuel than of running out of fuel and coasting down.

The probability assessment for outage length indicates that NYPA experts may be overconfident because the spread in the distribution narrows in the future

Table 27.2. *Probability estimates (tenth, fiftieth, and ninetieth percentiles) and target values for operating factors and outage lengths*

Cycle	Operating factor (%)				Outage length (days)			
	10th	50th	90th	*Target*	10th	50th	90th	*Target*
10	80	85	92	*90*	50	65	90	*50*
11	83	88	95	*90*	40	55	70	*50*
12	85	90	97	*95*	35	50	65	*50*
13	85	90	97	*95*	35	45	60	*35*
14	85	90	97	*95*	35	40	50	*35*

(Table 27.2). Generally, experts are less sure of events far into the future than they are of near events. In addition, they may show motivational bias because the actual values of operating factor and outage length move toward target values. We made the NYPA experts aware of these biases, but they stood by their assessments because they expect IP3 to become more efficient in the future.

Even though the NYPA could not forecast the precise timing of deregulation of the electric utility industry, we did not use the six-step probability assessment process because of time constraints. Instead, we assessed the tenth, fiftieth, and ninetieth percentiles directly from the NYPA senior managers serving in the core group, resulting in years 1999, 2000, and 2002. Approximating the probability distribution of a continuous variable with these three percentiles is common in practice. For future revisions of the analysis, we recommend a more thorough review of the factors surrounding the deregulation year and resulting purchase power prices.

The NYPA forecasts that replacement power cost will continue to vary monthly (Figure 27.7). These monthly estimates of the cost of buying replacement

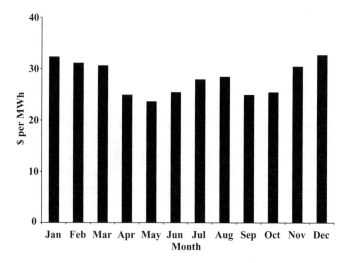

Figure 27.7. Replacement power cost.

power for the IP3 were forecast by the NYPA before deregulation of the electric utility industry. It expects the highest values from November through March. It also expects higher values during July and August than in April, May, June, September, and October. We thought it impractical to conduct probability assessments on replacement power cost for each month of each cycle.

The electric utility experts we interviewed, both within and outside of the NYPA, believed that the current seasonal differences in replacement power are likely to diminish in the area IP3 serves as energy providers try to capitalize on the higher price that they can get for power during certain seasons. As the supply of electricity increases to meet demand during the higher-priced seasons, prices will come down. Precisely how much seasonal replacement power costs will change will be known only after deregulation. For our analysis, we assumed that after deregulation the cost of replacement power would be constant throughout the year. We also assumed that the cost of replacement power after deregulation would be equal to the average across all months before deregulation. As a result, the month during which a refueling outage starts is a factor in determining the replacement power contribution to total NPV cost before, but not after, deregulation. We also assumed that the cost of replacement power after deregulation would not escalate during our ten-year planning horizon to reflect the price control that deregulation is expected to provide.

Evaluation – Performing Analyses to Generate New Insights

We performed a variety of analyses to explore the performance of each strategy against the two objectives of cost and fish protection. We presented the results to the NYPA decision makers and gave compelling evidence that highlighted the key drivers of the results and the differences between the strategies. Although the analysis accounted for the range of possible outcomes for each strategy, in our presentation we emphasized the expected values of the outcome distributions.

The rank order of the refueling strategies differs depending on the performance measure. The relative rank of five refueling strategies for the NYPA's IP3 nuclear power plant is based on both expected net present value of cost and fish protection, expressed as the expected cumulative average percent reduction in the conditional entrainment mortality rate (CAPR in CEMR). Both lower values of NPV cost and higher values of CAPR in CEMR are better. No single strategy simultaneously minimizes the expected NPV cost and maximizes the expected CAPR in CEMR (Figure 27.8). Early in the project, we tried to convince the NYPA decision makers to specify the trade-offs between cost and fish protection, but they were unable to do so. Rather than force this, we recognized that we could infer this trade-off later because the analysis was limited to two objectives.

We presented the rankings of the strategies to the NYPA decision makers without explicitly weighting cost and fish protection. The 16-week and 32-week strategies were dominated by the fixed 2001 strategy (Figure 27.8). Therefore, we compared the remaining three strategies. Unrestricted operation cost $5.3 million less than the fixed 2001 strategy because the savings associated with operating

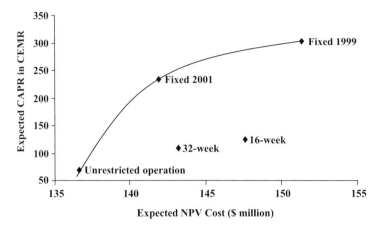

Figure 27.8. Pareto diagram.

until the end of FPDs outweighed the cost of buying more expensive replacement power. However, it provided fish protection well below a standard previously accepted by the NYPA, a CAPR in CEMR of 204 based on the Hudson River Cooling Tower Settlement Agreement (Barnthouse et al. 1988). Fish protection above this standard was provided by both the fixed 2001 and the fixed 1999 strategies. The NYPA decision makers chose the fixed 2001 strategy because it met the previously accepted standard for fish protection at a cost savings of nearly $10 million. Despite the absence of explicit weighting among objectives, the NYPA decision makers drew on the insights from the decision analysis modeling to reinforce their choice of a refueling strategy.

Stakeholder Reaction

The decision analysis provided new insights for scheduling refueling outages at IP3. Historically, the NYPA decision makers believed that strategies allowing refueling outages to start within a fixed period of many weeks were better than those that required refueling outages to start within a particular week. They wanted refueling outages to start when scheduled, and past refueling outages had often started at times very different from those initially scheduled. For the future, it seemed reasonable to assume that the probability of starting refueling outages at the end of FPDs within a fixed period of weeks was considerably higher than the probability of starting them during a particular week. However, the 16-week and 32-week strategies did not guarantee that IP3 could operate until the end of FPDs. These strategies also resulted in two of the five outages that occurred during weeks when replacement power was higher than during the weeks associated with the fixed 2001 strategy.

    Another insight from the analysis was that the NYPA nuclear plant operators and decision makers differed in their forecasts of operating factors and outage length durations. We identified these disagreements in the data collection phase, which then fueled discussion and attempts to resolve the differences among the NYPA staff.

Finally, even though NYPA decision makers had been comfortable with their assumptions about replacement power, they were surprised at how much replacement power affected the results of the analysis. Consequently, they are exploring further study of replacement-power forecasts.

Reflections

This was a very exciting decision analysis project in that it was important to the NYPA nuclear plant operators and passionate environmental stakeholders; it was fast-paced but defensible; and we were able to bring clarity to their issues through our analyses.

We had some difficulty in obtaining agreement from the NYPA decision makers in committing to a set of trade-off weights among cost and fish protection. However, we were able to make inferences as to the "value" placed on preserving fish for each of the strategies, thereby helping them to see how their choice implies a certain set of weights. We thought that this was a good compromise given the political tensions that existed. In the past eight years that each of us has spent inside major biopharmaceutical organizations applying decision analytic techniques to R&D priorities, we have also found it challenging to formally assess tradeoffs between financial and strategic objectives. Laying out the metrics on each dimension has usually proved adequate to drive consensus in this setting.

The short timelines required in this project forced us to be as efficient as possible in the use of a few of the powerful tools the decision analysis toolkit provides (decision pyramid, influence diagrams, objectives hierarchy, and software). However, had we more time, the NYPA could have benefited from a more external focus in terms of the long-term uncertainties in the electric power industry. We only touched the surface in thinking through (and modeling) future regulatory scenarios, ownership issues (the plant has since changed owners), operating improvements, power prices, etc. We have seen the overemphasis on internal issues, which ignore some of the more important but harder to grasp external risks, to be a barrier to high-quality decisions. Focusing only on internal issues often results in missed opportunities.

The NYPA accepted our insights and analytical results as a major improvement in the approach it used for scheduling outages to refuel IP3; the decision analysis accounted for key uncertainties in the refueling schedule and provided a systematic approach for simultaneously evaluating the cost of refueling outages and fish protection. It also provided the NYPA with a tool for explaining its selection of a refueling outage schedule to other stakeholders. As a result, the NYPA used our model in developing a schedule for refueling outages at IP3 over the ten-year period 1999 through 2008. We believe our approach is generally applicable to other electric utilities that must evaluate options for operating power plants when faced with competing objectives and significant uncertainty, and other organizations wrestling with similar tradeoffs between financial and nonfinancial objectives.

Appendix

The appendix contains the details of the quantitative model that computes cost and fish protection for any scenario in the decision tree, including the equations and variable definitions that describe the underlying cost model. We implemented the cost model in an Excel spreadsheet and evaluated the scenarios for each strategy with DPL linked to Excel. Refer to Figure 27.6 for the timing logic of the 730-day cycle at IP3.

$DaysBefore_i$ is the number of days in cycle i before the $Order_i date$, and it depends on the scheduled refueling outage date for cycle i ($RO_i date$), when the previous cycle ended ($OutEndAct_{i-1}$), and the number of days in cycle i after the $Order_i date$ ($DaysAfter$):

$$DaysBefore_i = RO_i date - OutEndAct_{i-1} - DaysAfter$$

FPD_i is the amount of fuel loaded into the nuclear reactor for cycle i at the $Order_{i-1} date$.

$$FPD_i = (DaysPerCycle - OutLen_{i-1}t - DaysXtra_{i-1}) * OF_i t$$

$DaysPerCycle$ is 730 days. $OutLen_i t$ is the target outage length for cycle i. $OF_i t$ is the target operating factor for cycle i. $DaysXtra_i$ estimates the number of extra fuel days in cycle i at the $Order_i date$ and depends on how much fuel is loaded into the core for cycle i (FPD_i), how well IP3 operates before the $Order_i date$, and how well IP3 is expected to operate after the $Order_i date$.

$$DaysXtra_i = [FPD_i - (DaysBefore_i * OF_i a1 + DaysAfter * OF_i t)]/OF_i t$$

$OutStartAct_i$ is when IP3 actually shuts down for its refueling, and it depends on how well IP3 operated relative to its target.

$$OutStartAct_i = \begin{cases} RO_i date + Balance_i + CoastDays_i, & balance_i < 0 \\ RO_i date + DaysOutWin_i, & balance_i \geq 0 \end{cases}$$

$BALANCE_i$ is the amount of fuel left in core at the completion of cycle i and $CoastDays_i$ is the number of days that IP3 can coast in cycle i. $BALANCE_i = FuelLeft_i - (DaysOutWin_i * OF_i a2)$.

$FuelLeft_i$ is the number of days of nuclear fuel left in the core in cycle i on the $RO_i date$ and is the difference between the amount loaded into the core in cycle i and the amount of fuel actually used. $FuelLeft_i = FPD_i - (DaysBefore_i * OF_i a1 + DaysAfter * OF_i a2)$.

$DaysOutWin_i$ is the number of days that IP3 could operate in cycle i beyond the $RO_i date$ but still remain within the window of a refueling strategy.

$$DaysOutWin_i = \begin{cases} FuelLeft_i / OF_i a2, \\ \text{unrestricted operation} \\ Min\{FuelLeft_i / OF_i t, Win - OutLen_i t, HiWin_i - RO_i date \\ -OutLen_i t\}, \\ \text{16-week and 32-week} \\ Min\{FuelLeft_i / OF_i t, HiWin_i - RO_i date - OutLen_i t\}, \\ \text{fixed 2001 and fixed 1999} \end{cases}$$

Win is the window of a refueling strategy. $LoWin_i$ and $HiWin_i$ are the earliest and latest dates in cycle i for this window.

We determine the amount of fish protection using $OutStartAct_i$ and $OutEndAct_i$ as inputs (Figure 27.6). Total cost is the sum of replacement-power cost, unused-fuel cost, and coast-down cost. We determine replacement-power cost before deregulation using monthly replacement-power cost values (Figure 27.7) with $OutStartAct_i$ and $OutEndAct_i$ as inputs. After deregulation, replacement power is a constant. Unused-fuel cost is the product of $Balance_i$ and a daily fuel value. Coast-down cost is the amount IP3 is derated using $CoastDays_i$ and replacement-power cost as inputs.

REFERENCES

Barnthouse, L. W., Boreman, J., Englert, T. L., Kirk, W. L., and Horn, E. G. (1988). Hudson River settlement agreement: Technical rationale and cost considerations. *American Fisheries Society Monograph, 4,* 267–273.

Clemen, R. T. (1996). *Making Hard Decisions: An Introduction to Decision Analysis.* (2nd ed.). Belmont, CA: Duxbury Press.

Coastal Environmental Services, Inc. (1996). Evaluation of alternative outage schedules based on a multispecies approach. Bowie, MD: Post, Buckley, Schuh, and Jernigan.

Fourcade, F., Johnson, E., Bara, M., and Cortey-Dumont, P. (1997). Optimizing nuclear power plant refueling with mixed-integer programming. *European Journal of Operations Research, 97,* 269–280.

Kahneman, D., Slovic P., and Tversky, R. (Eds.). (1982). *Judgment under Uncertainty: Heuristics and Biases.* New York: Cambridge University Press.

Keeney, R. (1992). *Value-Focused Thinking.* Cambridge, MA: Harvard University Press.

Manzella, A., and Dalton, C. (2004). *DPL 6.0 Professional User Guide.* Concord, MA: Syncopation Software, Inc.

Matheson, D., and Matheson, J. E. (1998). *The Smart Organization.* Boston, MA: Harvard Business School Press.

Merkhofer, M. W. (1987). Quantifying judgmental uncertainty: Methodology, experiences, and insights. *IEEE Transactions of Systems, Man, and Cybernetics, SMC-17*(5), 741–752.

Russo, J. E., and Schoemaker, P. J. H. (1990). *Decision Traps: The Ten Barriers to Brilliant Decision-Making and How to Overcome Them.* New York: Simon & Schuster.

Spetzler, C. S., and Staël von Holstein, C.-A. S. (1975). Probability encoding in decision analysis. *Management Science, 22*(3), 340–352.

28 Perspective on Decision-Analysis Applications[1]

Donald L. Keefer, Craig W. Kirkwood, and James L. Corner

ABSTRACT. This chapter identifies, and provides perspective on, trends and developments in decision-analysis applications, based primarily on an exhaustive survey of decision-analysis applications published in the period 1990–2001 in major English-language operations research and closely related journals. It serves as a guide to those interested in recent applications in specific areas or in applications that illustrate the use of particular methods. We compare the characteristics of the applications articles surveyed here with those of applications articles appearing in a similar set of journals between 1970 and 1989 and conclude that the overall rate of publication of decision-analysis applications has increased. In addition, we find that both the mix of application areas and the specific aspects of decision analysis that are emphasized in applications publications have shifted somewhat. We also identify and discuss noteworthy trends in, and developments affecting, published applications, including those in computer software and software-related tools, decision conferencing, stochastic trees, value-focused thinking, normative systems, organizational processes, and real options. We highlight several award-winning decision-analysis applications and discuss formation of a new practitioner-oriented professional group. Finally, we present some concerns and thoughts on future needs for advancing decision-analysis practice.

Introduction

This chapter provides our perspective on the state of decision-analysis applications, based primarily on a survey of applications articles published from 1990 to 2001 in major English-language operations research journals and other closely related journals. We compare the results of this survey with an earlier survey by Corner and Kirkwood (1991) that covered a similar set of journals for the period 1970–1989, and we identify noteworthy trends in, and developments affecting, decision-analysis applications. A companion technical report by Keefer et al. (2002) provides short summaries of the individual applications articles.

Based on our study, we believe that the state of decision-analysis applications is healthy, and that there was a substantial increase in the rate of publication of

---

[1] Reprinted by permission, with minor additions and corrections, D. L. Keefer, C. W. Kirkwood, J. L. Corner, Perspective on Decision Analysis Applications, 1990–2001, *Decision Analysis* 1(1), 2004, 4–22. Copyright 2004, the Institute for Operations Research and the Management Sciences, 7240 Parkway Drive, Suite 310, Hanover, MD 21076 USA.

decision-analysis applications over the period 1990–2001 relative to 1970–1989. Furthermore, there was also an expansion in the use of new methods, particularly those related to problem formulation, implementation, and computation. Thus, although certain decision-analysis application areas have matured and applications therein have become somewhat routine, there continue to be new types of applications and use of new methods.

This chapter also provides a guide to published applications of decision analysis for practitioners and instructors who are interested in specific areas of application or in applications illustrating specific decision-analysis methods. In addition, it provides useful information for researchers interested in learning more about which research topics have had an impact on decision-analysis applications.

We use the term *decision analysis* to refer to a set of quantitative methods for analyzing decisions based on the *axioms of consistent choice* (Clemen 1996, Chapter 14; Kirkwood 1997, Section 9.9). Decision analysis is *normative*, rather than *descriptive*. That is, it provides a systematic quantitative approach to making better decisions, rather than a description of how unaided decisions are made. There is some subjectivity in deciding whether a particular application qualifies as an application of decision analysis. To be included, an application generally had to explicitly analyze alternatives for a decision problem using judgmental probabilities and/or subjectively assessed utility/value functions. Ambiguous cases were resolved by including the article if, on balance, it took a decision-analysis approach. There is also some subjectivity in deciding whether an article reports an application. Many of the surveyed articles report case histories of the use of decision analysis to address a specific decision problem, although other articles report on analysis that provided background or insights for policy making.

This chapter does not address the analytic hierarchy process or multicriteria decision making, two approaches that are related to multiattribute decision analysis. See Mollaghasemi and Pet-Edwards (1997) or Yoon and Hwang (1995) for more information about these approaches. Brown (1992) and Howard (1992), who are both prominent decision analysts, present differing philosophical views from a decision-analysis perspective about the relationship between decision analysis and other decision-oriented methods, such as fuzzy logic and the analytic hierarchy process.

This chapter is organized as follows: The Background References section considers background decision-analysis references for applications work. The Applications Articles and Publications Trends section describes the applications articles that we surveyed for the period 1990–2001 by providing tables that show the application area and methods used for each application, and the overall characteristics of the set of applications, including a comparison with applications from the period 1970–1989 surveyed by Corner and Kirkwood (1991). The Additional Noteworthy Trends and Developments section provides our perspective relative to trends and developments in decision-analysis applications that we observed. The Needs and Concerns section presents our views for the future. In the last section, we present our concluding remarks.

Background References

The vigor and continued development of decision analysis is demonstrated by the substantial number of textbooks and other references on decision-analysis applications that were published between 1990 and 2001. Decision-analysis textbooks include Bell and Schleifer (1995), Clemen (1996), Golub (1997), Goodwin and Wright (1998), Marshall and Oliver (1995), McNamee and Celona (1990, 2001), and Skinner (1999). Kirkwood (1992, 1999) provides brief introductions to decision-analysis methods, whereas Hammond et al. (1999) provide a relatively nonquantitative introduction to systematic decision-analysis procedures. Keeney (1992) presents a value-focused approach to formulating decision problems, and Kirkwood (1997) reviews methods for analyzing decisions with multiple conflicting objectives, including spreadsheet procedures to implement these methods. Oliver and Smith (1990) address influence diagrams, which became widely used during the 1990s.

In addition to these publications of general decision-analysis methods, several publications specifically address probability assessment, approximation procedures, or utility/value function assessment. Shephard and Kirkwood (1994) provide an annotated transcript of a probability elicitation interview that illustrates standard probability elicitation procedures. Morgan and Henrion (1990) address specifics of probability assessment and communication about uncertainty in the context of policy analysis. Clemen et al. (2000) examine methods for assessing probabilistic dependence among pairs of random variables. Keefer (1994) discusses three-point approximations to represent continuous probability distributions in decision-analysis problems, including those where risk preferences are important. Poland (1999) reviews an approximate probabilistic analysis procedure to reduce the assessment and computational complexity of decision analyses with many uncertainties, some of which may be dependent. This work draws on "moment methods" described by Smith (1993), whereby an approximation to the distribution of an output variable is obtained from its moments, which are calculated from moments of the (assessed) input distributions. Keefer (1991) presents a framework for addressing resource allocation decisions with risk aversion and probabilistic dependence. Borcherding et al. (1991) and Lai (2001) provide empirical comparisons of different methods for assessing weights for multiattribute utility and value functions. Edwards (1992) reviews theory and applications issues associated with using expected-utility analysis.

A number of other sources from 1990 to 2001 provide additional reference material relevant for applications. Corner and Corner (1995) summarize the characteristics of decision-analysis applications from 1970 to 1989 that were surveyed by Corner and Kirkwood (1991). Zeckhauser et al. (1996) include some papers of interest for decision-analysis practice, including applications to public policy and medical decision making. Magat et al. (1996) review a general approach for establishing a death-equivalent metric for valuing long-term health effects. Noonan and Vidich (1992) present a decision-analysis framework for utilizing hazardous waste site assessment in real estate acquisition. Two websites were established that provide additional information about decision analysis and its applications, one by the Decision Analysis Society of INFORMS (www.informs.org/Society/DA) and one by the Decision Analysis Affinity Group (www.daag.net).

Applications Articles and Publications Trends

This section summarizes characteristics of the decision-analysis applications articles published in the operations research literature for the period 1990–2001, and compares these to characteristics of applications articles published during the period 1970–1989, as surveyed by Corner and Kirkwood (1991). Table 28.1 shows the journals that were surveyed and the number of decision-analysis applications articles in each journal. The first four rows of this table provide overall summary data for each of the two time periods, including the number of years in each period, the number of journals covered, the total number of applications articles in all of the journals, and the total number of articles in the journals that were covered for both time periods (the "common journals"). Note that the third row of Table 28.1 lists eighty-five applications articles for the period 1970–1989 even though Corner and Kirkwood (1991) show eighty-six applications for that period. This is because Corner and Kirkwood (1991) include one article in the medical category that is a survey, rather than an application, and that article is not included in these comparisons.

The remaining rows of the table relate to the number of applications articles for each journal. For these rows, the second column shows the number of applications articles identified in each journal by Corner and Kirkwood (1991) for the period 1970–1989, the third column shows the number of articles that we identified in each journal for the period 1990–2001, the fourth column shows the average number of applications articles published per year in each journal for the period 1970–1989, and the fifth column shows this average for the period 1990–2001. Finally, the sixth column shows the percent change in the average number of articles published each year from the period 1970–1989 to the period 1990–2001. For example, Table 28.1 shows that there were eighteen decision-analysis applications articles published in *Interfaces* between 1970 and 2001, and forty published in *Interfaces* between 1990 and 2001. Table 28.1 also shows that this corresponds to an average of $18/20 = 0.90$ articles per year between 1970 and 1989 and an average of $40/12 = 3.33$ articles per year between 1990 and 2001. Thus, as shown in the right-most column of the table, there was a $(3.33 - 0.90) / 0.90 = 270$ percent increase in the average number of decision-analysis applications articles published per year in *Interfaces* from 1970–1989 to 1990–2001.

As row 3 shows, we identified eighty-six application articles in the sixteen journals that we surveyed for the period 1990–2001. The set of journals that we surveyed is the same as the set covered for 1970–1989 by Corner and Kirkwood (1991), except that we added the following six journals: the *Journal of Multi-Criteria Decision Analysis* and *Military Operations Research* (two new journals that began publication in the 1990s); *Reliability Engineering and System Safety*, *Research • Technology Management*, and *Theory and Decision* were added to our

Table 28.1. Number of applications articles, by journal, with trends

	Number of articles		Average number of articles per year		
	1970–1989	1990–2001	1970–1989	1990–2001	Percent change
Number of years covered	20	12			
Number of journals covered	10	16			
Total number of articles	85	86	4.25	7.17	69
Total no. of articles (common journals)	85	63	4.25	5.25	24
Decision Sciences	4	1	0.20	0.08	−58
European Journal of OR	5	0	0.25	0.00	−100
IEEE Trans. on Engineering Mgt.	not covered	4		0.33	
IEEE Trans. on SMC	7	1	0.35	0.08	−76
Interfaces	18	40	0.90	3.33	270
Journal of MCDA	not published	6		0.50	
Journal of the OR Society	18	1	0.90	0.08	−91
Management Science	10	4	0.50	0.33	−33
Military OR	not published	8		0.67	
Omega	3	1	0.15	0.08	−44
Operations Research	15	11	0.75	0.92	22
OR Letters	0	0	0.00	0.00	0
Reliability Engr and Sys Safety	not covered	2		0.17	
Research • Tech Mgt	not covered	2		0.17	
Risk Analysis	6	4	0.30	0.33	11
Theory and Decision	not covered	1		0.08	

survey set at the recommendation of knowledgeable individuals; and *IEEE Transactions on Engineering Management,* which we feel is comparable to some of the other journals added. The third row in Table 28.1 shows that there was a 69 percent increase in the average number of decision-analysis applications articles published per year from 1970–1989 to 1990–2001. This substantial increase in the average publication rate may be somewhat overstated because of the six journals that were added for 1990–2001. However, the fourth row in Table 28.1 shows that even without considering those six journals the average annual publication rate increased by 24 percent.

This overall positive trend masks what may be a less positive trend, namely that applications publications appear to be concentrating in a smaller number of journals, most of which are published in the United States. In particular, 47 percent of the applications during the 1990–2001 period were published in *Interfaces*; however, only 21 percent of the applications during the 1970–1989 period were published in that journal. Another 13 percent of the 1990–2001 articles appeared in *Operations Research*, primarily in its OR Practice section (nine of eleven articles) – which, like *Interfaces*, explicitly targets applications. The new journal *Military Operations Research* came in third with 9 percent of the articles. There was a substantial drop in the number of decision-analysis applications articles published in the main European OR journals (*European Journal of Operational Research*, *Journal of the Operational Research Society*, and *Omega*), with decision-analysis applications virtually disappearing from those journals. Although the new *Journal of Multi-Criteria Decision Analysis*, which is based in the United Kingdom, is publishing decision-analysis applications, there appears to be an overall trend for a greater portion of the decision-analysis applications to be published in U.S. journals, and especially in the INFORMS practice journal *Interfaces*.

The increase in decision-analysis applications published by *Interfaces* is partially explained by two milestones. First, in 1995, the new regular column "Practice Abstracts," edited by one of the current authors, began soliciting submissions. This produced six of the forty *Interfaces* applications articles that we survey. Second, two special issues of *Interfaces* appeared between 1990 and 2001 (November–December 1992 and November–December 1999) that focused on decision-analysis applications. These special issues yielded an additional twelve of the forty applications articles published in *Interfaces*. Of course, some of those articles might have been published in *Interfaces* even without the special issues. Also, even if the Practice Abstracts and special issues are ignored, the annual rate of publication of decision-analysis applications in *Interfaces* increased substantially from 1970–1989 to 1990–2001. Note, also, that there were two special decision-analysis issues in journals during the period 1970–1989 (the January–February 1980 issue of *Operations Research* and the April 1982 issue of the *Journal of the Operational Research Society*). Therefore, the overall count of decision-analysis applications articles should not be significantly skewed by these special issues, and it is clear that there was a significant increase in the rate of publication of applications articles from 1970–1989 to 1990–2001.

Table 28.2. Application articles listed by application area

Energy
Bidding and Pricing: Keefer (1995), Keefer et al. (1991), Kidd and Prabhu (1990).

Environmental Risk: Balson et al. (1992), French (1996), Hämäläinen et al. (2000), Keeney and von Winterfeldt (1991), Procaccia et al. (1997).

Product and Project Selection: Borison (1995), Burnett et al. (1993), Dyer et al. (1990), Keeney et al. (1995), Parnell (2001), Smith and McCardle (1999), Walls et al. (1995).

Strategy: Keeney and McDaniels (1992), Keeney and McDaniels (1999), Skaf (1999).

Technology Choice: Dyer et al. (1998), Jackson et al. (1999), Perdue and Kumar (1999), Toland et al. (1998), von Winterfeldt and Schweitzer (1998).

Miscellaneous: Dunning et al. (2001), Rios Insua and Salewicz (1995), Taha and Wolf (1996).

Manufacturing and services
Finance: Engemann and Miller (1992), Mulvey (1994).

Product Planning: Beccue (2001), Dillon and Haimes (1996), Keeney (2000), Millet (1994), Yassine et al. (1999).

R&D Project Selection: Bruggink (1997), Hess (1993), Islei et al. (1991), Perdue et al. (1999), Rzasa et al. (1990), Spradlin and Kutoloski (1999), Stonebraker et al. (1997), Thurston (1990).

Strategy: Bodily and Allen (1999), Clemen and Kwit (2001), Keeney (1999b), Krumm and Rolle (1992), Kusnic and Owen (1992), Matheson and Matheson (1999), Quaddus et al. (1992).

Miscellaneous: Chien and Sainfort (1998).

Medical
Brown (1997), Feinstein (1990), Hazen et al. (1998), Smith and Winkler (1999), Winkler et al. (1995).

Military
Bresnick et al. (1997), Buede and Bresnick (1992), Burk and Parnell (1997), Davis et al. (1999), Davis et al. (2000), Doyle et al. (2000), Griggs et al. (1997), Jackson et al. (1997), Kerchner et al. (2001), Parnell et al. (1998), Parnell et al. (2001), Rayno et al. (1997), Stafira et al. (1997).

Public policy
Bana e Costa (2001), Hall et al. (1992), Heger and White (1997), Jones et al. (1990), Keeney (1997), Keeney and McDaniels (2001), Keeney and von Winterfeldt (1994), Keeney et al. (1990), Lehmkuhl et al. (2001), McDaniels (1995), Reagan-Cirincione et al. (1991), Spector (1993), Taylor et al. (1993).

General
Baker et al. (2000), Hurley (1998), Keller and Kirkwood (1999), Matzkevich and Abramson (1995), Paté-Cornell and Fischbeck (1994), Vári and Vecsenyi (1992).

Classification of Applications Areas, with Trends

In Table 28.2, each applications article that we surveyed for the period 1990–2001 is classified into exactly one of the applications areas or subareas shown in that table. The area/subarea selected for a particular article is the one that, on balance, is most emphasized in the article. This table is presented as a guide for readers who are interested in finding applications articles that address specific application

Table 28.3. Number of applications articles by application area, with trends

	Number of articles	
	1970–1989	1990–2001
Energy	**24**	**26**
Bidding (and pricing)	3	3
Environmental risk	NA*	5
Product and project selection	4	7
Regulation	5	NA
Site selection	8	NA
Strategy	NA	3
Technology choice	4	5
Miscellaneous	NA	3
Manufacturing and services	**16**	**23**
Budget allocation	3	NA
Finance	NA	2
Product planning	4	5
R&D project selection	NA	8
Strategy	5	7
Miscellaneous	4	1
Medical	**16**	**5**
Military	**NA**	**13**
Public policy	**20**	**13**
Standard setting	8	NA
Miscellaneous	12	13
General	**9**	**6**

* Not applicable.

areas. Brief summaries of all of these articles are included in the technical report by Keefer et al. (2002).

Table 28.3 compares the application area for the articles published during the period 1970–1989 (Corner and Kirkwood 1991) with the application area for the articles that we surveyed. There are some differences in our classification scheme relative to the scheme used by Corner and Kirkwood (1991) because of shifts in decision-analysis application areas between 1970–1989 and 1990–2001. (A classification category that is not used in one of the two survey articles is indicated in Table 28.3 with a "Not Applicable (NA)" entry.) However, we used similar classification areas to those in Corner and Kirkwood (1991) to the extent possible to facilitate comparisons between the two time periods.

Because of the slightly different classification categories, as well as the addition of some new journals and the differing lengths of the two time periods compared in Table 28.3, caution should be used in drawing conclusions about trends in applications. However, there are some significant points. First, within the energy area, there appears to have been a shift toward applications in environmental risk, product and project selection, and strategy, and away from regulation and site selection. Overall, energy continues to be a significant application area for decision analysis. Within manufacturing and services, R&D project selection applications increased during the period 1990–2001 to the extent that we include a separate category for these applications, which was not needed by Corner and Kirkwood (1991) for the period 1970–1989.

Medical applications published in the OR literature dropped substantially between 1970–1989 and 1990–2001. However, we believe this is because decision-analysis methods are now so well established within the medical community that most medical decision-analysis applications are published in medical journals and other journals focusing on medical decision making. Published military applications increased from virtually none in the period 1970–1989 to the extent that the numbers now justify a separate military category. This appears to be due in part to the new journal *Military Operations Research*, which has published a substantial number of decision-analysis applications since it was established in 1994. Finally, although public policy applications still continue at a substantial rate, there was not a sufficiently large number of these during the 1990–2001 period focused on standard setting to justify a separate subcategory for these.

Methodological and Implementation Issues, with Trends

Table 28.4 lists those application articles that present significant detail about a particular decision-analysis methodological or implementation issue. Many articles deal with nearly all of the methodological and implementation issues shown in that table, but an article is included in Table 28.4 only if it provides detailed information on a topic. Thus, this table can be used to identify articles that emphasize a particular methodological or implementation issue. Articles are included in the strategy and/or objectives generation category if they discuss overall decision strategy and/or present an objectives or value hierarchy, or discuss the decision structuring process in detail. Articles are included in the problem structuring/formulation category if they describe and present a decision tree and/or influence diagram and discuss its development and use. The probability assessment category includes articles that discuss the elicitation of subjective probabilities, probabilistic dependence or independence, and/or risk assessment. Similarly, articles are listed in the utility assessment category if subjective utility/value functions or trade-offs between attributes are discussed in depth. Articles are listed in the sensitivity analysis category if tornado or rainbow diagrams, or something similar, are presented and/or statistical or mathematical approaches to model sensitivity analysis are discussed.

The communication/facilitation category includes articles that discuss the role of the analyst, how decision analysis facilitates the decision process, and/or how communication channels are opened because of the use of the approach. Articles are included in the group issues category if there is discussion about aggregating individual preferences into a group function, or discussion of the solicitation and treatment of multiple individual inputs into the preference or probability model. Finally, the implementation category includes articles that discuss postmodeling issues related to implementing chosen alternatives or the value of decision-analysis techniques for the individuals or organization in their decision making efforts.

Table 28.4. Application articles addressing methodological and implementation issues

Strategy and/or objectives generation
Baker et al. (2000), Bana e Costa (2001), Bodily and Allen (1999), Bresnick et al. (1997), Brown (1997), Buede and Bresnick (1992), Burk and Parnell (1997), Burnett et al. (1993), Chien and Sainfort (1998), Davis et al. (1999), Davis et al. (2000), Doyle et al. (2000), Dyer et al. (1998), Dyer et al. (1990), French (1996), Hämäläinen et al. (2000), Islei et al. (1991), Jackson et al. (1997), Jackson et al. (1999), Jones et al. (1990), Keeney (1999b), Keeney and McDaniels (1992, 1999, 2001) Keeney et al. (1995), Keeney and von Winterfeldt (1994), Keeney et al. (1990), Keller and Kirkwood (1999), Kerchner et al. (2001), Krumm and Rolle (1992), Kusnic and Owen (1992), Lehmkuhl et al. (2001), McDaniels (1995), Parnell et al. (1998), Parnell et al. (2001), Perdue and Kumar (1999), Rayno et al. (1997), Reagan-Cirincione et al. (1991), Skaf (1999), Spector (1993), Spradlin and Kutoloski (1999), von Winterfeldt and Schweitzer (1998).

Problem structuring/formulation (via decision trees and influence diagrams)
Balson et al. (1992), Bodily and Allen (1999), Borison (1995), Brown (1997), Dillon and Haimes (1996), Dunning et al. (2001), Dyer et al. (1998), Dyer et al. (1990), Engemann and Miller (1992), Feinstein (1990), Griggs et al. (1997), Hazen et al. (1998), Heger and White (1997), Hess (1993), Jackson et al. (1999), Keefer (1995), Keefer et al. (1991), Keeney (1997), Keeney et al. (1995), Keeney and von Winterfeldt (1994), Krumm and Rolle (1992), Matheson and Matheson (1999), Matzkevich and Abramson (1995), Millet (1994), Perdue et al. (1999), Quaddus et al. (1992), Rzasa et al. (1990), Smith and McCardle (1999), Smith and Winkler (1999), Stafira et al. (1997), Stonebraker et al. (1997), Taylor et al. (1993), Walls et al. (1995), Yassine et al. (1999).

Probability assessment
Balson et al. (1992), Chien and Sainfort (1998), Dillon and Haimes (1996), Dunning et al. (2001), Dyer et al. (1990), Feinstein (1990), Keefer (1995), Keeney et al. (1995), Keeney and von Winterfeldt (1991), Keeney and von Winterfeldt (1994), McDaniels (1995), Paté-Cornell and Fischbeck (1994), Perdue et al. (1999), Procaccia et al. (1997), Smith and McCardle (1999), Smith and Winkler (1999), Stafira et al. (1997), Taha and Wolf (1996), Taylor et al. (1993), von Winterfeldt and Schweitzer (1998), Winkler et al. (1995), Yassine et al. (1999).

Utility/value assessment
Baker et al. (2000), Bana e Costa (2001), Bresnick et al. (1997), Burk and Parnell (1997), Doyle et al. (2000), Dyer et al. (1998), Dyer et al. (1990), Hall et al. (1992), Hämäläinen et al. (2000), Hazen et al. (1998), Jackson et al. (1997), Jackson et al. (1999), Keeney (2000), Keeney and McDaniels (1992), Keeney and McDaniels (1999), Keeney et al. (1995), Keeney and von Winterfeldt (1994), Keeney et al. (1990), Kerchner et al. (2001), Kidd and Prabhu (1990), Lehmkuhl et al. (2001), McDaniels (1995), Mulvey (1994), Parnell et al. (1998), Rayno et al. (1997), Rios Insua and Salewicz (1995), Thurston (1990), Walls et al. (1995).

Sensitivity analysis
Baker et al. (2000), Bana e Costa (2001), Bodily and Allen (1999), Brown (1997), Doyle et al. (2000), Dyer et al. (1998), Hess (1993), Jackson et al. (1999), Keeney and von Winterfeldt (1994), Kerchner et al. (2001), Lehmkuhl et al. (2001), McDaniels (1995), Millet (1994), Perdue et al. (1999), Quaddus et al. (1992), Reagan-Cirincione et al. (1991), Smith and Winkler (1999), Spradlin and Kutoloski (1999), Stafira et al. (1997), Taylor et al. (1993), Thurston (1990), Walls et al. (1995), Yassine et al. (1999).

(continued)

Table 28.4 (*continued*)

Communication/facilitation
Bodily and Allen (1999), Borison (1995), Bresnick et al. (1997), Feinstein (1990), French (1996), Hämäläinen et al. (2000), Islei et al. (1991), Jones et al. (1990), Keefer (1995), Keefer et al. (1991), Keeney (1999b), Keeney and McDaniels (1992), Keeney and McDaniels (1999), Keeney et al. (1995), Keeney et al. (1990), Keller and Kirkwood (1999), Kerchner et al. (2001), Krumm and Rolle (1992), Kusnic and Owen (1992), Lehmkuhl et al. (2001), McDaniels (1995), Quaddus et al. (1992), Reagan-Cirincione et al. (1991), Skaf (1999), Spector (1993), Spradlin and Kutoloski (1999), Vári and Vecsenyi (1992), von Winterfeldt and Schweitzer (1998), Winkler et al. (1995).

Group issues
Baker et al. (2000), Bana e Costa (2001), Bresnick et al. (1997), Hämäläinen et al. (2000), Keeney and McDaniels (1999), Keeney et al. (1990), Keller and Kirkwood (1999), Kusnic and Owen (1992), Quaddus et al. (1992), Reagan-Cirincione et al. (1991), Vári and Vecsenyi (1992), Winkler et al. (1995).

Implementation
Baker et al. (2000), Bodily and Allen (1999), Burk and Parnell (1997), Doyle et al. (2000), Dyer et al. (1990), Engemann and Miller (1992), Islei et al. (1991), Jackson et al. (1997), Keefer et al. (1991), Keeney and McDaniels (1992), Keeney and McDaniels (1999), Keeney et al. (1995), Keeney and von Winterfeldt (1994), Keeney et al. (1990), Keller and Kirkwood (1999), Kerchner et al. (2001), Kusnic and Owen (1992), Lehmkuhl et al. (2001), Parnell et al. (1998), Parnell et al. (2001), Paté-Cornell and Fischbeck (1994), Rzasa et al. (1990), Skaf (1999), Smith and Winkler (1999), Spradlin and Kutoloski (1999), Vári and Vecsenyi (1992), Walls et al. (1995).

Table 28.5 compares the classifications of articles by methodological and implementation issues in Corner and Kirkwood's (1991) survey of application during the 1970–1989 period with our classification for applications during the 1990–2001 period. As with the comparison of application areas in Table 28.3, caution is warranted in interpreting Table 28.5. Specifically, the classification categories that we use for our survey of 1990–2001 applications is somewhat different from Corner and Kirkwood's (1991) classification categories because of changes in methodological and implementation issues that are emphasized in the articles. However, some general conclusions can be drawn about trends in methodological and implementation issues.

First, Corner and Kirkwood's (1991) classification categories "problem structuring/formulation" and "decision trees" for the 1970–1989 applications do not adequately represent the corresponding topics in the 1990–2001 applications. A new classification category "strategy and/or objectives generation" was added primarily because of the expanded use of value-focused thinking approaches in a variety of applications. Corner and Kirkwood's (1991) category "decision trees" was expanded to "problem structuring/formulation (via decision trees and influence diagrams)," primarily because of the expanded use of influence diagrams during the 1990–2001 period. A new category, "sensitivity analysis," was added because of the expanded discussion in the 1990–2001 articles of such sensitivity analysis methods as tornado and rainbow diagrams. Of course, sensitivity analysis was well

Table **28.5.** Number of applications articles by methodological and implementation issue, with trends

	Number of articles	
	1970–1989	1990–2001
Strategy and/or objectives generation	NA*	42
Problem structuring/formulation	24	34
Decision trees	36	NA
Probability assessment	15	22
Utility/value assessment	28	28
Sensitivity analysis	NA	23
Communication/facilitation	23	29
Group decision making (issues)	13	12
Implementation	NA	27

* Not applicable.

recognized prior to 1990 as an important part of decision analysis, but it received substantially increased emphasis in the articles published in the 1990–2001 period relative to its emphasis in the 1970–1989 period. Although we cannot say for certain why this is true, it seems reasonable that the expanded use of spreadsheets and personal-computer decision-analysis packages may have facilitated conducting and reporting sensitivity analyses.

Finally, a new "implementation" category was added because of the expanded consideration of this topic in published applications. Of course, implementation has always been important in applications. The increase in emphasis on implementation in the 1990–2001 publications relative to the 1970–1989 publications may be due in part to the increased concentration of articles in *Interfaces*, as well as the substantial number of articles appearing in the new journal, *Military Operations Research*, which appears to encourage emphasis on implementation issues.

Additional Noteworthy Trends and Developments

In the preceding section, we discuss trends based primarily on counts and classifications of the applications articles that we surveyed. In this section, we draw more broadly on the contents of the applications articles to discuss a number of additional noteworthy trends and developments relevant to decision-analysis applications and practice between 1990 and 2001. In addition, we note developments in professional societies relevant to decision-analysis practice and cite award-winning entries in practice competitions. The specific sources highlighted in this section, some of which are not applications articles, are those that fit within these trends and developments. As indicated above, the companion technical report to this article (Keefer et al. 2002) contains brief summaries of *all* the applications articles that we surveyed, including additional information about those highlighted in this section.

General Trends and Developments

COMPUTER SOFTWARE AND RELATED TOOLS. During the period 1990–2001, increasingly powerful personal-computer decision-analysis software was developed, refined, and used in applications. This facilitated more widespread use of decision-analysis tools developed in the 1980s such as influence diagrams and strategy tables, and tornado diagrams for sensitivity analysis. It also facilitated structuring and analyzing larger decision-analysis models. For example, in an analysis to help the New York Power Authority develop a 10-year schedule for refueling its Indian Point 3 Nuclear Power Plant, Dunning et al. (2001) used software in applying a spectrum of decision-analysis tools including strategy tables, an influence diagram, and a decision tree with more than 200 million paths. Similarly, in a study to help Amgen select a strategy for developing and commercializing a new drug, Beccue (2001) employed a variety of software-based decision-analysis tools including an influence diagram, a tornado diagram, and a decision tree with approximately 500,000 scenarios for each of eight key strategies that were identified via a strategy table.

Regarding overall software developments, Call and Miller (1990) discuss computational approaches to automating decision-analysis calculation procedures. Stand-alone software packages using decision trees and/or influence diagrams that were developed or updated during the period 1990–2001 include DATA, DPL, and Supertree, and spreadsheet decision-analysis add-ins include PrecisionTree and TreePlan. Even stand-alone packages are often used in conjunction with spreadsheet models, which are used pervasively in practice. Development also continued on the stand-alone software package Logical Decisions that specifically focuses on decisions with multiple objectives. Several of these packages are now available in conjunction with decision analysis or basic OR textbooks. Current information about these and other software packages can be obtained from the Decision Analysis Society website or from the biennial surveys of decision-analysis software in *ORMS Today* (Maxwell 2002).

DECISION CONFERENCING. A decision conference is an intensive computer-assisted group meeting, or workshop, focused on a specific decision problem and utilizing outside facilitators skilled in decision analysis and group facilitation techniques. The idea is to generate and evaluate alternatives in a structured fashion and use real-time quantitative models to help the group reach consensus on a preferred alternative while avoiding "groupthink" pitfalls. Decision conferences typically last about two days. Although originated prior to the period surveyed in this article, decision conferencing has become more prominent in applications in the OR literature during the period covered by this survey, perhaps in part due to improvements in computer software and hardware. This approach offers a powerful synthesis of techniques from decision analysis, decision-support systems, and group management. (See Chapter 19 in this volume, "Decision Conferencing," by Lawrence Phillips for a detailed presentation of the approach and his pioneering work in the field.)

Decision conferencing is most often applied in conjunction with multiattribute value models, and typically in the public sector. Bresnick et al. (1997) and Buede and Bresnick (1992) describe military applications utilizing decision conferences and multiattribute models. French (1996) and Hämäläinen et al. (2000) discuss the use of decision conferences and multiattribute analysis for nuclear accident management in conjunction with the RODOS project, a European initiative to build a decision support system for emergency response. Reagan-Cirincione et al. (1991) and Quaddus et al. (1992) describe multiattribute applications involving, respectively, strategic policy options for medical malpractice insurance for the New York State Insurance Department and strategic planning in a volunteer organization providing services to the disabled. Vári and Vecsenyi (1992) discuss the use of decision-analysis methods in conjunction with twenty-six decision conferences on a variety of decision problems for manufacturing, services, and government organizations in Hungary.

STOCHASTIC TREES. Stochastic trees were developed during the period covered by our survey to aid medical decision making. They combine features of continuous-time Markov chains with those of decision trees and, in particular, enable time to be modeled as a continuum where health state transitions can occur at any instant. They retain the familiar rollback procedure for decision trees and can also accommodate risk preferences via utility functions. Hazen et al. (1998) and Pellissier et al. (1996) review stochastic tree analysis methods and their application to hip replacement surgery.

This is an exciting development for decision analysis in an important application area. The basic assumption that health state transitions can occur at any moment in continuous time appears to be natural in the medical context, and the case for applying stochastic trees more widely to medical decision problems seems persuasive. Understandably, additional medical applications are likely to appear primarily in the medical literature rather than the OR literature. Methodological developments continue in this relatively new area (see, for example, Hazen 2000).

VALUE-FOCUSED THINKING. Keeney (1992, 1994, 1999a, 2001) makes the case for using values as the primary driver for problem structuring and analysis, including the generation of alternatives, and provides methods to aid in this process, as well as illustrative examples. This *value-focused thinking* expands on earlier work on multiattribute utility and value models, and has been a major force in increasing the number and scope of multiattribute applications, as well as the quantity and quality of alternatives generated in decision analyses.

In particular, the book by Keeney (1992) on value-focused thinking, along with the spreadsheet-oriented text on multiobjective decision analysis by Kirkwood (1997), appears to have been influential in military applications during the survey period. For example, Burk and Parnell (1997), Davis et al. (2000), Doyle et al. (2000), Jackson et al. (1997), Kerchner et al. (2001), Parnell et al. (1998), and Parnell et al. (2001) all describe military applications that make prominent use of value-focused thinking and multiattribute value models. All of these articles cite Keeney (1992), and all except for Burk and Parnell (1997) cite Kirkwood (1997).

Baker et al. (2000), Keeney (1999b), Keeney and McDaniels (1992, 2001), and Lehmkuhl et al. (2001) describe applications of value-focused thinking in other areas, including strategy and public policy. Drawing on both the descriptive and prescriptive literature on decision making, Corner et al. (2001) suggest a dynamic synthesis of value-focused thinking with alternative-focused thinking.

Interdisciplinary Trends and Developments

Each of the following trends or developments links decision-analysis methods with another discipline and, thus, is a synthesis of traditional decision analysis with another established discipline. Because of the interdisciplinary nature of these trends and developments, we include several sources beyond the OR applications literature that was considered in our survey.

NORMATIVE SYSTEMS. Connections between decision analysis and artificial intelligence (AI) methods have been increasingly recognized, and this has led to significant research and applications, much of which has been published outside of the OR literature. There were a variety of creative applications involving combinations of decision analysis and AI methods over the period covered by our survey. Henrion et al. (1991) provide an extensive introduction to the connections between decision analysis and knowledge-based expert systems. Matzkevich and Abramson (1995) survey and synthesize research from the decision analysis and AI communities involving influence diagrams and belief networks. Their discussion of *normative systems*, which are AI systems based on influence diagrams or belief nets and thus on Bayesian principles, is of particular interest. They provide brief descriptions of several implemented systems in areas including medical diagnosis, energy price and demand forecasting, and machine vision. Silverman (1994) focuses on approaches to unifying expert systems methods with mathematical modeling approaches to decision making, including decision analysis. Hedbert (1998) reviews decision-analysis-oriented work at Microsoft Research, including development of a Bayesian-based system for automating more responsive interfaces that was applied to the Office Assistant in Microsoft Office.

This area appears to have great potential for additional applications. Further information about decision-analysis methods in AI can be found at the website of the Association for Uncertainty in Artificial Intelligence at www.auai.org.

ORGANIZATIONAL PROCESSES. As decision analysis has matured, increasing attention has been devoted to specifying procedures for conducting and implementing decision analysis successfully in organizations. In large-scale strategic decision analyses in particular, a well-defined process typically is used for managing the efforts of, and the interactions between, carefully constructed teams composed of analysts, managers, and executives. Such a process typically is used first in structuring and analyzing the decision problem at hand and then in following through to manage and carry out recommended action plans and accompanying changes. Organizational processes for decision analysis were developed within decision-analysis consulting and practitioner groups in the 1980s, but were not widely known outside these groups until the 1990s. Bodily and Allen (1999) review a dialogue process to manage the interaction between decision analysts and other stakeholders in a decision. Kusnic and Owen (1992), Krumm and Rolle (1992), and Skaf (1999) provide guidance on conducting and implementing large-scale decision analyses within major industrial firms, including the effective use of teams and large databases, as well as methods for dealing with multiple decision makers. Matheson and Matheson (1999) discuss the use of an *outside–in* approach to take better account of a company's external environment during strategic decision analysis. Clemen and Kwit (2001) review the history of decision and risk analysis at Eastman Kodak Company from the early 1980s to 2001 and summarize the characteristics of 178 projects conducted between 1990 and 1999.

In related work, Horowitz (1990) provides several different authors' perspectives on organizational decision making from a decision-analysis point of view. Bordley (2001) compares and contrasts conventional decision analysis as commonly applied in industrial practice with *soft OR* techniques and finds much in common between decision analysis and classical interactive planning. Kasanen et al. (2000) examine characteristics of six major real-world decision processes relative to common assumptions or myths in the multicriteria decision making and multiattribute utility fields, and suggest changes in assumptions and practices to make models from these fields more widely useful.

Decision-analysis frameworks for R&D organizational planning processes received particular attention. Bordley (1998) considers organizational issues related to using decision analysis for R&D project selection and emphasizes the benefits of stimulating researchers to develop better projects by improving communications. Matheson et al. (1994), Matheson and Menke (1994), and Menke (1994) review decision-analysis approaches to R&D planning. Matheson and Matheson (1998) present a framework for applying decision-analysis methods to R&D strategy.

As a result of the work cited above, considerable additional guidance is now available concerning processes for successfully conducting and implementing a major decision-analysis project within an organization.

REAL OPTIONS. During the period covered by this survey, the importance of modeling sequential decisions in conjunction with the resolution of uncertainties over time became more widely recognized. Downstream decision alternatives provide *real options* that can increase flexibility in managing real-world projects with evolving risks, and these real options are analogous to financial options. In R&D projects, for instance, the cost of conducting research can be viewed as the price of a call option to develop or commercialize a new product subsequently, and exercising this option incurs an additional cost (the exercise price). Relevant methodologies for addressing decisions with real options include larger decision trees, dynamic programming, and financial options methods (Amram and Kulatilaka 1999, Dixit and Pindyck 1994, and Trigeorgis 1996). Smith (1999) provides a concise nontechnical overview of the similarities and differences between conventional decision analysis and the real-options approach.

Several authors have pointed out the benefits of *options thinking* in providing more realistic evaluations than traditional analyses. For instance, Morris et al. (1991) use an options framework in conjunction with a simple decision tree to demonstrate that the riskier of two R&D projects having the same expected value is typically the better choice when sequencing is properly incorporated. Faulkner (1996) provides a brief, nontechnical introduction to real options, and based on several years of experience at Eastman Kodak, describes the advantages of evaluating R&D projects as sequential adaptive strategies. Pauwels et al. (2000) illustrate the advantages of applying options thinking along with conventional decision-analysis tools in emergency response situations by analyzing a simple two-period nuclear incident evacuation model. Benaroch (2001) presents methods for structuring and evaluating multiple, possibly interacting, operating options in technology investments and includes an illustrative example involving establishment of an internet-based sales channel. Howard (1996) provides an overview of various types of options in decision problems and emphasizes the importance of recognizing and creating, as well as modeling, these options, and he illustrates several evaluation methods.

Perdue et al. (1999) discuss a method using both options-pricing techniques and decision-analysis tools in R&D planning. Smith and McCardle (1999) provide a tutorial introduction to options-pricing methods and their integration with decision-analysis methods, with a focus on evaluating oil and gas investments. Real options have also received attention outside the traditional journal literature, such as in various conferences of the Society of Petroleum Engineers (SPE). (Abstracts, as well as ordering instructions, for SPE conference papers are on the web at www.spe.org.) For instance, Claeys and Walkup (1999) discuss framing techniques used to ensure that all key options and uncertainties are included and illustrate use of these on examples from several actual petroleum valuation efforts. Gallant et al. (1999) discuss learning models for analyzing dynamic complexity, that is, changes in information over time, and illustrate their use in exploration and production examples based on actual projects. Faiz (2000) discusses how real-options valuation, a combination of options-pricing theory and decision analysis, relates to other popular management tools, such as portfolio optimization, and provides illustrative real-world case studies.

As suggested by Smith (1999), both decision analysis and finance professionals could benefit from learning more about each other's tools and incorporating them into models appropriately. Although a number of applications in our survey used real-options thinking in generating downstream options, we found only two articles that provided in-depth descriptions of applications where real-options methods were combined with conventional decision-analysis methods (Perdue et al. 1999 and Smith and McCardle 1999). Hence, the potential synergism has not yet had a major impact on published applications.

Practice Competitions and Professional Societies

In this section, we highlight decision-analysis applications that achieved significant recognition in practice competitions held by professional societies during the survey period. In addition, we discuss the founding and progress of a new professional group for decision analysis practitioners.

EDELMAN AWARD COMPETITION. During the period covered by this survey, three applications of decision analysis became finalists in the Franz Edelman Award competition held annually by INFORMS to recognize and reward outstanding examples of management science and operations research practice worldwide. Burnett et al. (1993) describe the long-term use of a project appraisal methodology (PAM) within the Gas Research Institute's annual five-year R&D planning process. PAM calculates benefit-to-cost ratios for R&D projects at multiple levels of funding to aid in allocating the R&D budget, obtaining expected benefits at each level by using a multiattribute scoring function and judgmental probabilities for technical and commercial successes. The authors estimate that benefits from using PAM have been in the tens of billions of dollars.

Paté-Cornell and Fischbeck (1994) perform a probabilistic risk analysis of failure of the exterior surface tiles on the United States' space shuttle orbiter. Expert opinion and the experience of the first thirty shuttle flights were used to build a decomposed model of risk for various zones on the shuttle's tile-bearing surface. The analysis showed that roughly 15 percent of the tiles contribute 85 percent of the risk of failure. The study further highlighted organizational factors that contribute to potential tile failure risks and led to various policy changes in the management and maintenance of the tiles.

Von Winterfeldt and Schweitzer (1998) describe an analysis to help the U.S. Department of Energy choose which tritium-supply alternatives to pursue to replenish tritium for the U.S. nuclear weapons stockpile. Ten alternatives were evaluated with respect to production assurance, cost, and environmental impacts based in part on multiple-expert probability assessments and results from a dynamic production-simulation model. The analysis was influential in shaping the final choice by the U.S. Secretary of Energy, and its defensibility helped avoid lawsuits from vendors whose alternatives were not chosen.

As a result of his experience with this entry in the Edelman Award competition, von Winterfeldt worked to establish the Practice Award (see below) of the Decision Analysis Society of INFORMS (DAS), while serving as the DAS Chair. We anticipate that the DAS Practice Award competition will stimulate additional entries from decision analysis in the Edelman Award competition in the future.

DECISION ANALYSIS SOCIETY PRACTICE AWARD. In 1999, DAS inaugurated an annual Practice Award to recognize, promote, and publicize good decision-analysis practice. The competition for the award begins with submission of a brief written summary of a recent decision-analysis application and culminates with presentations by the finalists at a DAS-sponsored session at the annual INFORMS meeting. The winners of the first Practice Award in 1999 were Mazen A. Skaf of Navigant Consulting, Inc., and Donald W. Spillman of Shell (Oil) Offshore, Inc., for "A Portfolio Management Process and System for an Upstream Oil and Gas Organization." This project, described in Skaf (1999), produced a portfolio management process and system that was used to help manage a large portfolio of upstream oil and gas assets in the Gulf of Mexico through exploration, development, and production, and to provide analytical support for a variety of portfolio, lease-bidding, drilling, development, and resource-requirements decisions. The system uses a variety of decision-analysis tools and concepts, and its use has significantly impacted the client organization, including value added in the hundreds of millions of dollars.

The winner in 2000 was David A. Mauney of Structural Integrity Associates, Inc., for "Best Practices in the Application of Decision/Financial Analysis to Repair/Replacement Decisions of Plant Components." This work developed a process that uses optimization techniques in conjunction with a risk-based decision model to aid in planning the timing of major maintenance investments for fossil-fuel power plants. Where necessary, this process includes interviews tailored to obtain judgmental probability data from plant personnel most familiar with the components. Its application in the power industry has resulted in savings in the tens of millions of dollars.

The 2001 winner was Eric Johnson of Pharsight Corporation for "Life Cycle Strategy Analysis," which is described in Johnson and Petty (2003). In this study, consultants from Pharsight helped a client firm reach consensus on a development strategy for a cancer drug. They used a variety of decision-analysis methods to construct and evaluate a manageable number of candidate strategies, and they subsequently succeeded in constructing a hybrid strategy with an expected NPV $50 million greater than that of any of the original candidate strategies and $100 million greater than that of the status quo strategy.

DECISION ANALYSIS AFFINITY GROUP. No discussion of decision-analysis practice over the 1990–2001 period would be complete without mentioning the Decision Analysis Affinity Group (DAAG), which was founded in 1995 to promote the use of decision analysis in industry and to further the development and careers of industrial practitioners. Since 1995, DAAG has held annual conferences focusing on the use and implementation of decision analysis within major corporations. This has successfully filled an important niche for decision-analysis practitioners, and recent conferences have typically attracted 75 to 100 participants. Historically, to create an open and collegial atmosphere among peers, attendance by consultants and academics was discouraged and was limited to those explicitly invited for some purpose such as a presentation. Beginning with the 2002 conference, this policy was liberalized (Spradlin and Skinner 2001).

Although some DAAG members are also members of DAS and/or INFORMS, most are not and have no desire to become members. Furthermore, most DAAG members have little or no interest in, or motivation for, publishing. Despite the differences in focus between DAS and DAAG, we hope the change in attendance policy for DAAG conferences will lead to more interaction and collaboration between these two groups. Additional information about DAAG and its conferences, including abstracts and presentations, is available at the DAAG website (www.daag.net).

Needs and Concerns

In the preceding two sections, we identified a number of trends and developments in decision-analysis applications and practice based primarily on our survey of the OR literature. These are predominately positive, and thus, encouraging for the future of decision analysis. In this section, we describe some needs and potential pitfalls for the continued advancement of decision-analysis practice. These reflect our personal perspectives, and we hope what follows will stimulate discussion and debate, as well as additional research and action.

Status in Companies and Universities

It is well-documented that the number of internal OR groups within corporations has decreased in recent years (for example, see Fildes and Ranyard 2000), and there is evidence that decision-analysis groups are subject to the same factors that affect internal corporate OR groups. Recent examples where decision-analysis groups have in effect been disbanded include Eastman Kodak (Clemen and Kwit 2001) and General Motors (Lieberman 2002). Moreover, decision analysis itself, not just the corresponding internal group, has fallen in and out of favor in a number of corporations over the years. Spradlin (2001) suggests that many internal decision-analysis consulting groups are likely to disappear unless they redefine themselves to look like something else and that decision analyses, where done at all, will be done either by the business units themselves or by external consultants. Additional research into factors that influence the rise and fall of internal decision-analysis groups and of decision analysis itself within corporations could help strengthen the position of decision analysis within corporations.

Even among INFORMS members, "decision analysis" does not convey the unambiguous meaning that "linear programming" or "queueing" does. For instance, *Interfaces* classifies many articles under decision analysis, presumably because they involve some sort of analysis of decisions, that we would not recognize as decision analysis. (In fact, we found during our survey of applications that key word searches in indices and even article abstracts were of limited value because of the differing definitions that various authors use for the term "decision analysis.") The coverage of decision analysis in many OR/MS textbooks largely focuses on mechanics and mathematics and omits such important topics as problem structuring, probability assessment, cognitive biases, and discretization of continuous distributions. Computer scientists often do not mean what we mean when they use the term "decision trees." Hopefully, the contents of the new journal *Decision Analysis* will help to delineate the field more clearly.

Since the founding of decision analysis, a small group of institutions have been the primary sources of ideas, methodological tools, and well-trained graduate students. (See Raiffa 2002 for an interesting personal account of the origin and evolution of the field, including the origin of the "decision analysis" name.) Our concern is that education for decision analysis practitioners and faculty appears to depend on specific individuals; as retirements continue in academia and as acquisitions, reorientations, and retirements continue at decision analysis consulting firms, well-trained decision analysts may become harder to find – particularly those having both strong academic backgrounds and practical experience with applications. Development of tools, software, and innovations in organizational implementation, which have often come from the consulting firms, could also suffer. As an old country-music song asks, "Who's gonna fill those shoes?" It is worth noting that the Decision Education Foundation (www.decisioneducation.org) is focusing on educating high school students, as well as their teachers and parents, in better decision making approaches. This is certainly laudable, but it is not a replacement for strong decision analysis programs at the university level.

Better Tools

Here, we briefly highlight two additional areas where we think further developments could significantly enhance the applicability of decision analysis in practice. (The preceding section included discussion of several noteworthy methodological developments that had an impact on decision-analysis applications during the 1990–2001 period. Of course, further progress in those areas would also be welcome.)

First, better methods are needed for modeling and assessing probabilistic dependence among random variables. Whether the variables are discrete, continuous, or discrete representations of continuous variables, the size and complexity of the assessment task grows rapidly with the number of dependent random variables unless simplifying assumptions are made. In practice, independence is often assumed, and this typically is adequate if expected value is the sole criterion of choice and the output variable (e.g., NPV) is a linear, or nearly linear, function of the random variables. However, assuming independence can introduce significant errors if substantial nonlinearities are present – which can affect the accuracy of the expected value – or if the entire distribution of the output variable is of interest, for example, because of risk aversion. Keefer (1991) shows that conditional independence, perfect positive dependence, and combinations thereof can be useful in modeling dependence in the context of bidding for oil and gas leases. In the context of business portfolios, Poland (1999) addresses interbusiness dependencies by conditioning evaluations for individual businesses on "global" outcome scenarios for variables that have an impact on multiple businesses, and treats business-specific random variables as independent across businesses. Recently, constructing approximate joint probability distributions via multivariate functions called copulas, which use dependence information such as correlations to combine univariate marginal distributions, has received considerable attention (Clemen and Reilly 1999; Clemen et al. 2000; Reilly 2000; Yi and Bier 1998). This approach appears promising, especially for continuous variables, but we have not yet seen a decision-analysis application using copulas in the OR literature. Thus, despite some progress during the survey period in handling dependence, more work is needed in this area – especially work geared toward practitioners.

Second, we continue to need more realistic methods for dealing with the time dynamics of many decision problems. Sequential decision models have been part of the conceptual toolkit of decision analysis since its early days, and it is interesting to see the finance profession advancing real-options methods as an alternative to decision analysis for these types of decisions. The difficulty with using decision-analysis methods for such decisions seems to be the complexity and size of the models that are needed when conventional decision-analysis methods are used. In the preceding section, we cited the use of real-options methods, dynamic programming, and stochastic trees to address various types of time dynamics. Use of system dynamics methods has also been proposed (Howard et al. 1998). Additional work on these approaches, combined with the increased capabilities that modern decision-analysis software provides for constructing and analyzing large-scale decision-analysis models, will hopefully facilitate better analyses of decisions with time dynamics.

Concluding Remarks

Although there are some institutional, educational, and methodological needs that merit further attention, our analysis of the applications articles we surveyed and of other sources, as presented above, shows that the state of decision-analysis applications is healthy. Both the number of published applications and the rate of publication have increased. Furthermore, these applications cover a broad range of decisions in both the public and private sectors, and they demonstrate that decision analysis is used increasingly for a wide variety of strategic and tactical decisions. Readers interested in brief summaries for each of the surveyed applications articles are referred to the technical report by Keefer et al. (2002).

Acknowledgments

The authors thank Brian Bajuk, Daniel G. Brooks, Richard F. Deckro, Emilia Iovtcheva, Jeffrey M. Keisler, Jack M. Kloeber, Jr., Gregory S. Parnell, Robert K. Perdue, and James E. Smith for their assistance in providing material for the article on which this chapter is based. They thank the editors and referees of that article for their helpful comments and suggestions. They also thank the Departments of Management and Supply Chain Management at Arizona State University for their assistance.

REFERENCES

Amram, M., and Kulatilaka, N. (1999). *Real options: Managing strategic investment in an uncertain world*. Boston: Harvard Business School Press.

Baker, S. F., Green, S. G., Lowe, J. K., and Francis, V. E. (2000). A value-focused approach for laboratory equipment purchases. *Military Operations Research*, 5(4), 43–56.

Balson, W. E., Welsh, J. L., and Wilson, D. S. (1992). Using decision analysis and risk analysis to manage utility environmental risk. *Interfaces*, 22(6), 126–139.

Bana e Costa, C. A. (2001). The uses of multi-criteria decision analysis to support the search for less conflicting policy options in a multi-actor context: Case study. *Journal of Multi-Criteria Decision Analysis, 10*, 111–125.

Beccue, P. (2001). Choosing a development strategy for a new product at Amgen. In D. L. Keefer (Ed.), Practice abstracts. *Interfaces, 31*(5), 62–64.

Bell, D. E., and Schleifer, A., Jr. (1995). *Decision making under uncertainty.* Cambridge, MA: Course Technology, Inc.

Benaroch, M. (2001). Option-based management of technology investment risk. *IEEE Transactions on Engineering Management, 48*(4), 428–444.

Bodily, S. E., and Allen, M. S. (1999). A dialogue process for choosing value-creating strategies. *Interfaces, 29*(6), 16–28.

Borcherding, K., Eppel, T., and von Winterfeldt, D. (1991). Comparison of weighting judgments in multiattribute utility measurement. *Management Science, 37*, 1603–1619.

Bordley, R. F. (1998). R&D project selection versus R&D project generation. *IEEE Transactions on Engineering Management, 45*, 407–413.

Bordley, R. F. (2001). Relating value-focused thinking and interactive planning. *Journal of the Operational Research Society, 52*, 1315–1326.

Borison, A. (1995). Oglethorpe Power Corporation decides about investing in a major transmission system. *Interfaces, 25*(2), 25–36.

Bresnick, T. A., Buede, D. M., Pisani, A. A., Smith, L. L., and Wood, B. B. (1997). Airborne and space-borne reconnaissance force mixes: A decision analysis approach. *Military Operations Research, 3*(4), 65–78.

Brown, G. M. (1997). Evaluation of vision correction alternatives for myopic adults. *Interfaces, 27*(2), 66–84.

Brown, R. V. (1992). The state of the art of decision analysis: A personal perspective. *Interfaces, 22*(6), 5–14.

Bruggink, P. R. (1997). The contribution of project analysis to an R&D project at an industrial R&D center. In D. L. Keefer (Ed.), Practice abstracts. *Interfaces, 27*(2), 107–111.

Buede, D. M., and Bresnick, T. A. (1992). Applications of decision analysis to the military systems acquisition process. *Interfaces, 22*(6), 110–125.

Burk, R. C., and Parnell, G. (1997). Evaluating future military space technologies. *Interfaces, 27*(3), 60–73.

Burnett, W. M., Monetta, D. J., and Silverman, B. G. (1993). How the Gas Research Institute (GRI) helped transform the U.S. natural gas industry. *Interfaces, 23*(1), 44–58.

Call, H. J., and Miller, W. A. (1990). A comparison of approaches and implementations for automating decision analysis. *Reliability Engineering and System Safety, 30*, 115–162.

Chien, C.-F., and Sainfort, F. (1998). Evaluating the desirability of meals: An illustrative multiattribute decision analysis procedure to assess portfolios with interdependent items. *Journal of Multi-Criteria Decision Analysis, 7*, 230–238.

Claeys, J., and Walkup, G., Jr. (1999). Discovering real options in oilfield exploration and development. Paper 52956, *Society of Petroleum Engineers Hydrocarbon Economics and Evaluation Symposium*, Dallas, TX.

Clemen, R. T. (1996). *Making hard decisions: An introduction to decision analysis.* (2nd ed.). Belmont, CA: Duxbury Press.

Clemen, R.T., Fischer, G. W., and Winkler, R. L. (2000). Assessing dependence: Some experimental results. *Management Science, 46*(8), 1100–1115.

Clemen, R. T., and Kwit, R. C. (2001). The value of decision analysis at Eastman Kodak Company, 1990–1999. *Interfaces, 31*(5), 74–92.

Clemen, R. T., and Reilly, T. (1999). Correlations and copulas for decision and risk analysis. *Management Science, 45*(2), 208–224.

Corner, J. L., Buchanan, J., and Henig, M. (2001). Dynamic decision problem structuring. *Journal of Multi-Criteria Decision Analysis, 10*, 129–141.

Corner, J. L., and Corner, P. D. (1995). Characteristics of decisions in decision analysis practice. *Journal of the Operational Research Society*, *46*, 304–314.

Corner, J. L., and Kirkwood, C. W. (1991). Decision analysis applications in the operations research literature, 1970–1989. *Operations Research*, *39*, 206–219.

Davis, C. C., Deckro, R. F., and Jackson, J. A. (1999). A methodology for evaluating and enhancing C4 networks. *Military Operations Research*, *4*(2), 45–60.

Davis, C. C., Deckro, R. F., and Jackson, J. A. (2000). A value focused model for a C4 network. *Journal of Multi-Criteria Decision Analysis*, 9, 138–162.

Dillon, R., and Haimes, Y. Y. (1996). Risk of extreme events via multiobjective decision trees: Application to telecommunications. *IEEE Transactions on Systems, Man, and Cybernetics – Part A: Systems and Humans*, 26, 262–271.

Dixit, A. K., and Pindyck, R. S. (1994). *Investment under uncertainty*. Princeton NJ: Princeton University Press.

Doyle, M. P., Deckro, R. F., Kloeber, J. M., and Jackson, J. A. (2000). Measures of merit for offensive information operations courses of action. *Military Operations Research*, *5*(2), 5–18.

Dunning, D. J., Lockfort, S., Ross, Q. E., Beccue, P. C., and Stonebraker, J. S. (2001). New York Power Authority uses decision analysis to schedule refueling of its Indian Point 3 nuclear power plant. *Interfaces*, *31*(5), 121–135.

Dyer, J. S., Edmunds, T., Butler, J. C., and Jia, J. (1998). A multiattribute utility analysis of alternatives for the disposition of surplus weapons-grade plutonium. *Operations Research*, *46*, 749–762.

Dyer, J. S., Lund, R. N., Larsen, J. B., Kumar, V., and Leone, R. P. (1990). A decision support system for prioritizing oil and gas exploration activities. *Operations Research*, 38, 386–396.

Edwards, W., (Ed.). (1992). *Utility theories: Measurements and applications*. Boston: Kluwer.

Engemann, K. J., and Miller, H. E. (1992). Operations risk management at a major bank. *Interfaces*, *22*(6), 140–149.

Faiz, S. (2000). Real options application: From successes in asset valuation to challenges for an enterprise-wide approach. Paper 62964, *Society of Petroleum Engineers Annual Technical Conference and Exhibition*, Dallas, TX.

Faulkner, T. W. (1996). Applying "options thinking" to R&D valuation. *Research • Technology Management*, *39*(3), 50–56.

Feinstein, C. D. (1990). Deciding whether to test student athletes for drug use. *Interfaces*, *20*(3), 80–87.

Fildes, R., and Ranyard, J. (2000). Internal OR consulting: Effective practice in a changing environment. *Interfaces*, *30*(5), 34–50.

French, S. (1996). Multi-attribute decision support in the event of a nuclear accident. *Journal of Multi-Criteria Decision Analysis*, *5*, 39–57.

Gallant, L., Kieffel, H., and Chatwin, R. (1999). Using learning models to capture dynamic complexity in petroleum exploration. Paper 52954, *Society of Petroleum Engineers Hydrocarbon Economics and Evaluation Symposium*, Dallas, TX.

Golub, A. L. (1997). *Decision analysis: An integrated approach*. New York: Wiley.

Goodwin, P., and Wright, G. (1998). *Decision analysis for management judgment*. (2nd ed.). Chichester, England: Wiley.

Griggs, B. J., Parnell, G. S., and Lehmkuhl, L. J. (1997). An air mission planning algorithm using decision analysis and mixed integer programming. *Operations Research*, *45*, 662–676.

Hall, N. G., Hershey, J. C., Kessler, L. G., and Stotts, R. C. (1992). A model for making project funding decisions at the National Cancer Institute. *Operations Research*, *40*, 1040–1052.

Hämäläinen, R. P., Lindstedt, M. R. K., and Sinkko, K. (2000). Multiattribute risk analysis in nuclear emergency management. *Risk Analysis*, *20*(4), 455–467.

Hammond, J. S., Keeney, R. L., and Raiffa, H. (1999). *Smart choices: A practical guide to making better decisions*. Boston: Harvard Business School Press.

Hazen, G. (2000). Preference factoring for stochastic trees. *Management Science, 46*(3), 389–403.

Hazen, G., Pellissier, J. M., and Sounderpandian, J. (1998). Stochastic-tree models in medical decision making. *Interfaces, 28*(4), 64–80.

Hedbert, S. R. (1998). Executive insight: Is AI going mainstream at last? A look inside Microsoft Research. *IEEE Intelligent Systems, 13*(2), 21–25.

Heger, A. S., and White, J. E. (1997). Using influence diagrams for data worth analysis. *Reliability Engineering and System Safety, 55*, 195–202.

Henrion, M., Breese, J. S., and Horvitz, E. J. (1991). Decision analysis and expert systems. *AI Magazine, 12*(4), 64–91.

Hess, S. W. (1993). Swinging on the branch of a tree: Project selection applications. *Interfaces, 23*(6), 5–12.

Horowitz, I. (Ed.). (1990). *Organization and decision theory*. Boston: Kluwer Academic Publishers.

Howard, R. A. (1992). Heathens, heretics, and cults: The religious spectrum of decision aiding. *Interfaces, 22*(6), 15–27.

Howard, R. A. (1996). Options. In Zeckhauser et al. (Eds.) *Wise choices: Decisions, games, and negotiations*, pp. 81–101.

Howard, R. A., Conn, M. B., Paich, M., Smith, J. E., and Smith, J. M. (1998). *Panel discussion: Downstream decisions (options) and dynamic modeling*. Presented at INFORMS Annual Meeting, Seattle, WA. (Complete transcript is available at www.informs.org/Society/DA.)

Hurley, W. J. (1998). Optimal sequential decisions and the content of the fourth-and-goal conference. *Interfaces, 28*(6), 19–22.

Islei, G., Lockett, G., Cox, B., Gisbourne, S., and Stratford, M. (1991). Modeling strategic decision making and performance measurements at ICI Pharmaceuticals. *Interfaces, 21*(6), 4–22.

Jackson, J. A., Kloeber, Jr., J. M., Ralston, B. E., and Deckro, R. F. (1999). Selecting a portfolio of technologies: An application of decision analysis. *Decision Sciences, 30*, 217–238.

Jackson, J. A., Parnell, G. S., Jones, B. L., Lehmkuhl, L. J., Conley, H. W., and Andrew, J. M. (1997). *Air Force 2025* operational analysis. *Military Operations Research, 3*(4), 5–21.

Johnson, E., and Petty, N., 2003. Apimoxin development strategy analysis. In D. L. Keefer, (Ed.), Practice abstracts. *Interfaces, 33*(3), 57–59.

Jones, M., Hope, C., and Hughes, R. (1990). A multi-attribute value model for the study of UK energy policy. *Journal of the Operational Research Society, 41*, 919–929.

Kasanen, E., Wallenius, H., Wallenius, J., and Zionts, S. (2000). A study of high-level managerial decision processes, with implications for MCDM research. *European Journal of Operational Research, 120*, 496–510.

Keefer, D. L. (1991). Resource allocation models with risk aversion and probabilistic dependence: Offshore oil and gas bidding. *Management Science, 37*, 377–395.

Keefer, D. L. (1994). Certainty equivalents for three-point discrete-distribution approximations. *Management Science, 40*, 760–773.

Keefer, D. L. (1995). Facilities evaluation under uncertainty: Pricing a refinery. *Interfaces, 25*(6), 57–66.

Keefer, D. L. (1997). Practice abstracts. *Interfaces, 27*(2), 107–111.

Keefer, D. L. (1999). Practice abstracts. *Interfaces, 29*(4), 96–98.

Keefer, D. L. (2000). Practice abstracts. *Interfaces, 30*(5), 31–33.

Keefer, D. L. (2001a). Practice abstracts. *Interfaces, 31*(4), 109–111.

Keefer, D. L. (2001b). Practice abstracts. *Interfaces, 31*(5), 62–64.

Keefer, D. L. (2003). Practice abstracts. *Interfaces*, *33*(3), 57–59.

Keefer, D. L., Kirkwood, C. W., and Corner, J. L. (2002). Decision analysis applications in the operations research literature, 1990–2001. Technical report, Department of Supply Chain Management, Arizona State University, Tempe, AZ. (Available at http://da.pubs.informs.org/online-supp.html.)

Keefer, D. L., Smith, F. B. Jr., and Back, H. B. (1991). Development and use of a modeling system to aid a major oil company in allocating bidding capital. *Operations Research*, *39*, 28–41.

Keeney, R. L. (1992). *Value-focused thinking: A path to creative decision making*. Cambridge, MA: Harvard University Press.

Keeney, R. L. (1994). Using values in operations research. *Operations Research*, *42*, 793–813.

Keeney, R. L. (1997). Evaluating electromagnetic field implications for a transmission-line moratorium. *IEEE Transactions on Engineering Management*, *44*, 268–275.

Keeney, R. L. (1999a). The value of Internet commerce to the customer. *Management Science*, *45*, 533–542.

Keeney, R. L. (1999b). Developing a foundation for strategy at Seagate Software. *Interfaces*, *29*(6), 4–15.

Keeney, R. L. (2000). Evaluating customer acquisition at American Express using multiple objectives. In D. L. Keefer (Ed.), Practice abstracts. *Interfaces*, *30*(5), 31–33.

Keeney, R. L. (2001). Modeling values for telecommunications management. *IEEE Transactions on Engineering Management*, *48*(3), 370–379.

Keeney, R. L., and McDaniels, T. L. (1992). Value-focused thinking about strategic decisions at BC Hydro. *Interfaces*, *22*(6), 94–109.

Keeney, R. L., and McDaniels, T. L. (1999). Identifying and structuring values to guide integrated resource planning at BC Gas. *Operations Research*, *47*, 651–662.

Keeney, R. L., and McDaniels, T. L. (2001). A framework to guide thinking and analysis regarding climate change policies. *Risk Analysis*, *21*(6), 989–1000.

Keeney, R. L., McDaniels, T. L., and Swoveland, C. (1995). Evaluating improvements in electric utility reliability at British Columbia Hydro. *Operations Research*, *43*, 933–947.

Keeney, R. L, and von Winterfeldt, D. (1991). Eliciting probabilities from experts in complex technical problems. *IEEE Transactions on Engineering Management*, *38*, 191–201.

Keeney, R. L, and von Winterfeldt, D. (1994). Managing nuclear waste from power plants. *Risk Analysis*, *14*, 107–130.

Keeney, R. L., von Winterfeldt, D., and Eppel, T. (1990). Eliciting public values for complex policy decisions. *Management Science*, *36*, 1011–1030.

Keller, L. R., and Kirkwood, C. W. (1999). The founding of INFORMS: A decision analysis perspective. *Operations Research*, *47*, 16–28.

Kerchner, P. M., Deckro, R. F., and Kloeber, J. M. (2001). Valuing psychological operations. *Military Operations Research*, *6*(2), 45–65.

Kidd, J. B., and Prabhu, S. P. (1990). A practical example of a multi-attribute decision aiding technique. *Omega, The International Journal of Management Science*, *18*, 139–149.

Kirkwood, C. W. (1992). An overview of methods for applied decision analysis. *Interfaces*, *22*(6), 28–39.

Kirkwood, C. W. (1997). *Strategic decision making: Multiobjective decision analysis with spreadsheets*. Belmont, CA: Duxbury Press.

Kirkwood, C. W. (1999). Decision analysis. In Sage and Rouse (Eds.). *Handbook of systems engineering and management*, pp. 1119–1145.

Krumm, F. V., and Rolle, C. F. (1992). Management and application of decision and risk analysis in Du Pont. *Interfaces*, *22*(6), 84–93.

Kusnic, M. W., and Owen, D. (1992). The unifying vision process: Value beyond traditional decision analysis in multiple-decision-maker-environments. *Interfaces*, *22*(6), 150–166.

Lai, S.-K. (2001). An empirical study of equivalence judgments vs. ratio judgments in decision analysis. *Decision Sciences*, *32*(2), 277–302.

Lehmkuhl, L., Lucia, D., and Feldman, J. (2001). Signals from space: The next –generation global positioning system. *Military Operations Research*, *6*(4), 5–18.

Lieberman, J. (2002). *Marketing of DA at GM: Rise and fall*. Presented at Decision Analysis Affinity Group Conference, Las Vegas, NV.

Magat, W. A., Viscusi, W. K., and Huber, J. (1996). A reference lottery metric for valuing health. *Management Science*, *42*, 1118–1130.

Marshall, K. T., and Oliver, R. M. (1995). *Decision making and forecasting, with emphasis on model building and policy analysis*. New York: McGraw-Hill.

Matheson, D., and Matheson, J. (1998). *The smart organization: Creating value through strategic R&D*. Boston: Harvard Business School Press.

Matheson, D., and Matheson, J. (1999). Outside-in strategic modeling. *Interfaces*, *29*(6), 29–41.

Matheson, D., Matheson, J., and Menke, M. M. (1994). Making excellent R&D decisions. *Research • Technology Management*, *37*(6), 21–24.

Matheson, J. E., and Menke, M. M. (1994). Using decision quality principles to balance your R&D portfolio. *Research • Technology Management*, *37*(3), 38–43.

Matzkevich, I., and Abramson, B. (1995). Decision analytic networks in artificial intelligence. *Management Science*, *41*, 1–22.

Maxwell, D. T. (2002). Decision analysis: Aiding insight VI – It's not your grandfather's decision-analysis software. *OR/MS Today*, *29*(3), 44–51.

McDaniels, T. L. (1995). Using judgment in resource management: A multiple objective analysis of a fisheries management decision. *Operations Research*, *43*, 415–426.

McNamee, P., and Celona, J. (1990). *Decision analysis with Supertree*. (2nd ed.). South San Francisco, CA: Scientific Press.

McNamee, P., and Celona, J. (2001). *Decision analysis for the professional* (3rd ed.). Menlo Park, CA: SmartOrg Inc.

Menke, M. M. (1994). Improving R&D decisions and execution. *Research • Technology Management*, *37*(5), 25–32.

Millet, I. (1994). A novena to Saint Anthony, or how to find inventory by not looking. *Interfaces*, *24*(2), 69–75.

Mollaghasemi, M., and Pet-Edwards, J. (1997). *Technical briefing: Making multiple-objective decisions*. Los Alamitos, CA: IEEE Computer Society Press.

Morgan, M. G., and Henrion, M. (1990). *Uncertainty: A guide to dealing with uncertainty in quantitative risk and policy analysis*. Cambridge, UK: Cambridge University Press.

Morris, P. A., Teisberg, E. O., and Kolbe A. L. (1991). When choosing R&D projects, go with long shots. *Research • Technology Management*, *34*(1), 35–40.

Mulvey, J. M. (1994). An asset-liability investment system. *Interfaces*, *24*(3), 22–33.

Noonan, F., and Vidich, C. A. (1992). Decision analysis for utilizing hazardous waste site assessments in real estate acquisition. *Risk Analysis*, *12*, 245–251.

Oliver, R. M., and Smith, J. Q. (Eds.). (1990). *Influence diagrams, belief nets, and decision analysis*. Chichester, England: Wiley.

Parnell, G. S. (2001). Work-package-ranking system for the Department of Energy's Office of Science and Technology. In D. L. Keefer (Ed.), Practice abstracts. *Interfaces*, *31*(4), 109–111.

Parnell, G. S., Conley, H. W., Jackson, J. A., Lehmkuhl, L. J., and Andrew, J. M. (1998). Foundations 2025: A value model for evaluating future air and space forces. *Management Science*, *44*, 1336–1350.

Parnell, G. S., Gimeno, B. I., Westphal, D., Engelbrecht, J. A., and Szafranski, R. (2001). Multiple perspective R&D portfolio analysis for the National Reconnaissance Office's technology enterprise. *Military Operations Research*, *6*(3), 19–34.

Paté-Cornell, M.-E., and Fischbeck, P. S. (1994). Risk management for the tiles of the space shuttle. *Interfaces*, *24*(1), 64–86.

Pauwels, N., Van de Walle, B., Hardeman, F., and Soudan, K. (2000). The implications of irreversibility in emergency response decisions. *Theory and Decision*, *49*, 25–51.

Pellissier, J. M., Hazen, G. B., and Chang, R. W. (1996). A continuous-risk decision analysis of total hip replacement. *Journal of the Operational Research Society*, *47*(6), 776–793.

Perdue, R. K., and Kumar, S. (1999). Decision analysis of high-level radioactive waste cleanup end points at the West Valley Demonstration Project waste tank farm. In D. L. Keefer (Ed.), Practice abstracts. *Interfaces*, *29*(4), 96–98.

Perdue, R. K., McAllister, W. J., King, P. V., and Berkey, B. G. (1999). Valuation of R and D projects using options pricing and decision analysis models. *Interfaces*, *29*(6), 57–74.

Poland, W. B. (1999). Simple probabilistic evaluation of portfolio strategies. *Interfaces*, *29*(6), 75–83.

Procaccia, H., Cordier, R., and Muller, S. (1997). Application of Bayesian statistical decision theory for a maintenance optimization problem. *Reliability Engineering and System Safety*, *55*, 143–149.

Quaddus, M. A., Atkinson, D. J., and Levy, M. (1992). An application of decision conferencing to strategic planning for a voluntary organization. *Interfaces*, *22*(6), 61–71.

Raiffa, H. (2002). Decision analysis: A personal account of how it got started and evolved. *Operations Research*, *50*, 179–185.

Rayno, B., Parnell, G. S., Burk, R. C., and Woodruff, B. W. (1997). A methodology to assess the utility of future space systems. *Journal of Multi-Criteria Decision Analysis*, *6*, 344–354.

Reagan-Cirincione, P., Schuman, S., Richardson, G. P., and Dorf, S. A. (1991). Decision modeling: Tools for strategic thinking. *Interfaces*, *21*(6), 52–65.

Reilly, T. (2000). Sensitivity analysis for dependent variables. *Decision Sciences*, *31*(3), 551–572.

Rios Insua, D., and Salewicz, K. A. (1995). The operation of Lake Kariba: A multiobjective decision analysis. *Journal of Multi-Criteria Decision Analysis*, *4*, 203–222.

Rzasa, P. V., Faulkner, T. W., and Sousa, N. L. (1990). Analyzing R&D portfolios at Eastman Kodak. *Research • Technology Management*, *33*(1), 27–32.

Sage, A. P., and Rouse, W. B., (Eds.). (1999). *Handbook of systems engineering and management*. New York: Wiley.

Shephard, G. G., and Kirkwood, C. W. (1994). Managing the judgmental probability elicitation process: A case study of analyst/manager interaction. *IEEE Transactions on Engineering Management*, *41*, 414–425.

Silverman, B. G. (1994). Unifying expert systems and the decision sciences. *Operations Research*, *42*, 393–413.

Skaf, M. A. (1999). Portfolio management in an upstream oil and gas organization. *Interfaces*, *29*(6), 84–104.

Skinner, D. C. (1999). *Introduction to decision analysis*. (2nd ed.). Gainesville, FL: Probabilistic Publishing.

Smith, J. E. (1993). Moment methods for decision analysis. *Management Science*, *39*, 340–358.

Smith, J. E. (1999). Much ado about options?*Decision Analysis Newsletter*, *18*(2) 4–5, 8. Newsletter Archive, www.informs.org/Society/DA.

Smith, J. E., and McCardle, K. F. (1999). Options in the real world: Lessons learned in evaluating oil and gas investments. *Operations Research*, *47*, 1–15.

Smith, J. E., and Winkler, R. L. (1999). Casey's problem: Interpreting and evaluating a new test. *Interfaces*, *29*(3), 63–76.

Spector, B. I. (1993). Decision analysis for practical negotiation application. *Theory and Decision*, *34*, 183–199.

Spradlin, T. (2001). *Internal DA consultants; What's going to happen?* Presented at Decision Analysis Affinity Group Conference, Houston, TX.

Spradlin, T., and Kutoloski, D. M. (1999). Action-oriented portfolio management. *Research • Technology Management, 42*(2), 26–32.

Spradlin, T., and Skinner, D. C. (2001). Decision analysis affinity group. *Decision Analysis Newsletter* 20(2–3), 5. Newsletter Archive, www.informs.org/Society/DA.

Stafira, Jr., S. Parnell, G. S., and Moore, J. T. (1997). A methodology for evaluating military systems in a counterproliferation role. *Management Science, 43,* 1420–1430.

Stonebraker, J. S., Sage, J. J., and Leak, B. L. (1997). Decision analysis provides insight to Ford Microelectronics Incorporated. In D. L. Keefer, (Ed.), Practice abstracts. *Interfaces, 27*(2), 107–111.

Taha, H. A., and Wolf, H. M. (1996). Evaluation of generator maintenance schedules at Entergy Electric System. *Interfaces, 26*(4), 56–65.

Taylor, A. C., Evans, J. S., and McKone, T. E. (1993). The value of animal test information in environmental control decisions. *Risk Analysis, 13,* 403–412.

Thurston, D. H. (1990). Multiattribute utility analysis in design management. *IEEE Transactions on Engineering Management, 37*(4), 296–301.

Toland, R. J., Kloeber, J. M. Jr., and Jackson, J. A. (1998). A comparative analysis of hazardous waste remediation alternatives. *Interfaces, 28*(5), 70–85.

Trigeorgis, L. (1996). *Real options: Managerial flexibility and strategy in resource allocation.* Cambridge, MA: MIT Press.

Vári, A., and Vecsenyi, J. (1992). Experiences with decision conferencing in Hungary. *Interfaces, 22*(6), 72–83.

Von Winterfeldt, D., and Schweitzer, E. (1998). An assessment of tritium supply alternatives in support of the U.S. nuclear weapons stockpile. *Interfaces, 28*(1), 92–112.

Walls, M. R., Morahan, G. T., and Dyer, J. S. (1995). Decision analysis of exploration opportunities in the onshore US at Phillips Petroleum Company. *Interfaces, 25*(6), 39–56.

Winkler, R. L., Wallsten, T. S., Whitfield, R. G., Richmond, H. M., Hayes, S. R., and Rosenbaum, A. S. (1995). An assessment of the risk of chronic lung injury attributable to long-term ozone exposure. *Operations Research, 43,* 19–28.

Yassine, A. A., Chelst, K. R., and Falkenburg, D. R. (1999). A decision analytic framework for evaluating concurrent engineering. *IEEE Transactions on Engineering Management, 46*(2), 144–157.

Yi, W., and Bier, V. M. (1998). An application of copulas to accident precursor analysis. *Management Science, 44*(12, Part 2), S257–S270.

Yoon, K. P., and Hwang, C. (1995). *Multiple attribute decision making: An introduction.* Thousand Oaks, CA: Sage Publications.

Zeckhauser, R. J., Keeney, R. L., and Sebenius, J. K. (Eds.). (1996). *Wise choices: Decisions, games, and negotiations.* Boston: Harvard Business School Press.

Index

611